Vauxhall Corsa Owners Workshop Manual

Steve Rendle and Mark Coombs

Models covered

Vauxhall Corsa models with petrol engines, including GSi 16V and special/limited editions;
3- and 5-door Hatchback, Corsavan and Combo Van
1196 cc, 1389 cc & 1598 cc

Also covers Opel Corsa range
Does not cover Diesel engines

ABCDE
FGHIJ
KLMNO
PQRST

THE BOOK ®

Haynes Publishing
Sparkford Nr Yeovil
Somerset BA22 7JJ England

Haynes Publications, Inc
861 Lawrence Drive
Newbury Park
California 91320 USA

Acknowledgements

Thanks are due to Champion Spark Plug, who supplied the illustrations showing spark plug conditions, to Holt Lloyd Limited who supplied the illustrations showing bodywork repair, and to Duckhams Oils, who provided lubrication data. Certain other illustrations are the copyright of Vauxhall Motors Ltd, and are used with their permission. Thanks are also due to Sykes-Pickavant Limited, who provided some of the workshop tools, and to all those people at Sparkford and Newbury Park who helped in the production of this manual.

A book in the **Haynes Owners Workshop Manual Series**

Printed by J.H. Haynes & Co. Ltd., Sparkford, Nr Yeovil, Somerset BA22 7JJ, England

ISBN 1 85010 985 0

British Library Cataloguing in Publication Data
A catalogue record for this book is available from the British Library.

We take great pride in the accuracy of information given in this manual, but vehicle manufacturers make alterations and design changes during the production run of a particular vehicle of which they do not inform us. No liability can be accepted by the authors or publishers for loss, damage or injury caused by any errors in, or omissions from, the information given.

Restoring and Preserving our Motoring Heritage

Few people can have had the luck to realise their dreams to quite the same extent and in such a remarkable fashion as John Haynes, Founder and Chairman of the Haynes Publishing Group.

Since 1965 his unique approach to workshop manual publishing has proved so successful that millions of Haynes Manuals are now sold every year throughout the world, covering literally thousands of different makes and models of cars, vans and motorcycles.

A continuing passion for cars and motoring led to the founding in 1985 of a Charitable Trust dedicated to the restoration and preservation of our motoring heritage. To inaugurate the new Museum, John Haynes donated virtually his entire private collection of 52 cars.

Now with an unrivalled international collection of over 210 veteran, vintage and classic cars and motorcycles, the Haynes Motor Museum in Somerset is well on the way to becoming one of the most interesting Motor Museums in the world.

A 70 seat video cinema, a cafe and an extensive motoring bookshop, together with a specially constructed one kilometre motor circuit, make a visit to the Haynes Motor Museum a truly unforgettable experience.

Every vehicle in the museum is preserved in as near as possible mint condition and each car is run every six months on the motor circuit.

Enjoy the picnic area set amongst the rolling Somerset hills. Peer through the William Morris workshop windows at cars being restored, and browse through the extensive displays of fascinating motoring memorabilia.

From the 1903 Oldsmobile through such classics as an MG Midget to the mighty 'E' Type Jaguar, Lamborghini, Ferrari Berlinetta Boxer, and Graham Hill's Lola Cosworth, there is something for everyone, young and old alike, at this Somerset Museum.

Haynes Motor Museum

Situated mid-way between London and Penzance, the Haynes Motor Museum is located just off the A303 at Sparkford, Somerset (home of the Haynes Manual) and is open to the public 7 days a week all year round, except Christmas Day and Boxing Day.

Contents

Spark plug condition and bodywork repair colour section between pages 0-32 and 1-1

Vauxhall Corsa LS 3-door

Vauxhall Corsa GLS Auto 5-door

Vauxhall Corsa GSi 16V

Vauxhall Combo Van LS

About this manual

Its aim

The aim of this manual is to help you get the best value from your vehicle. It can do so in several ways. It can help you decide what work must be done (even should you choose to get it done by a garage), provide information on routine maintenance and servicing, and give a logical course of action and diagnosis when random faults occur. However, it is hoped that you will use the manual by tackling the work yourself. On simpler jobs it may even be quicker than booking the car into a garage and going there twice, to leave and collect it. Perhaps most important, a lot of money can be saved by avoiding the costs a garage must charge to cover its labour and overheads.

The manual has drawings and descriptions to show the function of the various components so that their layout can be understood. Then the tasks are described and photographed in a clear step-by-step sequence.

Its arrangement

The manual is divided into Chapters, each covering a logical sub-division of the vehicle. The Chapters are each divided into Sections, numbered with single figures, eg 5; and the Sections are divided into numbered paragraphs.

It is freely illustrated, especially in those parts where there is a detailed sequence of operations to be carried out. The reference numbers used in illustration captions pinpoint the pertinent Section and the paragraph within that Section. That is, illustration 3.2 means that the il-lustration refers to Section 3, and paragraph 2 within that Section.

There is an alphabetical index at the back of the manual, as well as a contents list at the front. Each Chapter is also preceded by its own individual contents list.

References to the "left" or "right" of the vehicle are in the sense of a person in the driver's seat, facing forward.

Unless otherwise stated, nuts and bolts are removed by turning anti-clockwise, and tightened by turning clockwise.

Vehicle manufacturers continually make changes to specifications and recommendations, and these, when notified, are incorporated into our manuals at the earliest opportunity.

We take great pride in the accuracy of information given in this manual, but vehicle manufacturers make alterations and design changes during the production run of a particular vehicle of which they do not inform us. No liability can be accepted by the authors or publishers for loss, damage or injury caused by any errors in, or omissions from, the information given.

Project vehicles

The main project vehicle used in the preparation of this manual, and appearing in many of the photographic sequences, was a 1994 Vauxhall Corsa GSi 16V. Additional work was carried out and photographed on a Vauxhall Corsa 1.2i (E-drive) Merit 3-door, a Vauxhall Combo Van 1.4i, and a Vauxhall Corsa 1.4 LS Automatic.

Introduction to the Vauxhall Corsa

The Corsa covered by this manual was first introduced to the European market in Spring 1993. Although mechanically there is a fundamental similarity to the previous Vauxhall Nova/Opel Corsa models, the later version is much-improved and more refined in all respects. This manual covers models fitted with petrol engines, but other models in the range are available with diesel engines.

Three sizes of petrol engines are available in the Corsa range; 1.2 and 1.4 litre single overhead camshaft (SOHC) units, and a 1.6 litre double overhead camshaft (DOHC) unit, fitted to the performance-orientated GSi 16V model. All of the engines have fuel injection, and are fitted with a range of emission control systems. All of the engines are of a well-proven design and, provided regular maintenance is carried out, are unlikely to give trouble.

The Corsa is available in 3- and 5-door Hatchback, Corsavan (3-door Van based on Hatchback), and Combo Van body styles, with a wide range of fittings and interior trim depending on the model specification.

Fully-independent front suspension is fitted; the rear suspension is semi-independent, with a torsion beam and trailing arms.

Four-and five-speed manual gearboxes are available, and a four-speed electronically-controlled transmission is available as an option on certain models.

A wide range of standard and optional equipment is available within the Corsa range to suit most tastes, including central locking, electric windows, an electric sunroof, an anti-lock braking system and an air bag.

For the home mechanic, the Corsa is a straightforward vehicle to maintain, and most of the items requiring frequent attention are easily accessible.

General dimensions and weights

Note: *All figures are approximate, and may vary according to model. Refer to manufacturer's data for exact figures.*

Dimensions

Overall length:
All models except Combo Van..	3730 mm
Combo Van models..	4231 mm

Overall width:

All models except Combo Van:
Excluding door mirrors	1608 mm
Including door mirrors...	1768 mm

Combo Van models:
Excluding door mirrors	1688 mm
Including door mirrors...	2060 mm

Overall height (unladen):
All models except Combo Van..	1420 mm
Combo Van models..	1805 mm

Wheelbase:
All models except Combo Van..	2443 mm
Combo Van models..	2480 mm
Front track	1387 mm

Rear track:
All except Combo Van models...	1388 mm
Combo Van models..	1427 mm

Weights

Kerb weight:

3-door Hatchback:
1.2 litre models	835 to 855 kg
1.4 litre manual gearbox models	840 to 905 kg
1.4 litre automatic transmission models.....................................	875 to 890 kg
GSi 16V model	945 to 975 kg

5-door Hatchback models:
1.2 litre models	860 to 885 kg
1.4 litre manual gearbox models	865 to 925 kg
1.4 litre automatic transmission models.....................................	900 to 925 kg
Corsavan models	940 to 950 kg
Combo Van models..	1030 to 1045 kg

Maximum gross vehicle weight:

3-door Hatchback:
1.2 litre models	1320 kg

1.4 litre manual gearbox models:
Without air conditioning	1335 kg
With air conditioning	1375 kg
1.4 litre automatic transmission models.....................................	1375 kg

GSi 16V model:
Without air conditioning	1415 kg
With air conditioning..	1430 kg

5-door Hatchback models:
1.2 litre models	1340 kg

1.4 litre manual gearbox models:
Without air conditioning	1355 kg
With air conditioning..	1395 kg
1.4 litre automatic transmission models.....................................	1395 kg

Corsavan models:
1.2 litre models	1330 kg
1.4 litre models	1345 kg
Combo Van models..	1600 kg
Maximum roof rack load..	100 kg

Maximum towing weight:

Braked trailer:
1.2 litre models*	500 to 650 kg
1.4 litre models	900 kg
GSi 16V model	1000 kg

Unbraked trailer:
1.2 litre models	400 kg
All except 1.2 litre models...	450 kg
Maximum trailer nose weight..	50 kg

*Refer to Vauxhall/Opel dealer for exact recommendations

Jacking, towing and wheel changing

Jacking

The jack supplied with the vehicle tool kit should only be used for changing the roadwheels - see *"Wheel changing"* later in this Section. When carrying out any other kind of work, raise the vehicle using a hydraulic jack, and always supplement the jack with axle stands positioned under the vehicle jacking points.

When using a hydraulic jack or axle stands, always position the jack head or axle stand head under one of the relevant jacking points (note that the jacking points for use with a hydraulic jack and axle stands are different to those for use with the vehicle jack) **(see illustrations)**. **Do not** jack the vehicle under the sump or any of the steering or suspension components. **Never** *work under, around, or near a raised vehicle, unless it is adequately supported in at least two places.*

Towing

Towing eyes are fitted to the front and rear of the vehicle for at-tachment of a tow rope. The towing eyes can be accessed through slots in the bumpers **(see illustrations)**. Always turn the ignition key to position "II" when the vehicle is being towed, so that the steering lock is released, and that the direction indicator and brake lights will work.

Before being towed, release the handbrake; select neutral on manual transmission models, or "N" on automatic transmission models. Note that greater-than-usual pedal pressure will be required to operate the brakes, since the vacuum servo unit is only operational with the engine running. Similarly, on models with power steering, greater-than-usual steering effort will be required.

Note that a vehicle with automatic transmission should always be towed forwards. To avoid damage to the automatic transmission, do not tow the vehicle any faster than 50 mph (80 km/h), or any further than 60 miles (100 km). Where it can be arranged, models with automatic transmission should ideally be towed with the front wheels off the ground, particularly if a transmission fault is suspected.

Front jacking point for hydraulic jack or axle stands

Rear jacking point for hydraulic jack or axle stands

Front towing eye

Rear towing eye

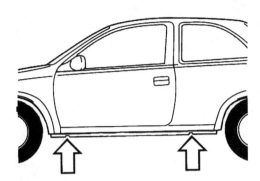

Jacking points for use with vehicle jack when wheel changing

Wheel changing

All except Combo Van models

On all except Combo Van models, the spare wheel is located under the carpet or cover panel in the luggage compartment, and the jack and wheel brace are located beneath the spare wheel. For access to the spare wheel, release the clips, and lift the carpet or cover panel, as applicable. Unscrew the plastic securing nut to remove the spare wheel.

Combo Van models

On Combo Van models, the spare wheel is located in a cradle under the rear of the vehicle. On models without a rear seat, the jack is secured by a bolt behind the driver's seat, and the wheel brace is located behind the passenger's seat. On models with a rear seat, the jack and wheel brace are located in a recess under the rear seat. For access to the spare wheel, proceed as follows.

(a)   Loosen the cradle securing bolt in the floor of the load area, using the wheel brace.
(b)   Lift the cradle sufficiently to disengage it from the latch.
(c)   Unhook the safety cord from the bracket under the vehicle.
(d)   Lower the cradle, and lift out the spare wheel.

All models

To change a wheel, remove the spare wheel, jack and wheel brace, as described previously, then proceed as follows.

Apply the handbrake, and place chocks at the front and rear of the wheel diagonally opposite the one to be changed. On automatic transmission models, place the selector lever in position "P", or with manual transmission models, select first or reverse gear. Make sure that the vehicle is located on firm, level ground, and then prise off, and remove, the wheel trim (if applicable). Slightly loosen the wheel nuts with the brace provided. Locate the jack head in the jacking point nearest to the wheel to be changed, and raise the jack by turning the handle. Note that the lug on the jack head must engage with the cut-out in the jacking point. On certain models, plastic covers must be unclipped for access to the jacking points **(see illustrations)**. When the wheel is

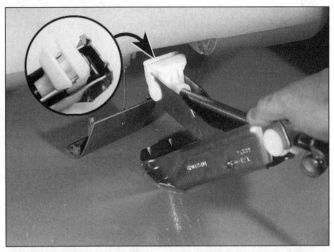

Locate the vehicle jack on firm, level ground, and engage the lug on the jack head with the cut-out in the jacking point

Removing a plastic cover for access to a jacking point - GSi 16V model

clear of the ground, remove the nuts and lift off the wheel. Fit the spare wheel and moderately tighten the nuts. Lower the vehicle, and then tighten the nuts fully in a diagonal sequence. Refit the wheel trim, where applicable. If possible, check the tyre pressure on the spare wheel. Remove the chocks and stow the jack, tools, and the damaged wheel (on Combo Van models, ensure that the safety cord is engaged with the bracket under the vehicle, and tighten the cradle securing bolt). Have the damaged tyre or wheel repaired, or renew it, as soon as possible.

Buying spare parts and vehicle identification numbers

Buying spare parts

Spare parts are available from many sources; for example, Vauxhall/Opel garages, other garages and accessory shops, and motor factors. Our advice regarding spare part sources is as follows.

Officially-appointed Vauxhall/Opel garages - This is the best source for parts which are peculiar to your car, and are not generally available (eg complete cylinder heads, internal gearbox components, badges, interior trim etc). It is also the only place at which you should buy parts if the vehicle is still under warranty. To be sure of obtaining the correct parts, it will be necessary to give the storeman your car's vehicle identification number, and if possible, take the old parts along for positive identification. Many   parts are available under a factory exchange scheme - any parts returned should always be clean. It obviously makes good sense to go straight to the specialists on your car for this type of part, as they are best equipped to supply you.

Other garages and accessory shops - These are often very good places to buy materials and components needed for the maintenance of your car (eg oil filters, spark plugs, bulbs, drivebelts, oils and greases, touch-up paint, filler paste, etc). They also sell general accessories, usually have convenient opening hours, charge lower prices, and can often be found not far from home.

Motor factors - Good factors will stock all the more important components which wear out comparatively quickly (eg exhaust systems, brake pads, seals and hydraulic parts, clutch components, bearing shells, pistons, valves etc). Motor factors will often provide new or reconditioned components on a part-exchange basis - this can save a considerable amount of money.

Vehicle identification numbers

Modifications are a continuing and unpublicised process in vehicle manufacture, quite apart from major model changes. Spare parts manuals and lists are compiled upon a numerical basis, the individual vehicle identification numbers being essential to correct identification of the component concerned.

When ordering spare parts, always give as much information as possible. Quote the car model, year of manufacture, body and engine numbers as appropriate.

The *Vehicle Identification Number (VIN)* plate is riveted to the top of the body front panel, and can be viewed once the bonnet is open. The plate carries the VIN, vehicle weight information, and paint and trim colour codes. The vehicle identification number is also stamped into the body floor panel between the right-hand front seat and the sill panel; lift the flap in the trim panel to reveal the number.

The *engine number* is stamped on a machined surface on the exhaust manifold side of the cylinder block, at the flywheel end. The first part of the engine number gives the engine code - eg "C 12 NZ" **(see illustrations)**.

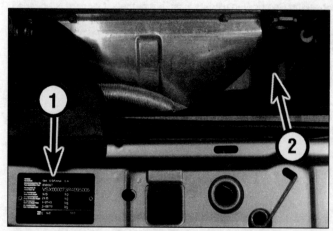

Vehicle Identification Number (VIN) plate (1) and engine number (2) locations

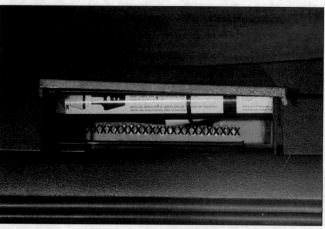

Vehicle Identification Number (VIN) stamped on body floor panel

Safety first!

However enthusiastic you may be about getting on with the job in hand, do take the time to ensure that your safety is not put at risk. A moment's lack of attention can result in an accident, as can failure to observe certain elementary precautions. There will always be new ways of having accidents, and the following points do not pretend to be a comprehensive list of all dangers; they are intended rather to make you aware of the risks and to encourage a safety-conscious approach to all work you carry out on your vehicle.

Essential DOs and DON'Ts

DON'T rely on a single jack when working underneath the vehicle. Always use reliable additional means of support, such as axle stands, securely placed under a structural part of the vehicle that you know will not give way.

DON'T attempt to loosen or tighten high-torque nuts (eg wheel hub nuts) while the vehicle is on a jack; it may be pulled off.

DON'T start the engine without first ascertaining that the transmission is in neutral (or "Park' where applicable) and the handbrake applied.

DON'T suddenly remove the filler cap from a hot cooling system - cover it with a cloth and release the pressure gradually first, or you may get scalded by escaping coolant.

DON'T attempt to drain oil, automatic transmission fluid, or coolant until you are sure it has cooled sufficiently to avoid scalding you.

DON'T grasp any part of the engine, exhaust or catalytic converter without first ascertaining that it is sufficiently cool to avoid burning you.

DON'T allow brake fluid or antifreeze to contact vehicle paintwork.

DON'T syphon toxic liquids such as fuel, brake fluid or antifreeze by mouth, or allow them to remain on your skin.

DON'T inhale dust - it may be injurious to health (see *Asbestos* below).

DON'T allow any spilt oil or grease to remain on the floor - wipe it up straight away, before someone slips on it.

DON'T use ill-fitting spanners or other tools which may slip and cause injury.

DON'T attempt to lift a heavy component which may be beyond your capability - get assistance.

DON'T rush to finish a job, or take unverified short cuts.

DON'T allow children or animals in or around an unattended vehicle.

DON'T park vehicles with catalytic converters over combustible materials such as dry grass, oily rags, etc if the engine has recently been run. As catalytic converters reach extremely high temperatures, any such materials in close proximity may ignite.

DON'T run vehicles equipped with catalytic converters without the exhaust system heat shields fitted.

DO wear eye protection when using power tools such as an electric drill, sander, bench grinder etc, and when working under the vehicle.

DO use a barrier cream on your hands prior to undertaking dirty jobs - it will protect your skin from infection as well as making the dirt easier to remove afterwards; but make sure your hands aren't left slippery. Note that long term contact with used engine oil can be a health hazard.

DO keep loose clothing (cuffs, tie etc) and long hair well out of the way of moving mechanical parts.

DO remove rings, wristwatch etc, before working on the vehicle - especially the electrical system.

DO ensure that any lifting tackle or jacking equipment used has a safe working load rating adequate for the job, and is used precisely as recommended by the manufacturer.

DO keep your work area tidy - it is only too easy to fall over articles left lying around.

DO get someone to check periodically that all is well when working alone on the vehicle.

DO carry out work in a logical sequence and check that everything is correctly assembled and tightened afterwards.

DO remember that your vehicle's safety affects that of yourself and others. If in doubt on any point, get specialist advice.

IF, in spite of following these precautions, you are unfortunate enough to injure yourself, seek medical attention as soon as possible.

Asbestos

Certain friction, insulating, sealing, and other products - such as brake linings, brake bands, clutch linings, gaskets, etc - contain asbestos. *Extreme care must be taken to avoid inhalation of dust from such products since it is hazardous to health.* If in doubt, assume that they *do* contain asbestos.

Fire

Remember at all times that petrol is highly flammable. Never smoke, or have any kind of naked flame around, when working on the vehicle. But the risk does not end there - a spark caused by an electrical short-circuit, by two metal surfaces contacting each other, by careless use of tools, or even by static electricity built up in your body under certain conditions, can ignite petrol vapour, which in a confined space is highly explosive. The vapour produced by spilling oil or hydraulic fluid onto hot metal, such as an exhaust manifold, can also be flammable or explosive.

Whenever possible, disconnect the battery earth terminal before working on any part of the fuel or electrical system, and never risk spilling fuel on to a hot engine or exhaust. Catalytic converters run at extremely high temperatures, and consequently can be an additional fire hazard. Observe the precautions outlined elsewhere in this section.

It is recommended that a fire extinguisher of a type suitable for fuel and electrical fires is kept handy in the garage or workplace at all times. Ideally, a suitable extinguisher should also be carried in the vehicle. Never try to extinguish a fuel or electrical fire with water. If a vehicle fire does occur, take note of the remarks below about hydrofluoric acid.

Note: *Any reference to a "torch" appearing in this manual should always be taken to mean a hand-held battery-operated electric lamp or flashlight. It does NOT mean a welding/gas torch or blowlamp.*

Hydrofluoric acid

Hydrofluoric acid is extremely corrosive. It is formed when certain types of synthetic rubber, which may be found in O-rings, oil seals, brake hydraulic system seals, fuel hoses etc, are exposed to temperatures above 400∞C. The obvious circumstance in which this could happen on a vehicle is in the case of a fire. The rubber does not burn, but changes into a charred or sticky substance which contains the acid. *Once formed, the acid remains dangerous for years. If it gets onto the skin, it may be necessary to amputate the limb concerned.*

When dealing with a vehicle which has suffered a fire, or with components salvaged from such a vehicle, always wear protective gloves, and discard them carefully after use. Bear this in mind if obtaining components from a car breaker.

Fumes

Certain fumes are highly toxic, and can quickly cause unconsciousness and even death if inhaled to any extent, especially if inhalation takes place through a lighted cigarette or pipe. Petrol vapour and air conditioning refrigerant vapour come into this category, as do the vapours from certain solvents such as trichloroethylene. Any draining or pouring of such volatile fluids should be done in a well-ventilated area (or, in the case of air conditioning refrigerant, should be left to a competent specialist).

When using cleaning fluids and solvents, read the instructions carefully. Never use materials from unmarked containers - they may give off poisonous vapours.

Never run the engine of a motor vehicle in an enclosed space, such as a garage. Exhaust fumes contain carbon monoxide, which is extremely poisonous; if you need to run the engine, always do so in the open air, or at least have the rear of the vehicle outside the workplace. Although vehicles fitted with catalytic converters have greatly-reduced toxic exhaust emissions, the above precautions should still be observed.

If you are fortunate enough to have the use of an inspection pit, never drain or pour petrol, and never run the engine, while the vehicle is standing over it; the fumes, being heavier than air, will concentrate in the pit, with possibly lethal results.

The battery

Batteries which are "sealed for life" require special precautions, which are normally outlined on a label attached to the battery. Such precautions are primarily related to situations involving battery charging, and jump-starting from another vehicle.

With a conventional battery, never cause a spark, or allow a naked light, in close proximity to it. It will normally be giving off a certain amount of hydrogen gas, which is highly explosive.

Whenever possible, disconnect the battery earth terminal before working on the fuel or electrical systems.

If possible, loosen the filler plugs or the filler cover when charging the battery from an external source. Do not charge at an excessive rate, or the battery may burst. Special care should be taken with the use of high charge-rate boost chargers, to prevent the battery from overheating.

Take care when topping-up and when carrying the battery. The acid electrolyte, even when diluted, is very corrosive, and should not be allowed to contact clothing, eyes or skin.

Always wear eye protection when cleaning the battery, to prevent the caustic deposits from entering your eyes.

The vehicle electrical system

Take care when making alterations or repairs to the vehicle wiring. Electrical faults are the commonest cause of vehicle fires. Make sure that any accessories are wired correctly, using an appropriately-rated fuse, and wire of adequate current-carrying capacity. When possible, avoid the use of "piggy-back" or self-splicing connectors to power additional electrical equipment from existing feeds; make up a new feed with its own fuse instead.

When considering the current which a new circuit will have to handle, do not overlook the switch, especially when planning to use an existing switch to control additional components - for instance, if spotlights are to be fed via the main lighting switch. For preference, a relay should be used to switch heavy currents. If in doubt, consult an auto-electrical specialist.

Any wire which passes through a body panel or bulkhead must be protected from chafing, using a grommet or similar device. A wire which is allowed to chafe bare against the bodywork will cause a short-circuit, and possibly a fire.

Mains electricity and electrical equipment

When using an electric power tool, inspection light, diagnostic equipment etc, which works from the mains, always ensure that the appliance is correctly connected to its plug and that, where necessary, it is properly earthed. Do not use such appliances in damp conditions. Beware of creating a spark or applying excessive heat in the vicinity of fuel or fuel vapour. Also ensure that the appliances meet the relevant national safety standards.

Ignition HT voltage

A severe electric shock can result from touching certain parts of the ignition system, such as the HT leads, when the engine is running or being cranked, particularly if components are damp or the insulation is defective. Where an electronic ignition system is fitted, the HT voltage is much higher and could prove fatal, especially to wearers of cardiac pacemakers.

Jacking and vehicle support

The jack provided with the vehicle is designed primarily for emergency wheel changing, and its use for servicing and overhaul work on the vehicle is best avoided. Instead, a more substantial workshop jack (trolley jack or similar) should be used. Whichever type is employed, it is essential that additional safety support is provided by means of axle stands designed for this purpose. Never use makeshift means such as wooden blocks or piles of house bricks, as these can easily topple or, in the case of bricks, disintegrate under the weight of the vehicle. Further information on the correct positioning of the jack and axle stands is provided in the *"Jacking, towing and wheel changing"* Section.

If removal of the wheels is not required, the use of drive-on ramps is recommended. Caution should be exercised to ensure that they are correctly aligned with the wheels, and that the vehicle is not driven too far along them so that it promptly falls off the other ends, or tips the ramps.

General repair procedures

Whenever servicing, repair or overhaul work is carried out on the car or its components, it is necessary to observe the following procedures and instructions. This will assist in carrying out the operation efficiently and to a professional standard of workmanship.

Joint mating faces and gaskets

When separating components at their mating faces, never insert screwdrivers or similar implements into the joint between the faces in order to prise them apart. This can cause severe damage which results in oil leaks, coolant leaks, etc upon reassembly. Separation is usually achieved by tapping along the joint with a soft-faced hammer in order to break the seal. However, note that this method may not be suitable where dowels are used for component location.

Where a gasket is used between the mating faces of two components, ensure that it is renewed on reassembly, and fit it dry unless otherwise stated in the repair procedure. Make sure that the mating faces are clean and dry, with all traces of old gasket removed. When cleaning a joint face, use a tool which is not likely to score or damage the face, and remove any burrs or nicks with an oilstone or fine file.

Make sure that tapped holes are cleaned with a pipe cleaner, and keep them free of jointing compound, if this is being used, unless specifically instructed otherwise.

Ensure that all orifices, channels or pipes are clear, and blow through them, preferably using compressed air.

Oil seals

Oil seals can be removed by levering them out with a wide flat-bladed screwdriver or similar implement. Alternatively, a number of self-tapping screws may be screwed into the seal, and these used as a purchase for pliers or some similar device in order to pull the seal free.

Whenever an oil seal is removed from its working location, either individually or as part of an assembly, it should be renewed.

The very fine sealing lip of the seal is easily damaged, and will not seal if the surface it contacts is not completely clean and free from scratches, nicks or grooves. If the original sealing surface of the component cannot be restored, and the manufacturer has not made provision for slight relocation of the seal relative to the sealing surface, the component should be renewed.

Protect the lips of the seal from any surface which may damage them in the course of fitting. Use tape or a conical sleeve where possible. Lubricate the seal lips with oil before fitting and, on dual-lipped seals, fill the space between the lips with grease.

Unless otherwise stated, oil seals must be fitted with their sealing lips toward the lubricant to be sealed.

Use a tubular drift or block of wood of the appropriate size to install the seal and, if the seal housing is shouldered, drive the seal down to the shoulder. If the seal housing is unshouldered, the seal should be fitted with its face flush with the housing top face (unless otherwise instructed).

Screw threads and fastenings

Seized nuts, bolts and screws are quite a common occurrence where corrosion has set in, and the use of penetrating oil or releasing fluid will often overcome this problem if the offending item is soaked for a while before attempting to release it. The use of an impact driver may also provide a means of releasing such stubborn fastening devices, when used in conjunction with the appropriate screwdriver bit or socket. If none of these methods works, it may be necessary to resort to the careful application of heat, or the use of a hacksaw or nut splitter device.

Studs are usually removed by locking two nuts together on the threaded part, and then using a spanner on the lower nut to unscrew the stud. Studs or bolts which have broken off below the surface of the component in which they are mounted can sometimes be removed using a proprietary stud extractor. Always ensure that a blind tapped hole is completely free from oil, grease, water or other fluid before installing the bolt or stud. Failure to do this could cause the housing to crack

due to the hydraulic action of the bolt or stud as it is screwed in.

When tightening a castellated nut to accept a split pin, tighten the nut to the specified torque, where applicable, and then tighten further to the next split pin hole. Never slacken the nut to align the split pin hole, unless stated in the repair procedure.

When checking or retightening a nut or bolt to a specified torque setting, slacken the nut or bolt by a quarter of a turn, and then retighten to the specified setting. However, this should not be attempted where angular tightening has been used.

For some screw fastenings, notably cylinder head bolts or nuts, torque wrench settings are no longer specified for the latter stages of tightening, "angle-tightening" being called up instead. Typically, a fairly low torque wrench setting will be applied to the bolts/nuts in the correct sequence, followed by one or more stages of tightening through specified angles.

Locknuts, locktabs and washers

Any fastening which will rotate against a component or housing in the course of tightening should always have a washer between it and the relevant component or housing.

Spring or split washers should always be renewed when they are used to lock a critical component such as a big-end bearing retaining bolt or nut. Locktabs which are folded over to retain a nut or bolt should always be renewed.

Self-locking nuts can be re-used in non-critical areas, providing resistance can be felt when the locking portion passes over the bolt or stud thread. However, it should be noted that self-locking stiffnuts tend to lose their effectiveness after long periods of use, and in such cases should be renewed as a matter of course.

Split pins must always be replaced with new ones of the correct size for the hole.

When thread-locking compound is found on the threads of a fastener which is to be re-used, it should be cleaned off with a wire brush and solvent, and fresh compound applied on reassembly.

Special tools

Some repair procedures in this manual entail the use of special tools such as a press, two or three-legged pullers, spring compressors, etc. Wherever possible, suitable readily-available alternatives to the manufacturer's special tools are described, and are shown in use. In some instances, where no alternative is possible, it has been necessary to resort to the use of a manufacturer's tool, and this has been done for reasons of safety as well as the efficient completion of the repair operation. Unless you are highly-skilled and have a thorough understanding of the procedures described, never attempt to bypass the use of any special tool when the procedure described specifies its use. Not only is there a very great risk of personal injury, but expensive damage could be caused to the components involved.

Environmental considerations

When disposing of used engine oil, brake fluid, antifreeze, etc, give due consideration to any detrimental environmental effects. Do not, for instance, pour any of the above liquids down drains into the general sewage system, or onto the ground to soak away. Many local council refuse tips provide a facility for waste oil disposal, as do some garages. If none of these facilities are available, consult your local Environmental Health Department for further advice.

With the universal tightening-up of legislation regarding the emission of environmentally-harmful substances from motor vehicles, most current vehicles have tamperproof devices fitted to the main adjustment points of the fuel system. These devices are primarily designed to prevent unqualified persons from adjusting the fuel/air mixture, with the chance of a consequent increase in toxic emissions. If such devices are encountered during servicing or overhaul, they should, wherever possible, be renewed or refitted in accordance with the vehicle manufacturer's requirements or current legislation.

Tools and working facilities

Introduction

A selection of good tools is a fundamental requirement for anyone contemplating the maintenance and repair of a motor vehicle. For the owner who does not possess any, their purchase will prove a considerable expense, offsetting some of the savings made by doing-it-yourself. However, provided that the tools purchased meet the relevant national safety standards and are of good quality, they will last for many years and prove an extremely worthwhile investment.

To help the average owner to decide which tools are needed to carry out the various tasks detailed in this manual, we have compiled three lists of tools under the following headings: *Maintenance and minor repair, Repair and overhaul*, and *Special*. Newcomers to practical mechanics should start off with the *Maintenance and minor repair* tool kit, and confine themselves to the simpler jobs around the vehicle. Then, as confidence and experience grow, more difficult tasks can be undertaken, with extra tools being purchased as, and when, they are needed. In this way, a *Maintenance and minor repair* tool kit can be built up into a *Repair and overhaul* tool kit over a considerable period of time, without any major cash outlays. The experienced do-it-yourselfer will have a tool kit good enough for most repair and overhaul procedures, and will add tools from the *Special* category when it is felt that the expense is justified by the amount of use to which these tools will be put.

Maintenance and minor repair tool kit

The tools given in this list should be considered as a minimum requirement if routine maintenance, servicing and minor repair operations are to be undertaken. We recommend the purchase of combination spanners (ring one end, open-ended the other); although more expensive than open-ended ones, they do give the advantages of both types of spanner.

Combination spanners:
*   Metric - 8, 9, 10, 11, 12, 13, 14, 15, 17 & 19 mm*
Adjustable spanner - 35 mm jaw (approx)
Spark plug spanner (with rubber insert)
Spark plug gap adjustment tool
Set of feeler gauges
Brake bleed nipple spanner
Screwdrivers:
*   Flat blade - approx 100 mm long x 6 mm dia*
*   Cross blade - approx 100 mm long x 6 mm dia*
Combination pliers
Hacksaw (junior)
Tyre pump
Tyre pressure gauge
Oil can
Oil filter removal tool
Fine emery cloth
Wire brush (small)
Funnel (medium size)

Repair and overhaul tool kit

These tools are virtually essential for anyone undertaking any major repairs to a motor vehicle, and are additional to those given in the *Maintenance and minor repair* list. Included in this list is a comprehensive set of sockets. Although these are expensive, they will be found invaluable as they are so versatile - particularly if various drives are included in the set. We recommend the half-inch square-drive type, as this can be used with most proprietary torque wrenches. If you cannot afford a socket set, even bought piecemeal, then inexpensive tubular box spanners are a useful alternative.

The tools in this list will occasionally need to be supplemented by tools from the *Special* list.

Sockets (or box spanners) to cover range in previous list (including
*   Torx sockets)*
Reversible ratchet drive (for use with sockets) **(see illustration)**
Extension piece, 250 mm (for use with sockets)
Universal joint (for use with sockets)
Torque wrench (for use with sockets)
Self-locking grips
Ball pein hammer
Soft-faced mallet (plastic/aluminium or rubber)

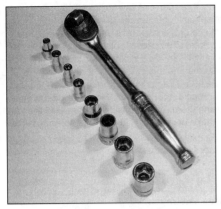

Sockets and reversible ratchet drive

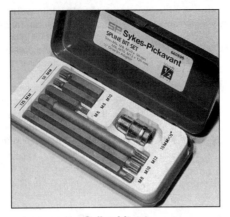

Spline bit set

Spline key set

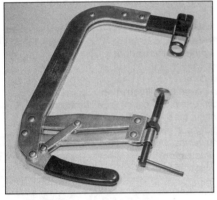

Valve spring compressor

Piston ring compressor

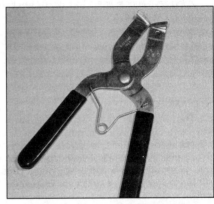

Piston ring removal/installation tool

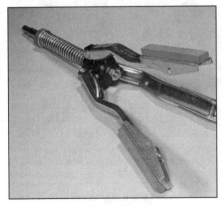

Cylinder bore hone

Three-legged hub and bearing puller

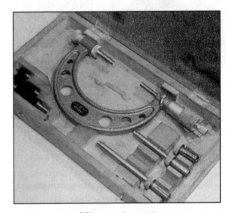

Micrometer set

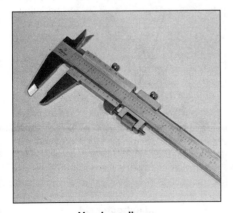

Vernier calipers

Dial test indicator and magnetic stand

Stroboscopic timing light

Screwdrivers:
  Flat blade - long & sturdy, short (chubby), and narrow
      (electricians) types
  Cross blade - Long & sturdy, and short (chubby) types
Pliers:
  Long-nosed
  Side cutters (electricians)
  Circlip (internal and external)
Cold chisel - 25 mm
Scriber
Scraper
Centre punch
Pin punch
Hacksaw
Brake hose clamp
Brake/clutch bleeding kit
Selection of twist drills
Steel rule/straight-edge
Allen keys (inc. splined/Torx type) **(see illustrations)**
Selection of files
Wire brush
Axle-stands
Jack (strong trolley or hydraulic type)
Light with extension lead

Special tools

The tools in this list are those which are not used regularly, are expensive to buy, or which need to be used in accordance with their manufacturers' instructions. Unless relatively difficult mechanical jobs are undertaken frequently, it will not be economic to buy many of these tools. Where this is the case, you could consider clubbing together with friends (or joining a motorists' club) to make a joint purchase, or borrowing the tools against a deposit from a local garage or tool hire

specialist. It is worth noting that many of the larger DIY superstores now carry a large range of special tools for hire at modest rates.

The following list contains only those tools and instruments freely available to the public, and not those special tools produced by the vehicle manufacturer specifically for its dealer network. You will find occasional references to these manufacturers' special tools in the text of this manual. Generally, an alternative method of doing the job without the vehicle manufacturers' special tool is given. However, sometimes there is no alternative to using them. Where this is the case and the relevant tool cannot be bought or borrowed, you will have to entrust the work to a franchised garage.

Valve spring compressor **(see illustration)**
Valve grinding tool
Piston ring compressor **(see illustration)**
Piston ring removal/installation tool **(see illustration)**
Cylinder bore hone **(see illustration)**
Balljoint separator
Coil spring compressors (where applicable)
Two/three-legged hub and bearing puller **(see illustration)**
Impact screwdriver
Micrometer and/or vernier calipers **(see illustrations)**
Dial gauge **(see illustration)**
Stroboscopic timing light **(see illustration)**
Dwell angle meter/tachometer
Universal electrical multi-meter
Cylinder compression gauge **(see illustration)**
Hand-operated vacuum pump and gauge **(see illustration)**
Clutch plate alignment set **(see illustration)**
Brake shoe steady spring cup removal tool **(see illustration)**
Bush and bearing removal/installation set **(see illustration)**
Stud extractors **(see illustration)**
Tap and die set **(see illustration)**
Lifting tackle
Trolley jack

Compression testing gauge

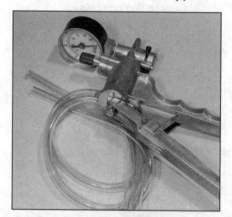

Vacuum pump and gauge

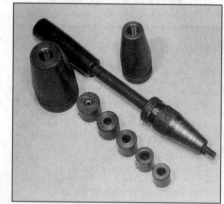

Clutch plate alignment set

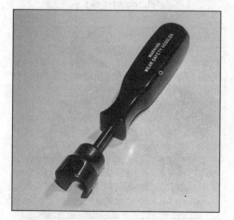

Brake shoe spring cup removal tool

Bush and bearing removal/installation set

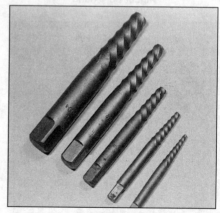

Stud extractor set

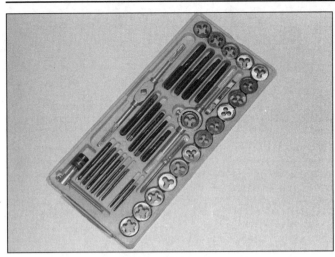

Tap and die set

Buying tools

For practically all tools, a tool factor is the best source, since he will have a very comprehensive range compared with the average garage or accessory shop. Having said that, accessory shops often offer excellent quality tools at discount prices, so it pays to shop around.

Remember, you don't have to buy the most expensive items on the shelf, but it is always advisable to steer clear of the very cheap tools. There are plenty of good tools around at reasonable prices, but always aim to purchase items which meet the relevant national safety standards. If in doubt, ask the proprietor or manager of the shop for advice before making a purchase.

Care and maintenance of tools

Having purchased a reasonable tool kit, it is necessary to keep the tools in a clean and serviceable condition. After use, always wipe off any dirt, grease and metal particles using a clean, dry cloth, before putting the tools away. Never leave them lying around after they have been used. A simple tool rack on the garage or workshop wall for items such as screwdrivers and pliers is a good idea. Store all normal spanners and sockets in a metal box. Any measuring instruments, gauges, meters, etc, must be carefully stored where they cannot be damaged or become rusty.

Take a little care when tools are used. Hammer heads inevitably become marked, and screwdrivers lose the keen edge on their blades from time to time. A little timely attention with emery cloth or a file will soon restore items like this to a good serviceable finish.

Working facilities

Not to be forgotten when discussing tools is the workshop itself. If anything more than routine maintenance is to be carried out, some form of suitable working area becomes essential.

It is appreciated that many an owner-mechanic is forced by circumstances to remove an engine or similar item without the benefit of a garage or workshop. Having done this, any repairs should always be done under the cover of a roof.

Wherever possible, any dismantling should be done on a clean, flat workbench or table at a suitable working height.

Spanner jaw gap and bolt size comparison table

Jaw gap – in (mm)	Spanner size	Bolt size
0.197 (5.00)	5 mm	M 2.5
0.216 (5.50)	5.5 mm	M 3
0.218 (5.53)	$\frac{7}{32}$ in AF	
0.236 (6.00)	6 mm	M 3.5
0.250 (6.35)	$\frac{1}{4}$ in AF	
0.275 (7.00)	7 mm	M 4
0.281 (7.14)	$\frac{9}{32}$ in AF	
0.312 (7.92)	$\frac{5}{16}$ in AF	
0.315 (8.00)	8 mm	M 5
0.343 (8.71)	$\frac{11}{32}$ in AF	
0.375 (9.52)	$\frac{3}{8}$ in AF	
0.394 (10.00)	10 mm	M 6
0.406 (10.32)	$\frac{13}{32}$ in AF	
0.433 (11.00)	11 mm	M 7
0.437 (11.09)	$\frac{7}{16}$ in AF	$\frac{1}{4}$ in SAE
0.468 (11.88)	$\frac{15}{32}$ in AF	
0.500 (12.70)	$\frac{1}{2}$ in AF	$\frac{5}{16}$ in SAE
0.512 (13.00)	13 mm	M8
0.562 (14.27)	$\frac{9}{16}$ in AF	$\frac{3}{8}$ in SAE
0.593 (15.06)	$\frac{19}{32}$ in AF	
0.625 (15.87)	$\frac{5}{8}$ in AF	$\frac{7}{16}$ in SAE
0.669 (17.00)	17 mm	M 10
0.687 (17.44)	$\frac{11}{16}$ in AF	
0.709 (19.00)	19 mm	M 12
0.750 (19.05)	$\frac{3}{4}$ in AF	$\frac{1}{2}$ in SAE
0.781 (19.83)	$\frac{25}{32}$ in AF	
0.812 (20.62)	$\frac{13}{16}$ in AF	
0.866 (22.00)	22 mm	M 14
0.875 (22.25)	$\frac{7}{8}$ in AF	$\frac{9}{16}$ in SAE
0.937 (23.79)	$\frac{15}{16}$ in AF	$\frac{5}{8}$ in SAE
0.945 (24.00)	24 mm	M 16
0.968 (24.58)	$\frac{31}{32}$ in AF	
1.000 (25.40)	1 in AF	$\frac{11}{16}$ in SAE
1.062 (26.97)	1 $\frac{1}{16}$ in AF	$\frac{3}{4}$ in SAE
1.063 (27.00)	27 mm	M 18
1.125 (28.57)	1 $\frac{1}{8}$ in AF	
1.182 (30.00)	30 mm	M 20
1.187 (30.14)	1 $\frac{3}{16}$ in AF	
1.250 (31.75)	1 $\frac{1}{4}$ in AF	$\frac{7}{8}$ in SAE
1.260 (32.00)	32 mm	M 22
1.312 (33.32)	1 $\frac{5}{16}$ in AF	
1.375 (34.92)	1 $\frac{3}{8}$ in AF	
1.418 (36.00)	36 mm	M 24
1.437 (36.49)	1 $\frac{7}{16}$ in AF	1 in SAE
1.500 (38.10)	1 $\frac{1}{2}$ in AF	
1.615 (41.00)	41 mm	M 27

Any workbench needs a vice; one with a jaw opening of 100 mm is suitable for most jobs. As mentioned previously, some clean dry storage space is also required for tools, as well as for any lubricants, cleaning fluids, touch-up paints and so on, which become necessary.

Another item which may be required, and which has a much more general usage, is an electric drill with a chuck capacity of at least 8 mm. This, together with a good range of twist drills, is virtually essential for fitting accessories.

Last, but not least, always keep a supply of old newspapers and clean, lint-free rags available, and try to keep any working area as clean as possible.

Booster battery (jump) starting

When jump-starting a car using a booster battery, observe the following precautions.

(a) *Before connecting the booster battery, make sure that the ignition is switched off.*

(b) *Ensure that all electrical equipment (lights, heater, wipers, etc) is switched off.*

(c) *Make sure that the booster battery is the same voltage as the discharged one in the vehicle.*

(d) *If the battery is being jump-started from the battery in another vehicle, the two vehicles MUST NOT TOUCH each other.*

(e) *Make sure that the transmission is in neutral (manual gearbox) or Park (automatic transmission).*

Connect one jump lead between the positive (+) terminals of the two batteries. Connect the other jump lead first to the negative (-) terminal of the booster battery, and then to a good earthing point on the vehicle to be started, such as a bolt or bracket on the engine block, at least 45 cm from the battery if possible **(see illustration)**. Make sure that the jump leads will not come into contact with the fan, drivebelts or other moving parts of the engine.

Start the engine using the booster battery, then with the engine running at idle speed, disconnect the jump leads in the reverse order of connection.

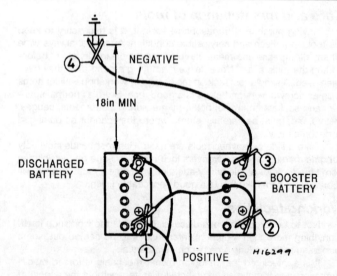

Jump start lead connections for negative-earth vehicles - connect leads in order shown

Radio/cassette unit anti-theft system - precaution

The radio/cassette unit fitted as standard equipment by Vauxhall/Opel is equipped with a built-in security code, to deter thieves. If the power source to the unit is cut, the anti-theft system will activate. Even if the power source is immediately reconnected, the radio/cassette unit will not function until the correct security code has been entered. Therefore, if you do not know the correct security code for the radio/cassette unit, **do not** disconnect the battery negative terminal of the battery, or remove the radio/cassette unit from the vehicle.

To enter the correct security code, follow the instructions provided with the radio/cassette player handbook.

If an incorrect code is entered, the unit will become locked, and cannot be operated.

If this happens, or if the security code is lost or forgotten, seek the advice of your Vauxhall/Opel dealer. On presentation of proof of ownership, a Vauxhall/Opel dealer will be able to unlock the unit and provide you with a new security code.

Conversion factors

Length (distance)

Inches (in)	25.4	= Millimetres (mm)	X 0.0394	= Inches (in)
Feet (ft)	0.305	= Metres (m)	X 3.281	= Feet (ft)
Miles	1.609	= Kilometres (km)	X 0.621	= Miles

Volume (capacity)

Cubic inches (cu in; in³)	X 16.387	= Cubic centimetres (cc; cm³)	X 0.061	= Cubic inches (cu in; in³)
Imperial pints (Imp pt)	X 0.568	= Litres (l)	X 1.76	= Imperial pints (Imp pt)
Imperial quarts (Imp qt)	X 1.137	= Litres (l)	X 0.88	= Imperial quarts (Imp qt)
Imperial quarts (Imp qt)	X 1.201	= US quarts (US qt)	X 0.833	= Imperial quarts (Imp qt)
US quarts (US qt)	X 0.946	= Litres (l)	X 1.057	= US quarts (US qt)
Imperial gallons (Imp gal)	X 4.546	= Litres (l)	X 0.22	= Imperial gallons (Imp gal)
Imperial gallons (Imp gal)	X 1.201	= US gallons (US gal)	X 0.833	= Imperial gallons (Imp gal)
US gallons (US gal)	X 3.785	= Litres (l)	X 0.264	= US gallons (US gal)

Mass (weight)

Ounces (oz)	X 28.35	= Grams (g)	X 0.035	= Ounces (oz)
Pounds (lb)	X 0.454	= Kilograms (kg)	X 2.205	= Pounds (lb)

Force

Ounces-force (ozf; oz)	X 0.278	= Newtons (N)	X 3.6	= Ounces-force (ozf; oz)
Pounds-force (lbf; lb)	X 4.448	= Newtons (N)	X 0.225	= Pounds-force (lbf; lb)
Newtons (N)	X 0.1	= Kilograms-force (kgf; kg)	X 9.81	= Newtons (N)

Pressure

Pounds-force per square inch (psi; lbf/in²; lb/in²)	X 0.070	= Kilograms-force per square centimetre (kgf/cm²; kg/cm²)	X 14.223	= Pounds-force per square inch (psi; lbf/in²; lb/in²)
Pounds-force per square inch (psi; lbf/in²; lb/in²)	X 0.068	= Atmospheres (atm)	X 14.696	= Pounds-force per square inch (psi; lbf/in²; lb/in²)
Pounds-force per square inch (psi; lbf/in²; lb/in²)	X 0.069	= Bars	X 14.5	= Pounds-force per square inch (psi; lbf/in²; lb/in²)
Pounds-force per square inch (psi; lbf/in²; lb/in²)	X 6.895	= Kilopascals (kPa)	X 0.145	= Pounds-force per square inch (psi; lbf/in²; lb/in²)
Kilopascals (kPa)	X 0.01	= Kilograms-force per square centimetre (kgf/cm²; kg/cm²)	X 98.1	= Kilopascals (kPa)
Millibar (mbar)	X 100	= Pascals (Pa)	X 0.01	= Millibar (mbar)
Millibar (mbar)	X 0.0145	= Pounds-force per square inch (psi; lbf/in²; lb/in²)	X 68.947	= Millibar (mbar)
Millibar (mbar)	X 0.75	= Millimetres of mercury (mmHg)	X 1.333	= Millibar (mbar)
Millibar (mbar)	X 0.401	= Inches of water (inH₂O)	X 2.491	= Millibar (mbar)
Millimetres of mercury (mmHg)	X 0.535	= Inches of water (inH₂O)	X 1.868	= Millimetres of mercury (mmHg)
Inches of water (inH₂O)	X 0.036	= Pounds-force per square inch (psi; lbf/in²; lb/in²)	X 27.68	= Inches of water (inH₂O)

Torque (moment of force)

Pounds-force inches (lbf in; lb in)	X 1.152	= Kilograms-force centimetre (kgf cm; kg cm)	X 0.868	= Pounds-force inches (lbf in; lb in)
Pounds-force inches (lbf in; lb in)	X 0.113	= Newton metres (Nm)	X 8.85	= Pounds-force inches (lbf in; lb in)
Pounds-force inches (lbf in; lb in)	X 0.083	= Pounds-force feet (lbf ft; lb ft)	X 12	= Pounds-force inches (lbf in; lb in)
Pounds-force feet (lbf ft; lb ft)	X 0.138	= Kilograms-force metres (kgf m; kg m)	X 7.233	= Pounds-force feet (lbf ft; lb ft)
Pounds-force feet (lbf ft; lb ft)	X 1.356	= Newton metres (Nm)	X 0.738	= Pounds-force feet (lbf ft; lb ft)
Newton metres (Nm)	X 0.102	= Kilograms-force metres (kgf m; kg m)	X 9.804	= Newton metres (Nm)

Power

Horsepower (hp)	X 745.7	= Watts (W)	X 0.0013	= Horsepower (hp)

Velocity (speed)

Miles per hour (miles/hr; mph)	X 1.609	= Kilometres per hour (km/hr; kph)	X 0.621	= Miles per hour (miles/hr; mph)

Fuel consumption*

Miles per gallon, Imperial (mpg)	X 0.354	= Kilometres per litre (km/l)	X 2.825	= Miles per gallon, Imperial (mpg)
Miles per gallon, US (mpg)	X 0.425	= Kilometres per litre (km/l)	X 2.352	= Miles per gallon, US (mpg)

Temperature

Degrees Fahrenheit = (°C x 1.8) + 32

Degrees Celsius (Degrees Centigrade; °C) = (°F - 32) x 0.56

It is common practice to convert from miles per gallon (mpg) to litres/100 kilometres (l/100km), where mpg (Imperial) x l/100 km = 282 and mpg (US) x l/100 km = 235

Fault diagnosis

Contents

Introduction

The vehicle owner who does his or her own maintenance according to the recommended service schedules should not have to use this section of the manual very often. Modern component reliability is such that, provided those items subject to wear or deterioration are inspected or renewed at the specified intervals, sudden failure is comparatively rare. Faults do not usually just happen as a result of sudden failure, but develop over a period of time. Major mechanical failures in particular are usually preceded by characteristic symptoms over hundreds or even thousands of miles. Those components which do occasionally fail without warning are often small and easily carried in the vehicle.

With any fault-finding, the first step is to decide where to begin investigations. Sometimes this is obvious, but on other occasions, a little detective work will be necessary. The owner who makes half a dozen haphazard adjustments or replacements may be successful in curing a fault (or its symptoms), but will be none the wiser if the fault recurs, and ultimately may have spent more time and money than was necessary.

A calm and logical approach will be found to be more satisfactory in the long run. Always take into account any warning signs or abnormalities that may have been noticed in the period preceding the fault - power loss, high or low gauge readings, unusual smells, etc - and remember that failure of components such as fuses or spark plugs may only be pointers to some underlying fault.

The pages which follow provide an easy-reference guide to the more common problems which may occur during the operation of the vehicle. These problems and their possible causes are grouped under headings denoting various components or systems, such as Engine, Cooling system, etc. The Chapter and/or Section which deals with the problem is also shown in brackets. Whatever the fault, certain basic principles apply. These are as follows:

Verify the fault. This is simply a matter of being sure that you know what the symptoms are before starting work. This is particularly important if you are investigating a fault for someone else, who may not have described it very accurately.

Don't overlook the obvious. For example, if the vehicle won't start, is there petrol in the tank? (Don't take anyone else's word on this particular point, and don't trust the fuel gauge either!) If an electrical fault is indicated, look for loose or broken wires before digging out the test gear.

Cure the disease, not the symptom. Substituting a flat battery with a fully-charged one will get you off the hard shoulder, but if the underlying cause is not attended to, the new battery will go the same way. Similarly, changing oil-fouled spark plugs for a new set will get you moving again, but remember that the reason for the fouling (if it wasn't simply an incorrect grade of plug) will have to be established and corrected.

Don't take anything for granted. Particularly, don't forget that a "new" component may itself be defective (especially if it's been rattling around in the boot for months), and don't leave components out of a fault diagnosis sequence just because they are new or recently-fitted. When you do finally diagnose a difficult fault, you'll probably realise that all the evidence was there from the start.

1   Engine

Engine fails to rotate when attempting to start
- Battery terminal connections loose or corroded (Chapter 1).
- Battery discharged or faulty (Chapter 5A).
- Broken, loose or disconnected wiring in the starting circuit (Chapter 5A).
- Defective starter solenoid or switch (Chapter 5A).
- Defective starter motor (Chapter 5A).
- Starter pinion or flywheel ring gear teeth loose or broken (Chapters 5A and 2A).
- Engine earth strap broken or disconnected (Chapter 5A).
- Automatic transmission not in Park/Neutral position or starter inhibitor switch faulty (Chapter 7B).

Engine rotates, but will not start
- Fuel tank empty.
- Battery discharged (engine rotates slowly) (Chapter 5A).
- Battery terminal connections loose or corroded (Chapter 1).
- Ignition components damp or damaged (Chapters 1, 5B and 5C).
- Broken, loose or disconnected wiring in the ignition circuit (Chapters 1, 5B and 5C).
- Worn, faulty or incorrectly-gapped spark plugs (Chapter 1).
- Fuel injection system fault (Chapter 4A).
- Major mechanical failure (eg camshaft drive) (Chapters 2A or 2B).

Engine difficult to start when cold
- Battery discharged (Chapter 5A).
- Battery terminal connections loose or corroded (Chapter 1).
- Worn, faulty or incorrectly-gapped spark plugs (Chapter 1).
- Fuel injection system fault (Chapter 4A).
- Other ignition system fault (Chapters 1, 5B and 5C).
- Low cylinder compressions (Chapter 2A).

Engine difficult to start when hot
- Air filter element dirty or clogged (Chapter 1).
- Fuel injection system fault (Chapter 4A).
- Low cylinder compressions (Chapter 2A).

Starter motor noisy or excessively-rough in engagement
- Starter pinion or flywheel ring gear teeth loose or broken (Chapters 5A and 2A).
- Starter motor mounting bolts loose or missing (Chapter 5A).
- Starter motor internal components worn or damaged (Chapter 5A).

Engine starts, but stops immediately
- Loose or faulty electrical connections in the ignition circuit (Chapters 1, 5B and 5C).
- Vacuum leak at the fuel injection unit/throttle body or inlet manifold (Chapter 4A).
- Fuel injection system fault (Chapter 4A).

Engine idles erratically
- Air filter element clogged (Chapter 1).
- Vacuum leak at the fuel injection unit/throttle body, inlet manifold or associated hoses (Chapter 4A).
- Worn, faulty or incorrectly-gapped spark plugs (Chapter 1).
- Uneven or low cylinder compressions (Chapter 2A).
- Camshaft lobes worn (Chapter 2A).
- Timing belt incorrectly tensioned (Chapter 2A).
- Fuel injection system fault (Chapter 4A).

Engine misfires at idle speed
- Worn, faulty or incorrectly-gapped spark plugs (Chapter 1).
- Faulty spark plug HT leads (Chapter 1).
- Engine management system fault (Chapters 1, 5B and 5C)
- Vacuum leak at the fuel injection unit/throttle body, inlet manifold or associated hoses (Chapter 4A).
- Distributor cap cracked or tracking internally - where applicable (Chapter 1).
- Uneven or low cylinder compressions (Chapter 2A).
- Disconnected, leaking, or perished crankcase ventilation hoses (Chapter 4B).
- Fuel injection system fault (Chapter 4A).

Engine misfires throughout the driving speed range
- Fuel filter choked (Chapter 1).
- Fuel pump faulty, or delivery pressure low (Chapter 4A).
- Fuel tank vent blocked, or fuel pipes restricted (Chapter 4A).
- Vacuum leak at the fuel injection unit/throttle body, inlet manifold or associated hoses (Chapter 4A).
- Worn, faulty or incorrectly-gapped spark plugs (Chapter 1).
- Faulty spark plug HT leads (Chapter 1).
- Distributor cap cracked or tracking internally - where applicable (Chapter 1).
- Faulty ignition coil or DIS module (Chapters 5B and 5C).
- Uneven or low cylinder compressions (Chapter 2A).
- Fuel injection system fault (Chapter 4A).

Engine hesitates on acceleration
- Worn, faulty or incorrectly-gapped spark plugs (Chapter 1).
- Vacuum leak at the fuel injection unit/throttle body, inlet manifold or associated hoses (Chapter 4A).
- Fuel injection system fault (Chapter 4A).

Engine stalls
- Vacuum leak at the fuel injection unit/throttle body, inlet manifold or associated hoses (Chapter 4A).
- Fuel filter choked (Chapter 1).
- Fuel pump faulty, or delivery pressure low (Chapter 4A).
- Fuel tank vent blocked, or fuel pipes restricted (Chapter 4A).
- Fuel injection system fault (Chapter 4A).

Engine lacks power
- Engine management system fault (Chapters 1, 5B and 5C)
- Timing belt incorrectly fitted or tensioned (Chapter 2A).
- Fuel filter choked (Chapter 1).
- Fuel pump faulty, or delivery pressure low (Chapter 4A).
- Uneven or low cylinder compressions (Chapter 2A).
- Worn, faulty or incorrectly-gapped spark plugs (Chapter 1).
- Vacuum leak at the fuel injection unit/throttle body, inlet manifold or associated hoses (Chapter 4A).
- Brakes binding (Chapters 1 and 9).
- Clutch slipping (Chapter 6).
- Automatic transmission fluid level incorrect (Chapter 1).
- Fuel injection system fault (Chapter 4A).

Engine backfires
- Engine management system fault (Chapters 1, 5B and 5C)
- Timing belt incorrectly fitted or tensioned (Chapter 2A).
- Vacuum leak at the fuel injection unit/throttle body, inlet manifold or associated hoses (Chapter 4A).
- Fuel injection system fault (Chapter 4A).

Oil pressure warning light illuminated with engine running
- Low oil level, or incorrect oil grade (Chapter 1).
- Faulty oil pressure sensor (Chapter 5A).
- Worn engine bearings and/or oil pump (Chapter 2B).
- High engine operating temperature (Chapter 3).
- Oil pressure relief valve defective (Chapter 2A).
- Oil pick-up strainer clogged (Chapter 2A).

Engine runs-on after switching off
- Excessive carbon build-up in engine (Chapter 2B).
- High engine operating temperature (Chapter 3).
- Fuel injection system fault (Chapter 4A).

Engine noises

Pre-ignition (pinking) or knocking during acceleration or under load
- Engine management system fault (Chapters 1, 5B and 5C)
- Incorrect grade of fuel (Chapter 1).
- Vacuum leak at the fuel injection unit/throttle body, inlet manifold or associated hoses (Chapter 4A).
- Excessive carbon build-up in engine (Chapter 2B).
- Worn or damaged distributor (where applicable) or other ignition system component (Chapters 5B and 5C).
- Fuel injection system fault (Chapter 4A).

Whistling or wheezing noises
- Leaking inlet manifold or fuel injection unit/throttle body gasket (Chapter 4A).
- Leaking exhaust manifold gasket or pipe-to-manifold joint (Chapter 4A).
- Leaking vacuum hose (Chapters 4A, 4B, 5A, 5B and 9).
- Blowing cylinder head gasket (Chapter 2A).

Tapping or rattling noises
- Worn valve gear or camshaft (Chapter 2A).
- Ancillary component fault (water pump, alternator, etc) (Chapters 3, 5A, etc).

Knocking or thumping noises
- Worn big-end bearings (regular heavy knocking, perhaps less under load) (Chapter 2B).
- Worn main bearings (rumbling and knocking, perhaps worsening under load) (Chapter 2B).
- Piston slap (most noticeable when cold) (Chapter 2B).
- Ancillary component fault (water pump, alternator, etc) (Chapters 3, 5A, etc).

2   Cooling system

Overheating
- Insufficient coolant in system (Chapter 1).
- Thermostat faulty (Chapter 3).
- Radiator core blocked, or grille restricted (Chapter 3).
- Electric cooling fan or thermoswitch faulty (Chapter 3).
- Pressure cap faulty (Chapter 3).
- Ignition timing incorrect (Engine management system fault) (Chapters 1, 5B and 5C).
- Inaccurate temperature gauge sender unit (Chapter 3).
- Airlock in cooling system (Chapter 1).

Overcooling
- Thermostat faulty (Chapter 3).
- Inaccurate temperature gauge sender unit (Chapter 3).

External coolant leakage
- Deteriorated or damaged hoses or hose clips (Chapter 1).
- Radiator core or heater matrix leaking (Chapter 3).
- Pressure cap faulty (Chapter 3).
- Water pump seal leaking (Chapter 3).
- Boiling due to overheating (Chapter 3).
- Core plug leaking (Chapter 2B).

Internal coolant leakage
- Leaking cylinder head gasket (Chapter 2A).
- Cracked cylinder head or cylinder bore (Chapter 2A).

Corrosion
- Infrequent draining and flushing (Chapter 1).
- Incorrect coolant mixture or inappropriate coolant type (Chapter 1).

3   Fuel and exhaust systems

Excessive fuel consumption
- Air filter element dirty or clogged (Chapter 1).
- Fuel injection system fault (Chapter 4A).
- Ignition timing incorrect (Engine management system fault) (Chapters 1, 5B and 5C).
- Tyres under-inflated (Chapter 1).

Fuel leakage and/or fuel odour
- Damaged or corroded fuel tank, pipes or connections (Chapter 4A).
- Fuel injection system fault (Chapter 4A).

Excessive noise or fumes from exhaust system
- Leaking exhaust system or manifold joints (Chapters 1 and 4A).
- Leaking, corroded or damaged silencers or pipe (Chapters 1 and 4A).
- Broken mountings causing body or suspension contact (Chapter 1).

4   Clutch

Pedal travels to floor - no pressure or very little resistance
- Broken clutch cable (Chapter 6).
- Incorrect clutch cable adjustment (Chapter 1).
- Broken clutch release bearing or fork (Chapter 6).
- Broken diaphragm spring in clutch pressure plate (Chapter 6).

Clutch fails to disengage (unable to select gears)
- Incorrect clutch cable adjustment (Chapter 1).

- Clutch disc sticking on gearbox input shaft splines (Chapter 6).
- Clutch disc sticking to flywheel or pressure plate (Chapter 6).
- Faulty pressure plate assembly (Chapter 6).
- Clutch release mechanism worn or incorrectly assembled (Chapter 6).

Clutch slips (engine speed increases, with no increase in vehicle speed)

- Incorrect clutch cable adjustment (Chapter 1).
- Clutch disc linings excessively worn (Chapter 6).
- Clutch disc linings contaminated with oil or grease (Chapter 6).
- Faulty pressure plate or weak diaphragm spring (Chapter 6).

Judder as clutch is engaged

- Clutch disc linings contaminated with oil or grease (Chapter 6).
- Clutch disc linings excessively worn (Chapter 6).
- Clutch cable sticking or frayed (Chapter 6).
- Faulty or distorted pressure plate or diaphragm spring (Chapter 6).
- Worn or loose engine or gearbox mountings (Chapter 2A).
- Clutch disc hub or gearbox input shaft splines worn (Chapter 6).

Noise when depressing or releasing clutch pedal

- Worn clutch release bearing (Chapter 6).
- Worn or dry clutch pedal bushes (Chapter 6).
- Faulty pressure plate assembly (Chapter 6).
- Pressure plate diaphragm spring broken (Chapter 6).
- Broken clutch disc cushioning springs (Chapter 6).

5 Manual gearbox

Noisy in neutral with engine running

- Input shaft bearings worn (noise apparent with clutch pedal released, but not when depressed) (Chapter 7A).*
- Clutch release bearing worn (noise apparent with clutch pedal depressed, possibly less when released) (Chapter 6).

Noisy in one particular gear

- Worn, damaged or chipped gear teeth (Chapter 7A).*

Difficulty engaging gears

- Clutch fault (Chapter 6).
- Worn or damaged gear linkage (Chapter 7A).
- Incorrectly-adjusted gear linkage (Chapter 7A).
- Worn synchroniser units (Chapter 7A).*

Jumps out of gear

- Worn or damaged gear linkage (Chapter 7A).
- Incorrectly-adjusted gear linkage (Chapter 7A).
- Worn synchroniser units (Chapter 7A).*
- Worn selector forks (Chapter 7A).*

Vibration

- Lack of oil (Chapter 1).
- Worn bearings (Chapter 7A).*

Lubricant leaks

- Leaking differential output oil seal (Chapter 7A).
- Leaking housing joint (Chapter 7A).*
- Leaking input shaft oil seal (Chapter 7A).*

*Although the corrective action necessary to remedy the symptoms described is beyond the scope of the home mechanic, the above information should be helpful in isolating the cause of the condition, so that the owner can communicate clearly with a professional mechanic.

6 Automatic transmission

Note: *Due to the complexity of the automatic transmission, it is difficult for the home mechanic to properly diagnose and service this unit. For problems other than the following, the vehicle should be taken to a dealer service department or automatic transmission specialist.*

Fluid leakage

- Automatic transmission fluid is usually deep red in colour. Fluid leaks should not be confused with engine oil, which can easily be blown onto the transmission by air flow.
- To determine the source of a leak, first remove all built-up dirt and grime from the transmission housing and surrounding areas, using a degreasing agent, or by steam-cleaning. Drive the vehicle at low speed, so air flow will not blow the leak far from its source. Raise and support the vehicle, and determine where the leak is coming from. The following are common areas of leakage.
  - (a) Oil pan.
  - (b) Dipstick tube (Chapter 1).
  - (c) Transmission-to-oil cooler fluid pipes/unions (Chapter 7B).

Transmission fluid brown, or has burned smell

- Transmission fluid level low, or fluid in need of renewal (Chapter 1).

General gear selection problems

- Chapter 7B deals with checking and adjusting the selector cable on automatic transmissions. The following are common problems which may be caused by a poorly-adjusted cable.
  - (a) Engine starting in gears other than Park or Neutral.
  - (b) Indicator on gear selector lever pointing to a gear other than the one actually being used.
  - (c) Vehicle moves when in Park or Neutral.
  - (d) Poor gearshift quality or erratic gearchanges.
- Refer to Chapter 7B for the selector cable adjustment procedure.

Transmission will not downshift (kickdown) with accelerator pedal fully depressed

- Low transmission fluid level (Chapter 1).
- Incorrect selector cable adjustment (Chapter 7B).

Engine will not start in any gear, or starts in gears other than Park or Neutral

- Incorrect starter inhibitor switch adjustment (Chapter 7B).
- Incorrect selector cable adjustment (Chapter 7B).

Transmission slips, shifts roughly, is noisy, or has no drive in forward or reverse gears

- There are many probable causes for the above problems, but the home mechanic should be concerned with only one possibility - fluid level. Before taking the vehicle to a dealer or transmission specialist, check the fluid level and condition of the fluid as described in Chapter 1. Correct the fluid level as necessary, or change the fluid and filter if needed. If the problem persists, professional help will be necessary.

7 Driveshafts

Clicking or knocking noise on turns (at slow speed on full-lock)

- Lack of constant velocity joint lubricant, possibly due to damaged gaiter (Chapter 8).
- Worn outer constant velocity joint (Chapter 8).

Vibration when accelerating or decelerating

- Worn inner constant velocity joint (Chapter 8).
- Bent or distorted driveshaft (Chapter 8).

8   Braking system

Note: *Before assuming that a brake problem exists, make sure that the tyres are in good condition and correctly inflated, that the front wheel alignment is correct, and that the vehicle is not loaded with weight in an unequal manner. Apart from checking the condition of all pipe and hose connections, any faults occurring on the anti-lock braking system should be referred to a Vauxhall/Opel dealer for diagnosis.*

Vehicle pulls to one side under braking

- Worn, defective, damaged or contaminated front brake pads or rear brake shoes on one side (Chapters 1 and 9).
- Seized or partially-seized front brake caliper or rear wheel cylinder piston (Chapters 1 and 9).
- A mixture of brake pad/shoe lining materials fitted between sides (Chapters 1 and 9).
- Front brake caliper mounting bolts loose (Chapter 9).
- Rear brake backplate mounting bolts loose (Chapter 9).
- Worn or damaged steering or suspension components (Chapters 1 and 10).

Noise (grinding or high-pitched squeal) when brakes applied

- Brake pad or shoe friction lining material worn down to metal backing (Chapters 1 and 9).
- Excessive corrosion of brake disc or drum. (May be apparent after the vehicle has been standing for some time (Chapters 1 and 9).
- Foreign object (stone chipping, etc) trapped between brake disc and shield (Chapters 1 and 9).

Excessive brake pedal travel

- Inoperative rear brake self-adjust mechanism (Chapters 1 and 9).
- Faulty master cylinder (Chapter 9).
- Air in hydraulic system (Chapters 1 and 9).
- Faulty vacuum servo unit (Chapter 9).

Brake pedal feels spongy when depressed

- Air in hydraulic system (Chapters 1 and 9).
- Deteriorated flexible rubber brake hoses (Chapters 1 and 9).
- Master cylinder mounting nuts loose (Chapter 9).
- Faulty master cylinder (Chapter 9).

Excessive brake pedal effort required to stop vehicle

- Faulty vacuum servo unit (Chapter 9).
- Disconnected, damaged or insecure brake servo vacuum hose (Chapter 9).
- Primary or secondary hydraulic circuit failure (Chapter 9).
- Seized brake caliper or wheel cylinder piston(s) (Chapter 9).
- Brake pads or brake shoes incorrectly fitted (Chapters 1 and 9).
- Incorrect grade of brake pads or brake shoes fitted (Chapters 1 and 9).
- Brake pads or brake shoe linings contaminated (Chapters 1 and 9).

Judder felt through brake pedal or steering wheel when braking

- Excessive run-out or distortion of front discs or rear drums (Chapters 1 and 9).
- Brake pad or brake shoe linings worn (Chapters 1 and 9).
- Brake caliper or rear brake backplate mounting bolts loose (Chapter 9).
- Wear in suspension or steering components or mountings (Chapters 1 and 10).

Brakes binding

- Seized brake caliper or wheel cylinder piston(s) (Chapter 9).
- Incorrectly-adjusted handbrake mechanism (Chapter 9).
- Faulty master cylinder (Chapter 9).

Rear wheels locking under normal braking

- Rear brake shoe linings contaminated (Chapters 1 and 9).
- Faulty brake pressure regulator (Chapter 9).

9   Suspension and steering

Note: *Before diagnosing suspension or steering faults, be sure that the trouble is not due to incorrect tyre pressures, mixtures of tyre types, or binding brakes.*

Vehicle pulls to one side

- Defective tyre (Chapter 1).
- Excessive wear in suspension or steering components (Chapters 1 and 10).
- Incorrect front wheel alignment (Chapter 10).
- Accident damage to steering or suspension components (Chapter 1).

Wheel wobble and vibration

- Front roadwheels out of balance (vibration felt mainly through the steering wheel) (Chapters 1 and 10).
- Rear roadwheels out of balance (vibration felt throughout the vehicle) (Chapters 1 and 10).
- Roadwheels damaged or distorted (Chapters 1 and 10).
- Faulty or damaged tyre (Chapter 1).
- Worn steering or suspension joints, bushes or components (Chapters 1 and 10).
- Wheel bolts loose (Chapters 1 and 10).

Excessive pitching and/or rolling around corners, or during braking

- Defective shock absorbers (Chapters 1 and 10).
- Broken or weak spring and/or suspension component (Chapters 1 and 10).
- Worn or damaged anti-roll bar or mountings (Chapter 10).

Wandering or general instability

- Incorrect front wheel alignment (Chapter 10).
- Worn steering or suspension joints, bushes or components (Chapters 1 and 10).
- Roadwheels out of balance (Chapters 1 and 10).
- Faulty or damaged tyre (Chapter 1).
- Wheel bolts loose (Chapters 1 and 10).
- Defective shock absorbers (Chapters 1 and 10).

Excessively-stiff steering

- Lack of steering gear lubricant (Chapter 10).
- Seized track rod end balljoint or suspension balljoint (Chapters 1 and 10).
- Broken or incorrectly-adjusted auxiliary drivebelt (Chapter 1).
- Incorrect front wheel alignment (Chapter 10).
- Steering rack or column bent or damaged (Chapter 10).

Excessive play in steering

- Worn steering column intermediate shaft universal joint (Chapter 10).
- Worn steering track rod end balljoints (Chapters 1 and 10).
- Worn rack-and-pinion steering gear (Chapter 10).
- Worn steering or suspension joints, bushes or components (Chapters 1 and 10).

Lack of power assistance

- Broken or incorrectly-adjusted auxiliary drivebelt (Chapter 1).
- Incorrect power steering fluid level (Chapter 1).
- Restriction in power steering fluid hoses (Chapter 1).
- Faulty power steering pump (Chapter 10).
- Faulty rack-and-pinion steering gear (Chapter 10).

Tyre wear excessive

Tyres worn on inside or outside edges
- Tyres under-inflated (wear on both edges) (Chapter 1).
- Incorrect camber or castor angles (wear on one edge only) (Chapter 10).
- Worn steering or suspension joints, bushes or components (Chapters 1 and 10).
- Excessively-hard cornering.
- Accident damage.

Tyre treads exhibit feathered edges
- Incorrect toe setting (Chapter 10).

Tyres worn in centre of tread
- Tyres over-inflated (Chapter 1).

Tyres worn on inside and outside edges
- Tyres under-inflated (Chapter 1).

Tyres worn unevenly
- Tyres/wheels out of balance (Chapter 1).
- Excessive wheel or tyre run-out (Chapter 1).
- Worn shock absorbers (Chapters 1 and 10).
- Faulty tyre (Chapter 1).

10   Electrical system

Note: *For problems associated with the starting system, refer to the faults listed under "Engine" earlier in this Section.*

Battery will not hold a charge for more than a few days
- Battery defective internally (Chapter 5A).
- Battery terminal connections loose or corroded (Chapter 1).
- Auxiliary drivebelt worn or incorrectly adjusted (Chapter 1).
- Alternator not charging at correct output (Chapter 5A).
- Alternator or voltage regulator faulty (Chapter 5A).
- Short-circuit causing continual battery drain (Chapters 5A and 12).

Ignition/no-charge warning light remains illuminated with engine running
- Auxiliary drivebelt broken, worn, or incorrectly adjusted (Chapter 1).
- Alternator brushes worn, sticking, or dirty (Chapter 5A).
- Alternator brush springs weak or broken (Chapter 5A).
- Internal fault in alternator or voltage regulator (Chapter 5A).
- Broken, disconnected, or loose wiring in charging circuit (Chapter 5A).

Ignition/no-charge warning light fails to come on
- Warning light bulb blown (Chapter 12).
- Broken, disconnected, or loose wiring in warning light circuit (Chapter 12).
- Alternator faulty (Chapter 5A).

Lights inoperative
- Bulb blown (Chapter 12).
- Corrosion of bulb or bulbholder contacts (Chapter 12).
- Blown fuse (Chapter 12).
- Faulty relay (Chapter 12).
- Broken, loose, or disconnected wiring (Chapter 12).
- Faulty switch (Chapter 12).

Instrument readings inaccurate or erratic

Instrument readings increase with engine speed
- Faulty voltage regulator (Chapter 12).

Fuel or temperature gauges give no reading
- Faulty gauge sender unit (Chapters 3 or 4A).
- Wiring open-circuit (Chapter 12).
- Faulty gauge (Chapter 12).

Fuel or temperature gauges give continuous maximum reading
- Faulty gauge sender unit (Chapters 3 or 4A).
- Wiring short-circuit (Chapter 12).
- Faulty gauge (Chapter 12).

Horn inoperative, or unsatisfactory in operation

Horn operates all the time
- Horn push either earthed or stuck down (Chapter 12).
- Horn cable-to-horn push earthed (Chapter 12).

Horn fails to operate
- Blown fuse (Chapter 12).
- Cable or cable connections loose, broken or disconnected (Chapter 12).
- Faulty horn (Chapter 12).

Horn emits intermittent or unsatisfactory sound
- Cable connections loose (Chapter 12).
- Horn mountings loose (Chapter 12).
- Faulty horn (Chapter 12).

Windscreen/tailgate wipers inoperative, or unsatisfactory in operation

Wipers fail to operate, or operate very slowly
- Wiper blades stuck to screen, or linkage seized or binding (Chapters 1 and 12).
- Blown fuse (Chapter 12).
- Cable or cable connections loose, broken or disconnected (Chapter 12).
- Faulty relay (Chapter 12).
- Faulty wiper motor (Chapter 12).

Wiper blades sweep over too large or too small an area of the glass
- Wiper arms incorrectly positioned on spindles (Chapter 1).
- Excessive wear of wiper linkage (Chapter 12).
- Wiper motor or linkage mountings loose or insecure (Chapter 12).

Wiper blades fail to clean the glass effectively
- Wiper blade rubbers worn or perished (Chapter 1).
- Wiper arm tension springs broken, or arm pivots seized (Chapter 12).
- Insufficient windscreen washer additive to adequately remove road film (Chapter 1).

Windscreen/tailgate washers inoperative, or unsatisfactory in operation

One or more washer jets inoperative
- Blocked washer jet (Chapter 1).
- Disconnected, kinked or restricted fluid hose (Chapter 12).
- Insufficient fluid in washer reservoir (Chapter 1).

Washer pump fails to operate
- Broken or disconnected wiring or connections (Chapter 12).
- Blown fuse (Chapter 12).
- Faulty washer switch (Chapter 12).
- Faulty washer pump (Chapter 12).

Washer pump runs for some time before fluid is emitted from jets
- Faulty one-way valve in fluid supply hose (Chapter 12).

Electric windows inoperative, or unsatisfactory in operation

Window glass will only move in one direction

- Faulty switch (Chapter 12)

Window glass slow to move

- Incorrectly-adjusted door glass guide channels (Chapter 11).
- Regulator seized or damaged, or in need of lubrication (Chapter 11).
- Door internal components or trim fouling regulator (Chapter 11).
- Faulty motor (Chapter 11).

Window glass fails to move

- Incorrectly-adjusted door glass guide channels (Chapter 11).
- Blown fuse (Chapter 12).
- Faulty relay (Chapter 12).
- Broken or disconnected wiring or connections (Chapter 12).
- Faulty motor (Chapter 11).

Central locking system inoperative, or unsatisfactory in operation

Complete system failure

- Blown fuse (Chapter 12).
- Faulty relay (Chapter 12).
- Broken or disconnected wiring or connections (Chapter 12).
- Faulty control unit (Chapter 11).

Latch locks but will not unlock, or unlocks but will not lock

- Faulty master switch (Chapter 12).
- Broken or disconnected latch operating rods or levers (Chapter 11).
- Faulty relay (Chapter 12).
- Faulty control unit (Chapter 11).

One solenoid/motor fails to operate

- Broken or disconnected wiring or connections (Chapter 12).
- Faulty solenoid/motor (Chapter 11).
- Broken, binding or disconnected latch operating rods or levers (Chapter 11).
- Fault in door latch (Chapter 11).

MOT test checks

Introduction

Motor vehicle testing has been compulsory in Great Britain since 1960, when the Motor Vehicle (Tests) Regulations were first introduced. At that time, testing was only applicable to vehicles ten years old or older, and the test itself only covered lighting equipment, braking systems and steering gear. Current vehicle testing is far more extensive and, in the case of private vehicles, is now an annual inspection commencing three years after the date of first registration. Test standards are becoming increasingly stringent; for details of changes consult the latest edition of the MOT Inspection Manual (available from HMSO or bookshops).

This section is intended as a guide to getting your vehicle through the MOT test. It lists all the relevant testable items, how to check them yourself, and what is likely to cause the vehicle to fail. Obviously it will not be possible to examine the vehicle to the same standard as the professional MOT tester, who will be highly experienced in this work, and will have all the necessary equipment available. However, working through the following checks will provide a good indication as to the condition of the vehicle, and will enable you to identify any problem areas before submitting the vehicle for the test. Where a component is found to need repair or renewal, reference should be made to the appropriate Chapter in the manual, where further information will be found.

The following checks have been sub-divided into four categories as follows.

(a) *Checks carried out from the driver's seat.*
(b) *Checks carried out with the vehicle on the ground.*
(c) *Checks carried out with the vehicle raised and with the wheels free to rotate.*
(d) *Exhaust emission checks.*

In most cases, the help of an assistant will be necessary to carry out these checks thoroughly.

Checks carried out from the driver's seat

Handbrake (Chapter 9)

Test the operation of the handbrake by pulling on the lever until the handbrake is in the normal fully-applied position. Ensure that the travel of the lever (the number of clicks of the ratchet) is not excessive before full resistance of the braking mechanism is felt. If so, this would indicate incorrect adjustment of the rear brakes, or incorrectly-adjusted handbrake cables.

With the handbrake fully applied, tap the lever sideways, and make sure that it does not release, which would indicate wear in the ratchet and pawl. Release the handbrake, and move the lever from side to side to check for excessive wear in the pivot bearing. Check the security of the lever mountings, and make sure that there is no corrosion of any part of the body structure within 30 cm of the lever mounting. If the lever mountings cannot be readily seen from inside the vehicle, carry out this check later when working underneath.

Footbrake (Chapter 9)

Check that the brake pedal is sound, without visible defects such as excessive wear of the pivot bushes, or broken or damaged pedal pad. Check also for signs of fluid leaks on the pedal, floor or carpets, which would indicate failed seals in the brake master cylinder.

Depress the brake pedal slowly at first, then rapidly until sustained pressure can be held. Maintain this pressure, and check that the pedal does not creep down to the floor, which would again indicate problems with the master cylinder. Release the pedal, wait a few seconds, then depress it once until firm resistance is felt. Check that this resistance occurs near the top of the pedal travel. If the pedal travels nearly to the floor before firm resistance is felt, this would indicate incorrect brake adjustment, resulting in "insufficient reserve travel" of the footbrake. If firm resistance cannot be felt, ie the pedal feels spongy, this would indicate that air is present in the hydraulic system, which will necessitate complete bleeding of the system.

Check that the servo unit is operating correctly, by depressing the brake pedal several times to exhaust the vacuum. Keep the pedal depressed, and start the engine. As soon as the engine starts, the brake pedal resistance will be felt to alter. If this is not the case, there may be a leak from the brake servo vacuum hose, or the servo unit itself may be faulty.

Steering wheel and column (Chapter 10)

Examine the steering wheel for fractures or looseness of the hub, spokes or rim. Move the steering wheel from side to side and then up and down, in relation to the steering column. Check that the steering wheel is not loose on the column, indicating wear in the column splines, or a loose steering wheel retaining nut. Continue moving the steering wheel as before, but also turn it slightly from left to right. Check that there is no abnormal movement of the steering wheel, indicating excessive wear in the column upper support bearing, universal joint(s) or flexible coupling.

Windscreen and mirrors (Chapter 11)

The windscreen must be free of cracks or other damage which will seriously interfere with the driver's field of view, or which will prevent the windscreen wipers from operating properly. Small stone chips are acceptable. Any stickers, dangling toys or similar items must also be clear of the field of view.

Rear view mirrors must be secure, intact, and capable of being adjusted. The nearside (passenger side) door mirror is not included in the test, unless the interior mirror cannot be used - for instance, in the case of a van with blacked-out rear windows.

Seat belts and seats (Chapter 11)

Note: *The following checks are applicable to all seat belts, front and rear. Front seat belts must be of a type that will restrain the upper part of the body; lap belts are not acceptable. Various combinations of seat belt types are acceptable at the rear.*

Carefully examine the seat belt webbing for cuts or any signs of serious fraying or deterioration. If the seat belt is of the retractable type, pull the belt all the way out, and examine the full extent of the webbing.

Fasten and unfasten the belt, ensuring that the locking mechanism holds securely and releases properly when intended. If the belt is of the retractable type, check also that the retracting mechanism operates correctly when the belt is released.

Check the security of all seat belt mountings and attachments which are accessible, without removing any trim or other components, from inside the vehicle **(see illustration)**. Any serious corrosion, fracture or distortion of the body structure within 30 cm of any mounting point will cause the vehicle to fail. Certain anchorages will not be accessible or even visible from inside the vehicle; in this instance, further

Check the security of all seat belt mountings - upper mounting shown, with trim cover removed

checks should be carried out later, when working underneath. If any part of the seat belt mechanism is attached to the front seat, then the seat mountings are treated as anchorages, and must also comply as above.

The front seats themselves must be securely attached so that they cannot move unexpectedly, and the backrests must lock in the upright position.

Doors (Chapter 11)

Both front doors must be able to be opened and closed from outside and inside, and must latch securely when closed. In the case of a pick-up, the tailgate must be securely attached, and capable of being securely fastened.

Electrical equipment (Chapter 12)

Switch on the ignition and operate the horn. The horn must operate, and produce a clear sound audible to other road users. Note that a gong, siren or two-tone horn fitted as an alternative to the manufacturer's original equipment is not acceptable.

Check the operation of the windscreen washers and wipers. The washers must operate with adequate flow and pressure, and with the jets adjusted so that the liquid strikes the windscreen near the top of the glass.

Operate the windscreen wipers in conjunction with the washers, and check that the blades cover their designed sweep of the windscreen without smearing. The blades must effectively clean the glass, so that the driver has an adequate view of the road ahead and to the front nearside and offside of the vehicle. If the screen smears or does not clean adequately, it is advisable to renew the wiper blades before the MOT test.

Depress the footbrake with the ignition switched on, and have your assistant check that both rear stop-lights operate, and are extinguished when the footbrake is released. If one stop-light fails to operate, it is likely that a bulb has blown, or that there is a poor electrical contact at, or near, the bulbholder. If both stop-lights fail to operate, check for a blown fuse, faulty or incorrectly-adjusted stop-light switch, or possibly two blown bulbs. If the lights stay on when the brake pedal is released, it is possible that the switch is at fault.

Checks carried out with the vehicle on the ground

Vehicle identification

Front and rear number plates must be in good condition, securely fitted, and easily read. Letters and numbers must be correctly spaced, with the gap between the group of numbers and the group of letters at least double the gap between adjacent numbers and letters.

The vehicle identification number on the plate under the bonnet must be legible. It will be checked during the test, as part of the measures taken to prevent the fraudulent acquisition of certificates.

Electrical equipment (Chapter 12)

Switch on the sidelights, and check that both front and rear sidelights and the number plate lights are illuminated, and that the lenses and reflectors are secure and undamaged. This is particularly important at the rear, where a cracked or damaged lens would allow a white light to show to the rear, which is unacceptable. Note in addition that any lens that is excessively dirty, either inside or out, such that the light intensity is reduced, could also constitute a fail.

Switch on the headlights, and check that both dipped beam and main beam units are operating correctly and at the same light intensity. If either headlight shows signs of dimness, this is usually attributable to a poor earth connection or severely corroded internal reflector. Inspect the headlight lenses for cracks or stone damage. Any damage to the headlight lens will normally constitute a fail, but this is very much down to the tester's discretion. Bear in mind that with all light units, they must operate correctly when first switched on. It is not acceptable to tap a light unit to make it operate.

The headlights must not only be aligned so as not to dazzle other road users when switched to dipped beam, but also so as to provide

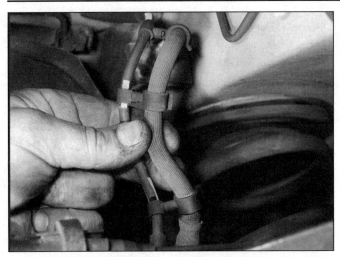

Check the braking system pipes and hoses for signs of damage or deterioration

Examine the steering rack rubber gaiters for condition and security

adequate illumination of the road. This can only be accurately checked using optical beam-setting equipment, so if you have any doubts about the headlight alignment, it is advisable to have this professionally checked and if necessary reset, before the MOT test.

With the ignition switched on, operate the direction indicators and check that they show amber lights to the front and to the rear, that they flash at the rate of between one and two flashes per second, and that the "tell-tale" on the instrument panel also functions. Operation of the sidelights and stop-lights must not affect the indicators - if it does, the cause is usually a bad earth at the rear light cluster. Similarly check the operation of the hazard warning lights, which must work with the ignition on and off. Examine the lenses for cracks or damage as described previously.

Check the operation of the rear foglight(s). The test only concerns itself with the statutorily-required foglight, which is the one on the offside (driver's side). The light must be secure, and emit a steady red light. The warning light on the instrument panel or in the switch must also work.

Footbrake (Chapter 9)

From within the engine compartment, examine the brake pipes for signs of leaks, corrosion, insecurity, chafing or other damage. Check the master cylinder and servo unit for leaks, security of their mountings, or excessive corrosion in the vicinity of the mountings. The master cylinder reservoir must be secure; if it is of the translucent type, the fluid level must be between the upper and lower level markings.

Turn the steering as necessary so that the right-hand front brake flexible hose can be examined. Inspect the hose carefully for any sign of cracks or deterioration of the rubber. This will be most noticeable if the hose is bent slightly, and is particularly common where the rubber portion enters the metal end fitting **(see illustration)**. Turn the steering onto full-left then full-right lock, and ensure that the hose does not contact the wheel, tyre, or any part of the steering or suspension mechanism. While your assistant depresses the brake pedal firmly, check the hose for any bulges or fluid leaks under pressure. Now repeat these checks on the left-hand front hose. Should any damage or deterioration be noticed, renew the hose.

Steering mechanism and suspension (Chapter 10)

Have your assistant turn the steering wheel from side to side slightly, up to the point where the steering gear just begins to transmit this movement to the roadwheels. Check for excessive free play between the steering wheel and the steering gear, which would indicate wear in the steering column joints, wear or insecurity of the steering column-to-steering gear coupling, or insecurity, incorrect adjustment, or wear in the steering gear itself. Generally speaking, free play greater than 1.3 cm for vehicles with rack-and-pinion type steering, or 7.6 cm for vehicles with steering box mechanisms, should be considered excessive.

Have your assistant turn the steering wheel more vigorously in each direction, up to the point where the roadwheels just begin to turn. As this is done, carry out a complete examination of all the steering joints, linkages, fittings and attachments. Any component that shows signs of wear, damage, distortion, or insecurity should be renewed or attended to accordingly. On vehicles equipped with power steering, also check that the power steering pump is secure, that the pump drivebelt is in satisfactory condition and correctly adjusted, that there are no fluid leaks or damaged hoses, and that the system operates correctly. Additional checks can be carried out later with the vehicle raised, when there will be greater working clearance underneath.

Check that the vehicle is standing level, and at approximately the correct ride height. Ensure that there is sufficient clearance between the suspension components and the bump stops to allow full suspension travel over bumps.

Shock absorbers (Chapter 10)

Depress each corner of the vehicle in turn, and then release it. If the shock absorbers are in good condition, the corner of the vehicle will rise and then settle in its normal position. If there is no noticeable damping effect from the shock absorber, and the vehicle continues to rise and fall, then the shock absorber is defective, and the vehicle will fail. A shock absorber which has seized will also cause the vehicle to fail.

Exhaust system (Chapter 4A)

Start the engine, and with your assistant holding a rag over the tailpipe, check the entire system for leaks, which will appear as a rhythmic fluffing or hissing sound at the source of the leak. Check the effectiveness of the silencer by ensuring that the noise produced is of a level to be expected from a vehicle of similar type. Providing that the system is structurally sound, it is acceptable to cure a leak using a proprietary exhaust system repair kit or similar method.

Checks carried out with the vehicle raised and with the wheels free to rotate

Jack up the front and rear of the vehicle, and securely support it on axle stands positioned at suitable load-bearing points under the vehicle structure. Position the stands clear of the suspension assemblies, ensure that the wheels are clear of the ground, and that the steering can be turned onto full-right and -left lock.

Steering mechanism (Chapter 10)

Examine the steering rack rubber gaiters for signs of splits, lubricant leakage, or insecurity of the retaining clips **(see illustration)**. If power steering is fitted, check for signs of deterioration, damage, chafing or leakage of the fluid hoses, pipes or connections. Also check for excessive stiffness or binding of the steering, a missing split pin or

Shake the roadwheel vigorously to check for excess play in the wheel bearings and suspension components

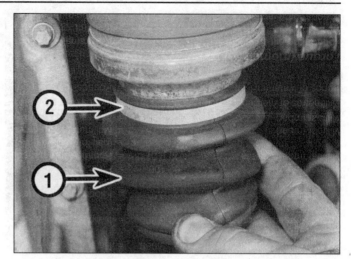

Inspect the constant velocity joint gaiters (1) and retaining clips (2)

locking device, or any severe corrosion of the body structure within 30 cm of any steering component attachment point.

Have your assistant turn the steering onto full-left then full-right lock. Check that the steering turns smoothly, without undue tightness or roughness, and that no part of the steering mechanism, including a wheel or tyre, fouls any brake flexible or rigid hose or pipe, or any part of the body structure.

On vehicles with four-wheel steering, similar considerations apply to the rear wheel steering linkages. However, it is permissible for a rear wheel steering system to be inoperative, provided that the rear wheels are secured in the straight-ahead position, and that the front wheel steering system is operating effectively.

Front and rear suspension and wheel bearings (Chapter 10)

Starting at the front right-hand side of the vehicle, grasp the road-wheel at the 3 o'clock and 9 o'clock positions, and shake it vigorously. Check for any free play at the wheel bearings, suspension balljoints, or suspension mountings, pivots and attachments. Check also for any serious deterioration of the rubber or metal casing of any mounting bushes, or any distortion, deformation or severe corrosion of any components. Look for missing split pins, tab washers or other locking devices on any mounting or attachment, or any severe corrosion of the vehicle structure within 30 cm of any suspension component attachment point.

If any excess free play is suspected at a component pivot point, this can be confirmed by using a large screwdriver or similar tool and levering between the mounting and the component attachment. This will confirm whether the wear is in the pivot bush, its retaining bolt, or in the mounting itself (the bolt holes can often become elongated).

Now grasp the wheel at the 12 o'clock and 6 o'clock positions, shake it vigorously, and repeat the previous inspection **(see illustration)**. Rotate the wheel, and check for roughness or tightness of the front wheel bearing such that imminent failure of the bearing is indicated.

Carry out all the above checks at the other front wheel, and then at both rear wheels.

Roadsprings and shock absorbers (Chapter 10)

On vehicles with strut type suspension units, examine the strut assembly for signs of serious fluid leakage, corrosion, or severe pitting of the piston rod or damage to the casing. Check also for security of the mounting points.

If coil springs are fitted, check that the spring ends locate correctly in their spring seats, that there is no severe corrosion of the spring, and that it is not cracked, broken, or in any way damaged.

If the vehicle is fitted with leaf springs, check that all leaves are intact, that the axle is securely attached to each spring, and that there is no wear or deterioration of the spring eye mountings, bushes, and shackles.

The same general checks apply to vehicles fitted with other suspension types, such as torsion bars, hydraulic displacer units, etc. In all cases, ensure that all mountings and attachments are secure, that there are no signs of excessive wear, corrosion, cracking, deformation or damage to any component or bush, and that there are no fluid leaks or damaged hoses or pipes (hydraulic types).

Inspect the shock absorbers for signs of serious fluid leakage. (Slight seepage of fluid is normal for some types of shock absorber, and is not a reason for failing.) Check for excessive wear of the mounting bushes or attachments, or damage to the body of the unit.

Driveshafts (Chapter 8)

With the steering turned onto full-lock, rotate each front wheel in turn, and inspect the constant velocity joint gaiters for splits or damage **(see illustration)**. Also check the gaiter is securely attached to its respective housings by clips or other methods of retention.

Continue turning the wheel, and check that each driveshaft is straight, with no sign of damage.

Braking system (Chapter 9)

If possible without dismantling, check for wear of the brake pads and the condition of the discs. Ensure that the friction lining material has not worn excessively, and that the discs are not fractured, pitted, scored or worn excessively.

Carefully examine all the rigid brake pipes underneath the vehicle, and the flexible hoses at the rear. Look for signs of excessive corrosion, chafing or insecurity of the pipes, and for signs of bulging under pressure, chafing, splits or deterioration of the flexible hoses.

Look for signs of hydraulic fluid leaks at the brake calipers or on the brake backplates, indicating failed hydraulic seals in the components concerned.

Slowly spin each wheel, while your assistant depresses the foot-brake then releases it. Ensure that each brake is operating, and that the wheel is free to rotate when the pedal is released. It is not possible to test brake efficiency without special equipment, but (traffic and local conditions permitting) a road test can be carried out to check that the vehicle pulls up in a straight line.

Examine the handbrake mechanism, checking for signs of frayed or broken cables, excessive corrosion, or wear or insecurity of the linkage **(see illustration)**. Have your assistant operate the handbrake, while you check that the mechanism works on each relevant wheel, and releases fully, without binding.

Fuel and exhaust systems (Chapter 4A)

Inspect the fuel tank, fuel pipes, hoses and unions (including the unions at the pump, filter and carburettor). All components must be secure, and free from leaks. The fuel filler cap must also be secure, and of an appropriate type.

Examine the exhaust system over its entire length checking for

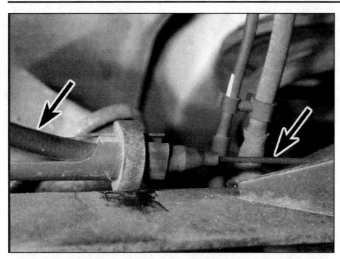

Check the handbrake cables (arrowed) for signs of fraying, and for secure mounting

Check the condition of the exhaust system, paying particular attention to the mountings (arrowed)

any damaged, broken or missing mountings, security of the pipe retaining clamps, and condition of the system with regard to rust and corrosion **(see illustration)**.

Wheels and tyres (Chapter 10)

Carefully examine each tyre in turn, on both the inner and outer walls, and over the whole of the tread area. Check for signs of cuts, tears, lumps, bulges, separation of the tread, and exposure of the ply or cord due to wear or other damage. Check also that the tyre bead is correctly seated on the wheel rim, and that the tyre valve is sound and properly seated. Spin the wheel, and check that it is not excessively distorted or damaged, particularly at the bead rim.

Check that the tyres are of the correct size for the vehicle, and that they are of the same size and type on each axle. (Having a "space saver" spare tyre in use is not acceptable.) The tyres should also be inflated to the specified pressures.

Using a suitable gauge, check the tyre tread depth. The current legal requirement states that the tread pattern must be visible over the whole tread area, and must be of a minimum depth of 1.6 mm over at least three-quarters of the tread width. It is acceptable for some wear of the inside or outside edges of the tyre to be apparent, but this wear must be in one even circumferential band, and the tread must be visible. Any excessive wear of this nature may indicate incorrect front wheel alignment, which should be checked before the tyre becomes excessively worn. See the appropriate Chapters for further information on tyre wear patterns and front wheel alignment.

Body corrosion (Chapter 11)

Check the condition of the entire vehicle structure for signs of corrosion in any load-bearing areas. For the purpose of the MOT test, all chassis box sections, side sills, crossmembers, pillars, suspension, steering, braking system and seat belt mountings and anchorages should all be considered as load-bearing areas. As a general guide, any corrosion which has seriously reduced the metal thickness of a load-bearing area to weaken it, is likely to cause the vehicle to fail. Should corrosion of this nature be encountered, professional repairs are likely to be needed.

Body damage or corrosion which causes sharp or otherwise dangerous edges to be exposed will also cause the vehicle to fail.

Exhaust emission checks

Have the engine at normal operating temperature, and make sure that the preliminary conditions for checking idle speed and mixture (ignition system in good order, air filter element clean, etc) have been met.

Before any measurements are carried out, raise the engine speed to around 2500 rpm, and hold it at this speed for 20 seconds. Allow the engine speed to return to idle, and watch for smoke emissions from the exhaust tailpipe. If the idle speed is obviously much too high, or if dense blue or clearly-visible black smoke comes from the tailpipe for more than 5 seconds, the vehicle will fail. As a rule of thumb, blue smoke signifies oil being burnt (worn valve stem oil seals, valve guides, piston rings or bores) while black smoke signifies unburnt fuel (dirty air cleaner element, mixture extremely rich, or other carburettor or fuel injection system fault).

If idle speed and smoke emission are satisfactory, an exhaust gas analyser capable of measuring carbon monoxide (CO) and hydrocarbons (HC) is now needed. The following paragraphs assume that such an instrument can be hired or borrowed - it is unlikely to be economic for the home mechanic to buy one. Alternatively, a local garage may agree to perform the check for a small fee.

CO emissions (mixture)

Current MOT regulations specify a maximum CO level at idle of 4.5% for vehicles first used after August 1983. The CO level specified by the vehicle maker is well inside this limit.

If the CO level cannot be reduced far enough to pass the test (and assuming that the fuel and ignition systems are otherwise in good condition) it is probable that the carburettor is badly worn, or that there is some problem in the fuel injection system. On carburettors with an automatic choke, it may be that the choke is not releasing as it should.

It is possible for the CO level to be within the specified maximum for MOT purposes, but well above the maximum specified by the manufacturer. The tester is entitled to draw attention to this, but it is not in itself a reason for failing the vehicle.

HC emissions

With the CO emissions within limits, HC emissions must be no more than 1200 ppm (parts per million). If the vehicle fails this test at idle, it can be re-tested at around 2000 rpm; if the HC level is then 1200 ppm or less, this counts as a pass.

Excessive HC emissions can be caused by oil being burnt, but they are more likely to be due to unburnt fuel. Possible reasons include:

(a) *Spark plugs in poor condition or incorrectly gapped.*
(b) *Ignition timing incorrect.*
(c) *Valve clearances incorrect.*
(d) *Engine compression low.*

Note that excessive HC levels in the exhaust gas can cause premature failure of the catalytic converter (when fitted).

Notes

Are your plugs trying to tell you something?

Normal.
Grey-brown deposits, lightly coated core nose. Plugs ideally suited to engine, and engine in good condition.

Heavy Deposits.
A build up of crusty deposits, light-grey sandy colour in appearance.
Fault: Often caused by worn valve guides, excessive use of upper cylinder lubricant, or idling for long periods.

Lead Glazing.
Plug insulator firing tip appears yellow or green/yellow and shiny in appearance.
Fault: Often caused by incorrect carburation, excessive idling followed by sharp acceleration. Also check ignition timing.

Carbon fouling.
Dry, black, sooty deposits.
Fault: over-rich fuel mixture.
Check: carburettor mixture settings, float level, choke operation, air filter.

Oil fouling.
Wet, oily deposits. Fault: worn bores/piston rings or valve guides; sometimes occurs (temporarily) during running-in period.

Overheating.
Electrodes have glazed appearance, core nose very white – few deposits. Fault: plug overheating. Check: plug value, ignition timing, fuel octane rating (too low) and fuel mixture (too weak).

Electrode damage.
Electrodes burned away; core nose has burned, glazed appearance. Fault: pre-ignition. Check: for correct heat range and as for 'overheating'.

Split core nose.
(May appear initially as a crack). Fault: detonation or wrong gap-setting technique. Check: ignition timing, cooling system, fuel mixture (too weak).

WHY DOUBLE COPPER IS BETTER FOR YOUR ENGINE.

Unique Trapezoidal Copper Cored Earth Electrode — 50% Larger Spark Area — Copper Cored Centre Electrode

Champion Double Copper plugs are the first in the world to have copper core in both centre <u>and</u> earth electrode. This innovative design means that they run cooler by up to 100°C – giving greater efficiency and longer life. These double copper cores transfer heat away from the tip of the plug faster and more efficiently. Therefore, Double Copper runs at cooler temperatures than conventional plugs giving improved acceleration response and high speed performance with no fear of pre-ignition.

TRAPEZOIDAL COPPER CORED EARTH ELECTRODE
50% INCREASE IN SPARK AREA

EARTH ELECTRODE TEMPERATURE VS ENGINE SPEED

Champion Double Copper plugs also feature a unique trapezoidal earth electrode giving a 50% increase in spark area. This, together with the double copper cores, offers greatly reduced electrode wear, so the spark stays stronger for longer.

 FASTER COLD STARTING

 **FOR UNLEADED OR LEADED FUEL**

 **ELECTRODES UP TO 100°C COOLER**

 BETTER ACCELERATION RESPONSE

 LOWER EMISSIONS

 50% BIGGER SPARK AREA

 THE LONGER LIFE PLUG

Plug Tips/Hot and Cold.
Spark plugs must operate within well-defined temperature limits to avoid cold fouling at one extreme and overheating at the other.
Champion and the car manufacturers work out the best plugs for an engine to give optimum performance under all conditions, from freezing cold starts to sustained high speed motorway cruising.
Plugs are often referred to as hot or cold. With Champion, the higher the number on its body, the hotter the plug, and the lower the number the cooler the plug.

Plug Cleaning
Modern plug design and materials mean that Champion no longer recommends periodic plug cleaning. Certainly don't clean your plugs with a wire brush as this can cause metal conductive paths across the nose of the insulator so impairing its performance and resulting in loss of acceleration and reduced m.p.g.
However, if plugs are removed, always carefully clean the area where the plug seats in the cylinder head as grit and dirt can sometimes cause gas leakage.
Also wipe any traces of oil or grease from plug leads as this may lead to arcing.

CHAMPION

D O U B L E 〓 C O P P E R

This photographic sequence shows the steps taken to repair the dent and paintwork damage shown above. In general, the procedure for repairing a hole will be similar; where there are substantial differences, the procedure is clearly described and shown in a separate photograph.

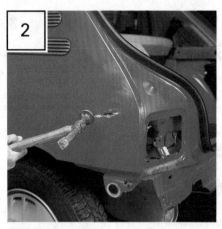

First remove any trim around the dent, then hammer out the dent where access is possible. This will minimise filling. Here, after the large dent has been hammered out, the damaged area is being made slightly concave.

Next, remove all paint from the damaged area by rubbing with coarse abrasive paper or using a power drill fitted with a wire brush or abrasive pad. 'Feather' the edge of the boundary with good paintwork using a finer grade of abrasive paper.

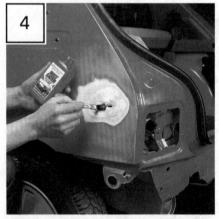

Where there are holes or other damage, the sheet metal should be cut away before proceeding further. The damaged area and any signs of rust should be treated with Turtle Wax Hi-Tech Rust Eater, which will also inhibit further rust formation.

For a large dent or hole mix Holts Body Plus Resin and Hardener according to the manufacturer's instructions and apply around the edge of the repair. Press Glass Fibre Matting over the repair area and leave for 20-30 minutes to harden. Then ...

... brush more Holts Body Plus Resin and Hardener onto the matting and leave to harden. Repeat the sequence with two or three layers of matting, checking that the final layer is lower than the surrounding area. Apply Holts Body Plus Filler Paste as shown in Step 5B.

For a medium dent, mix Holts Body Plus Filler Paste and Hardener according to the manufacturer's instructions and apply it with a flexible applicator. Apply thin layers of filler at 20-minute intervals, until the filler surface is slightly proud of the surrounding bodywork.

For small dents and scratches use Holts No Mix Filler Paste straight from the tube. Apply it according to the instructions in thin layers, using the spatula provided. It will harden in minutes if applied outdoors and may then be used as its own knifing putty.

Use a plane or file for initial shaping. Then, using progressively finer grades of wet-and-dry paper, wrapped round a sanding block, and copious amounts of clean water, rub down the filler until glass smooth. 'Feather' the edges of adjoining paintwork.

7

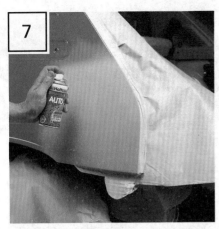

Protect adjoining areas before spraying the whole repair area and at least one inch of the surrounding sound paintwork with Holts Dupli-Color primer.

8

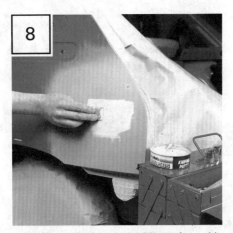

Fill any imperfections in the filler surface with a small amount of Holts Body Plus Knifing Putty. Using plenty of clean water, rub down the surface with a fine grade wet-and-dry paper – 400 grade is recommended – until it is really smooth.

9

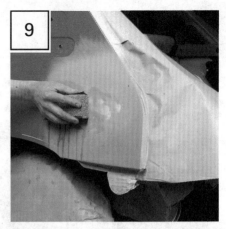

Carefully fill any remaining imperfections with knifing putty before applying the last coat of primer. Then rub down the surface with Holts Body Plus Rubbing Compound to ensure a really smooth surface.

10

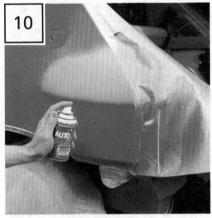

Protect surrounding areas from overspray before applying the topcoat in several thin layers. Agitate Holts Dupli-Color aerosol thoroughly. Start at the repair centre, spraying outwards with a side-to-side motion.

10A

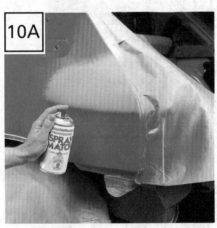

If the exact colour is not available off the shelf, local Holts Professional Spraymatch Centres will custom fill an aerosol to match perfectly.

10B

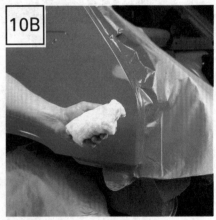

To identify whether a lacquer finish is required, rub a painted unrepaired part of the body with wax and a clean cloth.

11

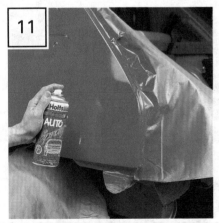

If *no* traces of paint appear on the cloth, spray Holts Dupli-Color clear lacquer over the repaired area to achieve the correct gloss level.

12

13

The paint will take about two weeks to harden fully. After this time it can be 'cut' with a mild cutting compound such as Turtle Wax Minute Cut prior to polishing with a final coating of Turtle Wax Extra.

14

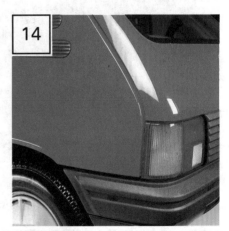

When carrying out bodywork repairs, remember that the quality of the finished job is proportional to the time and effort expended.

HAYNES No1 for DIY

Haynes publish a wide variety of books besides the world famous range of *Haynes Owners Workshop Manuals*. They cover all sorts of DIY jobs. Specialist books such as the *Improve and Modify* series and the *Purchase and DIY Restoration Guides* give you all the information you require to carry out everything from minor modifications to complete restoration on a number of popular cars. In addition there are the publications dealing with specific tasks, such as the *Car Bodywork Repair Manual* and the *In-Car Entertainment Manual*. The *Household DIY* series gives clear step-by-step instructions on how to repair everyday household objects ranging from toasters to washing machines.

Whether it is under the bonnet or around the home there is a Haynes Manual that can help you save money. Available from motor accessory stores and bookshops or direct from the publisher.

Chapter 1
Routine maintenance and servicing

Contents

Specifications

Note: Refer to "Buying spare parts and vehicle identification numbers" for details of engine identification.

Engine

Oil filter type - all models .... Champion G102

Cooling system

Antifreeze mixtures (antifreeze to Vauxhall/Opel
specification GME L6 368): ....

	Antifreeze	Water
Protection to -10°C	20%	80%
Protection to -20°C	34%	66%
Protection to -30°C	44%	56%
Protection to -40°C	52%	48%

Fuel grade

Note: On all except X 12 SZ and C 16 XE engines, the octane coding plug must be positioned correctly in accordance with the octane rating of the fuel being used - refer to Chapter 4A, Section 1 for details.

Fuel octane requirement*:

12 NZ engine	98 RON (Super), 95 RON (Premium) or 91 RON (Regular) unleaded
C 12 NZ engine	95 RON (Premium) or 91 RON (Regular) unleaded
X 12 SZ engine	98 RON (Super), 95 RON (Premium) or 91 RON (Regular)** unleaded
C 14 NZ engine	95 RON (Premium) or 91 RON (Regular) unleaded
C 14 SE engine	98 RON (Super), 95 RON (Premium) or 91 RON (Regular)*** unleaded
C 16 XE engine	98 RON (Super), 95 RON (Premium) or 91 RON (Regular)** unleaded

*For details of engine code location, refer to "Buying spare parts and vehicle identification numbers".
**If no higher-octane unleaded fuel is available, 91 RON (Regular) unleaded fuel can be used, provided severe engine loads (including towing and heavy payloads) and full-throttle operation are avoided.
***If no higher-octane unleaded fuel is available, 91 RON (Regular) unleaded fuel can be used, provided a special octane plug (available from a Vauxhall/Opel dealer) is used.

Fuel system

Air filter element type:
1.2 and 1.4 litre engines	Champion U640
1.6 litre (DOHC) engines	Champion U643
Fuel filter type (all engines)	Champion L225

Ignition system

Spark plugs:

Type:
1.2 litre engines	Champion RN9YCC
1.4 litre engines	Champion RN7YCC
1.6 litre (DOHC) engine	Champion RC9MCC
Electrode gap (all models)	0.8 mm

The spark plug gap quoted is that recommended by Champion for their specified plugs listed above. If spark plugs of any other type are to be fitted, refer to their manufacturer's spark plug gap recommendations.
HT leads	Champion type not available

Clutch

Clutch pedal travel	126.0 to 132.0 mm

Braking system

Minimum front brake pad lining thickness (including backing plate)	7.0 mm
Minimum rear brake shoe lining thickness	2.5 mm

Tyres

Pressures (tyres cold):	Front	Rear
Corsa and Corsavan:		
12 NZ, C 12 NZ, X 12 SZ and C 14 NZ engines:		
Normal load (up to 3 passengers)*	1.9 bars (27 psi)	1.7 bars (24 psi)
Full load	2.1 bars (30 psi)	2.4 bars (35 psi)
C 14 SE engine:		
Normal load (up to 3 passengers)**	2.1 bars (30 psi)	1.9 bars (27 psi)
Full load	2.3 bars (33 psi)	2.7 bars (39 psi)
C 16 XE engine:		
Normal load:		
185/60 R 14 tyres	2.1 bars (30 psi)	1.9 bars (27 psi)
165/65 R 14 tyres	2.4 bars (35 psi)	2.2 bars (31.5 psi)
Full load:		
185/60 R 14 tyres	2.3 bars (33 psi)	2.7 bars (39 psi)
165/65 R 14 tyres	2.5 bars (36 psi)	2.9 bars (42 psi)
Combo Van:		
Normal load (up to 2 passengers and 100 kg load)	1.9 bars (27 psi)	1.9 bars (27 psi)
Full load	2.0 bars (28.5 psi)	3.3 bars (48 psi)

Note: *Pressures apply only to original-equipment tyres, and may vary if any other make of tyre is fitted; check with the tyre manufacturer or supplier for correct pressures if necessary*
*Add 0.2 bars (3 psi) to both front and rear tyres on models with air conditioning and/or automatic transmission under normal load conditions.
**Add 0.1 bars (1.5 psi) to both front and rear tyres on models equipped with air conditioning under normal load conditions.

Wiper blades

Type (front and rear)	Champion X-4503

Torque wrench settings

	Nm	lbf ft
Sump drain plug:		
SOHC engines	55	41
DOHC engine	45	33
Spark plugs	25	18
Cooling system bleed screw (DOHC engine)	15	11
Roadwheel bolts	110	81

Lubricants, fluids and capacities

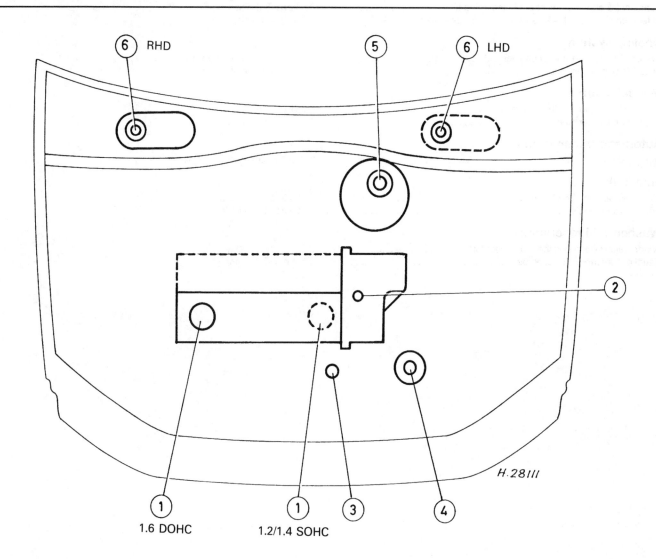

1.6 DOHC   1.2/1.4 SOHC

H.28111

Lubricants and fluids

Component or system	Lubricant type/specification	Duckhams recommendation
1 Engine	Multigrade engine oil, viscosity range SAE 10W/40 to 20W/50, to API SF/CC, SF/CD, SG/CC or SG/CD	Duckhams QXR, QS, Hypergrade Plus, or Hypergrade
2 Manual gearbox	Vauxhall/Opel gear oil No 90 001 777	Duckhams Hypoid 80W/90 or Hypoid 75W/90S
3 Automatic transmission	Dexron II type automatic transmission fluid	Duckhams Uni-Matic
4 Power steering fluid reservoir	Dexron II type automatic transmission fluid	Duckhams Uni-Matic
5 Cooling system	Clean water and antifreeze to Vauxhall/Opel specification GME L 6 368	Duckhams Universal Antifreeze and Summer Coolant
6 Brake fluid reservoir	Hydraulic fluid to DOT 4 or SAE J1703	Duckhams Universal Brake and Clutch Fluid

Capacities

Engine oil
Capacity (all engines - oil change, including filter) .... 3.5 litres (6.2 pints)
Difference between "MAX" and "MIN" dipstick marks.......................... 1.0 litre (1.8 pints)

Cooling system
All SOHC (1.2 and 1.4 litre) engines .... 5.9 litres (10.4 pints) approx.
DOHC (1.6 litre) engine... 5.8 litres (10.2 pints) approx.

Manual gearbox
All SOHC (1.2 and 1.4 litre) engines .... 1.6 litres (2.8 pints)
DOHC (1.6 litre) engine... 1.8 litres (3.2 pints)

Automatic transmission
Drain and refill... 3.0 to 3.5 litres (5.3 to 6.2 pints)

Fuel tank
All models except Combo Van .... 46.0 litres (10.1 gallons)
Combo Van models .... 50.0 litres (11.0 gallons)

Washer fluid reservoirs
Windscreen/tailgate washer fluid reservoir.. 2.6 litres (4.6 pints)
Headlight washer fluid reservoir .... 4.5 pints (7.9 pints)

1 Vauxhall Corsa maintenance schedule

1   The maintenance intervals in this manual are provided with the assumption that you, not the dealer, will be carrying out the work. These are the minimum maintenance intervals recommended by the manufacturer for vehicles driven daily. If you wish to keep your vehicle in peak condition at all times, you may wish to perform some of these procedures more often. We encourage frequent maintenance, because it enhances the efficiency, performance and resale value of your vehicle. If the vehicle is driven in dusty areas, used to tow a trailer, or driven frequently at slow speeds (idling in traffic) or on short journeys, more frequent maintenance intervals are recommended.

2   When the vehicle is new, it should be serviced by a factory-authorised dealer service department, in order to preserve the factory warranty.

Every 250 miles (400 km) or weekly

Check the engine oil level (Section 3)
Check the coolant level (Section 3)
Check the brake fluid level (Section 3)
Check the washer fluid level (Section 3)
Check the condition of the battery (Section 4)
Visually examine the tyres for tread depth, and for wear or damage (Section 5)
Check and if necessary adjust the tyre pressures (Section 5)

Every 9000 miles (15 000 km) or 12 months - whichever comes first

In addition to all the items listed previously, carry out the following:
Renew the engine oil and filter (Section 6)
Check all underbonnet and underbody components, pipes and hoses for leaks (Section 7)
Check the condition of the auxiliary drivebelt, and renew if necessary (Section 8)
Check the condition and security of the ignition HT system components (Section 9)
Check the operation of the engine management system (Section 10)
Check the operation and condition of the emission control system components (Section 11)
Renew the pollen filter (Section 12)
Check the operation of the horn, all lights, and the wipers and washers (Section 13)
Check the headlight beam alignment (Section 14)

Check the condition of the wiper blades (Section 15)
Check the tightness of the roadwheel bolts (Section 16)
Check the condition of the front brake pads (renew if necessary), and the calipers and discs (Section 17)
Check the rear brake pressure-regulating valve adjustment - 1.4 and 1.6 litre engine models (Section 18)
Check the condition of all brake fluid pipes and hoses (Section 19)
Check the bodywork and underbody for damage and corrosion, and check the condition of the underbody corrosion protection (Section 20)
Check the condition of the exhaust system components (Section 21)
Carry out a road test (Section 22)

Every 18 000 miles (30 000 km) or 2 years - whichever comes first

In addition to all the items listed previously, carry out the following:
Renew the air cleaner element (Section 23)
Renew the spark plugs - all except DOHC engine (Section 24)
Renew the fuel filter (Section 25)
Check the manual gearbox oil level - where applicable (Section 26)
Check the automatic transmission fluid level - where applicable (Section 27)
Check the power steering fluid level - where applicable (Section 28)
Check the operation of the automatic transmission system (Section 29)
Renew the coolant (Section 30)
Check the clutch cable adjustment (Section 31)
Lubricate all door, bonnet and tailgate hinges and locks (Section 32)
Check the condition of the rear brake shoes (renew if necessary), the drums and wheel cylinders (Section 33)
Renew the brake fluid (Section 34)
Check the condition of the front suspension and steering components, particularly the rubber gaiters and seals (Section 35)
Check the condition of the rear suspension components (Section 36)
Check the condition of the driveshaft joint gaiters, and the driveshaft joints (Section 37)

Every 36 000 miles (60 000 km) or 4 years - whichever comes first

In addition to all the items listed previously, carry out the following:
Renew the spark plugs - DOHC engine (Section 38)
Check the condition of the timing belt, and renew if necessary (Section 39)

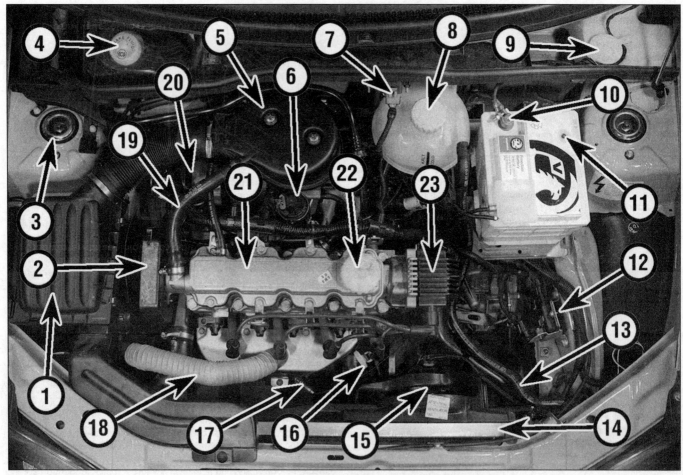

Underbonnet view of a Vauxhall Corsa 1.2 litre (X 12 SZ) engine

1	Air cleaner assembly	13	Coolant hose
2	Timing belt covers	14	Radiator
3	Front suspension strut top mounting	15	Cooling fan
4	Brake fluid reservoir	16	Oil level dipstick
5	Air box	17	Oxygen sensor
6	Exhaust gas recirculation (EGR) valve	18	Hot air tube
7	Manifold absolute pressure (MAP) sensor	19	Camshaft cover breather hose
8	Coolant expansion tank	20	Alternator
9	Washer fluid reservoir	21	Camshaft cover
10	Battery negative (earth) terminal	22	Oil filler cap
11	Battery condition indicator	23	Distributorless ignition system (DIS) module
12	Electronic modules		

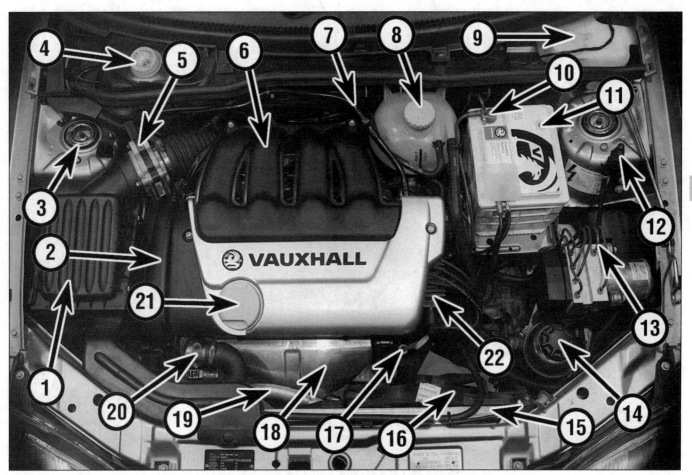

Underbonnet view of a Vauxhall Corsa GSi 16V model

1	Air cleaner assembly	12	Bonnet anti-theft alarm switch
2	Timing belt covers	13	ABS modulator assembly
3	Front suspension strut top mounting	14	Power steering fluid reservoir
4	Brake fluid reservoir	15	Radiator
5	Air mass meter	16	Cooling fan
6	Upper section of inlet manifold	17	Oil level dipstick
7	Brake servo vacuum hose	18	Exhaust manifold heat shield
8	Coolant expansion tank	19	Power steering fluid hose
9	Washer fluid reservoir	20	Thermostat housing
10	Battery negative (earth) terminal	21	Oil filler cap
11	Battery condition indicator	22	Distributorless ignition system (DIS) module

Front underbody view of a Vauxhall Corsa 1.2 litre (X 12 SZ) engine

1 Petrol pipes	12 Left-hand driveshaft
2 Front suspension lower arm	13 Driveshaft gaiter
3 Front brake caliper	14 Brake fluid pipes
4 Crankshaft speed/position sensor	15 Differential cover plate
5 Right-hand engine/gearbox mounting	16 Clutch bellhousing cover plate
6 Radiator hose	17 Rear engine/gearbox mounting
7 Oil filter	18 Engine oil drain plug
8 Cooling fan	19 Exhaust front section
9 Left-hand engine mounting	20 Steering rack
10 Front suspension tie-bar	21 Right-hand driveshaft
11 Brake fluid hose	

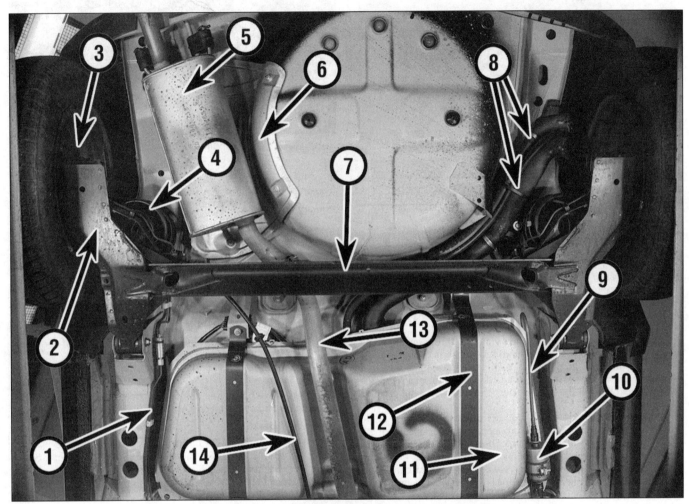

Rear underbody view of a Vauxhall Corsa Hatchback model

1 Brake fluid pipe
2 Rear suspension trailing arm
3 Rear brake backplate
4 Coil spring
5 Rear exhaust silencer
6 Exhaust heat shield
7 Rear axle

8 Fuel filler and vent pipes
9 Fuel pipe
10 Fuel filter
11 Fuel tank
12 Fuel tank securing strap
13 Exhaust rear section
14 Handbrake cable

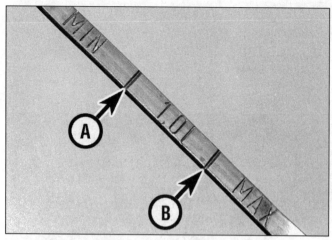

3.3 Engine oil level dipstick MIN (A) and MAX (B) marks

3.5 Topping-up the engine oil level

2   Introduction

General information

1   This Chapter is designed to help the home mechanic maintain his/her vehicle for safety, economy, long life and peak performance.

2   The Chapter contains a master maintenance schedule, followed by sections dealing specifically with each task on the schedule. Visual checks, adjustments, component renewal and other helpful items are included. Refer to the accompanying illustrations of the engine compartment and the underside of the vehicle for the locations of the various components.

3   Servicing of your vehicle in accordance with the mileage/time maintenance schedule and the following sections will provide a planned maintenance programme, which should result in a long and reliable service life. This is a comprehensive plan, so maintaining some items but not others at the specified service intervals, will not produce the same results.

4   As you service your vehicle, you will discover that many of the procedures can - and should - be grouped together, because of the particular procedure being performed, or because of the close proximity of two otherwise-unrelated components to one another. For example, if the vehicle is raised for any reason, the exhaust can be inspected at the same time as the suspension and steering components.

5   The first step in this maintenance programme is to prepare yourself before the actual work begins. Read through all the sections relevant to the work to be carried out, then make a list and gather together all the parts and tools required. If a problem is encountered, seek advice from a parts specialist, or a dealer service department.

Intensive maintenance

6   If, from the time the vehicle is new, the routine maintenance schedule is followed closely, and frequent checks are made of fluid levels and high-wear items, as suggested throughout this manual, the engine will be kept in relatively good running condition, and the need for additional work will be minimised.

7   It is possible that there will be times when the engine is running poorly due to the lack of regular maintenance. This is even more likely if a used vehicle, which has not received regular and frequent maintenance checks, is purchased. In such cases, additional work may need to be carried out, outside of the regular maintenance intervals.

8   If engine wear is suspected, a compression test (Chapter 2A) will provide valuable information regarding the overall performance of the main internal components. Such a test can be used as a basis to decide on the extent of the work to be carried out. If for example a compression test indicates serious internal engine wear, conventional maintenance as described in this Chapter will not greatly improve the performance of the engine, and may prove a waste of time and money, unless extensive overhaul work (Chapter 2B) is carried out first.

9   The following series of operations are those most often required to improve the performance of a generally poor-running engine:

Primary operations

(a)   Clean, inspect and test the battery (Section 4).
(b)   Check all the engine-related fluids (Section 3).
(c)   Check the condition and tension of the auxiliary drivebelt (Section 8).
(d)   Renew the spark plugs (Section 24 for SOHC engines, or 38 for DOHC engines).
(e)   Inspect the distributor cap and rotor arm - where applicable (Section 9).
(f)   Inspect the ignition HT leads (Section 9).
(g)   Check the condition of the air filter, and renew if necessary (Section 23).
(h)   Check the condition of all hoses, and check for fluid leaks (Section 7).

10   If the above operations do not prove fully effective, carry out the following secondary operations:

Secondary operations

All items listed under "Primary operations", plus the following:

(a)   Check the ignition system (Chapter 5B or 5C, as applicable).
(b)   Check the charging system (Chapter 5A).
(c)   Check the fuel system (Chapter 4A).
(d)   Renew the air filter (Section 23).
(e)   Renew the distributor cap and rotor arm - where applicable (Section 9).
(f)   Renew the ignition HT leads (Section 9).

3   Fluid level checks (every 250 miles/400 km or weekly)

Engine oil

1   The engine oil level is checked using a dipstick which extends through a tube and into the sump at the bottom of the engine. The dipstick is located at the front left-hand side of the engine.

2   The oil level should be checked with the vehicle standing on level ground. The check should be carried out before the vehicle is driven, or at least 5 minutes after the engine has been stopped. If the oil level is checked immediately after driving the vehicle, some of the oil will remain in the upper engine components and oil galleries, resulting in an inaccurate reading on the dipstick.

3   Withdraw the dipstick from the tube, and wipe all the oil from the end with a clean rag or paper towel. Insert the clean dipstick back into the tube as far as it will go, then withdraw it once more. Note the oil level on the end of the dipstick. Add oil as necessary until the level is between the upper (maximum) mark and lower (minimum) mark on the dipstick. Note that 1.0 litre of oil will be required to raise the level from the lower mark to the upper mark **(see illustration)**.

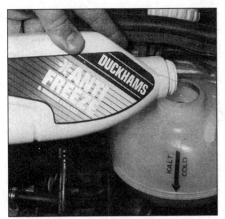

3.9 Topping-up the coolant level

3.12 Topping-up the brake fluid level

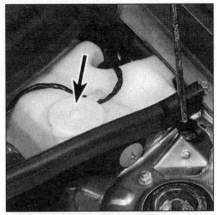

3.16a Windscreen and tailgate washer fluid reservoir location (arrowed)

4   Always maintain the level between the two dipstick marks. If the level is allowed to fall below the lower mark, oil starvation may result, which could lead to severe engine damage. If the engine is overfilled by adding too much oil, this may result in oil-fouled spark plugs, oil leaks, or oil seal failures.

5   Oil is added to the engine after removing the filler cap (twist it through a quarter-turn anti-clockwise and withdraw it) from the engine camshaft cover **(see illustration)**. It is advisable to use an oil can with a spout or a funnel, to avoid spillage. Always use the correct grade and type of oil as shown in *"Lubricants, fluids and capacities"*.

Coolant

Warning: *DO NOT attempt to remove the expansion tank pressure cap when the engine is hot, as there is a very great risk of scalding.*

6   All vehicles covered by this manual are equipped with a pressurised cooling system. A coolant expansion tank, located at the rear left-hand side of the engine compartment, is connected by hoses to the cooling system. The tank allows for expansion of the coolant as the engine temperature increases, and enables monitoring of the coolant level.

7   The coolant level in the expansion tank should be checked regularly. The level in the tank varies with the temperature of the engine. When the engine is cold, the coolant level should be slightly above the "KALT" (or "COLD") mark on the side of the tank. When the engine is hot, the level will rise.

8   If topping-up is necessary, wait until the engine is cold, then cover the expansion tank cap with a wad of rag, and slowly turn the cap anti-clockwise to relieve the pressure in the cooling system (a hissing sound will normally be heard). Wait until any pressure remaining in the system is released, then continue to turn the cap until it can be removed.

9   Add a mixture of water and antifreeze (see *"Antifreeze mixture"* in Section 30) through the expansion tank filler neck, until the coolant reaches the "COLD" level mark **(see illustration)**. Refit the cap, turning it clockwise as far as it will go to secure.

10   With a sealed-type cooling system, the addition of coolant should only be necessary at very infrequent intervals. If frequent topping-up is required, it is likely that there is a leak in the system. Check the radiator, all hoses and joint faces for any sign of staining or dampness, and rectify as necessary. If no leaks can be found, it is advisable to have the cooling system pressure-tested by a dealer or suitably-equipped garage, as this can often detect a small leak not previously visible.

Brake fluid

Note: *Hydraulic fluid is poisonous; wash off immediately and thoroughly in the case of skin contact, and seek immediate medical advice if any fluid is swallowed or gets into the eyes. Certain types of hydraulic fluid are inflammable, and may ignite when allowed into contact with hot components. When servicing any hydraulic system, it is safest to assume that the fluid IS inflammable, and to take precautions against the risk of fire as when handling petrol. Hydraulic fluid is also an effective paint stripper, and will attack certain plastics; if any is spilt, it should be washed off immediately using copious quantities of fresh*

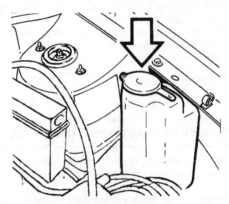

3.16b Headlight washer fluid reservoir location (arrowed)

water. Finally, it is hygroscopic (it absorbs moisture from the air) - old fluid may be contaminated and unfit for further use. When topping-up or renewing the fluid, always use the recommended type, and ensure that it comes from a freshly-opened, sealed container.

11   The brake fluid reservoir is mounted on the right-hand side of the engine compartment on right-hand drive models (on the left-hand side for left-hand drive models). The maximum and minimum fluid level marks are indicated on the side of the reservoir, and the fluid level should be maintained between these marks at all times.

12   If topping-up is necessary, first wipe the area around the filler cap with a clean rag before removing the cap. When adding fluid, pour it carefully into the reservoir to avoid spilling it on surrounding painted surfaces **(see illustration)**. Be sure to use only the specified brake hydraulic fluid, since mixing different types of fluid can cause damage to the system. See *"Lubricants, fluids and capacities"* at the beginning of this Chapter.

13   When adding fluid, it is a good idea to inspect the reservoir for contamination. The system should be drained and refilled if deposits, dirt particles or contamination can be seen in the fluid.

14   After filling the reservoir to the correct level, make sure that the cap is refitted securely, to avoid leaks and the entry of foreign matter.

15   The fluid level in the master cylinder reservoir will drop slightly as the brake pads and shoes wear down during normal operation. If the reservoir requires repeated replenishing to maintain the correct level, this is an indication of a hydraulic leak somewhere in the system, which should be investigated immediately.

Washer fluid

16   The fluid reservoir for the windscreen and tailgate washer system is located at the rear left-hand corner of the engine compartment scuttle. On models with a headlight washer system, a second reservoir is located on the left-hand side of the engine compartment, in front of the suspension strut top mounting **(see illustrations)**.

3.17 Topping-up the washer fluid level

5.1 Checking a tyre tread depth with a depth gauge

5.3 Checking a tyre pressure with a tyre pressure gauge

17   Check, and if necessary top-up, the fluid level in the reservoir(s). When topping-up, a suitable screenwash additive should be added in the quantities recommended on the bottle **(see illustration)**.
18   **Never** use engine antifreeze in the washer fluid, as it can damage the vehicle paintwork.

Power steering
19   Refer to Section 28.

4   Battery check (every 250 miles/400 km or weekly)

Caution: *Before carrying out any work on the vehicle battery, read through the precautions given in "Safety first!" at the beginning of this manual.*
1   A "maintenance-free" battery is standard equipment on all vehicles covered by this manual. Although this type of battery has many advantages over the older refillable type, and never requires the addition of distilled water, it should still be routinely maintained according to the following procedure.
2   The battery is located on the left-hand side and to the rear of the engine compartment. The exterior of the battery should be inspected periodically for damage such as a cracked case or cover.
3   Check the tightness of the battery cable clamps to ensure good electrical connections, and check the entire length of each cable for cracked insulation and frayed wiring.
4   If corrosion (visible as white, fluffy deposits) is evident, remove the cables from the battery terminals, clean them with a small wire brush, then refit them. Corrosion can be kept to a minimum by applying a layer of petroleum jelly to the clamps and terminals after they are reconnected.
5   Make sure that the battery tray is in good condition, and that the retaining clamp is tight.
6   Corrosion (white deposits) on the tray, retaining clamp and the battery itself can be removed with a solution of water and baking soda. Corrosion of this nature is caustic, so don't get any on your hands, or in your eyes. Thoroughly rinse all cleaned areas with plain water.
7   Any metal parts of the vehicle damaged by corrosion should be covered with a zinc-based primer, then painted.
8   Further information on the battery, charging, and jump-starting, can be found in Chapter 5A and in the preliminary sections of this manual.

5   Tyre checks (every 250 miles/400 km or weekly)

1   The original tyres on all Corsa vehicles have tread wear safety bands which will appear when the tread depth reaches approximately 1.6 mm. Tread wear can be monitored with a simple, inexpensive device known as a tread depth indicator gauge **(see illustration)**.
2   Wheels and tyres should give no real problems in use, provided that a close eye is kept on them with regard to excessive wear or damage. To this end, the following points should be noted.

3   Ensure that tyre pressures are checked regularly and maintained correctly. Checking should be carried out with the tyres cold, and **not** immediately after the vehicle has been in use **(see illustration)**. If the pressures are checked with the tyres hot, an apparently-high reading will be obtained, owing to heat expansion. **Under no circumstances** should an attempt be made to reduce the pressures to the quoted cold reading in this instance, or effective under-inflation will result.
4   Note any abnormal tread wear **(see illustration)**. Tread pattern irregularities such as feathering, flat spots, and more wear on one side than the other, are indications of front wheel alignment and/or balance problems. If any of these conditions are noted, they should be rectified as soon as possible.
5   Under-inflation will cause overheating of the tyre, owing to excessive flexing of the casing, and the tread will not sit correctly on the road surface. This will cause a consequent loss of adhesion and excessive wear, not to mention the danger of sudden tyre failure due to heat build-up.
6   Over-inflation will cause rapid wear of the centre part of the tyre tread, coupled with reduced adhesion, harsher ride, and the danger of shock damage occurring in the tyre casing.
7   Regularly check the tyres for damage in the form of cuts or bulges, especially in the sidewalls. Remove any nails or stones embedded in the tread before they penetrate the tyre to cause deflation. If removal of a nail does reveal that the tyre has been punctured, refit the nail, so that its point of penetration is marked. Then immediately change the wheel, and have the tyre repaired by a tyre dealer as soon as possible. Do not drive on a tyre in such a condition. If in any doubt as to the possible consequences of any damage found, consult your local tyre dealer for advice.
8   Periodically remove the wheels, and clean any dirt or mud from the inside and outside surfaces. Examine the wheel rims for signs of rusting, corrosion, or other damage. Light alloy wheels are easily damaged by "kerbing" whilst parking, and similarly, steel wheels may become dented or buckled. Renewal of the wheel is very often the only course of remedial action possible.
9   The balance of each wheel and tyre assembly should be maintained to avoid excessive wear, not only to the tyres, but also to the steering and suspension components. Wheel imbalance is normally signified by vibration through the vehicle's bodyshell, although in many cases it is particularly noticeable through the steering wheel. Conversely, it should be noted that wear or damage in suspension or steering components may cause excessive tyre wear. Out-of-round or out-of-true tyres, damaged wheels, and wheel bearing wear/maladjustment also fall into this category. Balancing will not usually cure vibration caused by such wear.
10   Wheel balancing may be carried out with the wheel either on or off the vehicle. If balanced on the vehicle, ensure that the wheel-to-hub relationship is marked in some way prior to subsequent wheel removal, so that the relationship can be maintained when the wheel is refitted.
11   General tyre wear is influenced to a large degree by driving style - harsh braking and acceleration, or fast cornering, will all produce more rapid tyre wear. Interchanging of tyres may result in more even wear. However, it is worth bearing in mind that if this is completely effective,

Condition	Probable cause	Corrective action	Condition	Probable cause	Corrective action
Shoulder wear	• Underinflation (wear on both sides) • Incorrect wheel camber (wear on one side) • Hard cornering	• Check and adjust pressure • Repair or renew suspension parts • Reduce speed	**Feathered edge** **Toe wear**	• Incorrect toe setting	• Adjust front wheel alignment
Centre wear	• Overinflation	• Measure and adjust pressure	**Uneven wear**	• Incorrect camber or castor • Malfunctioning suspension • Unbalanced wheel • Out-of-round brake disc/drum	• Repair or renew suspension parts • Repair or renew suspension parts • Balance tyres • Machine or renew disc/drum

5.4 Tyre tread wear patterns and causes

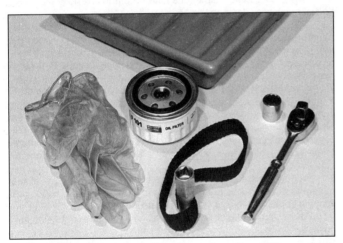

6.2 Tools and materials required for engine oil and filter renewal

6.4 Engine oil drain plug (arrowed) - SOHC engine

the added expense is incurred of replacing simultaneously a complete set of tyres - this may prove financially restrictive for many owners.

12 Front tyres may wear unevenly as a result of wheel misalignment. The front wheels should always be correctly aligned according to the settings specified by the vehicle manufacturer.

13 Legal restrictions apply to many aspects of tyre fitting and usage, and in the UK this information is contained in the Motor Vehicle Construction and Use Regulations. It is suggested that a copy of these regulations is obtained from your local police if in doubt as to current legal requirements with regard to tyre type and condition, minimum tread depth, etc.

6 Engine oil and filter renewal (every 9000 miles/15 000 km or 12 months)

1 Frequent oil and filter changes are the most important preventative maintenance procedures which can be undertaken by the DIY owner. As engine oil ages, it becomes diluted and contaminated, which leads to premature engine wear.

2 Before starting this procedure, gather together all the necessary tools and materials **(see illustration)**. Also make sure that you have plenty of clean rags and newspapers handy, to mop up any spills. Ideally, the engine oil should be warm, as it will drain more easily, and more built-up sludge will be removed with it. Take care not to touch the exhaust or any other hot parts of the engine when working under the vehicle. To avoid any possibility of scalding, and to protect yourself from possible skin irritants and other harmful contaminants in used engine oils, it is advisable to wear gloves when carrying out this work. Access to the underside of the vehicle will be greatly improved if it can be raised on a lift, driven onto ramps, or jacked up and supported on axle stands. Whichever method is chosen, make sure that the vehicle remains level, or if it is at an angle, that the drain plug is at the lowest point. The drain plug is located at the rear of the sump.

3 Remove the oil filler cap from the camshaft cover (twist it through a quarter-turn anti-clockwise and withdraw it).

4 Using a spanner, or preferably a suitable socket and bar, slacken the drain plug about half a turn **(see illustration)**. Position the draining

container under the drain plug, then remove the plug completely. If possible, try to keep the plug pressed into the sump while unscrewing it by hand the last couple of turns. As the plug releases from the threads, move it away sharply, so that the stream of oil from the sump runs into the container, not up your sleeve!

5   Allow some time for the oil to drain, noting that it may be necessary to reposition the container as the oil flow slows to a trickle.

6   After all the oil has drained, wipe the drain plug and the sealing washer with a clean rag. Examine the condition of the sealing washer, and renew it if it shows signs of scoring or other damage which may prevent an oil-tight seal. Clean the area around the drain plug opening, and refit the plug complete with the washer. Tighten the plug securely, preferably to the specified torque, using a torque wrench.

7   The oil filter is located at the front left-hand side of the engine. Note that on DOHC engine models, access is most easily obtained from underneath the front of the vehicle.

8   Move the container into position under the oil filter.

9   Use an oil filter removal tool to slacken the filter initially, then unscrew it by hand the rest of the way **(see illustration)**. Empty the oil from the old filter into the container.

10   Use a clean rag to remove all oil, dirt and sludge from the filter sealing area on the engine. Check the old filter to make sure that the rubber sealing ring has not stuck to the engine. If it has, carefully remove it.

11   Apply a light coating of clean engine oil to the sealing ring on the new filter, then screw the filter into position on the engine. Tighten the filter firmly by hand only - **do not** use any tools.

12   Remove the old oil and all tools from under the vehicle then, if applicable, lower the vehicle to the ground.

13   Fill the engine through the filler hole in the camshaft cover, using the correct grade and type of oil (refer to Section 3 for details of topping-up). Pour in half the specified quantity of oil first, then wait a few minutes for the oil to drain into the sump. Continue to add oil, a small quantity at a time, until the level is up to the lower mark on the dipstick. Adding a further 1.0 litre will bring the level up to the upper mark on the dipstick.

14   Start the engine and run it for a few minutes, while checking for leaks around the oil filter seal and the sump drain plug. Note that there may be a delay of a few seconds before the low oil pressure warning light goes out when the engine is first started, as the oil circulates through the new oil filter and the engine oil galleries before the pressure builds up.

15   Stop the engine, and wait a few minutes for the oil to settle in the sump once more. With the new oil circulated and the filter now completely full, recheck the level on the dipstick, and add more oil as necessary.

16   Dispose of the used engine oil safely, with reference to *"General repair procedures"* in the preliminary sections of this manual.

6.9 Using an oil filter removal tool to slacken the filter (viewed from underneath the vehicle)

components. Hose clips can pinch and puncture hoses, resulting in cooling system leaks. If wire-type hose clips are used, it may be a good idea to replace them with screw-type clips.

4   Inspect all the cooling system components (hoses, joint faces etc.) for leaks. A leak in the cooling system will usually show up as white- or rust-coloured deposits on the area adjoining the leak. Where any problems of this nature are found on system components, renew the component or gasket with reference to Chapter 3.

5   Where applicable, inspect the automatic transmission fluid cooler hoses for leaks or deterioration.

6   With the vehicle raised, inspect the petrol tank and filler neck for punctures, cracks and other damage. The connection between the filler neck and tank is especially critical. Sometimes, a rubber filler neck or connecting hose will leak due to loose retaining clamps or deteriorated rubber.

7   Carefully check all rubber hoses and metal fuel lines leading away from the petrol tank. Check for loose connections, deteriorated hoses, crimped lines and other damage. Pay particular attention to the vent pipes and hoses, which often loop up around the filler neck and can become blocked or crimped. Follow the lines to the front of the vehicle, carefully inspecting them all the way. Renew damaged sections as necessary.

8   From within the engine compartment, check the security of all fuel hose attachments and pipe unions, and inspect the fuel hoses and vacuum hoses for kinks, chafing and deterioration.

9   Where applicable, check the condition of the power steering fluid hoses and pipes.

7   Hose and fluid leak check (every 9000 miles/15 000 km or 12 months)

1   Visually inspect the engine joint faces, gaskets and seals for any signs of water or oil leaks. Pay particular attention to the areas around the camshaft cover, cylinder head, oil filter and sump joint faces. Bear in mind that, over a period of time, some very slight seepage from these areas is to be expected; what you are really looking for is any indication of a serious leak. Should a leak be found, renew the offending gasket or oil seal by referring to the appropriate Chapters in this manual.

2   Also check the security and condition of all the engine-related pipes and hoses. Ensure that all cable ties or securing clips are in place, and in good condition. Clips which are broken or missing can lead to chafing of the hoses pipes or wiring, which could cause more serious problems in the future.

3   Carefully check the radiator hoses and heater hoses along their entire length. Renew any hose which is cracked, swollen or deteriorated. Cracks will show up better if the hose is squeezed. Pay close attention to the hose clips that secure the hoses to the cooling system

8   Auxiliary drivebelt check and renewal (every 9000 miles/15 000 km or 12 months)

Models with V-belt

Checking and adjustment

1   Correct tensioning of the auxiliary drivebelt will ensure that it has a long life. Beware, however, of overtightening, as this can cause excessive wear in the alternator.

2   The auxiliary drivebelt drives the alternator, and the power steering pump and/or air conditioning compressor where applicable.

3   For improved access, remove the air cleaner assembly as described in Chapter 4A.

4   The belt should be inspected along its entire length, and if it is found to be worn, frayed or cracked, it should be renewed as a precaution against breakage in service. It is advisable to carry a spare drivebelt of the correct type in the vehicle at all times.

5   Although special tools are available for measuring the belt

8.6 Loosening the alternator upper mounting nut and bolt

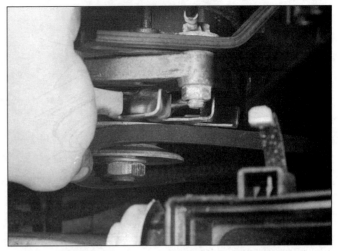

8.7 Removing the auxiliary drivebelt (V-belt type)

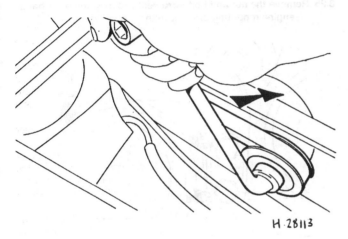

H.28113

8.13a Lever the tensioner roller against the spring pressure . . .

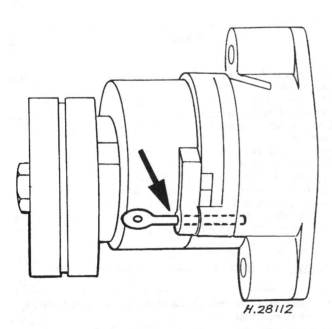

H.28112

8.13b . . . until the roller can be locked in position using
a suitable tool (arrowed)

tension, a good approximation can be achieved if the belt is tensioned so that there is approximately 13.0 mm of free movement under firm thumb pressure at the mid-point of the longest run between pulleys. If in doubt, err on the slack side, as an excessively-tight belt may cause damage to the alternator or other components.

6   If adjustment is required, loosen the alternator upper mounting nut and bolt - use two spanners, one to counterhold the bolt **(see illustration)**. Lever the alternator away from the engine using a wooden lever at the mounting bracket until the correct tension is achieved, then tighten the bolt securing the adjuster bracket, and the alternator mounting nuts and bolts. On no account lever at the free end of the alternator, as serious internal damage could be caused to the alternator.

Removal, renewal and refitting

7   To remove the belt, simply loosen the mounting nuts and bolts, and the bolt securing the adjuster bracket, as described previously, and slacken the belt sufficiently to slip it from the pulleys **(see illustration)**.

8   Refit the belt, and tension it as described previously.

Models with ribbed belt - models without power steering and air conditioning

Checking and adjustment

9   Proceed as described in paragraphs 1 to 4.

10   An automatic drivebelt tensioner is fitted, and there is no requirement to check the drivebelt tension.

Removal, renewal and refitting

11   To remove the drivebelt, remove the air cleaner assembly (if not already done) for improved access, as described in Chapter 4A.

12   Mark the running direction of the belt if it is to be refitted.

13   Using a suitable spanner or socket and wrench engaged with the tensioner roller bolt, lever the tensioner roller against the spring pressure. The roller can then be locked in position, using a suitable pin punch or similar tool inserted through the lug on the roller assembly, to engage with the corresponding hole in the tensioner backplate **(see illustrations)**.

14   With the tensioner locked in position, slip the drivebelt from the pulleys.

15   Refit the drivebelt by slipping the belt over the pulleys. If the original belt is being refitted, ensure that the running direction marks made on the belt are positioned as noted before removal.

16   Using the method described previously, lever the tensioner roller until the locking tool can be removed from the backplate. Use the spanner or wrench to gradually release the tensioner in order to tension the belt. **Do not** allow the tensioner to spring back unrestrained.

17   Check that the belt is correctly located on all the pulleys.

18   Refit the air cleaner assembly.

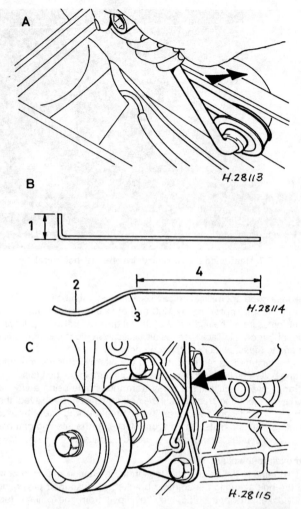

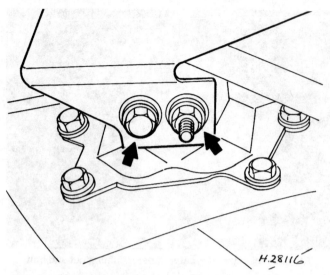

8.25 Remove the nut and bolt (arrowed) securing the right-hand engine mounting bracket to the mounting block

8.22 Tools used to lock tensioner in position - models with power steering and air conditioning

B	Dimensions of locking tool	1	30.0 mm
C	Locking tool (arrowed) in position	2	Radius 30.0 mm
		3	Radius 35.0 mm
		4	150.0 mm

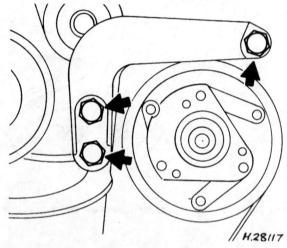

8.28 Unbolt the engine bracket (bolts arrowed) and withdraw it downwards

Models with ribbed belt - models with power steering and air conditioning

Checking and adjustment

19   Proceed as described in paragraphs 1 to 4.
20   An automatic drivebelt tensioner is fitted, and there is no requirement to check the drivebelt tension.

Removal, renewal and refitting

21   Proceed as described in paragraphs 11 and 12.
22   Obtain a wire rod of approximately 4 mm (0.16 in) diameter x 280 mm (11 ins). Make up a suitable tool as shown to lock the tensioner in position as the belt is removed **(see illustration)**.
23   Using a suitable spanner or socket and wrench engaged with the tensioner roller bolt, lever the tensioner roller against the spring pressure. The roller can then be locked in position, using the tool inserted through the lug on the roller assembly, to engage with the corresponding hole in the tensioner backplate.
24   Attach a suitable hoist and lifting tackle to the engine lifting brackets on the cylinder head, and support the weight of the engine.
25   Working under the vehicle, remove the nut and bolt securing the right-hand engine mounting bracket to the mounting block on the body **(see illustration)**.

26   Remove the right-hand front suspension tie-bar as described in Chapter 10.
27   Using the lifting tackle, lower the engine approximately 50.0 mm.
28   Unbolt the engine bracket from the power steering pump bracket **(see illustration)**, and withdraw it downwards from the engine compartment.
29   Withdraw the auxiliary drivebelt from the pulleys.
30   Proceed as described in paragraphs 15 to 17 inclusive.
31   Refit the engine bracket, and tighten the securing bolts.
32   Raise the engine, using the lifting tackle, and refit the right-hand front suspension tie-bar with reference to Chapter 10.
33   Refit the nut and bolt securing the right-hand engine mounting to the mounting block on the body, and tighten the nut and bolt to the specified torque (see Chapter 2A).
34   Disconnect the hoist and lifting tackle.
35   Refit the air cleaner assembly.

9   Ignition HT system check (every 9000 miles/15 000 km or 12 months)

1   To check the HT leads, proceed as follows.
2   On DOHC engine models, unscrew the two securing screws, and

9.9 Releasing a distributor cap securing clip

12.4 Withdrawing the pollen filter

lift off the plastic shield which fits over the camshaft cover.

3   Ensure that the leads are numbered before removing them, to avoid confusion when refitting (No 1 is at the timing belt end of the engine). Working on each HT lead in turn, pull the end of the lead from the spark plug by gripping the end connector, not the lead, otherwise the lead connection may be fractured. Note that on DOHC engines, a plastic tool is provided (attached to one of the HT leads) to pull the leads from the spark plugs.

4   Check inside the connector for signs of corrosion, which will look like a white crusty powder. Push the connector back onto the spark plug, ensuring that it is a tight fit on the plug. If it is not, remove the lead again, and use pliers to carefully crimp the metal terminal inside the connector until it fits securely on the end of the spark plug.

5   Using a clean rag, wipe the entire length of the lead to remove any built-up dirt and grease. Once the lead is clean, check for burns, cracks and other damage. Do not bend the lead excessively, or pull the lead lengthwise - the conductor inside might break.

6   Disconnect the other end of the lead from the distributor cap, or DIS module, as applicable. Again, pull only on the connector. Check for corrosion and a tight fit, as described previously for the spark plug end of the lead. Refit the lead securely on completion.

7   Check the remaining HT leads one at a time, in the same way, including the lead from the distributor cap to the coil, where applicable.

8   If new HT leads are required, purchase a set for your specific vehicle and engine type.

9   On models fitted with a distributor, loosen the securing screws, or release the securing clips, as applicable, and remove the distributor cap **(see illustration)**. Wipe the cap clean inside and out, and carefully inspect it for signs of cracks, "tracking" (indicated by thin black lines running between the contacts) and worn, corroded, burnt, or loose contacts. Check that the carbon brush in the centre of the cap is not

worn, that it moves freely, and stands proud of the surface of the cap. Renew the cap if any faults are found. When fitting a new cap, remove the HT leads from the old cap one at a time, and fit them to the new cap in the exact same location. Do not simultaneously remove all the leads from the old cap, as it is easy to fit the leads to the new cap in the wrong positions, resulting in the wrong cylinder firing order.

10   Where applicable, remove the rotor arm. Examine the rotor arm for corrosion, cracks or other damage. If the metal portion of the rotor arm is badly burnt or loose, renew the rotor arm. If slightly burnt or corroded, it may be cleaned with a fine file.

11   Note that it is common practice to renew the distributor cap and rotor arm whenever new HT leads are fitted.

12   Even with the ignition system in first-class condition, some engines may still occasionally experience poor starting, attributable to damp ignition components. To disperse moisture, Holts Wet Start can be very effective. Holts Damp Start can be used for providing a sealing coat to exclude moisture from the ignition system, and in extreme difficulty, Holts Cold Start will help to start a car when only a very poor spark occurs.

10   Engine management system check (every 9000 miles/15 000 km or 12 months)

1   This check is part of the manufacturer's maintenance schedule, and involves testing the engine management system using special dedicated test equipment. Such testing will allow the test equipment to read any fault codes stored in the electronic control unit memory.

2   Unless a fault is suspected, this test is not essential, although it should be noted that it is recommended by the manufacturers.

3   If access to suitable test equipment is not possible, make a thorough check of all ignition, fuel and emission control system components, hoses, and wiring, for security and obvious signs of damage. Further details of the fuel system, emission control system and ignition system can be found in Chapters 4 and 5.

11   Emission control system check (every 9000 miles/15 000 km or 12 months)

1   Check all emission control system components for condition and security, with reference to Chapter 4B. Pay particular attention to all wiring and hoses.

12   Pollen filter renewal (every 9000 miles/15 000 km or 12 months)

1   Peel the bonnet seal off the engine compartment bulkhead, and remove it from the vehicle.

2   Undo the retaining screws from the windscreen cowl panels, and remove the left-hand panel from the vehicle.

3   Lift the right-hand cowl panel, and prise out the two plugs from the centre of the water deflector shield.

4   Lift the water deflector shield, then release the two retaining clips and lift the pollen filter out from its housing, noting which way round it is fitted **(see illustration)**.

5   Wipe clean the filter housing and install the new filter, making sure it is the correct way up. Ensure that the filter is correctly seated, and secure it in position with the retaining clips.

6   Refitting is the reverse of the removal procedure.

13   Electrical system check (every 9000 miles/15 000 km or 12 months)

1   Check the operation of all the electrical equipment, ie lights, direction indicators, horn, etc. Refer to the appropriate sections of Chapter 12 for details if any of the circuits are found to be inoperative.

2   Note that stop-light switch adjustment is described in Chapter 9.
3   Check all accessible wiring connectors, harnesses and retaining clips for security, and for signs of chafing or damage. Rectify any faults found.

14 Headlight beam alignment check (every 9000 miles/15 000 km or 12 months)

1   Accurate adjustment of the headlight beam is only possible using optical beam-setting equipment, and this work should therefore be carried out by a Vauxhall/Opel dealer or service station with the necessary facilities.
2   Basic adjustments can be carried out in an emergency, and further details are given in Chapter 12.

15 Wiper blade check (every 9000 miles/15 000 km or 12 months)

1   Check the condition of the wiper blades. If they are cracked, or show any signs of deterioration, or if they fail to clean the glass effectively, renew the blades. Ideally, the wiper blades should be renewed annually as a matter of course.
2   To remove a wiper blade, pull the arm away from the glass until it locks. Swivel the blade through 90°, then squeeze the locking clip, and detach the blade from the arm **(see illustration)**. When fitting the new blade, make sure that the blade locks securely into the arm, and that the blade is orientated correctly.

16 Roadwheel bolt tightness check (every 9000 miles/15 000 km or 12 months)

1   Using a torque wrench on each wheel bolt in turn, ensure that the bolts are tightened to the specified torque.

17 Front brake pad, caliper and disc check (every 9000 miles/15 000 km or 12 months)

1   Apply the handbrake, then jack up the front of the vehicle and support securely on axle stands; remove the roadwheels (see "*Jacking, towing and wheel changing*").
2   For a quick check, the thickness of friction material remaining on each pad can be measured through the slot in the front of the caliper body. If any pad is worn to the specified minimum thickness or less, all four pads must be renewed (see Chapter 9).
3   For a comprehensive check, the brake pads should be removed and cleaned. This will allow the operation of the caliper to be checked, and the condition of the brake disc itself to be fully examined on both sides (see Chapter 9).

18 Rear brake pressure-regulating valve adjustment check - 1.4 and 1.6 litre engine models (every 9000 miles/15 000 km or 12 months)

Check the operation of the valve and adjust it as described in Section 17 of Chapter 9.

19 Brake fluid pipe and hose check (every 9000 miles/15 000 km or 12 months)

1   The brake hydraulic system includes a number of metal pipes, which run from the master cylinder to the front and rear brake assemblies, and the hydraulic modulator on models with an anti-lock braking

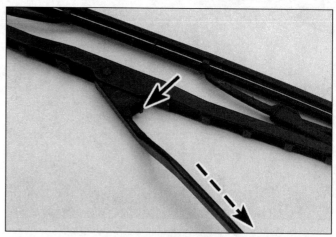

15.2 Depress the wiper blade locking clip (arrowed) and slide the blade from the arm in the direction shown

system (ABS). Flexible hoses are fitted between the pipes and the front and rear brake assemblies, to allow for steering and suspension movement.
2   When checking the system, first look for signs of leakage at the pipe or hose unions, then examine the flexible hoses for signs of cracking, chafing or deterioration of the rubber. Bend the hoses sharply between the fingers (but do not actually bend them double, or the casing may be damaged) and check that this does not reveal previously-hidden cracks, cuts or splits. Check that the pipes and hoses are securely fastened in their clips.
3   Carefully working along the length of the metal pipes, look for dents, kinks, damage of any sort, or corrosion. Light corrosion can be polished off, but if the depth of pitting is significant, the pipe must be renewed.

20 Bodywork and underbody condition check (every 9000 miles/15 000 km or 12 months)

Bodywork damage/corrosion check
1   Once the car has been washed, and all tar spots and other surface blemishes have been cleaned off, carefully check all paintwork, looking closely for chips or scratches. Pay particular attention to vulnerable areas such as the front panels (bonnet and spoiler), and around the wheel arches. Any damage to the paintwork must be rectified as soon as possible, to comply with the terms of the manufacturer's anti-corrosion warranties; check with a Vauxhall/Opel dealer for details.
2   If a chip or light scratch is found which is recent and still free from rust, it can be touched-up using the appropriate touch-up stick which can be obtained from Vauxhall/Opel dealers. Any more serious damage, or rusted stone chips, can be repaired as described in Chapter 11, but if damage or corrosion is so severe that a panel must be renewed, seek professional advice as soon as possible.
3   Always check that the door and ventilation opening drain holes and pipes are completely clear, so that water can drain out.

Underbody corrosion protection check
4   The wax-based underbody protective coating should be inspected annually, preferably just prior to Winter, when the underbody should be washed down as thoroughly as possible without disturbing the protective coating. Any damage to the coating should be repaired using a suitable wax-based sealer. If any of the body panels are disturbed for repair or renewal, do not forget to re-apply the coating. Wax should be injected into door cavities, sills and box sections, to maintain the level of protection provided by the vehicle manufacturer - seek the advice of a Vauxhall/Opel dealer.

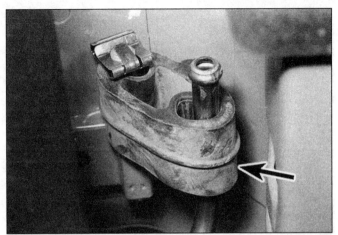

21.3 Check the condition of the exhaust system mountings (typical example arrowed)

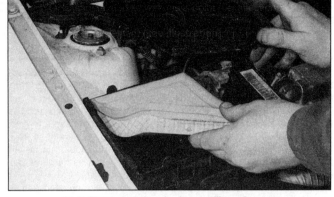

23.3 Removing the air cleaner filter element

21 Exhaust system check (every 9000 miles/15 000 km or 12 months)

1   With the engine cold (at least an hour after the vehicle has been driven), check the complete exhaust system from the engine to the end of the tailpipe. The exhaust system is most easily checked with the vehicle raised on a hoist, or suitably supported on axle stands, so that the exhaust components are readily visible and accessible.

2   Check the exhaust pipes and connections for evidence of leaks, severe corrosion and damage. Make sure that all brackets and mountings are in good condition, and that all relevant nuts and bolts are tight. Leakage at any of the joints or in other parts of the system will usually show up as a black sooty stain in the vicinity of the leak. Holts Flexiwrap and Holts Gun Gum exhaust repair systems can be used for effective repairs to exhaust pipes and silencer boxes, including ends and bends. Holts Flexiwrap is an MOT-approved permanent exhaust repair. Holts Firegum is suitable for the assembly of all exhaust system joints.

3   Rattles and other noises can often be traced to the exhaust system, especially the brackets and mountings **(see illustration)**. Try to move the pipes and silencers. If the components are able to come into contact with the body or suspension parts, secure the system with new mountings. Otherwise separate the joints (if possible) and twist the pipes as necessary to provide additional clearance.

22 Road test (every 9000 miles/15 000 km or 12 months)

Instruments and electrical equipment

1   Check the operation of all instruments and electrical equipment.

2   Make sure that all instruments read correctly, and switch on all electrical equipment in turn, to check that it functions properly.

Steering and suspension

3   Check for any abnormalities in the steering, suspension, handling or road "feel".

4   Drive the vehicle, and check that there are no unusual vibrations or noises.

5   Check that the steering feels positive, with no excessive "sloppiness", or roughness, and check for any suspension noises when cornering and driving over bumps.

Drivetrain

6   Check the performance of the engine, clutch (where applicable), gearbox/transmission and driveshafts.

7   Listen for any unusual noises from the engine, clutch and gearbox/transmission.

8   Make sure that the engine runs smoothly when idling, and that there is no hesitation when accelerating.

9   Check that, where applicable, the clutch action is smooth and progressive, that the drive is taken up smoothly, and that the pedal travel is not excessive. Also listen for any noises when the clutch pedal is depressed.

10   On manual gearbox models, check that all gears can be engaged smoothly without noise, and that the gear lever action is not abnormally vague or "notchy".

11   On automatic transmission models, make sure that all gearchanges occur smoothly, without snatching, and without an increase in engine speed between changes. Check that all the gear positions can be selected with the vehicle at rest. If any problems are found, they should be referred to a Vauxhall/Opel dealer.

12   Listen for a metallic clicking sound from the front of the vehicle, as the vehicle is driven slowly in a circle with the steering on full-lock. Carry out this check in both directions. If a clicking noise is heard, this indicates wear in a driveshaft joint, in which case renew the joint if necessary.

Check the operation and performance of the braking system

13   Make sure that the vehicle does not pull to one side when braking, and that the wheels do not lock prematurely when braking hard.

14   Check that there is no vibration through the steering when braking.

15   Check that the handbrake operates correctly without excessive movement of the lever, and that it holds the vehicle stationary on a slope.

16   Test the operation of the brake servo unit as follows. With the engine off, depress the footbrake four or five times to exhaust the vacuum. Hold the brake pedal depressed, then start the engine. As the engine starts, there should be a noticeable "give" in the brake pedal as vacuum builds up. Allow the engine to run for at least two minutes, and then switch it off. If the brake pedal is depressed now, it should be possible to detect a hiss from the servo as the pedal is depressed. After about four or five applications, no further hissing should be heard, and the pedal should feel considerably harder.

23 Air cleaner filter element renewal (every 18 000 miles/30 000 km or 2 years)

1   The air cleaner assembly is located at the front right-hand corner of the engine compartment.

2   Release the securing clips, and lift the air cleaner cover sufficiently to enable removal of the filter element. Where applicable, take care not to strain the wiring for the air mass meter, attached to the air cleaner cover (DOHC engine models), or the intake air temperature sensor (SOHC engine models with multi-point fuel injection), located in the air trunking.

3   Lift out the filter element **(see illustration)**.

4   Wipe out the casing and the cover. Fit the new filter, noting that the rubber locating flange should be uppermost, and secure the cover with the clips.

24   Spark plug check and renewal - SOHC engines (every 18 000 miles/30 000 km or 2 years)

1   The correct functioning of the spark plugs is vital for the correct running and efficiency of the engine. It is essential that the plugs fitted are appropriate for the engine, the suitable type being specified at the beginning of this Chapter. If the correct type of plug is used and the engine is in good condition, the spark plugs should not need attention between scheduled renewal intervals, except for adjustment of their gaps. Spark plug cleaning is rarely necessary, and should not be attempted unless specialised equipment is available, as damage can easily be caused to the firing ends.

2   To remove the plugs, first open the bonnet, then proceed as follows.

3   If necessary, mark the HT leads 1 to 4, to correspond to the cylinder the lead serves (No 1 cylinder is nearest the timing belt end of the engine). Pull the HT leads from the plugs by gripping the end connectors, not the leads, otherwise the lead connections may be fractured.

4   It is advisable to remove any dirt from the spark plug recesses using a clean brush, vacuum cleaner or compressed air, before removing the plugs, to prevent the dirt dropping into the cylinders.

5   Unscrew the plugs using a spark plug spanner, a suitable box spanner, or a deep socket and extension bar (see illustration). Keep the socket in alignment with the spark plugs, otherwise if it is forcibly moved to either side, the porcelain top of the spark plug may be broken off. As each plug is removed, examine it as follows.

6   Examination of the spark plugs will give a good indication of the condition of the engine. If the insulator nose of the spark plug is clean and white, with no deposits, this is indicative of a weak mixture or too hot a plug (a hot plug transfers heat away from the electrode slowly, while a cold plug transfers heat away quickly).

7   If the tip and insulator nose are covered with hard black-looking deposits, then this is indicative that the idle mixture is too rich. Should the plug be black and oily, then it is likely that the engine is fairly worn, as well as the mixture being too rich.

8   If the insulator nose is covered with light-tan to greyish-brown deposits, then the mixture is correct and it is likely that the engine is in good condition.

9   The spark plug gap is of considerable importance as, if it is too large or too small, the size of the spark and its efficiency will be seriously impaired. For the best results, the spark plug gap should be set in accordance with the Specifications at the beginning of this Chapter.

10   To set the spark plug gap, measure the gap between the electrodes with a feeler gauge, and then bend open, or close, the outer plug electrode until the correct gap is achieved (see illustrations). The

24.5 Removing a spark plug - SOHC engine

centre electrode should never be bent, as this may crack the insulation and cause plug failure, if nothing worse.

11   Special spark plug electrode gap adjusting tools are available from most motor accessory shops (see illustration).

12   Before fitting the new spark plugs, check that the threaded connector sleeves on the top of the plug are tight, and that the plug exterior surfaces and threads are clean.

13   Screw in the spark plugs by hand where possible, then tighten them to the specified torque. Take extra care to enter the plug threads correctly, as the cylinder head is of light alloy construction.

14   Reconnect the HT leads in their correct order.

25   Fuel filter renewal (every 18 000 miles/30 000 km or 2 years)

1   The fuel filter is located under the rear of the vehicle (see illustration).

2   Depressurise the fuel system as described in Chapter 4A.

3   Disconnect the battery negative lead.

4   Chock the front wheels, then jack up the rear of the vehicle, and support securely on axle stands (see "Jacking, towing and wheel changing").

5   Loosen the clamp nut and bolt, and withdraw the filter from its clamp (see illustration). Note the orientation of the fuel flow direction arrow.

6   Position a suitable container below the fuel filter, to catch spilt fuel.

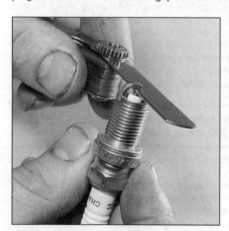

24.10a Measuring a spark plug electrode gap using a feeler gauge

24.10b Measuring a spark plug electrode gap using a wire gauge

24.11 Adjusting a spark plug electrode gap using a special tool

25.1 Fuel filter - Combo Van model

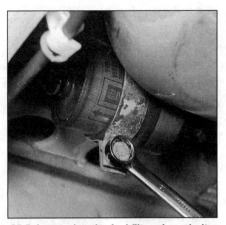

25.5 Loosening the fuel filter clamp bolt - Hatchback model

25.7a Release the connectors, . . .

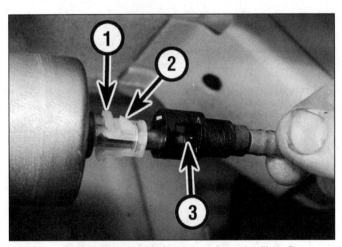

25.7b . . . and disconnect the fuel hoses from the filter. Depress the catches (1) to release the locking tags (2) from the locating holes (3)

7   Release the connectors and disconnect the fuel hoses from the fuel filter, noting their locations to ensure correct refitting **(see illustrations)**. A Vauxhall/Opel special tool is available to disconnect the hose connectors, but provided care is taken, the connections can be released using a pair of pliers. Be prepared for fuel spillage, and take adequate fire precautions.
8   Recover the mounting rubber from the old filter, and transfer it to

the new filter.
9   Fitting the new filter is a reversal of removal, bearing in mind the following points.

(a)   Ensure that the filter is fitted with the flow direction arrow on the filter body pointing in the direction of fuel flow (see illustration).

(b)   Ensure that the hoses are reconnected to their correct locations, as noted before removal.

(c)   On completion, run the engine and check for leaks. If leakage is evident, stop the engine immediately and rectify the problem without delay.

26   Manual gearbox oil level check (every 18 000 miles/30 000 km or 2 years)

1   Ensure that the vehicle is standing on level ground and the handbrake applied.
2   Working underneath the vehicle, unscrew the gearbox oil level plug, which is located in the rear left of the differential housing **(see illustration)**.
3   The oil level should be up to the lower edge of the level plug hole.
4   If necessary, top-up with oil through the breather/filler orifice in the gear selector cover. Unscrew the breather/filler plug, and top-up with the specified grade of oil, until oil just begins to run from the level plug hole. A funnel may be helpful, to avoid spillage **(see illustrations)**. Do not overfill - if too much oil is added, wait until the excess has run out of the level plug hole. Refit the level plug and the breather/filler plug on completion.

25.9 Ensure that the flow direction arrow points in the direction of fuel flow

26.2 Gearbox oil level plug (arrowed)

26.4a Unscrew the breather/filler plug . . .

26.4b . . . and top-up with the specified grade of oil

27.4 Automatic transmission fluid level dipstick location (arrowed)

27 Automatic transmission fluid level check (every 18 000 miles/30 000 km or 2 years)

1   To check the fluid level, the vehicle must be parked on level ground. Apply the handbrake.
2   If the transmission fluid is cold (ie, if the engine is cold), the level check must be completed with the engine idling, within one minute of the engine being started.
3   With the engine idling, fully depress the brake pedal, and move the gear selector lever smoothly through all positions, finishing in position "P".
4   With the engine still idling, withdraw the transmission fluid level dipstick (located at the left-hand side of the engine compartment, next to the engine oil level dipstick). Pull up the lever on the top of the dipstick to release it from the tube. Wipe the dipstick clean with a lint-free rag, re-insert it and withdraw it again **(see illustration)**.
5   If the transmission fluid was cold at the beginning of the procedure, the fluid level should be on the "MAX" mark on the side of the dipstick marked "+20°C". Note that 0.4 litres of fluid is required to raise the level from the "MIN" to the "MAX" mark **(see illustration)**.
6   If the transmission fluid was at operating temperature at the beginning of the procedure (ie, if the vehicle had been driven for at least 12 miles/20 km), the fluid level should be between the "MIN" and "MAX" marks on the side of the dipstick marked "+80°C". Note that 0.2 litres of fluid is required to raise the level from the "MIN" to the "MAX" mark.
7   If topping-up is necessary, stop the engine, and top-up with the specified type of fluid through the transmission dipstick tube.
8   Re-check the level, and refit the dipstick on completion.

28 Power steering fluid level check (every 18 000 miles/30 000 km or 2 years)

1   The power steering fluid level is checked with a dipstick attached to the reservoir filler cap. The reservoir is located in the front left-hand corner of the engine compartment, directly behind the headlight unit.
2   The fluid level should be checked with the engine stopped and the front wheels set in the straight-ahead position.
3   Unscrew the filler cap from the top of the reservoir, and wipe all fluid from the cap dipstick with a clean rag. Refit the filler cap, then re-move it again. Note the fluid level on the dipstick. When the engine is cold, the fluid level should be up to the lower mark on the dipstick. When the engine is at normal operating temperature, the fluid level should up to the upper mark on the dipstick **(see illustration)**.
4   If necessary, top-up with the specified type of fluid, then refit the filler cap securely **(see illustration)**.
5   If frequent topping-up of the system proves to be necessary, this indicates that there is a leak in the hydraulic system, which should be traced and rectified without delay.

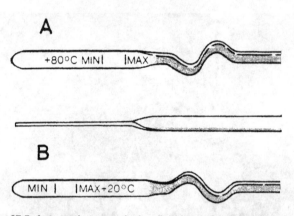

27.5 Automatic transmission fluid level dipstick markings

A   *Markings for fluid at operating temperature*
B   *Markings for cold fluid*

29 Automatic transmission system check (every 18 000 miles/30 000 km or 2 years)

1   This check is part of the manufacturer's maintenance schedule, and involves testing the automatic transmission control system using special dedicated test equipment. Such testing will allow the test equipment to read any fault codes stored in the electronic control unit memory.
2   Unless a fault is suspected, this test is not essential, although it should be noted that it is recommended by the manufacturers.
3   If access to suitable test equipment is not possible, make a thorough check of all control system components and wiring for security and obvious signs of damage. Further details of the control system can be found in Chapter 7B.

30 Coolant renewal (every 18 000 miles/30 000 km or 2 years)

Cooling system draining

Warning: *Wait until the engine is cold before starting this procedure. Do not allow antifreeze to come in contact with your skin, or with the painted surfaces of the vehicle. Rinse off spills immediately with plenty of water. Never leave antifreeze lying around in an open container, or in a puddle on the driveway or garage floor. Children and pets are attracted by its sweet smell, but antifreeze is fatal if ingested. Refer to the note at the beginning of the "Antifreeze mixture" sub-section before proceeding.*

28.3 Power steering fluid level marks (arrowed)

28.4 Topping-up the power steering fluid level

30.12 On SOHC engine models, remove the coolant temperature sender (arrowed) before filling the cooling system

30.15 Refitting the thermostat housing bleed screw - DOHC engine

1   To drain the cooling system, first cover the expansion tank cap with a wad of rag, and slowly turn the cap anti-clockwise to relieve the pressure in the cooling system (a hissing sound will normally be heard). Wait until any pressure remaining in the system is released, then continue to turn the cap until it can be removed.

2   Position a suitable container beneath the radiator bottom hose connection, then slacken the hose clip and ease the hose from the radiator stub. If the hose joint has not been disturbed for some time, it will be necessary to gently manipulate the hose to break the joint. Do not use excessive force, or the radiator stub could be damaged. Allow the coolant to drain into the container.

3   As no cylinder block drain plug is fitted, and the radiator bottom hose may be situated above the bottom of the radiator, the system cannot be drained completely. Care should therefore be taken when refilling the system, to maintain antifreeze strength. If the system is being drained for coolant renewal, it is recommended that the cooling fan switch is unscrewed from the radiator (see Chapter 3) in order to allow the maximum possible quantity of coolant to be drained.

4   If the coolant has been drained for a reason other than renewal, then provided it is clean and less than two years old, it can be re-used. Note that Vauxhall/Opel do not specify renewal intervals for the coolant installed in the system when the vehicle is new, so renewal is up to the discretion of the owner.

Cooling system flushing

5   If coolant renewal has been neglected, or if the antifreeze mixture has become diluted, then in time, the cooling system may gradually lose efficiency, as the coolant passages become restricted due to rust, scale deposits, and other sediment. The cooling system efficiency can be restored by flushing the system clean.

6   The radiator should be flushed independently of the engine, to avoid unnecessary contamination.

7   To flush the radiator, disconnect the top hose at the radiator, then insert a garden hose into the radiator top inlet. Direct a flow of clean water through the radiator, and continue flushing until clean water emerges from the radiator bottom outlet (the bottom radiator hose should have been disconnected to drain the system). If after a reasonable period, the water still does not run clear, the radiator can be flushed with a good proprietary cleaning agent such as Holts Radflush or Holts Speedflush. It is important that the cleaning agent manufacturer's instructions are followed carefully. If the contamination is particularly bad, insert the hose in the radiator bottom outlet, and flush the radiator in the reverse direction ("reverse-flushing").

8   To flush the engine block, the thermostat must be removed, because it will be shut, and would otherwise prevent the flow of water around the engine. On SOHC engine models, remove the thermostat as described in Chapter 3, then temporarily refit the thermostat cover. On DOHC engine models, the thermostat cannot be removed from the cover. In order to flush the block, the thermostat cover must be removed as described in Chapter 3, and the aperture temporarily covered over. Take care not to introduce dirt or debris into the system if this approach is used.

9   With the radiator top and bottom hoses disconnected from the radiator, insert a hose into the radiator bottom hose. Direct a clean flow of water through the engine, and continue flushing until clean water emerges from the radiator top hose.

10   On completion of flushing, refit the thermostat and/or cover with reference to Chapter 3, and reconnect the hoses.

Cooling system filling

11   Before attempting to fill the cooling system, make sure that all hoses and clips are in good condition, and that the clips are tight. Note that an antifreeze mixture must be used all year round, to prevent corrosion of the alloy engine components. Where applicable, also ensure that the cooling fan switch has been refitted to the radiator.

12   On SOHC engine models, disconnect the wire and unscrew the coolant temperature sender from the inlet manifold (see illustration). On DOHC models, unscrew the bleed screw which is situated in the thermostat housing cover.

13   Remove the expansion tank cap, and fill the system by slowly pouring the coolant into the expansion tank to prevent airlocks from forming.

14   If the coolant is being renewed, begin by pouring in a couple of litres of water, followed by the correct quantity of antifreeze, then top-up with more water.

15   When coolant free of air bubbles emerges from the orifice, refit the coolant temperature sender and tighten it securely (SOHC engines), or refit the bleed screw and tighten it to the specified torque setting (DOHC engines) (see illustration).

16   Top-up the coolant level to the "KALT" (or "COLD") mark on the expansion tank, then refit the expansion tank cap.

17   Start the engine and run it until it reaches normal operating temperature, then stop the engine and allow it to cool.

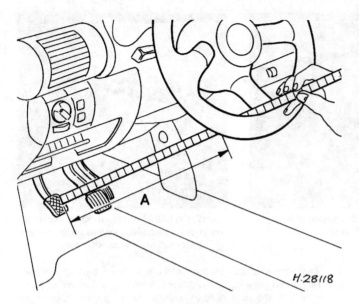

H.28118

31.1a Measure the dimension (A) from the top edge of the pedal to the lowest point of the steering wheel . . .

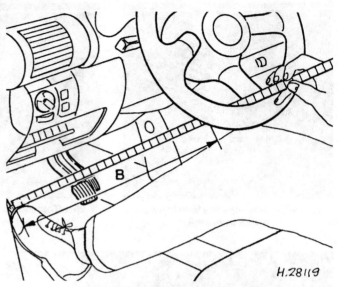

H.28119

31.1b . . . then fully depress the pedal and repeat the measurement (B)

18   Check for leaks, particularly around disturbed components. Check the coolant level in the expansion tank, and top-up if necessary. Note that the system must be cold before an accurate level is indicated in the expansion tank. If the expansion tank cap is removed while the engine is still warm, cover the cap with a thick cloth, and unscrew the cap slowly to gradually relieve the system pressure (a hissing sound will normally be heard). Wait until any pressure remaining in the system is released, then continue to turn the cap until it can be removed.

Antifreeze mixture

Note: *Vauxhall/Opel do not specify renewal intervals for the antifreeze mixture, as the mixture used to fill the system when the vehicle is new is designed to last the lifetime of the vehicle. However, it is strongly recommended that the coolant is renewed at the intervals specified in the "Maintenance schedule", as a precaution against possible engine corrosion problems. This is particularly advisable if the coolant has been renewed previously, using an antifreeze other than that specified by Vauxhall/Opel. With many antifreeze types, the corrosion inhibitors become progressively less effective with age. It is up to the individual owner whether or not to follow this advice.*

19   Always use an ethylene-glycol based antifreeze which is suitable for use in mixed-metal cooling systems. The quantity of antifreeze and levels of protection are indicated in the Specifications.

20   Before adding antifreeze, the cooling system should be completely drained, preferably flushed, and all hoses and clips checked for condition and security.

21   After filling with antifreeze, a label should be attached to the radiator or expansion tank, stating the type and concentration of antifreeze used, and the date installed. Any subsequent topping-up should be made with the same type and concentration of antifreeze.

22   Do not use engine antifreeze in the windscreen/tailgate washer system, as it will cause damage to the vehicle paintwork. A screen-wash such as Turtle Wax High Tech Screen Wash should be added to the washer system in the quantities recommended on the bottle.

31 Clutch cable adjustment check (every 18 000 miles/30 000 km or 2 years)

1   Working inside the vehicle, ensure that the clutch pedal is in its normal rest position, then measure the distance from the centre of the top edge of the pedal to the lowest point of the steering wheel. Fully depress the pedal, and repeat the measurement **(see illustrations)**. The measurements can be taken using a suitable strip of wood or

metal, as the important figure is the *difference* between the two measurements, ie the movement (stroke) of the pedal.

2   The difference between the two measurements must be as given in the Specifications - if not, adjust the clutch cable as follows to achieve the specified pedal movement.

3   Working in the engine compartment, remove the clip from the threaded rod at the clutch release arm on the gearbox, then turn the threaded rod as required, using a spanner on the flats provided **(see illustration)**. Turn the rod clockwise to increase pedal movement, or anti-clockwise to decrease pedal movement. Recheck the pedal movement, and then refit the clip to the threaded rod on completion.

4   On a vehicle in which the clutch has covered a high mileage, it may no longer be possible to adjust the cable to achieve the specified pedal movement, and this indicates that the clutch friction disc requires renewal. Note that when correctly adjusted, the clutch pedal will rest slightly higher than the brake pedal - it is incorrect for the two pedals to be in alignment. If the pedals are aligned, the clutch cable requires adjustment.

32 Hinge and lock lubrication (every 18 000 miles/30 000 km or 2 years)

1   Lubricate the hinges of the bonnet, doors and tailgate with a light general-purpose oil. Similarly, lubricate all latches, locks and lock strikers. At the same time, check the security and operation of all the locks, adjusting them if necessary (see Chapter 11).

2   Lightly lubricate the bonnet release mechanism and cable with a suitable grease.

33 Rear brake shoe, drum and wheel cylinder check (every 18 000 miles/30 000 km or 2 years)

1   Chock the front wheels, then jack up the rear of the vehicle, and support it securely on axle stands (see *"Jacking, towing and wheel changing"*).

2   For a quick check, the thickness of friction material remaining on one of the brake shoes can be observed through the hole in the brake backplate which is exposed by prising out the sealing grommet **(see illustration)**. If a rod of the same diameter as the specified minimum friction material thickness is placed against the shoe friction material, the amount of wear can be assessed. A torch or inspection light will probably be required. If the friction material on any shoe is worn down

31.3 Removing the clip from the clutch pedal threaded rod. Threaded rod adjuster flats arrowed

33.2 Removing the sealing grommet from a brake backplate

35.4 Rocking a roadwheel to check steering/suspension component wear

to the specified minimum thickness or less, all four shoes must be renewed as a set.

3   For a comprehensive check, the brake drum should be removed and cleaned. This will allow the wheel cylinders to be checked, and the condition of the brake drum itself to be fully examined (see Chapter 9).

34 Brake fluid renewal (every 18 000 miles/30 000 km or 2 years)

1   The procedure is similar to that for the bleeding of the hydraulic system as described in Chapter 9, except that the brake fluid reservoir should be emptied by siphoning, using a (clean) old battery hydrometer or similar before starting, and allowance should be made for the old fluid to be expelled from the circuit when bleeding each section of the circuit.

35 Front suspension and steering check (every 18 000 miles/30 000 km or 2 years)

1   Apply the handbrake, then raise the front of the vehicle and securely support it on axle stands (see *"Jacking, towing and wheel changing"*).

2   Inspect the balljoint dust covers and the steering gear gaiters for splits, chafing or deterioration. Any wear of these components will cause loss of lubricant, and may allow water to enter the components, resulting in rapid deterioration of the balljoints or steering gear.

3   On vehicles with power steering, check the fluid hoses for chafing or deterioration, and the pipe and hose unions for fluid leaks. Also check for signs of fluid leakage under pressure from the steering gear rubber gaiters, which would indicate failed fluid seals within the steering gear.

4   Grasp each roadwheel at the 12 o'clock and 6 o'clock positions, and try to rock it **(see illustration)**. Very slight free play may be felt, but if the movement is appreciable, further investigation is necessary to determine the source. Continue rocking the wheel while an assistant depresses the footbrake. If the movement is now eliminated or significantly reduced, it is likely that the hub bearings are at fault. If the free play is still evident with the footbrake depressed, then there is wear in the suspension joints or mountings.

5   Now grasp each wheel at the 9 o'clock and 3 o'clock positions, and try to rock it as before. Any movement felt now may again be caused by wear in the hub bearings or the steering track-rod end balljoints. If the track-rod end balljoint is worn, the visual movement will be obvious.

6   Using a large screwdriver or flat bar, check for wear in the suspension mounting bushes by levering between the relevant suspension component and its attachment point. Some movement is to be expected, as the mountings are made of rubber, but excessive wear should be obvious. Also check the condition of any visible rubber bushes, looking for splits, cracks or contamination of the rubber.

7   Check for any signs of fluid leakage around the suspension strut/shock absorber bodies, or from the rubber gaiters around the piston rods. Should any fluid be noticed, the suspension strut/shock absorber is defective internally, and should be renewed. **Note:** *Suspension struts/shock absorbers should always be renewed in pairs on the same axle.*

8   With the vehicle standing on its wheels, have an assistant turn the steering wheel back and forth about an eighth of a turn each way. There should be very little, if any, lost movement between the steering wheel and roadwheels. If this is not the case, closely observe the joints and mountings previously described, but in addition check the steering column rubber coupling for wear, and also check the steering gear itself.

9   The efficiency of each suspension strut/shock absorber may be checked by bouncing the vehicle at each corner. Generally speaking, the body will return to its normal position and stop after being depressed. If it rises and returns on a rebound, the suspension strut/shock absorber is probably suspect. Also examine the suspension strut/shock absorber upper and lower mountings for any signs of wear.

36 Rear suspension check (every 18 000 miles/30 000 km or 2 years)

1   Chock the front wheels, then jack up the rear of the vehicle and support securely on axle stands (see *"Jacking, towing and wheel changing"*).

2   Inspect the rear suspension components for any signs of obvious wear or damage. Pay particular attention to the rubber mounting bushes, and renew if necessary (see Chapter 10).

3   Grasp each roadwheel at the 12 o'clock and 6 o'clock positions, and try to rock it. Any excess movement indicates incorrect adjustment or wear in the wheel bearings. Wear may also be accompanied by a rumbling sound when the wheel is spun, or a noticeable roughness if the wheel is turned slowly. The wheel bearing can be renewed as described in Chapter 10.

4   Check the rear shock absorbers in a similar manner to that described previously for the front shock absorbers.

37 Driveshaft check (every 18 000 miles/30 000 km or 2 years)

1   With the vehicle raised and securely supported on stands, turn the steering onto full-lock, then slowly rotate each front roadwheel. Inspect the condition of the outer constant velocity (CV) joint rubber gaiters, while squeezing the gaiters to open out the folds. Check for signs of cracking, splits or deterioration of the rubber, which may allow the grease to escape and lead to water and grit entering the joint. Also check the security and condition of the retaining clips. Repeat these checks on the inner CV joints. If any damage or deterioration is found, the gaiters should be renewed as described in Chapter 8.

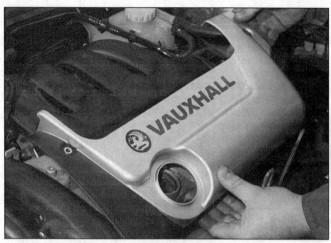

38.1a Removing the plastic cover from the camshaft cover -
DOHC engine

38.1b Using the plastic tool to pull an HT lead from a spark plug

38.1c Use a suitable long-reach socket to
remove the spark plugs

38.1d Tighten the spark plugs to the
specified torque

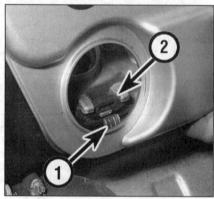

38.1e Ensure that the plastic cover lugs
(1) engage with the camshaft
cover rubbers (2)

2   At the same time, check the general condition of the CV joints themselves by first holding the driveshaft and attempting to rotate the wheel. Repeat this check by holding the inner joint and attempting to rotate the driveshaft. Any appreciable movement indicates wear in the joints, wear in the driveshaft splines, or a loose front hub nut.

38   Spark plug check and renewal - DOHC engine (every 36 000 miles/60 000 km or 4 years)

1   Proceed as described for SOHC engines in Section 24, noting the following points **(see illustrations)**.

(a) *For access to the spark plugs, the oil filler cap and the plastic cover must be removed from the top of the camshaft cover. The plastic cover is secured by two screws.*

(b) *A plastic tool is provided (attached to one of the spark plug leads) to pull the HT leads from the spark plugs.*

(c) *Take great care, when removing and refitting the spark plugs, to use a suitable long-reach socket, which locates in the spark plug hole (the manufacturers recommend the use of Vauxhall/Opel special tool KM-194-B). If a standard spark plug removal socket is used, which does not provide adequate guidance in the spark plug's hole, it is possible for the socket to touch the ceramic body of the spark plug, causing hairline cracks - this may cause intermittent misfiring and possible damage to the catalytic converter.*

(d) *Tighten the spark plugs to the specified torque.*

(e) *When refitting the plastic cover, ensure that the lugs on the plastic cover engage with the rubbers on the camshaft cover.*

39   Timing belt check (every 36 000 miles/60 000 km or 4 years)

Note: *Although Vauxhall/Opel do not specify an interval for checking the tension of the timing belt on SOHC engines, it is strongly recommended that the following checks are carried out for all models at the intervals specified in the "Maintenance schedule". Similarly, Vauxhall/Opel do not specify renewal intervals for the timing belt, but it is common practice to renew the timing belt on petrol engines after approximately 36 000 miles/60 000 km. The following precautionary checks are recommended to prevent the possibility of serious engine damage which may occur if the belt is worn, or if the belt breaks in service. It is up to the individual owner to decide whether or not to follow this advice. Consult a Vauxhall/Opel dealer for further advice if in doubt.*

1   Remove the upper outer timing belt cover, with reference to Chapter 2A if necessary.

2   Ensure that the gearbox/transmission is in neutral, then using a suitable spanner or socket on the crankshaft pulley bolt, rotate the crankshaft so that the full length of the timing belt can be progressively checked. Examine the belt carefully for any signs of uneven wear, splitting (particularly around the teeth), or oil contamination, and renew it if there is the slightest doubt about its condition.

3   There is no requirement to check the drivebelt tension (DOHC engines are fitted with an automatic tensioner), but if desired, the tension can be checked as described in Chapter 2A. It is recommended that a check on belt tension is made whenever the belt is inspected, but it is up to the individual owner to decide whether or not to follow this advice.

4   On completion, refit the timing belt cover.

Chapter 2 Part A:
In-car engine repair procedures

Contents

Specifications

General - SOHC engine

Engine type	Four-cylinder, in-line, water-cooled. Single overhead camshaft, belt-driven, acting on hydraulic valve lifters
Manufacturer's engine codes:*	
1.2 litre engine without catalytic converter	12 NZ
1.2 litre engine with catalytic converter, but no EGR system (see Chapter 4B)	C 12 NZ
1.2 litre engine with catalytic converter and EGR system (see Chapter 4B)	X 12 SZ
1.4 litre single-point fuel injection engine	C 14 NZ
1.4 litre multi-point fuel injection engine	C 14 SE
Bore:	
1.2 litre engines	72.00 mm
1.4 litre engines	77.60 mm
Stroke	73.40 mm
Capacity:	
1.2 litre engines	1196 cc
1.4 litre engines	1389 cc

General - SOHC engine (continued)

Firing order	1-3-4-2 (No 1 cylinder at timing belt end)
Direction of crankshaft rotation	Clockwise (viewed from timing belt end of engine)

Compression ratio:

12 NZ and C 12 NZ engines	9.1:1
X 12 SZ engine	10.0:1
C 14 NZ engine	9.4:1
C 14 SE engine	10.0:1

Maximum power:

12 NZ and C 12 NZ engines	33 kW at 5000 rpm
X 12 SZ engine	33 kW at 4600 rpm
C 14 NZ engine	44 kW at 5200 rpm
C 14 SE engine	60 kW at 5800 rpm

Maximum torque:

12 NZ engine	88 Nm at 2800 rpm
C 12 NZ engine	86 Nm at 2800 rpm
X 12 SZ engine	90 Nm at 2800 rpm
C 14 NZ engine	103 Nm at 2800 rpm
C 14 SE engine	114 Nm at 3400 rpm
Maximum compression pressure difference between cylinders	1.0 bar

For details of engine code location, see "Buying spare parts and vehicle identification numbers".

General - DOHC engine

Engine type	Four-cylinder, in-line, water-cooled. Double overhead camshafts, belt-driven, acting on hydraulic valve lifters
Manufacturer's engine code*	C 16 XE
Bore	79.00 mm
Stroke	81.50 mm
Capacity	1598 cc
Firing order	1-3-4-2 (No 1 cylinder at timing belt end)
Direction of crankshaft rotation	Clockwise (viewed from timing belt end of engine)
Compression ratio	11.0:1
Maximum power	80 kW at 5500 rpm
Maximum torque	150 Nm at 3500 rpm
Maximum compression pressure difference between cylinders	1.0 bar

For details of engine code location, see "Buying spare parts and vehicle identification numbers".

Camshaft - SOHC engines

Endfloat	0.090 to 0.210 mm

Camshaft bearing journal diameter:

No 1	39.435 to 39.455 mm
No 2	39.685 to 39.705 mm
No 3	39.935 to 39.955 mm
No 4	40.185 to 40.205 mm
No 5	40.435 to 40.455 mm

Camshaft bearing journal diameter in housing:

No 1	39.500 to 39.525 mm
No 2	39.750 to 39.775 mm
No 3	40.000 to 40.025 mm
No 4	40.250 to 40.275 mm
No 5	40.500 to 40.525 mm
Maximum permissible radial run-out	0.040 mm

Camshafts - DOHC engine

Endfloat	0.040 to 0.144 mm
Camshaft bearing journal diameter	27.939 to 27.960 mm
Maximum permissible radial run-out	0.040 mm

Lubrication system

Minimum permissible oil pressure at idle speed, with engine at operating temperature (oil pressure of at least 80°C)	1.5 bars
Oil pump type	Gear-type, driven directly from crankshaft

Oil pump clearances:

Inner-to-outer gear teeth clearance (backlash)	0.100 to 0.200 mm
Gear-to-housing clearance (endfloat)	0.080 to 0.150 mm

Flywheel

Maximum permissible lateral run-out of starter ring gear	0.500 mm
Refinishing limit - maximum depth of material which may be removed from clutch friction surface	0.300 mm

Torque wrench settings

	Nm	lbf ft
Plastic shield-to-camshaft cover screws (DOHC engine)	4	3
Camshaft cover bolts	8	6
Crankshaft pulley bolt:*		
Stage 1	95	70
Stage 2	Angle-tighten a further 30°	
Stage 3	Angle-tighten a further 15°	
Outer timing belt cover bolts	4	3
Rear timing belt cover bolts:		
SOHC engines	12	9
DOHC engine	6	4
Coolant pump bolts	8	6
Camshaft sprocket bolt:		
SOHC engines	45	33
DOHC engine	65	48
Timing belt tension indicator bolt (SOHC engines)	20	15
Timing belt tensioner bolt (DOHC engine)	20	15
Timing belt idler roller bolts (DOHC engine)	25	18
DIS module-to-mounting plate bolts	8	6
DIS module mounting plate-to-camshaft housing bolts (SOHC engines)	12	9
DIS module mounting plate-to-cylinder head bolts (DOHC engine)	8	6
Camshaft bearing cap bolts (DOHC engine)	8	6
Cylinder head bolts (all engines):*		
Stage 1	25	18
Stage 2	Angle-tighten a further 60°	
Stage 3	Angle-tighten a further 60°	
Stage 4	Angle-tighten a further 60°	
Camshaft thrust plate bolts (SOHC engines)	8	6
Sump drain plug:		
SOHC engines	55	41
DOHC engine	45	33
Oil pick-up pipe-to-oil pump bolts**	8	6
Oil pick-up pipe bracket-to-cylinder block bolt	8	6
Sump-to-cylinder block bolts**	8	6
Sump-to-gearbox bolts (DOHC engine)	60	44
Oil pump-to-cylinder block bolts	6	4
Oil pump cover screws	6	4
Oil pressure relief valve plug to oil pump	30	22
Clutch bellhousing cover plate	7	5
Flywheel/driveplate bolts:*		
Stage 1	35	26
Stage 2	Angle-tighten a further 30°	
Stage 3	Angle-tighten a further 15°	
Engine-to-gearbox/transmission bolts	75	55
Right-hand engine mounting block-to-body bolts:		
SOHC engine models without power steering	65	48
SOHC engine models with power steering	20	15
DOHC engine models	20	15
Right-hand engine mounting block-to-engine bracket bolt/nut	60	44
Right-hand engine mounting bracket-to-engine bolts:		
SOHC engine models without power steering	65	48
SOHC engine models with power steering	60	44
DOHC engine models	60	44
Left-hand engine/gearbox/transmission mounting block-to-body bolts**	65	48
Left-hand engine/gearbox/transmission mounting block-to-gearbox/transmission bracket bolts	60	44
Left-hand engine/gearbox/transmission mounting bracket-to-gearbox/transmission bolts	60	44
Rear engine/gearbox/transmission mounting block-to-body bolts	65	48
Rear engine/gearbox/transmission mounting block-to-gearbox/transmission bracket bolts	65	48
Rear engine/gearbox/transmission mounting bracket-to-gearbox/transmission bolts	70	52
Alternator mounting bracket-to-engine bolts - SOHC engines (M10)	40	30
Alternator mounting bracket-to-engine bolts - DOHC engine	35	26
Alternator-to-mounting bracket bolts - SOHC engines (M10)	40	30

2A

Torque wrench settings (continued)

	Nm	lbf ft
Alternator-to-mounting bracket bolts - SOHC engines (M8)...................	30	18
Alternator-to-mounting bracket bolts - DOHC engine	35	26
Alternator-to-adjuster bracket bolts (models with V-belt)	25	18
Alternator adjuster bracket -to-cylinder head bolts (models with V-belt)..	25	18
Alternator (auxiliary) drivebelt tensioner roller-to-engine bolt (models with ribbed belt)	20	15
Exhaust manifold hot-air shroud bolts	8	6
Inlet manifold nuts (SOHC engines).................................	22	16
Lower section of inlet manifold-to-cylinder head nuts (DOHC engine)...	20	15
Exhaust manifold nuts	22	16
Thermostat housing bolts (SOHC engines)	10	7
Thermostat cover-to-housing bolts (DOHC engine)..............	8	6
Thermostat housing-to-cylinder head bolts (DOHC engine)	20	15
Starter motor bolts...	25	18
Spark plugs..	25	18
Main bearing cap bolts:*		
Stage 1	50	37
Stage 2	Angle-tighten a further 45°	
Stage 3	Angle-tighten a further 15°	
Big-end bearing cap bolts:		
SOHC engines - bolts with 15.0 mm thread length	25	18
SOHC engines - bolts with 40.0 mm thread length:*		
Stage 1	25	18
Stage 2..	Angle-tighten a further 30°	
DOHC engine:*		
Stage 1	25	18
Stage 2..	Angle-tighten a further 30°	

*Use new bolts.
**Use thread-locking compound.

1   General information

How to use this Chapter

1   This Part of Chapter 2 describes the repair procedures which can reasonably be carried out on the engine while it remains in the vehicle. If the engine has been removed from the vehicle and is being dismantled as described in Chapter 2B, any preliminary dismantling procedures can be ignored.

2   Note that, while it may be *possible* physically to overhaul items such as the piston/connecting rod assemblies while the engine is in the vehicle, such tasks are not usually carried out as separate operations, and usually require the execution of several additional procedures (not to mention the cleaning of components and of oilways); for this reason, all such tasks are classed as major overhaul procedures, and are described in Chapter 2B.

3   Chapter 2B describes the removal of the engine/transmission unit from the vehicle, and the full overhaul procedures which can then be carried out.

Engine description

4   The engine is of four-cylinder in-line type, with a single overhead camshaft (SOHC) or double overhead camshafts (DOHC), depending on model. The engine is mounted transversely at the front of the vehicle **(see illustrations)**.

5   The crankshaft runs in five shell-type bearings, and the centre bearing incorporates thrust bearing shells to control crankshaft endfloat.

6   The connecting rods are attached to the crankshaft by horizontally-split shell-type big-end bearings. The pistons are attached to the connecting rods by gudgeon pins, which are an interference fit in the connecting rod small-end bores. The aluminium-alloy pistons are fitted with three piston rings - two compression rings and an oil control ring.

7   The camshaft on SOHC engines is driven from the crankshaft by a toothed composite-rubber belt. Each cylinder has two valves (on inlet and one exhaust), operated via rocker arms which are supported

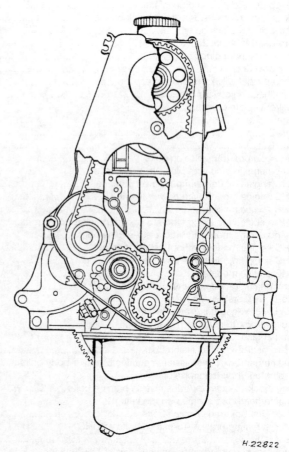

1.4a Front sectional view of SOHC engine

H.22822

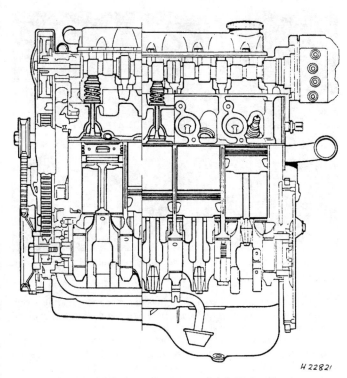

1.4b Side sectional view of SOHC engine

at their pivot ends by hydraulic self-adjusting valve lifters (tappets).

8   On DOHC engines, both camshafts are driven from the crankshaft by a toothed composite-rubber belt. Each cylinder has four valves (two inlet and two exhaust), operated directly from the camshafts via hydraulic self-adjusting valve lifters. One camshaft operates the inlet valves, and the other operates the exhaust valves.

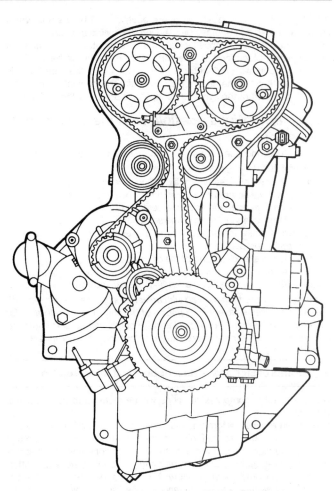

1.4c Front sectional view of DOHC engine

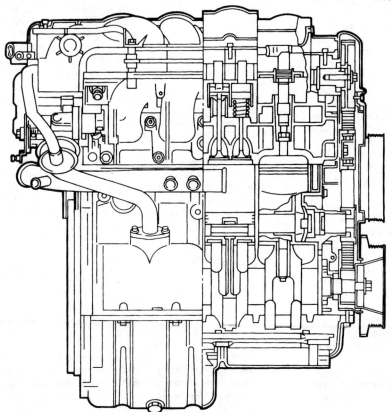

1.4d Side sectional view of DOHC engine

2A

9   The inlet and exhaust valves are each closed by a single valve spring, and operate in guides pressed into the cylinder head.
10   A gear-type oil pump is located in a housing attached to the front of the cylinder block, and is driven directly from the crankshaft.
11   On models with a distributor (see Chapter 5B), the distributor is driven directly from the end of the camshaft. The coolant pump is located at the front of the cylinder block, and is driven by the timing belt.

Repair operations possible with the engine in the vehicle

12   The following operations can be carried out without having to remove the engine from the vehicle.

(a)   Removal and refitting of the cylinder head.
(b)   Removal and refitting of the timing belt and sprockets.
(c)   Removal and refitting of the camshaft.
(d)   Removal and refitting of the sump.
(e)   Removal and refitting of the big-end bearings, connecting rods, and pistons*.
(f)   Removal and refitting of the oil pump.
(g)   Renewal of the engine mountings.
(h)   Removal and refitting of the flywheel/driveplate.

*Although the operation marked with an asterisk can be carried out with the engine in the vehicle (after removal of the sump), it is preferable for the engine to be removed, in the interests of cleanliness and improved access. For this reason, the procedure is described in Chapter 2B.

---

2   Compression test - description and interpretation

Note: A suitable compression gauge will be required to carry out this test.

1   When engine performance is down, or if misfiring occurs which cannot be attributed to the ignition or fuel systems, a compression test can provide diagnostic clues as to the engine's condition. If the test is performed regularly, it can give warning of trouble before any other symptoms become apparent. **Note:** The engine must be at normal operating temperature, and the battery must be fully-charged for this test. Refer to the precautions to be observed when working on models with a catalytic converter (see Chapter 4A, Section 1) before proceeding.
2   Remove all of the spark plugs from the engine (see Chapter 1).
3   Disconnect the wiring plug from the ignition coil/DIS module, and remove the fuel pump relay (see Chapter 4A - "Fuel system - depressurising").
4   Fit a compression tester to the No 1 spark plug hole (No 1 cylinder is nearest the timing belt end of the engine) - the type of tester which screws into the plug thread is to be preferred **(see illustration)**.
5   Have an assistant hold the accelerator pedal fully depressed, at the same time cranking the engine over for approximately four seconds on the starter motor. After one or two revolutions, the compression pressure reading on the gauge should build up to a maximum figure and then stabilise. Record the highest reading obtained.
6   Repeat the test on the remaining cylinders, recording the pressure in each.
7   All cylinders should produce very similar pressures; any difference greater than that specified indicates the existence of a fault. Note that the compression should build up quickly in a healthy engine; low compression on the first stroke, followed by gradually-increasing pressure on successive strokes, indicates worn piston rings. A low compression reading on the first stroke, which does not build up during successive strokes, indicates leaking valves or a blown head gasket (a cracked head could also be the cause). Deposits on the undersides of the valve heads can also cause low compression.
8   If the pressure in any cylinder is significantly lower than that in the remaining cylinders, carry out the following test to isolate the cause. Introduce a teaspoonful of clean engine oil into the relevant cylinder through its spark plug hole, and repeat the test.
9   If the addition of oil temporarily improves the compression pressure, this indicates that bore or piston wear is responsible for the pressure loss. No improvement suggests that leaking or burnt valves, or a blown head gasket may be to blame.

2.4   Compression tester fitted to No 1 spark plug hole

10   A low reading from two adjacent cylinders is almost certainly due to the head gasket having blown between them; the presence of coolant in the engine oil will confirm this.
11   If one cylinder is about 20 percent lower than the others, and the engine has a slightly rough idle, a worn camshaft lobe could be the cause.
12   If the compression reading is unusually high, the combustion chambers are probably coated with carbon deposits. If this is the case, the cylinder head should be removed and decarbonised (see Chapter 2B).
13   On completion of the test, refit the spark plugs, reconnect the ignition coil wiring, and refit the fuel pump relay.

---

3   Top dead centre (TDC) for No 1 piston - locating

1   Top dead centre (TDC) is the highest point in the cylinder that a piston reaches as the crankshaft turns. Each piston reaches TDC at the end of the compression stroke, and again at the end of the exhaust stroke. For the purpose of timing the engine, TDC refers to the position of No 1 piston at the end of its compression stroke. On all engines in this manual, No 1 piston and cylinder are at the timing belt end of the engine.
2   All engine overhaul procedures use the factory timing marks, which vary according to engine type.
3   Disconnect both battery leads.
4   Remove the upper outer timing belt cover as described in Section 6.
5   Using a suitable spanner or socket on the crankshaft pulley bolt (note that on manual gearbox models, the crankshaft can be turned by engaging top gear, and pushing the vehicle backwards or forwards as necessary), rotate the crankshaft to bring No 1 piston to TDC as follows, according to engine type. Whatever method is used, turning the engine will be made much easier if the spark plugs are removed first (see Chapter 1).

SOHC engines

6   The timing marks must be aligned as follows **(see illustrations)**.

(a)   The timing mark on the camshaft sprocket must be aligned with the notch in the rear timing belt cover.
(b)   The notch in the crankshaft pulley, or the timing mark on the TDC sensor wheel (as applicable) must be aligned with the pointer (raised line) on the timing belt cover. Note that if the crankshaft pulley and lower outer timing belt cover have been removed, the timing mark on the crankshaft sprocket can be used instead of the mark on the pulley. The mark on the crankshaft sprocket must align with the corresponding mark on the rear timing belt cover, and the oil pump lower flange.

3.6a Camshaft sprocket timing mark aligned with notch in rear timing belt cover (No 1 piston at TDC) - SOHC engines

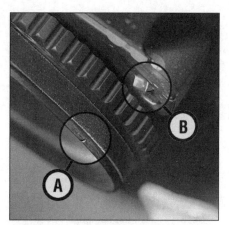

3.6b Notch in crankshaft pulley (A) aligned with timing pointer (B) on timing belt cover (No 1 piston at TDC) - SOHC engines

3.6c Crankshaft sprocket timing mark aligned with mark on rear timing belt cover and oil pump lower flange (No 1 piston at TDC) - SOHC engines

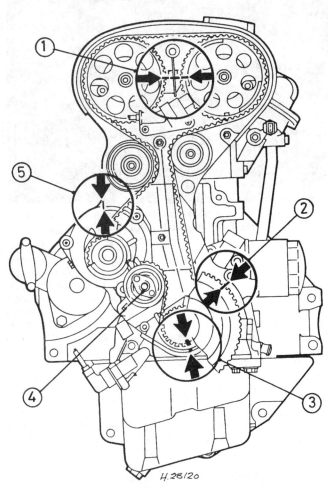

3.7a Timing mark positions with No 1 piston at TDC - DOHC engine

1   Camshaft sprocket timing marks aligned with top edge of cylinder head
2   TDC sensor wheel timing mark aligned with mark on timing belt cover
3   Crankshaft sprocket timing mark aligned with mark on timing belt cover
4   Timing belt tensioner bolt
5   Coolant pump mark aligned with mark on cylinder block (see Chapter 3)

DOHC engines

7   The timing marks must be aligned as follows **(see illustrations)**.

(a)   *The timing marks on the camshaft sprockets must be directly opposite each other, and aligned with the top edge of the cylinder head.*

3.7b Camshaft sprocket timing marks (A) aligned with top edge of cylinder head (B) - DOHC engine

3.7c Crankshaft sprocket timing mark (A) aligned with mark (B) on timing belt cover - DOHC engine

2A

4.1a Disconnect the breather hoses . . .

4.1b . . . from the camshaft cover - SOHC engines

4.3 Lifting the camshaft cover from the camshaft housing - SOHC engines

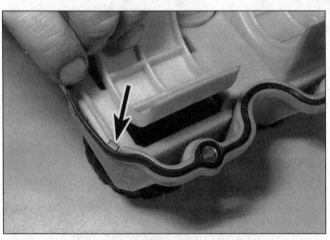

4.5 Tag on seal (arrowed) engages with notch in camshaft cover - SOHC engines

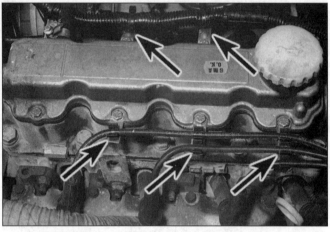

4.8 Ensure that the brackets (arrowed) are in place on the camshaft cover bolts - SOHC engines

(b)   The timing mark on the TDC sensor wheel must be aligned with the pointer (raised line) on the timing belt cover. Note that if the crankshaft pulley and lower outer timing belt cover have been removed, the timing mark on the crankshaft sprocket can be used instead of the mark on the pulley. The mark on the crankshaft sprocket must align with the corresponding mark on the rear timing belt cover (there may be two marks on the sprocket, in which case ignore the mark with a cross stamped across it).

4 Camshaft cover - removal and refitting

SOHC engines

Removal

1   Disconnect the breather hose(s) from the stub(s) on the camshaft cover **(see illustrations)**.
2   Take note of the positions of any brackets and/or clips secured by the camshaft cover bolts, then unscrew and remove the bolts, along with the clips and/or brackets, as applicable.
3   Lift the camshaft cover from the camshaft housing **(see illustration)**. If the cover is stuck, do not lever between the cover and camshaft housing mating surfaces - if necessary, gently tap the cover sideways to free it. Recover the cork gasket or rubber seal, as applicable.

Refitting

4   Before refitting, examine the inside of the cover for a build-up of oil sludge or any other contamination, and if necessary clean the cover with paraffin, or a water-soluble solvent. Where applicable, examine the condition of the crankcase ventilation filter inside the camshaft

cover, and clean as described for the inside of the cover if clogging is evident (if desired, the filter can be removed from the cover, after removing the securing bolts). Dry the cover thoroughly before refitting.
5   Where applicable, examine the condition of the rubber seal, and if necessary renew it. Note that on certain models, the seal rests in a groove in the cover, and a tag on the seal engages with the notch in the cover when the seal is correctly positioned **(see illustration)**. If a cork gasket was fitted, it should always be renewed on refitting.
6   Thoroughly clean the mating faces of the camshaft housing and the cover.
7   Position the cover on the camshaft housing, noting that the breather pipe stub(s) should be nearest the timing belt end of the engine.
8   Refit the securing bolts, ensuring that any clips and/or brackets are in place under their heads as noted before removal, and tighten the bolts to the specified torque in a diagonal sequence **(see illustration)**.
9   Reconnect the breather hose(s) to the stub(s) on the cover.

DOHC engines

Removal

10   Remove the upper section of the inlet manifold as described in Chapter 4A.
11   Disconnect the breather hoses from the flywheel end of the camshaft cover **(see illustration)**.
12   Using the tool provided (attached to one of the spark plug HT lead connectors), pull the HT leads from the spark plugs, and lay them to one side, clear of the camshaft cover.
13   Progressively loosen the camshaft cover securing bolts (preferably working from the ends of the cover towards the centre, in a spiral pattern), then withdraw the bolts **(see illustration)**.
14   Lift the camshaft cover from the cylinder head **(see illustration)**,

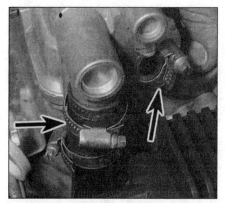

4.11 Disconnect the breather hoses (arrowed) from the camshaft cover

4.13 Unscrew the bolts . . .

4.14 . . . and lift the camshaft cover from the cylinder head

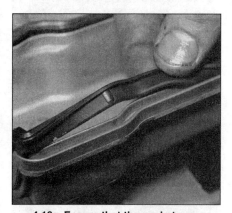

4.16a Ensure that the gaskets are correctly located

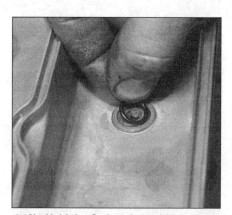

4.16b Hold the O-rings in position using a little grease

5.4 Removing the crankshaft pulley - note notch in pulley and locating lug on sprocket (arrowed)

2A

and recover the rubber gaskets and O-rings.

Refitting

15 Commence refitting by examining the condition of the rubber gaskets and O-rings. If necessary, renew the gaskets and O-rings.

16 Ensure that the gaskets and O-rings are correctly located on the camshaft cover **(see illustrations)**. **Tip:** *Smear the O-rings with a little light grease to hold them in position as the cover is refitted.*

17 Fit the cover to the cylinder head, then refit the securing bolts. Tighten the bolts to the specified torque, working from the centre to the ends of the cover, in a spiral pattern.

18 Reconnect the HT leads to the spark plugs.

19 Reconnect the breather hose to the camshaft cover.

20 Refit the upper section of the inlet manifold as described in Chapter 4A.

---

5 Crankshaft pulley - removal and refitting

Note: *Due to the high specified torque for the pulley securing bolt, it is suggested that consideration is given to renewing the bolt on refitting, although this is not specified by the manufacturers.*

Removal

1 Access is most easily obtained from under the wheel arch, after jacking up the vehicle and removing the right-hand front wheel (see *"Jacking, towing and wheel changing"*). If necessary for subsequent operations, rotate the crankshaft to position No 1 piston to TDC as described in Section 3.

2 Remove the auxiliary drivebelt as described in Chapter 1.

3 To prevent the crankshaft from turning as the pulley bolt is unscrewed, select top gear and have an assistant apply the brakes hard (manual gearbox models only). Alternatively, remove the starter motor, and lock the flywheel ring gear teeth using a suitable tool.

5.7 Using an angle gauge to tighten the crankshaft pulley bolt to the final stage

4 Unscrew the pulley bolt and recover the washer fitted behind it, then remove the pulley **(see illustration)**. Note that on DOHC engines, an E18 Torx socket will be required to unscrew the pulley bolt.

Refitting

5 On refitting, ensure that the notch in the pulley fits over the locating lug on the crankshaft sprocket.

6 Prevent the crankshaft from turning as during removal, then fit the pulley securing bolt (it is recommended that a new bolt is used - refer to the note at the beginning of this Section), ensuring that the washer is in place under the bolt head.

7 Tighten the bolt to the specified torque, in the stages given in the Specifications **(see illustration)**.

8 Refit and tension the auxiliary drivebelt, as described in Chapter 1.

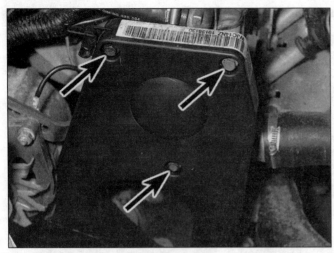

6.3 Upper timing belt cover securing bolts (arrowed) - SOHC engines

6.9a Unscrew the four securing bolts (arrowed) . . .

6.9b . . . and remove the lower timing belt cover - SOHC engines

6.14 Unscrewing a rear timing belt cover upper securing screw - SOHC engines

6.15 Crankshaft speed/position sensor wiring clipped to rear of rear timing belt cover - SOHC engines

6 Timing belt covers - removal and refitting

SOHC engines

Upper outer cover - removal

1   For improved access, remove the air cleaner assembly, and the air inlet trunking, as described in Chapter 4A.

2   Remove the auxiliary drivebelt, as described in Chapter 1.

3   Unscrew the three securing bolts, and unclip the lower edge of the upper cover from the lower cover. Withdraw the upper cover **(see illustrations)**.

Upper outer cover - refitting

4   Refitting is a reversal of removal, but refit and tension the auxiliary drivebelt as described in Chapter 1.

Lower outer cover - removal

5   For improved access, raise the front right-hand side of the vehicle, and support securely on axle stands (see *"Jacking, towing and wheel changing"*). Remove the roadwheel.

6   If desired, to further improve access, remove the underwing shield (see Chapter 11).

7   Remove the crankshaft pulley as described in Section 5.

8   Where applicable, unclip the TDC sensor wiring from the lower timing belt cover.

9   Unscrew the four securing bolts, and remove the lower timing belt cover **(see illustrations)**.

Lower outer cover - refitting

10   Refitting is a reversal of removal. Refit the crankshaft pulley as described in Section 5.

Rear cover - removal

11   Remove the outer covers as described previously in this Section.

12   Remove the timing belt and sprockets as described in Sections 7 and 8.

13   Unscrew the securing bolt, and remove the timing belt tension indicator assembly from the cylinder block.

14   Unscrew the two upper and two lower screws securing the rear timing belt cover **(see illustration)**.

15   Withdraw the rear cover, and where applicable, unclip the crankshaft speed/position sensor wiring from the rear of the cover **(see illustration)**.

Rear cover - refitting

16   Refitting is a reversal of removal, bearing in mind the following points.
   (a) Refit the timing belt sprockets as described in Section 8.
   (b) Refit and tension the timing belt as described in Section 7.
   (c) Refit the outer timing belt covers as described previously in this Section.

DOHC engine

Upper outer cover - removal

17   For improved access, remove the air cleaner assembly, complete with the air mass meter, as described in Chapter 4A.

6.19 Removing the upper outer timing belt cover - DOHC engine

6.25a Lower outer timing belt cover upper securing bolt (arrowed) . . .

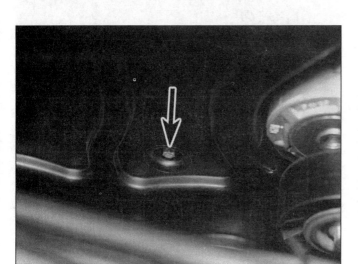

6.25b . . . and lower (arrowed) securing bolt - DOHC engine

6.30 Rear timing belt cover securing bolts - arrowed (seen with timing belt and sprockets still fitted)

18 Unclip the camshaft position sensor wiring from the timing belt cover, noting its routing.
19 Unscrew the three securing bolts, and remove the cover **(see illustration)**.

Upper outer cover - refitting
20 Refitting is a reversal of removal, ensuring that the camshaft position sensor wiring is routed as noted before removal.

Lower outer cover - removal
21 For improved access, raise the front right-hand side of the vehicle, and support securely on axle stands (see "Jacking, towing and wheel changing"). Remove the roadwheel.
22 If desired, to further improve access, remove the underwing shield (see Chapter 11).
23 Remove the upper outer timing belt cover, as described previously in this Section.
24 Remove the crankshaft pulley, as described in Section 5.
25 Remove the two securing bolts, then release the four clips, and withdraw the lower outer cover **(see illustrations)**.

Lower outer cover - refitting
26 Refitting is a reversal of removal, but refit the crankshaft pulley with reference to Section 5.

Rear cover - removal
27 Remove the outer covers as described previously in this Section.

28 Remove the timing belt, sprockets and inlet-side idler roller, as described in Sections 7 and 8.
29 Unscrew the securing bolt and remove the timing belt tensioner.
30 Unscrew the two upper and two lower securing screws, and withdraw the rear cover from the engine **(see illustration)**.

Rear cover - refitting
31 Refitting is a reversal of removal, bearing in mind the following points:

(a) Refit the timing belt sprockets as described in Section 8.
(b) Refit and tension the timing belt as described in Section 7.
(c) Refit the outer timing belt covers as described previously in this Section.

---

7   Timing belt - removal, refitting and adjustment

SOHC engines

Removal
1 Disconnect the battery negative lead.
2 Remove the outer timing belt covers as described in Section 6.
3 If not already done, turn the crankshaft to bring No 1 piston to top dead centre, as described in Section 3.

7.4a Insert a tool into the hole (arrowed) in the tension indicator arm . . .

7.4b . . . then lever the arm clockwise and lock in position - SOHC engines

7.5 Loosening a coolant pump securing bolt

7.6 Sliding the timing belt from the camshaft sprocket - SOHC engines

7.15 Using special tool KM-421-A to turn the coolant pump - SOHC engines

4   Insert a suitable tool (such as a pin punch) into the hole in the timing belt tension indicator arm, then lever the arm clockwise to its stop, and lock in position by inserting the tool into the corresponding hole in the tension indicator backplate **(see illustrations)**. Leave the tool in position to lock the tension indicator until the belt is refitted.

5   Loosen the three coolant pump securing bolts, using a suitable Allen key or hexagon bit, then turn the pump to relieve the tension in the timing belt **(see illustration)**.

6   Slide the timing belt from the sprockets, and withdraw it from the engine **(see illustration)**. Take note of any arrows marked on the belt to indicate the direction of rotation (if necessary, mark the belt to aid correct refitting).

Refitting

7   Ensure that No 1 piston is still positioned at top dead centre, as described in Section 3.

8   Refit the timing belt around the sprockets, starting at the crankshaft sprocket.

9   Adjust the timing belt tension, as described in paragraphs 11 to 20 inclusive.

10   On completion, reconnect the battery negative lead.

Adjustment

Note: *The engine must be cold when checking and adjusting the timing belt tension.*

11   With the outer timing belt covers removed as described in Section 6, proceed as follows.

12   If not already done, turn the crankshaft to bring No 1 piston to top dead centre, as described in Section 3.

13   If desired, to make the crankshaft easier to turn during the following

procedure, remove the spark plugs as described in Chapter 1.

14   Loosen the three coolant pump securing bolts, using a suitable Allen key or hexagon bit, but do not remove them.

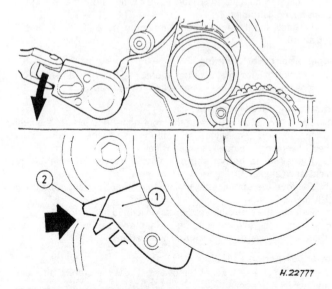

7.18 Turn the coolant pump (special tool shown) anti-clockwise until the tension indicator pointer (1) is positioned in the centre of the "V" (2) - SOHC engines

7.24 Withdraw the camshaft position sensor - DOHC engine

7.25 Timing belt tensioner securing bolt (1) and hexagon hole (2) in front plate - DOHC engine

7.26 Sliding the timing belt from the sprockets - DOHC engine

15 Turn the coolant pump clockwise to increase the belt tension until the tensioner indicator arm moves fully clockwise to its stop (ie the holes in the indicator arm and the tensioner backplate are aligned).

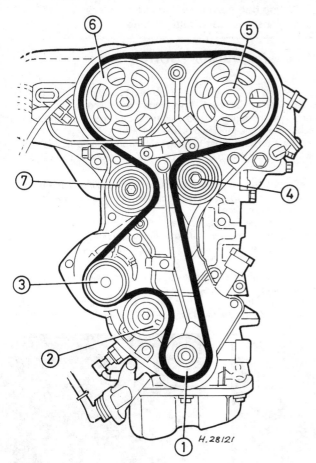

7.29 Fit the timing belt around the sprockets in the order shown - DOHC engine

1 Crankshaft sprocket
2 Timing belt tensioner
3 Coolant pump sprocket
4 Exhaust-side idler pulley
5 Exhaust camshaft sprocket
6 Inlet camshaft sprocket
7 Inlet-side idler pulley

2A

Note that a special tool is available to turn the coolant pump (Vauxhall/Opel tool KM-421-A or equivalent) **(see illustration)**.
16 Tighten the coolant pump securing bolts sufficiently to prevent the pump from moving during the following operation.
17 Using a suitable socket or spanner on the crankshaft pulley bolt, turn the crankshaft clockwise through two complete revolutions, until No 1 piston is again positioned at top dead centre. Turn the crankshaft smoothly without jerking, to avoid the belt jumping on the pulleys. Check that the timing marks are correctly aligned as described in Section 3.
18 Carefully turn the coolant pump anti-clockwise to slacken the belt, until the tension indicator pointer is positioned in the centre of the "V" on the tensioner backplate **(see illustration)**, then tighten the coolant pump securing bolts to the specified torque.
19 Turn the crankshaft clockwise through two complete revolutions, as described previously, and check that the tension indicator pointer is still positioned as described in paragraph 18 - if not, the procedure described in paragraphs 14 to 18 inclusive must be repeated until the pointer aligns correctly.
20 On completion, refit the spark plugs (where applicable), and refit the outer timing belt covers as described in Section 6.

DOHC engine

Removal
Note: *The engine must be cold when removing the timing belt.*
21 Disconnect the battery negative lead.
22 Remove the outer timing belt covers as described in Section 6.
23 If not already done, turn the crankshaft to bring No 1 piston to top dead centre, as described in Section 3.
24 Unscrew the two bolts securing the camshaft position sensor mounting bracket to the cylinder head, and move the sensor/bracket assembly to one side **(see illustration)**.
25 Loosen the belt tensioner securing bolt sufficiently to completely relieve the tension in the belt. If necessary, turn the tensioner clockwise to relieve the tension, using a suitable hexagon bit or Allen key engaged with the hole provided in the tensioner front plate **(see illustration)**.
26 Slide the timing belt from the sprockets, and withdraw it from the engine **(see illustration)**. Take note of any arrows marked on the belt to indicate the direction of rotation (if necessary, mark the belt to aid correct refitting).

Refitting
27 Ensure that No 1 piston is still positioned at top dead centre, as described in Section 3.
28 If the coolant pump has been disturbed, check the position of the pump. The mark on the edge of the pump must be aligned with the corresponding mark on the cylinder block (see Chapter 3). If necessary, loosen the securing bolts, and turn the pump as required to align the marks, then tighten the bolts to the specified torque.
29 Refit the timing belt around the sprockets, starting at the crankshaft sprocket, and working in the order shown **(see illustration)**.

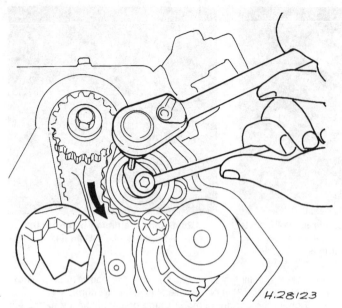

7.35 Turn the tensioner anti-clockwise until maximum tension is attained, with the pointer positioned to the right of the "V" (inset) - DOHC engine

Note: *When fitting the belt over the inlet camshaft sprocket, ensure that the belt does not jump a tooth on the sprocket, and make sure that the timing marks on both camshaft sprockets stay positioned directly opposite each other, and aligned with the top edge of the cylinder head.*

30   Adjust the timing belt tension, as described in paragraphs 32 to 40 inclusive.

31   On completion, reconnect the battery negative lead.

Adjustment

32   With the outer timing belt covers removed as described in Section 6, proceed as follows.

33   If not already done, turn the crankshaft to bring No 1 piston to top dead centre, as described in Section 3.

34   If desired, to make the crankshaft easier to turn during the following procedure, remove the spark plugs as described in Chapter 1.

35   With the tensioner securing bolt loosened, engage a suitable hexagon bit or Allen key with the hole provided in the tensioner front plate, and turn the tensioner anti-clockwise until maximum tension is attained. The tension indicator pointer should be positioned to the right of the "V" on the tensioner backplate **(see illustration)**. Note that there

is no stop on the tensioner front plate, so it is possible to turn the plate beyond the maximum tension position.

36   Tighten the tensioner securing bolt in this position.

37   Using a suitable socket or spanner on the crankshaft pulley bolt, turn the crankshaft clockwise through two complete revolutions, until No 1 piston is again positioned at top dead centre. Turn the crankshaft smoothly without jerking, to avoid the belt jumping on the pulleys. Check that the timing marks are correctly aligned as described in Section 3.

38   Engage the hexagon bit or Allen key with the hole in the tensioner front plate, then slacken the tensioner securing bolt, and carefully turn the front plate clockwise to slacken the belt until the tension indicator pointer is positioned in the centre of the "V" on the tensioner backplate **(see illustration)**. Tighten the tensioner securing bolt to the specified torque.

39   Turn the crankshaft clockwise through two complete revolutions, as described previously, and check that the tension indicator pointer is still positioned as described in paragraph 38 - if not, the procedure described in paragraphs 35 to 39 inclusive must be repeated until the pointer aligns correctly.

40   On completion, refit the spark plugs (where applicable), and refit the outer timing belt covers as described in Section 6.

---

8   Timing belt sprockets (and idler rollers - DOHC engines) - removal and refitting

Camshaft sprocket - SOHC engines

Removal

1   Remove the timing belt as described in Section 7. Note that if only the camshaft sprocket is to be removed, the timing belt can be left engaged with the remaining sprockets, and slipped from the camshaft sprocket once the tension has been relieved.

2   The camshaft must be prevented from turning as the sprocket bolt is unscrewed, and this can be achieved in one of two ways as follows.

(a)   *Make up a tool similar to that shown **(see illustration)**, and use it to hold the sprocket stationary by means of the holes in the sprocket face.*

(b)   *With the camshaft cover removed as described in Section 4, prevent the camshaft from turning by holding it with a suitable spanner on the flats provided between Nos 3 and 4 camshaft lobes.*

3   Unscrew the camshaft sprocket bolt and withdraw it, noting the washer under the bolt head.

4   Withdraw the sprocket from the end of the camshaft, where applicable manipulating the timing belt from the sprocket as it is withdrawn.

7.38 To set the belt tension, turn the tensioner clockwise until the pointer is positioned in the centre of the "V" - DOHC engine

8.2 Improvised tool being used to hold the camshaft sprocket stationary - SOHC engines

8.5 Lug (1) on camshaft engages with hole (2) in sprocket - SOHC engines

8.6 Tightening the camshaft sprocket securing bolt while holding the camshaft using a spanner on the camshaft flats - SOHC engines

8.10a Using a Torx bit engaged with the rear timing belt cover bolt hole to counterhold the inlet camshaft sprocket - DOHC engine

Refitting

5   Commence refitting by offering the camshaft sprocket to the camshaft, making sure that the lug on the end of the camshaft engages with the corresponding hole in the camshaft sprocket **(see illustration)**.

6   Refit the sprocket securing bolt, ensuring that the washer is in place, and tighten the bolt to the specified torque, preventing the camshaft from turning as during removal **(see illustration)**.

7   Where applicable, refit the camshaft cover as described in Section 4.

8   Refit and tension the timing belt as described in Section 7.

Camshaft sprockets - DOHC engine

Removal

9   Remove the timing belt as described in Section 7.

10   The camshaft sprocket bolt must be prevented from turning as the sprocket bolt is unscrewed, and this can be achieved in one of two ways as follows **(see illustrations)**.

(a) *Pass a suitable Torx bit and extension bar through one of the holes in the camshaft sprocket, to engage with the rear timing belt cover bolt. Use the Torx bit and extension bar to counterhold the sprocket as the bolt is loosened.*

(b) *With the camshaft cover removed as described in Section 4, prevent the camshaft from turning by holding it with a suitable spanner on the flats provided in front of No 1 cam lobe.*

11   Unscrew the camshaft sprocket bolt and withdraw it, noting the washer under the bolt head **(see illustration)**.

12   Withdraw the sprocket from the end of the camshaft.

Refitting

13   Proceed as described in paragraphs 5 to 8 inclusive, noting the following points:

(a) *Ensure that the sprocket is fitted so that the timing mark is visible on the outer face.*

(b) *If both camshaft sprockets have been removed, ensure that they are refitted to their correct camshafts - the exhaust camshaft sprocket is fitted with lugs which activate the camshaft position sensor.*

Crankshaft sprocket

Note: *It is recommended that a new securing bolt is used when refitting the crankshaft pulley - see Section 5.*

Removal

14   Remove the timing belt as described in Section 7.

15   Remove the sprocket from the end of the crankshaft.

Refitting

16   Refit the crankshaft sprocket with the locating flange and locating lug for the crankshaft pulley outermost **(see illustration)**.

17   Refit and tension the timing belt as described in Section 7.

2A

8.10b Counterholding the inlet camshaft using a spanner on the flats in front of No 1 cam lobe - DOHC engine

8.11 Removing the inlet camshaft sprocket - DOHC engine

8.16 Refit the crankshaft sprocket with the locating flange and locating lug for pulley outermost - SOHC engines

8.20 Timing belt idler rollers (arrowed) - DOHC engine

9.3 Withdrawing the timing belt tension indicator - SOHC engines

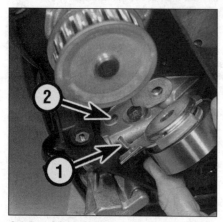

9.4 Lug (1) on tension indicator backplate must engage with hole (2) in oil pump - SOHC engines (shown with engine removed from vehicle)

10.3 Extracting the camshaft front oil seal using a self-tapping screw - SOHC engines

10.6a Fitting a new camshaft front oil seal using a socket and bolt - DOHC engine

Idler rollers - DOHC engine

Removal

18 Remove the timing belt as described in Section 7.
19 Unscrew the securing bolt, and remove the relevant idler roller.

Refitting

20 If both idler rollers have been removed, note that the larger-diameter roller fits on the inlet side of the engine **(see illustration)**.
21 Refit the relevant idler roller, and tighten the securing bolt to the specified torque.
22 Refit the timing belt as described in Section 7.

9 Timing belt tension indicator (SOHC engines) and tensioner (DOHC engine) - removal and refitting

Removal

1 On SOHC engines, the tension indicator simply provides a way of ensuring that the timing belt tension is correct - the belt is tensioned by adjusting the position of the coolant pump. On the DOHC engine, the tensioner is used to tension the timing belt, and it incorporates a tension indicator, similar to that used on the SOHC engines.
2 Remove the timing belt as described in Section 7.
3 Unscrew the central securing bolt, and withdraw the tension indicator/tensioner **(see illustration)**.

Refitting

4 Refit the tension indicator, ensuring that the lug on the

indicator/tensioner backplate engages with the corresponding hole in the oil pump **(see illustration)**.
5 Refit the indicator/tensioner securing bolt, and on SOHC engines, tighten it to the specified torque. On DOHC engines, do not tighten the bolt until the timing belt has been tensioned.
6 Refit and tension the timing belt, as described in Section 7.

10 Camshaft oil seals - renewal

Front oil seal

1 Remove the camshaft sprocket as described in Section 8.
2 Punch or drill a small hole in the centre of the now-exposed oil seal.
3 Screw in a self-tapping screw, and pull on the screw with pliers to extract the seal **(see illustration)**.
4 Clean the oil seal seat with a wooden or plastic scraper.
5 Wind a thin band of tape around the end of the camshaft, to protect the lips of the new oil seal as it is fitted.
6 Grease the lips of the new seal, then fit it to the housing. Ideally, the seal should be drawn into position using a suitable socket or tube and washer, and a suitable bolt. Alternatively, the seal can be tapped into position **(see illustrations)**. The seal should be fitted with its outer face flush with the housing. Take care not to damage the seal lips during fitting.
7 Carefully remove the tape from the end of the camshaft.
8 Refit the camshaft sprocket as described in Section 8.

Rear oil seal - SOHC engines

9 Remove the distributor, or DIS (Distributorless Ignition System) module, as applicable, from the end of the camshaft housing, as

10.6b Fitting a new camshaft front oil seal using a large socket - SOHC engines

10.10 Removing the O-ring/camshaft rear oil seal from the rear of the distributor

10.11 Coil mounting plate removed for access to O-ring/camshaft rear oil seal (arrowed)

11.7 Camshaft thrustplate and securing bolts - SOHC engines

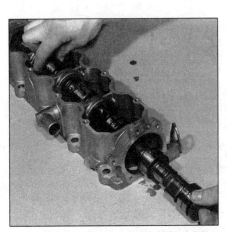

11.9 Withdrawing the camshaft from the housing - SOHC engines

11.10 Oil supply hole (arrowed) in camshaft housing - SOHC engines

described in Chapter 5B or 5C.

10   On models with a distributor, the camshaft rear oil seal takes the form of an O-ring on the rear of the distributor body. Prise off the old O-ring using a screwdriver **(see illustration)**, then fit the new O-ring, and refit the distributor as described in Chapter 5B.

11   On models with DIS, the camshaft rear oil seal takes the form of an O-ring on the rear of the DIS module mounting plate. Unscrew the three module mounting plate securing bolts, and withdraw the plate from the end of the camshaft housing **(see illustration)**. Prise off the old O-ring using a screwdriver, then fit the new O-ring, and refit the module mounting plate. Refit the DIS module to the mounting plate, with reference to Chapter 5C if necessary.

Rear oil seal - DOHC engine

12   No camshaft rear oil seals are fitted to the DOHC engine.

***

11   Camshaft(s) - removal, inspection and refitting

SOHC engines

Note: *The camshaft front oil seal should be renewed on refitting.*

Removal

1   The camshaft can only be removed without disturbing the housing if a special tool (Vauxhall/Opel No 603 850, or equivalent) is available to depress the cam followers whilst the camshaft is withdrawn.

2   Assuming that such a tool is not available, the camshaft housing must be removed. Since the cylinder head bolts must be removed, it is strongly recommended that a new cylinder head gasket is fitted. If the

gasket is not renewed, and it "blows" on reassembly, the cylinder head will have to be removed in order to renew the gasket, and another set of new bolts will have to be obtained for refitting. *You have been warned!*

3   Removal and refitting of the camshaft housing is described in Section 12 along with cylinder head removal and refitting. If it is decided not to disturb the cylinder head, the relevant paragraphs referring specifically to cylinder head removal and refitting can be ignored; it is strongly recommended that the cylinder head is clamped to the cylinder block using four head bolts and some spacers, to reduce the possibility of the seal between the head and the block being broken.

4   With the camshaft housing removed, proceed as follows.

5   Remove the distributor, or DIS (Distributorless Ignition System) module, as applicable, from the end of the camshaft housing, with reference to Chapter 5B or 5C if necessary.

6   Where applicable, unscrew the three securing bolts, and remove the DIS module mounting plate from the end of the camshaft housing.

7   Working at the distributor/DIS module end of the camshaft, unscrew the two camshaft thrustplate securing bolts, using a suitable Allen key or hexagon bit **(see illustration)**.

8   Withdraw the thrustplate, noting which way round it is fitted.

9   Carefully withdraw the camshaft from the distributor/DIS module end of the housing, taking care not to damage the bearing journals **(see illustration)**.

Inspection

10   With the camshaft removed, examine the bearings in the camshaft housing for signs of obvious wear or pitting. If evident, a new camshaft housing will probably be required. Also check that the oil supply holes in the camshaft housing are free from obstructions **(see illustration)**.

11.16 Checking the camshaft endfloat using a feeler gauge - SOHC engines

11.25b Camshaft bearing cap numbers (exhaust camshaft shown) - DOHC engine

11   The camshaft itself should show no marks or scoring on the journal or cam lobe surfaces. If evident, renew the camshaft. Note that if the camshaft is renewed, all the rocker arms should also be renewed.
12   Check the camshaft thrustplate for signs of wear or grooves, and renew if evident.

Refitting
13   It is advisable to renew the camshaft front oil seal as a matter of course if the camshaft has been removed. Prise out the old seal using a screwdriver, and tap in the new seal until it is flush with the housing, using a suitable socket or tube.
14   Commence refitting by liberally oiling the bearings in the housing, and also the oil seal lip.
15   Carefully insert the camshaft into the housing from the distributor/DIS module end, taking care to avoid damage to the bearings.
16   Refit the thrustplate, and tighten the securing bolts. Check the camshaft endfloat by inserting a feeler gauge between the thrustplate and the camshaft end flange. If the endfloat exceeds that specified, renew the thrustplate **(see illustration)**.
17   On models with DIS, examine the condition of the O-ring on the rear of the DIS module mounting plate, and renew it if necessary. Refit the mounting plate.
18   Refit the distributor, or DIS module, as applicable, as described in Chapter 5B or 5C.
19   Where applicable, remove the bolts and spacers clamping the cylinder head to the block.
20   Refit the camshaft housing, as described in Section 12.
21   If a new camshaft has been fitted, it is important to observe the

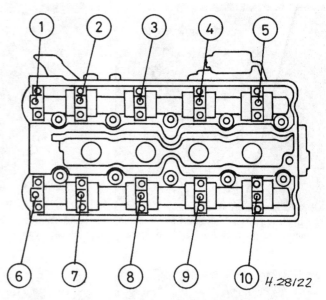

11.25a Camshaft bearing cap numbering sequence (No 1 at timing belt end) - DOHC engine

following running-in schedule (unless otherwise specified by the camshaft manufacturer) immediately after initially starting the engine.

(a)   *One minute at 2000 rpm.*
(b)   *One minute at 1500 rpm.*
(c)   *One minute at 3000 rpm.*
(d)   *One minute at 2000 rpm.*

22   Change the engine oil (but not the filter, unless due in any case) approximately 600 miles (1000 km) after fitting a new camshaft.

DOHC engine

Removal
23   Remove the camshaft cover as described in Section 4.
24   Remove the relevant camshaft sprocket as described in Section 8.
25   Check the camshaft bearing caps for identification marks, and if none are present, make corresponding marks on the bearing caps and the top surface of the cylinder head using a centre-punch (take care not to damage the cylinder head or bearing caps). Note the orientation of the bearing caps before removal, as they must be refitted in exactly the same positions from which they are removed. The inlet camshaft caps are usually numbered 1 to 5, and the exhaust camshaft caps 6 to 10, with corresponding numbers cast into the cylinder head **(see illustrations)**.
26   Before removing the camshaft, check the endfloat using a dial gauge or a feeler gauge. If the endfloat is outside the specified limits, the camshaft must be renewed.
27   If removing the inlet camshaft, loosen Nos 1, 3 and 5 bearing cap bolts progressively by half a turn, then by a full turn, then remove the bolts. Similarly, if removing the exhaust camshaft, loosen and then remove Nos 6, 8 and 10 bearing cap bolts. Lift the relevant bearing caps from the cylinder head **(see illustration)**.
28   Progressively loosen the remaining bearing cap bolts (bearing caps 2 and 4, or 7 and 9, as applicable) in half-turn stages, working in a crosswise pattern (this is necessary to progressively relieve the tension in the valve springs), then remove the bolts.
29   Lift the remaining bearing caps from the cylinder head, then lift out the camshaft, complete with the oil seal **(see illustration)**. If both camshafts are removed, identify them as exhaust and inlet.

Inspection
30   With the camshaft removed, examine the bearing surfaces in the cylinder head for signs of obvious wear or pitting. If evident, the cylinder head and all the bearing caps must be renewed as a matched set, as it is not possible to renew the bearings individually.

11.27 Removing a camshaft bearing cap - DOHC engine

11.29 Lifting the exhaust camshaft from the cylinder head -
DOHC engine

11.33 Lubricate the contact faces of the valve lifters with
molybdenum disulphide paste - DOHC engine

H.28/30

11.34 Coat the timing belt-end bearing cap mating faces of the
cylinder head (arrowed) with sealing compound - DOHC engine

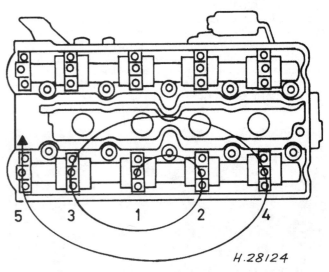

H.28124

11.39 Camshaft bearing cap bolt tightening sequence (exhaust
camshaft shown) - DOHC engine

31   The camshaft should show no marks or scoring on the journal or cam lobe surfaces. If evident, renew the camshaft.

32   It is advisable to renew the camshaft front oil seal as a matter of course. Prise the old seal from the front of the camshaft and discard it.

Refitting

33   Commence refitting by liberally coating the contact faces of the hydraulic valve lifters and the camshaft lobes with molybdenum disulphide paste **(see illustration)**.

34   Coat the timing belt-end bearing cap mating faces of the cylinder head (No 1 and/or 6, depending on the camshaft(s) removed) with sealing compound (Vauxhall/Opel No 15 04 201, or equivalent) **(see illustration)**.

35   Oil the bearing surfaces and the lobes of the camshaft, then place the camshaft in position on the cylinder head. Temporarily refit the camshaft sprocket, and check that the timing marks are still aligned with No 1 piston at TDC, as described in Section 3.

36   Loosely refit the bearing caps in their original positions as noted during removal.

37   If refitting the inlet camshaft, refit Nos 2 and 4 bearing cap bolts, and progressively tighten them in half-turn stages, working in a crosswise pattern. Tighten the bolts until the bearing caps just contact the mating faces of the cylinder head - **do not** fully tighten the bolts at this stage. Similarly, if refitting the exhaust camshaft, refit and tighten Nos 7 and 9 bearing cap bolts.

38   Refit the remaining bearing cap bolts, and tighten them progressively until the bearing caps just contact the mating faces of the cylinder head - **do not** fully tighten the bolts at this stage.

39   Working from the centre outwards in a spiral pattern, as shown, tighten the bearing cap bolts to the specified torque **(see illustration)**.

40   Lubricate the lips of a new camshaft oil seal with a little grease, and fit the oil seal as described in Section 10.

41   Refit the relevant camshaft sprocket as described in Section 8.

42   Refit the camshaft cover as described in Section 4.

12.6 Unbolting a wiring harness earth lead from the camshaft housing - SOHC engines

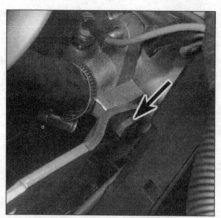

12.7 Unbolt the upper alternator mounting bracket bolt (arrowed) from the inlet manifold - SOHC engines

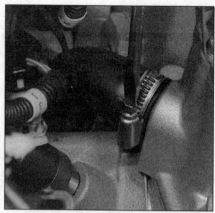

12.8 Loosening the crankcase breather hose clamp from the camshaft housing stub - SOHC engines

12 Cylinder head - removal and refitting

SOHC engines

Removal

Note: *The engine must be cold when removing the cylinder head. A new cylinder head gasket and new cylinder head bolts must be used on refitting, and a suitable sealant (Vauxhall/Opel No 15 03 166, or equivalent) will be required to coat the camshaft housing-to-cylinder head mating faces.*

1   Depressurise the fuel system as described in Chapter 4A .
2   Disconnect the battery negative lead.
3   Drain the cooling system as described in Chapter 1.
4   Remove the camshaft sprocket as described in Section 8.
5   Disconnect the exhaust front section from the manifold, with reference to Chapter 4A.
6   Where applicable, unbolt the wiring harness earth lead(s) from the camshaft housing **(see illustration)**.
7   Loosen the alternator mountings, then unbolt the upper alternator mounting bracket(s) from the inlet manifold and camshaft housing, as applicable **(see illustration)**. Note that on certain models it will be necessary to remove the upper alternator mounting nut and bolt, and pivot the alternator away from the upper mounting bracket, leaving the bracket attached to the inlet manifold (the bracket securing bolt cannot be reached with the manifold fitted to the cylinder head).
8   Disconnect the crankcase breather hose from the stub at the rear of the camshaft housing **(see illustration)**.
9   Where applicable, unclip the wiring harness from the brackets on

the camshaft cover, and move the harness to one side **(see illustration)**.
10   Where applicable, separate the two halves of the wiring harness connector, and release the connector from the clip on the camshaft cover **(see illustration)**.
11   On single-point fuel injection engines, disconnect the hot-air hose from the shroud on the exhaust manifold.
12   The cylinder head can be removed complete with the manifolds, or the manifolds can be detached from the cylinder head prior to removal, with reference to Chapter 4A. If no work is to be carried out on the inlet manifold, it can be unbolted from the cylinder head and supported to one side out of the way, thus avoiding the need to disconnect the relevant hoses, pipes and wiring.
13   If the cylinder head is to be removed complete with the manifolds, disconnect all relevant hoses, pipes and wiring from the inlet manifold and associated components, with reference to Chapter 4A.
14   If the inlet manifold is to be left in the engine compartment, proceed as follows - otherwise proceed to paragraph 18.
15   Disconnect the breather hose(s) from the camshaft cover.
16   Make a final check to ensure that all necessary hoses, pipes and wires have been disconnected. Unscrew the inlet manifold securing nuts, noting the location of any brackets (eg, engine lifting bracket) attached to the studs in the cylinder head, and lift the inlet manifold from the cylinder head. Ensure that the manifold is properly supported, taking care not to strain any of the hoses, pipes and wires, etc, which are still connected.
17   Recover the manifold gasket from the cylinder head.
18   If desired, remove the exhaust manifold with reference to Chapter 4.
19   Unscrew the two upper rear timing belt cover securing bolts from

12.9 Unclip the fuel injector wiring harness from the brackets on the camshaft cover

12.10 Separate the two halves of the wiring connector - SOHC engines

12.22 Disconnecting the coolant hose from the thermostat housing - SOHC engines

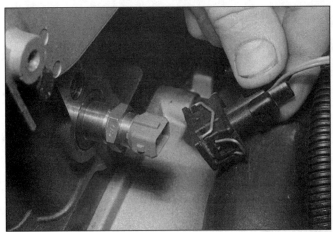

12.23 Disconnecting the wiring plug from the coolant temperature sensor - SOHC engines with multi-point fuel injection

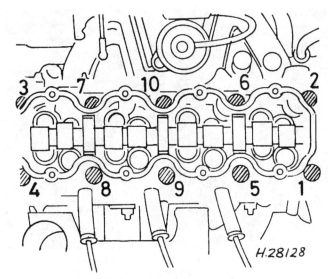

12.26 Cylinder head bolt loosening sequence - SOHC engines

12.27 Lifting the camshaft housing from the cylinder head - SOHC engines

wiring plug.

22 Disconnect the coolant hose from the thermostat housing **(see illustration)**.

23 On multi-point fuel injection models, disconnect the wiring plug from the coolant temperature sensor located in the end of the cylinder head **(see illustration)**.

24 On X 12 SZ engines, unscrew the nuts securing the fuel tank vent valve mounting bracket and the earth wiring to the left-hand end of the camshaft housing. Move the valve assembly and the wiring to one side, clear of the working area.

25 Make a final check to ensure that all relevant hoses, pipes and wires, etc, have been disconnected.

26 Working from the outside inwards in a spiral pattern as shown, loosen all the cylinder head bolts by a quarter of a turn, then loosen all the bolts by half a turn, and finally loosen and remove the bolts **(see illustration)**. Recover the washers.

27 Lift the camshaft housing from the cylinder head **(see illustration)**. If necessary, tap the housing gently with a soft-faced mallet to free it from the cylinder head, but **do not** lever at the mating faces. Note that the camshaft housing is located on dowels.

28 Lift the rocker arms and their thrust pads from the cylinder head, keeping them in order so that they can be refitted in their original positions **(see illustrations)**.

29 Lift the hydraulic valve lifters from the cylinder head, and keep the lifters in order, so that they can be refitted in their original positions **(see illustration)**.

the camshaft housing.

20 On models with a distributor, disconnect the HT leads from the spark plugs and the coil, labelling them if necessary to aid refitting, and remove the distributor cap. Disconnect the distributor wiring plug.

21 On models with DIS (see Chapter 5C), disconnect the HT leads from the spark plugs and the DIS module, and remove the leads, labelling them if necessary to aid refitting. Disconnect the DIS module

12.28a Lift the rocker arms . . .

12.28b . . . and their thrust pads from the cylinder head - SOHC engines

12.29 Lift the hydraulic valve lifters from the cylinder head - SOHC engines

12.30 Lifting the cylinder head from the cylinder block - SOHC engines

12.33a Cylinder head gasket `OBEN/TOP' markings

30   Lift the cylinder head from the cylinder block **(see illustration)**. If necessary, tap the cylinder head gently with a soft-faced mallet to free it from the block, but **do not** lever at the mating faces. Note that the cylinder head is located on dowels.
31   Recover the cylinder head gasket, and discard it.

Refitting
32   Clean the cylinder head and block mating faces, and the camshaft housing and cylinder head mating faces, by careful scraping. Take care not to damage the cylinder head and camshaft housing, which are made of light alloy, and are easily scored. Cover the coolant passages and other openings with masking tape or rag, to prevent dirt and carbon falling in. Mop out all the oil from the bolt holes; if oil is left in the holes, hydraulic pressure could crack the block when the bolts are refitted.
33   Commence refitting by locating a new cylinder head gasket on the block so that the word "OBEN" or "TOP" can be read from above **(see illustrations)**.
34   With the mating faces scrupulously clean, locate the cylinder head on the block so that the positioning dowels engage in their holes.
35   Before refitting the hydraulic valve lifters, it is advisable to dismantle and clean them as described in Section 10 in Chapter 2B.
36   Refit the hydraulic valve lifters, thrust pads and rocker arms to the cylinder head in their original positions. Liberally oil the valve lifter bores. Lubricate the contact faces of the valve lifters, thrust pads and rocker arms with a little molybdenum disulphide grease **(see illustration)**.
37   Temporarily refit the camshaft sprocket, and ensure that the

12.33b Cylinder head gasket correctly located over dowels (arrowed) in cylinder block - SOHC engines

timing marks are still positioned with No 1 piston at top dead centre (the mark on the sprocket should be uppermost - see Section 3).
38   Apply sealing compound (Vauxhall/Opel No 15 03 166, or equivalent) to the cylinder head top mating face, then refit the camshaft housing to the cylinder head **(see illustration)**.

12.36 Lubricate the valve lifter contact faces - SOHC engines

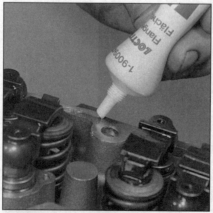

12.38 Apply sealing compound to the cylinder head top mating face - SOHC engines

12.39 Fit new cylinder head bolts, ensuring that the washers are in place - SOHC engines

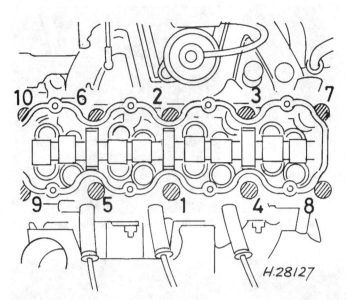

12.40a Cylinder head bolt tightening sequence - SOHC engines

12.40b Tighten the cylinder head bolts to the specified torque . . .

39   Fit the **new** cylinder head bolts, ensuring that the washers are in place under their heads, and screw the bolts in *by hand* as far as possible **(see illustration)**.

40   Tighten the cylinder head bolts, working from the inside outwards in a spiral pattern, as shown. Tighten the bolts in the four stages given in the Specifications - ie, tighten all bolts to the Stage 1 torque, then tighten all bolts to Stage 2, and so on **(see illustrations)**.

41   Further refitting is a reversal of the removal procedure, bearing in mind the following points.

42   Ensure that the ignition HT leads are reconnected to their correct cylinders.

43   Where applicable, refit the manifolds to the cylinder head with reference to Chapter 4A, using new gaskets.

44   Reconnect the exhaust front section to the manifold, using a new gasket, with reference to Chapter 4A.

45   Refit the camshaft sprocket as described in Section 8.

46   Refill the cooling system as described in Chapter 1.

47   On completion, check that all relevant hoses, pipes and wires, etc, have been reconnected.

48   When the engine is started, check for signs of leaks.

DOHC engine

Note: *A new cylinder head gasket and new cylinder head bolts must be used on refitting.*

Removal

49   Depressurise the fuel system as described in Chapter 4A .

50   Disconnect the battery negative lead.

51   Drain the cooling system as described in Chapter 1.

52   Remove the camshaft cover as described in Section 4.

53   Remove the camshaft sprockets and the timing belt idler rollers, as described in Section 8, and the timing belt tensioner as described in Section 9.

54   Remove the rear timing belt cover with reference to Section 6.

55   Unscrew the union nut, and disconnect the return hose from the fuel pressure regulator **(see illustration)**. Be prepared for fuel spillage, and clamp or plug the hose, to reduce fuel loss and to prevent dirt ingress.

56   Similarly, disconnect the fuel supply hose from the fuel rail.

57   Disconnect the throttle cable from the throttle body, with reference to Chapter 4A if necessary, and move the cable clear of the working area.

58   Unclip the oxygen sensor wiring connector from its bracket on the gearbox, and separate the two halves of the connector.

59   Disconnect the wiring plug and the spark plug HT leads from the DIS module. Disconnect the HT leads from the spark plugs, and remove them completely.

60   Disconnect the wiring from the coolant temperature sensor and the temperature gauge sender, located in the thermostat housing **(see illustration)**.

2A

12.40c . . . then through the specified angles - SOHC engines

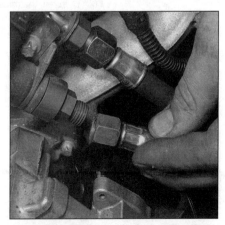

12.55 Disconnecting the fuel return hose from the fuel pressure regulator

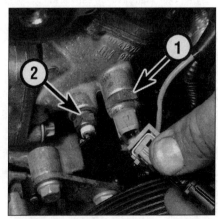

12.60 Disconnect the wiring from the coolant temperature sensor (1) and the temperature gauge sender (2)

12.61 Disconnect the coolant hose from the thermostat housing

12.64a Disconnect the wiring connectors for the fuel injector . . .

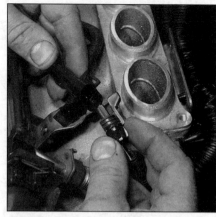

12.64b . . . camshaft position sensor . . .

12.64c . . . and crankshaft speed/position sensor

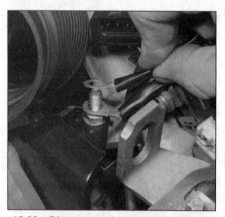

12.66a Disconnect the earth wiring from the stud on the alternator upper mounting bracket . . .

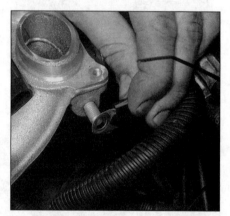

12.66b . . . and the inlet manifold

61   Disconnect the coolant hose from the thermostat housing **(see illustration)**.

62   Remove the front section of the exhaust system as described in Chapter 4A.

63   Disconnect the wiring plugs from the idle speed control motor and the throttle position sensor, located in the throttle body.

64   Unclip the following wiring connectors from their brackets, and separate the two halves of the connector in each case **(see illustrations)**:

   (a) *Fuel injector wiring connector.*
   (b) *Camshaft position sensor wiring connector.*

   (c) *Crankshaft speed/position sensor wiring connector.*

65   Unclip the crankshaft speed/position sensor wiring from the lower section of the inlet manifold, and feed the wiring down through the clips on the manifold, so that the wiring can be left in the engine compartment. Note the routing of the wiring.

66   Disconnect the earth wiring from the studs on the alternator upper mounting bracket, and the gearbox end of the inlet manifold **(see illustrations)**.

67   Disconnect the coolant hose from the timing belt end of the lower section of the inlet manifold **(see illustration)**.

68   Unscrew the three securing bolts, and remove the upper alternator

12.67 Disconnect the coolant hose (arrowed) from the timing belt end of the manifold

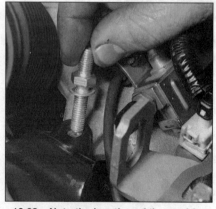

12.68a Note the location of the stud for the earth wiring . . .

12.68b . . . and remove the upper alternator mounting bracket

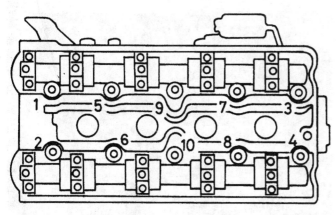

H.28/25

12.71a Cylinder head bolt loosening sequence - DOHC engine

mounting bracket (note that one of the bolts doubles as a stud for the earth wiring) **(see illustrations)**. Pivot the alternator away from the manifold.

69   Make a final check to ensure that all relevant hoses, pipes and wires have been disconnected.

70   Using a cable-tie, or a suitable length of wire or string, secure the throttle body to its mounting bracket on the inlet manifold.

71   Working in a spiral pattern from the centre outwards in the order shown, progressively loosen the cylinder head bolts. First loosen all the bolts by quarter of a turn, then loosen all the bolts by half a turn,

then finally slacken all the bolts fully and withdraw them from the cylinder head. Recover the washers **(see illustrations)**.

72   Lift the cylinder head from the cylinder block **(see illustration)**. If necessary, tap the cylinder head gently with a soft-faced mallet to free it from the block, but **do not** lever at the mating faces. Note that the cylinder head is located on dowels.

73   Recover the cylinder head gasket, and discard it.

Refitting

74   Clean the cylinder head and block mating faces by careful scraping. Take care not to damage the cylinder head, which is made of light alloy, and is easily scored. Cover the coolant passages and other openings with masking tape or rag, to prevent dirt and carbon falling in. Mop out all the oil from the bolt holes; if oil is left in the holes, hydraulic pressure could crack the block when the bolts are refitted.

75   Commence refitting by locating a new cylinder head gasket on the block, so that the word "OBEN" or "TOP" is uppermost at the timing belt end of the engine **(see illustration)**.

76   With the mating faces scrupulously clean, locate the cylinder head on the block so that the positioning dowels engage in their holes.

77   Temporarily refit the camshaft sprockets, and check that camshafts and the crankshaft are still positioned for No 1 piston at top dead centre (see Section 3).

78   Fit the **new** cylinder head bolts, ensuring that the washers are in place under their heads, and screw in the bolts *by hand* as far as possible.

79   Tighten the bolts in the order shown. Tighten the bolts in the four stages given in the Specifications - ie, tighten all bolts to the Stage 1 torque, then tighten all bolts to Stage 2, and so on **(see illustrations)**.

80   Further refitting is a reversal of removal, bearing in mind the following points.

2A

12.71b Remove the cylinder head bolts and washers

12.72 Lifting the cylinder head from the cylinder block

12.75 Cylinder head gasket `OBEN/TOP' marking should be at timing belt end of engine

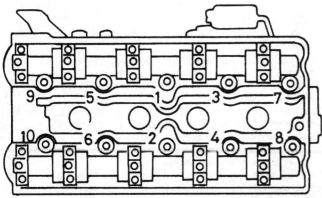

H.28/26

12.79a Cylinder head bolt tightening sequence - DOHC engine

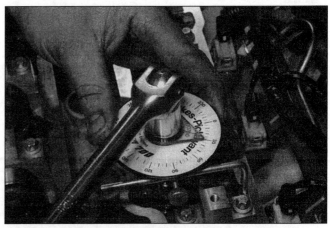

12.79b Tightening a cylinder head bolt using an angle gauge

13.6 Removing the engine-to-gearbox/transmission blanking plate - SOHC engines

13.7 Withdrawing the sump - SOHC engines

81   Ensure that all hoses, wires and cables are routed as noted during removal.

82   Refit the front section of the exhaust system as described in Chapter 4A.

83   Reconnect the throttle cable to the throttle body, and when the throttle body has been refitted to the upper section of the inlet manifold, check the cable adjustment as described in Chapter 4A.

84   Refit the camshaft sprockets and the timing belt idler rollers, as described in Section 8.

85   Refit the camshaft cover as described in Section 4.

86   Refill and bleed the cooling system as described in Chapter 1.

87   On completion, check that all relevant hoses, pipes and wires, etc, have been reconnected (check the security of the fuel hose connections)

88   When the engine is started, check for signs of leaks.

---

13 Sump and oil pick-up pipe - removal and refitting

Note: *A new sump gasket must be used on refitting. Suitable sealant (Vauxhall/Opel No 15 03 294, or equivalent) will be required to coat the cylinder block face (see text), and suitable thread-locking compound will be required to coat the sump securing bolt threads (and the oil pick-up pipe bolt threads, where applicable). If the oil pick-up pipe is removed, a new O-ring should be used on refitting.*

SOHC engines

Removal

1   Disconnect the battery negative lead.

2   Drain the engine oil, with reference to Chapter 1 if necessary, then refit and tighten the sump drain plug.

3   Apply the handbrake, then jack up the front of the vehicle and support securely on axle stands (see *"Jacking, towing and wheel changing"*).

4   Disconnect the exhaust system from the manifold, and disconnect the system from the forward rubber mountings, with reference to Chapter 4A. Lower the system sufficiently to enable removal of the sump (support the system using wire or string).

5   Where applicable, disconnect the wiring from the oil level sensor mounted in the sump.

6   Unscrew the securing bolts, and remove the engine-to-gearbox/transmission blanking plate from the bellhousing **(see illustration)**.

7   Unscrew the securing bolts, and withdraw the sump **(see illustration)**. If necessary, tap the sump with a soft-faced mallet to free it from the cylinder block - **do not** lever between the sump and cylinder block mating faces.

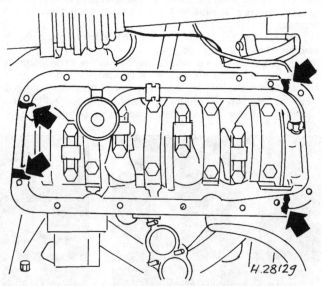

13.11 Apply sealing compound to oil pump and rear main bearing cap joints before refitting sump

8   Recover the gasket.

9   If desired, the oil pick-up pipe can be removed by unscrewing the single bolt securing the support bracket to the cylinder block, and the two bolts securing the end of the pipe to the oil pump. Recover the O-ring.

Refitting

10   Clean all traces of old gasket from the mating faces of the cylinder block and sump.

11   Commence refitting by applying sealing compound (Vauxhall/Opel No 15 03 294, or equivalent) to the joints between the oil pump and cylinder block, and the rear main bearing cap and cylinder block **(see illustration)**.

12   If the oil pick-up pipe has been removed, clean the threads of the securing bolts (including the bracket securing bolt), and coat them with thread-locking compound before refitting. Refit the pick-up pipe to the oil pump using a new O-ring, then refit the bracket securing the pipe to the cylinder block **(see illustration)**.

13   Coat the sump securing bolt threads with thread-locking compound, then refit the sump, using a new gasket, and tighten the securing bolts progressively to the specified torque.

14   Further refitting is a reversal of removal, but refit the front section of the exhaust system with reference to Chapter 4A, and on completion, refill the engine with oil as described in Chapter 1.

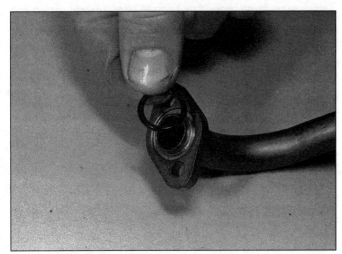

13.12 Fit a new O-ring to the oil pick-up pipe

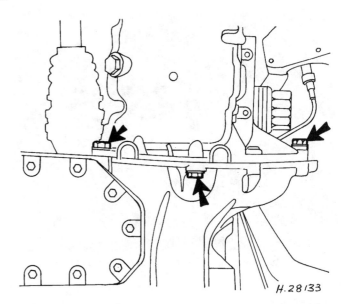

13.15a Sump-to-gearbox securing bolts (arrowed) - DOHC engine

13.15b Prising a plug from the cylinder block for access to a sump end securing bolt - DOHC engine

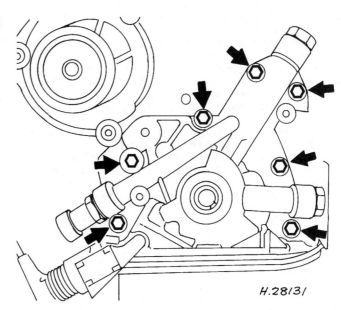

14.5 Oil pump securing bolts (arrowed) - SOHC engines

DOHC engine

Removal

15   Proceed as described previously for SOHC engines, noting the following points **(see illustrations)**:
  (a) *Remove the front section of the exhaust system, with reference to Chapter 4A.*
  (b) *Note that there is no engine-to-gearbox blanking plate.*
  (c) *Before unscrewing the bolts securing the sump to the cylinder block, remove the three bolts securing the sump to the gearbox.*
  (d) *The plastic plugs must be prised from the cylinder block (using a screwdriver or similar tool) for access to the two end bolts securing the sump to the cylinder block*

Refitting

16   Proceed as described previously for SOHC engines, but note the following.
17   To ensure a good seal between the sump and the gearbox, refit the sump-to-cylinder block bolts (coat the bolt threads with thread-locking compound), and the sump-to-gearbox bolts, and lightly tighten all bolts.
18   Tighten the sump-to-gearbox bolts to the specified torque, then tighten the sump-to-cylinder block bolts to the specified torque.

14 Oil pump - removal, inspection and refitting

Note: *A new oil pump gasket and a new front crankshaft oil seal must be used on refitting.*

Removal

1   Remove the rear timing belt cover as described in Section 6.
2   Remove the sump and oil pick-up pipe as described in Section 13.
3   Disconnect the wiring from the oil pressure switch mounted in the oil pump.
4   Where applicable, unbolt the crankshaft speed/position sensor bracket from the oil pump. Move the sensor/bracket assembly to one side, taking care not to damage the sensor.
5   Remove the securing bolts, and withdraw the oil pump from the cylinder block **(see illustration)**. Recover the gasket.

2A

14.7 Removing an oil pump rear cover securing screw

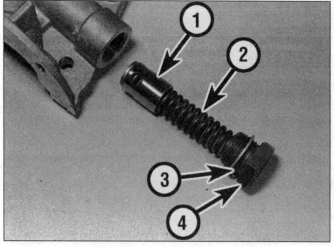

14.8 Oil pressure relief valve components

1	*Plunger*	3	*Sealing ring*
2	*Spring*	4	*Plug*

Inspection

Note: *A new pressure relief valve sealing ring should be used on re-assembly, and suitable sealing compound (Vauxhall/Opel No 15 03 166, or equivalent) will be required to coat the pump housing mating face.*

6   With the oil pump removed, proceed as follows.
7   Remove the securing screws and withdraw the rear cover **(see illustration)**. The screws may be very tight, in which case it may be necessary to use an impact driver to remove them.
8   The oil pressure relief valve components can be removed from the pump by unscrewing the cap. Withdraw the cap, sealing ring, spring and plunger **(see illustration)**.
9   Prise the crankshaft front oil seal from the pump using a screwdriver.
10   Check the clearance between the inner and outer gear teeth (backlash) using a feeler gauge **(see illustration)**.
11   Check the clearance between the end faces of the gears and the housing (endfloat) using a straight edge and a feeler gauge **(see illustration)**.
12   If any of the clearances are outside the specified limits, renew the components as necessary.
13   Examine the pressure relief valve spring and plunger, and renew if any sign of damage or wear is evident.
14   Ensure that the interior of the pump body is scrupulously clean before commencing reassembly.
15   Discard the old pressure relief valve sealing ring, then thoroughly clean the pressure relief valve components, and lubricate them with clean engine oil before refitting. Use a new sealing ring.
16   Ensure that the gears are clean, then lubricate them with clean

engine oil, and refit them to the pump body, noting that the outer gear is marked with a punch dot to indicate its outer face (ie, the face nearest the pump cover) **(see illustration)**.
17   Ensure that the mating faces of the rear cover and the pump housing are clean, then coat the pump housing mating face with sealing compound (Vauxhall/Opel No 15 03 166, or equivalent), and refit the rear cover. Refit and tighten the securing screws.
18   Fit a new crankshaft front oil seal to the recess in the pump body, using a suitable socket or tube, so that the seal is flush with the outer face of the housing **(see illustration)**.

Refitting

19   Thoroughly clean the mating faces of the oil pump and cylinder block, then locate a new gasket on the block.
20   Wind a thin layer of tape around the front edge of the crankshaft, to prevent damage to the oil seal lips as the pump is refitted.
21   With a new oil seal fitted to the pump, as described previously in this Section, grease the oil seal lips, then refit the pump, ensuring that the inner gear engages with the flats on the crankshaft **(see illustration)**.
22   Tighten the securing bolts to the specified torque, then carefully remove the tape from the front of the crankshaft.
23   Where applicable, refit the crankshaft speed/position sensor and its securing bracket, and tighten the securing bolt.
24   Reconnect the wiring to the oil pressure switch.
25   Refit the oil pick-up pipe and sump, as described in Section 13.
26   Refit the rear timing belt cover as described in Section 6.

14.10 Check the clearance between the inner and outer gear teeth . . .

14.11 . . . and between the end faces of the gears and the housing

14.16 Gear outer face identification mark (arrowed)

14.18 Fitting a new crankshaft front oil seal to the oil pump

14.21 Refitting the oil pump (shown with engine removed
from vehicle and inverted)

1   Tape wound around crankshaft
2   Flats on crankshaft engage with inner oil pump gear

15 Crankshaft oil seals - renewal

Front oil seal

1   Remove the crankshaft sprocket as described in Section 8.
2   Punch or drill a small hole in the centre of the now-exposed oil seal.
3   Screw in a self-tapping screw, and pull on the screw with pliers to extract the seal (see illustration). Several attempts may be necessary. Be careful not to damage the sealing face of the crankshaft.
4   Clean the oil seal seat with a wooden or plastic scraper.
5   Wind a thin band of tape around the end of the crankshaft, to protect the lips of the new oil seal as it is fitted.
6   Grease the lips of the new seal, and tap it into position until it is flush with the outer face of the oil pump body, using a suitable socket or tube (see illustration). Take care not to damage the seal lips during fitting.
7   Carefully remove the tape from the end of the crankshaft.
8   Refit the crankshaft sprocket, as described in Section 8.

Rear oil seal

9   Remove the flywheel/driveplate as described in Section 16.
10   Proceed as described in paragraphs 2 to 4 inclusive of this Section.
11   Grease the lips of the new seal, then tap the seal into position using a suitable tube, until flush with the outer faces of the cylinder block and rear main bearing cap. It is advisable to wind a length of tape around the end of the crankshaft to reduce the possibility of damage to

the lips of the oil seal as the seal is fitted.
12   Refit the flywheel/driveplate as described in Section 16.

16 Flywheel/driveplate - removal, inspection and refitting

Note: New flywheel/driveplate securing bolts must be used on refitting.

Removal

1   Remove the starter motor as described in Chapter 5A.
2   Remove the clutch as described in Chapter 6, or the automatic transmission as described in Chapter 7B, as applicable.
3   If the gearbox is still attached to the engine, remove the clutch release bearing and its guide sleeve, as described in Chapter 6.
4   Although the flywheel/driveplate bolt holes are offset so that the flywheel/driveplate can only be fitted in one position, it will make refitting easier if alignment marks are made between the flywheel/driveplate and the end of the crankshaft.
5   Prevent the flywheel/driveplate from turning by jamming the ring gear teeth using a suitable tool. If the engine and gearbox are still fitted to the vehicle, access is most easily obtained through the starter motor aperture.
6   Unscrew the securing bolts, and remove the flywheel/driveplate (see illustration). Take care, as the flywheel is heavy.

15.3 Using a self-tapping screw and a
pair of pliers to extract the
crankshaft front oil seal

15.6 Tapping a new crankshaft front oil
seal into position

16.6 Removing the flywheel

16.13a Tool for preventing the flywheel from turning, secured using an engine-to-gearbox bolt

16.13b Tighten the flywheel securing bolts to the specified torque . . .

16.13c . . . and then through the specified angle

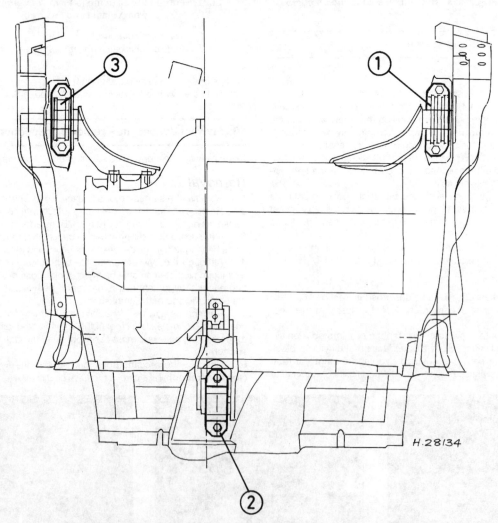

17.2a Engine/gearbox mountings - SOHC engine models without power steering

1 Right-hand mounting	*2 Rear mounting*	*3 Left-hand mounting*

Inspection

7   If the teeth on the flywheel starter ring are badly worn, or if some are missing, then it will be necessary to remove the ring and fit a new one.

8   The old ring can be split with a cold chisel, after making a cut with a hacksaw blade between two gear teeth. Take great care not to damage the flywheel during this operation, and wear eye protection at all times. Once the ring has been split, it will spread apart, and can be lifted from the flywheel.

9   The new ring gear must be heated evenly to between 180

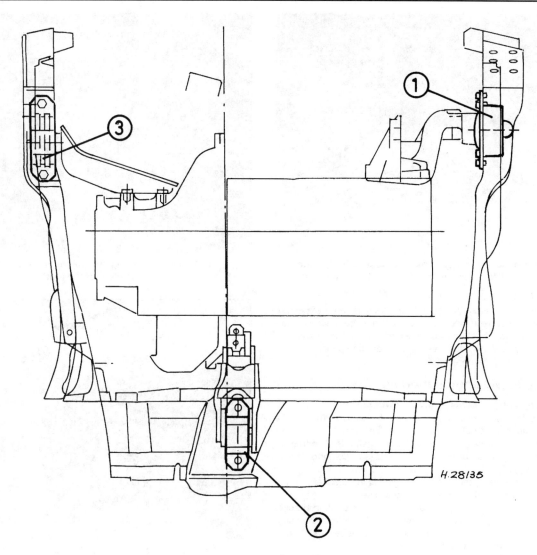

17.2b Engine/gearbox mountings - SOHC engine models with power steering, and DOHC engine models

1   *Right-hand mounting*   2   *Rear mounting*   3   *Left-hand mounting*

and 230°C. Unless facilities for heating by oven or flame are available, leave the fitting to a Vauxhall/Opel dealer or engineering works. The new ring gear must not be overheated during this work, or the temper of the metal will be affected.

10   The ring should be tapped gently down onto its register, and left to cool naturally - the contraction of the metal on cooling will ensure that it is a secure and permanent fit.

11   If the clutch friction disc contact surface of the flywheel is scored, or on close inspection, shows signs of small hair cracks (caused by overheating), it may be possible to have the flywheel surface-ground, provided the overall thickness of the flywheel is not reduced too much. Consult a Vauxhall/Opel dealer or a specialist engine repairer, and if grinding is not possible, renew the flywheel complete.

Refitting

12   Offer the flywheel to the end of the crankshaft, and align the previously-made marks on the flywheel and crankshaft.

13   Coat the threads of the new flywheel bolts with thread-locking compound (note that new bolts may be supplied ready-coated), then fit the bolts and tighten them to the three stages given in the Specifications, whilst preventing the flywheel from turning as during removal **(see illustrations)**.

14   Where applicable, refit the clutch release bearing and its guide sleeve, as described in Chapter 6.

15   Refit the clutch as described in Chapter 6, or the automatic transmission as described in Chapter 7B, as applicable.

16   Refit the starter motor as described in Chapter 5A.

---

17 Engine/gearbox/transmission mountings - inspection and renewal

---

Note: *References to "engine/gearbox" in this Section may be taken to be equally applicable for vehicles with automatic transmission.*

Inspection

1   To improve access, raise the front of the vehicle and support it securely on axle stands (see *"Jacking, towing and wheel changing"*).

2   Check the mounting blocks (rubbers) to see if they are cracked, hardened or separated from the metal at any point **(see illustrations)**. Renew the mounting block if any such damage or deterioration is evident.

3   Check that all the mounting securing nuts and bolts are securely tightened, using a torque wrench to check if possible.

4   Using a large screwdriver, or a similar tool, check for wear in the mounting blocks by carefully levering against them to check for free play. Where this is not possible, enlist the aid of an assistant to move the engine/gearbox unit back and forth, and from side to side, while

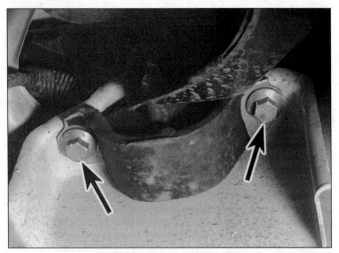

17.7 Right-hand engine/gearbox mounting-to-body bolts (arrowed) - SOHC engine model without power steering

17.17 Lower the engine until the mounting bracket is clear of the stud

you observe the mountings. While some free play is to be expected, even from new components, excessive wear should be obvious. If excessive free play is found, check first to see that the securing nuts and bolts are correctly tightened, then renew any worn components as described in the following paragraphs.

Renewal - SOHC engine models

Right-hand mounting - models without power steering

Note: *Suitable thread-locking compound will be required to coat the threads of the mounting block-to-body bolts on refitting.*

5   If not already done, apply the handbrake, then raise the front of the vehicle and support securely on axle stands (see *"Jacking, towing and wheel changing"*).

6   Attach suitable lifting tackle to the engine lifting brackets on the cylinder head, and support the weight of the engine.

7   Working under the vehicle, unbolt the engine mounting bracket from the cylinder block. Now unbolt the mounting block from the body, then withdraw the bracket/mounting block assembly **(see illustration)**.

8   Unbolt the mounting block from the bracket.

9   Fit the new mounting block to the bracket, and tighten the securing bolts to the specified torque.

10   Before refitting the bracket/mounting block assembly, clean the threads of the mounting block-to-body bolts, then check that the bolts rotate freely in their threaded holes in the body. If necessary, re-cut the threaded holes in the body using a suitable-size tap.

11   Refit the mounting bracket to the cylinder block, and tighten the securing bolts to the specified torque.

12   Coat the threads of the mounting block-to-body bolts with suitable thread-locking compound, then refit them and tighten to the specified torque.

13   Disconnect the lifting tackle and hoist from the engine.

14   Lower the vehicle to the ground.

Right-hand mounting - models with power steering

Note: *Suitable thread-locking compound will be required to coat the threads of the mounting block-to-body bolts on refitting.*

15   Proceed as described in paragraphs 5 and 6.

16   Working under the vehicle, remove the nut and bolt securing the engine mounting bracket to the mounting block.

17   Using the lifting tackle, carefully lower the right-hand side of the engine, until the engine mounting bracket is clear of the mounting block stud **(see illustration)**.

18   Unbolt the mounting block from the body.

19   Before refitting the mounting block, clean the threads of the mounting block-to-body bolts, then check that the bolts rotate freely in their threaded holes in the body. If necessary, re-cut the threaded holed in the body using a suitable tap.

20   Coat the threads of the mounting block-to-body bolts with

17.25 Unbolting the left-hand engine/gearbox mounting bracket from the gearbox

suitable thread-locking compound, then refit the mounting block to the body, and tighten the bolts to the specified torque.

21   Carefully raise the right-hand side of the engine until the mounting block stud protrudes through the bracket sufficiently to refit the nut.

22   Refit the nut and bolt securing the engine mounting bracket to the mounting block, and tighten them to the specified torque.

23   Proceed as described in paragraphs 13 and 14.

Left-hand mounting

Note: *Suitable thread-locking compound will be required to coat the threads of the mounting block-to-body bolts on refitting.*

24   Proceed as described in paragraphs 5 and 6.

25   Working under the vehicle, unbolt the mounting bracket from the gearbox, and from the mounting block, and withdraw the bracket **(see illustration)**.

26   Unbolt the mounting block from the body.

27   Before refitting the mounting block, clean the threads of the mounting block-to-body bolts, then check that the bolts rotate freely in their threaded holes in the body. If necessary, re-cut the threaded holes in the body using a suitable tap.

28   Coat the threads of the mounting block-to-body bolts with suitable thread-locking compound, then refit the mounting block to the body, and tighten the bolts to the specified torque.

29   Refit the mounting bracket, and tighten the securing bolts to the specified torque.

30   Proceed as described in paragraphs 13 and 14.

17.34 The arrow on the rear engine/gearbox mounting block must point towards the front of the vehicle

Rear mounting

31   Proceed as described in paragraphs 5 and 6.

32   Working under the vehicle, remove the nut and bolt securing the mounting block to the gearbox/transmission bracket.

33   Remove the bolts securing the mounting block to the body, and withdraw the mounting block.

34   Refitting is a reversal of removal, but ensure that the arrow on the mounting block points towards the front of the vehicle **(see illustration)**.

Renewal - DOHC engine models

Right-hand mounting - models without air conditioning

35   Remove the air cleaner and the air inlet trunking, as described in Chapter 4A.

36   Remove the two securing screws, and lift off the plastic shield with fits over the top of the camshaft cover.

37   If not already done, apply the handbrake, then raise the front of the vehicle and support securely on axle stands (see *"Jacking, towing and wheel changing"*).

38   Attach suitable lifting tackle to the engine lifting brackets on the cylinder head, and support the weight of the engine.

39   Depressurise the cooling system by removing the expansion tank cap. **Warning:** *Do not attempt to remove the expansion tank filler cap while the engine is hot, as there is a high risk of scalding. If the expansion tank filler cap must be removed before the engine and radiator have fully cooled (even thought this is NOT recommended) the*

pressure in the cooling system must be relieved as follows. Cover the cap with a thick layer of cloth, to avoid scalding, and slowly unscrew the filler cap until a hissing sound can be heard. When the hissing has stopped, indicating that the pressure has reduced, slowly unscrew the filler cap until it can be removed; if more hissing sounds are heard, wait until they have stopped before unscrewing the cap completely. At all times, keep well away from the filler cap opening.

40   Have a container ready to collect escaping coolant, then disconnect the radiator upper hose from the thermostat housing. If desired, the cooling system can be partially drained as described in Chapter 1 before disconnecting the hose.

41   Disconnect the exhaust front section from the manifold as described in Chapter 4A, and support the exhaust system using wire or string.

42   Proceed as described in paragraphs 16 to 22 inclusive. On models fitted with power steering, take care not to strain the power steering pump fluid hoses when lowering the engine.

43   Reconnect the front section of the exhaust system to the manifold, using a new gasket, with reference to Chapter 4A if necessary.

44   Reconnect the radiator top hose to the thermostat housing.

45   Disconnect the lifting tackle and hoist from the engine.

46   Lower the vehicle to the ground.

47   Refit the plastic shield to the camshaft cover.

48   Refit the air cleaner and the air inlet trunking.

49   Reconnect the battery negative lead.

50   Top-up and bleed the cooling system as described in Chapter 1.

Right-hand mounting - models with air conditioning

51   Proceed as described in paragraphs 35 to 41 inclusive, but completely remove the radiator top hose.

52   Remove the auxiliary drivebelt as described in Chapter 1.

53   Unbolt the power steering pump from its mounting bracket, as described in Chapter 10, and move the pump to one side, leaving the fluid lines connected. Support the pump (using wire or string if necessary) to avoid straining the fluid lines.

54   Remove the right-hand front suspension tie-bar as described in Chapter 10.

55   Proceed as described in paragraphs 16 to 22 inclusive.

56   Refit the front suspension tie-bar as described in Chapter 10.

57   Refit the power steering pump to its bracket as described in Chapter 10.

58   Refit the auxiliary drivebelt as described in Chapter 1.

59   Proceed as described in paragraphs 43 to 50 inclusive, but reconnect the radiator top hose to the thermostat housing and to the radiator.

Left-hand mounting

60   The procedure is as described previously for SOHC engine models.

Rear mounting

61   The procedure is as described previously for SOHC engine models.

2A

Notes

Chapter 2 Part B: Engine removal and general engine overhaul procedures

Contents

Specifications

Cylinder block

Material	Cast iron
Maximum cylinder bore ovality	0.013 mm
Maximum cylinder bore taper	0.013 mm
Maximum permissible rebore oversize	0.500 mm
Cylinder bore diameters:	**Bore diameter** **Identification mark**

	Bore diameter	Identification mark
1.2 litre engines:		
Production size 1	71.955 to 71.965 mm	6
	71.965 to 71.975 mm	7
	71.975 to 71.985 mm	8
Production size 2	71.985 to 71.995 mm	99
	71.995 to 72.005 mm	00
	72.005 to 72.015 mm	01
	72.015 to 72.025 mm	02
Production size 4	72.065 to 72.075 mm	07
0.500 mm oversize	72.465 to 72.475 mm	7 + 0.5
1.4 litre engines:		
Production size 1	77.555 to 77.565 mm	6
	77.565 to 77.575 mm	7
	77.575 to 77.585 mm	8
Production size 2	77.585 to 77.595 mm	99
	77.595 to 77.605 mm	00
	77.605 to 77.615 mm	01
	77.615 to 77.625 mm	02
Production size 4	77.665 to 77.675 mm	07
0.500 mm oversize	78.065 to 78.075 mm	7 + 0.5
1.6 litre engines	No information available at time of writing	

2B

Crankshaft and bearings

Number of main bearings 5
Main bearing journal diameter:
    Standard (all engines).. 54.980 to 54.997 mm
    0.250 mm undersize (all engines)... 54.730 to 54.747 mm
    0.500 mm undersize (all engines)... 54.482 to 54.495 mm

Main bearing shell colour codes:	Bearing cap shells	Cylinder block shells
Standard	Brown	Green
0.250 mm undersize	Brown/blue	Green/blue
0.500 mm undersize	Brown/white	Green/white

Centre (thrust) main bearing journal width:
    Standard... 26.000 to 26.052 mm
    0.250 mm undersize.. 26.200 to 26.252 mm
    0.500 mm undersize.. 26.400 to 26.452 mm
Big-end bearing journal diameter:
    Standard... 42.971 to 42.987 mm
    0.250 mm undersize.. 42.721 to 42.737 mm
    0.500 mm undersize.. 42.471 to 42.487 mm
Big-end bearing shell colour codes:
    Standard... None
    0.250 mm undersize.. Blue
    0.500 mm undersize.. White
Maximum main and big-end bearing journal out-of-round .... 0.040 mm
Main bearing running clearance .... 0.013 to 0.043 mm
Big-end bearing running clearance .... 0.019 to 0.071 mm
Crankshaft endfloat .... 0.100 to 0.200 mm
Connecting rod endfloat.. 0.110 to 0.240 mm

Pistons

Piston-to-bore clearance:
    New .... 0.020 mm
    After rebore (oversize) .... 0.010 to 0.030 mm
Note: *Piston diameters - pistons carry identification marks corresponding to those listed previously for cylinder bore diameters. The appropriate piston diameter is 0.020 mm less than the corresponding bore diameter.*

Piston rings

Number of rings (per piston).. 2 compression, 1 oil control
Ring end gap:
    Compression .... 0.300 to 0.500 mm
    Oil control (top and bottom sections)...................................... 0.400 to 1.400 mm
Ring gap offset (to gap of adjacent ring)*... 180°
For oil control ring sections, see text (Section 21).

Cylinder head

Material .... Light alloy
Maximum permissible distortion of sealing face .... 0.025 mm
Overall height of cylinder head (sealing surface-to-sealing surface):
    SOHC engines.. 95.250 ± 0.450 mm
    DOHC engine .... 134.700 to 135.000 mm
Valve seat width:
    SOHC engines:
        Inlet .... 1.300 to 1.500 mm
        Exhaust .... 1.600 to 1.800 mm
    DOHC engine:
        Inlet .... 1.000 to 1.400 mm
        Exhaust .... 1.400 to 1.800 mm

Valves and guides - SOHC engines

Stem diameter:	Inlet	Exhaust
Standard	6.998 to 7.012 mm	6.978 to 6.992 mm
0.075 mm oversize	7.073 to 7.087 mm	7.053 to 7.067 mm
0.150 mm oversize	7.148 to 7.162 mm	7.128 to 7.142 mm
0.250 mm oversize	7.248 to 7.262 mm	7.228 to 7.242 mm

Valve guide bore:
    Standard... 7.030 to 7.050 mm
    0.075 mm oversize .... 7.105 to 7.125 mm
    0.150 mm oversize .... 7.180 to 7.200 mm
    0.250 mm oversize .... 7.280 to 7.300 mm

Maximum permissible valve stem play in guide:

Inlet.. 0.018 to 0.052 mm

Exhaust... 0.038 to 0.072 mm

Valve seat angle... 46°

Valve clearances.. Automatic adjustment by hydraulic valve lifters

Valves and guides - DOHC engine

	Inlet	Exhaust
Stem diameter:		
Standard	5.955 to 5.970 mm	5.935 to 5.950 mm
0.075 mm oversize	6.030 to 6.045 mm	6.010 to 6.025 mm
0.150 mm oversize	6.105 to 6.120 mm	6.085 to 6.100 mm
Valve guide bore:		
Standard	6.000 to 6.012 mm	
0.075 mm oversize	6.075 to 6.090 mm	
0.150 mm oversize	6.150 to 6.165 mm	
Maximum permissible valve stem play in guide:		
Inlet	0.030 to 0.060 mm	
Exhaust	0.040 to 0.070 mm	
Valve seat angle	45°	
Valve clearances	Automatic adjustment by hydraulic valve lifters	

Torque wrench settings

Refer to Specifications for Chapter 2A.

1 General information

This Part of Chapter 2 includes details of engine removal and re-fitting, and general overhaul procedures for the cylinder head, cylinder block/crankcase, and internal engine components.

The information ranges from advice concerning preparation for an overhaul and the purchase of replacement parts, to detailed step-by-step procedures covering removal, inspection, renovation and refitting of internal engine components.

The following Sections have been compiled based on the assumption that the engine has been removed from the vehicle. For information concerning in-vehicle engine repair, as well as information on the removal and refitting of the external components necessary to facilitate overhaul, refer to Chapter 2A, and to Section 8 of this Part.

2 Engine overhaul - general information

It is not always easy to determine when, or if, an engine should be completely overhauled, as a number of factors must be considered.

High mileage is not necessarily an indication that an overhaul is needed, while low mileage does not preclude the need for an overhaul. Frequency of servicing is probably the most important consideration. An engine which has had regular and frequent oil and filter changes, as well as other required maintenance, will most likely give many thousands of miles of reliable service. Conversely, a neglected engine may require an overhaul very early in its life.

Excessive oil consumption is an indication that piston rings, valve seals and/or valve guides are in need of attention. Make sure that oil leaks are not responsible before deciding that the rings and/or guides are bad. Perform a cylinder compression check to determine the extent of the work required.

Check the oil pressure with a gauge fitted in place of the oil pressure sender, and compare it with the Specifications. If it is extremely low, the main and big end bearings and/or the oil pump are probably worn out.

Loss of power, rough running, knocking or metallic engine noises, excessive valve gear noise and high fuel consumption may also point to the need for an overhaul, especially if they are all present at the same time. If a complete tune-up does not remedy the situation, major mechanical work is the only solution.

An engine overhaul involves restoring the internal parts to the specifications of a new engine. During an overhaul, new pistons and/or rings are fitted, and the cylinder bores are reconditioned. New main bearings, connecting rod bearings and camshaft bearings are generally fitted, and if necessary, the crankshaft may be reground to restore the journals. The valves are also serviced as well, since they are usually in less-than-perfect condition at this point. While the engine is being overhauled, other components, such as the distributor, starter and alternator, can be overhauled as well. The end result should be a like-new engine that will give many trouble-free miles. **Note:** *Critical cooling system components such as the hoses, drivebelts, thermostat and water pump MUST be renewed when an engine is overhauled. The radiator should be checked carefully to ensure that it is not clogged or leaking. Also it is a good idea to renew the oil pump whenever the engine is overhauled.*

Before beginning the engine overhaul, read through the entire procedure to familiarise yourself with the scope and requirements of the job. Overhauling an engine is not difficult if you follow all of the instructions carefully, have the necessary tools and equipment, and pay close attention to all specifications; however, it can be time-consuming. Plan on the vehicle being tied up for a minimum of two weeks, especially if parts must be taken to an engineering works for repair or reconditioning. Check on the availability of parts, and make sure that any necessary special tools and equipment are obtained in advance. Most work can be done with typical hand tools, although a number of precision measuring tools are required for inspecting parts to determine if they must be renewed. Often the engineering works will handle the inspection of parts, and offer advice concerning reconditioning and renewal. **Note:** *Always wait until the engine has been completely dismantled and all components, especially the engine block, have been inspected before deciding what service and repair operations must be performed by an engineering works. Since the condition of the block will be the major factor to consider when determining whether to overhaul the original engine or buy a reconditioned unit, do not purchase parts or have overhaul work done on other components until the block has been thoroughly inspected. As a general rule, time is the primary cost of an overhaul, so it does not pay to fit worn or sub-standard parts.*

2B

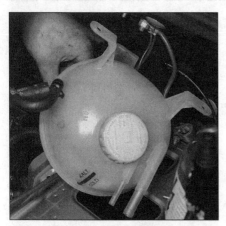

4.14 Removing the expansion tank - DOHC engine model

4.15 Disconnect the heater coolant hoses (arrowed) at the bulkhead

4.16 Disconnect the clutch cable from the release lever

As a final note, to ensure maximum life and minimum trouble from a reconditioned engine, everything must be assembled with care in a spotlessly-clean environment.

3 Engine removal - methods and precautions

If you have decided that an engine must be removed for overhaul or major repair work, several preliminary steps should be taken.

Locating a suitable place to work is extremely important. Adequate work space, along with storage space for the vehicle, will be needed. If a garage is not available, at the very least a flat, level, clean work surface is required.

Cleaning the engine compartment and engine before beginning the removal procedure will help keep tools clean and organised.

An engine hoist or A-frame will also be necessary. Make sure the equipment is rated in excess of the combined weight of the engine and transmission. Safety is of primary importance, considering the potential hazards involved in lifting the engine out of the vehicle.

If this is the first time you have removed an engine, an assistant should be available. Advice and aid from someone more experienced would also be helpful. There are many instances when one person cannot simultaneously perform all of the operations required when lifting the engine out of the vehicle.

Plan the operation ahead of time. Arrange for, or obtain, all of the tools and equipment you will need, prior to beginning the job. Some of the equipment necessary to perform engine removal and installation safely and with relative ease are (in addition to an engine hoist) a heavy-duty trolley jack, complete sets of spanners and sockets as described at the front of this manual, wooden blocks, and plenty of rags and cleaning solvent for mopping-up spilled oil, coolant and fuel. If the hoist must be hired, make sure that you arrange for it in advance, and perform all of the operations possible without it beforehand. This will save you money and time.

Plan for the vehicle to be out of use for quite a while. An engineering works will be required to perform some of the work which the do-it-yourselfer cannot accomplish without special equipment. These places often have a busy schedule, so it would be a good idea to consult them before removing the engine, in order to accurately estimate the amount of time required to rebuild or repair components that may need work.

Always be extremely careful when removing and refitting the engine. Serious injury can result from careless actions. Plan ahead, take your time, and you will find that a job of this nature, although major, can be accomplished successfully.

On all Corsa models, the engine must be removed complete with the gearbox/transmission as an assembly. There is insufficient clearance in the engine compartment to remove the engine leaving the gearbox/transmission in the vehicle. The assembly is removed by raising the front of the vehicle, and lowering the assembly from the engine compartment.

4 Engine/manual gearbox assembly - removal and refitting

Note: *Suitable equipment will be required to support the engine and gearbox during this procedure - see text.*

Removal

1   Depressurise the fuel system as described in Chapter 4A.
2   Disconnect both battery leads.
3   To improve access, remove the bonnet as described in Chapter 11.
4   Drain the cooling system as described in Chapter 1.
5   Drain the engine oil as described in Chapter 1.
6   Remove the air cleaner assembly, as described in Chapter 4A.
7   On right-hand-drive models, remove the battery, as described in Chapter 5A.
8   Disconnect the coolant hoses connecting the radiator to the thermostat housing, coolant gallery (at the gearbox end of the engine), and expansion tank.
9   Remove the radiator cooling fan and shroud assembly as described in Chapter 3.
10   Disconnect the throttle cable from the throttle linkage, as described in Chapter 4A, and move the cable clear of the engine, noting its routing.
11   Disconnect the vacuum pipe(s) from the fuel injection unit or the throttle body (as applicable), noting their locations.
12   Disconnect the brake servo vacuum hose from the inlet manifold.
13   Where applicable, disconnect the hoses and the wiring plug from the fuel tank vent valve (see Chapter 4B).
14   Unscrew the securing nuts, then remove the coolant expansion tank from the engine compartment bulkhead, disconnect the coolant hoses, and withdraw the expansion tank **(see illustration)**.
15   Disconnect the heater coolant hoses from the heater matrix pipes at the engine compartment bulkhead **(see illustration)**. Be prepared for coolant spillage.
16   Remove the retaining clip (where applicable), then slide the clutch cable from the release lever, pushing the release lever back towards the bulkhead if necessary, to allow the cable to be disconnected **(see illustration)**. Pull the cable support from the bracket on the gearbox casing, then move the cable to one side out of the way, taking note of its routing. **Tip:** *Measure the length of the threaded rod protruding through the plastic block at the release arm end of the cable. This will enable approximate presetting of the cable when refitting.*
17   Disconnect the wiring from the reversing light switch, located at the front of the gearbox, above the mounting bracket **(see illustration)**.
18   Unscrew the securing sleeve and disconnect the speedometer cable from the top of the gearbox, as described in Chapter 12. Note that on certain models, the cable is in two sections, joined by a connector near the engine compartment bulkhead - in this case, it may be

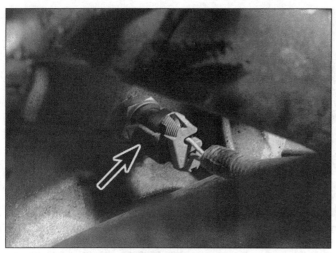

4.17 Disconnect the wiring from the reversing light switch (arrowed)

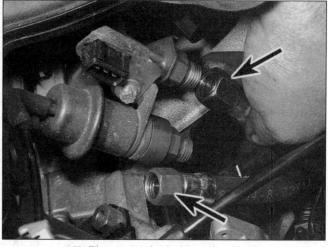

4.19 Disconnect the fuel lines (arrowed) - DOHC engine model shown

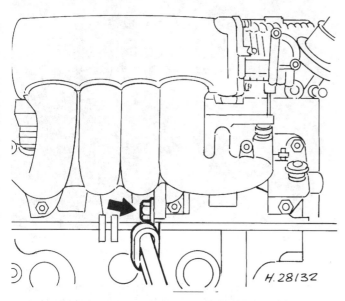

4.20 Fuel line bracket securing bolt location (arrowed) - SOHC engine models with multi-point fuel injection

easier to separate the two cable sections at the connector, rather than to disconnect the cable from the gearbox.

19   Identify the fuel supply and return lines, then unscrew the unions, or loosen the clamps, as applicable, and disconnect the fuel lines from the fuel injection unit (single-point fuel injection models) or the fuel rail/fuel pressure regulator (multi-point fuel injection models), as applicable **(see illustration)**. Be prepared for fuel spillage, and take adequate fire precautions. Plug or clamp the open ends of the pipes and hoses, to prevent dirt ingress and further fuel leakage.

20   On SOHC engine models with multi-point fuel injection, unbolt the fuel line bracket from the lower rear of the inlet manifold **(see illustration)**.

21   Identify and disconnect all relevant wiring from the engine and associated components, using the following list as a guide **(see illustrations)**. Make careful notes of the routing of the wiring, and the positions of any brackets or cable-ties. In some cases, it may be necessary to separate wiring harness connectors, in which case identify the connectors. **Tip:** *If the engine is to be removed for some time, making sketches or taking a few photographs of wire and hose runs and connections before disconnection will prove helpful when refitting.*

(a)   *Oil pressure warning light switch (see Chapter 5A).*
(b)   *Temperature gauge sender (see Chapter 3).*
(c)   *Distributor or DIS module (see Chapter 5B or 5C, as applicable).*
(d)   *Engine earth wiring (bolted to inlet manifold and/or cylinder head).*

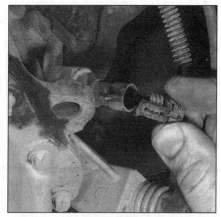

4.21a Disconnecting the wiring from the oil pressure warning light switch (viewed from underneath vehicle)

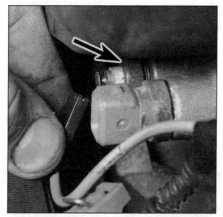

4.21b Disconnecting the wiring from the temperature gauge sender (arrowed) - DOHC engine model shown

4.21c Disconnect the auxiliary leads from the battery positive . . .

4.21d . . . and negative leads - DOHC engine model shown

4.21e Disconnecting the fuel injector wiring harness connector - DOHC engine model

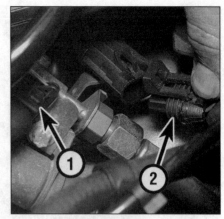

4.21f Disconnect the crankshaft speed/position sensor (1) and camshaft position sensor (2) wiring connectors - DOHC engine

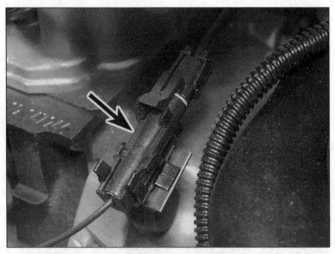

4.21g Oxygen sensor wiring connector location (arrowed) on engine-to-gearbox bolt bracket

4.24 The front of the vehicle must be raised approximately 650 mm to enable engine/gearbox removal

(e)   *Disconnect the auxiliary battery leads from the main battery leads (secured by nuts).*
(f)   *Fuel injectors (see Chapter 4A).*
(g)   *Throttle position sensor (see Chapter 4A).*
(h)   *Idle speed control motor (see Chapter 4A).*
(i)   *Coolant temperature sensor (see Chapter 4A).*
(j)   *Crankshaft speed/position sensor (see Chapter 4A).*
(k)   *Camshaft position sensor (see Chapter 4A).*
(l)   *Oxygen sensor (see Chapter 4A).*
(m) *Knock sensor (see Chapter 5C).*

22   On models with power steering, remove the auxiliary drivebelt as described in Chapter 1.
23   On models with power steering (but not power steering *and* air conditioning), unbolt the power steering pump from the bracket on the engine as described in Chapter 10. The pump can be moved to one side and left in the engine compartment, avoiding the need to disconnect the fluid hoses, but note the routing of the hoses to aid refitting.
24   Apply the handbrake, then jack up the front of the vehicle and support securely on axle stands (see *"Jacking, towing and wheel changing"*). Note that the vehicle must be raised sufficiently high (approximately 650 mm) to enable the engine/gearbox assembly to be withdrawn from under the front of the vehicle **(see illustration)**. Remove the roadwheels.
25   Attach a suitable hoist and lifting tackle to the engine lifting brackets on the cylinder head, and support the weight of the engine.
26   Working under the front of the vehicle, loosen the clamp nut and

bolt securing the gear selector rod to the linkage, then pull the selector tube towards the engine compartment bulkhead to separate it from the linkage.
27   Where applicable, unscrew the retaining nut, and disconnect the earth strap from the gearbox endplate.
28   Disconnect the wiring from the alternator and the starter motor.
29   Disconnect the exhaust front section from the manifold, with reference to Chapter 4A. Release the exhaust system from its forward rubber mountings, and move the system to one side, clear of the engine and gearbox. On DOHC engine models, remove the exhaust front section.
30   Remove the front suspension lower arms, tie-bars, and anti-roll bar, as described in Chapter 10.
31   Disconnect the inner ends of the driveshafts from the gearbox, as described in Chapter 8. There is no need to disconnect the driveshafts from the swivel hubs. Be prepared for oil spillage, and plug the openings in the gearbox to prevent dirt ingress and further oil loss. Do not allow the driveshafts to hang down under their own weight, or the joints may be damaged; support the driveshafts with wire or string.
32   Make a final check to ensure that all relevant pipes, hoses, wires, etc have been disconnected, and that they are positioned clear of the engine and gearbox.
33   To stabilise the engine/gearbox assembly as it is removed, it is advisable to support the assembly from underneath using a jack and interposed block of wood, in addition to the engine hoist and lifting tackle.

4.36 Pull the gear linkage pivot pin (arrowed) from the rear engine/gearbox mounting

34   Ensure that the engine/gearbox assembly is adequately supported, then proceed as follows.

35   Unscrew the through-bolt and nut securing the rear engine/gearbox mounting bracket to the mounting on the body.

36   Release the spring clip, then pull the gear linkage pivot pin from the bracket on the rear engine/gearbox mounting **(see illustration)**.

37   Remove the two bolts securing the rear engine/gearbox mounting bracket to the gearbox, and withdraw the mounting bracket.

38   Unbolt the left-hand and right-hand engine/gearbox mountings from the body, with reference to Chapter 2A if necessary.

39   On models with air conditioning and power steering, proceed as follows:

(a)   *Carefully lower the engine/gearbox assembly by approximately 100 mm.*

(b)   *Unbolt the compressor from the bracket on the engine (see Chapter 3), and move the compressor to one side, leaving the refrigerant lines connected. **Warning:** Do not under any circumstances attempt to disconnect the refrigerant lines. Suspend the compressor from the front body crossmember using wire or string.*

(c)   *Similarly, unbolt the power steering pump from the bracket (see Chapter 10), and suspend the pump in the engine compartment, leaving the fluid lines connected.*

40   Carefully lower the engine/gearbox assembly from the engine compartment.

41   Ensure that the assembly is adequately supported using jacks, or a suitable trolley, then disconnect the engine hoist and lifting tackle, and withdraw the engine/gearbox assembly from under the front of the vehicle.

42   With the engine/gearbox assembly removed, support the assembly on suitable blocks of wood positioned on a workbench, or failing that, on a clean area of the workshop floor.

43   Clean away any external dirt using paraffin or a water-soluble solvent and a stiff brush.

44   Where applicable, unscrew the securing bolts, and remove the engine-to-gearbox blanking plate from the bellhousing.

45   Ensure that both engine and gearbox are adequately supported, then unscrew and remove the engine-to-gearbox bolts, noting the locations of any brackets which may be secured by the bolts.

46   Carefully withdraw the gearbox from the engine, ensuring that the weight of the gearbox is not allowed to hang on the input shaft while it is engaged with the clutch friction disc. Note that the gearbox locates on dowels positioned in the cylinder block.

Refitting

47   On models where the clutch can be removed and refitted with the engine/gearbox in the vehicle (see Chapter 6), if the clutch has been removed, it will prove easier to refit after the engine/gearbox assembly has been refitted to the vehicle. If the clutch is fitted to the flywheel

before reconnecting the engine and gearbox, ensure that the friction disc is centred as described in Chapter 6.

48   Carefully offer the gearbox to the engine until the bellhousing is located on the dowels in the cylinder block, then refit the engine-to-gearbox bolts, and tighten them to the specified torque. Make sure that any brackets secured by the bolts are correctly positioned, as noted before removal. If the clutch is still bolted to the flywheel, ensure that the weight of the gearbox is not allowed to hang on the input shaft as it is engaged with the clutch friction disc.

49   Where applicable, if the clutch is in place, refit the gearbox bellhousing cover plate.

50   Where applicable, refit the engine-to-gearbox blanking plate to the bellhousing.

51   With the front of the vehicle raised and supported on axle stands, move the engine/gearbox assembly under the vehicle, ensuring that the assembly is adequately supported.

52   Reconnect the hoist and lifting tackle to the engine lifting brackets.

53   On models with air conditioning, proceed as follows:

(a)   *Raise the engine/gearbox assembly sufficiently to enable the power steering pump and air conditioning compressor to be refitted.*

(b)   *Refit the power steering pump, with reference to Chapter 10 if necessary.*

(c)   *Refit the air conditioning compressor, with reference to Chapter 3 if necessary.*

54   Raise the engine/gearbox assembly, and reconnect the left-hand and right-hand engine-gearbox mountings to the body, with reference to Chapter 2A if necessary.

55   Refit the rear engine/gearbox mounting bracket to the gearbox, and tighten the bolts to the specified torque.

56   Refit the through-bolt and nut securing the rear engine/gearbox mounting to the mounting on the body.

57   Refit the gear linkage to the bracket on the rear engine/gearbox mounting, and secure with the pivot pin.

58   Reconnect the inner ends of the driveshafts to the gearbox as described in Chapter 8.

59   Refit the front suspension anti-roll bar, tie-bars and lower arms, as described in Chapter 10.

60   Reconnect the exhaust front section to the manifold, or refit the exhaust front section, as applicable, as described in Chapter 4A. Where applicable, reconnect the exhaust system to the forward rubber mountings.

61   Reconnect the wiring to the alternator and the starter motor.

62   Where applicable, reconnect the gearbox earth strap.

63   Reconnect the gear selector rod to the gear linkage, and adjust the linkage as described in Chapter 7A.

64   Disconnect the hoist and lifting tackle from the engine lifting brackets.

65   Refit the roadwheels, and lower the vehicle to the ground.

66   On models with power steering, refit the power steering pump to the bracket on the engine, routing the fluid hoses as noted before removal.

67   Where applicable, refit and tension the auxiliary drivebelt as described in Chapter 1.

68   Reconnect all relevant wiring to the engine and associated components, ensuring that the wiring is routed and secured as noted before removal.

69   On SOHC engine models with multi-point fuel injection, refit the fuel line bracket to the inlet manifold.

70   Reconnect the fuel lines, ensuring that they are connected to their correct locations, and tighten the unions or hose clamps, as applicable.

71   Reconnect the speedometer cable to the gearbox, or reconnect the speedometer cable connector (as applicable), with reference to Chapter 10 if necessary.

72   Reconnect the reversing light switch wiring

73   If not already done, refit the clutch unit as described in Chapter 6; refit the gearbox bellhousing cover plate.

74   Reconnect and if necessary adjust the clutch cable, as described in Chapter 6.

75   Reconnect the heater coolant hoses to the pipes at the engine

compartment bulkhead.

76   Reconnect the coolant hoses to the expansion tank, and refit the expansion tank to the bulkhead.

77   Where applicable, reconnect the hoses and the wiring plug to the fuel tank vent valve.

78   Reconnect the brake servo vacuum hose to the inlet manifold.

79   Reconnect the vacuum pipe(s) to the fuel injection unit or the throttle body, as applicable.

80   Reconnect the throttle cable to the throttle linkage, and if necessary adjust the cable, as described in Chapter 4A.

81   Refit the radiator cooling fan and shroud assembly as described in Chapter 3.

82   Reconnect the coolant hoses to the radiator, thermostat housing, coolant gallery, and expansion tank.

83   On right-hand drive models, refit the battery.

84   Refit the air cleaner assembly.

85   Refill the engine with oil, as described in Chapter 1.

86   Refill and bleed the cooling system as described in Chapter 1.

87   Check and if necessary top-up the gearbox oil level as described in Chapter 1.

88   Make a final check to ensure that all relevant hoses, pipes and wires have been correctly reconnected.

89   Refit the bonnet as described in Chapter 11.

90   Reconnect the battery leads.

---

5   Engine/automatic transmission assembly - removal and refitting

Note: Suitable equipment will be required to support the engine and transmission during this procedure - see text. New torque converter-to-driveplate bolts must be used on refitting.

Removal

1   Proceed as described in Section 4, paragraphs 1 to 23 inclusive, ignoring paragraphs 16 and 17.

2   Working in the engine compartment, remove the retaining clip, and disconnect the selector cable from the actuating lever on the transmission **(see illustration)**. Unclip the cable sheath from the bracket on the transmission, then move the cable to one side, clear of the transmission.

3   Disconnect the vent hose from the front of the transmission.

4   Disconnect the transmission wiring harness plugs, and unbolt the wiring harness brackets from the transmission.

5   Apply the handbrake, then jack up the front of the vehicle and support securely on axle stands (see *"Jacking, towing and wheel changing"*). Note that the vehicle must be raised sufficiently high (approximately 650 mm) to enable the engine/transmission assembly to be withdrawn from under the front of the vehicle. Remove the roadwheels.

6   Attach a suitable hoist and lifting tackle to the engine lifting brackets on the cylinder head, and support the weight of the engine.

7   Place a suitable container beneath the transmission fluid cooler hose connections at the transmission. Clamp the transmission fluid cooler hoses, then disconnect them from the transmission, noting their locations. Be prepared for fluid spillage, and plug the open ends of the hoses and transmission connections, to minimise fluid loss and prevent dirt ingress.

8   Proceed as described in Section 4, paragraphs 28 to 43 inclusive, ignoring paragraph 36, and substituting "transmission" for "gearbox".

9   Unscrew the securing bolts, and remove the transmission bell-housing cover plate.

10   If the original torque converter and driveplate are to be refitted, make alignment marks between the torque converter and the drive-plate, to ensure that the components are reassembled in their original positions.

11   Working through the bottom of the bellhousing, unscrew the three torque converter-to-driveplate bolts. It will be necessary to turn the crankshaft using a suitable spanner or socket on the crankshaft pulley or sprocket bolt (as applicable), to gain access to each bolt in turn through the aperture. Use a screwdriver or a similar tool to jam the driveplate ring gear, preventing the driveplate from rotating as the bolts

5.2 Remove the retaining clip (arrowed) and disconnect the selector cable

are loosened. Discard the bolts.

12   Ensure that the engine and transmission are adequately supported, then unscrew and remove the engine-to-transmission bolts (note the location of any brackets secured by the bolts). Carefully pull the engine and transmission apart, ensuring that the torque converter is held firmly in place in the transmission casing as the engine and transmission are separated, otherwise it could fall out, resulting in fluid spillage and possible damage. Retain the torque converter while the transmission is removed by bolting a strip of metal across the transmission bellhousing end face.

Refitting

13   Before refitting begins, check that the left-hand engine/transmission mounting-to-body bolts rotate freely in their threaded holes in the body. If necessary, re-cut the threaded holes in the body, using a suitable tap.

14   If the original torque converter is being refitted, commence refitting by recutting the torque converter-to-driveplate bolt threads in the torque converter, using an M10 x 1.25 mm tap.

15   If a new transmission is being fitted, the manufacturers recommend that the radiator fluid cooler passages are flushed clean before the new transmission is installed. Ideally, compressed air should be used (in which case, ensure that adequate safety precautions are taken). Alternatively, the cooler can be flushed with clean automatic transmission fluid, until all the old fluid has been expelled, and fresh fluid runs clear from the cooler outlet.

16   Carefully offer the transmission to the engine until the bellhousing is located on the dowels in the cylinder block (ensure that the torque converter is held firmly in place in the transmission casing as the engine and transmission are connected), then refit the engine-to-transmission bolts, and tighten them to the specified torque. Make sure that any brackets secured by the bolts are correctly positioned, as noted before removal.

17   If the original torque converter and driveplate are being refitted, carefully turn the crankshaft to align the marks made before removal, before refitting the torque converter-to-driveplate bolts.

18   Fit **new** torque converter-to-driveplate bolts, and tighten them to the specified torque (see Chapter 7B). Turn the crankshaft for access to each bolt in turn, and prevent the driveplate from turning as during removal.

19   Refit the transmission bellhousing cover plate.

20   Proceed as described in Section 4, paragraphs 51 to 61 inclusive, substituting "transmission" for "gearbox", and ignoring paragraph 57.

21   Reconnect the transmission fluid cooler hoses to the transmission, ensuring that they are correctly reconnected, as noted before removal.

22   Disconnect the hoist and lifting tackle from the engine lifting brackets.

23   Refit the roadwheels, and lower the vehicle to the ground.

24   Reconnect the transmission wiring harness plugs, and secure the

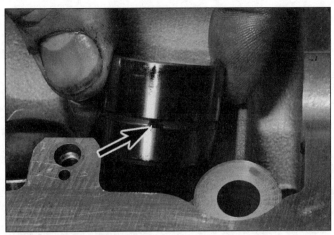

7.2 Remove the valve lifters from the cylinder head, and store with the oil groove (arrowed) at the bottom - DOHC engine

wiring harness brackets to the transmission.

25   Reconnect the vent hose to the transmission.

26   Reconnect the selector cable to the actuating lever on the transmission, and refit the cable sheath to the transmission bracket.

27   On models with power steering, refit the power steering pump to the bracket on the engine, routing the fluid hoses as noted before removal.

28   Where applicable, refit and tension the auxiliary drivebelt as described in Chapter 1.

29   Reconnect all relevant wiring to the engine and associated components, ensuring that the wiring is routed and secured as noted before removal.

30   On SOHC engine models with multi-point fuel injection, refit the fuel line bracket to the inlet manifold.

31   Reconnect the fuel lines, ensuring that they are connected to their correct locations, and tighten the unions or hose clamps, as applicable.

32   Reconnect the speedometer cable to the transmission, or reconnect the speedometer cable connector (as applicable), with reference to Chapter 10 if necessary.

33   Proceed as described in Section 4, paragraphs 75 to 86 inclusive.

34   Check and if necessary top-up the transmission fluid level as described in Chapter 1.

35   Check the adjustment of the selector cable as described in Chapter 7B.

36   Make a final check to ensure that all relevant hoses, pipes and wires have been correctly reconnected.

37   Refit the bonnet as described in Chapter 11.

38   Reconnect the battery leads.

6   Engine overhaul - dismantling sequence

1   It is far easier to dismantle and work on the engine if it is mounted on a portable engine stand. These stands can often be hired from a tool hire shop. Depending on the type of stand used, the flywheel/driveplate may have to be removed from the engine to allow the engine stand bolts to be tightened into the end of the cylinder block.

2   If a stand is not available, it is possible to dismantle the engine while supported on blocks on a sturdy workbench or on the floor. Be extra-careful not to tip or drop the engine when working without a stand.

3   Before starting the overhaul procedure, the external ancillary components must be removed (this is the case even if a reconditioned engine is to be fitted, in which case, the components from the old engine must be transferred to the reconditioned unit). These components include the following:

(a)   *Alternator and mounting bracket (see Chapter 5A).*
(b)   *Starter motor (see Chapter 5A).*
(c)   *Rear coolant gallery and hoses.*
(d)   *Inlet and exhaust manifolds (see Chapter 4A).*

(e)   *Oil filter (see Chapter 1).*
(f)   *Distributor/DIS module components (as applicable), HT leads and spark plugs (see Chapters 1, 5B and 5C).*
(g)   *Engine mountings (where applicable) (see Chapter 2A).*
(h)   *Oil pressure switch (see Chapter 5A).*
(i)   *Crankcase breather tube.*
(j)   *Engine lifting brackets.*
(k)   *Crankshaft speed/position sensor and bracket (where applicable) (see Chapter 4A).*
(l)   *Coolant temperature sensor (see Chapter 4A).*
(m)   *Knock sensor (X 12 SZ and C 16 XE engines) (see Chapter 5C).*
(n)   *Power steering pump and mounting bracket (where applicable) (see Chapter 10).*
(o)   *Wiring harnesses.*
(p)   *Dipstick.*
(q)   *Coolant pump and thermostat (the timing belt and rear timing belt cover must be removed for access to these components) (see Chapter 3).*

Note: *When removing the ancillary components from the engine, pay close attention to details which may be helpful or important during refitting. Note the fitted position of gaskets, seals, spacers, washers, bolts and other small items.*

4   If a "short" engine is being obtained (which consists of the cylinder block, crankshaft, pistons and connecting rods all assembled as a unit), then the cylinder head, sump, timing belt, and possibly other components (such as the oil pump) will have to be removed from the old unit and fitted to the new unit.

5   If a complete overhaul is being planned, the engine can be dismantled using the following sequence.

(a)   *Inlet and exhaust manifolds (see Chapter 4A).*
(b)   *Timing belt and sprockets (see Chapter 2A).*
(c)   *Cylinder head, valve lifters, camshaft(s) and rocker components (as applicable) (see Chapter 2A).*
(d)   *Flywheel/driveplate (see Chapter 2A).*
(e)   *Sump (see Chapter 2A).*
(f)   *Oil pump (see Chapter 2A).*
(g)   *Piston/connecting rod assemblies (see Section 10).*
(h)   *Crankshaft (see Section 11).*

6   Before beginning the dismantling and overhaul procedures, make sure that all the correct tools have been obtained. Refer to the preliminary Sections of this manual for further information.

7   Cylinder head - dismantling

Note: *New and reconditioned cylinder heads are available from the manufacturers, and from engine overhaul specialists. Due to the fact that some specialist tools are required for the dismantling and inspection procedures, and new components may not be readily available, it may be more practical and economical for the home mechanic to purchase a reconditioned head rather than to dismantle, inspect and recondition the original head. A valve spring compressor tool will be required for this operation.*

1   With the cylinder head removed as described in Chapter 2A, clean away all external dirt, and remove the following components, if not already done:

(a)   *Manifolds (see Chapter 4A).*
(b)   *Spark plugs (see Chapter 1).*
(c)   *Thermostat housing, and the thermostat (see Chapter 3).*
(d)   *On DOHC engines, remove the camshafts (see Chapter 2A), the DIS module and its bracket (see Chapter 5C), and the coolant housing (mounted on the inlet manifold side of the cylinder head).*

2   On DOHC engines, remove the hydraulic valve lifters from their bores, using a rubber suction plunger tool - do not invert the cylinder head in order to remove the valve lifters. Keep the valve lifters upright at all times, with the oil groove at the bottom **(see illustration)**. Immerse them, in order of removal, in a container of clean engine oil until they are to be refitted.

2B

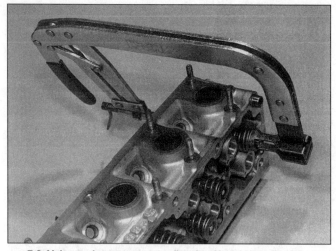

7.3 Valve spring compressor fitted to No 1 exhaust valve - SOHC engines

3   To remove a valve, fit a valve spring compressor tool. Ensure that the arms of the compressor tool are securely positioned on the head of the valve and the spring cap **(see illustration)**. The valves on the DOHC engine are deeply-recessed, and a suitable extension piece may be required for the spring compressor.
4   Compress the valve spring to relieve the pressure of the spring cap acting on the collets. If the spring cap sticks to the valve stem, support the compressor tool, and give the end a light tap with a soft-faced mallet to help free the spring cap.

5   Extract the two split collets, then slowly release the compressor tool **(see illustration)**.
6   Remove the spring cap, spring, valve stem oil seal (using long-nosed pliers if necessary), and the spring seat, then withdraw the valve through the combustion chamber **(see illustrations)**.
7   Repeat the procedure for the remaining valves, keeping all components in strict order so that they can be refitted in their original positions, unless all the components are to be renewed. If the components are to be kept and used again, place each valve assembly in a labelled polythene bag or a similar small container **(see illustration)**. Note that as with cylinder numbering, the valves are normally numbered from the timing belt end of the engine. Make sure that on DOHC engines, the valve components are identified as inlet and exhaust, as well as numbered.

8   Cylinder head and valve components - cleaning and inspection

1   Thorough cleaning of the cylinder head and valve components, followed by a detailed inspection, will enable a decision to be made on whether further work is necessary before reassembling the components.

Cleaning

2   Scrape away all traces of old gasket material and sealing compound from the cylinder head surfaces. Take care not to damage the cylinder head surfaces, as the head is made of light alloy.
3   Scrape away the carbon from the combustion chambers and ports, then wash the cylinder head thoroughly with paraffin or a suitable solvent.
4   Scrape off any heavy carbon deposits that may have formed on the valves, then use a power-operated wire brush to remove deposits from the valve heads and stems.

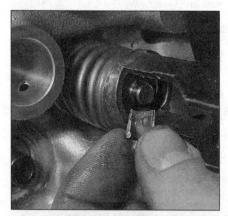

7.5 Extracting a split collet - SOHC engines

7.6a Remove the spring cap . . .

7.6b . . . spring . . .

7.6c . . . valve stem oil seal . . .

7.6d . . . and the spring seat - DOHC engine shown

7.7 Place each valve assembly in a labelled polythene bag

8.6 Checking the cylinder head surface for distortion

8.9a Valve lifter oil holes (arrowed) in cylinder head - DOHC engine

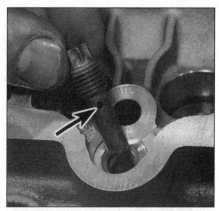

8.9b Check the oil holes (arrowed) in the oil jets for obstructions - DOHC engine

Inspection

Note: *Be sure to perform all the following inspection procedures before concluding that the services of a machine shop or engine overhaul specialist are required. Make a list of all items that require attention.*

Cylinder head

5   Inspect the head very carefully for cracks, evidence of coolant leakage, and other damage. If cracks are found, a new cylinder head should be obtained.

6   Use a straight-edge and feeler blade to check that the cylinder head surface is not distorted **(see illustration)**. If the specified distortion limit is exceeded, it may be possible to have the cylinder head resurfaced, provided that the overall height of the head is not reduced to less than the specified minimum.

7   Examine the valve seats in each of the combustion chambers. If the seats are severely pitted, cracked or burned, then they will need to be re-cut by an engine overhaul specialist. If only slight pitting is evident, this can be removed by grinding the valve heads and seats together with coarse, then fine, grinding paste, as described later in this Section.

8   If the valve guides are worn, indicated by a side-to-side motion of the valve, the guides can be reamed, and valves with oversize stems can be fitted. This work is best carried out by an engine overhaul specialist. A dial gauge may be used to determine whether the amount of side play of a valve exceeds the specified maximum.

9   Check the valve lifter bores in the cylinder head for wear. If excessive wear is evident, the cylinder head must be renewed. Also check the valve lifter oil holes in the cylinder head for obstructions. On DOHC engines, unscrew the oil jets from the cylinder head, and check the oil holes for obstruction. Clean the jets if necessary, then refit and tighten them. If desired, the oil gallery plugs (where applicable) can be removed, and the oil galleries can be cleaned by blowing through with

compressed air **(see illustrations)**. **Warning:** *Wear eye protection when using compressed air!*

Valves

Warning: *The exhaust valves fitted to DOHC engines are filled with sodium, to improve heat transfer. Sodium is a highly-reactive metal, which will ignite or explode spontaneously on contact with water (including water vapour in the air). Valves containing sodium must NOT be disposed of with ordinary scrap - seek advice from a Vauxhall/Opel dealer if the valves are to be disposed of.*

10   Examine the head of each valve for pitting, burning, cracks and general wear, and check the valve stem for scoring and wear ridges. Rotate the valve, and check for any obvious indication that it is bent. Look for pitting and excessive wear on the end of each valve stem. If the valve appears satisfactory at this stage, measure the valve stem diameter at several points using a micrometer **(see illustration)**. Any significant difference in the readings obtained indicates wear of the valve stem. Should any of these conditions be apparent, the valve(s) must be renewed. If the valves are in satisfactory condition, they should be ground (lapped) onto their respective seats to ensure a smooth gas-tight seal.

11   Valve grinding is carried out as follows. Place the cylinder head upside-down on a bench, with a block of wood at each end to give clearance for the valve stems.

12   Smear a trace of coarse carborundum paste on the seat face in the cylinder head, and press a suction grinding tool onto the relevant valve head. With a semi-rotary action, grind the valve head to its seat, lifting the valve occasionally to redistribute the grinding paste **(see illustration)**. When a dull, matt, even surface is produced on the faces of both the valve seat and the valve, wipe off the paste and repeat the process with fine carborundum paste. A light spring placed under the valve head will greatly ease this operation. When a smooth unbroken

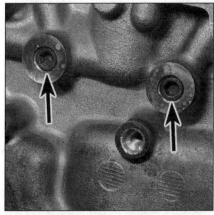

8.9c Cylinder head oil gallery plugs (arrowed) - DOHC engine

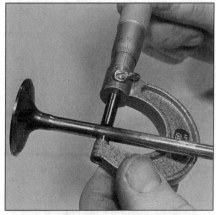

8.10 Measuring a valve stem diameter

8.12 Grinding-in a valve seat

2B

ring of light grey matt finish is produced on both the valve and seat faces, the grinding operation is complete. Carefully clean away every trace of grinding paste, taking great care to leave none in the ports or in the valve guides. Clean the valves and valve seats with a paraffin-soaked rag, then with a clean rag, and finally, if an air line is available, blow the valves, valve guides and cylinder head ports clean.

Valve springs

13   Check that all the valve springs are intact. If any one is broken, all should be renewed.

14   If possible, check the free height of the springs against new ones, then stand each spring on a flat surface and check it for squareness. If a spring is found to be too short, or damaged in any way, renew all the springs as a set. Springs suffer from fatigue, and it is a good idea to re-new them even if they look serviceable.

Rocker arm components - SOHC engines

15   Check the rocker arm and thrust pad faces (the areas that contact the valve lifters and valve stems) for pits, wear, score-marks or any in-dication that the surface-hardening has worn through. Check the rocker arm camshaft contact faces in the same manner. Clean the oil hole in the top of each rocker arm using a length of wire. Renew any rocker arms or thrust pads which appear suspect.

Valve lifters - SOHC engines

16   Proceed as described in paragraph 9.

17   On engines which have covered a high mileage, or for which the service history (particularly oil changes) is suspect, it is possible for the valve lifters to suffer internal contamination, which in extreme cases may result in increased engine top-end noise and wear. To minimise the possibility of problems occurring later in the life of the engine, it is

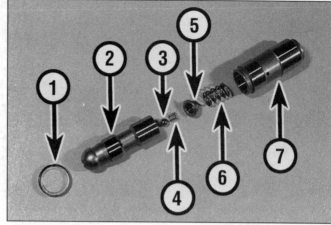

8.17 Hydraulic valve lifter components - SOHC engines

1	Collar	5	Plunger cap
2	Plunger	6	Large spring
3	Ball	7	Cylinder
4	Small spring		

advisable to dismantle and clean the hydraulic valve lifters as follows whenever the cylinder head is overhauled. Note that this procedure is not recommended by the manufacturers, and no spare parts are avail-able for the valve lifters - if any of the components are unserviceable, the complete assembly must be renewed **(see illustration)**.

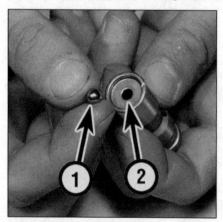

8.23 Locate the ball (1) on its seat (2) in the base of the plunger

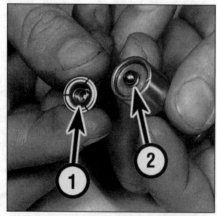

8.24a Spring (1) located in plunger cap, and ball (2) located on seat in plunger

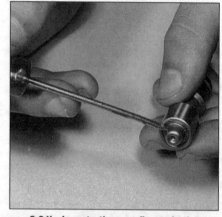

8.24b Locate the cap flange in the plunger groove

8.25a Locate the spring over the plunger cap . . .

8.25b . . . then slide the plunger and spring assembly into the cylinder

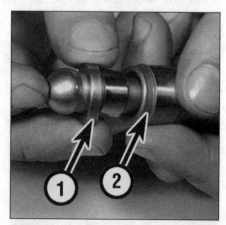

8.26 Slide the collar (1) over the top of the plunger and engage with the groove (2) in the cylinder

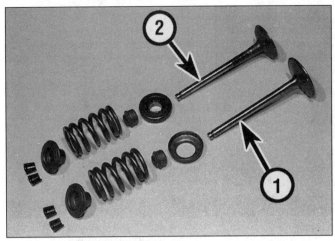

9.1 Inlet (1) and exhaust (2) valve components - SOHC engines

18   Carefully pull the collar from the top of the valve lifter cylinder. It should be possible to remove the collar by hand - if a tool is used, take care not to distort the collar.
19   Withdraw the plunger from the cylinder, and recover the spring.
20   Using a small screwdriver, carefully prise the cap from the base of the plunger. Recover the spring and ball from under the cap, taking care not to lose them as the cap is removed.
21   Carefully clean all the components using paraffin or a suitable

9.2 Inserting an exhaust valve into its guide - SOHC engines

solvent, paying particular attention to the machined surfaces of the cylinder (internal surfaces), and piston (external surfaces). Thoroughly dry all the components using a lint-free cloth. Carefully examine the springs for damage or distortion - the complete valve lifter must be renewed if the springs are not in perfect condition.
22   Lubricate the components sparingly with clean engine oil of the correct grade (see Chapter 1), then reassemble as follows.
23   Invert the plunger, and locate the ball on its seat in the base of the plunger **(see illustration)**.
24   Locate the smaller spring on its seat in the plunger cap, then carefully refit the cap and spring, ensuring that the spring locates on the ball. Carefully press around the flange of the cap, using a small screwdriver if necessary, until the flange is securely located in the groove in the base of the plunger **(see illustrations)**.
25   Locate the larger spring over the plunger cap, ensuring that the spring is correctly seated, and slide the plunger and spring assembly into the cylinder **(see illustrations)**.
26   Slide the collar over the top of the plunger, and carefully compress the plunger by hand, until the collar can be pushed down to engage securely with the groove in the cylinder **(see illustration)**.

Valve lifters - DOHC engines

Note: *The valve lifters should always be stored upright in a container of clean engine oil while removed from the cylinder head.*
27   Inspect the valve lifters for obvious signs of wear on the contact faces, and check the valve lifter oil holes for obstructions, particularly for oil sludge. If excessive wear is evident (this is unlikely), all the valve lifters must be renewed as a set.

9   Cylinder head - reassembly

2B

Note: *New valve stem oil seals should be used on reassembly. A valve spring compressor tool will be required for this operation.*
1   With all the components cleaned, starting at one end of the cylinder head, fit the valve components as follows **(see illustration)**.
2   Insert the appropriate valve into its guide (if new valves are being fitted, insert each valve into the location to which it has been ground), ensuring that the valve stem is well-lubricated with clean engine oil **(see illustration)**. If the original components are being refitted, all components must be refitted in their original positions.
3   Fit the spring seat **(see illustration)**.
4   New valve stem oil seals should be supplied with a fitting sleeve, which fits over the collet groove in the valve stem, to prevent damage to the oil seal as it is slid down the valve stem **(see illustration)**. If no sleeve is supplied, wind a short length of tape round the top of the valve stem to cover the collet groove.
5   Lubricate the valve stem oil seal with clean engine oil, then push the oil seal down the valve stem using a suitable tube or socket, until the seal is fully engaged with the spring seat **(see illustrations)**. Remove the fitting sleeve or the tape, as applicable, from the valve stem.

9.3 Fitting a spring seat (exhaust valve shown) - SOHC engines

9.4 Slide the oil seal fitting sleeve down the valve stem . . .

9.5a . . . then fit the valve stem oil seal . . .

9.5b . . . and push onto the spring seat using a suitable socket - SOHC engines

9.6a Fit the valve spring . . .

9.6b . . . and spring cap - SOHC engine shown

9.8a Apply a little grease to the split collets . . .

9.8b . . . then refit the split collets - DOHC engine shown

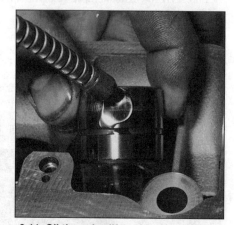

9.11 Oil the valve lifters before refitting - DOHC engine

10.3 Big-end cap centre-punched identification marks. Note that lug on bearing cap faces flywheel end of engine

settle the components.

10   Repeat the procedure for the remaining valves, ensuring that if the original components are being used, they are all refitted in their original positions.

11   On DOHC engines, refit the hydraulic valve lifters to the cylinder head in their original positions. Liberally oil the valve lifters and their bores **(see illustration)**. If new valve lifters are being fitted, initially immerse each one in a container of clean engine oil, and compress it (by hand) several times to charge it.

12   Refit the following components as applicable (if desired, these components can be refitted after refitting the cylinder head).

   (a)   *On DOHC engines, refit the camshafts (see Chapter 2A), the DIS module and its mounting bracket (see Chapter 5C), and the coolant housing (see illustration).*

   (b)   *Refit the thermostat housing and thermostat, using a new sealing ring, where applicable - see Chapter 3.*

   (c)   *Refit the spark plugs (see Chapter 1).*

   (d)   *Refit the manifolds (see Chapter 4A).*

10 Piston/connecting rod assemblies - removal

Note: *On DOHC engines, the mating faces of the connecting rods and the big-end bearing caps are "rough" (not machined), which ensures perfect mating of each individual rod and bearing cap. When the components have been removed from the engine, extreme care should be taken not to damage the mating surfaces - eg do not rest the bearing caps on the mating faces. Ensure that each bearing cap is kept together with its respective rod, to prevent any possibility of the components being refitted incorrectly.*

1   Remove the cylinder head as described in Chapter 2A.

6   Fit the valve spring and the spring cap **(see illustrations)**.

7   Fit the spring compressor tool, and compress the valve spring until the spring cap passes beyond the collet groove in the valve stem.

8   Refit the split collets to the groove in the valve stem, with the narrow ends nearest the spring. **Tip:** *Apply a little grease to the split collets, then fit the split collets into the groove. The grease should hold the collets in the groove* **(see illustrations)**.

9   Slowly release the compressor tool, ensuring that the collets are not dislodged from the groove. When the compressor is fully released, give the top of the valve assembly a tap with a soft-faced mallet to

11.5 Check the crankshaft endfloat using a dial gauge . . .

11.6 . . . or a feeler gauge

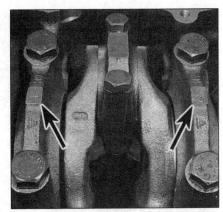

11.7 Main bearing cap identification marks (arrowed)

11.9 Lifting the crankshaft from the crankcase

2   Remove the sump and oil pick-up pipe, as described in Chapter 2A.

3   If the connecting rods and big-end caps are not marked to indicate their positions in the cylinder block (ie marked with cylinder numbers), centre-punch them at adjacent points either side of the cap/rod joint. Note to which side of the engine the marks face **(see illustration)**.

4   Unscrew the big-end cap bolts from the first connecting rod, and remove the cap. If the bearing shells are to be re-used, tape the cap and the shell together.

5   Check the top of the cylinder bore for a wear ridge. If evident, carefully scrape it away with a ridge reamer tool, otherwise the piston rings may jam against the ridge as the piston is pushed out of the block.

6   Place the wooden handle of a hammer against the bottom of the connecting rod, and push the piston/rod assembly up and out of the cylinder bore. Recover the bearing shell, and tape it to the connecting rod if it is to be re-used.

7   Remove the remaining three assemblies in a similar way. Rotate the crankshaft as necessary to bring the big-end bolts to the most accessible position.

11 Crankshaft - removal

1   Remove the flywheel/driveplate as described in Chapter 2A.

2   Remove the pistons and connecting rods, as described in Section 10.

3   Remove the oil pump as described in Chapter 2A.

4   Invert the engine so that the crankshaft is uppermost.

5   Before removing the crankshaft, check the endfloat using a dial gauge in contact with the end of the crankshaft. Push the crankshaft

fully one way, and then zero the gauge. Push the crankshaft fully the other way, and check the endfloat **(see illustration)**. The result should be compared with the specified limit, and will give an indication as to whether new thrust bearing shells are required.

6   If a dial gauge is not available, a feeler gauge can be used to measure crankshaft endfloat. Push the crankshaft fully towards one end of the crankcase, and insert a feeler gauge between the thrust flange of the centre main bearing shell and the machined surface of the crankshaft web **(see illustration)**. Before measuring, ensure that the crankshaft is fully forced towards one end of the crankcase, to give the widest possible gap at the measuring location.

7   The main bearing caps are normally numbered 1 to 4 from the timing belt end of the engine. The rear (flywheel end) cap is not marked. The numbers are read from the coolant pump side of the engine **(see illustration)**. If the bearing caps are not marked, centre-punch them to indicate their locations, and note to which side of the engine the marks face.

8   Unscrew and remove the main bearing cap bolts, and withdraw the bearing caps. If the bearing caps are stuck, tap them gently with a soft-faced mallet to free them. If the bearing shells are to be re-used, tape them to their respective caps.

9   Lift the crankshaft from the crankcase **(see illustration)**.

10   Extract the upper bearing shells, and identify them for position if they are to be re-used.

12 Cylinder block/crankcase - cleaning and inspection

Cleaning

1   For complete cleaning, ideally the core plugs should be removed, where fitted. Drill a small hole in the plugs, then insert a self-tapping screw, and pull out the plugs using a pair of grips or a slide hammer. Also remove all external components (senders, sensors, brackets, etc).

2   Note that, where applicable, the rubber plug located next to the bellhousing flange on the cylinder block covers the aperture for the installation of a diagnostic TDC sensor (used by Vauxhall/Opel dealers). The sensor, when connected to a suitable monitoring unit, indicates TDC from the position of the pins set into the crankshaft balance weight.

3   Scrape all traces of gasket from the cylinder block, taking particular care not to damage the cylinder head and sump mating faces.

4   Remove all oil gallery plugs, where fitted. The plugs are usually very tight - they may have to be drilled out and the holes re-tapped. Use new plugs when the engine is reassembled.

5   If the block is extremely dirty, it should be steam-cleaned.

6   If the block has been steam-cleaned, clean all oil holes and oil galleries one more time on completion. Flush all internal passages with warm water until the water runs clear. Dry the block thoroughly, and wipe all machined surfaces with a light oil. If you have access to compressed air, use it to speed the drying process, and to blow out all the

2B

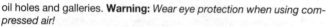

12.17 Piston diameter marking (arrowed) on piston crown

13.2 Using a feeler gauge to aid removal of a piston ring

oil holes and galleries. **Warning:** *Wear eye protection when using compressed air!*

7   If the block is relatively clean, an adequate cleaning job can be achieved with hot soapy water and a stiff brush. Take plenty of time, and do a thorough job. Regardless of the cleaning method used, be sure to clean all oil holes and galleries very thoroughly, dry the block completely, and coat all machined surfaces with light oil.

8   The threaded holes in the cylinder block must be clean, to ensure accurate torque readings when tightening fixings during reassembly. Run the correct-size tap (which can be determined from the size of the relevant bolt) into each of the holes to remove rust, corrosion, thread sealant or other contamination, and to restore damaged threads. If possible, use compressed air to clear the holes of debris produced by this operation. Do not forget to clean the threads of all bolts and nuts as well.

9   After coating the mating surfaces of the new core plugs with suitable sealant, fit them to the cylinder block. Make sure that they are driven in straight and seated correctly, or leakage could result. Special tools are available for this purpose, but a large socket, with an outside diameter which will just fit into the core plug, will work just as well.

10   Where applicable, apply suitable sealant to the new oil gallery plugs, and insert them into the relevant holes in the cylinder block. Tighten the plugs securely.

11   If the engine is to be left dismantled for some time, refit the main bearing caps, tighten the bolts finger-tight, and cover the cylinder block with a large plastic bag to keep it clean and prevent corrosion.

Inspection

12   Visually check the block for cracks, rust and corrosion. Look for stripped threads in the threaded holes (it may be possible to re-cut stripped threads using a suitable tap). If there has been any history of internal coolant leakage, it may be worthwhile asking an engine overhaul specialist to check the block using special equipment. If defects are found, have the block repaired if possible, otherwise a new block may be the only option.

13   Examine the cylinder bores for taper, ovality, scoring and scratches. Start by carefully examining the top of the cylinder bores. If they are at all worn, a very slight ridge will be found on the thrust side. This marks the top of the piston ring travel.

14   Measure the bore diameter of each cylinder at the top (just under the wear ridge), centre and bottom of the cylinder bore, parallel to the crankshaft axis.

15   Next, measure the bore diameter at the same three locations, at right-angles to the crankshaft axis. Compare the results with the figures given in the Specifications.

16   Repeat the procedure for the remaining cylinders.

17   If the cylinder wear exceeds the permitted tolerances, or if the cylinder walls are badly scored or scuffed, then the cylinders will have to be rebored by a suitably-qualified specialist, and new oversize pistons will have to be fitted. In this case, note the following points:

(a)   *Pistons and cylinder bores are closely matched in production. The actual diameter of the piston is indicated by numbers on its crown **(see illustration)**; the same numbers on the crankcase indicate the cylinder bore diameter.*

(b)   *After reboring has taken place, the cylinder bores should be measured accurately, and oversize pistons selected from the grades available to give the specified piston-to-bore clearance.*

(c)   *For grading purposes, the piston diameter is measured across the bottom of the skirt.*

18   If the bore wear is marginal, and within the specified tolerances, new special piston rings can be fitted to offset the wear.

19   If this is the case, the bores should be honed in order to allow the new rings to bed in correctly and provide the best possible seal. The conventional type of hone has spring-loaded stones, and is used with a power drill. You will also need some paraffin or honing oil, and rags. The hone should be moved up and down the cylinder bore to produce a crosshatch pattern, and plenty of honing oil should be used. Ideally, the cross-hatch lines should intersect at approximately a 60° angle. Do not remove more material than is necessary to produce the required finish. If new pistons are being fitted, the piston manufacturers may specify a finish with a different angle, so their instructions should be followed. Do not withdraw the hone from the cylinder while it is still being turned - stop it first. After honing a cylinder, wipe out all traces of the honing oil. An engine overhaul specialist will be able to carry out this work at moderate cost, if required.

13 Piston/connecting rod assembly - inspection

1   Before the inspection process can begin, the piston/connecting rod assemblies must be cleaned, and the original piston rings removed from the pistons.

2   Carefully expand the old rings over the top of the pistons. The use of two or three old feeler gauges will be helpful in preventing the rings dropping into empty grooves **(see illustration)**. Take care, however, as piston rings are sharp.

3   Scrape away all traces of carbon from the top of the piston. A hand-held wire brush, or a piece of fine emery cloth, can be used once the majority of the deposits have been scraped away.

4   Remove the carbon from the ring grooves in the piston, using an old ring. Break the ring in half to do this (be careful not to cut your fingers - piston rings are sharp). Be very careful to remove only the carbon deposits - do not remove any metal, and do not nick or scratch the sides of the ring grooves.

14.7 Measuring the diameter of a crankshaft journal

15.1a Typical main bearing shell . . .

15.1b . . . and main thrust bearing shell identification marks

5   Once the deposits have been removed, clean the piston/connecting rod assembly with paraffin or a suitable solvent, and dry thoroughly. Make sure that the oil return holes in the ring grooves are clear.

6   If the pistons and cylinder bores are not damaged or worn excessively, and if the cylinder block does not need to be rebored, the original pistons can be refitted. Normal piston wear shows up as even vertical wear on the piston thrust surfaces, and slight looseness of the top ring in its groove. New piston rings should always be used when the engine is reassembled.

7   Carefully inspect each piston for cracks around the skirt, at the gudgeon pin bosses, and at the piston ring lands (between the ring grooves).

8   Look for scoring and scuffing on the thrust faces of the piston skirt, holes in the piston crown, and burned areas at the edge of the crown. If the skirt is scored or scuffed, the engine may have been suffering from overheating, and/or abnormal combustion ("pinking") which caused excessively-high operating temperatures. The cooling and lubrication systems should be checked thoroughly. A hole in the piston crown, or burned areas at the edge of the piston crown indicates that abnormal combustion (pre-ignition, "pinking", knocking, or detonation) has been occurring. If any of the above problems exist, the causes must be investigated and corrected, or the damage will occur again. The causes may include leaks in the intake air tracts, incorrect fuel/air mixture, incorrect grade of spark plug, or incorrect ignition timing.

9   Corrosion of the piston, in the form of pitting, indicates that coolant has been leaking into the combustion chamber and/or the crankcase. Again, the cause must be corrected, or the problem may persist in the rebuilt engine.

10   Check the piston-to-bore clearance by measuring the cylinder bore (see Section 12) and the piston diameter. Measure the piston across the bottom of the skirt, at a 90° angle to the gudgeon pin. Subtract the piston diameter from the bore diameter to obtain the clearance. If this is greater than the figures given in the Specifications, the block will have to be rebored, and new pistons and rings fitted.

11   Check the fit of the gudgeon pin by twisting the piston and connecting rod in opposite directions. Any noticeable play indicates excessive wear, which must be corrected. If the pistons or connecting rods are to be renewed, it is necessary to have this work carried out by a Vauxhall/Opel dealer or a suitable engine overhaul specialist, who will have the necessary tooling to remove the gudgeon pins.

12   Check the alignment of the connecting rods visually, and if the rods are not straight, take them to an engine overhaul specialist for a more detailed check.

14 Crankshaft - inspection

1   Clean the crankshaft using paraffin or a suitable solvent, and dry it, preferably with compressed air if available. **Warning:** *Wear eye protection when using compressed air!* Be sure to clean the oil holes with

a pipe cleaner or similar probe, to ensure that they are not obstructed.

2   Check the main and big-end bearing journals for uneven wear, scoring, pitting and cracking.

3   Big-end bearing wear is accompanied by distinct metallic knocking when the engine is running (particularly noticeable when the engine is pulling from low revs), and some loss of oil pressure.

4   Main bearing wear is accompanied by severe engine vibration and rumble - getting progressively worse as engine revs increase - and again by loss of oil pressure.

5   Check the bearing journal for roughness by running a finger lightly over the bearing surface. Any roughness (which will be accompanied by obvious bearing wear) indicates the that the crankshaft requires regrinding.

6   If the crankshaft has been reground, check for burrs around the crankshaft oil holes (the holes are usually chamfered, so burrs should not be a problem unless regrinding has been carried out carelessly). Remove any burrs with a fine file or scraper, and thoroughly clean the oil holes as described previously.

7   Using a micrometer, measure the diameter of the main and big-end bearing journals, and compare the results with the Specifications at the beginning of this Chapter **(see illustration)**. By measuring the diameter at a number of points around each journal's circumference, you will be able to determine whether or not the journal is out-of-round. Take the measurement at each end of the journal, near the webs, to determine if the journal is tapered. If the crankshaft journals are damaged, tapered, out-of-round or excessively-worn, the crankshaft will have to be reground and undersize bearings fitted.

8   Check the oil seal contact surfaces at each end of the crankshaft for wear and damage. If the seal has worn an excessive groove in the surface of the crankshaft, consult an engine overhaul specialist, who will be able to advise whether a repair is possible, or whether a new crankshaft is necessary.

9   Where applicable, check the condition of the pins in the front crankshaft balance weight, which serve as detent points for the plug-in diagnostic sensor used by Vauxhall/Opel dealers.

15 Main and big-end bearings - inspection

1   Even though the main and big-end bearing shells should be renewed during engine overhaul, the old bearing shells should be retained for close examination, as they may reveal valuable information about the condition of the engine. The bearing shells carry identification marks to denote their size in the form of a colour code, or a letter/number code marked on the back of the shell **(see illustrations)**. If the shells are to be renewed, without carrying out any crankshaft regrinding, the old shells should be taken along when obtaining new shells, to ensure that the correct shells are obtained.

2   Bearing failure occurs because of lack of lubrication, the presence of dirt or other foreign particles, overloading the engine, or corrosion. If a

2B

bearing fails, the cause must be found and eliminated before the engine is reassembled, to prevent the failure from happening again.

3   To examine the bearing shells, remove them from the cylinder block, the main bearing caps, the connecting rods and the big-end bearing caps, and lay them out on a clean surface in the same order as they were fitted to the engine. This will enable any bearing problems to be matched with the corresponding crankshaft journal.

4   Dirt and other foreign particles can enter the engine in a variety of ways. Contamination may be left in the engine during assembly, or it may pass through filters or the crankcase ventilation system. Normal engine wear produces small particles of metal, which can eventually cause problems. If particles find their way into the lubrication system, it is likely that they will eventually be carried to the bearings. Whatever the source, these foreign particles often end up embedded in the soft bearing material, and are easily recognised. Large particles will not embed in the bearing, and will score or gouge the bearing and journal. To prevent possible contamination, clean all parts thoroughly, and keep everything spotlessly-clean during engine assembly. Once the engine has been installed in the vehicle, ensure that engine oil and filter changes are carried out at the recommended intervals.

5   Lack of lubrication (or lubrication breakdown) has a number of interrelated causes. Excessive heat (which thins the oil), overloading (which squeezes the oil from the bearing face), and oil leakage (from excessive bearing clearances, worn oil pump or high engine speeds) all contribute to lubrication breakdown. Blocked oil passages, which may be the result of misaligned oil holes in a bearing shell, will also starve a bearing of oil and destroy it. When lack of lubrication is the cause of bearing failure, the bearing material is wiped or extruded from the steel backing of the bearing. Temperatures may increase to the point where the steel backing turns blue from overheating.

6   Driving habits can have a definite effect on bearing life. Full-throttle, low-speed operation (labouring the engine) puts very high loads on bearings, which tends to squeeze out the oil film. These loads cause the bearings to flex, which produces fine cracks in the bearing face (fatigue failure). Eventually the bearing material will loosen in places, and tear away from the steel backing. Regular short journeys can lead to corrosion of bearings, because insufficient engine heat is produced to drive off the condensed water and corrosive gases which form inside the engine. These products collect in the engine oil, forming acid and sludge. As the oil is carried to the bearings, the acid attacks and corrodes the bearing material.

7   Incorrect bearing installation during engine assembly will also lead to bearing failure. Tight-fitting bearings leave insufficient bearing lubrication clearance, and will result in oil starvation. Dirt or foreign particles trapped behind a bearing shell results in high spots on the bearing which can lead to failure.

8   If new bearings are to be fitted, the bearing running clearances should be measured before the engine is finally reassembled, to ensure that the correct bearing shells have been obtained (see Sections 18 and 19). If the crankshaft has been reground, the engineering works should be able to advise on the correct-size bearing shells to suit the work carried out. If there is any doubt as to which bearing shells should be used, seek advice from a Vauxhall/Opel dealer.

16   Engine overhaul - reassembly sequence

1   Before reassembly begins, ensure that all necessary new parts have been obtained (particularly gaskets, and various bolts which must be renewed), and that all the tools required are available. Read through the entire procedure to familiarise yourself with the work involved, and to ensure that all items necessary for reassembly of the engine are to hand. In addition to all normal tools and materials, a thread-locking compound will be required. A tube of RTV sealing compound will also be required, to seal certain joint faces which are not fitted with gaskets.

2   In order to save time and avoid problems, engine reassembly can be carried out in the following order:

    (a)   Piston rings (see Section 17).
    (b)   Crankshaft and main bearings (see Section 18).
    (c)   Piston/connecting rod assemblies (see Section 19).

17.5 Measuring a piston ring end gap using a feeler gauge

    (d)   Oil pump (see Chapter 2A).
    (e)   Sump (see Chapter 2A).
    (f)   Flywheel/driveplate (see Chapter 2A).
    (g)   Cylinder head, valve lifters, camshaft(s) and rocker components (as applicable) (see Chapter 2A).
    (h)   Timing belt and sprockets (see Chapter 2A).
    (i)   Engine external components.

17   Piston rings - refitting

1   Before refitting the new piston rings, the ring end gaps must be checked as follows.

2   Lay out the piston/connecting rod assemblies and the new piston ring sets, so that the ring sets will be matched with the same piston and cylinder during the end gap measurement and subsequent engine reassembly.

3   Insert the top ring into the first cylinder, and push it down the bore using the top of the piston. This will ensure that the ring remains square with the cylinder walls. Position the ring near the bottom of the cylinder bore, at the lower limit of ring travel.

4   Measure the end gap using feeler gauges.

5   Repeat the procedure with the ring at the top of the cylinder bore, at the upper limit of its travel, and compare the measurements with the figures given in the Specifications **(see illustration)**.

6   If the gap is too small (unlikely if genuine Vauxhall/Opel parts are used), it must be enlarged or the ring ends may contact each other during engine operation, causing serious damage. Ideally, new piston rings providing the correct end gap should be fitted, but as a last resort, the end gap can be increased by filing the ring ends very carefully with a fine file. Mount the file in a vice equipped with soft jaws, slip the ring over the file with the ends contacting the file face, and slowly move the ring to remove material from the ends - take care, as piston rings are sharp, and are easily broken.

7   With new piston rings, it is unlikely that the end gap will be too large. If they are too large, check that you have the correct rings for your engine and for the particular cylinder bore size.

8   Repeat the checking procedure for each ring in the first cylinder, and then for the rings in the remaining cylinders. Remember to keep rings, pistons and cylinders matched up.

9   Once the ring end gaps have been checked and if necessary corrected, the rings can be fitted to the pistons.

10   The oil control ring (lowest one on the piston) is composed of three sections, and should be installed first. Fit the lower steel ring, then the spreader ring, followed by the upper steel ring **(see illustration)**.

11   With the oil control ring components installed, the second (middle) ring can be fitted. It is usually stamped with a mark ("TOP") which

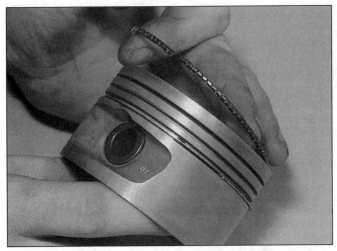

17.10 Fitting an oil control spreader ring

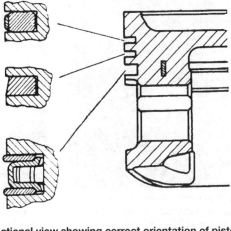

17.12 Sectional view showing correct orientation of piston rings

2B

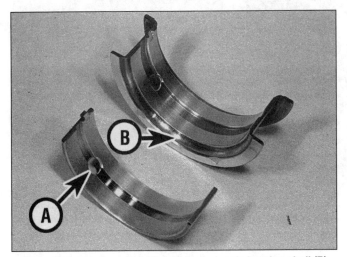

**18.4a Main bearing shell (A) and central main bearing shell (B)
with thrust flange**

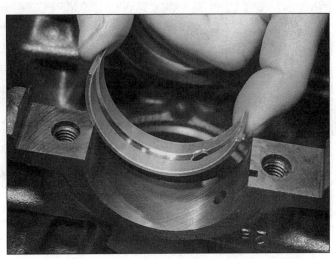

18.4b Fitting a main bearing shell to the cylinder block

must face up, towards the top of the piston. **Note:** *Always follow the instructions supplied with the new piston ring sets - different manufacturers may specify different procedures. Do not mix up the top and middle rings, as they have different cross-sections.* Using two or three old feeler blades, as for removal of the old rings, carefully slip the ring into place in the middle groove.

12   Fit the top ring in the same manner, ensuring that, where applicable, the mark on the ring is facing up. If a stepped ring is being fitted, fit the ring with the smaller diameter of the step uppermost **(see illustration)**.

13   Repeat the procedure for the remaining pistons and rings.

18   Crankshaft - refitting and main bearing running clearance check

1   Refitting the crankshaft is the first step in the engine reassembly procedure. It is assumed at this point that the cylinder block and crankshaft have been cleaned, inspected and repaired or reconditioned as necessary.

2   Position the cylinder block with the sump mating face uppermost.

Main bearing running clearance check

Note: *When finally refitting the crankshaft, new main bearing cap bolts must be used. However, when checking the bearing running clearance,* the original bolts should be used, and then discarded. A vernier dial indicator, an internal micrometer, or "Plastigage" will be required for this check - see text.

3   Clean the bearing shells and the bearing recesses in both the cylinder block and main bearing caps. If new shells are being fitted, ensure that all traces of the protective grease are cleaned off using paraffin. Wipe the shells dry with a clean lint-free cloth.

4   Note that the central bearing shells have thrust flanges which control crankshaft endfloat. If the original bearing shells are being re-used, they must be refitted to their original locations in the block and caps **(see illustrations)**.

5   Before the crankshaft can be permanently installed, the main bearing running clearance should be checked, and this can be done in either of two ways. One method is to fit the main bearing caps to the cylinder block, with bearing shells in place. With the original cap retaining bolts tightened to the specified torque, measure the internal diameter of each assembled pair of bearing shells using a vernier dial indicator or an internal micrometer. If the diameter of each corresponding crankshaft journal is measured and then subtracted from the bearing internal diameter, the result will give the main bearing running clearance. The second (and more accurate) method is to use a product known as "Plastigage". This consists of a fine thread of perfectly-round plastic, which is compressed between the bearing cap shell and the crankshaft journal. When the bearing cap is removed, the deformed plastic can be measured with a special card gauge supplied with the Plastigage kit. The running clearance is determined from this gauge.

18.7 Lay the length of Plastigage on the journal to be measured, parallel to the crankshaft centre-line

18.11 Using the scale on the envelope provided to check the width of the crushed Plastigage (at its widest point)

18.16 Lubricate the main bearing shells before fitting the crankshaft

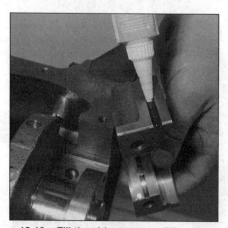

18.19a Fill the side grooves of the rear main bearing cap with RTV jointing compound . . .

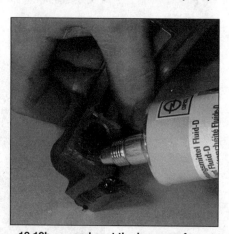

18.19b . . . and coat the lower surfaces with sealing compound

18.19c Fitting the centre main bearing cap

Plastigage is sometimes difficult to obtain in this country, but enquiries at one of the larger specialist chains of quality motor factors should produce the name of a stockist in your area. The procedure for using Plastigage is as follows.

6   With the upper main bearing shells in place in the cylinder block, carefully lay the crankshaft in position. Do not use any lubricant; the crankshaft journals and bearing shells must be perfectly clean and dry.

7   Cut several pieces of the appropriate-size Plastigage (they should be slightly shorter than the width of the main bearings) and place one piece on each crankshaft journal axis **(see illustration)**.

8   With the bearing shells in position in the caps, fit the caps to their original locations. Take care not to disturb the Plastigage.

9   Starting with the centre main bearing and working outwards, tighten the main bearing cap bolts (use the original bolts) progressively to their specified torque. Do not rotate the crankshaft at any time during this operation.

10   Remove the bearing cap bolts and carefully lift off the caps, keeping them in order. Do not disturb the Plastigage or rotate the crankshaft. If any of the bearing caps are difficult to remove, free them by carefully tapping with a soft-faced mallet.

11   Compare the width of the deformed Plastigage on each journal with the scale printed on the card gauge to obtain the main bearing running clearance **(see illustration)**.

12   If the clearance is not as specified, the bearing shells may be the wrong size (or excessively-worn if the original shells are being re-used). Before deciding that different shells are required, make sure that no dirt or oil was trapped between the bearing shells and the caps or block when the clearance was measured. If the Plastigage was wider at one end than at the other, the crankshaft journal may be tapered.

13   Carefully remove all traces of the Plastigage material from the crankshaft and bearing shells, using a fingernail or other improvised tool which is unlikely to score the shells.

Final crankshaft refitting

Note: *New main bearing cap bolts must be used when refitting the crankshaft. Suitable sealants (Vauxhall/Opel Nos 15 03 294 and 15 04 201, or equivalents) will be required to coat the front and rear main bearing caps.*

14   Carefully lift the crankshaft out of the cylinder block once more.

15   Lubricate the lips of a new crankshaft rear oil seal, and carefully slip it over the rear of the crankshaft. Do this carefully, as the seal lips are very delicate. Ensure that the open side of the seal faces the inside of the engine.

16   Liberally lubricate each bearing shell in the cylinder block **(see illustration)**, and lower the crankshaft into position. Check that the rear oil seal is positioned correctly.

17   If necessary, seat the crankshaft using light taps from a soft-faced mallet on the crankshaft balance webs.

18   Lubricate the bearing shells in the bearing caps, and the crankshaft journals, then fit Nos 2, 3 and 4 bearing caps, and tighten the new bolts as far as possible by hand.

19   Fill the side grooves of the front (where applicable - not all engines have grooves in the front main bearing cap) and rear main bearing caps with RTV jointing compound (Vauxhall/Opel part No 15 03 294, or equivalent). Coat the lower surfaces of the bearing caps with sealing compound (Vauxhall/Opel part No 15 04 201, or equivalent). Fit the bearing caps, and tighten the new bolts as far as possible by hand **(see illustrations)**. Ensure that the front main bearing

18.20a Tighten the main bearing cap bolts to the specified torque, . . .

18.20b . . . then through the specified angle

19.5a Piston crown arrow must point towards timing belt end of engine - SOHC engine shown

2B

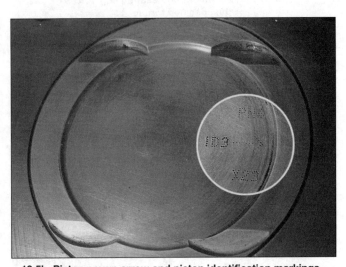

19.5b Piston crown arrow and piston identification markings - DOHC engine

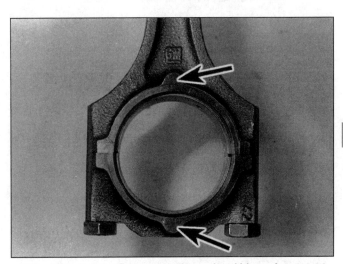

19.5c Lugs (arrowed) on connecting rod and big-end cap must point towards flywheel end of engine

cap is exactly flush with the end face of the cylinder block.

20 Working from the centre main bearing cap outwards, tighten the bearing cap bolts to the specified torque in the three stages given in the Specifications; ie tighten all bolts to Stage 1, then tighten all bolts to Stage 2, and so on **(see illustrations)**.

21 When all bolts have been fully tightened, inject further RTV jointing compound into the side grooves of the front (where applicable) and rear main bearing caps until it is certain that they are full.

22 Now rotate the crankshaft, and check that it turns freely, with no signs of binding or tight spots.

23 Check the crankshaft endfloat with reference to Section 11.

24 Refit the pistons and connecting rods as described in Section 19.

25 Refit the oil pump as described in Chapter 2A.

26 Refit the sump and oil pick-up pipe as described in Chapter 2A.

27 Refit the flywheel/driveplate as described in Chapter 2A.

28 Refit the cylinder head as described in Chapter 2A.

19 Piston/connecting rod assemblies - refitting and big-end bearing running clearance check

1 Clean the backs of the big-end bearing shells and the recesses in the connecting rods and big-end caps. If new shells are being fitted, ensure that all traces of the protective grease are cleaned off using paraffin. Wipe the shells, caps and connecting rods dry with a lint-free cloth.

2 Press the bearing shells into the connecting rods and caps in their correct positions.

Big-end bearing running clearance check

Note: *When finally refitting the piston/connecting rod assemblies, new big-end bearing cap bolts must be used. However, when checking the bearing running clearance, the original bolts should be used, and then discarded. A piston ring compressor tool will be required for this operation. On DOHC engines, ensure that the mating faces of the connecting rods and big-end bearing caps are clean before refitting (refer to the note at the beginning of Section 10 .*

3 Lubricate No 1 piston and piston rings, and check that the ring gaps are correctly positioned. The gap in the lower steel ring of the oil control ring should be offset 25.0 to 50.0 mm to the right of the spreader ring gap, and the upper steel ring gap should be offset by the same distance to the left of the spreader ring gap. The upper compression ring should be positioned with the ring gap offset by 180° to the lower compression ring gap.

4 Liberally lubricate the cylinder bore with clean engine oil.

5 Fit a ring compressor to No 1 piston, then insert the piston and connecting rod into the cylinder bore so that the base of the compressor stands on the block. With the crankshaft big-end bearing journal positioned at its lowest point, tap the piston carefully into the cylinder bore with the wooden handle of a hammer, and at the same time guide the connecting rod onto the bearing journal. Note that the arrow or notch, as applicable, on the piston crown should point towards the timing belt end of the engine, and the lugs on the connecting rod and big-end bearing cap should point towards the flywheel end of the engine **(see illustrations)**. The oil spray hole in the connecting rod should

19.5d Tapping a piston into its bore

19.9a Tighten the big-end bearing cap bolts to the specified torque . . .

be on the coolant pump side of the engine.

6   To measure the big-end bearing running clearance, refer to the information contained in Section 18, as the same general procedures apply. If the Plastigage method is being used, ensure that the big-end bearing journal and the bearing shells are clean and dry, then engage the connecting rod with the bearing journal. Lay the Plastigage strip on the bearing journal, fit the bearing cap in its original location (noting that the lug on the bearing cap should point towards the flywheel end of the engine), then tighten the original bearing cap bolts to the specified torque. Do not rotate the crankshaft during this operation. Remove the bearing cap, and check the running clearance by measuring the Plastigage as previously described.

7   Repeat the checking procedures on the remaining piston/connecting rod assemblies.

Final piston/connecting rod assembly refitting

Note: New big-end bearing cap bolts must be used when refitting the piston/connecting rod assemblies.

8   After checking the running clearance of all the big-end bearings and taking any corrective action necessary, clean off all traces of Plastigage from the bearing shells and journals.

9   Liberally lubricate the bearing journals and bearing shells, and refit the bearing caps once more, ensuring correct positioning as previously described. Tighten the new bearing cap bolts to the specified torque (where two stages are specified, tighten all bolts to Stage 1, then tighten all bolts to Stage 2) **(see illustrations)**.

10   After refitting each piston/connecting rod assembly, rotate the crankshaft, and check that it turns freely, with no signs of binding or tight spots.

11   Refit the oil pick-up pipe and sump, as described in Chapter 2A.

12   Refit the cylinder head as described in Chapter 2A.

20   Engine - initial start-up after overhaul

1   With the engine refitted to the vehicle, check the engine oil and coolant levels.

2   With the spark plugs removed and the ignition system disabled by disconnecting the coil or DIS module LT lead, or wiring plug (as applicable), crank the engine over on the starter until the oil pressure light goes out. This may take a few seconds as the new oil filter fills with oil.

3   Refit the spark plugs, and reconnect all ignition wiring.

4   Start the engine, noting that this may take a little longer than usual

19.9b . . . then through the specified angle

as fuel is pumped to the engine. If a new camshaft has been fitted to SOHC engine models, pay careful attention to the running-in procedure given in Chapter 2A.

5   While the engine is idling, check for fuel, coolant and oil leaks. Where applicable, check the power steering and/or automatic transmission fluid pipe/hose unions for leakage. Do not be alarmed if there are some odd smells and smoke from parts getting hot and burning off oil deposits.

6   Keep the engine idling until hot coolant is felt circulating through the radiator top hose, indicating that the engine is at normal operating temperature, then check as far as possible that the engine is running smoothly. Ideally, the engine management system should be checked using suitable diagnostic equipment with reference to Chapter 4A.

7   Stop the engine.

8   Allow the engine to cool, then recheck the oil and coolant levels, and top-up as necessary.

9   If new pistons, rings or bearings have been fitted, the engine must be run-in at reduced speeds and loads for the first 500 miles (800 km). Do not operate the engine at full-throttle, or allow it to labour in any gear during this period. It is beneficial to change the engine oil and filter at the end of this period.

Chapter 3
Cooling, heating and ventilation systems

Contents

3

Specifications

General

Expansion tank cap opening pressure	1.20 to 1.35 bars

Thermostat

Opening temperatures:

1.2 and 1.4 litre engines:

Starts to open	88°C
Fully-open	106°C

1.6 litre DOHC engine:

Starts to open	92°C
Fully-open	107°C

Electric cooling fan(s) operating temperatures

Cooling fan(s) on:

Models without air conditioning	100°C

Models with air conditioning:

Slow speed	100°C
Fast speed	105°C

Cooling fan(s) off:

Models without air conditioning	95°C

Models with air conditioning:

Slow speed	95°C
Fast speed	100°C

Torque wrench settings

	Nm	lbf ft
Thermostat:		
Housing bolts (1.2 and 1.4 litre engines)	10	7
Cover bolts (1.6 litre DOHC engine)	8	6
Coolant pump bolts	8	6

**3.5 Cooling fan switch is screwed into the right-hand
end of the radiator**

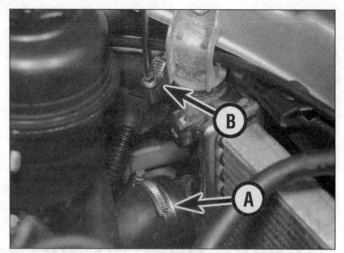

**3.8a Slacken the retaining clips, and disconnect the coolant hose
(A) and expansion tank hose (B) from the left-hand
end of the radiator . . .**

---

1   General information and precautions

General information

1   The cooling system is of pressurised type, comprising a pump
driven by the timing belt, an aluminium crossflow radiator, electric
cooling fan, and a thermostat. The system functions as follows. Cold
coolant from the radiator passes through the hose to the coolant
pump, where it is pumped around the cylinder block and head passages. After cooling the cylinder bores, combustion surfaces and valve
seats, the coolant reaches the underside of the thermostat, which is
initially closed. The coolant passes through the heater, and is returned
via the cylinder block to the coolant pump.
2   When the engine is cold, the coolant circulates only through the
cylinder block, cylinder head, expansion tank and heater. When the
coolant reaches a predetermined temperature, the thermostat opens
and the coolant passes through to the radiator. As the coolant circulates through the radiator, it is cooled by the inrush of air when the car
is in forward motion. Airflow is supplemented by the action of the electric cooling fan when necessary. Once the coolant has passed through
the radiator, and has cooled, the cycle is repeated.
3   The electric cooling fan, mounted on the rear of the radiator, is
controlled by a thermostatic switch. At a predetermined coolant temperature, the switch actuates the fan.
4   Refer to Section 11 for information on the air conditioning system.

Precautions

Warning: *Do not attempt to remove the expansion tank filler cap, or
disturb any part of the cooling system, while the engine is hot; there is a
high risk of scalding. If the expansion tank filler cap must be removed
before the engine and radiator have fully cooled (even though this is not
recommended) the pressure in the cooling system must first be relieved. Cover the cap with a thick layer of cloth, to avoid scalding, and
slowly unscrew the filler cap until a hissing sound can be heard. When
the hissing has stopped, indicating that the pressure has reduced,
slowly unscrew the filler cap until it can be removed; if more hissing
sounds are heard, wait until they have stopped before unscrewing the
cap completely. At all times, keep well away from the filler cap opening.*
Warning: *Do not allow antifreeze to come into contact with skin, or with
the painted surfaces of the vehicle. Rinse off spills immediately, with
plenty of water. Never leave antifreeze lying around in an open container, or in a puddle on the driveway or garage floor. Children and pets
are attracted by its sweet smell, but antifreeze can be fatal if ingested.*
Warning: *If the engine is hot, the electric cooling fan may start rotating
even if the engine is not running; be careful to keep hands, hair and
loose clothing well clear when working in the engine compartment.*

Warning: *Refer to Section 11 for precautions to be observed when
working on models equipped with air conditioning.*

2   Cooling system hoses - disconnection and renewal

Note: *Refer to the warnings given in Section 1 of this Chapter before
proceeding. Do not attempt to disconnect any hose while the system is
still hot.*
1   If the checks described in Chapter 1 reveal a faulty hose, it must
be renewed as follows.
2   First drain the cooling system (see Chapter 1). If the coolant is not
due for renewal, it may be re-used if it is collected in a clean container.
3   Before disconnecting a hose, first note its routing in the engine
compartment, and whether it is secured by any clips or ties. Use a
screwdriver to slacken the clips, then move the clips along the hose,
clear of the relevant inlet/outlet union. Carefully work the hose free.
4   Note that the radiator inlet and outlet unions are fragile; do not
use excessive force when attempting to remove the hoses. If a hose
proves to be difficult to remove, try to release it by rotating the hose
ends before attempting to free it. If all else fails, cut the hose with a
sharp knife, then slit it so that it can be peeled off in two pieces. Although this may prove expensive if the hose is otherwise undamaged,
it is preferable to buying a new radiator.
5   When fitting a hose, first slide the clips onto the hose, then work
the hose into position. If clamp-type clips were originally fitted, it is a
good idea to replace them with screw-type clips when refitting the
hose. If the hose is stiff, use a little soapy water (washing-up liquid is
ideal) as a lubricant, or soften the hose by soaking it in hot water.
6   Work the hose into position, checking that it is correctly routed
and secured. Slide each clip along the hose until it passes over the
flared end of the relevant inlet/outlet union, before tightening the clips
securely.
7   Refill the cooling system with reference to Chapter 1.
8   Check thoroughly for leaks as soon as possible after disturbing
any part of the cooling system.

3   Radiator - removal, inspection and refitting

Tip: *If leakage is the reason for wanting to remove the radiator, bear in
mind that minor leaks can be often be cured using a radiator sealant,
such as Holts Radweld, without removing the radiator.*

Removal

1   Disconnect the battery negative lead.
2   Drain the cooling system as described in Chapter 1.

3.8b . . . and the coolant hose from the right-hand end of the radiator

3.9a Unscrew the retaining bolt . . .

3.9b . . . and remove each radiator upper mounting bracket and rubber

3.10 Free the radiator from its lower mounting rubbers, and lift it out of the engine compartment

3.16 Inspect the mounting rubbers for signs of damage, and renew if necessary

3.17 On refitting, ensure that the radiator pegs engage with lower mounting rubbers (arrowed)

3   Prise out the retaining clip, and remove the air intake duct from the air cleaner housing.

4   Disconnect the wiring connector from the cooling fan motor.

5   Disconnect the wiring connector(s) from the cooling fan switch(es) on the right-hand end of the radiator **(see illustration)**.

6   On 1.2 and 1.4 litre models with air conditioning, and all 1.6 litre DOHC models, remove the cooling fan assembly as described in Section 5.

7   To improve clearance on models with power steering, unbolt the power steering fluid reservoir, and place it clear of the radiator.

8   Slacken the retaining clips, and disconnect the coolant and expansion tank hoses from the left-hand end of the radiator. Also disconnect the coolant hose from the radiator right-hand end **(see illustrations)**.

9   Undo the retaining bolts, and remove the left- and right-hand mounting brackets from the top of the radiator **(see illustrations)**.

10   Free the radiator from its lower mounting rubbers, and lift it out of the engine compartment **(see illustration)**.

Inspection

11   If the radiator has been removed due to suspected blockage, reverse-flush it as described in Chapter 1. Clean dirt and debris from the radiator fins, using an air line (in which case, wear eye protection) or a soft brush. Be careful, as the fins are easily damaged, and are sharp.

12   If necessary, a radiator specialist can perform a "flow test" on the radiator, to establish whether an internal blockage exists.

13   A leaking radiator must be referred to a specialist for permanent repair. Do not attempt to weld or solder a leaking radiator, as damage may result.

14   In an emergency, minor leaks from the radiator can be cured by using a suitable radiator sealant (in accordance with its manufacturer's

instructions) with the radiator *in situ*.

15   If the radiator is to be sent for repair, or is to be renewed, remove the cooling fan switch(es).

16   Inspect the radiator mounting rubbers, and renew them if necessary **(see illustration)**.

Refitting

17   Refitting is a reversal of removal, bearing in mind the following points:

(a)   Ensure that the lower lugs on the radiator are correctly engaged with the mounting rubbers in the body panel **(see illustration)**.

(b)   Ensure that all hoses are correctly reconnected, and their retaining clips securely tightened.

(c)   On completion, refill the cooling system as described in Chapter 1.

4   Thermostat - removal, testing and refitting

Removal

1.2 and 1.4 litre engines

1   Disconnect the battery negative lead.

2   Drain the cooling system as described in Chapter 1.

3   Remove the rear timing belt cover as described in Chapter 2.

4   Slacken the retaining clip, and disconnect the coolant hose from the thermostat housing.

5   Slacken and remove the two retaining bolts, and remove the thermostat housing from the engine.

4.10 On 1.6 litre DOHC engines, slacken the retaining clip and disconnect the coolant hose from the thermostat housing . . .

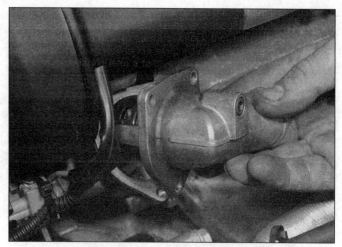

4.11 . . . then undo the three bolts and remove the thermostat housing cover from the engine. The thermostat is integral with the cover

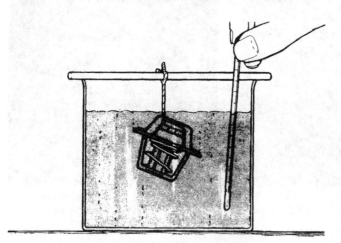

4.14 Testing the thermostat opening temperature

6   Withdraw the thermostat from the cylinder head.
7   Remove the sealing ring from the edge of the thermostat and discard it; a new one should be used on refitting.

1.6 litre DOHC engine

8   Disconnect the battery negative lead.
9   Drain the cooling system as described in Chapter 1.
10   Slacken the retaining clip, and disconnect the coolant hose from the thermostat housing **(see illustration)**.
11   Slacken and remove the three retaining bolts, and remove the thermostat housing cover from the front of the cylinder head **(see illustration)**. The thermostat is an integral part of the cover, and cannot be removed.
12   Recover the housing cover sealing ring, and discard it; a new one should be used on refitting.

Testing

13   A rough test of the thermostat's operation may be made by suspending it with a piece of string in a container full of water. Heat the water to bring it to the boil - the thermostat must open by the time the water boils. If not, renew it.
14   If a thermometer is available, the precise opening temperature of the thermostat may be determined, and compared with the figures given in the Specifications **(see illustration)**. The opening temperature is also marked on the thermostat.
15   A thermostat which fails to close as the water cools must also be renewed.

Refitting

1.2 and 1.4 litre engines

16   Refitting is a reversal of removal, bearing in mind the following points:

   (a)   Fit the new sealing ring to the thermostat, and fit the thermostat to the cylinder head. Ensure that the thermostat is fitted the correct way round, and that its lugs are correctly engaged with the slots in the cylinder head.
   (b)   Tighten the thermostat housing bolts to the specified torque setting.
   (c)   On completion, refill the cooling system as described in Chapter 1.

1.6 litre DOHC engine

17   Refitting is the reverse of the removal sequence, noting the following points:

   (a)   Fit a new sealing ring to the thermostat cover **(see illustration)**.
   (b)   Tighten the thermostat cover bolts to the specified torque setting.
   (c)   On completion, refill the cooling system as described in Chapter 1.

5   Electric cooling fan - testing, removal and refitting

Testing

1   The cooling fan is supplied with current via the ignition switch, relay(s) and a fuse (see Chapter 12). The circuit is completed by the cooling fan thermostatic switch, which is mounted in the right-hand end of the radiator. **Note:** *On models with air conditioning, there are two switches fitted to the radiator; both switches operate the cooling fan and the air conditioning auxiliary cooling fan simultaneously. The lower switch operates at 100°C, switching the fans on at a slow speed. If the coolant temperature reaches 105°C, the upper switch operates both fans at full speed.*
2   If a fan does not appear to work, run the engine until normal operating temperature is reached, then allow it to idle. If the fan does not cut in within a few minutes (or before the temperature gauge indicates overheating), switch off the ignition and disconnect the wiring plug from the cooling fan switch. Bridge the two contacts in the wiring plug using a length of spare wire, and switch on the ignition. If the fan now operates, the switch is probably faulty, and should be renewed.
3   If the fan still fails to operate, check that full battery voltage is available at the feed wire to the switch; if not, then there is a fault in the feed wire (possibly due to a fault in the fan motor, or a blown fuse). If there is no problem with the feed, check that there is continuity

4.17 Fitting a new sealing ring to the thermostat cover groove

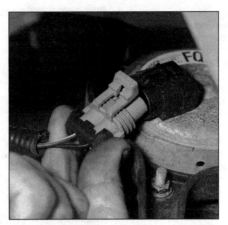

5.7 Disconnecting the wiring connector from the cooling fan motor (viewed from underneath)

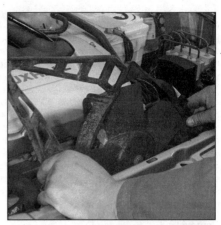

5.8 Undo the retaining bolts, and lift the cooling fan assembly out from the engine compartment

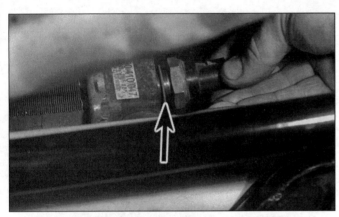

6.6 Unscrew the cooling fan switch from the radiator, and recover the sealing washer (arrowed)

between the switch earth terminal and a good earth point on the body. If not, then the earth connection is faulty, and must be re-made.

4   If the switch and the wiring are in good condition, the fault must lie in the motor itself. The motor can be checked by disconnecting the motor wiring connector and connecting a 12-volt supply directly to the motor terminals. If the motor fails this test, it is proved faulty, and must be renewed complete.

Removal

5   Disconnect the battery negative lead.
6   Prise out the retaining clip, and remove the air intake duct from the air cleaner housing.
7   Disconnect the wiring connector from the cooling fan **(see illustration)**.
8   Unscrew the fan shroud retaining bolts, then tilt the assembly back slightly towards the engine, and withdraw it upwards away from the radiator **(see illustration)**.
9   To separate the fan motor from the shroud, unscrew the three retaining nuts, and release the retaining clip. Slide off the retaining clip, and remove the fan blade from the motor.
10   No spare parts are available for the motor, and if the unit is faulty, it must be renewed complete.

Refitting

11   Refitting is a reversal of removal, ensuring that the fan blade (where removed) is correctly engaged with the motor pin, and that the shroud is correctly located in the radiator clips.
12   On completion, start the engine and run it until it reaches normal operating temperature; continue to run the engine, and check that the cooling fan cuts in and functions correctly.

6   Cooling system electrical switches - testing, removal and refitting

Electric cooling fan thermostatic switch(es)

Testing

1   Testing of the switch(es) is described in Section 5, as part of the electric cooling fan test procedure.

Removal

2   The switch(es) is/are located in the right-hand side of the radiator (see illustration 3.5). The engine and radiator should be cold before removing the switch.
3   Disconnect the battery negative lead. Firmly apply the handbrake, then jack up the front of the vehicle and support it on axle stands. Access to the switch can then be gained from underneath the vehicle.
4   Either drain the cooling system to below the level of the switch (as described in Chapter 1), or have ready a suitable plug which can be used to block the switch aperture in the radiator whilst the switch is removed. If a plug is used, take great care not to damage the radiator, and do not use anything which will allow foreign matter to enter the radiator.
5   Disconnect the wiring plug from the switch.
6   Carefully unscrew the switch from the radiator, and recover the sealing ring/washer **(see illustration)**.

Refitting

7   Refitting is a reversal of removal, using a new sealing ring/washer. Securely tighten the switch, and top-up/refill the cooling system as described in Chapter 1.
8   On completion, start the engine and run it until it reaches normal operating temperature; continue to run the engine, and check that the cooling fan cuts in and functions correctly.

Coolant temperature gauge sender

Testing

9   The coolant temperature gauge is fed with a stabilised voltage supply from the instrument panel feed (via the ignition switch and a fuse), and its earth is controlled by the sender.
10   The sender is screwed into the inlet manifold on 1.2 and 1.4 litre engines, or into the thermostat housing on 1.6 litre DOHC engines. The sender contains a thermistor (thermal resistor), an electronic component whose electrical resistance decreases at a predetermined rate as its temperature rises. When the coolant is cold, the sender resistance is high, current flow through the gauge is reduced, and the gauge needle points towards the "cold" end of the scale. If the sender is faulty, it must be renewed.
11   If the gauge develops a fault, first check the other instruments; if they do not work at all, check the instrument panel electrical feed. If

3

the readings are erratic, there may be a fault in the voltage stabiliser, which will necessitate renewal of the stabiliser (see Chapter 12). If the fault lies in the temperature gauge alone, check it as follows.

12   If the gauge needle remains at the "cold" end of the scale, disconnect the sender wire, and earth it to the cylinder head. If the needle then deflects when the ignition is switched on, the sender unit is proved faulty, and should be renewed. If the needle still does not move, remove the instrument panel (Chapter 12) and check the continuity of the wiring between the sender unit and the gauge, and the feed to the gauge unit. If continuity is shown, and the fault still exists, then the gauge is faulty, and the gauge unit should be renewed.

13   If the gauge needle remains at the "hot" end of the scale, disconnect the sender wire. If the needle then returns to the "cold" end of the scale when the ignition is switched on, the sender unit is proved faulty, and should be renewed. If the needle still does not move, check the remainder of the circuit as described previously.

Removal

14   Either partially drain the cooling system to just below the level of the sender (as described in Chapter 1), or have ready a suitable plug which can be used to block the sender aperture whilst it is removed. If a plug is used, take great care not to damage the internal threads, and do not use anything which will allow foreign matter to enter the cooling system.

15   Disconnect the battery negative lead.

16   Disconnect the wiring from the sender, then unscrew the unit from its location.

Refitting

17   Ensure the sender threads are clean, and apply a smear of suitable sealant to them.

18   Refit the sender, tightening it securely, and reconnect the wiring.

19   Top-up/refill the cooling system as described in Chapter 1.

20   On completion, start the engine and check the operation of the temperature gauge. Also check for coolant leaks.

Fuel injection system coolant temperature sensor

21   Refer to Chapter 4.

---

7   Coolant pump - removal and refitting

Removal

1   Drain the cooling system with reference to Chapter 1.

2   On 1.2 and 1.4 litre engines, remove the timing belt and rear timing belt cover as described in Chapter 2.

3   On 1.6 litre DOHC engines, remove the timing belt as described in Chapter 2.

4   Unscrew and remove the three coolant pump securing bolts.

5   Withdraw the coolant pump from the cylinder block, noting that it may be necessary to tap the pump lightly with a soft-faced hammer to free it from the cylinder block.

6   Recover the pump sealing ring, and discard it; a new one must be used on refitting.

7   Note that it is not possible to overhaul of the pump. If it is faulty, the unit must be renewed complete.

Refitting

8   Ensure that the pump and cylinder block mating surfaces are clean and dry, and apply a smear of silicone grease to the pump mating surface in the cylinder block. Vauxhall/Opel recommend the use of their grease (Part No 19 70 206); in the absence of this, ensure a good-quality equivalent is used.

9   Fit a new sealing ring to the pump, and install the pump in the cylinder block.

10   On 1.2 and 1.4 litre engines, refit the pump retaining bolts, tightening them by hand only at this stage. Refit the rear timing belt cover and install the timing belt as described in Chapter 2.

11   On 1.6 litre DOHC engines, align the edge of the coolant pump flange with the mark on the cylinder block, then tighten the coolant

7.11 On 1.6 litre DOHC engines, align the flange edge with the mark on the cylinder block (arrowed) when refitting the coolant pump

pump bolts to the specified torque setting **(see illustration)**. Refit the timing belt as described in Chapter 2.

12   On all models, refill the cooling system as described in Chapter 1.

---

8   Heater/ventilation system - general information

1   The heater/ventilation system consists of a four-speed blower motor (housed in the engine compartment), face-level vents in the centre and at each end of the facia, and air ducts to the front footwells.

2   The control unit is located in the facia, and the controls operate flap valves to deflect and mix the air flowing through the various parts of the heater/ventilation system. The flap valves are contained in the air distribution housing, which acts as a central distribution unit, passing air to the various ducts and vents.

3   Cold air enters the system through the grille at the rear of the engine compartment. On most models (depending on specification) a pollen filter is fitted to the ventilation intake, to filter out dust, soot, pollen and spores from the air entering the vehicle.

4   The air (boosted by the blower fan if required) then flows through the various ducts, according to the settings of the controls. Stale air is expelled through ducts behind the doors. If warm air is required, the cold air is passed through the heater matrix, which is heated by the engine coolant.

5   A recirculation lever enables the outside air supply to be closed off, while the air inside the vehicle is recirculated. This can be useful to prevent unpleasant odours entering from outside the vehicle, but should only be used briefly, as the recirculated air inside the vehicle will soon deteriorate.

6   Certain models may be fitted with heated front seats. The heat is produced by electrically-heated mats in the seat and backrest cushions (see Chapter 12). The temperature is regulated automatically by a thermostat, and cannot be adjusted.

---

9   Heater/ventilation components - removal and refitting

Heater/ventilation control unit

Removal

1   Disconnect the battery negative lead.

2   Remove the two centre vents from the facia panel as described in Section 10.

3   Remove the hazard warning light and heated rear window switches as described in Chapter 12. On models with heated front seats, also remove the seat heating switches.

4   Carefully lever the knob off the air recirculation lever, then prise the lever surround out of the centre facia panel, taking great care not to mark the panel **(see illustrations)**.

9.4a Lever off the knob from the air recirculation lever . . .

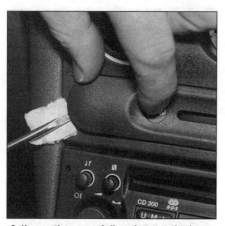

9.4b . . . then carefully prise out the lever surround. Note the use of a piece of card to avoid marking the facia panel

9.5a Undo the four retaining screws (arrowed) . . .

9.5b . . . then withdraw the centre facia panel from the facia

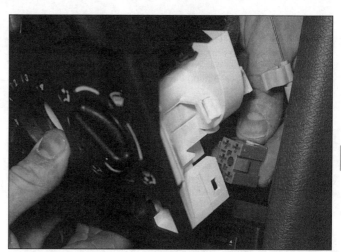

9.7 Free the wiring connectors from the rear of the centre facia panel and control unit, and remove the assembly from the facia

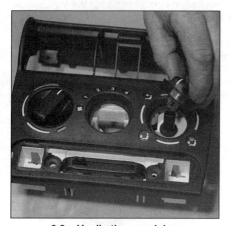

9.8a Unclip the remaining control knobs . . .

9.8b . . . then undo the two retaining screws (arrowed) . . .

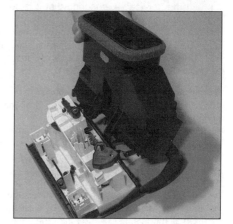

9.8c . . . and separate the vent and control unit from the facia panel

5   Undo the four retaining centre facia panel retaining screws, then withdraw the panel from the facia until access can be gained to the rear of the control panel **(see illustrations)**.
6   Unclip the four control cables, and release each cable from the control unit, noting each cable's correct fitted location and routing. **Note:** *The control cable end fittings are colour-coded for identification purposes.* The outer cables are released by simply lifting the retaining clips.
7   Disconnect the wiring connectors from the control panel, and un-clip the switch wiring connectors from the rear of the centre facia panel **(see illustration)**. Remove the centre facia panel from the vehicle.
8   If necessary, carefully prise off the remaining control knobs, then undo the two retaining screws, and unclip the heater control unit and vent from the centre facia panel **(see illustrations)**.

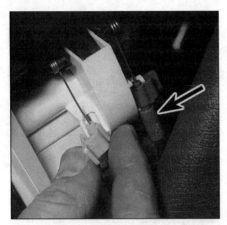

9.11 Unclipping the lower air distribution cable from the heater control unit. The rear cable (arrowed) is the upper air distribution cable

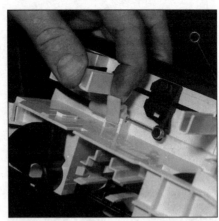

9.30 Disconnecting the air recirculation cable from the rear of the control unit

9.40a Undo the two left-hand retaining screws (arrowed) . . .

Refitting

9   Refitting is reversal of removal. Ensure that the control cables are correctly routed and reconnected to the control panel, as noted before removal. Clip the outer cables in position, and check the operation of each knob/lever before refitting the centre facia panel.

Heater/ventilation control cables - renewal

Lower air distribution control cable

10   Remove the heater/ventilation control unit from the facia, as described above in paragraphs 1 to 5.
11 .   Unclip the lower air distribution cable (with the grey end fitting) and free the cable from the right-hand side of the control unit. The outer cable is released by simply lifting the retaining clip **(see illustration)**.
12   Follow the run of the cable behind the facia, taking note of its routing, and disconnect the cable from the lever on the air distribution housing. Note that the method of fastening is the same as that used at the control unit. On right-hand drive models, if necessary, undo the two screws and remove the trim panel from the right-hand side of the facia centre panel to improve access to the cable.
13   Fit the new cable, ensuring that it is correctly routed, and free from kinks and obstructions.
14   Connect the cable to the control unit and air distribution housing, making sure the outer cable is clipped securely in position.
15   Check the operation of the control knob, then refit the control unit as described previously in this Section.

Upper air distribution control cable

16   Remove the heater/ventilation control unit from the facia, as described above in paragraphs 1 to 5.
17   Unclip the upper air distribution cable (with the brown end fitting) and free the cable from the right-hand side of the control unit (see illustration 9.11). The outer cable is released by simply lifting the retaining clip.
18   On left-hand drive models, remove the storage compartment (where fitted) from underneath the passenger side of the facia. The compartment is secured in position by a retaining screw and clip.
19   On all models, follow the run of the cable behind the facia, taking note of its routing, and disconnect the cable from the lever on the air distribution housing. Note that the method of fastening is the same as that used at the control unit. Release the cable from its retaining clip on the air distribution housing, and remove it from behind the facia.
20   Fit the new cable as described in paragraphs 13 to 15.

Air temperature control cable

21   Remove the heater/ventilation control unit from the facia, as described above in paragraphs 1 to 5.
22   Unclip and detach the upper and lower air distribution cables from the control unit (see paragraphs 11 and 17), noting the correct fitted location of each cable. Swing the control panel away from the facia, and disconnect the air temperature cable (with the black end fitting) from the left-hand side of the control unit.
23   On right-hand drive models, remove the storage compartment (where fitted) from underneath the passenger side of the facia. The compartment is secured in position by a retaining screw and clip.
24   On all models, follow the run of the cable behind the facia, taking note of its routing, and disconnect the cable from the lever on the air distribution housing. Note that the method of fastening is the same as that used at the control unit. Release the cable from its retaining clip on the air distribution housing, and remove it from behind the facia.
25   Fit the new cable, ensuring that it is correctly routed, and free from kinks and obstructions.
26   Connect the cable to the control unit and air distribution housing, making sure the outer cable is clipped securely in position. Also clip the air distribution cables into their correct positions.
27   Check the operation of the control knobs, then refit the control unit as described previously in this Section.

Air recirculation control cable

28   Remove the heater/ventilation control unit from the facia, as described above in paragraphs 1 to 5.
29   Unclip and detach the upper and lower air distribution cables from the control unit (see paragraphs 11 and 17), noting the correct fitted location of each cable.
30   Swing the control panel away from the facia, and disconnect the air recirculation cable (with the blue or yellow end fitting) from the rear of the control unit **(see illustration)**.
31   On left-hand drive models, remove the storage compartment (where fitted) from underneath the passenger side of the facia. The compartment is secured in position by a retaining screw and clip.
32   On all models, remove the cable and install the new one as described in paragraphs 24 to 27. Note that, on models with air conditioning, it will also be necessary to remove the glovebox (see Chapter 11, Section 26) and detach the cable from the evaporator housing.

Heater matrix

Removal

33   With the engine cold, unscrew the expansion tank cap (referring to the warning note in Section 1) to release any pressure present in the cooling system, then securely refit the cap.
34   On right-hand drive vehicles, remove the battery as described in Chapter 5.
35   Undo the expansion tank retaining nuts, and free the tank from the engine compartment bulkhead. Place the tank clear of the bulkhead to gain access to the heater matrix hose unions.
36   Clamp both heater hoses as close to the bulkhead as possible, to

9.40b . . . and the three right-hand screws (arrowed) . . .

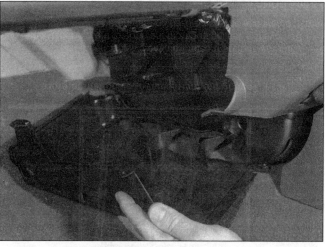

9.40c . . . then detach the air distribution housing base, and remove it from the left-hand side

9.41 Unclip the air distribution intermediate housing, and remove it from the left-hand side

9.43 Lower the heater matrix out of position, and swing it to the left to disengage its unions from the bulkhead

minimise coolant loss. Alternatively, drain the cooling system as described in Chapter 1.

37   Slacken the retaining clips, and disconnect both hoses from the heater matrix unions. Unscrew the retaining screw which is situated between the unions.

38   Working inside the vehicle, remove the storage compartment (where fitted) from underneath the passenger side of the facia. The compartment is secured in position by a retaining screw and clip.

39   On left-hand drive models, undo the two screws and remove the trim panel from the centre of the facia, on the driver's side. Unbolt the support strut (where fitted, this is situated on the driver's side of the air distribution housing) from the floor, and swing the strut away from the housing.

40   Undo the five retaining screws (two on the left-hand side, and three on the right-hand side) securing the lower cover to the base of the air distribution housing. Unclip the cover and remove it from the vehicle (see illustrations).

41   Detach the intermediate housing from bottom of the distribution housing, and remove it towards the left-hand side of the vehicle (see illustration). On left-hand drive models, it may be necessary to depress the brake and clutch pedals to allow the housing to be removed.

42   Cover the carpet directly underneath the air distribution housing, to catch any coolant which may be spilt from the matrix as it is removed. Alternatively, release the carpet fasteners, and fold the carpet back from the bulkhead so that any spilt coolant will go behind the carpet.

43   Lower the heater matrix out from the air distribution housing,

swing it to the left, then disengage the matrix unions from the bulkhead and remove the matrix from the vehicle (see illustration). Note: Keep the matrix unions uppermost as the matrix is removed, to prevent coolant spillage. Mop up any spilt coolant immediately, and wipe the affected area with a damp cloth to prevent staining.

44   Where necessary, recover the sealing grommets from the matrix unions, and refit them to the bulkhead.

Refitting

45   Refitting is a reversal of the removal procedure, bearing in mind the following points:

(a)   Apply a smear of oil to the matrix sealing grommets, to ease installation.

(b)   Ensure that the heater hose retaining clips are securely tightened.

(c)   On completion, top-up/refill the cooling system as described in Chapter 1.

Heater blower motor - models without air conditioning

Removal

46   Disconnect the battery negative lead.

47   Remove both windscreen wiper arms as described in Chapter 12.

48   Carefully prise out the wiper spindle sealing grommets from the windscreen cowl panel.

9.53 Where necessary, remove the pollen filter from the heater/ventilation intake

9.54a Undo the four retaining screws (arrowed) ...

9.54b ... and lift out the frame

49   Undo the retaining screws, and remove both halves of the windscreen cowl panel from the vehicle.

50   Peel the bonnet seal off the engine compartment bulkhead, and remove it from the vehicle.

51   Unscrew the large plastic nut from each wiper spindle.

52   Prise out the two clips from the centre of the water deflector shield. Release the deflector from the engine compartment bulkhead and wiper spindles, and remove it from the vehicle.

53   Where necessary, release the retaining clips and lift out the pollen filter **(see illustration)**.

54   Undo the screws, and remove the frame from the top of the heater/ventilation intake duct **(see illustrations)**.

55   Set the air recirculation control to the fresh air position.

56   Release the retaining clips, and remove the blower motor right-hand, then left-hand, covers from inside the intake duct **(see illustrations)**. **Note:** *Left and right are as seen from the driver's seat, throughout.*

57   Unhook the blower motor retaining clip, noting how the wiring is routed through the clip **(see illustration)**.

58   Disconnect the motor wiring connectors from the resistor, noting the correct routing of the wiring, and manoeuvre the blower motor out from its housing **(see illustration)**.

Refitting

59   Refitting is a reversal of the removal procedure, noting the following points:

    (a)   Make sure that the motor wiring is correctly routed underneath the blower motor retaining clip **(see illustration)** so that there is no danger of the wiring contacting the fan blades.

    (b)   Make sure that the blower motor covers are correctly engaged with each other, and clipped securely in position.

Heater blower motor - models with air conditioning

Removal

60   Remove the windscreen wiper motor as described in Chapter 12.

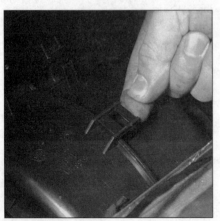

9.56a Release the retaining clips ...

9.56b ... and remove the right-hand ...

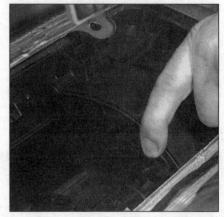

9.56c ... and left-hand covers from the blower motor

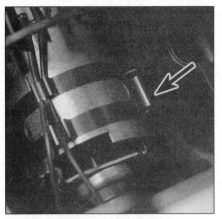

9.57 Unhook the retaining clip (arrowed) . . .

9.58 . . . and lift the blower motor out from its housing

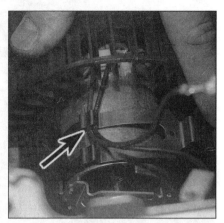

9.59 Secure the blower motor in position with the retaining clip, making sure its wiring is correctly routed through the clip (arrowed)

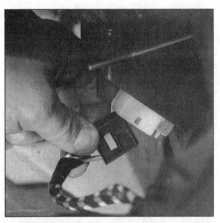

9.69 Disconnecting the wiring connector from the blower motor resistor (viewed through glovebox aperture)

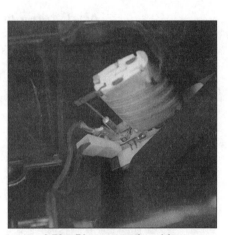

9.70a Disconnect the wiring connectors . . .

9.70b . . . then undo the retaining screw (arrowed) . . .

3

61 Where necessary, release the retaining clips and remove the pollen filter.

62 Undo the screws, and remove the frame from the top of the heating/ventilation intake duct. Where necessary, also cut the intake mesh to allow access to the motor assembly.

63 Set the air recirculation control to the fresh air position.

64 Undo the retaining screws, and remove both halves of the blower motor cover.

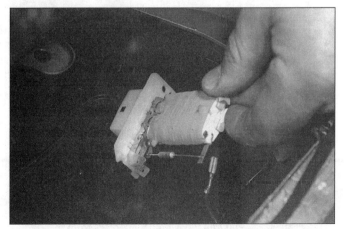

9.70c . . . and lift the blower motor resistor out of position

65 Disconnect the wiring connectors from the resistor, then undo the two screws and remove the blower motor retaining clamp.

66 Lift the blower motor assembly out of position.

Refitting

67 Refitting is a reverse of the removal procedure, noting the following points:

(a) Make sure that the motor wiring is correctly routed underneath the blower motor retaining clamp, so that there is no danger of the wiring contacting the fan blades.

(b) Make sure that the blower motor covers are correctly engaged with each other, and clipped securely in position.

Heater blower motor resistor

Removal

68 On models without air conditioning, carry out the operations described above in paragraphs 46 to 56. On models with air conditioning, carry out the operations described in paragraphs 60 to 64.

69 From inside the vehicle, reach up behind the facia, and disconnect the wiring connector from the underside of the blower motor resistor, which is on the left-hand side of the air distribution housing **(see illustration)**.

70 Return to the engine compartment, then undo the retaining screw and disconnect the blower motor wiring connectors from the resistor. Remove the resistor from the vehicle **(see illustrations)**.

Refitting

71 Refitting is the reverse of removal.

9.78 Removing the air distribution housing

73   Carry out the operations described in paragraphs 33 to 37.

74   Where necessary, release the retaining clips and remove the pollen filter.

75   Undo the screws, and remove the frame from the top of the heating/ventilation intake duct.

76   Cover the carpet directly underneath the air distribution housing, to catch any coolant which may be spilt from the matrix as the housing assembly is removed.

77   Disconnect the wiring connector from the blower motor resistor on the left-hand side of the housing.

78   Disconnect the duct from the driver's side of the housing, and remove the housing from the vehicle **(see illustration)**. **Note:** *Keep the matrix unions uppermost as the housing is removed, to prevent coolant spillage.* Mop up any spilt coolant immediately, and wipe the affected area with a damp cloth to prevent staining. Recover the foam spacers from behind the housing.

Refitting

79   Refitting is the reverse of removal. On completion, top-up the cooling system as described in Chapter 1.

Air distribution housing - models without air conditioning

Removal

72   Remove the facia assembly as described in Chapter 11.

Air distribution housing - models with air conditioning

80   On models with air conditioning, it is not possible to remove the air distribution housing without opening the refrigerant circuit (see Section 11). Therefore, this task must be entrusted to a Vauxhall/Opel dealer.

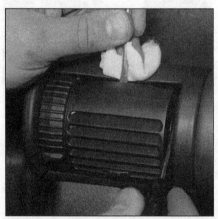

10.2 Remove the heater/ventilation ducts as described in text . . .

10.3 . . . to release them from their locating pegs (arrow)

10.9a Undo the four retaining screws (arrowed) . . .

10.9b . . . then withdraw the vent housing/switch assembly from the facia . . .

10.9c . . . and free the wiring connectors from the rear of the housing

10.12a Undo the three retaining screws (arrowed) . . .

10.12b . . . and remove the vent housing from the facia

10 Heater/ventilation vents and ducts - removal and refitting

Vents

1   Point the vent fully downwards then, using a suitable screwdriver, carefully lever between the top of the vent and the vent housing until a gap of approximately 2 mm appears. Position a piece of card behind screwdriver blade, to avoid damaging the housing.

2   Insert a small, flat-bladed screwdriver in through the gap, and carefully lever between the sides of the vent and the housing to release the vent from its locating pegs **(see illustration)**.

3   Once the vent is free from both its locating pegs, it can be withdrawn from the facia **(see illustration)**.

4   On refitting, carefully manoeuvre the vent back into the facia, ensuring it is correctly engaged with the locating pegs.

Driver's side heater/ventilation housing

5   Disconnect the battery negative lead.

6   Remove the cover from the fusebox.

7   Remove the driver's side vent as described in paragraphs 1 to 3.

8   Remove the lighting switch as described in Chapter 12.

9   Undo the four retaining screws, and withdraw the vent

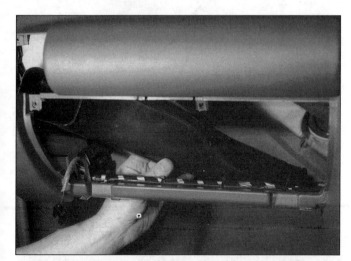

10.13 Disconnect the duct from the air distribution housing, and remove it from underneath the facia

housing/switch assembly from the facia, disconnecting its wiring connectors as they become accessible **(see illustrations)**.

10   Refitting is a reversal of the removal procedure, ensuring that the housing is correctly located with the duct.

Passenger side duct

11   Remove the glovebox as described in Section 26 of Chapter 11.

12   Undo the three retaining screws, and remove the vent housing from the facia **(see illustrations)**.

13   Disconnect the duct from the air distribution housing, and manoeuvre the duct out through the glovebox aperture, or from underneath the facia **(see illustration)**.

14   Refitting is a reversal of the removal procedure, ensuring that the duct is securely reconnected to the air distribution housing.

11 Air conditioning system - general information and precautions

General information

1   Air conditioning is available on certain models **(see illustration)**. It enables the temperature of incoming air to be lowered, and also dehumidifies the air, which makes for rapid demisting and increased comfort.

2   The cooling side of the system works in the same way as a domestic refrigerator. Refrigerant gas is drawn into a belt-driven compressor, and passes into a condenser mounted in front of the radiator, where it loses heat and becomes liquid. The liquid passes through an expansion valve to an evaporator, where it changes from liquid under high pressure to gas under low pressure. This change is accompanied by a drop in temperature, which cools the evaporator. The refrigerant returns to the compressor, and the cycle begins again.

3   Air blown through the evaporator passes to the air distribution unit, where it is mixed with hot air blown through the heater matrix, to achieve the desired temperature in the passenger compartment.

4   The heating side of the system works in the same way as on models without air conditioning (see Section 8).

5   The operation of the system is controlled electronically by the coolant temperature switches (see Section 5), which are screwed into the right-hand end of the radiator, and pressure switches which are screwed into the compressor high-pressure line. Any problems with the system should be referred to a Vauxhall/Opel dealer.

Precautions

6   It is necessary to observe special precautions whenever dealing with any part of the system, its associated components, and any items

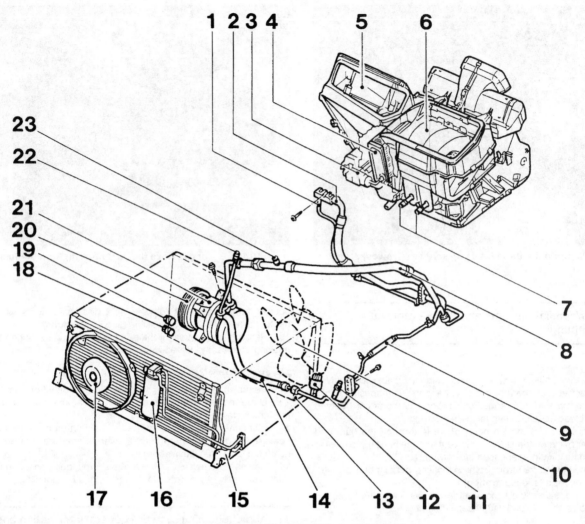

11.1 Air conditioning system components

1	High-pressure refrigerant pipe	13	Radiator
2	Low-pressure refrigerant hose	14	High-pressure refrigerant hose
3	Thermostatically-controlled expansion valve	15	Condenser
4	Evaporator	16	Accumulator
5	Recirculation air duct	17	Auxiliary cooling fan
6	Blower motor	18	Coolant temperature switch
7	Heater matrix unions	19	Coolant temperature switch
8	Low-pressure refrigerant hose	20	Compressor drive pulley with integral clutch
9	High pressure refrigerant hose	21	Compressor
10	Cooling fan	22	Low-pressure service connection
11	Idle-up switch	23	High-pressure service connection
12	Auxiliary cooling fan switch		

which necessitate disconnection of the system. **Warning:** *The refrigeration circuit contains a liquid refrigerant (Freon). This refrigerant is potentially dangerous, and should only be handled by qualified persons. If it is splashed onto the skin, it can cause frostbite. It is not itself poisonous, but in the presence of a naked flame it forms a poisonous gas; inhalation of the vapour through a lighted cigarette could prove fatal. Uncontrolled discharging of the refrigerant is dangerous, and potentially damaging to the environment. It is therefore dangerous to disconnect any part of the system without specialised knowledge and equipment. If for any reason the system must be disconnected, entrust this task to your Vauxhall/Opel dealer or a refrigeration engineer.*

7   Do not operate the air conditioning system if it is known to be short of refrigerant, as this may damage the compressor.

12 Air conditioning system components - removal and refitting

Warning: *Do not attempt to open the refrigerant circuit. Refer to the precautions given in Section 11.*

1   The only operation which can be carried out easily, without discharging the refrigerant, is renewal of the compressor drivebelt, which is covered in Chapter 1. All other operations must be referred to a Vauxhall/Opel dealer or an air conditioning specialist.

2   Where required for improved access, the compressor can be unbolted and moved aside, **without disconnecting its flexible hoses**, after removing the drivebelt.

Chapter 4 Part A:
Fuel and exhaust systems

Contents

4A

Specifications

General

System type:*
12 NZ, C 12 NZ, X 12 SZ, and C 14 NZ engines	Multec single-point fuel injection
C 14 SE engine	Multec "M" multi-point fuel injection
C 16 XE engine	Multec "S" sequential multi-point fuel injection

*For details of engine code location, refer to "Buying spare parts and vehicle identification numbers".

Fuel pump

Type	Electric, mounted in fuel tank

Multec single-point fuel injection system data

Idle speed (not adjustable - for reference only):
12 NZ and C 12 NZ engines	840 to 1000 rpm
X 12 SZ engine	820 to 980 rpm
C 14 NZ engine	830 to 990 rpm
Idle mixture CO content (all engines)	0.4% maximum (not adjustable)
Crankshaft speed/position sensor-to-sensor wheel air gap (X 12 SZ engine)	1.0 ± 0.7 mm

Multec "M" multi-point fuel injection system data (C 14 SE engine)

Idle speed (not adjustable - for reference only)	850 to 1010 rpm
Idle mixture CO content	0.4% maximum (not adjustable)
Crankshaft speed/position sensor-to-sensor wheel air gap	1.0 ± 0.7 mm

Multec "S" sequential multi-point fuel injection system data (C 16 XE engine)

Idle speed (not adjustable - for reference only)	820 to 980 rpm
Idle mixture CO content	0.4 % maximum (not adjustable)
Crankshaft speed/position sensor-to-sensor wheel air gap	1.0 ± 0.7 mm

Torque wrench settings

	Nm	lbf ft
Single-point fuel injection system		
Fuel line-to-fuel injection unit union nuts..	30	22
Fuel injection unit-to-inlet manifold nuts	22	16
Coolant temperature sensor...	20	15
Oxygen sensor..	30	22
Exhaust manifold securing nuts	22	16
Exhaust front section-to-manifold nuts	25	18
Inlet manifold nuts/bolts	22	16
Multec "M" multi-point fuel injection system		
Coolant temperature sensor...	20	15
Oxygen sensor..	30	22
Exhaust manifold securing nuts	22	16
Exhaust front section-to-manifold nuts	25	18
Inlet manifold nuts/bolts	22	16
Multec "S" sequential multi-point fuel injection system		
Coolant temperature sensor...	14	10
Oxygen sensor..	30	22
Exhaust manifold securing nuts	22	16
Exhaust front section-to-manifold nuts	25	18
Lower section of inlet manifold-to-cylinder head nuts	20	15

1   General information and precautions

General information

1   Three different basic types of fuel injection system are used in the Corsa range, these being Multec single-point fuel injection, Multec "M" multi-point fuel injection, and Multec "S" sequential multi-point fuel injection. The systems are described in more detail in Section 10.

2   Fuel is supplied from a tank mounted under the rear of the vehicle, by an electric fuel pump mounted in the tank. The fuel passes through a filter, to the fuel injection system, which incorporates various sensors, actuators, and an electronic control unit.

3   The inducted air passes through an air cleaner, which incorporates a paper filter element to filter out potentially-harmful particles (serious internal engine damage can be caused if foreign particles enter through the air intake system). On single-point fuel injection engines, the air cleaner has a vacuum-controlled air intake, supplying a blend of hot and cold air to suit the prevailing engine operating conditions.

4   The electronic control unit controls both the fuel injection system and the ignition system, integrating the two into a complete engine management system. Refer to Chapters 5B, or 5C, as applicable, for details of the ignition side of the system.

5   The exhaust system on all models, except those with the 12 NZ engine, incorporates a catalytic converter to reduce exhaust gas emissions. Further details can be found in Chapter 4B, along with details of the other emission control systems and components.

Octane plug adjustment

6   The fuel octane recommendations for each engine are given in Chapter 1 Specifications.

7   On all except X 12 SZ and C 16 XE engines, an octane coding plug is provided. The plug is located in the engine compartment, in a bracket attached to the right-hand suspension strut top mounting (see illustration). The coding plug allows the engine management system to optimise the ignition timing for the type of fuel in use.

8   By reversing the position of the octane coding plug in its connector, it is possible to choose between two octane ratings. The number visible on the plug should correspond to the octane rating of the fuel in use.

9   On C 14 SE engines, it is also possible to select a third octane rating by using a special coding plug, available from a Vauxhall/Opel dealer.

10   If the octane rating of the fuel being used is to be changed, allow

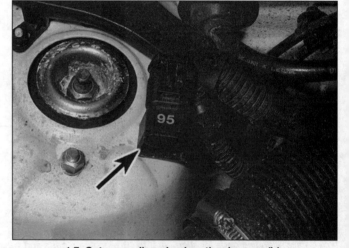

1.7 Octane coding plug location (arrowed) in engine compartment

the fuel tank to become practically empty, then fill the tank with the new type of fuel. Ensure that the ignition is switched off, then release the octane coding plug from its bracket and reverse the position of the plug in its connector to correspond with the octane rating of the new type of fuel.

11   On X 12 SZ and C 16 XE engines, the engine management system automatically adjusts the ignition timing for the type of fuel in use, via the knock control system (see Chapter 5C).

Precautions

12   Before disconnecting any fuel lines, or working on any part of the fuel system, the system must be depressurised as described in Section 6.

13   Care must be taken when disconnecting the fuel lines. When disconnecting a fuel union or hose, loosen the union or clamp screw slowly, to avoid sudden uncontrolled fuel spillage. Take adequate fire precautions.

14   When working on fuel system components, scrupulous cleanliness must be observed, and care must be taken not to introduce any foreign matter into fuel lines or components.

2.3 Intake air temperature control flap valve (arrowed) in air cleaner casing

3.4 Disconnect the wiring plug from the air mass meter - DOHC engine models

15   After carrying out any work involving disconnection of fuel lines, it is advisable to check the connections for leaks; pressurise the system by switching the ignition on and off several times.

16   Electronic control units are very sensitive components, and certain precautions must be taken to avoid damage to these units as follows.

17   When carrying out welding operations on the vehicle using electric welding equipment, the battery and alternator should be disconnected.

18   Although the underbonnet-mounted modules will tolerate normal underbonnet conditions, they can be adversely affected by excess heat or moisture. If using welding equipment or pressure-washing equipment in the vicinity of an electronic module, take care not to direct heat, or jets of water or steam, at the module. If this cannot be avoided, remove the module from the vehicle, and protect its wiring plug with a plastic bag.

19   Before disconnecting any wiring, or removing components, always ensure that the ignition is switched off.

20   Do not attempt to improvise fault diagnosis procedures using a test light or multi-meter, as irreparable damage could be caused to the module.

21   After working on fuel injection/engine management system components, ensure that all wiring is correctly reconnected before reconnecting the battery or switching on the ignition.

Warning: *Many of the procedures in this Chapter require the disconnection of fuel line connections, and the removal of components, which may result in some fuel spillage. Before carrying out any operation on the fuel system, refer to the precautions given in "Safety first!" at the beginning of this manual, and follow them implicitly. Petrol is a highly-dangerous and volatile liquid, and the precautions necessary when handling it cannot be overstressed.*

Precautions for models fitted with catalytic converter (all except 12 NZ engine)

22   Leaded fuel will damage the catalytic converter, and unleaded fuel must be used at all times. In addition, if unburnt fuel enters the catalytic converter, this may result in overheating and irreparable damage to the catalytic converter.

23   Damage to the catalytic converter may result if the following precautions are not observed:

(a)   *Consult a Vauxhall/Opel dealer as soon as possible in the event of misfiring, irregular engine running after a cold start, a significant loss of engine power, or any other malfunction which may indicate a fault in the ignition system. If it is necessary to continue driving, do so for a short time at low engine speed, without labouring the engine.*

(b)   *Avoid frequent cold starts one after another.*

(c)   *Avoid actuation of the starter for an unnecessarily long time during starting.*

(d)   *Do not allow the fuel tank to become empty.*

(e)   *Do not attempt to start the engine by push- or tow-starting - use jump leads (see "Booster battery (jump) starting").*

2   Air cleaner intake air temperature control system (single-point fuel injection engines) - testing

1   The air cleaner is thermostatically-controlled, to provide air at the most suitable temperature for combustion with minimum exhaust emission levels.

2   The optimum air temperature is achieved by drawing in cold air from an air intake at the front of the vehicle, and blending it with hot air from a shroud on the exhaust manifold. The proportion of hot air and cold air is varied by the position of a flap valve in the air cleaner intake spout, which is controlled by a vacuum diaphragm unit. The vacuum applied to the diaphragm is regulated by a heat sensor located within the air cleaner body.

3   To check the operation of the air temperature control, the engine must be cold. First check the position of the flap valve. The air cleaner cover and the air filter element must be removed in order to view the flap valve **(see illustration)**. Check that the flap is initially closed, to admit only cold air from outside the vehicle. Start the engine, and check that the flap now opens to admit only hot air from the exhaust manifold.

4   Temporarily refit the filter element and the air cleaner cover.

5   Run the engine until it reaches normal operating temperature.

6   Remove the cover and the filter element once more, and check that the flap is now closed, to admit only cold air from outside the vehicle, or in cold weather, a mixture of hot and cold air. Refit the filter element and the cover after making the check.

7   If the flap does not function correctly, the air cleaner must be renewed, as parts are not available individually.

3   Air cleaner assembly - removal and refitting

Removal

1   Disconnect the battery negative lead.

2   Where applicable, disconnect the wiring plug from the intake air temperature sensor, located in the air inlet trunking.

3   Disconnect the air inlet trunking from the airbox on the fuel injection unit (single-point fuel injection models), or the throttle body (multi-point fuel injection models), as applicable.

4   Release the securing clips, then lift off the air cleaner cover, and remove it from the vehicle. On DOHC engine models, disconnect the wiring plug from the air mass meter **(see illustration)**.

4A

3.6 Disconnecting the intake air temperature control vacuum pipe from the air cleaner

3.7 Disconnecting the hot-air trunking from the exhaust manifold hot-air shroud

3.8a Remove the air intake trunking securing clip from the crossmember . . .

3.8b . . . and disconnect the trunking from the air cleaner casing

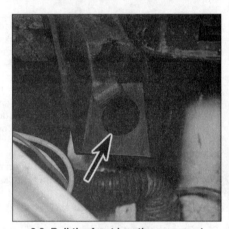

3.9 Pull the front locating grommet (arrowed) upwards . . .

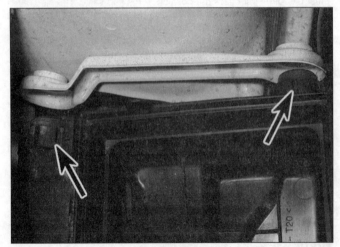

3.10a . . . then pull the air cleaner assembly forwards to release the rear locating rubbers (arrowed) . . .

5   Lift out the air cleaner element.
6   Where applicable, disconnect the intake air temperature control vacuum pipe from the air cleaner casing **(see illustration)**.
7   Where applicable, disconnect the hot-air trunking from the exhaust manifold hot-air shroud **(see illustration)**.

8   Remove the clip securing the air intake trunking to the engine compartment front crossmember, then disconnect the trunking from the front of the air cleaner casing, and withdraw the trunking **(see illustrations)**.
9   Pull the air cleaner front locating grommet to release it from the hole in the air cleaner casing, then pull the casing upwards over the grommet **(see illustration)**.
10   Pull the assembly forwards to release the rear locating rubbers, and withdraw the assembly from the engine compartment **(see illustrations)**.

Refitting

11   Refitting is a reversal of removal.

---

4   Throttle cable - removal, refitting and adjustment

SOHC engine models

Removal

1   On models with single-point fuel injection, remove the airbox from the top of the fuel injection unit, with reference to Section 12 if necessary.
2   Release the securing clip, and disconnect the cable end balljoint from the throttle linkage **(see illustration)**.
3   Release the cable grommet from its bracket on the inlet manifold **(see illustration)**.

3.10b ... and withdraw the assembly

4.2 Releasing the throttle cable end balljoint clip (arrowed)

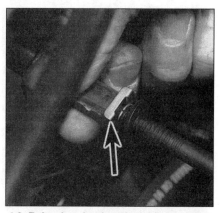

4.3 Releasing the throttle cable grommet from the bracket. Note clip (arrowed) provided for cable adjustment

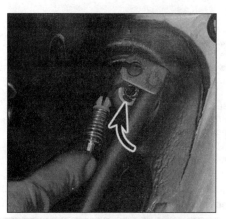

4.4 Pull the end of the throttle cable from the pedal - note cable grommet securing circlip (arrowed) at bulkhead

4.13 Disconnect the throttle cable end balljoint from the linkage ...

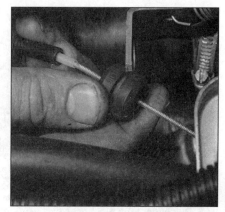

4.14 ... and release the throttle cable grommet from the throttle body bracket - DOHC engine

4A

4   Working inside the driver's footwell, pull the cable end from the top of the throttle pedal **(see illustration)**.
5   Where applicable, remove the circlip securing the cable grommet at the bulkhead in the footwell.
6   Make a careful note of the cable routing, then pull the cable through the bulkhead into the engine compartment.

Refitting
7   Refitting is a reversal of removal, bearing in mind the following points:

    (a) *Ensure that the cable is correctly routed, as noted during re-moval.*
    (b) *Ensure that the bulkhead grommet is correctly seated in its aperture, and that, where applicable, the circlip is engaged with the grommet.*
    (c) *On completion, check the throttle mechanism for satisfactory operation, and if necessary adjust the cable as described in the following paragraphs.*

Adjustment
8   The cable adjustment is controlled by the position of the metal clip on the cable sheath at the bracket on the inlet manifold.
9   The cable should be adjusted so that when the throttle pedal is released, there is very slight free play in the cable at the fuel injection unit/throttle body end.
10   Check that when the throttle pedal is fully depressed, the throttle valve is fully open.
11   Adjust the position of the clip on the cable sheath to achieve the desired results.

DOHC engine models

Removal
12   If desired, for improved access to the throttle body end of the ca-ble, remove the battery as described in Chapter 5A, and reach down through the hole in the battery tray.
13   Release the securing clip, and disconnect the cable end balljoint from the throttle linkage **(see illustration)**.
14   Release the cable grommet from the throttle body bracket **(see il-lustration)**.
15   Release the cable from the clips in the engine compartment. Note that the cable is routed around the front of the engine compartment, above the radiator.
16   Proceed as described in paragraphs 4 to 6 inclusive.

Refitting
17   Refitting is a reversal of removal, bearing in mind the following points:

    (a) *Ensure that the cable is correctly routed, as noted during re-moval.*
    (b) *Ensure that the bulkhead grommet is correctly seated in its aperture, and that, where applicable, the circlip is engaged with the grommet.*
    (c) *On completion, check the throttle mechanism for satisfactory operation, and if necessary adjust the cable with reference to paragraph 18.*

Adjustment
18   Proceed as described in paragraphs 8 to 11 inclusive, noting that the adjustment is controlled by the position of the metal clip on the ca-ble sheath at the throttle body bracket.

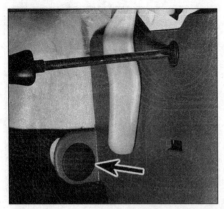

6.5 Remove the screw and the plastic clip (arrowed) securing the footwell trim panel

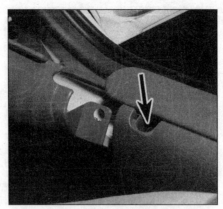

6.6 Withdraw the trim panel from the footwell. Note sill panel front securing screw has been removed from location arrowed

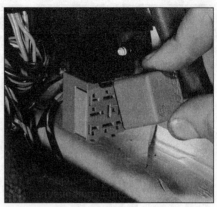

6.7 Removing the fuel pump relay from its socket

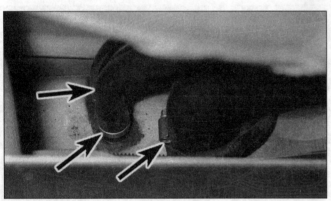

7.8 Disconnect the fuel hoses (arrowed) from the rear of the tank - Hatchback models

---

5   Throttle pedal - removal and refitting

Removal

1   Unclip the throttle cable end from the top of the pedal.
2   Remove the spring clip from the end of the throttle pedal pivot shaft.
3   Unhook the return spring from the pedal, and slide the pedal from the end of the pivot shaft.

Refitting

4   Refitting is a reversal of removal, but on completion, check and if necessary adjust the throttle cable free play as described in Section 4.

---

6   Fuel system - depressurising

Warning: *The fuel system is pressurised all the time the ignition is switched on, and will remain so for a considerable time after switching off. It is therefore essential to depressurise the system as follows, before disconnecting fuel lines, or carrying out any work on the fuel system components. Failure to observe this before carrying out work may result in a sudden release of pressure which may cause fuel spray - this constitutes a serious fire hazard, and a health risk. Note that, even when the system has been depressurised, fuel will still be present in the system fuel lines and components, and adequate precautions should still be taken when carrying out work.*

1   The simplest method of depressurising the fuel system is to remove the fuel pump relay, which is located behind the right-hand footwell trim panel, as follows.
2   Open the right-hand front door.

3   Where applicable, remove the storage tray from under the facia.
4   Remove the screw securing the front of the sill trim panel, and lift up the front edge of the sill trim panel.
5   Remove the screw and the plastic clip securing the footwell trim panel **(see illustration)**.
6   Carefully pull back the weatherstrip from the front edge of the door aperture to expose the edge of the footwell trim panel, then withdraw the trim panel from the footwell **(see illustration)**.
7   Remove the fuel pump relay from its socket **(see illustration)**.
8   Start the engine, run it for at least 5 seconds, then stop the engine.
9   Disconnect the battery negative lead.
10   Refit the fuel pump relay, and the trim panel.

---

7   Fuel tank - removal and refitting

Hatchback models

Note*: During this procedure, the rear of the vehicle must be raised sufficiently to enable the fuel tank securing straps to be lowered far enough to allow the fuel tank to pass below the rear axle - the front ends of the tank securing straps are mounted on hinge pins on the vehicle underside, and cannot be removed.*

Removal

1   Depressurise the fuel system as described in Section 6.
2   Disconnect the battery negative lead if not already done.
3   Siphon out any remaining fuel in the tank through the filler pipe. Siphon the fuel into a clean metal container which can be sealed.
4   Chock the front wheels, then jack up the rear of the vehicle and support securely on axle stands (see *"Jacking, towing and wheel changing"*).
5   Disconnect the rear of the exhaust system from its rubber mountings, and lower the system, or move it to one side sufficiently to enable removal of the fuel tank. On certain models, it may be necessary to remove the exhaust system completely to allow sufficient clearance - refer to Section 17 for details on removing the exhaust mountings and components.
6   Where applicable, remove the handbrake cable heat shield.
7   Slacken the handbrake cable adjuster with reference to Chapter 9, then pull the rubber grommet from the connecting link under the vehicle floor, and disconnect the rear section of the handbrake cable from the connecting link. Release the cable from the brackets on the underbody and fuel tank, as applicable, and move the cable clear of the working area.
8   Working under the vehicle, release the hose clamps, and disconnect the fuel hoses from the rear of the fuel tank **(see illustration)**.
9   Release the connectors and disconnect the fuel hoses from the fuel filter, noting their locations to ensure correct refitting. A Vauxhall/Opel special tool is available to disconnect the hose connectors, but provided care is taken, the connections can be released using a pair of pliers. Be

7.10 Fuel filter-to-fuel tank securing bolt (arrowed) - Hatchback models

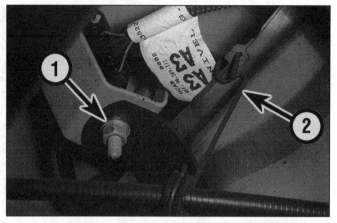

7.17 Fuel tank strap securing nut (1) and handbrake cable bracket (2)

7.24 Disconnect the fuel hoses (arrowed) from the rear of the tank - Combo Van models

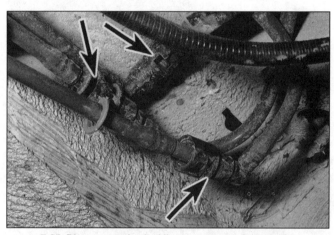

7.25 Disconnect the fuel line connectors (arrowed) - Combo Van models

4A

prepared for fuel spillage, and take adequate fire precautions.

10   Unscrew the securing bolt and remove the fuel filter, complete with its clamp, from the fuel tank **(see illustration)**.

11   Fold the rear sear cushions forwards.

12   Lift the carpet panel on the right-hand side of the floor to expose the plastic fuel pump cover.

13   Carefully prise the plastic cover from the floor to expose the fuel pump.

14   Disconnect the pump wiring plug.

15   Clamp the fuel feed and return hoses to prevent fuel spillage, then release the hose clips, and carefully disconnect the fuel hoses from the top of the pump. Be prepared for fuel spillage, and take adequate fire precautions.

16   Support the weight of the fuel tank on a jack with interposed block of wood.

17   Remove the two nuts from the securing straps at the rear of the fuel tank **(see illustration)**. Lower the straps clear of the rear axle to allow sufficient clearance to withraw the fuel tank.

18   Lower the tank sufficiently to enable access to the fuel hoses clipped to the tank. Unclip the relevant hoses from the tank, noting their locations to ensure correct refitting.

19   Continue to lower the tank until it can be removed from under the vehicle.

Refitting

20   If the tank contains sediment or water, it may cleaned out with two or three rinses of clean fuel. Remove the fuel filter, fuel gauge sender unit and fuel pump as described in Sections 8 and 9 respectively. Shake the tank vigorously, and change the fuel as often as is necessary to remove all contamination from the tank. *This procedure should be carried out in*

a well-ventilated area, and it is vital to take adequate fire precautions.

21   Any repairs to the fuel tank should be carried out by a professional. **Do not** under any circumstances attempt to weld or solder a fuel tank. Removal of all residual fuel vapours requires several hours of specialist cleaning.

22   Refitting is a reversal of removal, bearing in mind the following points:

(a)   *Ensure that all hoses are securely reconnected to their correct locations, as noted before removal.*

(b)   *Check the handbrake cable adjustment, as described in Chapter 9.*

(c)   *On completion, fill the fuel tank, then run the engine and check for leaks. If leakage is evident, stop the engine immediately and rectify the problem without delay.*

Combo Van models

Note: *During this procedure, the rear of the vehicle must be raised sufficiently to enable the fuel tank securing straps to be lowered far enough to allow the fuel tank to pass below the rear axle - the front ends of the tank securing straps are mounted on hinge pins on the vehicle underside, and cannot be removed.*

Removal

23   Proceed as described in paragraphs 1 to 4 inclusive.

24   Working under the vehicle, release the hose clamps, and disconnect the fuel hoses from the rear of the fuel tank **(see illustration)**.

25   Working at the front right-hand corner of the fuel tank, release the connectors, and disconnect the fuel lines which run around the side of the tank, noting their locations to ensure correct refitting **(see illustration)**. Be prepared for fuel spillage, and take adequate fire precautions. A

8.3a Prise the plastic cover from the floor . . .

8.3b . . . to expose the fuel pump cover. Locking ring arrowed

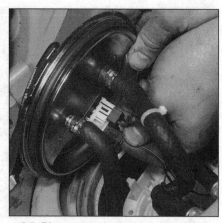

8.5 Disconnect the fuel gauge sender wiring plug

8.6a Using the hook . . .

8.6b . . . pull the sender unit from the fuel pump housing

Vauxhall/Opel special tool is available to release the fuel line connectors, but in the absence of this tool, the connectors can be released using a pair of long-nosed pliers, or similar tool, to depress the retaining tangs.

26 Unscrew the securing nut and withdraw the fuel filter, complete with its bracket, from the fuel tank securing strap stud at the rear of the fuel tank. Support the filter to one side, clear of the working area.

27 Support the weight of the fuel tank on a jack with interposed block of wood.

28 Remove the two nuts from the securing straps at the rear of the fuel tank. Lower the straps clear of the rear axle to allow sufficient clearance to withdraw the fuel tank.

29 Lower the tank sufficiently to enable access to the fuel pump wiring plug, and disconnect the plug.

30 Continue to lower the tank until it can be removed from under the vehicle.

Refitting

31 Refer to paragraphs 20 and 21.

32 Refitting is a reversal of removal, bearing in mind the following points:

(a) Ensure that all hoses are securely reconnected to their correct locations, as noted before removal.

(b) On completion, fill the fuel tank, then run the engine and check for leaks. If leakage is evident, stop the engine immediately and rectify the problem without delay.

8 Fuel gauge sender unit - removal and refitting

Hatchback models

Removal

Note: *The fuel tank should be as empty as possible when carrying out this procedure. If the fuel level in the tank is high, fuel should be siphoned out through the filler pipe to avoid any possibility of spillage - siphon the fuel into a clean metal container which can be sealed.*

1 Disconnect the battery negative lead.

2 Working inside the vehicle, fold the rear seat cushion forwards, and where applicable lift the carpet panel to expose the plastic fuel pump cover.

3 Carefully prise the plastic cover from the floor to expose the fuel pump cover **(see illustrations)**.

4 Release the fuel pump cover locking ring. A special tool (Vauxhall/Opel tool No KM-797) is available for this, but the ring can be removed by tapping anti-clockwise until the locking clips release. **Warning**: *To prevent the possibility of any sparks which could ignite fuel vapour, use a plastic, wooden or brass tool to release the locking ring.*

5 Withdraw the cover locking ring, then lift the pump cover from the top of the pump, and disconnect the fuel gauge sender unit wiring plug from the underside of the pump cover **(see illustration)**.

6 Using the hook provided, pull the sender unit from the clips on the side of the fuel pump housing **(see illustrations)**.

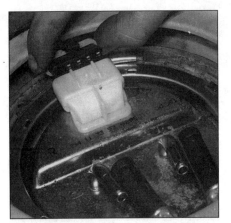

9.9 Disconnect the pump wiring plug

9.10 Releasing the fuel pump locking ring using a brass drift

9.11 Disconnect the wiring plugs from the underside of the cover

Refitting

7 Refitting is a reversal of removal, bearing in mind the following points:

(a) *Ensure that the sender unit engages correctly with the clips on the fuel pump housing.*

(b) *Check the condition of the sealing ring on the underside of the fuel pump cover, and renew if necessary.*

(c) *Refit the fuel pump cover locking ring by tapping it anti-clockwise until the locking clips "click" into position.*

Combo Van models

Removal

8 Remove the fuel tank as described in Section 7.
9 Release the connectors, and disconnect the fuel lines from the fuel pump cover, noting their locations to ensure correct refitting. Be prepared for fuel spillage, and take adequate fire precautions. A Vauxhall/Opel special tool is available to release the fuel line connectors, but in the absence of this tool, the connectors can be released using a pair of long-nosed pliers, or similar tool, to depress the retaining tangs.
10 Proceed as described in paragraphs 4 to 6 inclusive.

Refitting

11 Proceed as described in paragraph 7.
12 On completion, refit the fuel tank as described in Section 7.

---

9 Fuel pump - testing, removal and refitting

Hatchback models

Testing

1 If the pump is functioning, it should be possible to hear it "buzzing" by listening under the rear of the vehicle when the ignition is switched on. Unless the engine is started, the fuel pump should switch off after approximately two seconds. If the noise produced is excessive, this may indicate a faulty pump.
2 If the pump appears to have failed completely, check the wiring to the pump, and check the appropriate fuse and relay.
3 To test the performance of the pump, special equipment is required, and it is recommended that any suspected faults are referred to a Vauxhall/Opel dealer.

Removal

Note: *The fuel tank should be as empty as possible when carrying out this procedure. If the fuel level in the tank is high, fuel should be siphoned out through the filler pipe to avoid any possibility of spillage - siphon the fuel into a clean metal container which can be sealed.*

4 Depressurise the fuel system as described in Section 6.

9.13a Press the three pump housing retaining lugs (1 - one shown), and pull the housing from the tank using a hook engaged with the eyelet (2)

5 Disconnect the battery negative lead.
6 Working inside the vehicle, fold the rear seat cushion forwards, and where applicable, lift the carpet panel to expose the plastic fuel pump cover.
7 Carefully prise the plastic cover from the floor to expose the fuel pump cover.
8 Release the hose clips, and carefully disconnect the fuel hoses from the top of the pump cover. Be prepared for fuel spillage, and take adequate fire precautions. Clamp or plug the open ends of the hoses, to prevent dirt ingress and further fuel spillage.
9 Disconnect the pump wiring plug **(see illustration)**.
10 Release the fuel pump locking ring. A special tool (Vauxhall/Opel tool No KM-797) is available for this, but the ring can be removed by tapping anti-clockwise until the locking clips release. **Warning:** *To prevent the possibility of any sparks which could ignite fuel vapour, use a plastic, wooden or brass tool to release the locking ring* **(see illustration)**.
11 Lift the pump cover from the housing, then disconnect the two wiring plugs from the underside of the cover **(see illustration)**.
12 Loosen the hose clip, and disconnect the fuel hose from the top of the fuel pump.
13 Press the three pump housing retaining lugs to release them, and simultaneously pull the pump housing from the tank using a wire hook engaged with the eyelet provided **(see illustrations)**.

4A

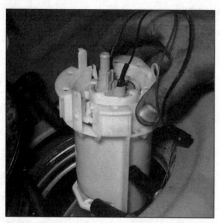

9.13b Withdrawing the fuel pump housing from the fuel tank

9.14 Removing the fuel filter from the base of the fuel pump

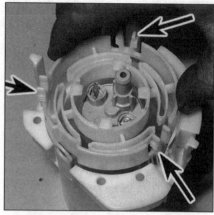

9.15a Compress the three locking tabs (arrowed) . . .

14   To remove the pump from the housing, first pull the filter from the base of the pump **(see illustration)**, and disconnect the wires from the pump. Note the wire locations to ensure correct refitting.
15   Compress the three locking tabs, and pull the pump mounting plate and the pump from the housing **(see illustrations)**.

Refitting

16   Refitting is a reversal of removal, bearing in mind the following points:

   (a)   *Before refitting the filter to the bottom of the pump, inspect the filter for contamination or blockage, and renew if necessary.*
   (b)   *Ensure that the pump mounting plate engages correctly with the retaining clips on the housing.*
   (c)   *Check the condition of the sealing ring on the underside of the fuel pump cover, and renew if necessary.*
   (d)   *Refit the fuel pump cover locking ring by tapping it anti-clock-wise until the locking clips "click" into position.*

Combo Van models

Testing

17   Proceed as described in paragraphs 1 to 3 inclusive.

Removal

18   Remove the fuel tank as described in Section 7.
19   Release the connectors, and disconnect the fuel lines from the top of the fuel pump cover, noting their locations to ensure correct refitting. Be prepared for fuel spillage, and take adequate fire precautions. A Vauxhall/Opel special tool is available to release the fuel line connectors, but in the absence of this tool, the connectors can be released using a pair of long-nosed pliers, or similar tool, to depress the retaining tangs. Be prepared for fuel spillage, and take adequate fire precautions.
20   Proceed as described in paragraphs 10 to 15 inclusive.

Refitting

21   Proceed as described in paragraph 16.
22   On completion, refit the fuel tank as described in Section 7.

10 Fuel injection systems - general information

Single-point fuel injection (Multec)

1   The system is under the overall control of the Multec engine man-agement system, which also controls the ignition system (see Chapter 5B or 5C, as applicable) **(see illustration)**.
2   Fuel is supplied from the rear-mounted fuel tank by an electric pump mounted in the tank, via a fuel filter, to the Multec injection unit. A fuel pressure regulator mounted on the injection unit maintains a constant fuel pressure to the fuel injector. Excess fuel is returned from the regulator to the tank.
3   The fuel injection unit (resembling a carburettor) houses the

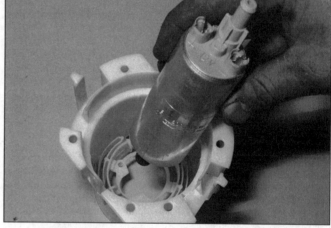

9.15b . . . and withdraw the pump from the housing

throttle valve, idle speed control motor, throttle position sensor, fuel in-jector, and pressure regulator.
4   The duration of the electrical pulse supplied to the fuel injector determines the time for which the injector is open, and hence the quantity of fuel injected. Pulse duration is computed by the Multec electronic control unit (ECU) on the basis of information received from the following sensors:

   (a)   *Throttle position sensor - informs the ECU of throttle position, and the rate of throttle opening/closing.*
   (b)   *Manifold absolute pressure (MAP) sensor - informs the ECU of the load on the engine (expressed in terms of inlet manifold vacuum).*
   (c)   *Distributor "Hall-effect" sensor (all except X 12 SZ engine) - in-forms the ECU of the crankshaft speed and position.*
   (d)   *Crankshaft speed/position sensor (X 12 SZ engine) - informs the ECU of the crankshaft speed and position.*
   (e)   *Coolant temperature sensor - informs the ECU of engine tem-perature.*
   (f)   *Exhaust gas oxygen sensor - informs the ECU of the oxygen content of the exhaust gases (explained in greater detail in Chapter 4B).*
   (g)   *Vehicle speed sensor - informs the ECU of the vehicle speed.*
   (h)   *Knock sensor (X 12 SZ engine only) - informs the ECU when engine "knock" (pre-ignition) occurs (explained in greater detail in Chapter 5C).*

5   The signals from the various sensors are processed by the ECU, and the optimum fuelling and ignition settings are selected for the prevailing engine operating conditions.
6   Idle speed is controlled by the idle speed control motor, which

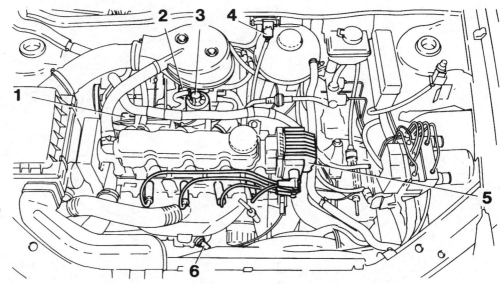

10.1 Layout of single-point fuel injection system/engine management system components (Multec) - X 12 SZ engine

1   Fuel tank vent valve (see Chapter 4B)
2   Fuel injection unit
3   Exhaust gas recirculation (EGR) valve (see Chapter 4B)
4   Manifold absolute pressure (MAP) sensor
5   Distributorless ignition system (DIS) module (see Chapter 5C)
6   Exhaust gas oxygen sensor

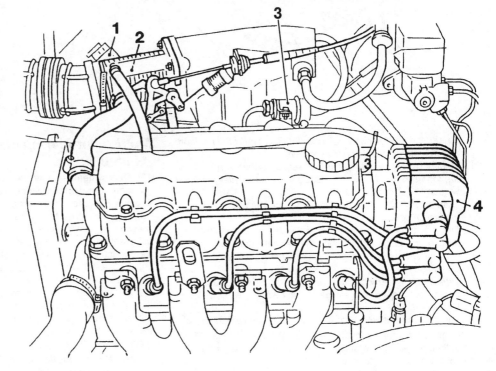

10.10 Layout of multi-point fuel injection system/engine management system components (Multec "M") - C 14 SE engine

1   Idle speed control motor
2   Throttle body
3   Fuel pressure regulator
4   Distributorless ignition system (DIS) module

4A

regulates the quantity of air bypassing the throttle valve. The motor is controlled by the electronic control unit; there is no provision for direct adjustment of idle speed.

7   Similarly, the fuel/air mixture is controlled within fine limits (to avoid damage to the catalytic converter) by the electronic control unit, via the fuel injector. No manual adjustment of fuel/air mixture is possible.

8   A catalytic converter is fitted, to reduce harmful exhaust gas emissions. Details of this and other emissions control system equipment are given in Chapter 4B.

9   If certain sensors fail, and send abnormal signals to the ECU, the ECU has a back-up programme. In this event, the abnormal signals are ignored, and a pre-programmed value is substituted for the sensor signal, allowing the engine to continue running, albeit at reduced efficiency. If the ECU enters its back-up mode, a warning light on the instrument panel will illuminate, and a fault code will be stored in the ECU memory. This fault code can be read using suitable specialist test equipment.

Multi-point fuel injection - SOHC engines (Multec "M")

10   The system is under the overall control of the Multec "M" engine management system, which also controls the ignition system (see Chapter 5C) **(see illustration)**.

11   Fuel is supplied from the rear-mounted fuel tank, via a fuel filter and a pressure regulator, to the fuel rail. Excess fuel is returned from the regulator to the tank. The fuel rail acts as a reservoir for the four fuel injectors, which inject fuel into the cylinder inlet tracts, upstream of the inlet valves. The fuel injectors operate in pairs. The injectors for cylinder Nos 1 and 2 operate simultaneously, as do the injectors for cylinder Nos 3 and 4.

12   The duration of the electrical pulses to the fuel injectors determines the quantity of fuel injected. The pulse duration is computed by the Multec "M" electronic control unit (ECU) on the basis of information received from the following sensors:

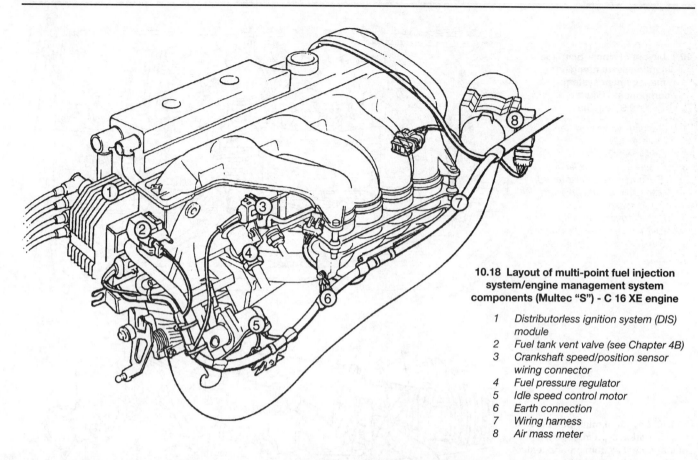

10.18 Layout of multi-point fuel injection system/engine management system components (Multec "S") - C 16 XE engine

1   *Distributorless ignition system (DIS) module*
2   *Fuel tank vent valve (see Chapter 4B)*
3   *Crankshaft speed/position sensor wiring connector*
4   *Fuel pressure regulator*
5   *Idle speed control motor*
6   *Earth connection*
7   *Wiring harness*
8   *Air mass meter*

(a)   *Throttle position sensor - informs the ECU of throttle position, and the rate of throttle opening/closing.*
(b)   *Manifold absolute pressure (MAP) sensor - informs the ECU of the load on the engine (expressed in terms of inlet manifold vacuum).*
(c)   *Crankshaft speed/position sensor - informs the ECU of the crankshaft speed and position.*
(d)   *Intake air temperature sensor - informs the ECU of the temperature of the air passing through the air intake ducting.*
(e)   *Coolant temperature sensor - informs the ECU of engine temperature.*
(f)   *Exhaust gas oxygen sensor - informs the ECU of the oxygen content of the exhaust gases (explained in greater detail in Chapter 4B).*
(g)   *Vehicle speed sensor - informs the ECU of the vehicle speed.*

13   The signals from the various sensors are processed by the ECU, and the optimum fuelling and ignition settings are selected for the prevailing engine operating conditions.
14   Idle speed is controlled by the idle speed control motor, which regulates the quantity of air bypassing the throttle valve. The motor is controlled by the electronic control unit; there is no provision for direct adjustment of the idle speed.
15   Similarly, the fuel/air mixture is controlled within fine limits (to avoid damage to the catalytic converter) by the electronic control unit, via the fuel injector. No manual adjustment of fuel mixture is possible.
16   A catalytic converter is fitted, to reduce harmful exhaust gas emissions. Details of this and other emissions control system equipment are given in Chapter 4B.
17   If certain sensors fail, and send abnormal signals to the ECU, the ECU has a back-up programme. In this event, the abnormal signals are ignored, and a pre-programmed value is substituted for the sensor signal, allowing the engine to continue running, albeit at reduced efficiency. If the ECU enters its back-up mode, a warning light on the instrument panel will illuminate, and a fault code will be stored in the ECU memory. This fault code can be read using suitable specialist test equipment.

Multi-point fuel injection - DOHC engine (Multec "S")

18   The system is under the overall control of the Multec "S" engine management system, which also controls the ignition system (see Chapter 5C) **(see illustration)**.
19   Fuel is supplied from the rear-mounted tank, via a fuel filter and a pressure regulator, to the fuel rail. Excess fuel is returned from the regulator to the tank. The fuel rail acts as a reservoir for the four fuel injectors, which inject fuel into the cylinder inlet tracts, upstream of the inlet valves. The Multec "S" system is a "sequential" fuel injection system. This means that each of the four fuel injectors is triggered individually, just before the inlet valve on the relevant cylinder opens.
20   The duration of the electrical pulses to the fuel injectors determines the quantity of fuel injected. The pulse duration is computed by the Multec "S" electronic control unit (ECU) on the basis of information received from the following sensors:

(a)   *Throttle position sensor - informs the ECU of throttle position, and the rate of throttle opening/closing.*
(b)   *Air mass meter - informs the ECU of the load on the engine (expressed in terms of the mass of air passing from the air cleaner to the throttle body).*
(c)   *Crankshaft speed/position sensor - informs the ECU of the crankshaft speed and position.*
(d)   *Camshaft position sensor - informs the ECU when No 1 cylinder is at top dead centre (TDC) on the firing stroke (expressed in terms of the position of the exhaust camshaft).*
(e)   *Coolant temperature sensor - informs the ECU of engine temperature.*
(f)   *Exhaust gas oxygen sensor - informs the ECU of the oxygen content of the exhaust gases (explained in greater detail in Chapter 4B).*
(g)   *Vehicle speed sensor - informs the ECU of the vehicle speed.*
(h)   *Knock sensor - informs the ECU when engine "knock" (pre-ignition) occurs (explained in greater detail in Chapter 5C).*

21   The signals from the various sensors are processed by the ECU,

12.1 Disconnecting the breather hose from the camshaft cover

and the optimum fuelling and ignition settings are selected for the prevailing engine operating conditions.

22   Idle speed is controlled by the idle speed control motor, which regulates the quantity of air bypassing the throttle valve. The motor is controlled by the electronic control unit; there is no provision for direct adjustment of the idle speed.

23   Similarly, the fuel/air mixture is controlled within fine limits (to avoid damage to the catalytic converter) by the electronic control unit, via the fuel injectors. No manual adjustment of fuel/air mixture is possible.

24   A catalytic converter is fitted, to reduce harmful exhaust gas emissions. Details of this and other emissions control system equipment are given in Chapter 4B.

25   If certain sensors fail, and send abnormal signals to the ECU, the ECU has a back-up programme. In this event, the abnormal signals are ignored, and a pre-programmed value is substituted for the sensor signal, allowing the engine to continue running, albeit at reduced efficiency. If the ECU enters its back-up mode, a warning light on the instrument panel will illuminate, and a fault code will be stored in the ECU memory. This fault code can be read using suitable specialist test equipment.

11   Fuel injection system components - testing

General

In order to safely test the fuel injection system components without the risk of damage to the components or electronic control unit,

12.3a Remove the securing screws . . .

specialist test equipment is required.

The systems have a self-diagnosis function, and any faults are stored as codes in the electronic control unit memory. These fault codes can be read using suitable test equipment. At the time of writing, no information was available regarding a method for reading the fault codes using equipment readily available to the DIY mechanic. The fault codes are given below purely for reference purposes.

System sensors and actuators can be tested for continuity and resistance using a suitable multi-meter, but always ensure that the ignition is switched off, and that the relevant sensor or actuator is disconnected from the engine management system. Refer to the precautions given in Section 1 before attempting to carry out any fault diagnosis.

In the event of a suspected fault, the best course of action is to seek advice from a Vauxhall/Opel dealer, who will have access to suitable specialist test equipment.

Engine management system fault codes

Code	Cause of fault
13	Oxygen sensor (open-circuit)
14	Coolant temperature sensor (voltage low)
15	Coolant temperature sensor (voltage high)
16	Knock sensor
18	Knock control system module
19	Incorrect engine speed (rpm) signal
21	Throttle position sensor (voltage high)
22	Throttle position sensor (voltage low)
24	No vehicle speed signal
25	Fuel injector (voltage low)
28	Fuel pump relay (faulty contact)
29	Fuel pump relay (voltage low)
32	Fuel pump relay (voltage high)
33	MAP sensor (voltage high)
34	MAP sensor (voltage low)
35	Idle speed control
44	Exhaust gases lean
45	Exhaust gases rich
46	EST (ignition system) lines (voltage high)
49	Battery (voltage high)
51	Electronic control unit
55	Electronic control unit
63	EST (ignition system) line coil (cylinders 2 and 3)
64	EST (ignition system) line coil (cylinders 1 and 4)
67	Airflow sensor (sensor range)
68	Airflow sensor (sensor frequency)
69	Intake air temperature sensor (voltage low)
71	Intake air temperature (voltage high)
72	EST (ignition system) lines (open-circuit)
75	Torque control (voltage low)
76	Continuous torque control
81	Fuel injector (voltage high)
92	Hall sensor
93	Electronic control unit

12   Fuel injection system components (single-point fuel injection) - removal and refitting

Airbox

Removal

1   Disconnect the breather hose from the airbox or the camshaft cover, as desired **(see illustration)**.

2   Loosen the clamp screw, and disconnect the air trunking from the end of the airbox, or from the air cleaner casing, as desired.

3   Remove the two securing screws, and lift the airbox from the fuel injection unit. Recover the sealing ring **(see illustrations)**.

4A

12.3b . . . and lift off the airbox and sealing ring

12.4 Disconnecting the vacuum pipe (arrowed) from the fuel injection unit

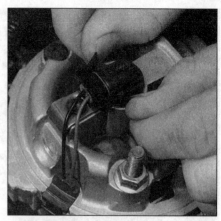

12.9 Releasing the fuel injector wiring plug retaining lugs

12.10 Sliding the fuel injector wiring rubber grommet from the fuel injection unit

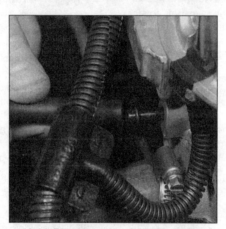

12.14 Disconnecting the MAP sensor hose from the fuel injection unit

12.15 Disconnect the operating rod (arrowed) from the throttle valve lever

4   Disconnect the two vacuum pipes from the rear of the airbox, or from the fuel injection unit and the air cleaner casing, as desired, noting their locations, then withdraw the airbox **(see illustration)**.

Refitting

5   Refitting is a reversal of removal, bearing in mind the following points:
(a)   *Inspect the sealing ring for damage or deterioration, and renew if necessary. Ensure that the sealing ring locates correctly in the grooves in the base of the airbox.*
(b)   *Ensure that the vacuum pipes are correctly reconnected, as noted before removal.*

Fuel injection unit

Note: *Refer to the precautions given in Section 1 before proceeding. All gaskets and seals must be renewed on refitting, and suitable thread-locking compound will be required to coat the fuel injection unit securing nut threads.*

Removal

6   Depressurise the fuel system as described in Section 6.
7   Disconnect the battery negative lead if not already done.
8   Remove the airbox from the top of the fuel injection unit, as described earlier in this Section.
9   Release the securing lugs, and disconnect the wiring plug from the fuel injector **(see illustration)**.
10   Remove the rubber seal from the top of the fuel injection unit (if not already done), then slide the fuel injector wiring rubber grommet from the slot in the side of the fuel injection unit **(see illustration)**.

Move the wiring to one side.
11   Disconnect the wiring plugs from the idle speed control motor and the throttle position sensor.
12   Disconnect the fuel feed and return hoses from the fuel injection unit, noting their locations to aid refitting. Be prepared for fuel spillage, and take adequate fire precautions. Clamp or plug the open ends of the hoses, to minimise further fuel loss.
13   Disconnect the vacuum hoses from the fuel injection unit, noting their locations and routing to ensure correct refitting.
14   Disconnect the MAP sensor hose from the rear of the fuel injection unit **(see illustration)**.
15   Disconnect the operating rod from the throttle valve lever **(see illustration)**.
16   Make a final check to ensure that all relevant hoses and wires have been disconnected to facilitate removal of the fuel injection unit.
17   Unscrew the two securing nuts, recovering the washers and the sleeves which fit over the manifold studs, then carefully lift the fuel injection unit from the inlet manifold **(see illustrations)**. Recover the gasket.
18   If desired, the fuel injection unit may now be split into its upper and lower sections by removing the two securing screws **(see illustration)**. The vacuum hose flange and the fuel hose unions can also be removed if desired.

Refitting

19   Refitting is a reversal of removal, bearing in mind the following points.
20   Where applicable, when reassembling the two sections of the fuel injection unit, use a new gasket. Similarly, where applicable, use a new

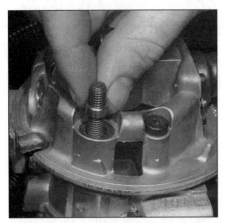

12.17a Recover the sleeves which fit over the manifold studs

12.17b Lifting the fuel injection unit from the inlet manifold

12.18 Removing a fuel injection unit upper-to-lower section securing screw

12.27 Disconnecting the wiring plug from the fuel injector

12.28a Remove the securing screw . . .

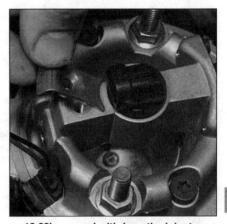

12.28b . . . and withdraw the injector clamp bracket

4A

12.29 Removing the fuel injector. Note the O-rings (arrowed)

gasket when refitting the vacuum hose flange. If the fuel hose unions have been removed, make sure that the washers are in place when re-fitting.

21   Refit the fuel injection unit to the manifold using a new gasket, ensuring that the sleeves are in place over the manifold studs. Coat the threads of the securing nuts with a suitable thread-locking compound before fitting. Ensure that the washers are in place under the nuts.

22   Ensure that all hoses are reconnected and routed correctly, as noted before removal.

23   On completion, check and if necessary adjust the throttle cable free play as described in Section 4.

Fuel injector

Note: *Refer to the precautions given in Section 1 before proceeding. If the original injector is being refitted, new O-rings must be used. Suitable thread-locking compound will be required to coat the clamp bracket screw threads.*

Removal

24   Depressurise the fuel system as described in Section 6.'

25   Disconnect the battery negative lead if not already done.

26   Remove the airbox from the top of the fuel injection unit, as described earlier in this Section.

27   Squeeze the securing lugs, and disconnect the wiring plug from the fuel injector **(see illustration)**.

28   Remove the Torx type securing screw, and withdraw the injector clamp bracket **(see illustrations)**.

29   Carefully withdraw the injector from the fuel injection unit **(see illustration)**.

Refitting

30   If the original injector is to be refitted, renew the two O-rings at the base of the injector.

31   Carefully install the injector in the fuel injection unit, with the wiring socket pointing towards the clamp bracket screw hole.

32   Refit the injector clamp bracket, ensuring that it engages correctly with the injector (the bracket should engage with the slot below the wiring socket in the injector).

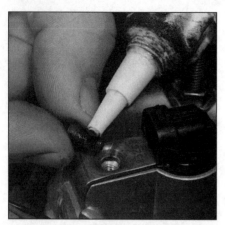

12.33 Coat the fuel injector clamp bracket screw with thread-locking compound

12.39a Unscrew the fuel pressure regulator securing screws (arrowed) . . .

12.39b . . . and remove the cover

33   Coat the threads of the clamp bracket screw with a suitable thread-locking compound, then refit and tighten the screw **(see illustration)**.
34   Reconnect the injector wiring plug.
35   Refit the airbox to the fuel injection unit.
36   Reconnect the battery negative lead.

Fuel pressure regulator

Note: *Refer to the precautions given in Section 1 before proceeding. The pressure regulator diaphragm must be renewed whenever the regulator cover is removed. Suitable thread-locking compound will be required to coat the regulator cover securing bolts.*

Removal

37   Depressurise the fuel system as described in Section 6.
38   Remove the airbox from the top of the fuel injection unit, as described earlier in this Section.
39   Unscrew the four Torx type pressure regulator cover securing screws, and carefully withdraw the cover **(see illustrations)**.
40   Recover the spring seat and spring assembly, and lift out the diaphragm **(see illustration)**.

Refitting

41   Refitting is a reversal of removal, but ensure that the diaphragm is correctly located in the groove in the fuel injection unit, and coat the threads of the cover securing screws with a suitable thread-locking compound before fitting.

Idle speed control motor

Note: *A new O-ring must be used on refitting, and suitable thread-locking compound will be required to coat the motor securing bolt threads.*

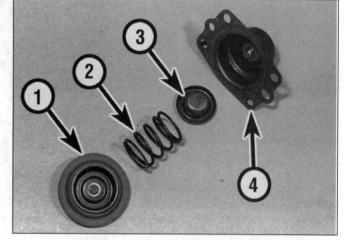

12.40 Fuel pressure regulator components

1 Diaphragm	3 Spring seat
2 Spring	4 Cover

Removal

42   Disconnect the battery negative lead.
43   Remove the airbox from the top of the fuel injection unit, as described earlier in this Section.
44   Release the securing lugs, and disconnect the wiring plug from the idle speed control motor **(see illustration)**.
45   Remove the two securing screws, and withdraw the motor from

12.44 Disconnecting the wiring plug from the idle speed control motor

12.45a Remove the securing screws . . .

12.45b . . . and withdraw the idle speed control motor. Note O-ring (arrowed)

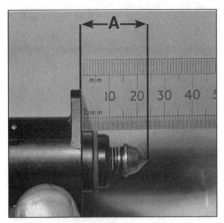

12.46 Measure the distance (A) between the end of the idle speed control motor piston and the end face of the motor body flange

12.49 Disconnecting the wiring plug from the throttle position sensor

12.50 Removing the throttle position sensor

the side of the fuel injection unit. Where applicable, recover the O-ring seal **(see illustrations)**.

Refitting

46   Refitting is a reversal of removal, bearing in mind the following points:

(a) *To avoid damaging the housing or the motor during refitting, the distance between the end of the motor piston and the end face of the motor body flange should not be greater than 28.0 mm. Measure the distance shown, and if greater than 28.0 mm, carefully push the piston into the motor body as far as its stop* **(see illustration)**.

(b) *Refit the motor using a new O-ring seal, with the wiring socket facing downwards.*

(c) *Coat the threads of the motor securing bolts with a suitable thread-locking compound before fitting.*

Throttle position sensor

Note: *Suitable thread-locking compound will be required to coat the sensor securing bolt threads on refitting.*

Removal

47   Disconnect the battery negative lead.

48   Remove the airbox from the top of the fuel injection unit, as described earlier in this Section.

49   Disconnect the wiring plug from the throttle position sensor **(see illustration)**.

50   Remove the two securing screws, and withdraw the sensor from its housing in the fuel injection unit **(see illustration)**.

Refitting

51   Ensure that the throttle valve is closed, then refit the sensor to the housing, making sure that the sensor arm is correctly engaged with the throttle valve shaft.

52   Coat the sensor securing bolts with suitable thread-locking compound, then insert and tighten them.

53   Further refitting is a reversal of removal.

Manifold absolute pressure (MAP) sensor

Removal

54   The sensor is located on the engine compartment bulkhead, under the scuttle flange.

55   Disconnect the battery negative lead.

56   Disconnect the sensor wiring plug and the vacuum pipe **(see illustration)**. Note the routing of the vacuum pipe.

57   Unscrew the two securing nuts, and withdraw the sensor from the bulkhead **(see illustrations)**.

Refitting

58   Refitting is a reversal of removal. It is important to ensure that when reconnecting the vacuum pipe, the pipe is routed with a downward slope from the sensor to the fuel injection housing. This is to prevent the possibility of the pipe becoming blocked from condensation freezing in the pipe during cold weather.

Distributor "Hall-effect" sensor (all except X 12 SZ engine)

59   The sensor is integral with the distributor assembly, and no individual spare parts are available. If the sensor is faulty, the distributor

4A

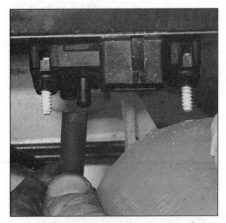

12.56 Disconnecting the vacuum pipe from the MAP sensor

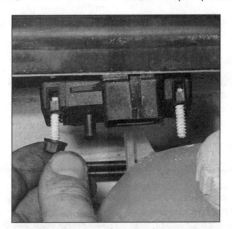

12.57a Unscrew the securing nuts . . .

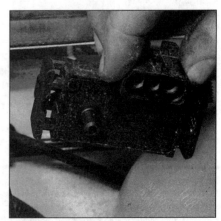

12.57b . . . and withdraw the MAP sensor

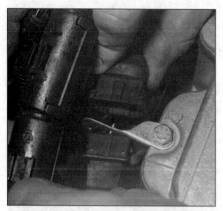

12.63 Separating the two halves of the crankshaft speed/position sensor wiring connector - X 12 SZ engine

12.65 Crankshaft speed/position sensor securing bolt (arrowed) - viewed from underneath vehicle

12.71 Disconnecting the wiring plug from the coolant temperature sensor (arrowed)

must be renewed complete. Details of distributor removal and refitting are given in Chapter 5B.

Crankshaft speed/position sensor (X 12 SZ engine only)

Removal

60   The sensor is located in a bracket attached to the oil pump at the lower timing belt end of the engine.

61   Access is most easily obtained from underneath the vehicle.

62   Disconnect the battery negative lead.

63   Separate the two halves of the sensor wiring connector, located in the bracket attached to the camshaft cover (see illustration).

64   Feed the wiring down behind the rear timing belt cover, and un-clip the wiring from the lugs on the cover.

65   Remove the securing bolt, and withdraw the sensor from the bracket on the oil pump (see illustration).

Refitting

66   Refitting is a reversal of removal, but ensure that the sensor and bracket are scrupulously clean before refitting, as any contamination may affect the air gap between the sensor and the toothed sensor wheel.

67   On completion, check the air gap between the end face of the sensor and the toothed sensor wheel, using a suitable feeler gauge. If the air gap is outside the specified limits (see Specifications), the sensor bracket must be renewed.

Coolant temperature sensor

Note: *A new sealing ring must be used on refitting.*

Removal

68   The sensor is located in the rear right-hand side of the inlet manifold.

69   Disconnect the battery negative lead.

70   Partially drain the cooling system, as described in Chapter 1.

71   Disconnect the sensor wiring plug (see illustration).

72   Unscrew the sensor, and withdraw it from the inlet manifold. Recover the sealing ring.

Refitting

73   Refitting is a reversal of removal, but use a new sealing ring, and on completion, top-up the cooling system as described in Chapter 1.

Exhaust gas oxygen sensor

Note: *The sensor must be removed and refitted with the exhaust system at normal operating temperature; take great care to avoid burns, and damage to tools or surrounding components during the procedure - the exhaust system and sensor will be very hot! If the original sensor is to be re-used, the threads must be lubricated with special grease on refitting - see text.*

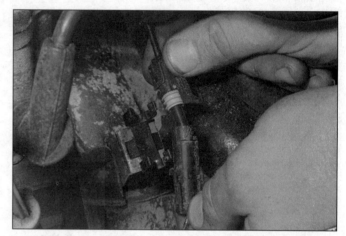

12.76 Disconnecting the oxygen sensor wiring connector

Removal

74   If the engine is cold, start the engine, and run it until it reaches normal operating temperature. Stop the engine.

75   Disconnect the battery negative lead.

76   Unclip the sensor wiring connector from the bracket on the gearbox/transmission, then separate the two halves of the connector (see illustration).

77   Using a suitable spanner, unscrew the sensor from the exhaust manifold. It is advisable to wear suitable gloves, as the exhaust system will be extremely hot (see illustration).

78   Withdraw the sensor and its wiring, taking care not to burn the wiring on the exhaust system.

Refitting

79   The sensor must be refitted with the engine and exhaust system still at normal operating temperature.

80   If a new sensor is being fitted, it will be supplied with the threads coated in a special grease, to prevent the sensor seizing in the exhaust manifold.

81   If the original sensor is being refitted, clean the threads carefully. The threads must be coated with Vauxhall/Opel special grease (No 19 48 602). Use only the specified grease, which consists of liquid graphite and glass beads. As the exhaust system heats up, the graphite will burn off, leaving the glass beads between the threads to prevent the sensor from seizing.

82   Refitting is a reversal of removal.

Vehicle speed sensor

83   The sensor is an integral part of the speedometer assembly, and no individual spare parts are available. If the sensor is faulty, the

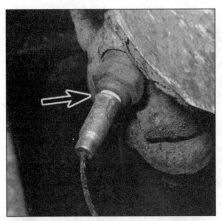

12.77 Oxygen sensor location (arrowed) in exhaust manifold - SOHC engines

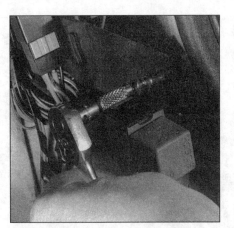

12.92a Remove the side . . .

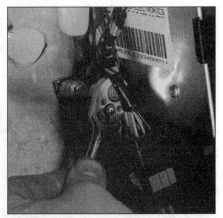

12.92b . . . and rear nuts securing the wiring connector/relay bracket assembly

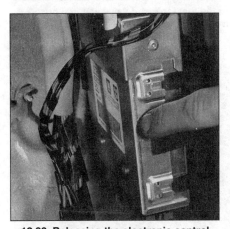

12.93 Releasing the electronic control unit securing clip

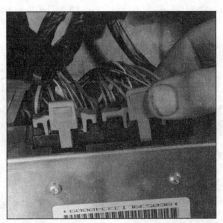

12.94 Disconnecting an electronic control unit wiring connector

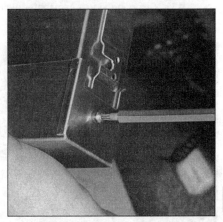

12.95a Remove the control unit rear cover . . .

4A

complete speedometer assembly must be renewed. Removal and refitting details for the speedometer are given in Section 10 of Chapter 12.

Knock sensor (X 12 SZ engine only)

84   The sensor is part of the knock control system, details of which are given in Chapter 5C.

Electronic control unit (ECU)

Note: *On X 12 SZ engine models, the control unit consists of two components - the basic control unit, and the programme memory, which clips into a circuit board in the control unit. The two components can be renewed independently, if a fault is suspected, but the source of the fault can only be established using specialist test equipment available to a Vauxhall/Opel dealer. On other models, the two components cannot be separated, and the complete unit must be renewed if a fault is suspected.*

Removal

85   The control unit is located behind the right-hand footwell trim panel.

86   Disconnect the battery negative lead.

87   Open the right-hand front door.

88   Where applicable, remove the storage tray from under the facia.

89   Remove the screw securing the front of the sill trim panel, and lift up the front edge of the sill trim panel.

90   Remove the screw and the plastic clip securing the footwell trim panel.

91   Carefully pull back the weatherstrip from the front edge of the door aperture to expose the edge of the footwell trim panel, then withdraw the trim panel from the footwell.

92   Remove the two securing nuts, and move the wiring

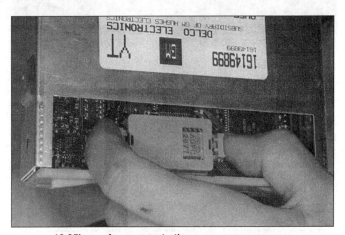

12.95b . . . for access to the programme memory

connector/relay bracket assembly to one side, clear of the control unit. It may be necessary to pull back the edge of the footwell rubber for access to the rear nut **(see illustrations)**.

93   Release the clip at the front of the control unit bracket, then pull the control unit forwards from the bracket **(see illustration)**.

94   Disconnect the wiring connectors, and withdraw the unit from the footwell **(see illustration)**.

95   On X 12 SZ engine models, the programme memory can be unclipped from its circuit board in the control unit, after removing the cover from the rear of the control unit. The cover is secured by two screws **(see illustrations)**. **Do not** touch the memory plug contacts.

13.4 Disconnecting a camshaft cover breather hose from the throttle body

13.5 Disconnecting the fuel tank vent valve vacuum hose from the throttle body

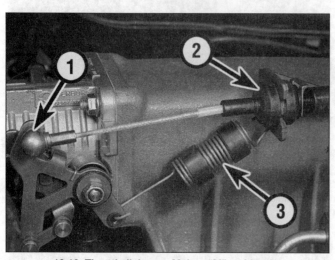

13.10 Throttle linkage - Multec "M" multi-point fuel injection system

    1   Cable end balljoint
    2   Cable grommet
    3   Throttle return spring (note orientation)

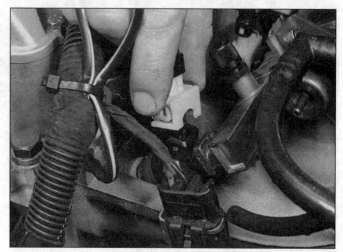

13.18 Disconnecting a fuel injector wiring plug

Refitting

96   Refitting is a reversal of removal.

Emission control system components

97   Details are given in Chapter 4B. Removal and refitting details for the oxygen sensor are given earlier in this Section.

---

13 Fuel injection system components (multi-point fuel injection - SOHC engines) - removal and refitting

---

Throttle body

Note: *A new gasket must be used on refitting.*

Removal

1   Disconnect the battery negative lead.
2   Disconnect the wiring plug from the intake air temperature sensor located in the inlet air trunking.
3   Loosen the clamp screw securing the air trunking to the throttle body, then release the air cleaner cover securing clips, and withdraw the air cleaner cover complete with the air trunking. If desired, to

improve access, the complete air cleaner assembly can be removed, as described in Section 3.
4   Disconnect the camshaft cover breather hoses from the throttle body **(see illustration)**.
5   Disconnect the fuel tank vent valve vacuum hose from the throttle body **(see illustration)**.
6   Disconnect the manifold absolute pressure (MAP) sensor vacuum hose from the throttle body.
7   Disconnect the coolant hoses from the throttle body. Be prepared for coolant spillage, and clamp or plug the open ends of the hoses, to prevent further coolant loss.
8   Disconnect the wiring plugs from the throttle position sensor and the idle speed control motor.
9   Release the securing clip, then disconnect the throttle cable end balljoint from the throttle valve lever.
10   Slide the throttle cable grommet from the bracket on the inlet manifold, then unhook the throttle return spring from the bracket. If desired, unhook the spring from the grommet in the throttle valve linkage, and lay the spring to one side out of the way (in this case, note the orientation of the spring to enable correct refitting) **(see illustration)**.
11   Make a final check to ensure that all relevant hoses and wires have been disconnected to facilitate removal of the throttle body.
12   Unscrew the four securing nuts, and withdraw the throttle body from the inlet manifold.
13   Recover the gasket.
14   If desired, the throttle position sensor and the idle speed control

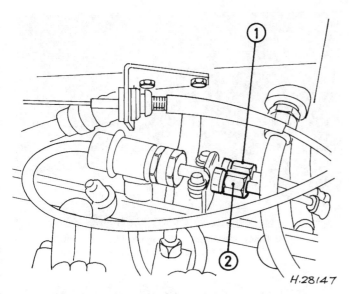

13.20 Disconnect the fuel feed (1) and fuel return (2) lines from the end of the fuel rail

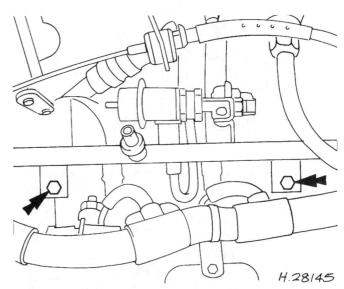

13.21 Fuel rail securing bolts (arrowed)

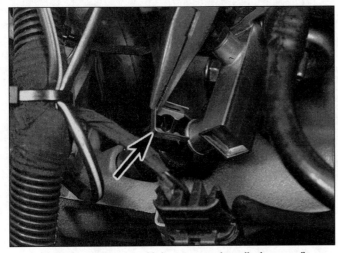

13.22 Removing a fuel injector securing clip (arrowed)

13.24 Fitting a new seal to a fuel injector

motor can be removed from the throttle body, as described later in this Section.

Refitting

15   Refitting is a reversal of removal, bearing in mind the following points:

(a) *Where applicable, refit the throttle position sensor and/or the idle speed control motor, as described later in this Section.*

(b) *Thoroughly clean the mating faces of the throttle body and inlet manifold, and refit the throttle body using a new gasket.*

(c) *Ensure that all wires and hoses are correctly reconnected and routed.*

(d) *Check and if necessary top-up the coolant level, as described in Chapter 1.*

(e) *On completion, check and if necessary adjust the throttle cable free play as described in Section 4.*

Fuel injectors

Note: *Refer to the precautions given in Section 1 before proceeding. The seals at both ends of the fuel injectors must be renewed on refitting.*

Removal

16   Depressurise the fuel system as described in Section 6.

17   Disconnect the battery negative lead if not already done.

18   Disconnect the wiring plugs from the fuel injectors, then move the wiring clear of the fuel rail **(see illustration)**.

19   Disconnect the vacuum pipe from the end of the fuel pressure regulator.

20   Unscrew the union nuts, and disconnect the fuel supply and return lines from the unions at the end of the fuel rail **(see illustration)**. Be prepared for fuel spillage, and take adequate fire precautions. Plug the open ends of the fuel lines, to prevent dirt ingress and further fuel spillage.

21   Remove the two fuel rail securing bolts, then lift the fuel rail, complete with fuel injectors, from the inlet manifold **(see illustration)**.

22   To remove an injector from the fuel rail, prise out the metal securing clip using a screwdriver or pair of pliers, then pull the injector from the fuel rail **(see illustration)**.

23   Overhaul of the fuel injectors is not possible, as no spares are available. If faulty, an injector must be renewed.

Refitting

24   Commence refitting by fitting new seals to both ends of the fuel injectors. Coat the seals with a thin layer of petroleum jelly before fitting **(see illustration)**.

25   Refitting is a reversal of removal.

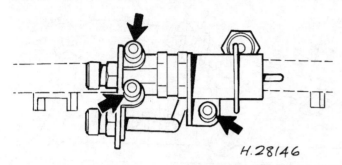

13.27 Fuel pressure regulator securing bolts (arrowed)

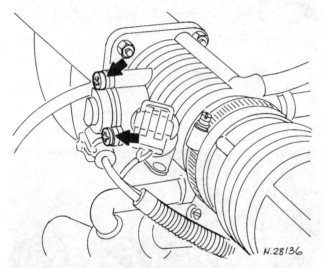

13.36 Throttle position sensor securing screws (arrowed)

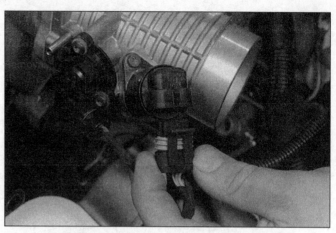

13.30 Disconnecting the wiring plug from the idle speed control motor

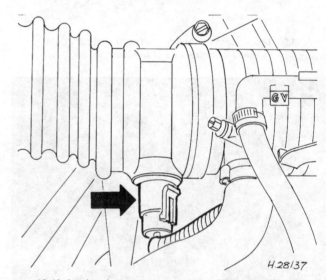

13.40 Intake air temperature sensor location (arrowed)

Fuel pressure regulator

Removal

Note: *Refer to the precautions given in Section 1 before proceeding. New fuel injector sealing rings, and a new pressure regulator sealing ring, must be used on refitting.*

26   Proceed as described in paragraphs 16 to 21 inclusive.

27   Unscrew the three securing bolts, and withdraw the fuel pressure regulator from the fuel rail **(see illustration)**. Recover the sealing ring.

Refitting

28   Refitting is a reversal of removal, bearing in mind the following points:

(a)   *Use a new sealing ring when refitting the pressure regulator, and coat the sealing ring with a thin layer of petroleum jelly before fitting.*

(b)   *Ensure that all pipes and wires are correctly reconnected.*

Idle speed control motor

Note: *A new sealing ring may be required on refitting.*

Removal

29   Disconnect the battery negative lead.

30   Release the securing clip, and disconnect the wiring plug from the idle speed control motor **(see illustration)**.

31   Remove the two securing screws, and withdraw the motor from the throttle body. Recover the O-ring seal.

Refitting

32   Before refitting the motor, examine the condition of the sealing ring, and renew if necessary.

33   Refitting is a reversal of removal, ensuring that the sealing ring is correctly located, and that the motor wiring socket faces downwards.

Throttle position sensor

Removal

34   Disconnect the battery negative lead.

35   Release the securing clips, and disconnect the wiring plug from the throttle position sensor.

36   Remove the securing screws, and withdraw the sensor from the throttle body **(see illustration)**.

Refitting

37   Refitting is a reversal of removal. Ensure that the sensor wiper engages correctly with the throttle valve shaft, and that the sensor is correctly seated in its location on the throttle body.

Manifold absolute pressure (MAP) sensor

38   Proceed as described in Section 12 for models with single-point fuel injection.

Crankshaft speed/position sensor

39   Proceed as described in Section 12 for models with single-point fuel injection.

Intake air temperature sensor

Removal

40   The sensor is located in the air inlet trunking, upstream of the

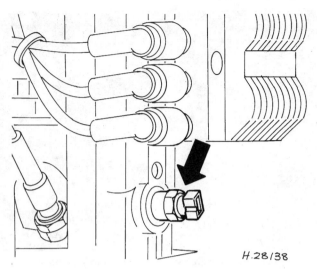

13.45 Coolant temperature sensor location (arrowed) in end of cylinder head

14.2a Withdrawing the throttle cable. Pull the grommet (arrowed) from the bracket

14.2b Note the orientation of the throttle return spring (arrowed) if it is to be disconnected

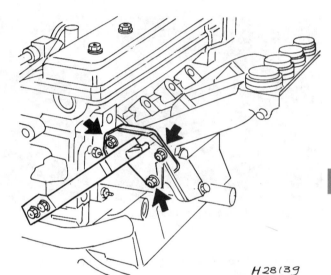

14.3 Throttle body mounting bracket securing bolts (arrowed) - viewed with throttle body removed

4A

throttle body **(see illustration)**.
41   Disconnect the battery negative lead.
42   Disconnect the sensor wiring plug.
43   Pull the sensor from the housing in the air inlet trunking.

Refitting
44   Refitting is a reversal of removal, but ensure that the sensor is pushed in to the stop in the air inlet trunking.

Coolant temperature sensor
45   Proceed as described in Section 12 for models with single-point fuel injection, but note that the sensor is located in the left-hand end face of the cylinder head, below the DIS module **(see illustration)**.

Exhaust gas oxygen sensor
46   Proceed as described in Section 12 for models with single-point fuel injection.

Vehicle speed sensor
47   The sensor is an integral part of the speedometer assembly, and no individual spare parts are available. If the sensor is faulty, the complete speedometer assembly must be renewed. Removal and refitting details for the speedometer are given in Section 10 of Chapter 12.

Electronic control unit
48   Proceed as described in Section 12 for models with single-point

fuel injection, noting that the programme memory and basic control unit can be renewed independently, as described for the X 12 SZ engine.

Emission control system components
49   Details are given in Chapter 4B. Removal and refitting details for the oxygen sensor are given earlier in this Section.

---

14   Fuel injection system components (multi-point fuel injection - DOHC engines) - removal and refitting

---

Throttle body

Removal
1   Remove the upper section of the inlet manifold, as described in Section 15.
2   Disconnect the throttle return spring and the throttle cable from the linkage on the throttle body (see Section 4). Position the throttle cable to one side, clear of the working area, noting its routing. If desired, the throttle return spring can be removed completely (in this case, note the orientation of the spring to enable correct refitting) **(see illustrations)**.
3   Unscrew the securing bolts, and remove the throttle body mounting bracket from the lower section of the inlet manifold **(see illustration)**.

14.11a Unscrew the fuel rail securing bolts . . .

14.11b . . . then lift the fuel rail from the inlet manifold

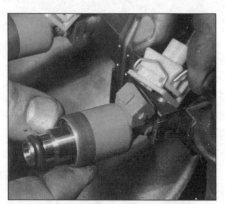

14.12a Disconnect the wiring plug . . .

14.12b . . . then remove the
securing clip . . .

14.12c . . . and withdraw the injector

4   Disconnect the wiring plugs from the throttle position sensor, and the idle speed control motor.

5   Plug the opening in the air intake trunking (disconnected from the throttle body when removing the upper section of the inlet manifold), to prevent the possibility of coolant entering the trunking during the following procedure.

6   Disconnect the coolant hoses from the throttle body. Be prepared for coolant spillage. Clamp or plug the open ends of the hoses, to reduce coolant spillage.

7   Lift the throttle body from the engine compartment.

Refitting

8   Refitting is a reversal of removal, bearing in mind the following points:

(a) Where applicable, ensure that the throttle return spring is refitted correctly.

(b) Refit the upper section of the inlet manifold as described in Section 15.

(c) On completion, check and if necessary adjust the throttle cable free play as described in Section 4. Check and if necessary top-up the coolant level as described in Chapter 1.

Fuel injectors

Note: Refer to the precautions given in Section 1 before proceeding. The seals at both ends of the fuel injectors must be renewed on refitting.

Removal

9   Depressurise the fuel system as described in Section 6.

10   Remove the upper section of the inlet manifold as described in Section 15.

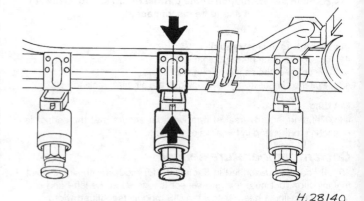

14.16 The metal tabs must engage with the cut-outs
in the injectors (arrowed)

11   Remove the two fuel rail securing bolts, then lift the fuel rail complete with the injectors sufficiently to enable the injectors to be removed **(see illustrations)**. Take care not to strain the fuel hoses and the wiring.

12   To remove an injector from the fuel rail, first disconnect the wiring plug. Prise out the metal securing clip using a screwdriver or a pair of pliers, and pull the injector from the fuel rail **(see illustrations)**.

13   Overhaul of the fuel injectors is not possible, as no spares are

14.21 Separate the two halves of the wiring connector

14.22 Fuel pressure regulator securing bolt (arrowed)

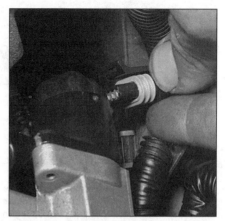

14.30 Disconnecting the wiring plug from the idle speed control motor

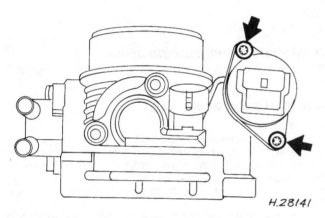

H.28141

14.31 Idle speed control motor securing bolts (arrowed) - viewed with throttle body removed for clarity

available. If faulty, an injector must be renewed.

14　The fuel rail assembly can be removed from the vehicle after disconnecting the two fuel lines, which are connected to the pipe on the fuel rail, and to the pressure regulator. Mark the hoses for position before disconnecting them, to ensure correct refitting. Similarly, disconnect all wiring, noting its routing and the position of the clips.

Refitting

15　Commence refitting by fitting new seals to both ends of the fuel injectors. Coat the seals with a thin layer of petroleum jelly before fitting.

16　Refitting is a reversal of removal, bearing in mind the following points:

(a) When refitting the injectors to the fuel rail, note that the metal tabs on the fuel rail must engage with the corresponding cutouts in the fuel injectors **(see illustration)** - the injectors can only be fitted in one position.

(b) Ensure that all wiring connectors are securely reconnected, and that the wiring is secured in the relevant brackets as noted before removal.

(c) Refit the upper section of the inlet manifold, as described in Section 15.

Fuel pressure regulator

Note: Refer to the precautions given in Section 1 before proceeding. A new sealing ring must be used on refitting.

Removal

17　Depressurise the fuel system as described in Section 6.
18　Disconnect the battery negative lead.

19　Disconnect the vacuum hose from the fuel pressure regulator.
20　Unscrew the union nut, and disconnect the fuel return line from the fuel pressure regulator, Be prepared for fuel spillage, and take adequate fire precautions. Plug the open end of the fuel line, to prevent dirt ingress and further fuel spillage.
21　Separate the two halves of the connector located above the pressure regulator **(see illustration)**, then unclip the wiring connector from its bracket.
22　Unscrew the pressure regulator securing bolt **(see illustration)**, and withdraw the regulator from the fuel rail, complete with the wiring connector bracket. Recover the sealing ring.

Refitting

23　Refitting is a reversal of removal, but use a new seal when refitting the pressure regulator to the fuel rail, and coat the seal with a thin layer of petroleum jelly before fitting.

Idle speed control motor

Note: Refer to the precautions given in Section 1 before proceeding. A new O-ring seal must be used when refitting the motor. Suitable thread-locking compound will be required to coat the threads of the motor securing bolts on refitting.

Removal

24　The idle speed control motor is located on the throttle body, under the inlet manifold at the rear of the engine.
25　Depressurise the fuel system as described in Section 6.
26　Disconnect the battery negative lead if not already done.
27　Partially drain the cooling system as described in Chapter 1 (drain sufficient coolant to empty the coolant expansion tank).
28　Disconnect the hoses from the coolant expansion tank, then unscrew the securing nuts, and withdraw the expansion tank.
29　Unscrew the union nut, and disconnect the fuel return line from the fuel pressure regulator. Be prepared for fuel spillage, and take adequate fire precautions. Plug the open end of the fuel line, to prevent dirt ingress and further fuel spillage. Move the fuel line to one side, clear of the working area.
30　Disconnect the wiring plug from the idle speed control motor **(see illustration)**.
31　Remove the two securing bolts, and withdraw the motor from the throttle body **(see illustration)**. Recover the O-ring seal.

Refitting

32　Refitting is a reversal of removal, bearing in mind the following points:

(a) To avoid damaging the housing or the motor during refitting, the distance between the end of the motor piston and the end face of the motor body flange should not be greater than 33.0 mm. Measure the distance shown, and if greater than specified, carefully push the piston into the motor body as far as its stop **(see illustration)**.

4A

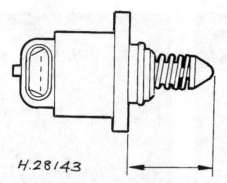

14.32 The distance between the end of the motor piston and the end face of the motor body flange should be a maximum of 33.0 mm

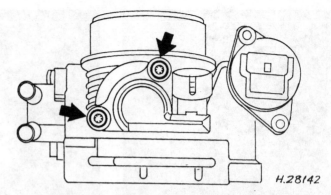

14.34 Throttle position sensor securing screws (arrowed)

(b) *Refit the motor, using a new O-ring seal.*
(c) *Coat the threads of the motor securing bolts with a suitable thread-locking compound before fitting.*
(d) *On completion, top-up and bleed the cooling system as described in Chapter 1.*

Throttle position sensor

Note: *Suitable thread-locking compound will be required to coat the threads of the sensor securing screws on refitting.*

Removal
33   Remove the throttle body as described earlier in this Section.
34   Remove the two securing screws, and withdraw the sensor from the throttle body **(see illustration)**.

Refitting
35   Refit the sensor to the throttle body, ensuring that the sensor wiper engages correctly with the throttle valve shaft, and ensuring that the sensor is correctly seated in its location in the throttle body. Coat the threads of the securing screws with suitable thread-locking compound before refitting.
36   Refit the throttle body as earlier in this Section.

Air mass meter

Removal
37   Disconnect the battery negative lead, then disconnect the air mass meter wiring plug **(see illustration)**.
38   Loosen the hose clamp, and disconnect the air trunking from the air mass meter.
39   Release the securing clips, then lift off the air cleaner cover, complete with the air mass meter.
40   Unscrew the securing bolts (recover the nuts if they are loose),

then separate the air mass meter from the air cleaner cover **(see illustration)**.

Refitting
41   Refitting is a reversal of removal.

Crankshaft speed/position sensor

42   Proceed as described in Section 12 for models with single-point fuel injection.

Camshaft position sensor

Removal
43   Disconnect the battery negative lead.
44   Unclip the sensor wiring connector from its bracket on the fuel rail (at the timing belt end of the engine), and separate the two halves of the wiring connector.
45   Remove the upper outer timing belt cover, with reference to Chapter 2A.
46   Unscrew the two securing bolts, and withdraw the sensor from the rear timing belt cover **(see illustration)**.

Refitting
47   Refitting is a reversal of removal.

Coolant temperature sensor

48   Proceed as described in Section 12 for models with single-point fuel injection, but note that the sensor is located in the thermostat housing **(see illustration)**.

Exhaust gas oxygen sensor

49   Proceed as described in Section 12 for models with single-point fuel injection, but note that the exhaust heat shield must be unbolted from the exhaust manifold for access to the sensor.

14.37 Disconnecting the air mass meter wiring plug

14.40 Air mass meter securing bolts (arrowed)

14.46 Removing the camshaft position sensor

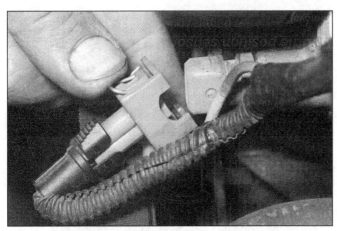

14.48 Disconnecting the wiring plug from the coolant temperature sensor

Vehicle speed sensor

50   The sensor is an integral part of the speedometer assembly, and no individual spare parts are available. If the sensor is faulty, the complete speedometer assembly must be renewed. Removal and refitting details for the speedometer are given in Section 10 of Chapter 12.

Knock sensor

51   The sensor is part of the knock control system, details of which are given in Chapter 5C.

Electronic control unit

52   Proceed as described in Section 12 for models with single-point fuel injection, noting that the programme memory and control unit can be renewed independently, as described for the X 12 SZ engine.

Emission control system components

53   Details are given in Chapter 4B. Removal and refitting details for the oxygen sensor are given earlier in this Section.

---

15   Inlet manifold - removal and refitting

Models with single-point fuel injection

Note: *A new manifold gasket must be used on refitting.*

Removal

1   Proceed as described for removal of the fuel injection unit in Section 12, paragraphs 6 to 14.

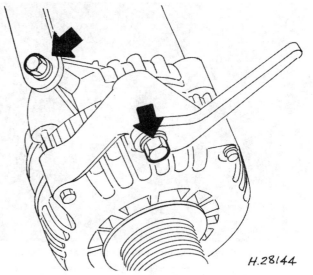

15.5 Remove the two upper alternator securing bolts (arrowed)

2   For improved access, remove the air cleaner assembly, as described in Section 3.
3   Remove the auxiliary drivebelt as described in Chapter 1.
4   On models with a "V-belt" alternator drive, unscrew the bolt securing the top of the alternator to the adjuster strut, and recover any washers and insulating bushes, noting their locations. Note the earth strap attached to the bolt. Pivot the alternator downwards, clear of the inlet manifold.
5   On models with a "ribbed belt" alternator drive, remove the two upper alternator securing bolts **(see illustration)**.
6   Disconnect the throttle cable end from the throttle linkage, then slide the cable grommet from the bracket on the inlet manifold, and move the throttle cable to one side out of the way (refer to Section 4 if necessary).
7   Unscrew the union nut, and disconnect the brake servo vacuum hose from the inlet manifold **(see illustration)**.
8   On X 12 SZ engines, disconnect the wiring plug from the exhaust gas recirculation valve.
9   Disconnect the wiring plug from the temperature gauge sender **(see illustration)**.
10   Where applicable, disconnect the wiring from the coolant temperature sensor, located at the right-hand rear of the inlet manifold.
11   Where applicable, separate the two halves of the wiring connector located in the bracket attached to the left-hand end of the inlet manifold **(see illustration)**. Unclip the connector from the bracket.

4A

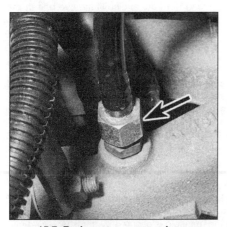

15.7 Brake servo vacuum hose connection (arrowed) at inlet manifold

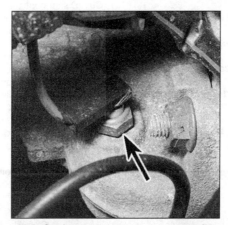

15.9 Coolant temperature gauge sender location (arrowed) in inlet manifold

15.11 Separate the two halves of the wiring connector (arrowed) located on the inlet manifold

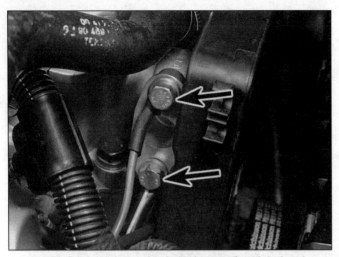

15.29 Earth lead securing bolts (arrowed) at right-hand end of cylinder head

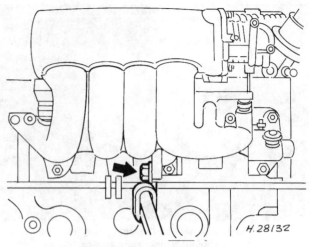

15.35 Fuel hose bracket securing bolt (arrowed) on unde side of inlet manifold

12   Partially drain the cooling system as described in Chapter 1, then disconnect the coolant hose from the rear of the inlet manifold. Be prepared for coolant spillage, and clamp or plug the open end of the hose, to reduce coolant loss.

13   Make a final check to ensure that all relevant hoses, pipes and wires have been disconnected.

14   Unscrew the securing nuts, and withdraw the manifold from the cylinder head. Note the locations of any brackets secured by the nuts. Recover the gasket.

15   It is possible that some of the manifold studs may be unscrewed from the cylinder head when the manifold securing screws are unscrewed. In this event, the studs should be screwed back into the cylinder head once the manifold has been removed, using two manifold nuts locked together on the stud.

16   If desired, the fuel injection unit and manifold-mounted ancillary components can be removed from the manifold, with reference to the relevant Sections of this Chapter.

Refitting

17   Refitting is a reversal of removal, bearing in mind the following points:

(a)   Clean the gasket faces of the manifold and cylinder head.

(b)   Where applicable, refit any ancillary components to the manifold, with reference to the relevant Sections of this Chapter.

(c)   If the alternator mounting bracket has been unbolted from the manifold, refit it before refitting the manifold, as access is limited once the manifold is in place.

(d)   Refit the manifold using a new gasket.

(e)   Ensure that all relevant hoses, pipes and wires are correctly reconnected and routed.

(f)   Refit and tension the auxiliary drivebelt with reference to Chapter 1.

(g)   On completion, top-up and bleed the cooling system as described in Chapter 1.

(h)   Check and if necessary adjust the throttle cable free play, as described in Section 4.

SOHC engine models with multi-point fuel injection

Note: On models where the inlet manifold is secured by studs (screwed into the cylinder head) and nuts, the studs and nuts should be replaced with bolts on refitting. A new manifold gasket must be used on refitting.

Removal

18   Depressurise the fuel system as described in Section 6.

19   Disconnect the battery negative lead if not already done.

20   Remove the auxiliary drivebelt as described in Chapter 1.

21   On models with a "V-belt" alternator drive, unscrew the bolt securing the top of the alternator to the adjuster strut, and recover any washers and insulating bushes, noting their locations. Note the earth strap attached to the bolt. Pivot the alternator downwards, clear of the inlet manifold.

22   On models with a "ribbed belt" alternator drive, remove the two upper alternator securing bolts.

23   Release the securing clip, then disconnect the throttle cable end balljoint from the throttle linkage. Slide the throttle cable grommet from the bracket on the inlet manifold, and move the throttle cable to one side out of the way.

24   Unscrew the union nut, and disconnect the brake servo vacuum hose from the inlet manifold.

25   Disconnect the camshaft cover breather hoses from the throttle body.

26   Disconnect the vacuum hoses from the throttle body, noting their locations to aid refitting.

27   Disconnect the coolant hoses from the throttle body (two hoses) and the inlet manifold (one hose), noting their locations to aid refitting. Be prepared for coolant spillage, and clamp or plug the open ends of the hoses, to prevent further coolant loss. Unclip the coolant hose from the rear of the manifold.

28   Disconnect the wiring plugs from the throttle position sensor, and from the idle speed control motor on the throttle body.

29   Unscrew the two securing bolts, and disconnect the earth leads from the right-hand end of the cylinder head **(see illustration)**.

30   Disconnect the earth lead from the engine lifting eye bolt at the left-hand end of the inlet manifold.

31   Disconnect the wiring from the coolant temperature gauge sender in the inlet manifold.

32   Disconnect the wiring plugs from the fuel injectors.

33   Where applicable, separate the two halves of the wiring connector located in the bracket attached to the upper left-hand inlet manifold stud (or bolt, as applicable).

34   Place a wad of rag beneath the fuel line unions on the fuel pressure regulator and the fuel rail, then slowly loosen the unions. Be prepared for fuel spillage, and take adequate fire precautions. Clamp or plug the open ends of the hoses, to prevent fuel spillage and dirt ingress.

35   Unscrew the bolt securing the fuel hose bracket to the underside of the inlet manifold **(see illustration)**.

36   Make a final check to ensure that all relevant hoses, pipes and wires have been disconnected.

37   On models where the manifold is secured by studs (screwed into the cylinder head) and nuts, the studs must be unscrewed from the cylinder head before the manifold can be removed **(see illustration)**.

15.37 Inlet manifold securing stud/bolt locations (arrowed) -
SOHC engines with multi-point fuel injection

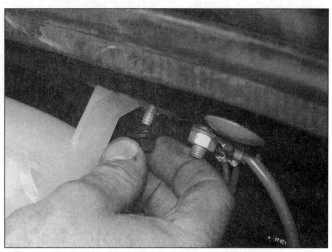

15.44a Removing an expansion tank securing nut

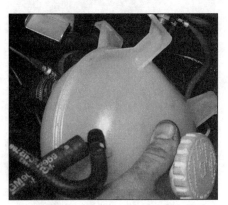

15.44b Access to the lower hose is easier
once the tank has been removed

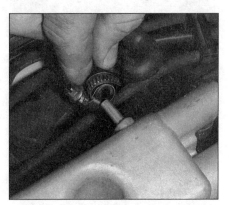

15.46a Disconnect the breather hose
from the camshaft cover . . .

15.46b . . . and the brake servo vacuum
hose from the upper section
of the inlet manifold

The studs can be removed using two of the manifold nuts locked together on the studs. Note the location of any brackets secured by the
nuts and studs.

38   On models where the manifold is secured by bolts, unscrew the
bolts, noting the location of any brackets secured by the bolts.

39   With the securing studs and nuts, or bolts (as applicable) removed, lift the manifold from the cylinder head. Recover the gasket.

40   If desired, the throttle body and manifold-mounted ancillary components can be removed from the manifold, with reference to the relevant Sections of this Chapter.

Refitting

41   Refitting is a reversal of removal, bearing in mind the following
points:

(a) Clean the gasket faces of the manifold and cylinder head.

(b) Where applicable, refit any ancillary components to the manifold, with reference to the relevant Sections of this Chapter.

(c) If the alternator mounting bracket has been unbolted from the
manifold, refit it before refitting the manifold, as access is limited once the manifold is in place.

(d) Refit the manifold using a new gasket.

(e) If studs and nuts were originally used to secure the manifold,
discard the studs and nuts, and use suitable bolts on refitting.

(f) Ensure that all relevant hoses, pipes and wires are correctly reconnected and routed.

(g) Refit and tension the auxiliary drivebelt with reference to
Chapter 1.

(h) On completion, top-up and bleed the cooling system as described in Chapter 1.

(i) Check and if necessary adjust the throttle cable free play, as
described in Section 4.

DOHC engine models - upper section of inlet manifold

Note: A new throttle body-to-mounting bracket gasket must be used
on refitting. A new O-ring and gasket may be required when refitting
the upper section of the inlet manifold to the throttle body mounting
bracket and the lower section of the inlet manifold.

Removal

42   Disconnect the battery negative lead.

43   Partially drain the cooling system as described in Chapter 1 (drain
sufficient coolant to empty the coolant expansion tank).

44   Disconnect the hoses from the coolant expansion tank, then unscrew the securing nuts, and withdraw the expansion tank. Note that
the lower hose is more easily disconnected once the tank has been removed **(see illustrations)**

45   Remove the oil filler cap, then remove the two securing screws,
and lift off the plastic shield which fits over the top of the camshaft
cover.

46   Disconnect the breather hose from the camshaft cover, and the
brake servo vacuum hose from the upper section of the inlet manifold
(see illustrations).

15.49 Move the fuel tank vent valve
to one side

15.52a Three of the four throttle body
securing bolts (arrowed) - viewed from
underneath with engine removed

15.52b Throttle body securing
bolt (arrowed)

15.53a Remove the securing bolts . . .

15.53b . . . and withdraw the upper
section of the inlet manifold

15.53c Recover the gasket

47 Disconnect the manifold vacuum hoses from the fuel pressure regulator and the evaporative emission control solenoid valve, located at the flywheel end of the upper section of the inlet manifold. Alternatively, disconnect these hoses from the manifold itself.

48 Disconnect the breather hose (which runs across the top of the fuel tank vent valve) from the camshaft cover.

49 Release the fuel tank vent valve retaining clip (using a screwdriver or similar tool), and withdraw the valve upwards from its mounting bracket. Leave the remaining hose(s) connected, and place the valve to one side, clear of the working area **(see illustration)**.

50 Remove the starter motor as described in Chapter 5A.

51 Loosen the clamp screw, and disconnect the air trunking from the lower end of the throttle body. Move the air trunking away from the throttle body, to gain access to the throttle body securing bolts (if desired, the bolt securing the air trunking to the bracket on the inlet manifold can be removed).

52 Working underneath the vehicle, remove the four bolts which secure the throttle body to its mounting bracket and the upper section of the inlet manifold **(see illustrations)**.

53 Unscrew the four securing bolts, and withdraw the upper section of the inlet manifold. Note that the throttle body will now be loose - ensure that none of the hoses or wiring connectors are strained. Recover the gasket between the upper and lower sections of the manifold if it is loose **(see illustrations)**.

54 Recover the O-ring between the throttle body mounting bracket and the upper section of the inlet manifold, and the gasket between the throttle body and the mounting bracket.

Refitting

55 Commence refitting by checking the condition of the rubber gasket which fits between the upper and lower sections of the inlet manifold. Renew the gasket if necessary. Similarly, check the condition of the O-ring between the throttle body mounting bracket and the upper section of the inlet manifold, and renew if necessary **(see illustration)**.

56 Clean the gasket faces of the throttle body and its mounting bracket. Ensure that no dirt enters the throttle body.

57 Refit the upper section of the inlet manifold, ensuring that the gasket between the upper and lower manifold sections locates correctly. Make sure that the O-ring between the throttle body mounting bracket and the upper section of the inlet manifold is in position.

58 Fit a new gasket between the throttle body and its mounting bracket **(see illustration)**. Refit and tighten the bolts securing the throttle body to its mounting bracket and the upper section of the inlet manifold.

59 Reconnect the air trunking to the lower end of the throttle body, and tighten the securing clamp.

60 Refit the starter motor, with reference to Chapter 5A if necessary.

61 Refit the fuel tank vent valve to its bracket, and reconnect the vacuum hose.

62 Reconnect the breather hose to the camshaft cover.

63 Reconnect the fuel pressure regulator vacuum hose.

64 Reconnect the breather hose and the brake servo vacuum hose to the upper section of the inlet manifold.

65 Refit the plastic shield which fits over the top of the camshaft cover, and refit the oil filler cap.

66 Reconnect the hoses to the coolant expansion tank, then refit the expansion tank.

67 Reconnect the battery negative lead.

68 Top-up and bleed the cooling system as described in Chapter 1.

15.55 Check the condition of the O-ring

15.58 Fit a new gasket between the throttle body and its mounting bracket

DOHC models - lower section of inlet manifold

Removal

69   Depressurise the fuel system as described in Section 6.

70   Remove the upper section of the inlet manifold as described previously in this Section. It should be noted however, that the cooling system should be drained completely.

71   Place a wad of rag beneath the fuel line unions on the fuel pressure regulator and the fuel rail, then slowly loosen the unions. Be prepared for fuel spillage, and take adequate fire precautions. Clamp or plug the open ends of the hoses, to prevent fuel spillage and dirt ingress.

72   Unclip the fuel injector wiring harness, crankshaft speed/position sensor, and camshaft position sensor wiring connectors from their brackets, and separate the two halves of the respective connectors **(see illustration)**.

73   Unscrew the securing nut, and disconnect the earth lead from the stud on the lower section of the inlet manifold **(see illustration)**.

74   Remove the auxiliary drivebelt, as described in Chapter 1.

75   Remove the securing nut, and disconnect the earth wiring from the upper alternator bracket stud **(see illustration)**. Unscrew the two securing bolts, and the stud, and remove the upper alternator bracket.

76   Pivot the alternator towards the rear of the engine compartment.

77   Unscrew the two securing bolts, and remove the wiring harness support bracket from the lower section of the inlet manifold, noting that one of the bolts also secures the air intake ducting **(see illustration)**.

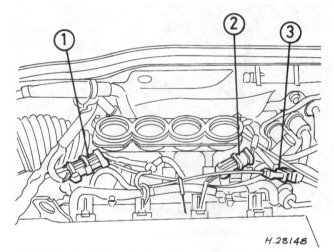

15.72 Injector (1), camshaft position sensor (2), and crankshaft speed/position sensor (3) wiring connector locations

78   Remove the screw securing the cable bracket to the air intake ducting.

79   Unscrew the three bolts securing the throttle body mounting

15.73 Disconnect the earth lead from the stud on the manifold

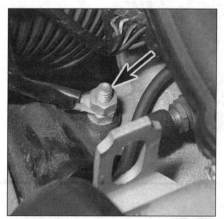

15.75 Disconnect the earth wiring from the upper alternator bracket stud (arrowed)

15.77 Wiring harness support bracket bolts (1) and cable bracket securing screw (2) - viewed with engine removed for clarity

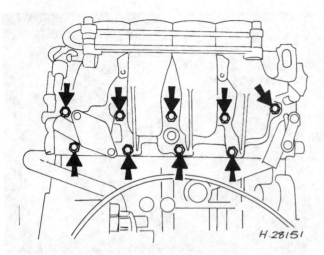

15.80 Inlet manifold (lower section) securing nuts (arrowed)

15.81 Unbolt the coolant housing to enable the gasket
to be removed

16.3a Exhaust manifold hot-air shroud upper . . .

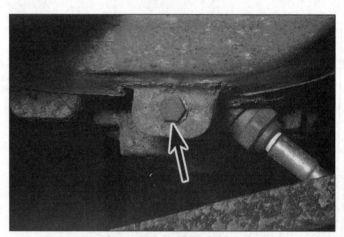

16.3b . . . and lower securing bolts (arrowed)

16.7 Exhaust manifold securing nuts (arrowed) - DOHC engine,
viewed with engine removed for clarity

Refitting

82   Refitting is a reversal of removal, bearing in mind the following points:

    (a)   *Clean the gasket faces of the lower section of the inlet manifold and the cylinder head.*

    (b)   *Refit the lower section of the manifold and the coolant housing to the cylinder head, using a new gasket.*

    (c)   *Refit and tension the auxiliary drivebelt as described in Chapter 1.*

    (d)   *Ensure that all wiring and hoses are correctly reconnected and routed.*

    (e)   *Refit the upper section of the inlet manifold as described previously in this Section.*

16 Exhaust manifold - removal and refitting

Removal

Note: *A new gasket must be used on refitting.*

1   Disconnect the battery negative lead.

2   Unclip the oxygen sensor wiring plug from its bracket on the gearbox/transmission, then separate the two halves of the connector.

3   Where applicable, disconnect the hot-air hose from the hot-air shroud on the exhaust manifold. Remove the securing bolts, and remove the hot-air shroud from the manifold **(see illustrations)**.

4   On DOHC engine models, unscrew the securing bolts, and remove the exhaust manifold heat shield.

bracket to the lower section of the inlet manifold (see illustration 14.3).

80   Unscrew the nuts securing the lower section of the inlet manifold to the cylinder head **(see illustration)**, then lift the lower section of the manifold from the engine compartment.

81   Unbolt the coolant housing from the timing belt end of the cylinder head, to enable the inlet manifold gasket to be removed from the cylinder head **(see illustration)**. Recover the gasket.

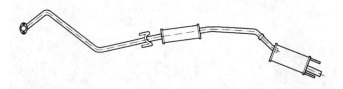

17.5a Exhaust system layout - 12 NZ SOHC engine

17.5b Exhaust system layout - all SOHC engines except 12 NZ

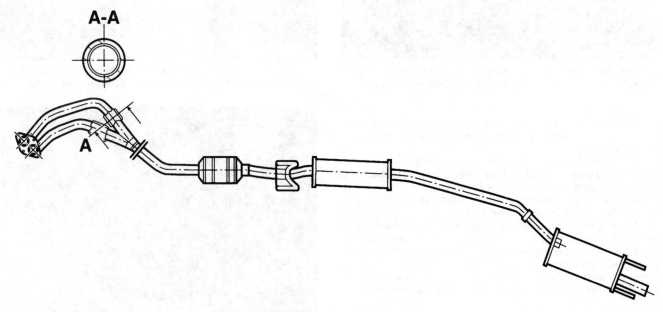

17.5c Exhaust system layout - DOHC engine

5   On DOHC engine models with air conditioning, remove the cooling fan and shroud assembly from the radiator as described in Chapter 3.
6   Disconnect the exhaust front section from the manifold, with reference to Section 17.
7   Unscrew the securing nuts, and lift the manifold from the cylinder head **(see illustration)**. Where applicable, note the location of the engine lifting bracket secured by one of the manifold studs. Recover the gasket.

Refitting

8   Refitting is a reversal of removal, bearing in mind the following points:

(a) Clean the gasket faces of the manifold and the cylinder head.
(b) Refit the manifold using a new gasket.
(c) Reconnect the front section of the exhaust system to the manifold with reference to Section 17.
(d) On DOHC engine models with air conditioning, refit the cooling fan and shroud to the radiator, with reference to Chapter 3.

---

17 Exhaust system - general information and component renewal

---

General information

1   Periodically, the exhaust system should be checked for signs of leaks or damage. Also inspect the system rubber mountings, and renew if necessary.

2   Small holes or cracks can be repaired using proprietary exhaust repair products, such as Holts Flexiwrap and Holts Gun Gum.
3   On SOHC engine models, the original factory-fitted exhaust system is a one-piece unit, with the exception of the rear silencer. On DOHC engine models, a separate exhaust front section is fitted.
4   Before renewing an individual section of the exhaust system, it is wise to inspect the remaining sections. If corrosion or damage is evident on more than one section of the system, it may prove more economical to renew the entire system.

Component renewal

Note: *All relevant gaskets and/or sealing rings should be renewed on refitting.*
5   With the exception of the rear silencer box (SOHC engine models), or the rear silencer box and the exhaust front section (DOHC engine models), the exhaust system originally fitted to the vehicle at the factory is a single-section welded unit, which includes the integral catalytic converter **(see illustrations)**.
6   With the exception of the rear silencer box, and the front section (DOHC engines), individual sections of the system can only be removed by cutting the system, and using suitable clamps and sleeves to join the new section to the remainder of the system. Individual sections of the exhaust system are available from Vauxhall/Opel dealers.
7   If any part of the system is to be renewed, it is important to ensure that the correct replacement components are obtained for the particular model concerned.
8   If it proves necessary to cut the system in order to renew a particular components, it is strongly recommended that any such work is entrusted to a Vauxhall/Opel dealer, or exhaust specialist.

4A

17.10a Recover the springs (arrowed) from the exhaust front section-to-intermediate section joint - DOHC engine model

17.10b Use a new gasket (arrowed) when reconnecting the exhaust front section to the manifold - DOHC engine model shown

9   If work is to be carried out on the exhaust system, first jack up the vehicle and support securely on axle stands (see *"Jacking, towing and wheel changing"*).

10   The exhaust front section can be disconnected from the manifold after removing the securing bolts. Recover the springs (where applicable) and the gasket. Renew the gasket on refitting. Similarly, on DOHC engine models, the exhaust front section can be disconnected from the intermediate section **(see illustrations)**.

11   To remove the entire exhaust system, disconnect the joints, or cut the system as necessary (with regard to the spare sections available), then unhook the rubber mountings, and withdraw the relevant section of the system. Note that it may be necessary to remove the spring clips from the exhaust mountings before the rubber mountings can be unhooked from the body or the exhaust system **(see illustration)**.

17.11 Exhaust system rubber mounting spring clip (arrowed)

Chapter 4 Part B:
Emissions control systems

Contents

Specifications

Torque wrench setting

	Nm	lbf ft
Exhaust gas recirculation valve-to-inlet manifold bolts..........................	20	15

1 General information and precautions

All models in the Corsa range run on unleaded petrol. Additionally, various systems may be fitted (depending on model) to reduce the emission of pollutants into the atmosphere. The systems are described in more detail in the following paragraphs.

Crankcase emissions control system

A crankcase ventilation system is fitted to all models, but the systems differ in detail according to model.

Oil fumes and blow-by gases (combustion gases which have passed by the piston rings) are drawn from the crankcase into the area of the cylinder head above the camshaft(s) via a hose. From here, the gases are drawn into the inlet manifold/throttle body (as applicable) and/or the airbox on the throttle body, where they are mixed with fresh air/fuel mixture and burnt, reducing harmful exhaust emissions.

Certain models may have a mesh filter inside the camshaft cover, which should be cleaned in paraffin if clogging is evident.

Exhaust emissions control system

To minimise the level of exhaust gas pollutants released into the atmosphere, all except 12 NZ engine models are fitted with a catalytic converter, located in the exhaust system. A "closed-loop" system is used; an exhaust gas oxygen sensor, mounted in the exhaust manifold, provides a signal to the fuel system electronic control unit, to enable it adjust the air/fuel mixture ratio within very fine limits. This enables the catalytic converter to operate at optimum efficiency at all times.

The oxygen sensor senses the level of oxygen in the exhaust gas, which is proportional to the air/fuel mixture ratio. A rich mixture produces exhaust gases with a low oxygen content, the oxygen content rising as the mixture weakens. The catalyst operates at maximum efficiency when the air/fuel mixture ratio is at the chemically-correct ratio for the complete combustion of petrol (14.7 parts of air to 1 part of fuel). The output voltage produced by the oxygen sensor alters sharply when this ratio is achieved. The electronic control unit uses this information to maintain the air/fuel ratio very close to the optimum value under all engine operating conditions, by varying the amount of fuel injected.

Fuel evaporation control system

To minimise the escape into the atmosphere of unburnt hydrocarbons, a fuel evaporation control system is fitted to all except 12 NZ engine models. The fuel tank filler cap is sealed, to prevent the release of fuel vapour into the atmosphere, and a charcoal canister is mounted under the front right-hand wheel arch, to collect the fuel vapours which would otherwise be released from the tank when the vehicle is parked. The vapours are stored in the canister until a vent valve is operated by manifold vacuum, or by the fuel system electronic control unit (depending on engine type). The vent valve releases the vapours into the engine inlet tract, where they are burnt during the normal combustion process.

2.9 Disconnecting the fuel vapour vent hose from the fuel injection unit - single-point fuel injection model shown

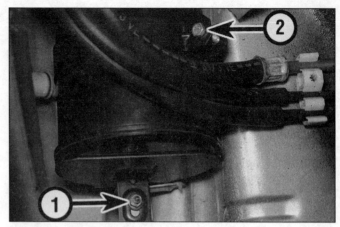

2.14 Charcoal canister bracket securing nut (1) and clamp bolt (2)

Exhaust gas recirculation system

This system is fitted to the X 12 SZ engine.

The exhaust gas recirculation system is designed to recirculate small quantities of exhaust gas into the inlet tract, and therefore into the combustion process. This process reduces the level of oxides of nitrogen present in the final exhaust gas which is released into the atmosphere. The volume of exhaust gas recirculated is controlled by the fuel system electronic control unit, via a valve mounted on the inlet manifold.

A tract in the cylinder head allows exhaust gas to pass from the exhaust side of the cylinder head to the exhaust gas recirculation valve in the inlet manifold.

2 Emissions control system components - testing and renewal

Crankcase emissions control system

Testing

1   If the system is thought to be faulty, first check that the hoses are unobstructed. High-mileage vehicles, particularly those regularly used for short journeys, are likely to develop a jelly-like deposit inside the crankcase emissions control system hoses. If excessive deposits are present, the relevant hose(s) should be removed and cleaned.

2   Periodically inspect the system hoses for security and damage, and renew them as necessary. Note that damaged or loose hoses can cause various engine running problems (erratic idle speed, stalling, etc) which can be difficult to trace.

Component renewal

3   The crankcase breather tube can be unbolted from the cylinder block (remove the starter motor for access) after disconnecting the hose. Use a new gasket when refitting.

4   Certain models have a mesh filter inside the camshaft cover, which should be cleaned in paraffin if clogging is evident. For access to the filter, remove the camshaft cover as described in Chapter 2A. The filter can be removed from the camshaft cover for cleaning after unscrewing the securing screws.

Exhaust emissions control system

Testing

5   The system can only be tested accurately using specialist Vauxhall/Opel diagnostic equipment. Any suspected faults should be referred to a Vauxhall/Opel dealer.

Catalytic converter - renewal

6   The catalytic converter is located in the exhaust system, and is an integral part of either the exhaust front section or (on DOHC engine models) the exhaust intermediate section.

7   Removal and refitting details for the exhaust system components

are given in Chapter 4A.

Oxygen sensor - renewal

8   Renewal of the oxygen sensor is described in the relevant fuel system Section of Chapter 4A.

Fuel evaporation control system

Testing

9   If the system is thought to be faulty, disconnect the hoses from the charcoal canister and vent valve, and check that the hoses are clear by blowing through them. If necessary, clean or renew the hoses **(see illustration)**.

10   If the vent valve or the charcoal canister itself are thought to be faulty, the only course of action available is renewal.

Charcoal canister - renewal

11   The charcoal canister is located under the front right-hand wheel arch.

12   Apply the handbrake, then jack up the front of the vehicle and support securely on axle stands (see *"Jacking, towing and wheel changing"*). Remove the front right-hand roadwheel.

13   Remove the wheel arch liner (see Chapter 11, Section 22) to expose the charcoal canister.

14   Remove the nut securing the canister bracket to the bracket on the body **(see illustration)**.

15   Unscrew the canister clamp bolt, and withdraw the canister from the clamp bracket.

16   Loosen the hose clamps, and disconnect the hoses from the top of the canister, noting their locations to ensure correct refitting **(see illustration)**.

17   Withdraw the canister from under the wheel arch.

18   Fit the new canister using a reversal of the removal procedure. Make sure that the hoses are correctly reconnected, as noted before removal. Ensure that the upper end of the canister clamp bracket locates in the cut-out in the body panel.

Fuel tank vent valve (all except X 12 SZ and C 16 XE engines) - renewal

19   The valve is located at the rear of the engine compartment, behind the inlet manifold **(see illustration)**.

20   Disconnect the three hoses from the valve, noting their locations to ensure correct refitting, and withdraw the valve.

21   Refitting is a reversal of removal, ensuring that the hoses are reconnected correctly, as noted before removal.

Fuel tank vent valve (X 12 SZ engine) - renewal

22   The valve is located at the timing belt end of the camshaft housing, at the rear.

23   Disconnect the battery negative lead.

24   For improved access, remove the breather hose connecting the airbox to the camshaft cover **(see illustration)**.

2.16 Note the locations of the charcoal canister hoses

2.19 Fuel tank vent valve (arrowed) - all except X 12 SZ and C 16 XE engines

2.24 Remove the breather hose . . .

2.25 . . . and lift the wiring harness clear for access to the fuel tank vent valve (arrowed) - X 12 SZ engine

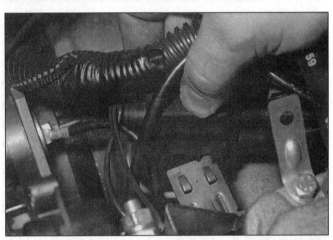

2.26 Slide the valve from its mounting bracket . . .

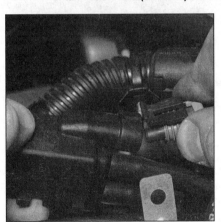

2.27 . . . and disconnect the wiring and hoses - X 12 SZ engine

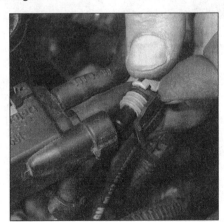

2.31 Disconnecting the wiring plug . . .

2.32 . . . and the hoses from the fuel tank vent valve - C 16 XE engine

25   Release the wiring harness from the brackets on the camshaft cover, and lift the harness clear of the fuel tank vent valve **(see illustration)**.

26   Depress the retaining lugs, and slide the valve rearwards from its mounting bracket **(see illustration)**.

27   Disconnect the valve wiring plug, and the two hoses, noting their locations to ensure correct refitting **(see illustration)**.

28   Withdraw the valve.

29   Refitting is a reversal of removal, ensuring that the hoses are reconnected correctly, as noted before removal.

Fuel tank vent valve (C 16 XE engine) - renewal

30   The valve is located on a bracket attached to the upper section of the inlet manifold. To improve access, disconnect the breather hose (which runs across the top of the valve) from the camshaft cover.

31   Disconnect the battery negative lead, then disconnect the wiring plug from the valve **(see illustration)**.

32   Disconnect the hoses from the valve, noting their locations to ensure correct refitting **(see illustration)**.

33   Using a screwdriver, release the valve retaining clip, and withdraw the valve upwards from its bracket.

2.38 Disconnecting the exhaust gas recirculation valve wiring plug

2.39 Exhaust gas recirculation valve securing bolts (arrowed)

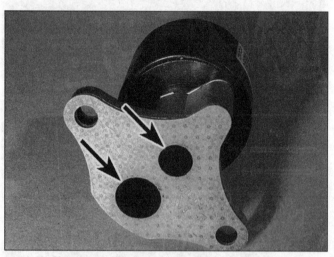

2.40 Check the exhaust gas recirculation valve vent holes (arrowed) for contamination

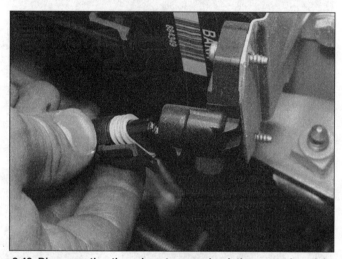

2.43 Disconnecting the exhaust gas recirculation control module wiring plug

34   Refitting is a reversal of removal, ensuring that the hoses are reconnected correctly, as noted before removal.

Exhaust gas recirculation system

Testing

35   The system can only be tested accurately using specialist Vauxhall/Opel diagnostic equipment. The wiring to the solenoid valve on the inlet manifold can be checked for condition and security, but any further testing should be referred to a Vauxhall/Opel dealer.

Exhaust gas recirculation valve - renewal

Note: *A new gasket must be used on refitting.*
36   The valve is located on top of the inlet manifold.
37   Remove the airbox from the top of the fuel injection unit, as described in Chapter 4A.
38   Disconnect the battery negative lead, then disconnect the wiring

plug from the valve **(see illustration)**.
39   Unscrew the two securing bolts, and withdraw the valve from the inlet manifold **(see illustration)**. Recover the gasket.
40   Check the valve vent holes for contamination, and clean if necessary **(see illustration)**.
41   Refitting is a reversal of removal. Thoroughly clean the mating faces of the valve and manifold, then refit the valve using a new gasket.

Exhaust gas recirculation control module - renewal

42   The module is located on a bracket mounted on the front left-hand wing panel.
43   Disconnect the battery negative lead, then disconnect the wiring plug from the module **(see illustration)**.
44   Remove the two securing bolts, and withdraw the module from its mounting bracket.
45   Refitting is a reversal of removal.

Chapter 5 Part A:
Starting and charging systems

Contents

5A

Specifications

General

Electrical system type.. 12-volt negative earth

Battery

Type... Lead-acid, "maintenance-free" (sealed for life)
Battery capacity... 36, 44, 55 or 60 Ah (depending on model)

Alternator

Type... Bosch or Delco-Remy
Maximum output.. 55, 70 or 100 amps (depending on model)
Regulated voltage.. 13.7 to 14.7 volts (approximately)
Brush minimum length:
    Delco-Remy 55-amp type .... 12.0 mm
    Delco-Remy 70- and 100-amp types.. 20.0 mm
    Bosch type .... 5.0 mm

Starter motor

Type... Pre-engaged, Delco-Remy or Valeo
Brush minimum length:
    Delco-Remy (except code number 09 000 756) .... 4.0 mm
    Delco-Remy (code number 09 000 756) .... 8.5 mm
    Valeo type.. 13.0 mm

Torque wrench settings

	Nm	lbf ft
Alternator mounting bracket-to-engine bolts (M10)	40	30
Alternator-to-mounting bracket bolts (M10)	40	30
Alternator-to-mounting bracket bolts (M8)	30	22
Alternator-to-adjuster bracket bolts (models with V-belt)	25	18
Alternator adjuster bracket -to-cylinder head bolts (models with V-belt)	25	18
Alternator (auxiliary) drivebelt tensioner roller-to-engine bolt (models with ribbed belt)	20	15
Starter motor bolts	25	18

1   General information and precautions

General information

The engine electrical system includes all charging, starting and ignition system components and engine oil sensors. Because of their engine-related functions, these components are covered separately from the body electrical devices such as the lights, instruments, etc (which are covered in Chapter 12).

The electrical system is of the 12-volt negative earth type.

The battery is of the "maintenance-free" (sealed for life) type, and is charged by the alternator, which is belt-driven from a crankshaft-mounted pulley.

The starter motor is of the pre-engaged type, incorporating an integral solenoid. On starting, the solenoid moves the drive pinion into engagement with the flywheel ring gear before the starter motor is energised. Once the engine has started, a one-way clutch prevents the motor armature being driven by the engine until the pinion disengages from the flywheel.

The ignition systems are covered in Parts B and C of this Chapter.

Further details of the various systems are given in the relevant Sections of this Chapter. While some repair procedures are given, the usual course of action is to renew the component concerned. The owner whose interest extends beyond mere component renewal should obtain a copy of the *"Automobile Electrical & Electronic Systems Manual"*, available from the publishers of this manual.

Precautions

It is necessary to take extra care when working on the electrical system, to avoid damage to semi-conductor devices (diodes and transistors), and to avoid the risk of personal injury. In addition to the precautions given in *"Safety first!"* at the beginning of this manual, observe the following when working on the system:

Always remove rings, watches, etc before working on the electrical system. Even with the battery disconnected, capacitive discharge could occur if a component's live terminal is earthed through a metal object. This could cause a shock or nasty burn.

Do not reverse the battery connections. Components such as the alternator, ignition system components, or any other components having semi-conductor circuitry, could be irreparably damaged.

If the engine is being started using jump leads and a slave battery, connect the batteries as shown in the preliminary section of this manual (see *"Booster battery (jump) starting"*). This also applies when connecting a battery charger.

Never disconnect the battery terminals, the alternator, any electrical wiring, or any test instruments, when the engine is running.

Do not allow the engine to turn the alternator when the alternator is not connected.

Never "test" for alternator output by "flashing" the output lead to earth.

Never use an ohmmeter of the type incorporating a hand-cranked generator for circuit or continuity testing.

Always ensure that the battery negative lead is disconnected when working on the electrical system.

Before using electric arc-welding equipment on the vehicle, disconnect the battery, alternator and components such as electronic

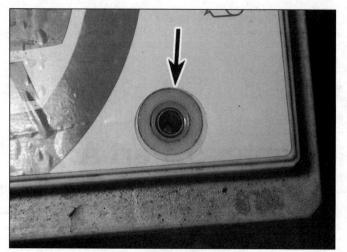

3.2 Battery condition indicator (arrowed)

control units, to protect them from the risk of damage.

The radio/cassette unit fitted as standard equipment by Vauxhall/Opel is equipped with a built-in security code, to deter thieves. If the power source to the unit is cut, the anti-theft system will activate. Even if the power source is immediately reconnected, the radio/cassette unit will not function until the correct security code has been entered. Therefore, if you do not know the correct security code for the radio/cassette unit, **do not** disconnect the battery negative lead or remove the radio/cassette unit from the vehicle. Refer to the *"Radio/cassette unit anti-theft system - precaution"* section at the beginning of this manual for details of how to enter the security code.

Refer to the precautions given in Chapter 4A, Section 1, when working on models equipped with a catalytic converter.

2   Electrical fault finding - general information

Refer to Chapter 12.

3   Battery - testing and charging

Note: *The following information refers only to the maintenance-free type battery fitted as original equipment.*

1 Topping-up and testing of the electrolyte in each battery cell is not possible. The condition of the battery can therefore only be tested by observing the battery condition indicator.

2 The battery condition indicator is located in the top of the battery casing, and indicates the condition of the battery by its colour **(see illustration)**. If the indicator shows green, then the battery is in a good state of charge. If the indicator turns darker, eventually to black, then the battery requires charging, as described later in this Section. If the indicator shows clear/yellow, then the electrolyte level in the battery is

4.4 Unscrewing the battery clamp bolt

too low to allow further use, and the battery should be renewed. **Do not** attempt to charge, load or jump-start a battery when the indicator shows clear/yellow.

3   If the battery is to be charged, remove it from the vehicle, as described in Section 4, and charge it as follows.

4   The maintenance-free type battery takes considerably longer to fully recharge than the standard type, the time taken being dependent on the extent of discharge.

5   A constant-voltage type charger is required; connect it up and set it to 13.9 to 14.9 volts, with a charge current below 25 amps.

6   If the battery is to be charged from a fully-discharged state (less than 12.2 volts output), have it recharged by a Vauxhall/Opel dealer or a competent automotive electrician, as the charge rate is high, and constant supervision during charging is necessary.

---

4   Battery - removal and refitting

Note: *Refer to the precautions in Section 1 before starting work. In particular, ensure that the security code for the radio/cassette unit is known before disconnecting the battery.*

Removal

1   The battery is located on the left-hand side of the engine compartment, towards the rear.

2   Disconnect the lead(s) at the negative (earth) terminal by unscrewing the retaining nut and removing the terminal clamp.

3   Disconnect the positive terminal lead(s) in the same way.

4   Unscrew the clamp bolt sufficiently to enable the battery to be lifted from its location **(see illustration)**. Keep the battery upright.

Refitting

5   Refitting is a reversal of removal, but smear petroleum jelly on the terminals when reconnecting the leads, and always reconnect the positive lead first, and the negative lead last.

---

5   Charging system - testing

Note: *Refer to the precautions given in "Safety first!" and in Section 1 of this Chapter before starting work.*

1   If the ignition/no-charge warning light fails to illuminate when the ignition is switched on, first check the alternator wiring connections for security. If satisfactory, check that the warning light bulb has not blown, and that the bulbholder is secure in its location in the instrument panel. If the light still fails to illuminate, check the continuity of the warning light feed wire from the alternator to the bulbholder. If all is

satisfactory, the alternator is at fault, and should be renewed, or taken to an auto-electrician for testing and repair.

2   If the ignition warning light illuminates when the engine is running, stop the engine and check that the drivebelt is correctly tensioned (see Chapter 1) and that the alternator connections are secure. If all is so far satisfactory, check the alternator brushes and slip rings (see Section 7). If the fault persists, the alternator should be renewed, or taken to an auto-electrician for testing and repair.

3   If the alternator output is suspect even though the warning light functions correctly, the regulated voltage may be checked as follows.

4   Connect a voltmeter across the battery terminals, and start the engine.

5   Increase the engine speed until the voltmeter reading remains steady; the reading should be approximately 12 to 13 volts, and no more than 14 volts.

6   Switch on as many electrical accessories (eg, the headlights, heated rear window and heater blower) as possible, and check that the alternator maintains the regulated voltage at around 13.5 to 14.5 volts.

7   If the regulated voltage is not as stated, the fault may be due to worn brushes, weak brush springs, a faulty voltage regulator, a faulty diode, a severed phase winding, or worn or damaged slip rings. The brushes and slip rings may be checked (see Section 7), but if the fault persists, the alternator should be renewed, or taken to an auto-electrician for testing and repair.

---

6   Alternator - removal and refitting

SOHC engines with "V-belt" alternator drive

Removal

1   Disconnect the battery negative lead.

2   Remove the auxiliary drivebelt as described in Chapter 1.

3   Disconnect the wires from their terminals on the rear of the alternator, noting their locations, or disconnect the wiring plug, as applicable. Note that on certain models, access to the alternator wiring may be easier from underneath the vehicle.

4   On models with multi-point fuel injection, remove the throttle body as described in Chapter 4A.

5   Unscrew the bolt securing the top of the alternator to the adjuster strut, and recover any washers and insulating bushes, noting their locations. Note the earth strap attached to the bolt.

6   Loosen the bolt securing the adjuster strut to the inlet manifold, and pivot the strut upwards to leave sufficient space to remove the alternator.

7   Support the alternator, then remove the nut and through-bolt securing the alternator to the engine bracket. Again, recover any washers and insulating bushes, noting their locations.

8   Withdraw the alternator from the engine.

Refitting

9   Refitting is a reversal of removal, bearing in mind the following points:

    (a)   *Ensure that all washers and insulating bushes are refitted in their correct locations, as noted before removal.*

    (b)   *Ensure that the earth lead is refitted to the top alternator securing bolt.*

    (c)   *Where applicable, refit the throttle body as described in Chapter 4A.*

    (d)   *Refit and tension the auxiliary drivebelt as described in Chapter 1.*

SOHC engines with "ribbed belt" alternator drive

Removal

10   Proceed as described in paragraphs 1 to 3 inclusive.

11   Remove the nut and through-bolt securing the alternator to the lower bracket. Recover any washers and insulating bushes, noting their locations.

5A

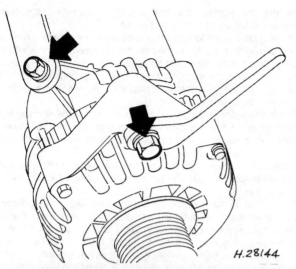

H.28144

6.12 Unbolt the two upper alternator mounting brackets (arrowed) - SOHC engines with "ribbed belt" alternator drive

6.18 Unbolt the crankshaft speed/position sensor bracket from the oil pump. Securing bolt arrowed

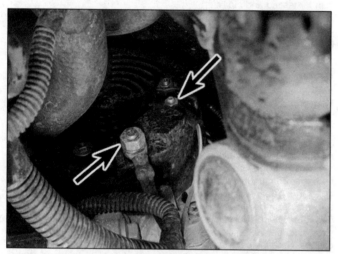

6.20 Alternator wiring securing nuts (arrowed) - DOHC engine (viewed from underneath vehicle)

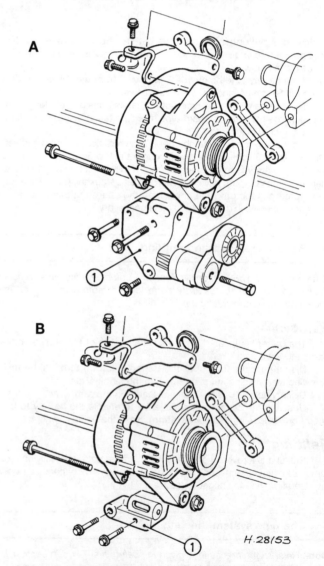

H.28153

6.24 Unbolt the alternator lower mounting bracket from the cylinder block - DOHC engine

A　Models without power steering or air conditioning
B　Models with power steering and/or air conditioning
1　Alternator lower mounting bracket

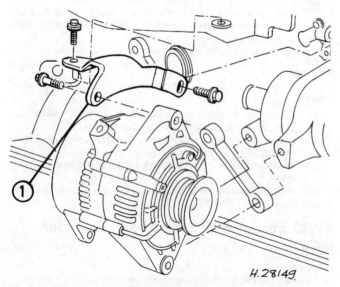

H.28149

6.22 Remove the upper alternator mounting bracket (1) - DOHC engine

7.1 Exploded view of "standard" Bosch alternator

1   Pulley nut
2   Pulley
3   Fan
4   Drive end housing
5   Bearing
6   Bearing retainer
7   Through-bolts
8   Brush holder/voltage regulator assembly
9   Slip ring end housing
10 Stator endplate
11 Stator
12 Bearing
13 Rotor

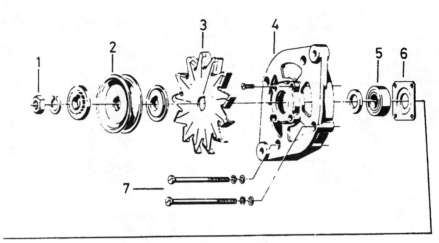

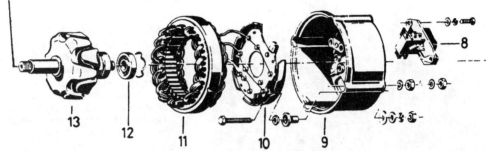

12   Support the alternator, then unbolt the two upper mounting brackets from the alternator, cylinder head and inlet manifold, and withdraw the brackets **(see illustration)**. Again, recover any washers and insulating bushes, noting their locations. Note the earth strap attached to the front mounting bracket bolts.

13   Withdraw the alternator from the engine.

Refitting

14   Refitting is a reversal of removal, bearing in mind the following points:

(a)   Ensure that any washers and insulating bushes are refitted in their correct locations, as noted before removal.

(b)   Ensure that the earth lead is refitted to the front mounting bracket.

(c)   Do not fully tighten any of the mounting bolts until the alternator and all mounting brackets are in position.

(d)   Refit and tension the auxiliary drivebelt as described in Chapter 1.

DOHC engine

Removal

15   Disconnect the battery negative lead.

16   Remove the auxiliary drivebelt as described in Chapter 1.

17   Apply the handbrake, then jack up the front of the vehicle and support securely on axle stands (see "Jacking, towing and wheel changing"). Remove the right-hand front roadwheel.

18   Unbolt the crankshaft speed/position sensor bracket from the oil pump, and move the bracket/sensor assembly to one side (take care not to damage the sensor or the wiring) **(see illustration)**.

19   Disconnect the wiring from the oil pressure switch, located in the end of the oil pump.

20   Disconnect the wires from their terminals on the rear of the alternator, noting their locations, or disconnect the wiring plug, as applicable **(see illustration)**.

21   Disconnect the outer end of the driveshaft from the front swivel hub assembly, as described in Chapter 8. There is no need to withdraw the driveshaft from the transmission. Support the end of the driveshaft using wire or string - do not allow the driveshaft to hang down under its own weight, or the joint may be damaged.

22   Unscrew the three securing bolts and remove the upper alternator mounting bracket **(see illustration)**. Note the location of the earth strap secured by the mounting bracket bolts.

23   Remove the nut and through-bolt securing the alternator to the lower mounting bracket. Recover any washers and insulating bushes, noting their locations.

24   Support the alternator, and unbolt the lower mounting bracket from the cylinder block **(see illustration)**. Withdraw the lower mounting bracket to allow sufficient clearance to remove the alternator.

25   Manipulate the driveshaft as necessary to allow sufficient clearance for the alternator to pass out through the wheel arch, then withdraw the alternator.

Refitting

26   Refitting is a reversal of removal, bearing in mind the following points:

(a)   Refit the nut and through-bolt securing the alternator to the lower mounting bracket before bolting the mounting bracket to the cylinder block. Ensure that any washers and insulating bushes are positioned as noted before removal.

(b)   Ensure that the earth strap is in position when refitting the upper alternator mounting bracket.

(c)   Reconnect the driveshaft to the front swivel hub assembly as described in Chapter 8.

(d)   Refit and tension the auxiliary drivebelt as described in Chapter 1.

5A

7   Alternator brushes and regulator - inspection and renewal

"Standard" Bosch alternator

1   The brush holder and voltage regulator are combined in a single assembly, which is bolted to the rear of the alternator **(see illustration)**. If the voltage regulator is faulty, the complete assembly must be renewed.

2   Disconnect the battery negative lead.

3   If desired, to improve access further, the alternator can be

7.4a Remove the securing screws . . .

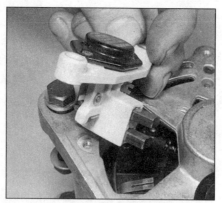

**7.4b . . . and withdraw the brush
holder/voltage regulator -
"standard" Bosch alternator**

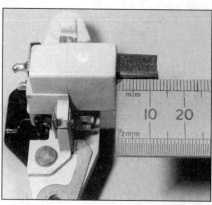

**7.5 Measuring the length of an alternator
brush - "standard" Bosch alternator**

7.10 Alternator slip rings (arrowed) - "standard" Bosch alternator

removed, as described in Section 6.

4   Remove the two securing screws, and withdraw the brush holder/voltage regulator assembly **(see illustrations)**.

5   Check that the brushes move freely in their guides, and that the brush lengths are within the limits given in the Specifications **(see illustration)**. If any doubt exists regarding the condition of the brushes, the best policy is to renew them as follows.

6   Hold the brush wire with a suitable pair of pliers, and unsolder it from the brush holder. Lift away the brush. Repeat for the remaining brush.

7   Note that whenever new brushes are fitted, new brush springs should also be fitted.

8   With the new springs fitted to the brush holder, insert the new brushes, and check that they move freely in their guides. If they bind, polish them lightly with a very fine file or glass paper.

**7.14 Exploded view of "compact"
Bosch alternator**

1   Pulley nut
2   Washer
3   Pulley
4   Bolt
5   Spacer
6   Drive end housing
7   Bearing
8   Bearing cover
9   Rotor
10 Bearing
11 Dust cover
12 Through-bolt
13 Plastic cover
14 Bolt
15 Voltage regulator/
    brush holder
16 Bolt
17 Nut
18 Through-bolt
19 Rectifier
20 Slip ring end housing
21 Bush
22 Stator

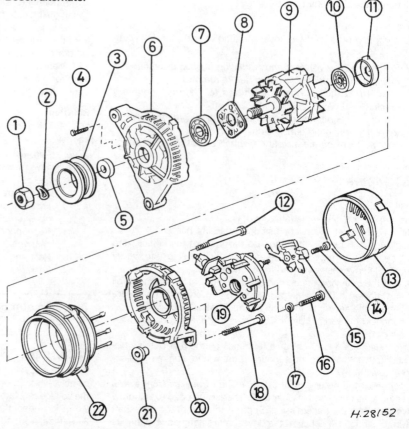

H.28152

7.15a Unscrew the securing nuts . . .

7.15b . . . and withdraw the plastic cover
- "compact" Bosch alternator

7.16a Removing the securing screws . . .

9   Solder the brush wire ends to the brush holder, taking care not to allow solder to pass to the stranded wire.
10   Check the condition of the slip rings, and if necessary clean them with a rag or very fine glass paper (see illustration).
11   Refit the brush holder/voltage regulator assembly, and tighten the securing screws.
12   If the alternator was removed, refit it as described in Section 6.
13   Reconnect the battery negative lead.

7.16b . . . and withdraw the brush holder/voltage regulator -
"compact" Bosch alternator

"Compact" Bosch alternator

14   The brush holder and voltage regulator are combined as a single assembly (see illustration). With the alternator removed as described in Section 6, proceed as follows.
15   Remove the three securing nuts, and withdraw the plastic cover from the rear of the alternator (see illustrations). Note that it is possible that the studs may be withdrawn as the nuts are unscrewed - in this case, the studs can be refitted using two nuts locked together on the studs.
16   Remove the two securing screws, and withdraw the brush holder/voltage regulator assembly from the rear of the alternator (see illustrations).
17   Check that the brushes move freely in their guides, and that the brush lengths are within the limits given in the Specifications. If any doubt exists regarding the condition of the brushes, the complete brush holder/voltage regulator assembly must be renewed.
18   Refitting is a reversal of removal.
19   Refit the alternator as described in Section 6.

"Standard" Delco-Remy alternator

Note: *No spare parts are available for Delco-Remy alternators marked "Made in Korea".*
20   The brush holder and voltage regulator are combined in a single assembly (see illustration). For access to the assembly, the alternator

5A

7.20 Exploded view of "standard" Delco-Remy alternator

1   Pulley nut (not fitted to all models)
2   Pulley
3   Fan
4   Drive end housing
5   Bearing
6   Bearing retainer
7   Rotor
8   Through-bolt
9   Slip ring end housing
10   Brush holder/voltage regulator assembly
11   Diode assembly
12   Stator

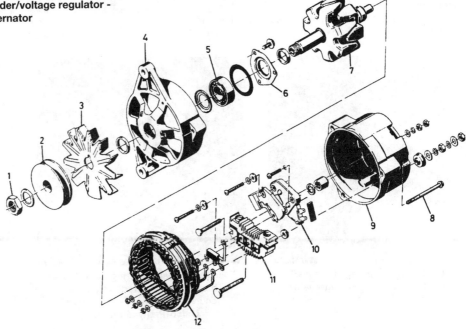

must be partially dismantled as follows. If the voltage regulator is faulty, the complete assembly must be renewed.

21   Remove the alternator as described in Section 6.

22   Scribe a line across the drive end housing and the slip ring end housing, to ensure correct alignment when reassembling.

23   Unscrew the three through-bolts, and prise the drive end housing and rotor away from the slip ring end housing and stator **(see illustration)**.

24   Check the condition of the slip rings, and if necessary clean them with a rag or very fine glass paper **(see illustration)**.

25   Remove the three nuts and washers securing the stator leads to the rectifier, and lift away the stator assembly **(see illustration)**.

26   Remove the terminal screw, and lift out the diode assembly.

27   Extract the two screws securing the brush holder and voltage regulator to the slip ring end housing, and remove the brush holder assembly. Note the insulation washers under the screw heads.

28   Check that the brushes move freely in their guides, and that the brush lengths are within the limits given in the Specifications. If any doubt exists regarding the condition of the brushes, the best policy is to renew them.

29   To fit new brushes, unsolder the old brush leads from the brush holder, and solder on the new leads in exactly the same place.

30   Check that the new brushes move freely in the guides.

31   Before refitting the brush holder assembly, retain the brushes in the retracted position using a stiff piece of wire or a twist drill.

32   Refit the brush holder assembly so that the wire or drill protrudes through the slot in the slip ring end housing, and tighten the securing screws.

33   Refit the diode assembly and the stator assembly to the housing, ensuring that the stator leads are in their correct positions, and refit the terminal screw and nuts.

34   Assemble the drive end housing and rotor to the slip ring end housing, ensuring that the previously-made marks are still aligned. Insert and tighten the three through-bolts.

35   Pull the wire or drill (as applicable) from the slot in the slip ring end housing, so that the brushes rest on the rotor slip rings **(see illustration)**.

36   Refit the alternator as described in Section 6.

"Compact" Delco-Remy alternator

37   With the alternator removed as described in Section 6, proceed as follows **(see illustration)**.

38   Unscrew the securing nuts, and remove the plastic cover from the rear of the alternator.

39   Unscrew the two brush holder securing screws, noting their different lengths. Note that one of the screws also secures the suppressor **(see illustration)**.

40   Unscrew the remaining suppressor securing nut, and lift the suppressor from the rear of the alternator.

7.23 Separating the drive end housing from the slip ring end housing - "standard" Delco-Remy alternator

41   Using a small screwdriver, or a similar tool, prise up the securing tag at the side of the brush holder, then lift the assembly from the rear of the alternator **(see illustration)**.

42   Check that the brushes move freely in their guides, and that the brush lengths are within the limits given in the Specifications. If any doubt exists regarding the condition of the brushes, the best policy is to renew them. If the brushes are renewed, it is wise to renew the brush springs at the same time.

43   To fit new brushes, unsolder the old brush leads from the brush holder, and solder on the new leads in exactly the same place.

44   Check that the new brushes move freely in the guides.

45   Refitting is a reversal of removal.

46   Refit the alternator as described in Section 6.

8   Starting system - testing

Note: *Refer to the precautions given in "Safety first!" and in Section 1 of this Chapter before starting work.*

1   If the starter motor fails to operate when the ignition key is turned to the appropriate position, the possible causes are as follows:

(a)   *The battery is faulty.*

(b)   *The electrical connections between the switch, solenoid, battery and starter motor are somewhere failing to pass the necessary current from the battery through the starter to earth.*

7.24 Alternator slip rings (arrowed) - "standard" Delco-Remy alternator

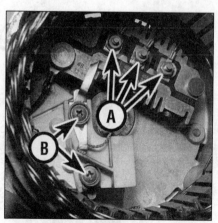

7.25 Stator lead securing nuts (A) and brush holder/voltage regulator securing screws (B) - "standard" Delco-Remy alternator

7.35 Removing the drill bit used to hold brushes in retracted position - "standard" Delco-Remy alternator

7.37 Sectional view of "compact" Delco-Remy alternator

1 *Drive end housing*
2 *Stator*
3 *Rotor*
4 *Slip rings*
5 *Fan*
6 *Rectifier*

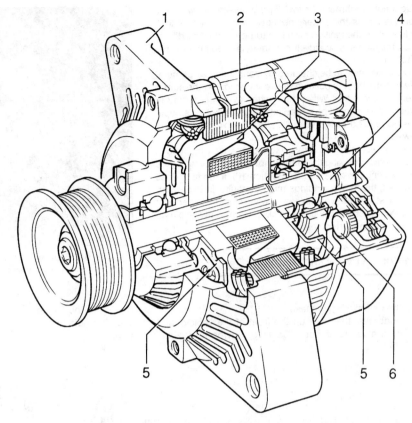

(c) *The solenoid is faulty.*
(d) *The starter motor is mechanically or electrically defective.*

2   To check the battery, switch on the headlights. If they dim after a few seconds, this indicates that the battery is discharged - recharge (see Section 3) or renew the battery. If the headlights glow brightly, operate the starter switch while watching the headlights. If they dim, then this indicates that current is reaching the starter motor, therefore the fault must lie in the starter motor. If the lights continue to glow brightly (and no clicking sound can be heard from the starter motor solenoid), this indicates that there is a fault in the circuit or solenoid - see the following paragraphs. If the starter motor turns slowly when operated, but the battery is in good condition, then this indicates either that the starter motor is faulty, or there is considerable resistance somewhere in the circuit.

3   If a fault in the circuit is suspected, disconnect the battery leads (including the earth connection to the body), the starter/solenoid wiring and the engine/transmission earth strap. Thoroughly clean the connections, and reconnect the leads and wiring. Use a voltmeter or test light to check that full battery voltage is available at the battery positive lead connection to the solenoid. Smear petroleum jelly around the battery terminals to prevent corrosion - corroded connections are among the most frequent causes of electrical system faults.

4   If the battery and all connections are in good condition, check the circuit by disconnecting the switched feed wire from the solenoid (the

5A

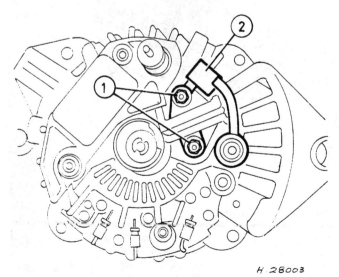

H 28003

7.39 Brush holder securing screws (1) and suppressor (2) - "compact" Delco-Remy alternator

H28004

7.41 Withdraw the brush holder (1) by after releasing the securing tag (2) - "compact" Delco-Remy alternator

thinner wire). Connect a voltmeter or test light between the wire end and a good earth (such as the battery negative terminal), and check that the wire is live when the ignition switch is turned to the "start" position. If it is, then the circuit is sound - if not, there is a fault in the ignition/starter switch or wiring.

5   The solenoid contacts can be checked by connecting a voltmeter or test light between the battery positive feed connection on the starter side of the solenoid, and earth. When the ignition switch is turned to the "start" position, there should be a reading or lighted bulb, as applicable. If there is no reading or lighted bulb, the solenoid is faulty and should be renewed.

6   If the circuit and solenoid are proved sound, the fault must lie in the starter motor. Begin checking the starter motor by removing it (see Section 9), and checking the brushes (see Section 10). If the fault does not lie in the brushes, the motor windings must be faulty. In this event, the starter motor must be renewed, unless an auto-electrical specialist can be found who will overhaul the unit at a cost significantly less than that of a new or exchange starter motor.

9   Starter motor - removal and refitting

Removal

1   Disconnect the battery negative lead.

2   Apply the handbrake, then jack up the front of the vehicle, and support securely on axle stands (see *"Jacking, towing and wheel changing"*).

9.3 Starter motor wiring securing nut (arrowed) - viewed from underneath vehicle

3   Note the wiring connections on the solenoid, then unscrew the securing nuts (where applicable) and disconnect them **(see illustration)**.

4   Where applicable, unscrew nut securing the earth cable to the

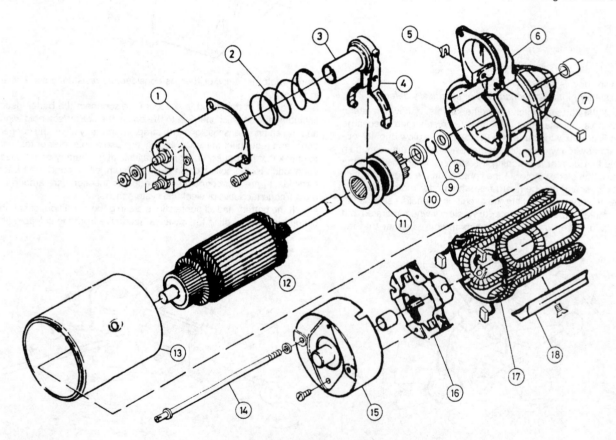

10.1 Exploded view of Delco-Remy type starter motor

1	Solenoid yolk	7	Actuating arm pivot pin	13	Main motor casing
2	Solenoid return spring	8	Shim	14	Through-bolt
3	Solenoid armature	9	C-clip	15	Commutator end housing
4	Actuating arm	10	Thrust collar	16	Brush plate
5	Pivot pin clip	11	Drive pinion and clutch assembly	17	Field coils
6	Drive end housing	12	Armature	18	Permanent magnet

10.3 Unscrew the through-bolts . . .

10.4 . . . and extract the two small screws
- Delco-Remy type starter motor

10.5 Lift the brush plate from the
commutator - Delco-Remy
type starter motor

10.17 Removing the rear cover - Valeo
type starter motor

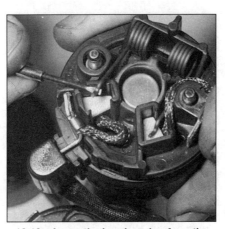

10.18a Lever the brush spring from the
brush plate . . .

10.18b . . . and recover the insulator
plates - Valeo type starter motor

5A

upper starter motor mounting stud. Recover the washer, and disconnect the cable from the stud.

5   Unscrew the starter motor mounting stud and bolt, or the two bolts, as applicable, and withdraw the motor from under the vehicle.

Refitting

6   Refitting is a reversal of removal, but where applicable, ensure that the earth cable is reconnected to the stud.

10 Starter motor - brush renewal

Delco-Remy starter motor

1   With the starter motor removed from the vehicle as described in Section 9 and cleaned, grip the unit in a vice fitted with soft jaw protectors **(see illustration)**.

2   Make alignment marks between the main motor casing and the commutator end housing.

3   Unscrew and remove the two through-bolts which hold the components of the starter motor assembly together **(see illustration)**.

4   Extract the two small screws which secure the commutator end housing to the brush plate, then lift off the commutator end housing **(see illustration)**.

5   Lift the brush retaining springs to remove the field brushes from the brush holders, then lift the brush plate from the commutator **(see illustration)**.

6   Remove the remaining springs and brushes from the brush holder.

7   If the brushes have worn to less than the specified minimum

length, renew them as a set. To renew the brushes, the leads must be unsoldered from their terminals, and the new brushes must be soldered in place.

8   Clean the brush holder assembly, and wipe the commutator with a petrol-moistened cloth. If the commutator is dirty, it may be cleaned with fine glass paper, then wiped with the cloth.

9   Check that the brush retaining springs provide adequate pressure on the brushes to maintain good contact with the commutator. Renew any worn springs.

10   Refit the brushes to the brush holder, and refit the retaining springs. To aid refitting of the brush holder assembly, the brushes can be retained in position using a socket or suitable tube of approximately 38.0 mm diameter.

11   Slide the brush holder over the commutator, and where applicable, withdraw the socket or tube.

12   Fit the commutator end housing, ensuring that the marks made on the end housing and the main motor casing are aligned.

13   Fit the two screws securing the end housing to the brush plate.

14   Refit and tighten the two through-bolts.

15   Refit the starter motor as described in Section 9.

Valeo starter motor

16   With the starter motor removed from the vehicle as described in Section 9 and cleaned, proceed as follows.

17   Unscrew the two securing nuts, and withdraw the rear cover from the starter motor **(see illustration)**.

18   Using a suitable screwdriver, lever the brush spring from the brush plate. Recover the insulator plates from under the ends of the spring **(see illustrations)**.

10.19a Lift the negative brush terminal from the stud . . .

10.19b . . . and the positive brush terminal (arrowed) from the insulator - Valeo type starter motor

10.20 Lifting a brush from the brush plate - Valeo type starter motor

10.23 Remove the brush plate to enable cleaning of the commutator (arrowed) - Valeo type starter motor

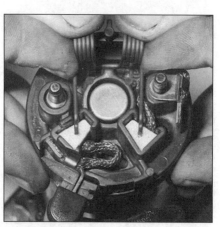

10.27 Refitting the brush spring - Valeo type starter motor

12.1 Oil pressure warning light switch location (arrowed)

19 Lift the negative brush wiring terminal from the stud on the brush plate, and lift the positive brush terminal from the insulator in the motor body **(see illustrations)**.
20 Lift the brushes from the brush plate. Note the locations of the brushes to ensure correct reassembly **(see illustration)**.
21 If the brushes have worn to less than the minimum specified length, they must be renewed.
22 If the positive brush is to be renewed, it must be unsoldered from the terminal on the solenoid wiring.
23 If desired, the brush plate can be lifted from the motor to enable the commutator to be cleaned **(see illustration)**. Clean the brush plate assembly, and wipe the commutator with a petrol-moistened cloth. If the commutator is very dirty, it may be cleaned with fine glass paper, then wiped with the cloth.
24 Check that the brush retaining spring provides adequate pressure on the brushes to maintain good contact with the commutator. Renew the spring if it is worn.
25 Commence refitting by refitting the brush plate (where applicable), and placing the brushes in position in the brush plate.
26 Locate the negative brush wiring terminal over the stud on the brush plate, and locate the positive brush terminal in the insulator in the motor body.
27 Fit the insulator plates to the ends of the brushes, then fit the brush spring **(see illustration)**.
28 Ensure that the insulator is in place in the wiring grommet cut-out in the motor rear cover, then refit the cover to the motor.
29 Refit the rear cover securing nuts.
30 Refit the starter motor as described in Section 9.

11 Ignition switch - removal and refitting

The switch is integral with the steering column lock, and removal and refitting is described in Section 18 of Chapter 10.

12 Oil pressure warning light switch - removal and refitting

Removal

1 The switch is screwed into the end of the oil pump, on the inlet manifold side of the engine **(see illustration)**. Access is most easily obtained from underneath the vehicle.
2 Disconnect the battery negative lead.
3 Disconnect the wiring from the switch.
4 Place a suitable container under the switch, to catch the oil which will be released as the switch is removed.
5 Using a suitable spanner, unscrew the switch. Be prepared for oil spillage, and plug the hole in the oil pump immediately, to minimise oil loss and prevent dirt ingress.

Refitting

6 Refitting is a reversal of removal. On completion, check and if necessary top-up the engine oil level as described in Chapter 1.

Chapter 5 Part B:
Multec MSTS-h ignition system

Contents

Specifications

General

System application*	12 NZ, C12 NZ and C 14 NZ (SOHC) engines
Location of No 1 cylinder	Timing belt end of engine
Firing order	1-3-4-2
Direction of distributor rotor arm rotation	Anti-clockwise (viewed from cap)

*For details of engine code locations, see "Buying spare parts and vehicle identification numbers".

Ignition timing (at idle speed, without vacuum)

All engines	10°BTDC

Ignition coil

Primary winding resistance	$0.45 \pm 0.05 \ \Omega$
Secondary winding resistance	$6000 \pm 1000 \ \Omega$

Torque wrench setting

	Nm	lbf ft
Spark plugs	25	18

1   General information and precautions

General information

Ignition system function

The ignition system is responsible for igniting the air/fuel mixture in each cylinder at the correct moment, in relation to engine speed and load.

The ignition system is based on feeding low-tension voltage from the battery to the coil, where it is converted into high-tension voltage. The high-tension voltage is powerful enough to jump the spark plug gap in the cylinders many times a second under high compression pressures, providing that the system is in good condition.

The low-tension (or primary) circuit consists of the following:

(a) *The battery.*
(b) *The lead to the ignition switch.*
(c) *The lead from the ignition switch to the low-tension coil windings.*
(d) *The lead to the supply terminals on the electronic control unit and the amplifier module.*
(e) *The amplifier module.*
(f) *The lead from the low-tension coil windings to the control terminal on the amplifier module.*
(g) *The lead from the electronic control unit to the amplifier module.*

The high-tension (or secondary) circuit consists of the following:

(a) *The high-tension (HT) coil windings.*
(b) *The HT lead from the coil to the distributor cap.*
(c) *The rotor arm.*
(d) *The HT leads to the spark plugs.*
(e) *The spark plugs.*

The system functions in the following manner. Current flowing through the low-tension coil windings produces a magnetic field around the high-tension windings. The electronic control unit produces a signal (amplified by the amplifier module) used to switch off the low-tension circuit.

The subsequent collapse of the magnetic field over the high-tension windings produces a high-tension voltage, which is then fed to the relevant spark plug, via the distributor cap and rotor arm. The low-tension circuit is automatically switched on again by the electronic control unit, to allow the magnetic field to build up again before the firing of the next spark plug. The ignition is advanced and retarded automatically, to ensure that the spark occurs at the correct instant in relation to the engine speed and load.

Multec MSTS-h (Microprocessor-controlled Spark Timing System - Hall effect)

This system is fitted to models with the 12 NZ, C 12 NZ, and C 14 NZ engines (see *"Buying spare parts and vehicle identification numbers"* for details of engine code locations).

The system is under the overall control of the Multec electronic control unit, which controls both the ignition and fuel injection systems. The system comprises a "Hall-effect" distributor, various sensors (whose inputs also provide data to control the fuel injection system), and the Multec electronic control unit, in addition to the amplifier module, coil, and spark plugs. Details of the system sensors and the electronic control unit are given in Chapter 4A (single-point fuel injection).

A "Hall-effect" sensor in the distributor provides the signal used to switch off the low-tension circuit. This signal is modified by the electronic control unit, in order to control the degree of ignition advance, according to information received from the other system sensors.

Engine load information is supplied to the Multec electronic control unit via inputs from the various system sensors (primarily the manifold absolute pressure (MAP) sensor and throttle position sensor - see Chapter 4A).

The electronic control unit selects the optimum ignition advance setting, based on the information received from the sensors. The degree of advance can thus be constantly varied to suit the prevailing engine operating conditions.

Precautions

Refer to the precautions given in Chapter 4A, Section 1 when carrying out work on models equipped with a catalytic converter.

Refer to the precautions to be observed when working on models fitted with an electronic control unit, given in Chapter 4A, Section 1.
Warning: *The HT voltage generated by an electronic ignition system is extremely high and, in certain circumstances, could prove fatal. Take care to avoid receiving electric shocks from the HT side of the ignition system. Do not handle HT leads, or touch the distributor or coil, when the engine is running. If tracing faults in the HT circuit, use well-insulated tools to manipulate live leads. Persons with surgically-implanted cardiac pacemaker devices should keep well clear of the ignition circuits, components and test equipment.*

2   Ignition system - testing

General

1   The components of the electronic ignition system are normally very reliable; most faults are far more likely to be due to loose or dirty connections or to "tracking" of HT voltage due to dirt, dampness or damaged insulation, than to the failure of any of the system components. **Always** check all wiring thoroughly before condemning an electrical component, and work methodically to eliminate all other possibilities before deciding that a particular component is faulty.
2   The practice of checking for a spark by holding the live end of an HT lead a short distance away from the engine is **not** recommended - not only is there a high risk of a powerful electric shock, but the coil, amplifier module, or electronic control unit may be damaged.
3   Extreme care should be taken when testing the system, as the electronic control unit is very sensitive, and if damaged, it may prove very costly to renew.
4   If in any doubt as to test procedures, or if the correct equipment is not available, entrust testing and fault diagnosis to a Vauxhall/Opel dealer. It is far better to pay the labour charges involved in having the vehicle checked by someone suitably qualified, than to risk damage to the system or yourself. The engine management system has a self-diagnostic function, and any problems with the system are stored as fault codes, which can be read using suitable specialist diagnostic equipment. Brief details are given in Chapter 4A.

Engine fails to start

5   If the engine either will not turn over at all, or only turns over very slowly, check the battery and starter motor. Connect a voltmeter across the battery terminals (meter positive probe to battery positive terminal), disconnect the ignition coil HT lead from the distributor cap and earth it, then note the voltage reading obtained while turning over the engine on the starter for around ten seconds (no more). If the reading obtained is less than approximately 8 volts, check the battery, starter motor and charging system (see Chapter 5A).
6   If the engine turns over at normal speed, but will not start, check the HT circuit by connecting a timing light (following the equipment manufacturer's instructions) and turning the engine over on the starter motor; if the light flashes, voltage is reaching the spark plugs, so these should be checked first. If the light does not flash, check the HT leads themselves, followed by the distributor cap, carbon brush and rotor arm (see Section 3). Additionally, use an ohmmeter or continuity tester to check that there is no continuity between any of the distributor cap contacts. Similarly, check that there is no continuity between the rotor arm body and its metal contact - note that the arm has a built-in resistance.
7   If the HT circuit appears to be sound, check the voltage at the ignition coil "+" terminal (black wires), which should be the same as the battery voltage (ie, at least 11.5 volts). If the voltage at the coil is significantly (more than 1.0 volt) less than that at the battery, it is likely that there is a fault in the feed to the coil. Note that the electronic control unit controls the coil feed. **Do not** attempt to "test" the electronic control unit with anything other than the appropriate test equipment, which will be available only at a suitably-equipped Vauxhall/Opel dealer. If

3.4 Removing the distributor cap

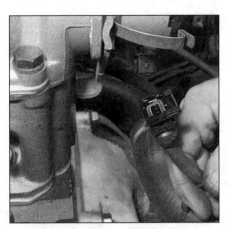

3.5 Disconnecting the distributor wiring plug

3.6 Distributor alignment mark on camshaft housing

any of the wires are to be checked which run to the electronic control unit (although this is not recommended without the correct test equipment), always unplug the relevant connector from the control unit (with the ignition switched off) first, so that there is no risk of the unit being damaged by the application of incorrect voltages from the test equipment.

8   If the feed to the coil is sound, check the coil itself, as described in Section 4.

9   If the relevant components have no obvious faults, such as dirty or loose connections, damp, or "tracking", and have been tested as far as possible, the vehicle must be taken to a Vauxhall/Opel dealer for testing using the appropriate equipment.

Engine misfires

10   Misfires are usually the result of partial or temporary failures in the system components, and the possible causes are too numerous to be eliminated without the use of special test equipment. The ignition system components can be checked for signs of obvious faults as described in the following paragraphs, but if these checks do not reveal the source of the problem, take the vehicle to a Vauxhall/Opel dealer, who will be able to test the full engine management system using the appropriate equipment.

11   An irregular misfire suggests either a loose/dirty connection or intermittent fault in the primary circuit, or an HT fault somewhere between the coil and the rotor arm.

12   With the ignition switched off, check carefully through the system, ensuring that all connections are clean and securely fastened. Check the feed to the coil, with reference to paragraph 7, and check the coil, as described in Section 4.

13   Regular misfiring is almost certainly due to a fault in the distributor cap, HT leads or spark plugs. Use a timing light (see paragraph 6) to check whether HT voltage is present at all leads.

14   Check that the coil, the distributor cap and the HT leads are clean and dry. Check the leads themselves and the spark plugs (by substitution if necessary - refer to Chapter 1 for details), then check the distributor cap, carbon brush and rotor arm (see Section 3).

15   If HT voltage is not present on any particular lead, the fault will be in that lead or in the distributor cap. If HT voltage is present on all leads, the fault will be in the spark plugs; check and renew them if there is any doubt about their condition.

3   Distributor - removal, overhaul and refitting

Removal

1   Disconnect the battery negative lead.

2   If necessary, identify each HT lead for position to aid correct refitting, then disconnect the leads from the spark plugs by pulling on the connectors, not on the leads. Similarly, disconnect the HT lead from

the coil. Pull the leads from the clips on the camshaft cover.

3   Note that various types of distributor may be fitted, depending on model.

4   Loosen the securing screws, or release the securing clips using a screwdriver, as applicable, and remove the distributor cap, complete with HT leads, from the distributor **(see illustration)**.

5   Disconnect the distributor wiring plug **(see illustration)**.

6   If the original distributor is to be refitted, check to see if there are alignment marks on the distributor body and camshaft housing **(see illustration)**. If no marks are present, make suitable marks so that the distributor can be refitted in its original position.

7   Using a suitable socket or spanner on the crankshaft pulley bolt, or by engaging top gear (manual gearbox models) and pushing the vehicle backwards or forwards as necessary (with the handbrake released!), turn the crankshaft to bring No 1 piston to the firing point. Turning the engine will be much easier if all the spark plugs are removed first (see Chapter 1). No 1 piston is at the firing point when the following conditions are met:

(a)   The timing pointer on the rear timing belt cover is aligned with the notch in the crankshaft pulley.

(b)   The tip of the rotor arm is pointing to the position occupied by the No 1 cylinder HT lead terminal in the distributor cap.

(c)   The rotor arm is aligned with the notch in the distributor body (remove the rotor arm and plastic shield, then refit the rotor arm to check the alignment with the notch), or the TDC arrow stamped on the distributor body, as applicable **(see illustrations)**.

3.7a Remove the plastic shield . . .

5B

3.7b ... and check that the rotor arm is aligned with notch in the distributor body

3.7c Rotor arm aligned with TDC arrow stamped on distributor body - alternative distributor type

3.8a Removing the clamp plate ...

3.8b ... and withdrawing the distributor

8   Unscrew the clamp nut and remove the clamp plate, then withdraw the distributor from the camshaft housing (see illustrations).

Overhaul

9   Check the distributor cap for corrosion of the segments, and for signs of tracking, indicated by a thin black line between the segments. Make sure that the carbon brush in the centre of the cap moves freely, and stands proud of the surface of the cap. Renew the cap if necessary.

10   If the metal portion of the rotor arm is badly burnt or loose, renew it. If slightly burnt or corroded, it may be cleaned with a fine file.

11   Examine the seal ring at the rear of the distributor body, and renew if necessary.

12   If desired, the plastic drive collar at the rear of the distributor can be renewed after driving out the securing roll pin (see illustration). Otherwise, no spare parts are available for the distributors, and if faulty, the complete unit must be renewed.

Refitting

13   Commence refitting by checking that No 1 cylinder is still at the firing point (see paragraph 7). The relevant timing marks should be aligned. If the engine has been turned whilst the distributor has been removed, check that No 1 cylinder is on its firing stroke by removing No 1 cylinder spark plug (if not already done) and placing a finger over the plug hole. Turn the crankshaft until compression can be felt, which indicates that No 1 piston is rising on its compression stroke. Continue turning the crankshaft until the relevant timing marks are in alignment.

14   Turn the rotor arm to the position noted in paragraph 7c, and hold the rotor arm in this position as the distributor is fitted, noting that the distributor driveshaft will only engage with the camshaft in one position. If the original distributor is being refitted, align the marks made on the distributor body and camshaft housing before removal.

15   Refit the clamp plate, and tighten the nut.

16   Remove the rotor arm, then refit the plastic shield and the rotor arm.

17   Reconnect the distributor wiring plug.

18   Refit the distributor cap, ensuring that the HT leads are correctly reconnected.

19   Reconnect the battery negative lead.

20   On completion, the ignition timing should ideally be checked by a Vauxhall/Opel dealer, using the appropriate test equipment.

4   Ignition coil - testing, removal and refitting

Testing

1   The coil is mounted on the left-hand side of the engine compartment, in front of the suspension turret.

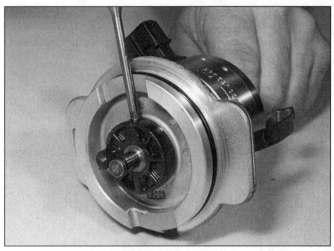

3.12 Driving out the distributor drive collar roll pin

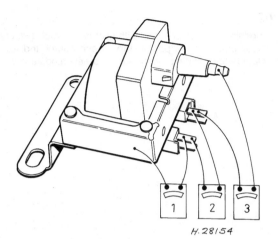

H.28154

4.3 Testing the ignition coil using an ohmmeter

1   *Checking for a short-circuit to earth*
2   *Checking the primary windings*
3   *Checking the secondary windings*

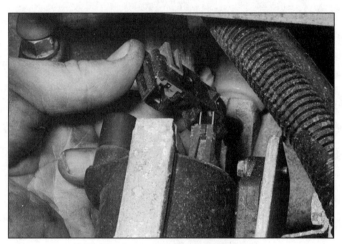

4.10 Disconnecting the coil wiring plug

4.12 Coil mounting details

1   *Coil mounting bracket securing bolt*
2   *Coil securing nuts*
3   *Suppressor*

2   Disconnect the battery negative lead, then disconnect the wiring plug and the HT lead from the coil.
3   Connect an ohmmeter between one of the LT terminals and the coil body, and check that there is no continuity (the ohmmeter should indicate infinity) **(see illustration)**. If there is continuity, the coil should be renewed.
4   Connect an ohmmeter between the coil LT terminals, and check that the resistance of the primary windings is within the specified limits.
5   Connect the ohmmeter between the HT terminal and one of the LT terminals, and check that the resistance of the secondary windings is within the specified limits.
6   If the readings are not as specified, the coil should be renewed.
7   Reconnect the coil wiring and the battery negative lead on completion.

Removal

8   Disconnect the battery negative lead.
9   Disconnect the HT lead from the coil.
10   Disconnect the coil wiring plug **(see illustration)**.
11   Disconnect the wiring plug from the ignition amplifier module mounted under the coil.
12   Unscrew the two coil mounting bracket securing bolts, and withdraw the coil, complete with the amplifier module and mounting plate **(see illustration)**. Note that on certain models fitted with power steering, one of the coil securing bolts also secures the power steering fluid reservoir bracket.

13   Unscrew the two securing nuts, and separate the coil from the mounting bracket/amplifier module mounting plate assembly. Note the location of the coil suppressor, which may be secured by one of the coil securing nuts on certain models.

Refitting

14   Refitting is a reversal of removal, ensuring that (where applicable) the coil suppressor is in position before fitting the coil securing bolts.

---

5   Ignition amplifier module - removal and refitting

Removal

1   The amplifier module is located on a bracket under the ignition coil.
2   Remove the ignition coil and amplifier module mounting bracket, as described in Section 4.
3   The module can be removed from the mounting plate after removing the two securing screws. Note that a heat-sink compound may be applied between the module and the mounting plate to improve heat dissipation.

Refitting

4   If the module was originally fitted with heat-sink compound, clean off the old compound, and apply suitable fresh compound to the mounting plate before refitting the module. If a new module is being fitted, it should be supplied with suitable heat-sink compound. Similar compounds can be purchased from DIY electrical shops.

5   Refit the coil mounting plate and coil assembly, as described in Section 4.

Chapter 5 Part C:
Multec DIS (Distributorless Ignition System)

Contents

Specifications

General

System application*	X 12 SZ and C 14 SE (SOHC) engines, and C 16 XE (DOHC) engine
Location of No 1 cylinder	Timing belt end of engine
Firing order	1-3-4-2

For details of engine code locations, see "Buying spare parts and vehicle identification numbers".

Ignition timing (at idle speed, without vacuum)**

X 12 SZ (SOHC) engine	10°BTDC
C 14 SE (SOHC) engine	5°BTDC
C 16 XE (DOHC) engine	Not specified

**For reference only - controlled by electronic control module, no adjustment possible.*

DIS module

Primary winding resistance	$0.56 \pm 0.05 \, \Omega$
Secondary winding resistance	$6000 \, \Omega$ approx.

Torque wrench settings

	Nm	lbf ft
DIS module bolts	7	5
Knock sensor	13	10
Spark plugs	25	18

5C

1 General information and precautions

General information

Ignition system function

The ignition system is responsible for igniting the air/fuel mixture in each cylinder at the correct moment, in relation to engine speed and load.

The ignition system is based on feeding low-tension voltage from the battery to the coil, where it is converted into high-tension voltage. The high-tension voltage is powerful enough to jump the spark plug gap in the cylinders many times a second under high compression pressures, providing that the system is in good condition.

The low-tension (or primary) circuit consists of the following:

(a) The battery.
(b) The lead to the ignition switch.
(c) The leads from the ignition switch to the DIS module, to the electronic control unit, and to the low-tension coil windings (integral with the DIS module).

The high-tension (or secondary) circuit consists of the following:

(a) The high-tension (HT) coil windings (integral with the DIS module).
(b) The HT leads from the DIS module to the spark plugs.
(c) The spark plugs.

The system functions in the following manner. Current flowing through the low-tension coil windings produces a magnetic field around the high-tension windings. The electronic control unit produces a signal used to switch off the low-tension circuit.

The subsequent collapse of the magnetic field over the high-tension windings produces a high-tension voltage, which is then fed directly from the coil to the relevant spark plugs. The low-tension circuit is automatically switched on again by the electronic control unit, to allow the magnetic field to build up again before the firing of the next pair of spark plugs. The ignition is advanced and retarded automatically, to ensure that the spark occurs at the correct instant in relation to the engine speed and load.

Multec DIS (Distributorless Ignition System)

This system is fitted to models with the X 12 SZ, C 14 SE and C 16 XE engines(see *"Buying spare parts and vehicle identification numbers"* for details of engine code locations).

The system is under the overall control of the Multec electronic control unit, which controls both the ignition and fuel injection systems. The system comprises various sensors (whose inputs also provide data to control the fuel injection system), and the Multec electronic control unit, in addition to the DIS module and spark plugs. Details of the system sensors and the electronic control unit are given in Chapter 4A.

The DIS module is attached to the camshaft housing in the position normally occupied by the distributor, and consists of two ignition coils and an electronic control module, housed in a common casing. Each ignition coil supplies two spark plugs with HT voltage - thus, one spark is provided in a cylinder with its piston on the compression stroke, and one in a cylinder with its piston on the exhaust stroke. This results in a "wasted spark" being supplied to one cylinder during each ignition cycle, but this has no detrimental effect. This system has the advantage that there are no moving parts - therefore there is no wear, and the system is largely maintenance-free.

Information on crankshaft position and engine speed and load is supplied to the Multec electronic control unit via inputs from the various system sensors (see Chapter 4A).

The electronic control unit selects the optimum ignition advance setting based on the information received from the various sensors. The degree of advance can thus be constantly varied to suit the prevailing engine operating conditions.

Precautions

Refer to the precautions given in Chapter 4A, Section 1 when carrying out work on models equipped with a catalytic converter.

Refer to the precautions to be observed when working on models fitted with an electronic control unit, given in Chapter 4A, Section 1.
Warning: *The HT voltage generated by an electronic ignition system is extremely high and, in certain circumstances, could prove fatal. Take care to avoid receiving electric shocks from the HT side of the ignition system. Do not handle HT leads, or touch the DIS module, when the engine is running. If tracing faults in the HT circuit, use well-insulated tools to manipulate live leads. Persons with surgically-implanted cardiac pacemaker devices should keep well clear of the ignition circuits, components and test equipment.*

2   Ignition system - testing

General

1   The components of the DIS system are normally very reliable; most faults are far more likely to be due to loose or dirty connections, or to "tracking" of HT voltage due to dirt, dampness or damaged insulation, than to the failure of any of the system components. **Always** check all wiring thoroughly before condemning an electrical component, and work methodically to eliminate all other possibilities before deciding that a particular component is faulty.

2   The practice of checking for a spark by holding the live end of an HT lead a short distance away from the engine is **not** recommended -

3.4 Disconnecting the DIS module wiring plug - SOHC engine

not only is there a high risk of a powerful electric shock, but the DIS module or electronic control unit may be damaged.

3   Extreme care should be taken if attempts are to be made to test the system, as the electronic control unit is very sensitive, and if damaged, it may prove very costly to renew.

4   Unless the correct special test equipment is available, entrust testing and fault diagnosis to a Vauxhall/Opel dealer. It is far better to pay the labour charges involved in having the vehicle checked by someone suitably qualified, than to risk damage to the system or yourself. The engine management system has a self-diagnostic function, and any problems with the system are stored as fault codes, which can be read using suitable specialist diagnostic equipment. Brief details are given in Chapter 4A.

Engine fails to start

5   If the engine either will not turn over at all, or only turns over very slowly, check the battery and starter motor. Connect a voltmeter across the battery terminals (meter positive probe to battery positive terminal). Disconnect the wiring plug from the DIS module, then note the voltage reading obtained while turning over the engine on the starter for around ten seconds (no more). If the reading obtained is less than approximately 8 volts, check the battery, starter motor and charging system (see Chapter 5A).

6   Testing of the ignition LT and HT circuits can only be carried out safely and effectively using special test equipment, and should be entrusted to a Vauxhall/Opel dealer.

Engine misfires

7   Misfires are usually the result of partial or temporary failures in the system components, and the possible causes are too numerous to be eliminated without the use of special test equipment. The ignition system wiring and the spark plugs can be checked for signs of obvious faults as described in the following paragraphs, but if these checks do not reveal the source of the problem, take the vehicle to a Vauxhall/Opel dealer, who will be able to test the full engine management system using the appropriate equipment.

8   An irregular misfire suggests a loose or dirty connection. With the ignition switched off, check the security and condition of the DIS module wiring, and the HT leads.

9   Regular misfiring is most likely to be due to a fault in the HT leads or spark plugs. Check that the HT leads are clean and dry. Check the leads themselves and the spark plugs (by substitution if necessary). Renew the spark plugs as a matter of course, if there is any doubt about their condition (refer to Chapter 1 for details of checking spark plugs).

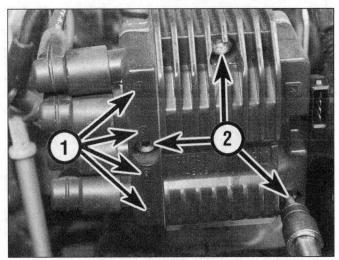

3.5 HT lead cylinder number identification marks (1) and DIS module securing screws (2)

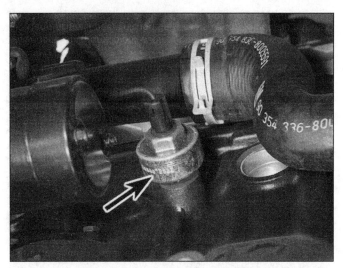

5.1 Knock sensor location (arrowed) - X 12 SZ engine (viewed from underneath vehicle)

3   DIS module - testing, removal and refitting

Testing

1   Testing of the DIS module can only be carried out safely, and without the risk of damage to the module, using the appropriate special test equipment. Testing should therefore be entrusted to a Vauxhall/Opel dealer.

Removal

2   The DIS module is mounted on the left-hand end of the camshaft housing.
3   Disconnect the battery negative lead.
4   Disconnect the module wiring plug **(see illustration)**.
5   Disconnect the HT leads from the module, noting their locations to ensure correct refitting. The HT lead cylinder numbers are stamped into the module casing **(see illustration)**.
6   Unscrew the three Torx type securing screws, and remove the module from its mounting plate.

Refitting

7   Refitting is a reversal of removal.

4   Knock control system (X 12 SZ and C 16 XE engines) - general information

Note: *For details of engine code locations, refer to "Buying spare parts and vehicle identification numbers".*

The knock control system forms part of the ignition system, and allows the ignition timing to be advanced to the point at which "knocking" or "pre-ignition" is about to occur. This contributes to improved engine efficiency and reduced exhaust emission levels, as it allows the engine to run as close as possible to the "knock limit" (the point at which "pre-ignition" or "pinking" occurs) without the risk of engine damage. The ignition timing is set to a pre-determined value (stored in the memory of the electronic control unit), which is very close to the knock limit for the engine. Due to slight changes in the combustion process during varying engine operating conditions, and possible slight fuel irregularities, engine knock may occur, and this is detected and controlled by the knock control system.

The system comprises a knock sensor, a knock module, and the Multec engine management electronic control unit (see Chapter 4A).

The knock sensor is located on the cylinder block, and contains a piezoelectric crystal, which has a resonance frequency which corresponds to the engine knock frequency. Mechanical vibrations in the cylinder block are converted by the sensor into an electrical signal. The output signal provided by the sensor increases with an increase in the vibrations in the cylinder block. If the signal increases beyond a preset limit, the sensor indicates the onset of "knock" to the knock module.

The knock module acts as a signal processor, and modifies the signal produced by the sensor before providing an output to the electronic control module.

The electronic control module processes the signals received from the knock module, and retards the ignition timing to prevent knock. From the signals provided by other engine management sensors (see Chapter 4A), the control unit can determine the cylinder which fired most recently before the knocking occurred, and hence can trace the knocking to that particular cylinder. The ignition timing for the particular cylinder concerned is thus retarded ("selective knock control"), giving independent ignition timing control over all four cylinders. Once knocking has been detected and prevented, the ignition timing is progressively advanced to the pre-determined value, or until knocking recurs. The system processes signals many times per second, and is able to react to changes sufficiently quickly to prevent engine damage, with no perceptible effect on engine performance.

If the system develops a fault, the ignition timing is automatically retarded by 5 degrees as a safety precaution, and this may be detected as a slight reduction in engine performance.

On models with the C 16 XE engine, the knock module is integral with the Multec electronic control unit.

5   Knock control system components (X 12 SZ and C 16 XE engines) - removal and refitting

Knock sensor

Note: *When refitting the sensor, to ensure correct operation, it is essential to tighten the sensor to the specified torque. Vauxhall/Opel specify the use of tool KM-728 to achieve this. If this tool is not available, it will be necessary to obtain or improvise a suitable alternative.*

Removal

1   The sensor is located at the rear of the engine, below the inlet manifold, between cylinders 2 and 3 **(see illustration)**.
2   Disconnect the battery negative lead.
3   Access is most easily obtained from underneath the vehicle. Apply the handbrake, then jack up the front of the vehicle and support securely on axle stands (see *"Jacking, towing and wheel changing"*).

5C

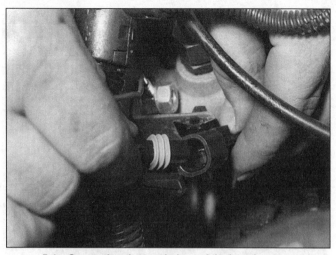

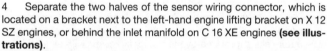

5.4a Separating the two halves of the knock sensor wiring connector - X 12 SZ engine

5.4b Knock sensor wiring connector location - C 16 XE engine

4   Separate the two halves of the sensor wiring connector, which is located on a bracket next to the left-hand engine lifting bracket on X 12 SZ engines, or behind the inlet manifold on C 16 XE engines **(see illustrations)**.
5   Unbolt the sensor from the cylinder block, using a suitable slotted socket or an open-ended spanner.

Refitting

6   Refitting is a reversal of removal, but ensure that the sensor is tightened to the specified torque, bearing in mind the note at the beginning of this Section.

Knock control system module (X 12 SZ engine)

Removal

7   The module is located on a bracket attached to the left-hand side of the engine compartment, in front of the suspension strut turret.
8   Disconnect the battery negative lead.
9   Disconnect the module wiring plug **(see illustration)**.
10   Remove the two securing screws, and withdraw the module from its bracket.

Refitting

11   Refitting is a reversal of removal.

5.9 Disconnecting the wiring plug from the knock control system module - X 12 SZ engine

Chapter 6 Clutch

Contents

6

Specifications

General

Type	Single dry plate, cable-operated

Clutch disc

Diameter:

SOHC engines	190.0 mm
DOHC engine	200.0 mm
Lining thickness (new - all models)	3.5 mm

Torque wrench settings

	Nm	lbf ft
Clutch bellhousing cover plate bolts	7	5
Input shaft socket-headed screw	15	11
Clutch cover-to-flywheel bolts	15	11
Clutch release fork-to-pivot shaft bolt	35	26
Gearbox endplate bolts:		
M7 bolts	15	11
M8 bolts	20	15

2.1 Unbolt the ignition coil bracket from the body panel for improved access to the clutch cable

2.2 Measuring the length of protruding threaded rod at the end of the clutch cable

2.3 Remove the clip (1) from the threaded rod, slide the threaded rod (2) from the release arm, and pull the assembly from the lug (3)

1 General information

All manual gearbox models are fitted with a single dry plate clutch, which consists of five main components; friction disc, pressure plate, diaphragm spring, cover and release bearing.

The friction disc is free to slide along the splines of the gearbox input shaft, and is held in position between the flywheel and the pressure plate by the pressure exerted on the pressure plate by the diaphragm spring. Friction lining material is riveted to both sides of the friction disc, and spring cushioning between the friction linings and the hub absorbs transmission shocks, and helps to ensure a smooth take-up of power as the clutch is engaged.

The diaphragm spring is mounted on pins, and is held in place in the cover by annular fulcrum rings.

The release bearing is located on a guide sleeve at the front of the gearbox. The bearing is free to slide on the sleeve, under the action of the release arm, which pivots inside the clutch bellhousing.

The release arm is operated by the clutch pedal, via a cable. As wear takes place on the friction disc over a period of time, the clutch pedal will rise progressively, relative to its original position. No periodic adjustment of the clutch cable is specified by the manufacturers.

When the clutch pedal is depressed, the release arm is actuated by means of the cable. The release arm pushes the release bearing forwards, to bear against the centre of the diaphragm spring, thus pushing the centre of the diaphragm spring inwards. The diaphragm spring acts against the fulcrum rings in the cover. As the centre of the spring is pushed in, the outside of the spring is pushed out, so allowing the pressure plate to move backwards away from the friction disc.

When the clutch pedal is released, the diaphragm spring forces the pressure plate into contact with the friction linings on the friction disc, and simultaneously pushes the friction disc forwards on its splines, forcing it against the flywheel. The friction disc is now firmly sandwiched between the pressure plate and the flywheel, and drive is taken up.

On certain SOHC engine models, the clutch assembly, release bearing and guide sleeve oil seal can be renewed without removing the engine or gearbox from the vehicle.

2 Clutch cable - removal and refitting

Removal

1 If desired, to improve access to the clutch cable at the gearbox end, the bracket securing the electronic modules/ignition coil can be unbolted from the side of the engine compartment **(see illustration)**.

2 Working in the engine compartment, measure the length of the threaded rod protruding through the plastic block at the release arm end of the cable **(see illustration)**. This will enable approximate presetting of the cable when refitting.

3 Remove the clip from the threaded rod at the release arm, then slide the rod from the release arm **(see illustration)**. Push the release arm towards the engine; if necessary, slacken the cable adjuster to aid removal.

4 Pull the cable assembly from the lug on the clutch bellhousing.

5 Unhook the return spring from the clutch pedal, and disconnect the cable end from the pedal. Note that the end of the return spring retains the cable end in the pedal. Access is limited, and it may prove easier to remove the clutch pedal, as described in Section 3, before disconnecting the cable.

6 The cable assembly can now be withdrawn into the engine compartment, by pulling it through the bulkhead. Take care not to damage the bulkhead grommet as the cable is withdrawn. Unclip the cable from any support brackets, and take note of the cable routing to aid refitting.

Refitting

7 Refitting is a reversal of removal, bearing in mind the following points:

(a) Ensure that the cable is routed as noted before removal.
(b) Position the threaded rod so that the length of thread protruding through the plastic block is as noted before removal, then adjust the cable as described in Chapter 1.
(c) Ensure that the bulkhead grommet is correctly seated.

3 Clutch pedal - removal and refitting

Removal

1 Proceed as described in paragraphs 1 to 4 in the previous Section. Then, working in the driver's footwell, remove the locking clip from the right-hand end of the clutch pedal pivot shaft, then unscrew the pedal retaining nut and recover the washer(s).

2 Push the pivot shaft out of the pedal bracket (to the left), then lower the pedal and return spring. Note the position of any washers and/or spacers on the pivot shaft, so that they can be refitted in their original positions.

3 Disconnect the cable end from the pedal by releasing the return spring, and withdraw the pedal and return spring from the vehicle **(see illustrations)**.

Refitting

4 Refitting is a reversal of removal, but before inserting the pedal pivot shaft, smear the surface with a little molybdenum disulphide grease.

5 On completion, adjust the clutch cable if necessary, as described in Chapter 1.

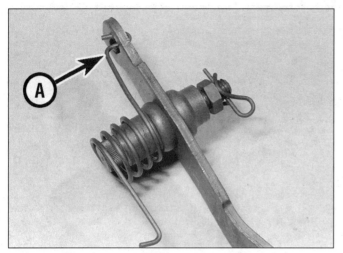

3.3a Clutch pedal components assembled as when in place in vehicle. Clutch cable is retained by return spring at "A"

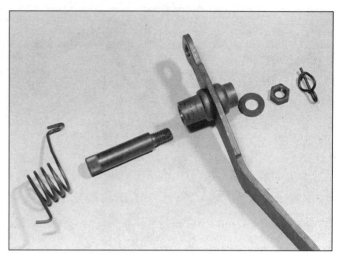

3.3b Clutch pedal pivot components

4.5 Removing the gearbox endplate

4.7 Extract the circlip (arrowed) from the end of the gearbox input shaft

4.8 Unscrew the screw from the end of the input shaft

4   Clutch assembly - removal, inspection and refitting

Warning: *Dust created by clutch wear (which gets deposited on the clutch components) may contain asbestos, which is a health hazard. DO NOT blow it out with compressed air, or inhale any of it. DO NOT use petrol (or petroleum-based solvents) to clean off the dust. Brake system cleaner or methylated spirit should be used to flush the dust into a suitable receptacle. After the clutch components are wiped clean with rags, dispose of the contaminated rags and cleaner in a sealed, marked container.*

Note: *On models fitted with a "standard" flywheel, the clutch can be removed and refitted without removing the engine or the gearbox, provided certain special tools can be obtained or improvised. C 14 SE SOHC and all DOHC engines are fitted with a "pot" flywheel during production, and this practice may be adopted on other models in the future. The "pot" flywheel is significantly thicker than the "standard" item, and the clutch assembly is recessed into the flywheel. Consequently there is insufficient clearance between the flywheel and the clutch bellhousing to enable the clutch to be removed with the engine and gearbox in the vehicle. On SOHC engines, before attempting to remove the clutch, remove the clutch bellhousing cover plate and examine the flywheel to ascertain which type is fitted, then proceed as follows, according to flywheel type.*

Models with "standard" flywheel

Note: *The manufacturers recommend the use of special tools for this procedure, although suitable alternatives can be improvised as described in the text. It is suggested that this Section is read thoroughly*

before work commences, in order that suitable tools can be made available as required. The circlip in the end of the input shaft, and the gearbox endplate gasket, should be renewed on reassembly. If the special tools required cannot be obtained or improvised, the clutch can be removed as described later in this Section for models with a "pot" flywheel, after removing the gearbox.

Removal

1   Where applicable, remove the left-hand front wheel trim, then loosen the roadwheel bolts. Apply the handbrake, jack up the front of the vehicle, and support securely on axle stands (see *"Jacking, towing and wheel changing"*). Remove the roadwheel for improved access.

2   Unscrew the securing bolts, and remove the cover plate from the base of the clutch bellhousing.

3   For improved access, remove the wheel arch liner, as described in Chapter 11, Section 22.

4   Where applicable, unscrew the retaining nut, and disconnect the earth strap from the gearbox endplate.

5   Place a suitable container beneath the gearbox endplate, to catch the oil which will be released, then unscrew the securing bolts and remove the endplate **(see illustration)**. Note the location of the bolts (including the stud for the earth strap, where applicable), as two different lengths are used.

6   Recover the gasket.

7   Extract the circlip from inside the end of the gearbox input shaft, using a pair of circlip pliers **(see illustration)**.

8   Using a twelve-point splined key, unscrew the screw from the end of the input shaft **(see illustration)**.

6

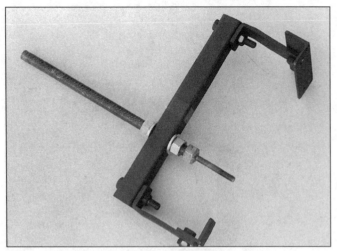

4.9a Improvised tool for disengaging gearbox input shaft from clutch

4.9b Disengaging the input shaft from the clutch using the improvised tool

9   The input shaft can now be pulled out of engagement with the splined hub of the clutch friction disc. The manufacturers specify the use of special tools for this operation (tool Nos KM-556-A and KM-556-4), but an alternative can be improvised as shown **(see illustrations)**. The tool bolts into place on the end of the gearbox, using the endplate securing bolts. Tool dimensions will vary according to gearbox type.

10   Alternatively, screw an M7 bolt into the end of the input shaft, and use the bolt to pull the shaft out to its stop. It is likely that the input shaft will be a very tight fit, in which case it may prove difficult to withdraw, without using the special tool previously described. In extreme cases, a slide hammer can be attached to the end of the shaft to enable it to be withdrawn - although this is not recommended, as damage to the gearbox components may result.

11   Before the clutch assembly can be removed, the pressure plate must be compressed against the tension of the diaphragm spring, otherwise the assembly will be too thick to be withdrawn through the space between the flywheel and the edge of the bellhousing.

12   Three special clamps are available from the manufacturers for this purpose (tool No KM-526-A), but suitable alternatives can be made up from strips of metal 3 mm thick. The clamps should be U-shaped, and made to the dimensions shown **(see illustration)**. Bevel the edges of the clamps to ease fitting, and cut a slot in one of the U-legs to clear the pressure plate rivets.

13   Have an assistant depress the clutch pedal fully, then fit each clamp securely over the edge of the cover/pressure plate, engaging the clamps in the apertures around the rim of the cover **(see illustrations)**. Turn the crankshaft using a suitable socket or spanner on the crankshaft pulley/sprocket bolt, to bring each clamp location into view.

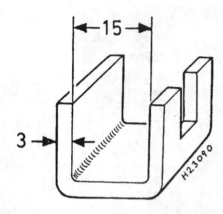

4.12 Clutch pressure plate retaining clamp dimensions - in mm

14   Once the clamps have been fitted, have the assistant release the clutch pedal.

15   Progressively loosen and remove the six bolts and spring washers which secure the clutch cover to the flywheel. As before when fitting the clamps, turn the crankshaft to bring each bolt into view. Where applicable (and if the original clutch is to be refitted), note the position of the mark on the flywheel which aligns with the notch in the rim of the clutch cover **(see illustrations)**.

16   The clutch assembly can now be withdrawn downwards from the

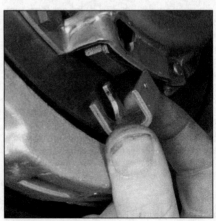

4.13a Fitting a suitable clamp . . .

4.13b . . . to compress the clutch pressure plate prior to removal

4.15a Loosening a clutch cover-to-flywheel bolt

4.15b Stamped mark on flywheel (arrowed) aligned with notch in clutch cover

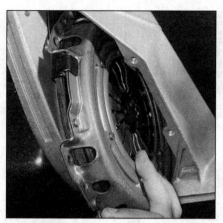

4.16 Withdrawing the clutch assembly from the bellhousing

4.25 Using the improvised tool to engage the input shaft with the clutch friction disc

bellhousing (see illustration). Be prepared to catch the clutch friction disc, which may drop out of the cover as it is withdrawn, and note which way round the friction disc is fitted. The greater-projecting side of the hub faces away from the flywheel.

17   In order to remove the clamps, the pressure plate can be compressed against the tension of the diaphragm spring in a vice fitted with soft jaw protectors.

Inspection

18   With the clutch assembly removed, clean off all traces of dust using a dry cloth. Although most friction discs now have asbestos-free linings, some do not, and it is wise to take suitable precautions; *asbestos dust is harmful, and must not be inhaled.*

19   Examine the linings of the clutch disc for wear and loose rivets, and the disc for distortion, cracks, broken torsion springs and worn splines. The surface of the friction linings may be highly glazed, but, as long as the friction material pattern can be clearly seen, this is satisfactory. If there is any sign of oil contamination, indicated by a continuous, or patchy, shiny black discolouration, the disc must be renewed. The source of the contamination must be traced and rectified before fitting new clutch components; typically, a leaking crankshaft oil seal or gearbox input shaft oil seal - or both - will be to blame (renewal procedures are given in Chapters 2A and 7A respectively). The disc must also be renewed if the lining thickness has worn down to, or just above, the level of the rivet heads.

20   Check the machined faces of the flywheel and pressure plate. If either is grooved, or heavily scored, renewal is necessary. The pressure plate must also be renewed if any cracks are apparent, or if the diaphragm spring is damaged, or its pressure suspect.

21   With the clutch removed, it is advisable to check the condition of the release bearing, as described in Section 5.

Refitting

22   Some replacement clutch assemblies are supplied with the pressure plate already compressed using the three clamps described in paragraph 12. If this is not the case, the pressure plate should first be compressed against the tension of the diaphragm spring. Use a vice fitted with soft jaw protectors, and fit the clamps used during removal.

23   It is important to ensure that no oil or grease gets onto the friction disc linings, or the pressure plate and flywheel faces. It is advisable to refit the clutch assembly with clean hands, and to wipe down the pressure plate and flywheel faces with a clean rag before assembly begins.

24   Apply a smear of molybdenum disulphide grease to the splines of the friction disc hub, then offer the disc to the flywheel, with the greater-projecting side of the hub facing away from the flywheel. Hold the friction disc against the flywheel while the cover/pressure plate assembly is offered into position.

25   The input shaft must now be pushed through the hub of the friction disc, until its end engages in the end of the crankshaft. **Under no circumstances** must the shaft be hammered home, as gearbox

damage may result. If the input shaft cannot be pushed home by hand, steady pressure should be exerted on the end of the shaft. The manufacturers specify the use of a special tool for this operation (tool No KM-564), but the improvised tool used to withdraw the shaft during the removal procedure can be used by repositioning the nut as shown (see illustration).

26   With the input shaft pushed fully home, position the cover/pressure plate assembly so that the mark on the flywheel is in alignment with the notch on the rim of the clutch cover, then refit and progressively tighten the six clutch cover-to-flywheel bolts (ensuring that the spring washers are fitted) in a diagonal sequence. Turn the crankshaft, using a suitable socket or spanner on the crankshaft pulley/sprocket bolt, to gain access to each bolt in turn, and finally tighten all the bolts to the specified torque.

27   Have an assistant depress the clutch pedal, then remove the three clamps from the edge of the cover/pressure plate, again turning the crankshaft for access to each clamp.

28   Once the clamps have been removed, have the assistant release the clutch pedal.

29   Refit and tighten the gearbox input shaft screw to the specified torque, then fit a new circlip.

30   Using a new gasket, refit the gearbox endplate, and tighten the securing bolts to the specified torque. Where applicable, ensure that the studded bolt which retains the earth strap is fitted to its correct location, as noted during removal.

31   Where applicable, reconnect the gearbox earth strap, and fit the retaining nut.

32   Refit the cover plate to the base of the clutch bellhousing, and tighten the securing bolts. Where applicable, refit the wheel arch liner.

33   Refit the roadwheel, then lower the vehicle to the ground and finally tighten the roadwheel bolts. Refit the wheel trim, where applicable.

34   Check the clutch cable adjustment, as described in Chapter 1.

35   Check and if necessary top-up the gearbox oil level, as described in Chapter 1.

Models with "pot" flywheel

Removal

36   Due to the size of the "pot" flywheel, there is insufficient space for the clutch to be withdrawn through the aperture in the clutch bellhousing, as described previously for models with a "standard" flywheel.

37   Unless the complete engine/gearbox assembly is to be removed from the vehicle and separated for major overhaul (see Chapter 2B), access to the clutch can be obtained by removing either the gearbox (Chapter 7A) or the engine (Chapter 2B).

38   With the engine or gearbox removed, proceed as follows.

39   Where applicable (and if the original clutch is to be refitted), note the position of the mark on the flywheel which aligns with the notch in the rim of the clutch cover, then progressively unscrew the six bolts and spring washers which secure the clutch cover to the flywheel (see

6

4.39 Unscrew the clutch cover securing bolts - note alignment marks (arrowed) . . .

4.40 . . . and withdraw the clutch assembly - model with "pot" flywheel

illustration).

40   With all the bolts removed, lift off the clutch assembly **(see illustration)**. Be prepared to catch the friction disc as the cover assembly is lifted from the flywheel, and note which way round the friction disc is fitted. The greater-projecting side of the hub should face away from the flywheel.

Inspection

41   Proceed as described in paragraphs 18 to 21 inclusive for models with a "standard" flywheel.

Refitting

42   Proceed as described in paragraphs 23 and 24.

43   Fit the clutch cover assembly, where applicable aligning the mark on the flywheel with the notch in the rim of the clutch cover. Insert the six bolts and spring washers, and tighten them finger-tight, so that the friction disc is gripped, but can still be moved.

44   The friction disc must now be centralised, so that when the engine and gearbox are mated, the gearbox input shaft splines will pass through the splines in the friction disc hub.

45   Centralisation can be carried out by inserting a round bar or a long screwdriver through the hole in the centre of the friction disc, so that the end of the bar rests in the spigot bearing in the centre of the crankshaft **(see illustration)**. Where possible, use a blunt instrument - if a screwdriver or similar is used, wrap tape around the blade to prevent damage to the bearing surface. Moving the bar/screwdriver sideways or up-and-down as necessary, move the friction disc as necessary to achieve centralisation. With the bar removed, view the friction disc hub in relation to the hole in the centre of the crankshaft and the circle created by the ends of the diaphragm spring fingers. When the hub appears exactly in the centre, all is correct. Alternatively, if a suitable clutch alignment tool can be obtained, this will eliminate all the guesswork, and obviate the need for visual alignment.

46   Tighten the cover retaining bolts gradually in a diagonal sequence, to the specified torque. Remove the alignment tool.

47   Refit the engine or the gearbox, as described in the relevant Chapter.

48   On completion, check the clutch cable adjustment, as described in Chapter 1.

---

5   Clutch release bearing - removal, inspection and refitting

---

Note: *Refer to the note and warning at the beginning of Section 4 before proceeding.*

Removal

1   On models with a "standard" flywheel, access to the release

4.45 Centralising the clutch friction disc using a socket and extension bar

bearing can be obtained with the engine and gearbox in the vehicle, after removing the clutch assembly as described in Section 4, although access is improved if the gearbox is removed.

2   On models with a "pot" flywheel, the gearbox must be removed for access to the release bearing. Unless the complete engine/gearbox assembly is to be removed from the vehicle and separated for major overhaul (see Chapter 2B), access to the clutch is most easily obtained by removing the gearbox, as described in Chapter 7A.

3   Unscrew the clamp bolt securing the release fork to the release arm pivot shaft **(see illustration)**.

4   If not already done, disconnect the clutch cable from the release arm, by removing the clip from the threaded rod, and then sliding the threaded rod from the release arm.

5   Pull the release arm pivot shaft up and out of the bellhousing, then withdraw the release fork and the bearing **(see illustration)**. Where necessary, slide the bearing from the release fork, and where applicable, pull the bearing from the plastic collar.

6   If desired, the gearbox input shaft oil seal can be renewed after removing the release bearing guide sleeve, as described in Chapter 7A.

Inspection

7   Spin the release bearing, and check it for excessive roughness. Hold the outer race, and attempt to move it laterally against the inner race. If any excessive movement or roughness is evident, renew the bearing. If a new clutch has been fitted, it is wise to renew the release

5.3 Unscrewing the clamp bolt securing the release fork to the release arm pivot shaft (model with "standard" flywheel)

5.5 Withdrawing the clutch release bearing (model with "standard" flywheel)

bearing as a matter of course.

8   The nylon bushes supporting the release arm pivot shaft can be renewed if necessary (this is likely to be difficult if the gearbox is still in the vehicle), by tapping them from their lugs in the bellhousing using a suitable drift. Drive the new bushes into position, ensuring that their locating tabs engage with the slots in the bellhousing lugs.

Refitting

9   Refitting of the release bearing and arm is a reversal of the removal procedure, bearing in mind the following points:

(a)   *Lightly smear the inner surfaces of the release arm pivot bushes, and the outer surfaces of the release bearing guide sleeve, with molybdenum disulphide grease.*

(b)   *Where applicable, fit the release bearing to the plastic collar, then fit the release bearing and fork together, and tighten the release fork clamp bolt to the specified torque.*

(c)   *Refit the clutch as described in Section 4, or refit the gearbox as described in Chapter 7A, as applicable.*

(d)   *On completion, check the clutch cable adjustment as described in Chapter 1.*

6

Notes

Chapter 7 Part A: Manual gearbox

Contents

Specifications

General

Type	Four or five forward speeds and one reverse, synchromesh on all forward gears. Integral differential

Manufacturer's designation:

12 NZ engine	F 10/5 WR
C 12 NZ engine	F 10/4 WR (four-speed) or F 10/5 WR (five-speed)
X 12 SZ engine	F 10/5 WR
C 14 NZ engine	F 10/5 WR
C 14 SE engine:	
Combo van models..	F 10/5 WR
Hatchback models	F 13/5 CR
C 16 XE engine...	F 15/5 CR

Gear ratios

F 10/4 WR gearbox:

1st...	3.55:1
2nd	1.96:1
3rd	1.30:1
4th	0.89:1
Reverse	3.31:1

F 10/5 WR gearbox:

1st...	3.55:1
2nd	1.96:1
3rd	1.30:1
4th	0.89:1
5th	0.71:1
Reverse	3.31:1

F 13/5 CR gearbox:

1st...	3.55:1
2nd	2.14:1
3rd	1.43:1
4th	1.12:1
5th	0.89:1
Reverse	3.31:1

F 15/5 CR gearbox:

1st...	3.73:1
2nd	2.13:1
3rd	1.41:1
4th	1.12:1
5th	0.89:1
Reverse	3.31:1

Final drive ratios

F 10/4 WR gearbox..	3.94:1
F 10/5 WR gearbox:	
All except X 12 SZ engine models	4.18:1
X 12 SZ engine models	3.74:1
F 13/5 CR gearbox	3.94:1
F 15/5 CR gearbox	3.74:1

Torque wrench settings

	Nm	lbf ft
Clutch bellhousing cover plate bolts	7	5
Gearchange lever housing-to-floorpan bolts.................................	6	4
Speedometer drivegear retaining plate bolt	4	3
Clutch release bearing guide sleeve bolts...................................	5	4
Reversing light switch...	20	15
Gearbox-to-engine bolts	75	55
Left-hand engine/gearbox mounting block-to-body bolts*.....................	65	48
Left-hand engine/gearbox mounting block-to-gearbox		
bracket bolts	60	44
Left-hand engine/gearbox mounting bracket-to-gearbox bolts.............	60	44
Rear engine/gearbox mounting block-to-body bolts	65	48
Rear engine/gearbox mounting block-to-gearbox		
bracket bolts	65	48
Rear engine/gearbox mounting bracket-to-gearbox bolts....................	70	52
Differential housing cover plate bolts:		
Steel plate	30	22
Alloy plate	18	13
Gearbox endplate bolts:		
M7 bolts	15	11
M8 bolts	20	15
Input shaft socket-headed screw	15	11

Use thread-locking compound.

1 General information

One of four different manual gearboxes may be fitted, with four or five forward speeds, depending on the model and the power output of the engine fitted (see Specifications); there are only minor internal differences between the gearbox types.

Drive from the clutch is picked up by the input shaft, which runs in parallel with the mainshaft. The input shaft and mainshaft gears are in constant mesh, and selection of gears is by sliding synchromesh hubs, which lock the appropriate mainshaft gear to the mainshaft.

Where applicable, the 5th speed components are located in an extension housing at the end of the gearbox.

Reverse gear is obtained by sliding an idler gear into mesh with two straight-cut gears on the input shaft and mainshaft.

All the forward gear teeth are helically-cut, to reduce noise and to improve wear characteristics.

The differential is mounted in the main gearbox casing, and drive is transmitted to the differential by a pinion gear on the end of the mainshaft. The inboard ends of the driveshafts locate directly into the differential. The gearbox and differential unit share the same lubricating oil.

Gear selection is by a floor-mounted gearchange lever, via a remote control linkage.

2 Gearbox oil - draining and refilling

Draining

1　Place a suitable container under the differential cover plate. Unscrew the securing bolts and withdraw the cover plate, allowing the gearbox oil to drain into the container **(see illustration)**.

2　Refit the differential cover plate, and tighten the securing bolts when the oil has drained.

Refilling

3　Proceed as described for the gearbox oil level check in Chapter 1.

2.1 Differential cover plate securing bolts (arrowed)

3 Gearchange linkage/mechanism - adjustment

Note: A new plug should be fitted to the gear linkage adjuster hole in the gear selector cover on completion of adjustment.

1　To improve access, jack up the front of the vehicle and support securely on axle stands (see *"Jacking, towing and wheel changing"*).

2　Working underneath the vehicle, loosen the clamp nut and bolt securing the gear selector rod to the clamp sleeve **(see illustration)**.

3　To allow access to the adjuster hole in the gearbox, remove the battery with reference to Chapter 5A.

4　Working at the rear of the gear selector housing, extract the plug from the adjuster hole **(see illustration)**.

5　Looking towards the engine compartment bulkhead, with the selector rod in the neutral plane, grip the gear selector rod, and twist it

3.2 Gear selector rod-to-clamp sleeve clamp nut (arrowed)

3.4 Extract the plug from the djuster hole . . .

3.5 . . . and insert a twist drill to engage with the selector lever - viewed with gearbox removed for clarity

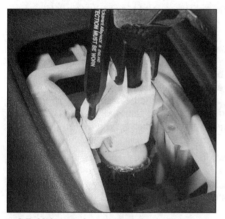

3.7 Using a pin punch to lock the gear lever in position

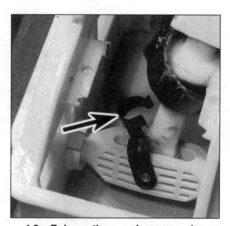

4.3a Release the gear lever securing clip (arrowed) . . .

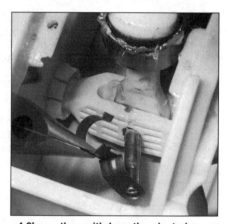

4.3b . . . then withdraw the pivot pin . . .

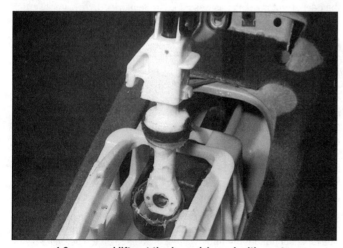

4.3c . . . and lift out the lever (viewed with centre console removed)

clockwise until a 4.5 mm diameter twist drill can be inserted through the adjuster hole in the gear selector cover, to engage with the hole in the selector lever (see illustration).

6   Working inside the vehicle, pull back on the front edge of the gearchange lever gaiter, and free its lower end from the centre console, to allow access to the base of the gearchange lever.

7   Move the gearchange lever to the neutral position in the 1st/2nd gear plane. Adjust the position of the lever until a suitable tool can be inserted through the holes in the base of the lever assembly and the

lever housing to lock the lever in position (see illustration).

8   Without moving the gearchange lever, tighten the clamp bolt and nut securing the gear selector rod to the clamp sleeve in the engine compartment.

9   Refit the gearchange lever gaiter to the centre console.

10   Remove the twist drill from the adjuster hole in the gear selector cover, and seal the hole with a new plug.

11   Refit the battery, and reconnect the battery leads.

12   Finally check that all gears can be engaged easily, first with the engine off, then with the engine running.

7A

4   Gearchange linkage/mechanism - removal, overhaul and refitting

Gearchange lever

Removal

1   Ensure that the lever is in neutral.

2   Pull back on the front edge of the gearchange lever gaiter, and free its lower end from the centre console to allow access to the base of the lever.

3   Release the clip from the base of the lever shaft, then withdraw the pivot pin, and lift out the lever (see illustrations).

Overhaul

4   To renew the gearchange lever gaiter and/or the knob, proceed as follows.

5   On models with a plastic lever knob, immerse the knob in hot water (approximately 80°C) for a few minutes, then twist the knob and tap it from the lever. On models with a leather-covered lever knob, clamp the

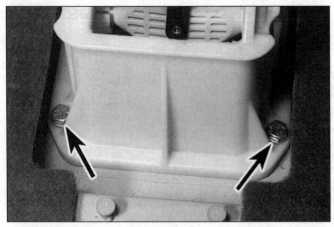

4.12 Two of the gear lever housing securing bolts (arrowed)

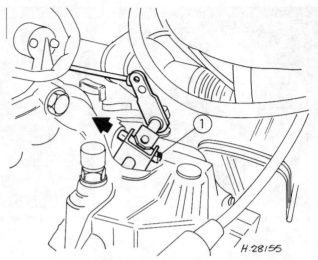

4.18 Gear linkage universal joint pin retaining lug (1)

lever in a vice fitted with soft jaw protectors, and place an open-ended spanner under the metal insert at the bottom of the knob; tap the knob from the lever, using the spanner as an insulator to protect the knob. There is a strong possibility that the knob will be destroyed during the removal process.

6   If renewing the gaiter, slide the old gaiter from the lever, and fit the new one. Use a little liquid detergent (eg washing-up liquid) to aid fitting if necessary.

7   Refit the knob (or fit the new knob, as applicable). When fitting a plastic knob, preheat it in hot water, as during removal. When fitting a leather-covered knob, preheat the metal insert at the base of the knob using a hair drier or hot-air gun. Ensure that the knob is fitted the correct way round.

Refitting

8   Refitting is a reversal of removal.

Gearchange lever housing assembly

Removal

9   Working in the engine compartment, loosen the clamp bolt securing the gear selector rod to the clamp sleeve.

10   Remove the gearchange lever, as described previously in this Section.

11   Remove the centre console, as described in Chapter 11.

12   Unscrew the four bolts securing the gearchange lever housing to the floorpan (see illustration).

13   The housing and clamp sleeve can now be withdrawn. Pull the assembly towards the rear of the vehicle, to feed the clamp sleeve through the bulkhead. As the clamp sleeve is fed through the bulkhead, have an assistant remove the clamp from the end of the clamp sleeve in the engine compartment, to avoid damage to the rubber boot on the bulkhead.

Overhaul

14   If desired, the rubber boot can be renewed by pulling the old boot from the bulkhead, and pushing the new boot into position, ensuring that it is correctly seated.

15   The clamp sleeve bush in the gearchange lever housing can be renewed after sliding the clamp sleeve from the housing. Prise the bush insert from the front of the housing, then prise the bush from the insert. Fit the new bush using a reversal of the removal procedure, but lubricate the inside of the bush with a little silicone grease.

Refitting

16   Refitting of the assembly is a reversal of removal, but before tightening the clamp bolt, adjust the gear selector linkage as described in Section 3.

Gear selector linkage

Removal

17   Ensure that the gearchange lever is in neutral.

18   Remove the securing pin (squeeze the two retaining lugs to

release the pin), and separate the two sections of the linkage universal joint (see illustration).

19   Loosen the clamp bolt securing the clamp sleeve to the linkage, and pull the clamp sleeve from the selector rod.

20   Release the spring clip, then pull the bellcrank pivot pin from the bracket on the rear engine/gearbox mounting.

21   Withdraw the linkage from the vehicle.

Overhaul

22   Check the linkage components for wear, and renew as necessary. The pivot bushes can be renewed by prising out the old bushes and pressing in the new, and the link can be renewed by pulling it from the balljoints. Further dismantling is not recommended.

Refitting

23   Refitting is a reversal of removal, but lubricate all moving components with a little grease, and before tightening the clamp bolt, adjust the gear selector linkage as described in Section 3.

---

5   Speedometer drive - removal and refitting

Removal

1   Unscrew the securing sleeve, and disconnect the speedometer cable from the top of the gearbox (see illustration), with reference to Chapter 12.

2   Unbolt the retaining plate, and withdraw the speedometer drive assembly (see illustrations).

3   If desired, the speedometer driven gear can be withdrawn from its sleeve, in which case note the thrustwasher under the gear (see illustration).

Refitting

4   If the driven gear has been removed from the sleeve, lubricate the gear shaft with a little silicone grease, then slide the gear into the sleeve, ensuring that the thrustwasher is in place on the gear shaft.

5   Inspect the O-ring seal on the sleeve, and renew if worn or damaged.

6   Further refitting is a reversal of removal.

---

6   Oil seals - renewal

Differential side (driveshaft) oil seals

1   Apply the handbrake, then jack up the front of the vehicle and support securely on axle stands (see *"Jacking, towing and wheel changing"*). Remove the relevant front roadwheel.

2   Disconnect the inner end of the relevant driveshaft from the

5.1 Disconnecting the speedometer cable from the gearbox

5.2a Unbolt the retaining plate . . .

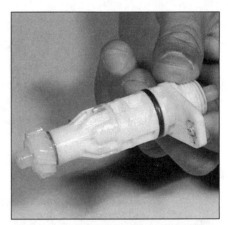

5.2b . . . and withdraw the speedometer drive assembly

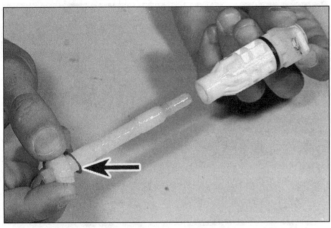

5.3 Withdrawing the speedometer driven gear from its sleeve. Note thrustwasher (arrowed)

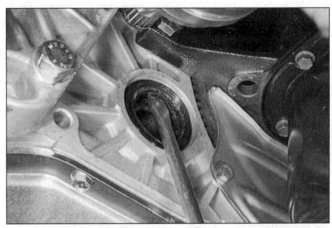

6.3 Prising out a differential side oil seal

6.4 Driving a new differential side oil seal into position

6.8a Withdraw the clutch release bearing guide sleeve . . .

7A

differential as described in Chapter 8. There is no need to disconnect the driveshaft from the swivel hub. Support the driveshaft by suspending it with wire or string - do not allow the driveshaft to hang down under its own weight, or the joints may be damaged.

3   Prise the now-exposed oil seal from the differential housing, using a screwdriver or similar instrument **(see illustration)**.

4   Smear the sealing lip of the new oil seal with a little gearbox oil, then using a metal tube or socket of suitable diameter, drive the new seal into the differential casing until the outer surface of the seal is flush with the outer surface of the differential casing **(see illustration)**.

5   Reconnect the driveshaft to the differential as described in Chapter 8.

6   Refit the roadwheel, then lower the vehicle to the ground.

Input shaft (clutch) oil seal

7   Remove the clutch release bearing and fork, as described in Chapter 6.

8   Unscrew the securing bolts, and withdraw the clutch release bearing guide sleeve from the bellhousing. Recover the O-ring which fits between the guide sleeve and the bellhousing **(see illustrations)**.

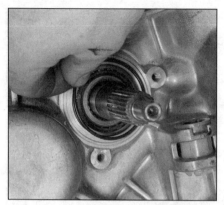

6.8b . . . and recover the O-ring

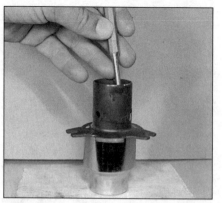

6.9 Driving the oil seal from the clutch release bearing guide sleeve

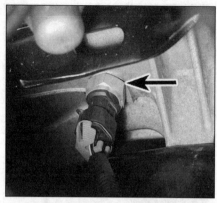

7.4 Disconnect the wiring from the reversing light switch (arrowed) - DOHC engine model shown

9   Drive the old seal from the guide sleeve **(see illustration)**, and fit a new seal using a suitable tube or socket. Press the new seal into position - do not drive it in, as the seal is easily damaged.
10   Fill the space between the lips of the new seal with lithium-based grease, then refit the guide sleeve using a new O-ring. The O-ring should be fitted dry.
11   Refit the guide sleeve to the bellhousing, and tighten the securing bolts.
12   Refit the clutch release bearing and fork as described in Chapter 6.

7   Reversing light switch - testing, removal and refitting

Testing
1   The reversing light circuit is operated by a plunger-type switch, mounted in the front of the gearbox casing.
2   To test the switch, disconnect the wiring, and use a suitable meter or a battery-and-bulb test circuit to check for continuity between the switch terminals. Continuity should only exist when reverse gear is selected. If this is not the case, and there are no obvious breaks or other damage to the wires, the switch is faulty and must be renewed.

Removal
3   The reversing light switch is located in the front of the gearbox casing, and is accessible from the engine compartment.
4   Disconnect the battery negative lead, then disconnect the wiring from the switch **(see illustration)**.
5   Unscrew the switch from the gearbox.

Refitting
6   Refitting is a reversal of removal.

8   Manual gearbox - removal and refitting

Note: *This is an involved procedure, and it may prove easier in many cases (particularly with DOHC engine models) to remove the gearbox complete with the engine as an assembly, as described in Chapter 2B. If removing the gearbox on its own, it is suggested that this Section is read through thoroughly before commencing work. Suitable equipment will be required to support the engine and gearbox, and the help of an assistant will be required.*

Removal
1   Disconnect the battery negative lead.
2   Remove the retaining clip (where applicable), then slide the clutch cable from the release lever, pushing the release lever back towards the bulkhead if necessary, to allow the cable to be disconnected. Pull the cable support from the bracket on the gearbox casing, then move the cable to one side out of the way, taking note of its routing **(see illustrations)**.

8.2a Slide the clutch cable from the release lever . . .

3   Disconnect the wiring from the reversing light switch, located at the front of the gearbox, above the mounting bracket (see Section 7).
4   Unscrew the securing sleeve, and disconnect the speedometer cable from the top of the gearbox, as described in Chapter 12. Note that on certain models, the cable is in two sections, joined by a connector near the engine compartment bulkhead - in this case, it may be easier to separate the two cable sections at the connector, rather than to disconnect the cable from the gearbox **(see illustration)**.
5   On DOHC engine models, to gain better access to the upper engine-to-gearbox bolts, proceed as follows:

(a)   *Drain the cooling system as described in Chapter 1, then disconnect the coolant hoses from the side of the expansion tank. Remove the expansion tank securing nuts, then move the tank to allow the lower coolant hose to be disconnected. Withdraw the tank.*
(b)   *Remove the two securing screws, and withdraw the plastic shield from the camshaft cover.*
(c)   *Disconnect the HT leads from the spark plugs, using the tool provided (attached to one of the leads).*
(d)   *Disconnect the breather hose which runs across the HT leads at the left-hand end of the cylinder head, to allow the HT leads to be moved clear of the engine.*
(e)   *Disconnect the wiring plug from the DIS ignition module, located at the left-hand end of the cylinder head. Unscrew the three securing bolts and remove the module, complete with the HT leads.*

6   Unscrew and remove the three upper engine-to-gearbox bolts, noting the locations of any brackets secured by the bolts. On certain models (DOHC engine models in particular), the plastic coolant gallery may prevent access to the centre upper bolt **(see illustrations)** in

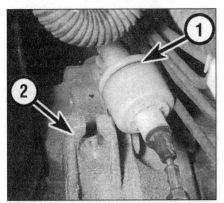

8.2b ... and pull the cable support (1) from the bracket (2) on the gearbox casing

8.4 Speedometer cable connector (arrowed) - DOHC engine model (viewed with engine removed)

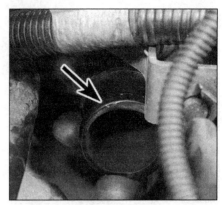

8.6a It may be necessary to move the coolant gallery (arrowed) ...

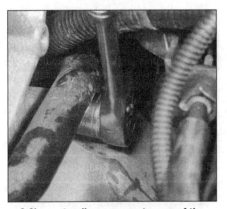

8.6b ... to allow access to one of the engine-to-gearbox bolts

8.6c Oxygen sensor bracket ...

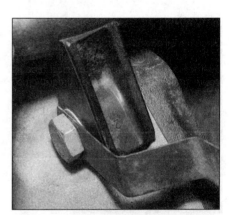

8.6d ... and coolant gallery and clutch cable brackets located on upper engine-to-gearbox bolts

which case, proceed as follows:

(a) Drain the cooling system as described in Chapter 1 (if not already done), then disconnect the radiator hose from the front of the coolant gallery.

(b) Remove the rear upper engine-to-gearbox bolt, which also secures the coolant gallery and a clutch cable bracket. Note that on DOHC engine models, access to this bolt is most easily obtained by reaching down through the hole in the battery tray.

(c) Move the coolant gallery as necessary to enable access to the centre upper engine-to-gearbox bolt.

7   Apply the handbrake, then jack up the front of the vehicle, and support securely on axle stands (see "Jacking, towing and wheel changing"). Note that the vehicle must be raised sufficiently high to enable the gearbox be withdrawn from under the front of the vehicle. Remove the roadwheels.

8   The engine must now be supported. Ideally, the engine should be supported using chains suspended from a strong wooden or metal beam, resting on blocks positioned securely in the channels at the sides of the engine compartment. A Vauxhall/Opel special tool is available for this purpose (see illustration). Alternatively, the engine can be supported using a suitable hoist and lifting tackle, but the hoist must be capable of supporting the engine with the front of the vehicle raised off the ground, leaving sufficient clearance to withdraw the gearbox from under the front of the vehicle (see previous paragraph). As a further alternative, the engine can be supported using a jack and interposed block of wood under the sump, but great care must be taken when removing the gearbox, not to move the engine off the jack - it is strongly recommended that the engine is additionally supported using a hoist or bar as described previously, to avoid any possibility of injury. Note that if a hoist is used to support the engine, a further hoist will be required to carry out removal of the gearbox safely. (The alternative to

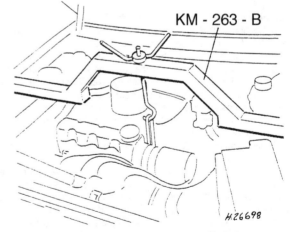

8.8 Vauxhall/Opel special tool No KM-263-B used to support engine

all this is to remove the engine and gearbox as an assembly, as described in Chapter 2B.)

9   With the engine supported, proceed as follows.

10   Where applicable, unbolt the earth strap from the end of the gearbox.

11   On SOHC engine models, unscrew the securing bolts, and remove the engine-to-gearbox blanking plate from the bellhousing (see illustration).

12   On models with a standard flywheel, if any work is to be carried out which involves removal of the clutch, at this stage, the gearbox input

7A

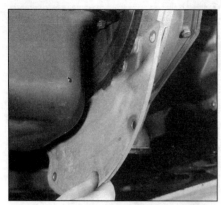

8.11 Removing the engine-to-gearbox blanking plate

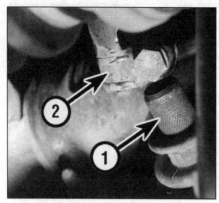

8.13 Pull the selector tube (1) from the gear linkage (2)

8.21 Strap passed through battery tray and around gearbox casing to support gearbox

8.22 Removing the left-hand engine/gearbox mounting bracket

8.23 Remove the nut and through-bolt securing the rear engine/gearbox mounting

8.28 Removing one of the lower engine-to-gearbox bolts

shaft can be withdrawn from the clutch friction disc as described in Chapter 6, Section 4. The clutch can then be installed after the gearbox has been refitted, which will ease centring of the clutch friction disc.

13   Loosen the clamp nut and bolt securing the gear selector rod to the linkage, then pull the selector tube towards the engine compartment bulkhead to separate it from the linkage **(see illustration)**.

14   On SOHC engine models, disconnect the exhaust front section from the manifold as described in Chapter 4A, and release the system from the forward rubber mountings - this will allow the engine to be lowered later in the procedure.

15   On DOHC engine models, remove the exhaust front section as described in Chapter 4A.

16   Place a suitable container under the differential cover plate, then remove the securing bolts, and withdraw the cover plate to drain the gearbox oil. Refit the differential cover plate on completion of draining

17   Remove the front anti-roll bar as described in Chapter 10.

18   Remove the left-hand front suspension lower arm and tie-bar as described in Chapter 10.

19   Disconnect the inner ends of the driveshafts from the gearbox as described in Chapter 8. There is no need to disconnect the driveshafts from the swivel hubs. Be prepared for oil spillage, and plug the openings in the gearbox, to prevent dirt ingress and further oil loss. Do not allow the driveshafts to hang down under their own weight, or the joints may be damaged - support the driveshafts with wire or string.

20   Support the gearbox with a trolley jack, with an interposed block of wood to spread the load. Ensure that the engine is adequately supported as described in paragraph 8.

21   Additionally, the gearbox should be supported from above, using a hoist. Fit a suitable strap around the gearbox casing, passing it through the hole in the battery tray (remove the battery as described in Chapter 5A, if not already done), and suspend the strap from the hoist

(see illustration). This will enable the gearbox to be lowered safely during removal.

22   Remove the left-hand engine/gearbox mounting bracket completely, by unscrewing the two bolts securing the bracket to the rubber mounting, and the three bolts securing the mounting bracket to the gearbox **(see illustration)**.

23   Remove the nut and through-bolt securing the rear engine/gearbox mounting bracket to the mounting on the body **(see illustration)**.

24   Release the spring clip, then pull the gear linkage pivot pin from the bracket on the rear engine/gearbox mounting.

25   Remove the two bolts securing the rear engine/gearbox mounting bracket to the gearbox, and withdraw the mounting bracket.

26   Make a final check to ensure that all relevant wiring, hoses, etc, have been disconnected to facilitate gearbox removal. Note that on certain models, the wiring for the oxygen sensor may be secured to the lug on the gearbox with a cable-tie.

27   Using the lifting tackle, and the jack(s), lower the engine and gearbox slightly.

28   Unscrew and remove the remaining engine-to-gearbox bolts **(see illustration)**, noting the locations of any brackets secured by the bolts.

29   With the aid of an assistant, carefully separate the gearbox from the engine (use the hoist to take the weight of the gearbox). It may be necessary to rock the gearbox a little to release it from the engine. If the gearbox input shaft is still engaged with the clutch (see paragraph 12), take care not to allow the weight of the gearbox to hang on the input shaft as the gearbox is separated from the engine.

30   Lower the gearbox from the engine compartment, taking care not to damage surrounding components.

Refitting

31   Before refitting, check that the left-hand engine/gearbox mounting-

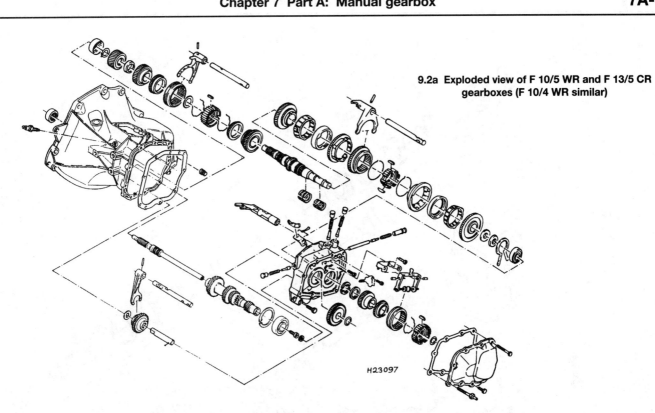

9.2a Exploded view of F 10/5 WR and F 13/5 CR gearboxes (F 10/4 WR similar)

H23097

to-body bolts rotate freely in their threaded holes in the body. If necessary, re-cut the threaded holes in the body using a suitable tap.

32   If the gearbox input shaft was not withdrawn from the clutch friction disc during removal (see paragraph 12), ensure that the friction disc is centred in the clutch cover, as described in Chapter 6, Section 4.

33   Commence refitting by positioning the gearbox under the front of the vehicle, supporting with the hoist and strap, and the trolley jack and interposed block of wood, as during removal.

34   Raise the gearbox sufficiently to enable the engine and gearbox to be mated together. Where applicable, ensure that the gearbox input shaft engages correctly with the clutch friction disc as the gearbox is joined to the engine.

35   Refit the lower engine-to-gearbox bolts, but do not fully tighten them at this stage. Ensure that any brackets or clips noted during removal are in place on the bolts.

36   Coat the threads of the left-hand engine/gearbox mounting-to-body bolts with thread-locking compound, then raise the engine and gearbox sufficiently to enable the mounting bracket to be refitted.

37   Refit the left-hand engine/gearbox mounting, and tighten the mounting bolts to the specified torque.

38   Refit the rear engine/gearbox mounting bracket to the gearbox, and tighten the bolts to the specified torque.

39   Refit the through-bolt and nut securing the rear engine/gearbox mounting to the mounting on the body.

40   Refit the gear linkage to the bracket on the rear engine/gearbox mounting, and secure with the pivot pin.

41   The hoist and jack used to support the gearbox can now be withdrawn.

42   Tighten the lower engine-to-gearbox bolts to the specified torque.

43   Refit the left-hand front suspension lower arm and tie-bar as described in Chapter 10.

44   Refit the front anti-roll bar as described in Chapter 10.

45   Reconnect the inner ends of the driveshafts to the gearbox as described in Chapter 8.

46   On DOHC engine models, refit the exhaust front section as described in Chapter 4A.

47   On SOHC engine models, reconnect the front section of the exhaust system to the manifold as described in Chapter 4A, and reconnect the system to the forward rubber mountings.

48   Reconnect the gear selector rod to the gear linkage, and adjust the linkage as described in Section 3.

49   Where applicable, engage the gearbox input shaft with the clutch friction disc as described in Chapter 6, Section 4.

50   On SOHC engine models, refit the engine-to-gearbox blanking plate to the bellhousing.

51   Where applicable, reconnect the earth strap to the end of the gearbox.

52   Remove or disconnect the equipment used to support the engine, and lower the vehicle to the ground.

53   Refit and tighten the three upper engine-to-gearbox bolts (where necessary, gaining access as described during removal); ensure that the coolant gallery (where applicable) and any brackets noted during removal are in place on the bolts. Where applicable, reconnect the radiator hose to the coolant gallery.

54   On DOHC engine models, refit the DIS module and HT leads, and the expansion tank, using a reversal of the removal procedure.

55   Reconnect the speedometer cable to the gearbox, or reconnect the two sections of the cable, as applicable, with reference to Chapter 12.

56   Reconnect the reversing light switch wiring.

57   Reconnect the clutch cable to the release lever, and check the clutch cable adjustment as described in Chapter 1. Ensure that the cable is routed as noted during removal.

58   Where applicable, refill the cooling system as described in Chapter 1.

59   Refill the gearbox with oil as described in Section 2.

60   Where applicable, refit the battery, then reconnect the battery negative lead.

7A

9   Manual gearbox overhaul - general information

1   The complete overhaul of a manual gearbox is a complicated task, requiring a number of special tools, and previous experience is a great help. It is therefore recommended that owners remove the gearbox themselves, if wished, but then either fit a new or reconditioned unit, or have the existing unit overhauled by a Vauxhall/Opel dealer or gearbox specialist.

2   The dismantling of the gearbox into its major assemblies is a reasonably straightforward operation, and can be carried out to enable an assessment of wear or damage to be made (suitable exploded views of the gearboxes are provided to assist owners who wish to do this) **(see illustrations)**. From this assessment, a decision can be taken on

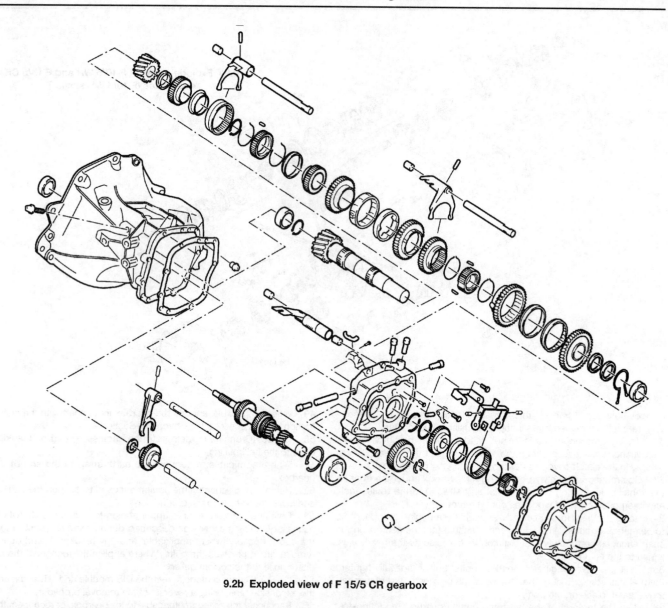

9.2b Exploded view of F 15/5 CR gearbox

whether or not to proceed with a full overhaul. Note, however, that any overhaul work will require the dismantling and reassembly of many small and intricate assemblies, as well as taking several precise measurements to assess wear. This will require a number of special tools, and previous experience will prove invaluable. As a minimum, the following tools will be required:

    (a)   *Internal and external circlip pliers.*
    (b)   *A selection of pin punches.*
    (c)   *A selection of Torx and splined bits.*
    (d)   *A bearing puller.*
    (e)   *A hydraulic press.*
    (f)   *A slide hammer.*
    (g)   *A selection of heat-sensitive marker pencils.*

3   While the *"Fault diagnosis"* Section at the beginning of this manual should help to isolate most gearbox faults to enable a decision to be taken on what course of action to follow, remember that economic considerations may rule out an apparently-simple repair. For example, a common reason for gearbox dismantling is to renew the synchromesh units, wear or faults in these assemblies being indicated by noise when changing gear. Jumping out of gear or similar gear selection faults may be due to worn selector forks, or synchro-sleeves. General noise during operation may be due to worn bearings, shafts or gears. The cumulative cost of renewing all worn components may make it more economical to renew the gearbox complete.

4   To establish whether gearbox overhaul is economically viable, first establish the cost of a complete replacement gearbox, comparing the cost of a new unit with that of an exchange reconditioned unit (if available), or even a good secondhand unit (with a guarantee) from a vehicle breaker. Compare these costs with the likely cost of the replacement parts which will be required if the existing gearbox is overhauled; do not forget to include all items which must be renewed when they are disturbed, such as oil seals, O-rings, roll pins, circlips, snap-rings, etc.

Chapter 7 Part B: Automatic transmission

Contents

Specifications

General

Type	Hydrodynamic torque converter with electronically-controlled mechanical lock-up system, two epicyclic gearsets giving four forward speeds and reverse, integral final drive. Gearchanging under full electronic control, with three "driving" modes selectable
Manufacturer's designation	AF 13

Gear ratios

1st	2.81:1
2nd	1.48:1
3rd	1.00:1
4th	0.74:1
Reverse	2.77:1
Final drive	4.05:1

Torque wrench settings

	Nm	lbf ft
Fluid cooler pipe union bolts	22	16
Torque converter-to-driveplate bolts*	50	37
Transmission bellhousing cover plate bolts	7	5
Transmission-to-engine bolts	75	55
Left-hand engine/transmission mounting block-to-body bolts**	65	48
Left-hand engine/transmission mounting block-to-transmission bracket bolts	60	44
Left-hand engine/transmission mounting bracket-to-transmission bolts	60	44
Rear engine/transmission mounting block-to-body bolts	65	48
Rear engine/transmission mounting block-to-transmission bracket bolts	65	48
Rear engine/transmission mounting bracket-to-transmission bolts	70	52

*Use new bolts
**Use thread-locking compound

7B

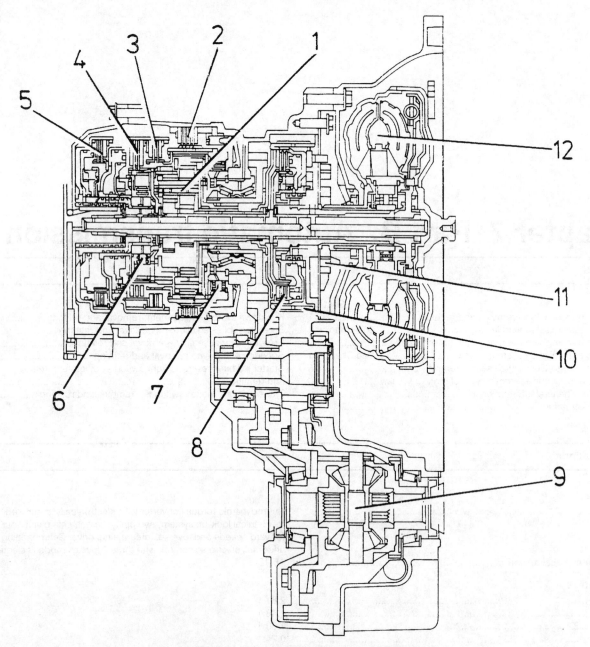

1.1 Cutaway view of AF 13 automatic transmission

1	Gear assembly	5	Multi-plate clutch	9	Differential
2	Multi-disc brake	6	Freewheel assembly	10	Brake band
3	Multi-plate clutch	7	Freewheel assembly	11	Fluid pump
4	Multi-plate clutch	8	Multi-plate clutch	12	Torque converter

1   General information

1   A 4-speed fully-automatic transmission is available as an option on certain Corsa models. The transmission consists of a torque converter, an epicyclic geartrain and hydraulically-operated clutches and brakes. The differential is integral with the transmission, and is similar to that used in manual gearbox models **(see illustration)**.

2   The torque converter provides a fluid coupling between the engine and transmission which acts as an automatic "clutch", and also provides a degree of torque multiplication when accelerating.

3   The epicyclic geartrain provides either one of the four forward gear ratios, or reverse gear, according to which of its component parts

are held stationary or allowed to turn. The components of the geartrain are held or released by brakes and clutches, which are activated by a hydraulic control unit. A fluid pump within the transmission provides the necessary hydraulic pressure to operate the brakes and clutches.

4   The transmission is electronically-controlled, and three driving modes - "Economy", "Sport" and "Winter" - are provided. The transmission electronic control unit (ECU) operates in conjunction with the engine management ECU to control the gearchanges. The transmission ECU receives information on transmission fluid temperature, throttle position, engine coolant temperature, and input-versus-output speed. The ECU controls the hydraulically-operated clutches and brakes via four solenoids. The control system can also retard the engine ignition timing, via the engine management ECU, to permit

1.4 Automatic transmission electronic control system

1   Diagnostic plug
2   Brake light switch
3   Kickdown switch
4   Transmission input speed sensor
5   Speedometer cable connection
6   "Economy/Sport" mode switch
7   "Winter" mode switch
8   Automatic transmission electronic control unit
9   Engine management electronic control unit
10 Throttle position sensor
11 DIS ignition module
12 Selector lever position switch
13 Solenoid valve connection
14 Transmission output speed sensor

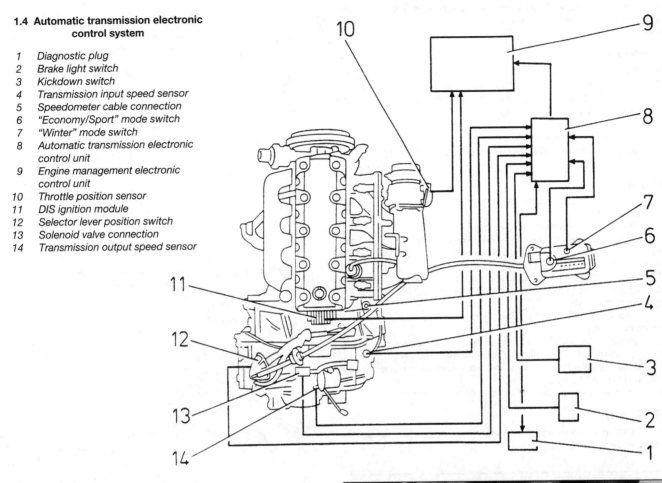

smoother gearchanges **(see illustration)**.
5   Due to the complexity of the automatic transmission, any repair or overhaul work must be entrusted to a Vauxhall/Opel dealer, who will have the necessary specialist equipment and knowledge for fault diagnosis and repair. Refer to the *"Fault diagnosis"* section at the beginning of this manual for further information.

2   Selector cable - adjustment, removal and refitting

Adjustment

1   Working in the engine compartment, check that the actuating lever on the transmission moves to the appropriate position, while an assistant moves the selector lever inside the vehicle through the full range of positions. Note that positions "P" and "N" are marked on the transmission, but the remaining positions are unmarked.
2   If adjustment is required, move the selector lever to position "P". Check that the lever is locked in position "P" by attempting to move the lever backwards and forwards without lifting the lever knob.
3   Working inside the vehicle, remove the centre console (as described in Chapter 11) for access to the cable clamp bolt.
4   Using a suitable socket, slacken the cable clamp bolt.
5   Again working in the engine compartment, move the actuating lever on the transmission forwards (io, towards the front of the vehicle), until it reaches its stop.
6   Attempt to turn the front roadwheels, and check that the parking pawl engages, locking the wheels in position.
7   Have the assistant hold the actuating lever against the stop, while the cable clamp bolt inside the vehicle is tightened.
8   Recheck the selector operation, as described in paragraph 1.
9   Refit the centre console on completion.

2.12 Transmission selector cable securing clip (arrowed)

Removal

10 Apply the handbrake, and ensure that the transmission selector lever is in position "P".
11 Disconnect the battery negative lead.
12 Remove the retaining clip and the washer, and disconnect the selector cable from the actuating lever on the transmission **(see illustration)**.
13 Unscrew the securing bolts, and withdraw the cable mounting bracket from the transmission.
14 Remove the centre console, as described in Chapter 11.

7B

15   Slacken the cable clamp bolt and unscrew the cable locknut, then withdraw the cable, and pull it through the bulkhead into the engine compartment, prising out the bulkhead grommet where necessary **(see illustration)**.

Refitting

16   Refitting is a reversal of the removal procedure. Make sure that the bulkhead grommet is correctly located, and before tightening the cable clamp bolt and refitting the centre console, adjust the cable as described previously in this Section.

3   Selector lever assembly - removal and refitting

Removal

1   Apply the handbrake, and ensure that the transmission selector lever is in position "P".
2   Disconnect the battery negative lead.
3   Remove the centre console as described in Chapter 11. Pull the illumination bulbholder from the selector cover, and disconnect the transmission "Winter" mode switch wiring connector.
4   Slacken the selector cable clamp bolt and unscrew the cable locknut, then disconnect the cable from the selector lever assembly (see illustration 2.15).
5   Disconnect the transmission "Economy/Sport" mode switch wiring connector.
6   Unscrew the securing nut, and withdraw the selector cable lever from the end of the selector lever pivot shaft. Recover the washer(s).
7   Slide the selector lever assembly from the housing, and recover the pivot bushes if they are loose.
8   No attempt should be made to dismantle the assembly.

Refitting

9   Refitting is a reversal of removal, but on completion, adjust the cable as described in Section 2.

4   Speedometer drive - removal and refitting

The procedure is as described for manual gearbox models in Chapter 7A.

5   Differential side (driveshaft) oil seals - renewal

The procedure is as described for manual gearbox models in Chapter 7A, bearing in mind the following points:

(a)   *Drain the transmission fluid into a suitable container by removing the drain plug located at the lower right-hand side of the transmission housing* **(see illustration)**.
(b)   *Smear the sealing ring of the new oil seal with transmission fluid.*
(c)   *On completion, refill the transmission through the dipstick tube with the correct quantity and type of fluid, and check the level as described in Chapter 1.*

6   Fluid cooler - general information

The transmission fluid cooler is an integral part of the radiator assembly; radiator removal and refitting is described in Chapter 3.
The hoses running from the transmission to the cooler should be checked at regular intervals, and renewed if there is any doubt about their condition.
Always take note of the pipe and hose connections before disturbing them, and take note of the hose routing.
To minimise the loss of fluid, and to prevent the entry of dirt into

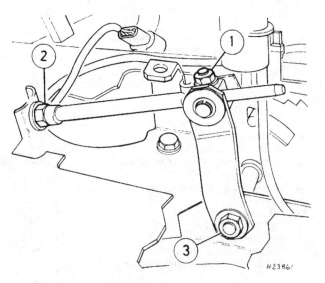

2.15 Automatic transmission selector cable connection at selector lever

1   Cable clamp bolt   3   Lever pivot nut
2   Cable locknut

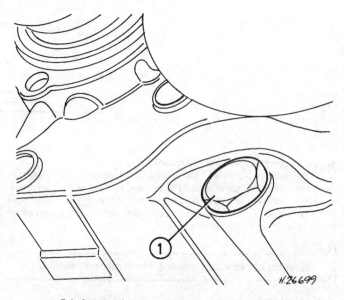

5.1 Automatic transmission fluid drain plug (1)

the system, clamp the hoses before disconnecting them, and plug the unions once the hoses have been disconnected.
When reconnecting the hoses, ensure that they are connected to their original locations, and route them so that they are not kinked or twisted. Also allow for the movement of the engine on its mountings, ensuring that the hoses will not be stretched or fouled by surrounding components.
Always renew the sealing washers if the banjo union bolts are disturbed, and tighten the bolts to their specified torque wrench setting. Be particularly careful when tightening the cooler unions.

7   Kickdown switch - adjustment, removal and refitting

Adjustment

1   Working in the engine compartment, remove the airbox from the

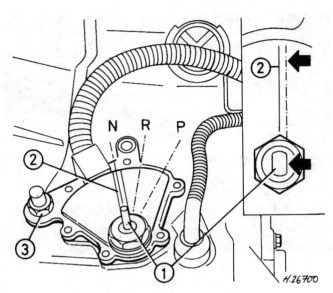

8.2 Starter inhibitor/reversing light switch adjustment

1   *Selector lever shaft*
2   *Groove in switch housing*
3   *Switch securing nut*
    Arrows (inset) show shaft in alignment with groove in switch housing

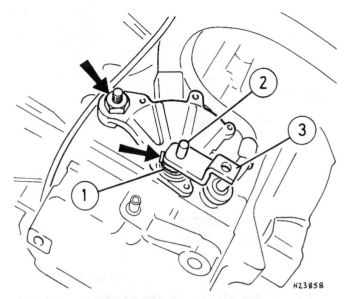

8.10 Starter inhibitor/reversing light switch

1   *Large nut*
2   *Selector lever shaft*
3   *Actuating lever*
    Arrows indicate switch mountings

top of the fuel injection unit, so that the throttle valve can be observed.

2   Have an assistant depress the throttle pedal until it contacts the switch on the vehicle floor. Check that the throttle valve is fully open, and that the pedal acts squarely on the centre of the switch button.

3   If the pedal/switch button contact point requires adjustment, this must be carried out by adjusting the throttle cable free play - see Chapter 4A.

Removal

4   Disconnect the battery negative lead.

5   Release the carpet from the retainer under the throttle pedal, and lift the carpet to expose the switch mounting.

6   Disconnect the switch wiring, then unclip the switch.

Refitting

7   Refitting is a reversal of removal, but push the switch into the retainer as far as the stop, and check the switch adjustment as described previously in this Section.

8   Starter inhibitor/reversing light switch - adjustment, removal and refitting

Adjustment

1   Remove the retaining clip, and disconnect the selector cable from the actuating lever on the transmission.

2   Move the actuating lever fully to the right against the stop, then turn the lever back two notches to position "N" **(see illustration)**.

3   Observe the end of the selector lever shaft. The shaft's flattened surface should be aligned with the groove in the switch housing. If necessary, loosen the nut securing the switch to the transmission, and turn the switch until the alignment is correct (see illustration 8.2).

4   Tighten the switch securing nut securely on completion.

5   Reconnect the selector cable to the actuating lever on the transmission, and adjust the cable as described in Section 2.

Removal

6   Apply the handbrake, and select position "N" with the gear

selector lever.

7   Disconnect the battery negative lead.

8   Remove the retaining clip and washer, and disconnect the selector cable from the actuating lever on the transmission.

9   Disconnect the wiring from the switch.

10   Using pliers to counterhold the shaft, unscrew the nut securing the actuating lever to the selector lever shaft. Remove the locking plate, and unscrew the large nut and washer securing the switch to the shaft **(see illustration)**.

11   Unscrew the nut securing the switch to the transmission, and withdraw the switch.

Refitting

12   Ensure that the selector lever shaft is in position "N" (the third detent from the front). Lower the switch onto the shaft, and rotate it until the shaft's flattened surface is aligned with the groove in the switch housing. Refit the nut which secures the switch to the transmission, and tighten it securely.

13   Refit the washer, then refit the large nut securing the switch to the selector lever shaft. Tighten the nut securely, then refit the locking plate.

14   Refit the nut securing the actuating lever to the selector lever shaft. Use pliers to counterhold the shaft as the nut is tightened, as during removal.

15   Refit the dipstick tube, using a new O-ring, then refit and tighten the securing nut.

16   Reconnect the switch wiring, and the battery negative lead.

17   Reconnect the selector cable to the actuating lever on the transmission, and adjust the cable as described in Section 2.

9   Transmission "mode" switches - removal and refitting

"Economy/Sport" mode switch

Removal

1   Remove the selector lever assembly as described in Section 3.

2   Using a length of welding rod or a similar tool inserted through the

7B

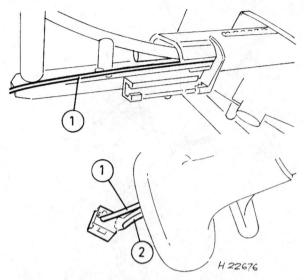

11.3 Transmission vent hose (arrowed)

9.2 Using welding rod (1) to push "Economy/Sport" switch from top of selector lever - unsolder wire connections (2)

lower end of the selector lever, push out the switch **(see illustration)**.
3   Note the wiring connections, then carefully unsolder the wires from the switch.

Refitting

4   Refitting is a reversal of removal, but ensure that the wiring connections are correct, as noted before removal, and refit the selector lever assembly as described in Section 3.

"Winter" mode switch

Removal

5   Disconnect the battery negative lead.
6   Remove the centre console as described in Chapter 11, then carefully push the switch from the console, and disconnect the wiring plug.

Refitting

7   Refitting is a reversal of removal.

11.6 Unscrew the three upper engine-to-transmission bolts (arrowed)

10   Electronic control unit - removal and refitting

Removal

1   The electronic control unit is located behind the glovebox on the passenger's side of the facia.
2   Disconnect the battery negative lead.
3   Remove the glovebox as described in Chapter 11, Section 26.
4   Release the control unit from its securing bracket, then disconnect the wiring plug, and withdraw the unit from the facia.

Refitting

5   Refitting is a reversal of removal.

11   Automatic transmission - removal and refitting

Removal

Note: *This is an involved procedure, and it may prove easier in many cases to remove the transmission complete with the engine as an assembly, as described in Chapter 2B. If removing the transmission on its own, it is suggested that this Section is read through thoroughly before commencing work. Suitable equipment will be required to support the engine and transmission, and the help of an assistant will be required. New torque converter-to-driveplate bolts must be used on refitting,*

and if the original torque converter is being used, an M10 x 1.25 mm tap will be required.
1   Disconnect the battery negative lead.
2   Working in the engine compartment, remove the retaining clip, and disconnect the selector cable from the actuating lever on the transmission. Unclip the cable sheath from the bracket on the transmission, then move the cable to one side, clear of the transmission.
3   Disconnect the vent hose from the front of the transmission **(see illustration)**.
4   Disconnect the transmission wiring harness plugs, and unbolt the wiring harness brackets from the transmission.
5   Unclip the oxygen sensor wiring connector from the bracket on the transmission, and separate the two halves of the connector.
6   Unscrew and remove the three upper engine-to-transmission bolts **(see illustration)**, noting the locations of any brackets or clips attached to the bolts. Note that on certain models, one of the bolts secures the dipstick tube. On certain models, the plastic coolant gallery may prevent access to the centre upper bolt, in which case, proceed as follows:

(a) *Drain the cooling system as described in Chapter 1 (if not already done), then disconnect the radiator hose from the front of the coolant gallery.*
(b) *Remove the rear upper engine-to-transmission bolt, which also secures the coolant gallery and a clutch cable bracket.*

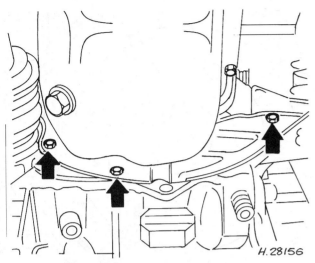

11.16 Transmission bellhousing cover plate securing bolts (arrowed)

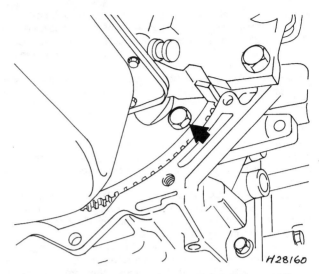

11.18 Torque converter-to-driveplate bolt (arrowed)

(c) Move the coolant gallery as necessary to enable access to the centre upper engine-to-transmission bolt.

7   Remove the dipstick and its tube from the transmission casing. Recover the O-ring.

8   Apply the handbrake, then jack up the front of the vehicle, and support securely on axle stands (see *"Jacking, towing and wheel changing"*). Note that the vehicle must be raised sufficiently high to enable the transmission to be withdrawn from under the front of the vehicle. Remove the roadwheels.

9   The engine must now be supported. Ideally, the engine should be supported using chains suspended from a strong wooden or metal beam, resting on blocks positioned securely in the channels at the sides of the engine compartment. A Vauxhall/Opel special tool is available for this purpose (see illustration 8.8 in Chapter 7A). Alternatively, the engine can be supported using a suitable hoist and lifting tackle, but the hoist must be capable of supporting the engine with the front of the vehicle raised off the ground, leaving sufficient clearance to withdraw the transmission from under the front of the vehicle (see previous paragraph). A further alternative is to support the engine using a jack and interposed block of wood under the sump, but great care must be taken when removing the transmission, not to move the engine off the jack - it is strongly recommended that the engine is additionally supported using a hoist or bar as described previously, to avoid any possibility of injury. Note that if a hoist is used to support the engine, a further hoist will be required to carry out removal of the transmission safely. (The alternative to all this is to remove the engine and transmission as an assembly, as described in Chapter 2B.)

10   Disconnect the speedometer cable from the top of the transmission, with reference to Chapter 12. Note that on certain models, the cable is in two sections, joined by a connector near the engine compartment bulkhead - in this case, it may be easier to separate the two cable sections at the connector, rather than to disconnect the cable from the transmission.

11   Disconnect the exhaust front section from the manifold as described in Chapter 4A, and release the system from the forward rubber mountings - this will allow the engine to be lowered later in the procedure.

12   Remove the front anti-roll bar as described in Chapter 10.

13   Remove the left-hand front suspension lower arm and tie-bar as described in Chapter 10.

14   Disconnect the inner ends of the driveshafts from the transmission as described in Chapter 8. There is no need to disconnect the driveshafts from the swivel hubs. Be prepared for transmission fluid spillage, and plug the openings in the transmission, to prevent dirt ingress and further fluid loss. Do not allow the driveshafts to hang down under their own weight, or the joints may be damaged - support the driveshafts with wire or string.

15   Place a suitable container beneath the transmission fluid cooler hose connections at the transmission. Clamp the transmission fluid cooler hoses, then disconnect them from the transmission, noting their locations. Be prepared for fluid spillage, and plug the open ends of the hoses and transmission, to minimise fluid loss and prevent dirt ingress.

16   Unscrew the securing bolts, and remove the transmission bellhousing cover plate **(see illustration)**.

17   If the original torque converter and driveplate are to be refitted, make alignment marks between the torque converter and the driveplate, to ensure that the components are reassembled in their original positions.

18   Working through the bottom of the bellhousing, unscrew the three torque converter-to-driveplate bolts. It will be necessary to turn the engine, using a suitable spanner or socket on the crankshaft pulley or sprocket bolt (as applicable), to gain access to each bolt in turn through the aperture **(see illustration)**. Turning the engine will be much easier if the spark plugs are removed first (see Chapter 1). Use a screwdriver or a similar tool to jam the driveplate ring gear, preventing the driveplate from rotating as the bolts are loosened. Discard the bolts.

19   Support the transmission with a trolley jack, with an interposed block of wood to spread the load. Ensure that the engine is adequately supported as described in paragraph 9.

20   Additionally, the transmission should be supported from above, using a hoist. Fit a suitable strap around the transmission casing, passing it through the hole in the battery tray (remove the battery as described in Chapter 5A, if not already done), and suspend the strap from the hoist. This will enable the transmission to be lowered safely during removal.

21   Remove the left-hand engine/transmission mounting bracket completely, by unscrewing the two bolts securing the bracket to the rubber mounting, and the three bolts securing the mounting bracket to the transmission.

22   Remove the nut and through-bolt securing the rear engine/transmission mounting bracket to the mounting on the body.

23   Remove the two bolts securing the rear engine/transmission mounting bracket to the transmission, and withdraw the mounting bracket.

24   Make a final check to ensure that all relevant wiring, hoses, etc, have been disconnected to facilitate transmission removal. Note that on certain models, the wiring for the oxygen sensor may be secured to the lug on the transmission with a cable-tie.

25   Using the lifting tackle and the jack(s), lower the engine and transmission slightly.

26   Ensure that the transmission is adequately supported, then unscrew and remove the three lower engine-to-transmission bolts (note the location of any brackets secured by the bolts). Ensure that the

7B

torque converter is held firmly in place in the transmission casing as the engine and transmission are separated, otherwise it could fall out, resulting in fluid spillage and possible damage. Retain the torque converter while the transmission is removed by bolting a strip of metal across the transmission bellhousing end face.

27   The transmission can now be lowered and withdrawn from under the front of the vehicle. The help of an assistant will greatly ease this operation.

Refitting

28   Before refitting, check that the left-hand engine/transmission mounting-to-body bolts rotate freely in their threaded holes in the body. If necessary, re-cut the threaded holes in the body using a suitable tap.

29   If the original torque converter is being refitted, commence refitting by recutting the torque converter-to-driveplate bolt threads in the torque converter using an M10 x 1.25 mm tap **(see illustration)**.

30   If a new transmission is being fitted, the manufacturers recommend that the radiator's fluid cooler passages are flushed clean before the new transmission is installed. Ideally, compressed air should be used (in which case, ensure that adequate safety precautions are taken; in particular, eye protection should be worn). Alternatively, the cooler can be flushed with clean automatic transmission fluid until all the old fluid has been expelled, and fresh fluid runs clear from the cooler outlet.

31   Commence refitting by positioning the transmission under the front of the vehicle, and support with a trolley jack and interposed block of wood, as during removal.

32   Where applicable, remove the strip of metal retaining the torque converter in the transmission, and hold the torque converter in position as the transmission is mated to the engine.

33   On models where the dipstick tube is secured by one of the engine-to-transmission bolts, fit the dipstick tube to the transmission, using a new O-ring.

34   Raise the engine and transmission sufficiently to enable the lower engine-to-transmission bolts to be fitted, but do not tighten them fully at this stage. Ensure that any brackets or clips (as applicable) noted during removal are in place on the bolts.

35   Coat the threads of the left-hand engine/transmission mounting-to-body bolts with suitable thread-locking compound, then raise the engine and transmission sufficiently to enable the mounting bracket to be refitted.

36   Refit the left-hand engine/transmission mounting, and tighten the bolts to the specified torque.

37   Refit the rear engine/transmission mounting bracket to the transmission, and tighten the bolts to the specified torque.

38   Refit the nut and through-bolt securing the rear engine/transmission mounting to the mounting on the body.

39   Tighten the previously-fitted engine-to-transmission bolts to the specified torque, then withdraw the trolley jack and the hoist used to support the transmission.

40   If the original torque converter and driveplate have been refitted, carefully turn the engine to align the marks made before removal, before fitting the torque converter-to-driveplate bolts.

41   Fit **new** torque converter-to-driveplate bolts, and tighten them to the specified torque. Turn the engine for access to each bolt in turn, and prevent the driveplate from turning as during removal.

42   Refit the transmission bellhousing cover plate.

43   Reconnect the fluid cooler hoses to the transmission. Ensure that the hoses are reconnected to their correct locations, as noted before removal.

44   Refit the suspension lower arm and tie-bar as described in Chapter 10.·

45   Refit the front anti-roll bar as described in Chapter 10.

46   Reconnect the inner end of the driveshafts to the transmission as described in Chapter 8.

47   Reconnect the front section of the exhaust system to the manifold

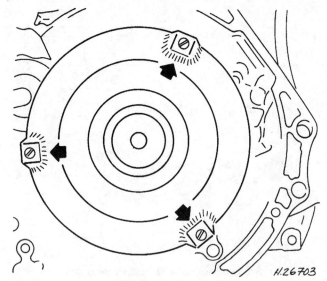

11.29 Torque converter-to-driveplate bolt threads (arrowed) must be recut on refitting

as described in Chapter 4A, and reconnect the system to the forward rubber mountings.

48   Reconnect the speedometer cable to the top of the transmission, or reconnect the two halves of the cable at the connector, as applicable.

49   Refit the roadwheels, then lower the vehicle to the ground.

50   Remove or disconnect the equipment used to support the engine, if not already done.

51   Refit and tighten the three upper engine-to-transmission bolts (where necessary gaining access as described during removal), ensuring that the coolant gallery, dipstick tube, and any brackets (as applicable) noted during removal are in place on the bolts. Where applicable, reconnect the radiator hose to the coolant gallery.

52   Reconnect the oxygen sensor wiring connector, and refit it to its bracket.

53   Reconnect the transmission wiring harness plugs, and secure the wiring harness brackets to the transmission.

54   Reconnect the transmission vent hose.

55   If not already done, refit the dipstick tube, using a new O-ring.

56   Refit the selector cable sheath to the bracket on the transmission. Reconnect the selector cable to the actuating lever on the transmission, fit the securing clip, then check the cable adjustment as described in Section 2.

57   Where applicable, refill the cooling system as described in Chapter 1.

58   Refit the battery, where applicable, then reconnect the battery negative lead.

59   Check the automatic transmission fluid level, and top-up if necessary as described in Chapter 1.

12   Automatic transmission overhaul - general information

In the event of a fault occurring on the transmission, it is first necessary to determine whether it is of an electrical, mechanical or hydraulic nature, and to achieve this, special test equipment is required. It is therefore essential to have the work carried out by a Vauxhall/Opel dealer if a transmission fault is suspected.

Do not remove the transmission from the car for possible repair before professional fault diagnosis has been carried out, since most tests require the transmission to be in the vehicle.

Chapter 8 Driveshafts

Contents

Specifications

Type .... Unequal length shafts with ball-and-cage type constant velocity joint at each end

Lubrication (overhaul only - see text)

Lubricant type/specification .... Vauxhall/Opel grease No 90 007 999/19 41 552 - joints are otherwise pre-packed with grease and sealed

Torque wrench settings

	Nm	lbf ft
Driveshaft retaining nut:		
Stage 1	100	74
Stage 2	Slacken the nut completely	
Stage 3	20	15
Stage 4	Angle-tighten through a further 90°	
Lower arm balljoint clamp bolt nut	30	22
Roadwheel bolts	110	81

8

2.2 **Extract the split pin from the driveshaft retaining nut**

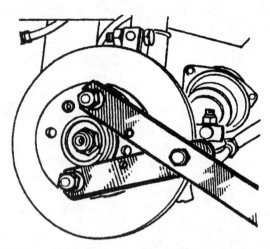

2.3 **Using a fabricated tool to hold the front hub stationary whilst the driveshaft retaining nut is slackened**

2.5 **Withdraw the clamp bolt, and free the lower arm balljoint from the swivel hub**

2.8a **Lever the driveshaft out from the transmission to release its circlip from the differential . . .**

2.8b **. . . then withdraw the shaft, taking great care not to damage the oil seal in the transmission**

1 General information

1   Drive is transmitted from the differential to the front wheels by means of two solid steel driveshafts of unequal length. The right-hand driveshaft is longer than the left-hand one, due to the position of the transmission unit.

2   Both driveshafts are splined at their outer ends to accept the wheel hubs, and are threaded so that each hub can be fastened by a large nut. The inner end of each driveshaft is splined to accept the differential sun gear.

3   Constant velocity (CV) joints are fitted to each end of the driveshafts, to ensure the smooth and efficient transmission of drive at all the angles possible as the roadwheels move up and down with the suspension, and as they turn from side to side under steering. Both inner and outer constant velocity joints are of the ball-and-cage type.

2 Driveshafts - removal and refitting

Note: *A new driveshaft retaining nut and balljoint clamp bolt nut will be needed on refitting.*

Removal

Tip: *If work is being carried out without the aid of an assistant, remove the wheel trim/hub cap (as applicable) then withdraw the split pin and slacken the driveshaft retaining nut with the vehicle resting on its wheels.*

1   Chock the rear wheels of the car, firmly apply the handbrake, then jack up the front of the car and support it on axle stands. Remove the appropriate front roadwheel, marking the correct fitted position of the wheel on the hub.

2   Extract the split pin from the driveshaft retaining nut and discard it; a new one must be used on refitting **(see illustration)**.

3   Refit at least two roadwheel bolts to the front hub, and tighten them securely. Have an assistant firmly depress the brake pedal to prevent the front hub from rotating, then using a socket and extension bar, slacken and remove the driveshaft retaining nut. Alternatively, a tool can be fabricated from two lengths of steel strip (one long, one short) and a nut an bolt; the nut and bolt forming the pivot of a forked tool. Bolt the tool to the hub using two wheel bolts, and hold the tool to prevent the hub from rotating as the driveshaft retaining nut is undone **(see illustration)**.

4   Unscrew the driveshaft retaining nut, and remove the washer. Discard the nut; a new one must be used on refitting.

5   Slacken and remove the lower arm balljoint clamp nut and bolt, and free the lower arm from the swivel hub **(see illustration)**. Discard the clamp bolt nut; a new one must be used on refitting.

6   Carefully pull the swivel hub assembly outwards, and withdraw the driveshaft outer constant velocity joint from the hub assembly. If necessary, the shaft can be tapped out of the hub using a soft-faced mallet. Support the driveshaft by suspending it with wire or string; do not allow it to hang under its own weight, or the joints may be damaged.

7   A suitable tool will now be required to release the inner end of the driveshaft from the differential. To release the right-hand driveshaft, a

2.12 Prior to refitting, ensure that the circlip (arrowed) is correctly located in the inner constant velocity joint groove

2.18a Working in the stages given in the Specifications, tighten the driveshaft retaining nut to the specified torque setting . . .

2.18b . . . and then through the specified angle (note the use of an angle gauge)

2.19a Insert a new split pin . . .

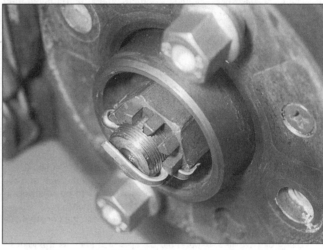

2.19b . . . and secure in position by bending over the split pin ends as shown

flat steel bar with a good chamfer on one end can be used. The left-hand driveshaft may prove more difficult to release, and a suitable square- or rectangular-section bar may be required.

8   Lever between the driveshaft and the differential housing to re-lease the driveshaft circlip from the differential. Carefully withdraw the driveshaft from the transmission unit, taking great care not to damage the driveshaft oil seal, and remove the driveshaft from underneath the vehicle **(see illustrations)**.

9   Plug the opening in the differential, to prevent further oil loss and dirt ingress.

10   **Do not** *allow the vehicle to rest on its wheels with one or both driveshaft(s) removed, as damage to the wheel bearing(s) may result.* If moving the vehicle is unavoidable, temporarily insert the outer end of the driveshaft(s) in the hub(s), and tighten the hub nut(s): in this case, the inner end(s) of the driveshaft(s) must be supported, for example by suspending with string from the vehicle underbody. **Do not** *allow the driveshaft to hang down under its own weight, or the joints may be damaged.*

Refitting

11   Before installing the driveshaft, examine the driveshaft oil seal in the transmission for signs of damage or deterioration. Renew if neces-sary, referring to the relevant Part of Chapter 7 for further information.

12   Check the circlip fitted to the inner constant velocity joint splines for signs of damage, and renew if necessary. Ensure that the circlip is correctly seated in its groove **(see illustration)**.

13   Thoroughly clean the driveshaft splines, and the apertures in the transmission unit and hub assembly. Apply a thin film of grease to the oil seal lips, and to the driveshaft splines and shoulders. Check that all gaiter clips are securely fastened.

14   Remove the plug from the transmission (see paragraph 9) and of-fer up the driveshaft. Locate the joint splines with those of the differen-tial sun gear, taking great care not to damage the oil seal.

15   Place a screwdriver or similar tool on the weld bead of the inner driveshaft joint, **not** the metal cover, and drive the shaft into the differen-tial until the retaining snap-ring engages positively. Pull on the joint, **not** the shaft, to make sure that the joint is securely retained by the circlip.

16   Locate the outer constant velocity joint splines with those of the swivel hub, and slide the joint back into position in the hub. Fit the washer and new driveshaft retaining nut, tightening it by hand only at this stage.

17   Locate the lower arm balljoint in the swivel hub, and insert the clamp bolt from the rear of the swivel hub, so that its threads are facing forwards. Fit a new nut to the clamp bolt, and tighten it to the specified torque setting.

18   Using the method employed on removal to prevent rotation, tighten the driveshaft retaining nut through the stages given in the Specifications at the start of this Chapter **(see illustrations)**.

19   With the nut correctly tightened, secure it in position with a new split pin **(see illustrations)**. If the holes in the driveshaft are not aligned with any of the slots in the nut, loosen (**do not** tighten) the nut by the *smallest possible amount* until the split pin can be inserted.

8

3.4 Expand the constant velocity joint circlip, and tap the joint off the end of the driveshaft

3.9 Examine the constant velocity joint balls and cage for signs of wear or damage

20   Refit the roadwheel, aligning the marks made on removal, then lower the vehicle to the ground and tighten the roadwheel bolts to the specified torque.

21   Top-up the transmission with the specified type of oil/fluid using the information given in Chapter 1.

3   Driveshaft rubber gaiters - renewal

Note: *If both driveshaft gaiters are to renewed at the same time, it is only necessary to remove one of the constant velocity joints. The second gaiter can then be slid along and removed from the exposed end of the driveshaft.*

1   Remove the driveshaft from the car as described in Section 2.

2   Secure the driveshaft in a vice equipped with soft jaws, and release the two retaining clips on the gaiter which is to be renewed. If necessary, the retaining clips can be cut to release them.

3   Slide the rubber gaiter down the shaft to expose the constant velocity joint. Scoop out any excess grease.

4   Using circlip pliers, expand the circlip which secures the joint to the driveshaft **(see illustration)**.

5   Using a soft-faced mallet, tap the joint off the end of the driveshaft.

6   Slide the rubber gaiter off the driveshaft, and discard it.

7   If both gaiters are to be renewed, release the retaining clips, then slide the second gaiter along the driveshaft and remove it.

8   Thoroughly clean the constant velocity joint(s) using paraffin, or a suitable solvent, and dry thoroughly. Carry out a visual inspection as follows.

9   Move the inner splined driving member from side to side, to expose each ball in turn at the top of its track. Examine the balls for cracks, flat spots, or signs of surface pitting **(see illustration)**.

10   Inspect the ball tracks on the inner and outer members. If the tracks have widened, the balls will no longer be a tight fit. At the same time, check the ball cage windows for wear or cracking between the windows.

11   If on inspection any of the constant velocity joint components are found to be worn or damaged, it will be necessary to renew the complete joint assembly (refer to the Note at the end of Section 4). If the joint is in satisfactory condition, obtain a new gaiter and retaining clips, a constant velocity joint circlip, and the correct type and quantity of grease **(see illustration)**.

12   Wind tape around the splines on the end of the driveshaft, to protect the gaiter as it is slid into place.

13   Where both gaiters have been removed, slide on the first gaiter and proceed as described in paragraphs 16 to 18.

14   Slide the (second) gaiter onto the end of the driveshaft **(see illustration)**, then remove the tape from the driveshaft splines.

15   Fit a new circlip to the constant velocity joint, then tap the joint onto the driveshaft until the circlip engages in its groove **(see illustrations)**. Make sure that the joint is securely retained by the circlip, by pulling on the joint, **not** the shaft.

16   Pack the joint with the specified type of grease **(see illustration)**. Work the grease well into the bearing tracks whilst twisting the joint, and fill the rubber gaiter with any excess.

17   Ease the gaiter over the joint, and ensure that the gaiter lips are correctly located in the grooves on both the driveshaft and constant velocity joint. Lift the outer sealing lip of the gaiter, to equalise air pressure within the gaiter.

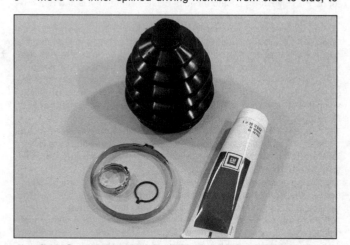

3.11 Components required for driveshaft gaiter renewal

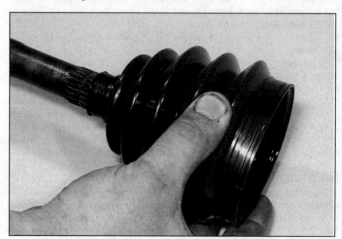

3.14 Slide the gaiter onto the end of the driveshaft

3.15a Fit a new circlip . . .

3.15b . . . ensuring it is correctly located in the constant velocity joint inner member

3.15c Slide the joint onto the driveshaft until the circlip is correctly located in the driveshaft groove

18   Fit the large metal retaining clip to the gaiter. Pull the clip as tight as possible, and locate the hooks on the clip in their slots. Remove any slack in the gaiter retaining clip by carefully compressing the raised section of the clip. In the absence of the special tool, a pair of side cutters may be used. Secure the small retaining clip using the same procedure **(see illustrations)**.
19   Check that both constant velocity joints move freely in all directions, then refit the driveshaft to the vehicle as described in Section 2.

3.16 Pack the constant velocity joint and gaiter with the grease supplied

4   Driveshaft overhaul - general information

1   If any of the checks described in Chapter 1 reveal wear in a driveshaft joint, first remove the roadwheel trim or centre cap (as appropriate).
2   If the split pin is in position, the driveshaft nut should be correctly tightened. If in doubt, remove the split pin and slacken the nut, then tighten it through all the stages listed in the Specifications at the start of this Chapter. Once tightened, secure the nut in position with a new split pin, and refit the centre cap or trim. Repeat this check on the other driveshaft nut.
3   Road-test the vehicle, and listen for a metallic clicking from the front as the vehicle, is driven slowly in a circle on full-lock. If a clicking noise is heard, this indicates wear in the outer constant velocity joint. This means that the joint must be renewed; as reconditioning is not possible.
4   If vibration, consistent with road speed, is felt through the car when accelerating, there is a possibility of wear in the inner constant

velocity joints.
5   To check the joints for wear, remove the driveshafts, then dismantle them as described in Section 3; if any wear or free play is found, the affected joint must be renewed. **Note:** *If driveshaft joint wear is apparent on a vehicle which has covered in excess of 50 000 miles (80 000 km), the manufacturer recommends that the complete driveshaft is renewed.*

8

3.18a Hook the large outer retaining clip ends together . . .

3.18b . . . then secure the clip in position by compressing the raised section of the clip

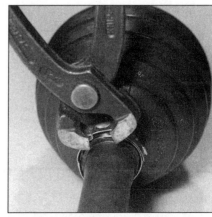

3.18c Small inner retaining clip is secured in position in the same way

Notes

Chapter 9 Braking system

Contents

Specifications

Front brakes

Type	Disc, with single-piston sliding caliper
Disc diameter:	
1.2 and 1.4 litre models	236 mm
1.6 litre DOHC models	256 mm
Disc thickness:	
New:	
Solid disc	12.7 mm
Ventilated disc	20.0 mm
Minimum thickness:	
Solid disc	9.7 mm
Ventilated disc	17.0 mm
Maximum disc runout	0.1 mm
Brake pad minimum thickness	7.0 mm

9

Rear brakes

Type	Single leading shoe drum

Drum diameter:

New:

Corsa and Corsavan models	200 mm
Combo Van models	230 mm

Maximum diameter:

Corsa and Corsavan models	201 mm
Combo Van models	231 mm
Maximum drum out-of-round	0.1 mm
Minimum friction material thickness	2.5 mm
Minimum friction material-to-rivet depth	0.5 mm

Torque wrench settings

	Nm	lbf ft
Front brake caliper:		
Guide bolts	30	22
Mounting bracket-to-swivel hub bolts	95	70
Front brake disc screw	4	3
Rear hub nut	25	18
Brake hose union bolt	40	30
Brake pipe union nut	16	12
Rear wheel cylinder bolts	9	7
Master cylinder mounting nuts	22	16
Master cylinder reservoir support bracket:		
Bracket-to-bulkhead nut	20	15
Bracket-to-reservoir bolt	12	9
Brake pedal pivot shaft nut	18	13
Servo unit mounting nuts	22	16
Pressure-regulating valve - 1.4 and 1.6 litre:		
Mounting bolts	20	15
Spring bolt (Corsa and Corsavan)	20	15
Spring clamp nuts (Combo Van)	20	15
ABS components:		
Modulator block nuts	8	6
Front wheel sensor bolt	8	6
Rear wheel sensor screw	4	3
Roadwheel bolts	110	81

1 General information

1 The braking system is of the servo-assisted, dual-circuit hydraulic type. The arrangement of the hydraulic system is such that each circuit operates one front and one rear brake from a tandem master cylinder. Under normal circumstances, both circuits operate in unison. However, in the event of hydraulic failure in one circuit, full braking force will still be available at two wheels.

2 All models have front disc brakes and rear drum brakes. An Antilock Braking System (ABS) is fitted as standard to the GSi 16V model, and was offered as an option on some other models (refer to Section 19 for further information on ABS operation).

3 The front disc brakes are actuated by single-piston sliding type calipers, which ensure that equal pressure is applied to each disc pad.

4 The rear drum brakes incorporate leading and trailing shoes, which are actuated by twin-piston wheel cylinders. A self-adjust mechanism is incorporated to automatically compensate for brake shoe wear. As the brake shoe linings wear, the footbrake operation automatically operates the adjuster mechanism, which effectively lengthens the shoe strut, and repositions the brake shoes to maintain the lining-to-drum clearance.

5 Pressure-regulating valves are situated in the hydraulic lines to control the pressure applied to the rear brakes. The regulating valves help to prevent rear wheel lock-up during emergency braking. On 1.2 litre models, the valves are of the pressure-dependent type; on all other models, they are of the load-dependent type, which actually alter the pressure to suit the load being carried by the vehicle.

6 The cable-operated handbrake provides an independent mechanical means of rear brake application.

Note: *When servicing any part of the system, work carefully and methodically; also observe scrupulous cleanliness when overhauling any part of the hydraulic system. Always renew components (in axle sets, where applicable) if in doubt about their condition, and use only genuine Vauxhall/Opel replacement parts, or at least those of known good quality. Note the warnings given in "Safety first" and at relevant points in this Chapter concerning the dangers of asbestos dust and hydraulic fluid.*

2 Hydraulic system - bleeding

Note: *Hydraulic fluid is poisonous; wash off immediately and thoroughly in the case of skin contact, and seek immediate medical advice if any fluid is swallowed or gets into the eyes. Certain types of hydraulic fluid are inflammable, and may ignite when allowed into contact with hot components. When servicing any hydraulic system, it is safest to assume that the fluid IS inflammable, and to take precautions against the risk of fire as though it is petrol that is being handled. Hydraulic fluid is also an effective paint stripper, and will attack plastics; if any is spilt, it should be washed off immediately using copious quantities of water. Finally, it is hygroscopic (it absorbs moisture from the air) - old fluid may be contaminated, and unfit for further use. When topping-up or renewing the fluid, always use the recommended type, and ensure that it comes from a freshly-opened sealed container.*

General

1   Any hydraulic system will only function correctly once all the air has been removed from the components and circuit; this is achieved by bleeding the system.

2   During the bleeding procedure, add only clean, fresh hydraulic fluid of the recommended type; never use old fluid, nor re-use any which has already been bled from the system. Ensure that sufficient fresh fluid is available before starting work.

3   If there is any possibility of the wrong fluid being in the system, the brake components and circuit must be flushed completely with un-contaminated, correct fluid, and new seals should be fitted to the various components.

4   If hydraulic fluid has been lost from the system (or if air has en-tered) because of a leak, ensure that the fault is cured before proceeding further.

5   Park the vehicle on level ground, switch off the engine and select first or reverse gear, then chock the wheels and release the handbrake.

6   Check that all pipes and hoses are secure, that the pipe unions are tight, and that the bleed screws are closed. Clean any dirt from around the bleed screws.

7   Unscrew the master cylinder reservoir cap, and top the master cylinder reservoir up to the "MAX" level line; refit the cap loosely, and remember to maintain the fluid level at least above the "MIN" level line throughout the procedure, to avoid the risk of further air entering the system.

8   There are a number of one-man, do-it-yourself brake bleeding kits currently available from motor accessory shops. It is recommended that one of these kits is used whenever possible, as they greatly sim-plify the bleeding operation, and also reduce the risk of expelled air and fluid being drawn back into the system. If such a kit is not avail-able, the basic (two-man) method must be used, which is described in detail below.

9   If a kit is to be used, prepare the vehicle as described previously, and follow the kit manufacturer's instructions, as the procedures may vary slightly according to the type being used; generally, they will be as outlined below in the relevant sub-section.

10   Whichever method is used, the same sequence must be followed (paragraphs 11 and 12) to ensure the removal of all air from the sys-tem.

Bleeding sequence

11   If the system has been only partially disconnected, and suitable precautions were taken to minimise fluid loss, it should only be neces-sary to bleed that part of the system (ie. the primary or secondary cir-cuit).

12   If the complete system is to be bled, then it should be done work-ing in the following sequence:
   (a) *Left-hand rear brake.*
   (b) *Right-hand front brake.*
   (c) *Right-hand rear brake.*
   (d) *Left-hand front brake.*

Bleeding - basic (two-man) method

13   Collect a clean glass jar, a suitable length of plastic or rubber tub-ing which is a tight fit over the bleed screw, and a ring spanner to fit the bleed screw. The help of an assistant will also be required.

14   Remove the dust cap from the first screw in the sequence. Fit the spanner and tube to the screw, place the other end of the tube in the jar, and pour in sufficient fluid to cover the end of the tube.

15   Ensure that the master cylinder reservoir fluid level is maintained at least above the "MIN" level line throughout the procedure.

16   Have the assistant fully depress the brake pedal several times to build up pressure, then maintain it on the final stroke.

17   While pedal pressure is maintained, unscrew the bleed screw (ap-proximately one turn) and allow the compressed fluid and air to flow into the jar. The assistant should maintain pedal pressure, following it down to the floor if necessary, and should not release it until instructed to do so. When the flow stops, tighten the bleed screw again; the pedal should then be released slowly, and the reservoir fluid level checked and topped-up.

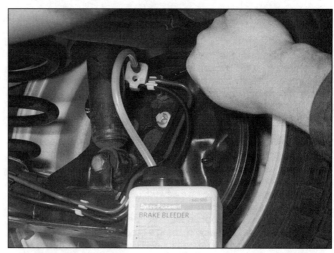

2.22 Using a one-way valve kit to bleed the rear brake

18   Repeat the steps given in paragraphs 16 and 17 until the fluid emerging from the bleed screw is free from air bubbles. If the master cylinder has been drained and refilled, and air is being bled from the first screw in the sequence, allow approximately five seconds between cycles for the master cylinder passages to refill.

19   When no more air bubbles appear, tighten the bleed screw se-curely, remove the tube and spanner, and refit the dust cap. Do not overtighten the bleed screw.

20   Repeat the procedure on the remaining screws in the sequence, until all air is removed from the system and the brake pedal feels firm again.

Bleeding - using a one-way valve kit

21   As their name implies, these kits consist of a length of tubing with a one-way valve fitted, to prevent expelled air and fluid being drawn back into the system; some kits include a translucent container, which can be positioned so that the air bubbles can be more easily seen flowing from the end of the tube.

22   The kit is connected to the bleed screw, which is then opened **(see illustration)**. The user returns to the driver's seat, depresses the brake pedal with a smooth, steady stroke, then slowly releases it; this is repeated until the expelled fluid is clear of air bubbles.

23   These kits simplify work so much that it is easy to forget the mas-ter cylinder reservoir fluid level; ensure that this is maintained at least above the "MIN" level line at all times, or air will be drawn into the sys-tem.

Bleeding - using a pressure bleeding kit

24   These kits are usually operated by the reservoir of pressurised air contained in the spare tyre, noting that it will probably be necessary to reduce the pressure to less than normal; refer to the instructions sup-plied with the kit.

25   By connecting a pressurised, fluid-filled container to the master cylinder reservoir, bleeding can be carried out simply by opening each screw in turn (in the specified sequence) and allowing the fluid to flow out until no more air bubbles can be seen in the expelled fluid.

26   This method has the advantage that the large reservoir of fluid provides an additional safeguard against air being drawn into the sys-tem during bleeding.

27   Pressure bleeding is particularly effective when bleeding "diffi-cult" systems, or when bleeding the complete system at the time of routine fluid renewal.

All methods

28   When bleeding is complete and firm pedal feel is restored, wash off any spilt fluid, tighten the bleed screws securely, and refit their dust caps.

29   Check the hydraulic fluid level, and top-up if necessary (Chap-ter 1).

9

30   Discard any hydraulic fluid that has been bled from the system; it will not be fit for re-use. Bear in mind that this fluid may be inflammable.

31   Check the feel of the brake pedal. If it feels at all spongy, air must still be present in the system, and further bleeding is required. Failure to bleed satisfactorily after a reasonable repetition of the bleeding procedure may be due to worn master cylinder seals.

3   Hydraulic pipes and hoses - renewal

Note: *Before starting work, refer to the note at the beginning of Section 2 concerning the dangers of hydraulic fluid.*

1   If any pipe or hose is to be renewed, minimise fluid loss by first removing the master cylinder reservoir cap, then tightening it down onto a piece of polythene to obtain an airtight seal. Alternatively, flexible hoses can be sealed, if required, using a proprietary brake hose clamp. Metal brake pipe unions can be plugged (if care is taken not to allow dirt into the system) or capped immediately they are disconnected. Place a wad of rag under any union that is to be disconnected, to catch any spilt fluid.

2   If a flexible hose is to be disconnected, unscrew the brake pipe union nut before removing the spring clip which secures the hose to its mounting bracket.

3   To unscrew the union nuts, it is preferable to obtain a brake pipe spanner of the correct size; these are available from most large motor accessory shops. Failing this, a close-fitting open-ended spanner will be required, though if the nuts are tight or corroded, their flats may be rounded-off if the spanner slips. In such a case, a self-locking wrench is often the only way to unscrew a stubborn union, but it follows that the pipe and the damaged nuts must be renewed on reassembly. Always clean a union and surrounding area before disconnecting it. If disconnecting a component with more than one union, make a careful note of the connections before disturbing any of them.

4   If a brake pipe is to be renewed it can be obtained, cut to length and with the union nuts and end flares in place, from Vauxhall/Opel dealers. All that is then necessary is to bend it to shape, following the line of the original, before fitting it to the car. Alternatively, most motor accessory shops can make up brake pipes from kits, but this requires very careful measurement of the original to ensure that the replacement is of the correct length. The safest answer is usually to take the original to the shop as a pattern.

5   On refitting, do not overtighten the union nuts. It is not necessary to exercise brute force to obtain a sound joint.

6   Ensure that the pipes and hoses are correctly routed, with no kinks, and that they are secured in the clips or brackets provided. After fitting, remove the polythene from the reservoir, and bleed the hydraulic system as described in Section 2. Wash off any spilt fluid, and check carefully for fluid leaks.

4   Front brake pads - renewal

Warning: *Renew BOTH sets of front brake pads at the same time - NEVER renew the pads on only one wheel, as uneven braking may result. Note that the dust created by wear of the pads may contain asbestos, which is a health hazard. Never blow it out with compressed air, and don't inhale any of it. An approved filtering mask should be worn when working on the brakes. DO NOT use petroleum-based solvents to clean brake parts - use brake cleaner or methylated spirit only.*

1   Chock the rear wheels, apply the handbrake, then jack up the front of the vehicle and support it on axle stands. Remove the front roadwheels, marking the correct fitted position of each wheel on its hub.

2   Using a screwdriver, prise the pad retaining spring from the outer edge of the caliper, noting its correct fitted position **(see illustration)**.

3   Prise out the two guide bolt dust caps from the inner edge of the caliper **(see illustration)**.

4   Unscrew the guide bolts from the caliper, and lift the caliper and inner pad away from the mounting bracket. Tie the caliper to the suspension strut using a suitable piece of wire **(see illustrations)**. Do not allow the caliper to hang unsupported on the flexible brake hose.

5   Remove the inner pad from the caliper piston, noting that it is retained by a clip attached to the pad backing plate, and recover the outer pad from the mounting bracket.

6   Brush the dirt and dust from the caliper, but take care not to inhale it. Carefully remove any rust from the edge of the brake disc.

7   First measure the thickness of each brake pad (friction material and backing plate) **(see illustration)**. If either pad is worn at any point to the specified minimum thickness or less, **all four** pads must be renewed. The pads should also be renewed if any are fouled with oil or grease; there is no satisfactory way of degreasing friction material, once contaminated. If any of the brake pads are worn unevenly, or fouled with oil or grease, trace and rectify the cause before reassembly. The pad retaining spring should also be renewed if new pads are to be fitted. New brake pads and retaining springs are available from Vauxhall/Opel dealers.

8   If the brake pads are still serviceable, carefully clean them using a clean, fine wire brush or similar, paying particular attention to the sides and back of the metal backing. Clean out the grooves in the friction material, and pick out any large embedded particles of dirt or debris. Carefully clean the pad locations in the caliper body/mounting bracket.

9   Prior to fitting the pads, check that the guide bolts are a snug fit in the caliper bushes. Brush the dust and dirt from the caliper and piston, but **do not** inhale it, as it is injurious to health. Inspect the dust seal around the piston for damage, and the piston for evidence of fluid leaks, corrosion or damage. If attention to any of these components is necessary, refer to Section 8.

10   If new brake pads are to be fitted, the caliper piston must be pushed back into the cylinder to make room for them. Either use a G-

4.2 Using a screwdriver, carefully prise out the pad retaining spring from the caliper

4.3 Remove the guide bolt dust caps . . .

4.4a . . . then unscrew the guide bolts . . .

4.4b . . . and slide off the caliper and inner pad assembly

4.4c Tie the caliper to the suspension strut, to avoid placing any strain on the hydraulic brake hose

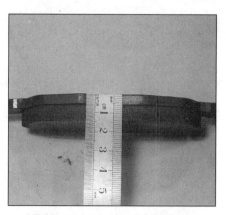

4.7 Measuring brake pad thickness

4.11 Clip the inner pad securely into the caliper piston . . .

4.12 . . . and fit the outer pad to the caliper mounting bracket

4.14 Slide the caliper into position and install the guide bolts, tightening them to the specified torque setting

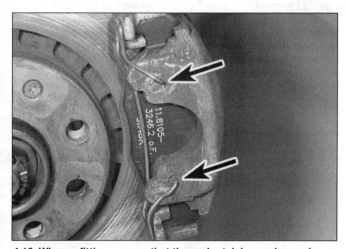

4.16 When refitting, ensure that the pad retaining spring ends are correctly located in the caliper holes (arrowed)

12 Fit the outer pad to the caliper mounting bracket, ensuring that its friction material is facing the brake disc (see illustration).
13 Slide the caliper and inner pad into position over the outer pad, and locate it in the mounting bracket.
14 Install the caliper guide bolts, and tighten them to the specified torque setting (see illustration).
15 Refit the guide bolt dust caps to the caliper.
16 Refit the pad retaining spring to the caliper, ensuring that its ends are correctly located in the caliper holes (see illustration).
17 Depress the brake pedal repeatedly, until normal (non-assisted) pedal pressure is restored, and the pads are pressed into firm contact with the brake disc.
18 Repeat the above procedure on the remaining front brake caliper.
19 Refit the roadwheels, aligning the marks made on removal, then lower the vehicle to the ground and tighten the roadwheel bolts to the specified torque setting.
20 Check the hydraulic fluid level as described in Chapter 1.

5 Rear brake shoes - renewal

clamp or similar tool, or use suitable pieces of wood as levers. Provided that the master cylinder reservoir has not been overfilled with hydraulic fluid, there should be no spillage, but keep a careful watch on the fluid level while retracting the piston. If the fluid level rises above the "MAX" level line at any time, the surplus should be syphoned off or ejected via a plastic tube connected to the bleed screw (see Section 2). **Note:** *Do not syphon the fluid by mouth, as it is poisonous; use a syringe or an old poultry baster.*
11 Fit the inner pad to the caliper, ensuring that its clip is correctly located in the caliper piston (see illustration).

Warning: *Brake shoes must be renewed on BOTH rear wheels at the same time - NEVER renew the shoes on only one wheel, as uneven braking may result. The dust created as the shoes wear may contain asbestos, which is a health hazard. Never blow it out with compressed air, and don't inhale any of it. An approved filtering mask should be worn when working on the brakes. DO NOT use petroleum-based solvents to clean brake parts - use brake cleaner or methylated spirit only.*
1 Remove the brake drum as described in Section 7.
2 Working carefully and taking the necessary precautions, remove all traces of brake dust from the brake drum, backplate and shoes.

9

5.3a Brake shoe wear can be assessed by measuring the thickness of the friction material . . .

5.3b . . . or by measuring the depth from the friction material surface to the rivet heads (a tyre tread depth indicator may be used, as shown)

5.5 Prior to disturbing the shoes, note the correct fitted locations of all components, paying particular attention to the adjuster strut components

5.6 Unhook the upper return spring, and remove it from the brake shoes

5.7 Remove the retaining spring, followed by the lever and return spring (arrowed)

5.9a Using pliers, remove the spring cup . . .

5.9b . . . then lift off the spring and retainer pin

3   Measure the thickness of the friction material of each brake shoe, at several points. If the friction material thickness or the depth from the friction material surface to any of the of rivet heads is equal to or less than the specified minimum, **all four** shoes must be renewed as a set **(see illustrations)**. Also, the shoes should be renewed if any are fouled with oil or grease; there is no satisfactory way of degreasing friction material, once contaminated.

4   If any of the brake shoes are worn unevenly, or fouled with oil or grease, trace and rectify the cause before reassembly. If the shoes are

to be renewed proceed as described below. If all is well refit the drums as described in Section 7.

5   Note the location and orientation of all components before dismantling, as an aid to reassembly **(see illustration)**.

6   Using a pair of pliers, carefully unhook the upper shoe return spring, and remove it from the brake shoes **(see illustration)**.

7   Prise the adjusting lever retaining spring out of the front shoe, and remove the retaining spring, lever and return spring from the brake shoe, noting each component's correct fitted position **(see illustration)**.

8   Prise the upper ends of the brake shoes apart, and withdraw the adjuster strut from between the shoes.

9   Using a pair of pliers, remove the front shoe retainer spring cup by depressing and turning it through 90∞. With the cup removed, lift off the spring and withdraw the retainer pin **(see illustrations)**.

10   Detach the front shoe from the lower return spring, and remove both the shoe and return spring.

11   Remove the rear shoe retainer spring cup, spring and retainer pin as described in paragraph 9, then remove the shoe, detaching it from the handbrake cable.

12   **Do not** depress the brake pedal until the brakes are reassembled. As a precaution, wrap a strong elastic band around the wheel cylinder pistons to retain them.

13   Although linings are available separately (without shoes), renewal of the shoes complete with linings is to be preferred, unless the necessary skills and equipment are available to fit new linings to the old shoes.

14   If both brake assemblies are dismantled at the same time, take care not to mix up the components. Note that the left-hand and right-hand adjuster components are marked as such; the threaded rod is marked "L" or "R", and the other "handed" components are colour-

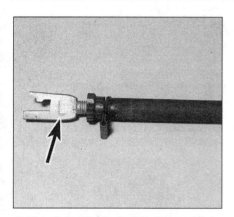

5.14 Left-hand adjuster strut assembly is marked "L" (arrow)

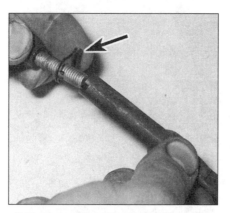

5.15 Dismantling the adjuster strut. The thermoclip (arrowed) should be renewed

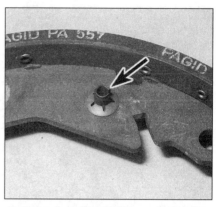

5.17 It may be necessary to transfer the adjusting lever pivot pin and clip (arrowed) from the original shoes to the new ones

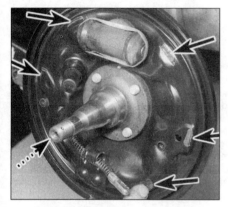

5.19 Apply a smear of anti-seize compound to the contact surfaces of the backplate (arrowed). Note the elastic band wrapped around the wheel cylinder

5.20 Engage the rear brake shoe with the handbrake cable, and locate the shoe on the backplate

5.22a Install the front shoe and lower return spring . . .

5.22b . . . and secure it in position with the retainer pin, spring and spring cup

coded black for the left-hand side, and silver for the right-hand side **(see illustration)**.

15　Dismantle and clean the adjuster strut. Apply a smear of silicone-based grease to the adjuster threads. If new brake linings or shoes are to be fitted, the thermoclip on the adjuster strut must also be renewed **(see illustration)**.

16　Examine the return springs. If they are distorted, or if they have seen extensive service, renewal is advisable. Weak springs may cause the brakes to bind.

17　If a new handbrake operating lever was not supplied with the new shoes (where applicable), transfer the lever from the old shoes. The lever may be secured with a pin and circlip, or by a rivet, which will have to be drilled out. It may also be necessary to transfer the adjusting lever pivot pin and clip from the original front shoe to the new shoe **(see illustration)**.

18　Peel back the rubber protective caps, and check the wheel cylinder for fluid leaks or other damage. Ensure that both cylinder pistons are free to move easily. Refer to Section 9, if necessary, for information on wheel cylinder overhaul.

19　Prior to installation, clean the backplate thoroughly. Apply a thin smear of high-temperature copper-based brake grease or anti-seize compound (eg Duckhams Copper 10) to all those surfaces of the backplate which bear on the shoes, particularly the wheel cylinder pistons and lower pivot point **(see illustration)**. Do not allow the lubricant to foul the friction material.

20　Ensure that the handbrake cable is correctly retained by the clip on the lower brake shoe pivot point, then engage the rear shoe with the cable. Locate the shoe on the backplate **(see illustration)**.

21　Install the rear shoe retainer pin and spring, and secure it in position with the spring cup.

22　Hook the lower return spring onto the rear shoe, then engage the front shoe with the return spring. Locate the front shoe on the backplate, and secure it in position with its retainer pin, spring and spring cup **(see illustrations)**.

23　Screw the adjuster strut wheel fully onto the forked end of the adjuster, so that the adjuster strut is set to its shortest possible length. Back the wheel off a half a turn, and check that it is free to rotate easily.

9

5.24 Refit the adjuster strut, noting that the longer, straight part of the fork (arrowed) must be behind the shoe

5.25 Refit the adjusting lever and spring, making sure that the spring is correctly engaged in the front brake shoe hole (arrowed)

5.26 Make sure that both shoes are correctly aligned with the wheel cylinder, then install the upper return spring

24 Manoeuvre the adjuster strut assembly into position between the brake shoes. Make sure that both ends of the strut are correctly engaged with the shoes, noting that the forked end of the strut must be positioned so that its longer, straight fork is to the rear of the shoe **(see illustration)**.

25 Engage the adjusting lever return spring with the front shoe and adjusting lever, and locate the lever on its pivot pin **(see illustration)**. Check that the lever and spring are correctly located, and secure them the lever in position with the retaining spring, making sure the spring ends are securely located in the retaining pin and shoe **(see illustration 5.5)**.

26 Remove the rubber band from the wheel cylinder. Make sure that both shoes are correctly positioned on the wheel cylinder pistons, then fit the upper return spring **(see illustration)**.

27 Ensure that the handbrake operating lever stop peg is correctly positioned against the edge of the shoe web, then refit the brake drum as described in Section 7.

28 Repeat the operation on the remaining brake.

29 Once both sets of rear shoes have been renewed, with the handbrake fully released, adjust the lining-to-drum clearance by repeatedly depressing the brake pedal at least 20 to 25 times. Whilst depressing the pedal, have an assistant listen to the rear drums, to check that the adjuster strut is functioning correctly; if so, a clicking sound will be emitted by the strut as the pedal is depressed.

30 Check and, if necessary, adjust the handbrake as described in Section 14.

31 On completion, check the hydraulic fluid level as described in Chapter 1.

---

6 Front brake disc - inspection, removal and refitting

Note: *Before starting work, refer to the note at the beginning of Section 4 concerning the dangers of asbestos dust.*

Inspection

Note: *If either disc requires renewal, BOTH should be renewed at the same time, to ensure even and consistent braking.*

1 Chock the rear wheels, firmly apply the handbrake, then jack up the front of the car and support it on axle stands. Remove the appropriate front roadwheel, marking its correct fitted position on the hub.

2 Slowly rotate the brake disc so that the full area of both sides can be checked; remove the brake pads if better access is required to the inner surface. Light scoring is normal in the area swept by the brake pads, but if heavy scoring is found, the disc must be renewed.

3 It is normal to find a lip of rust and brake dust around the disc's perimeter; this can be scraped off if required. If, however, a lip has formed due to excessive wear of the brake pad swept area, then the

disc's thickness must be measured using a micrometer. Take measurements at several places around the disc, at the inside and outside of the pad swept area; if the disc has worn at any point to the specified minimum thickness or less, the disc must be renewed.

4 If the disc is thought to be warped, it can be checked for run-out either using a dial gauge mounted on any convenient fixed point, while the disc is slowly rotated, or by using feeler gauges to measure (at several points all around the disc) the clearance between the disc and a fixed point such as the caliper mounting bracket. To ensure that the disc is squarely seated on the hub, fit two wheel bolts, complete with spacers approximately 10 mm thick, and tighten them securely. If the measurements obtained are at the specified maximum or beyond, the disc is excessively warped and must be renewed; however, it is worth checking first that the hub bearing is in good condition (Chapters 1 and/or 10).

5 Check the disc for cracks, especially around the wheel bolt holes, and for any other wear or damage, and renew if necessary.

Removal

Note: *New brake caliper-to-swivel hub bolts will be required when refitting.*

6 Unscrew the two bolts securing the brake caliper assembly to the swivel hub, and slide the caliper assembly off the disc **(see illustrations)**. Using a piece of wire or string, tie the caliper to the front suspension coil spring, to avoid placing any strain on the hydraulic brake hose. Discard the caliper mounting bolts; they must be renewed whenever they are disturbed.

6.6a Slacken and remove the two bolts (arrowed) securing the brake caliper to the hub . . .

6.6b . . . then slide the caliper assembly
off the brake disc

6.7a Undo the retaining screw . . .

6.7b . . . and remove the brake disc from
the hub

6.8a Apply thread-locking compound to
the threads of the brake caliper
mounting bolts . . .

6.8b . . . and tighten them to the specified
torque setting

7.2 Remove the cap from the centre of
the drum to gain access to the hub nut

7   Remove the screw securing the brake disc to the hub, and re-move the disc. If it is tight, lightly tap its rear face with a hide or plastic mallet **(see illustrations)**.

Refitting

8   Refitting is the reverse of the removal procedure, noting the fol-lowing points:
  (a) *Ensure that the mating surfaces of the disc and hub are clean and flat.*
  (b) *Tighten the disc retaining screw to the specified torque set-ting.*
  (c) *If a new disc has been fitted, use a suitable solvent to wipe any preservative coating from the disc before refitting the caliper.*
  (d) *Remove all traces of old thread-locking compound from the brake caliper holes in the swivel hub, ideally by running a tap of the correct size and pitch through them (or refer to the tip in Chapter 10, Section 2). If the threads of the new caliper mounting bolts are not already pre-coated with compound, apply a suitable thread-locking compound to them. Slide the caliper assembly into position over the disc, then fit the mount-ing bolts and tighten them to the specified torque setting (see illustrations).*
  (e) *Refit the roadwheel, aligning the marks made on removal, then lower the vehicle to the ground and tighten the roadwheel bolts to the specified torque. On completion, repeatedly de-press the brake pedal until normal (non-assisted) pedal pres-sure returns.*

7   Rear brake drum - removal, inspection and refitting

Note: *Before starting work, refer to the note at the beginning of Section 5 concerning the dangers of asbestos dust.*

Removal

1   Chock the front wheels, then jack up the rear of the vehicle and support it on axle stands. Remove the appropriate rear wheel, marking its correct fitted position on the drum, and release the handbrake. Pro-ceed as described under the relevant sub-heading.

Corsa and Corsavan

2   Prise out the cap from the centre of the drum **(see illustration)**.
3   Extract the split pin from the hub nut and discard it; a new one must be used on refitting.
4   Slacken and remove the rear hub nut, then slide off the toothed washer and remove the outer bearing from the centre of the drum **(see illustrations)**.

7.4a Slacken and remove the hub nut and washer . . .

9

7.4b . . . followed by the outer bearing

7.7a If necessary, release the handbrake lever stop-peg by inserting a screwdriver in through the hole in the rear of the backplate . . .

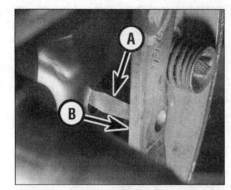

7.7b . . . and use screwdriver (A) to push handbrake lever away from the brake shoe in the direction of arrow (B) - shown with drum removed

7.14 Prior to refitting the drum, check that the handbrake lever is correctly positioned on the shoe

7.15 Fit the toothed washer, making sure its tooth is correctly engaged with the stub axle slot

7.16a Tighten the hub nut to the specified torque setting while rotating the drum

5   It should now be possible to withdraw the brake drum assembly from the stub axle by hand. It may be difficult to remove the drum, due to the brake shoes binding on the inner circumference of the drum. If the brake shoes are binding, first check that the handbrake is fully released, then proceed as follows.

6   Referring to Section 14 for further information, fully slacken the handbrake cable adjuster nut to obtain maximum free play in the cable.

7   Remove the plug from the inspection hole in the brake backplate, and push the handbrake operating lever outwards away from the brake shoe. This will release the handbrake lever stop-peg from the edge of the brake shoe, and further collapse the shoes **(see illustrations)**. The brake drum can then be withdrawn from the stub axle.

Combo Van

8   Slacken and remove the drum retaining screw, and remove the drum from the vehicle. It may be difficult to remove the drum due to the brake shoes binding on the inner circumference of the drum. If the brake shoes are binding, first check that the handbrake is fully released, then proceed as described above in paragraphs 6 and 7.

Inspection

Note: *If either drum requires renewal, BOTH should be renewed at the same time, to ensure even and consistent braking.*

9   Working carefully, remove all traces of brake dust from the drum, but *avoid inhaling the dust, as it is a health-hazard.*

10   Scrub clean the outside of the drum, and check it for obvious signs of wear or damage (such as cracks around the roadwheel bolt holes); renew the drum if necessary.

11   Examine the inside of the drum carefully. Light scoring of the friction surface is normal, but if heavy scoring is found, the drum must be renewed. It is usual to find a lip on the drum's inboard edge which consists of a mixture of rust and brake dust; this should be scraped away, to leave a smooth surface which can be polished with fine (120- to

150-grade) emery paper. If, however, the lip is due to the friction surface being recessed by excessive wear, then the drum must be renewed.

12   If the drum is thought to be excessively worn, or oval, its internal diameter must be measured at several points using an internal micrometer. Take measurements in pairs, the second at right-angles to the first, and compare the two to check for signs of ovality. Provided that it does not enlarge the drum to beyond the specified maximum diameter, it may be possible to have the drum refinished by skimming or grinding; if this is not possible, the drums on **both** sides must be renewed. Note that if the drum is to be skimmed, **both** drums must be refinished, to maintain a consistent internal diameter on both sides.

Refitting

13   If a new brake drum is to be installed, use a suitable solvent to remove any preservative coating that may have been applied to its interior. Note that it may also be necessary to shorten the adjuster strut length by rotating the strut wheel, to allow the new drum to pass over the brake shoes.

Corsa and Corsavan

14   Ensure that the handbrake lever stop peg is correctly repositioned against the edge of the brake shoe web **(see illustration)**, and apply a smear of grease to the drum oil seal.

15   Slide the drum into position, then refit the outer bearing and toothed thrustwasher, ensuring that its tooth is correctly engaged in the axle slot **(see illustration)**.

16   Refit the hub nut, and tighten it to the specified torque setting, while rotating the brake drum to settle the hub bearings in position. Gradually slacken the hub nut until the position is found where it is just possible to move the toothed washer from side to side using a screwdriver **(see illustrations)**. **Note:** *Only a small amount of force should be needed to move the washer.* When the hub nut is correctly positioned,

7.16b Gradually slacken the hub nut until the position is found where it is just possible to move the toothed washer

7.17 When the hub bearing is correctly adjusted, secure the nut in position with a new split pin

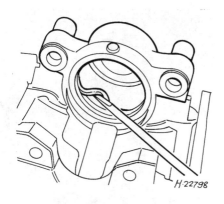

8.7 Removing the piston seal from the caliper body

secure it in position with a new split pin.

17   If the stub axle holes are not aligned with any of the slots in the hub nut, tighten the nut by the *smallest amount possible* until the split pin can be inserted. With the nut in this position, check that it is still possible to move the toothed washer. If it is, insert the split pin and secure it in position. If it is not possible to move the washer, slacken the nut slightly until the next hub nut slot/axle hole aligns. Check that it is possible to move the toothed washer, then secure the hub nut in position with the new split pin **(see illustration)**.

18   Fit the cap to the centre of the brake drum.

19   With the handbrake fully released, adjust the lining-to-drum clearance by repeatedly depressing the brake pedal at least 20 to 25 times. Whilst depressing the pedal, have an assistant listen to the rear drums, to check that the adjuster strut is functioning correctly; if so, a clicking sound will be emitted by the strut as the pedal is depressed.

20   With the lining-to-drum clearance set, check and, if necessary, adjust the handbrake as described in Section 14.

21   Refit the roadwheel, aligning the marks made on removal, then lower the vehicle to the ground and tighten the roadwheel bolts to the specified torque setting.

Combo Van

22   Ensure that the drum and hub flange mating surfaces are clean and dry, and remove all traces of corrosion.

23   Ensure that the handbrake lever stop peg is correctly repositioned against the edge of the brake shoe web, and locate the drum on the hub. Refit the drum retaining screw, and tighten it securely.

24   Carry out the operations described in paragraphs 19 to 21.

8   Front brake caliper - removal, overhaul and refitting

Note: *New brake hose sealing washers will be required when refitting. Before starting work, refer to the note at the beginning of Section 2 concerning the dangers of hydraulic fluid, and to the warning at the beginning of Section 4 concerning the dangers of asbestos dust.*

Removal

1   Chock the rear wheels, apply the handbrake, then jack up the front of the vehicle and support it on axle stands. Remove the appropriate roadwheel, marking its correct fitted position on the wheel hub.

2   Minimise fluid loss by first removing the master cylinder reservoir cap, then tightening it down onto a piece of polythene to obtain an air-tight seal. Alternatively, use a brake hose clamp, a G-clamp or a similar tool to clamp the flexible hose.

3   Clean the area around the caliper brake hose union. Slacken and remove the union bolt, and recover the sealing washer from either side of the hose union. Discard the washers; new ones must be used on refitting. Plug the hose end and caliper hole, to minimise fluid loss and prevent the ingress of dirt into the hydraulic system.

4   Remove the brake pads as described in paragraphs 2 to 5 of Section 4, and remove the caliper from the vehicle.

Overhaul

5   With the caliper on the bench, wipe away all traces of dust and dirt, but *avoid inhaling the dust, as it is a health hazard.*

6   Withdraw the partially-ejected piston from the caliper body, and remove the dust seal. The piston can be withdrawn by hand, or if necessary pushed out by applying compressed air to the brake hose union hole. Only low pressure should be required, such as is generated by a foot pump.

7   Using a small screwdriver, carefully remove the piston seal from the caliper, taking great care not mark the bore **(see illustration)**.

8   Carefully press the guide bushes out of the caliper body.

9   Thoroughly clean all components, using only methylated spirit, isopropyl alcohol or clean hydraulic fluid as a cleaning medium. Never use mineral-based solvents such as petrol or paraffin, which will attack the hydraulic system's rubber components. Dry the components immediately, using compressed air or a clean, lint-free cloth. Use compressed air to blow clear the fluid passages, if available (wear eye protection).

10   Check all components, and renew any that are worn or damaged. Check particularly the cylinder bore and piston; these should be renewed (note that this means the renewal of the complete body assembly) if they are scratched, worn or corroded in any way. Similarly check the condition of the guide bushes and bolts; both bushes and bolts should be undamaged and (when cleaned) a reasonably tight sliding fit in each other. If there is any doubt about the condition of any component, renew it.

11   If the assembly is fit for further use, obtain the necessary components from your Vauxhall/Opel dealer. Renew the caliper seals as a matter of course; these should never be re-used.

12   On reassembly, ensure that all components are absolutely clean and dry.

13   Soak the piston and the new piston (fluid) seal in clean hydraulic fluid. Smear clean fluid on the cylinder bore surface.

14   Fit the new piston (fluid) seal, using only the fingers to manipulate it into the cylinder bore groove.

15   Fit the new dust seal to the piston, refit it to the cylinder bore using a twisting motion, and ensure that the piston enters squarely into the bore. Press the dust seal fully into the caliper body, and push the piston fully into the caliper bore.

16   Ease the guide bushes into position in the caliper body.

Refitting

17   Refit the caliper and brake pads as described in paragraphs 11 to 16 of Section 4.

18   Position a new sealing washer on each side of the hose union, and connect the brake hose to the caliper. Ensure that the hose is correctly positioned against the caliper body lug, then install the union bolt and tighten it to the specified torque setting.

9

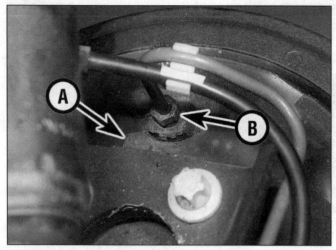

9.4 Rear wheel cylinder retaining bolt (A) and brake pipe union nut (B)

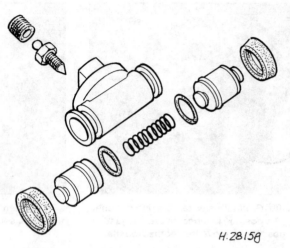

9.6 Exploded view of a rear brake wheel cylinder

19   Remove the brake hose clamp or the polythene, where fitted, and bleed the hydraulic system as described in Section 2. Note that, providing the precautions described were taken to minimise brake fluid loss, it should only be necessary to bleed the relevant front brake.

20   Refit the roadwheel, aligning the marks made on removal, then lower the vehicle to the ground and tighten the roadwheel bolts to the specified torque.

9   Rear wheel cylinder - removal, overhaul and refitting

Note: *Before starting work, refer to the note at the beginning of Section 2 concerning the dangers of hydraulic fluid, and to the warning at the beginning of Section 5 concerning the dangers of asbestos dust.*

Removal

1   Remove the brake drum as described in Section 7.

2   Using pliers, carefully unhook the upper brake shoe return spring, and remove it from both brake shoes. Pull the upper ends of the shoes away from the wheel cylinder to disengage them from the pistons.

3   Minimise fluid loss by first removing the master cylinder reservoir cap, then tightening it down onto a piece of polythene to obtain an airtight seal. Alternatively, use a brake hose clamp, a G-clamp or a similar tool to clamp the flexible hose at the nearest convenient point to the wheel cylinder.

4   Wipe away all traces of dirt around the brake pipe union at the rear of the wheel cylinder, and unscrew the union nut. Carefully ease the pipe out of the wheel cylinder, and plug or tape over its end to prevent dirt entry. Wipe off any spilt fluid immediately **(see illustration)**.

5   Unscrew the two wheel cylinder retaining bolts from the rear of the backplate, and remove the cylinder, taking great care not to allow surplus hydraulic fluid to contaminate the brake shoe linings.

Overhaul

6   Brush the dirt and dust from the wheel cylinder, but take care not to inhale it **(see illustration)**.

7   Pull the rubber dust seals from the ends of the cylinder body.

8   The pistons will normally be ejected by the pressure of the coil spring, but if they are not, tap the end of the cylinder body on a piece of wood, or apply low air pressure (eg, from a foot pump) to the hydraulic fluid union hole to eject the pistons from their bores.

9   Inspect the surfaces of the pistons and their bores in the cylinder body for scoring, or evidence of metal-to-metal contact. If evident, renew the complete wheel cylinder assembly.

10 - If the pistons and bores are in good condition, discard the seals and obtain a repair kit, which will contain all the necessary renewable items.

11   Lubricate the piston seals with clean brake fluid, and insert them

into the cylinder bores, with the spring between them, using finger pressure only.

12   Dip the pistons in clean brake fluid, and insert them into the cylinder bores.

13   Fit the dust seals, and check that the pistons can move freely in their bores.

Refitting

14   Ensure that the backplate and wheel cylinder mating surfaces are clean, then spread the brake shoes and manoeuvre the wheel cylinder into position.

15   Engage the brake pipe, and screw in the union nut two or three turns to ensure that the thread has started.

16   Insert the two wheel cylinder retaining bolts, and tighten them to the specified torque setting. Now tighten the brake pipe union nut to the specified torque.

17   Remove the clamp from the flexible brake hose, or the polythene from the master cylinder reservoir (as applicable).

18   Ensure that the brake shoes are correctly located in the cylinder pistons, then carefully refit the brake shoe upper return spring, using a screwdriver to stretch the spring into position.

19   Refit the brake drum as described in Section 7.

20   Bleed the brake hydraulic system as described in Section 2. Providing suitable precautions were taken to minimise loss of fluid, it should only be necessary to bleed the relevant rear brake.

10   Master cylinder - removal, overhaul and refitting

Note: *New master cylinder retaining nuts will be required when refitting. Before starting work, refer to the warning at the beginning of Section 2 concerning the dangers of hydraulic fluid.*

Removal

1   Remove the master cylinder reservoir cap, and syphon the hydraulic fluid from the reservoir. **Note:** *Do not syphon the fluid by mouth, as it is poisonous; use a syringe or an old poultry baster.* Alternatively, open any convenient bleed screw in the system, and gently pump the brake pedal to expel the fluid through a plastic tube connected to the screw (see Section 2).

2   Disconnect the battery negative lead, and the wiring connector from the brake fluid level sender unit **(see illustration)**. Proceed as described under the relevant sub-heading.

Left-hand drive models

3   Wipe clean the area around the brake pipe unions on the side of the master cylinder, and place absorbent rags beneath the pipe unions to catch any surplus fluid. Make a note of the correct fitted positions of

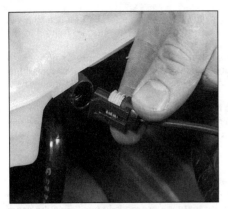

10.2 Disconnecting the master cylinder brake fluid level sender wiring connector

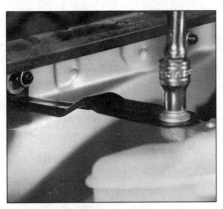

10.12a On right-hand drive models, unscrew the retaining bolt and nut . . .

10.12b . . . and remove the support bracket from the master cylinder

10.13a Undo the two retaining nuts (arrowed) . . .

10.13b . . . and remove the master cylinder from the servo unit

10.13c Where necessary, recover the pushrod . . .

the unions, then unscrew the union nuts and carefully withdraw the pipes. Plug or tape over the pipe ends and master cylinder orifices, to minimise the loss of brake fluid and to prevent the entry of dirt into the system. Wash off any spilt fluid immediately with cold water.

4   Slacken and remove the two nuts securing the master cylinder to the vacuum servo unit and discard them; new ones must be used on refitting. Withdraw the master cylinder assembly from the engine compartment, noting that on models with ABS, it will be necessary to undo the two retaining nuts securing the fluid reservoir to the engine compartment bulkhead.

5   Recover the seal which is fitted between the master cylinder and servo. If the servo unit pushrod has come away with the master cylinder, remove it and refit it to the centre of the servo.

Right-hand drive models

6   Remove both windscreen wiper arms as described in Chapter 12.
7   Carefully prise out the wiper spindle sealing grommets from the windscreen cowl panel.
8   Undo the retaining screws, and remove both halves of the windscreen cowl panel from the vehicle.
9   Peel the bonnet seal off the engine compartment bulkhead, and remove it from the vehicle.
10   Unscrew the large plastic nut from each wiper spindle.
11   Prise out the two retaining clips from the centre of the water deflector shield, then release the shield from the engine compartment bulkhead and wiper spindles, and remove it from the vehicle.
12   Unscrew the nut and bolt, and remove the support bracket from the top of the master cylinder fluid reservoir (see illustrations).
13   Remove the master cylinder as described above in paragraphs 3 to 5, ignoring the note concerning models fitted with ABS (see illustrations).

10.13d . . . and rubber seal from the servo unit

Overhaul

Models with ABS

14   At the time of writing, master cylinder overhaul on models with ABS is not possible, as no spares are available. If the cylinder is thought to be faulty, it must be renewed.

15   The only parts available individually are the fluid reservoir and its mounting seals. These can be renewed as described below for the non-ABS models.

9

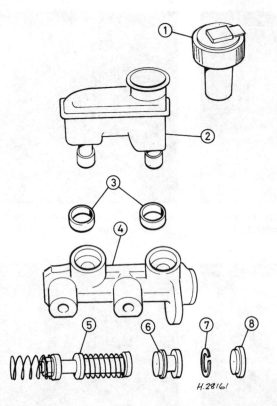

10.16 Exploded view of the master cylinder - models without ABS

1 Cap	5 Primary piston and springs
2 Reservoir	6 Secondary piston
3 Seals	7 Circlip
4 Master cylinder body	8 Seal

Models without ABS

16   Unhook the clip (where necessary), and remove the fluid reservoir and reservoir seals from the master cylinder body **(see illustration)**.

17   Carefully prise the seal out of the end of the master cylinder.

18   Using a wooden dowel, press the piston assembly into the master cylinder body, then extract the circlip from the end of the master cylinder bore.

19   Noting the order of removal and the direction of fitting of each component, withdraw the piston assemblies, complete with springs and seals. Tap the body on to a clean wooden surface to dislodge them. If necessary, clamp the master cylinder body in a vice (fitted with soft jaw covers) and use compressed air (applied through the one of the fluid ports) to assist the removal of the piston assemblies. Wear eye protection if compressed air is used.

20   Thoroughly clean all components, using only methylated spirit, isopropyl alcohol or clean hydraulic fluid as a cleaning medium. Never use mineral-based solvents such as petrol or paraffin, which will attack the hydraulic system's rubber components. Dry the components immediately, using compressed air (wear eye protection) or a clean, lint-free cloth.

21   Check all components, and renew any that are worn or damaged. Check particularly the cylinder bores and pistons; the complete assembly should be renewed if these are scratched, worn or corroded. If there is any doubt about the condition of the assembly or of any of its components, renew it. Check that the body's fluid passages are clear.

22   If the assembly is fit for further use, obtain a repair kit from your Vauxhall/Opel dealer. The kit consists of both piston assemblies and springs, as well as a new circlip. Renew all seals disturbed on dismantling, and the piston circlip, as a matter of course; these should never be re-used.

23   On reassembly, soak the piston assemblies in clean hydraulic fluid. Smear clean fluid into the cylinder bore.

24   Insert the pistons into the bore, using a twisting motion to avoid trapping the seal lips. Ensure that all components are refitted in the correct order and the right way round.

25   Press the piston assemblies fully into the bore using a clean wooden dowel, and secure them in position with the new circlip. Ensure that the circlip is correctly located in the groove in the cylinder bore.

26   Fit the new seal to the end of the master cylinder bore.

27   Fit the new mounting seals to the master cylinder body, then refit the reservoir, ensuring it's clipped securely in position.

Refitting

Left-hand drive models

28   Remove all traces of dirt from the master cylinder and servo unit mating surfaces, and check that the pushrod is in position in the servo unit. Inspect the master cylinder seal for signs of wear or damage, and renew if necessary.

29   Fit the seal to the servo and refit the master cylinder, ensuring that the pushrod enters the master cylinder bore centrally. Fit the new master cylinder mounting nuts, and tighten them to the specified torque. On models with ABS, securely tighten the fluid reservoir retaining nuts.

30   Wipe clean the brake pipe unions, refit them to the master cylinder ports, and tighten them to the specified torque.

31   Refill the master cylinder reservoir with new fluid, and bleed the complete hydraulic system as described in Section 2.

Right-hand drive models

32   Refit the master cylinder as described in paragraphs 28 to 30, ignoring the note concerning models with ABS.

33   Refit the fluid reservoir support bracket, tightening its retaining nut and bolt to the specified torque setting.

34   Install the components removed for access by reversing the removal procedure.

11   Brake pedal - removal and refitting

Removal

Left-hand drive models

1   Unhook the return spring from the brake pedal.

2   Slide off the spring clip, and withdraw the clevis pin securing the pedal to the servo unit pushrod **(see illustration)**.

3   Remove the locking clip from the brake pedal pivot shaft, then slacken and remove the nut and washer from the shaft **(see illustrations)**.

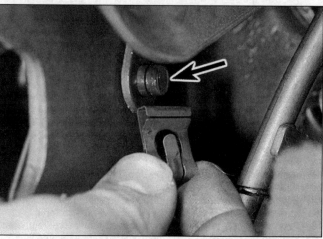

11.2 Slide off the spring clip, and withdraw the clevis pin (arrowed) securing the servo pushrod to the pedal

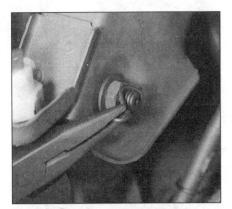

11.3a Withdraw the locking clip . . .

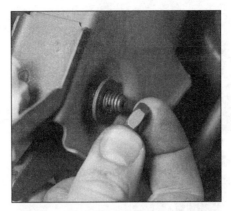

11.3b . . . then slacken and remove the
pivot shaft nut and washer

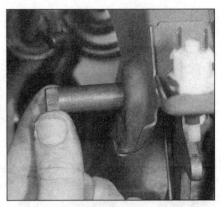

11.4a Withdraw the pivot shaft . . .

11.4b . . . and remove the pedal and
return spring from the mounting bracket

11.7 On right-hand drive models, it will be
necessary to first remove the clutch pedal
bracket in order to remove the
brake pedal

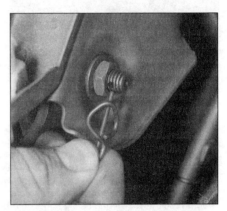

11.10 Tighten the pivot shaft nut to the
specified torque setting, and secure it in
position with the locking clip

4   Slide the pivot shaft to the left, and remove the brake pedal and return spring from underneath the facia **(see illustrations)**.

5   Inspect the pedal pivot bush and shaft for signs of wear, and renew if necessary.

Right-hand drive models

6   On models with manual transmission, detach the clutch cable from the pedal as described in Chapter 6, and unhook the return spring from the pedal.

7   Working in the engine compartment, unscrew the clutch pedal mounting bracket retaining nuts and washers. From inside the vehicle, undo the bracket retaining bolt(s) and remove the bracket assembly from the vehicle **(see illustration)**. **Note:** *This bracket is fitted on models with automatic transmission, even though the clutch pedal is not present.*

8   Remove the brake pedal as described above in paragraphs 1 to 5.

Refitting

Left-hand drive models

9   Apply a smear of multi-purpose grease to the pedal pivot bush, and fit the return spring to the pedal.

10   Manoeuvre the pedal and spring into position, ensuring it is correctly engaged with the servo pushrod, and insert the pivot shaft bolt from the left-hand side. Fit the washer and nut. Tighten the pivot shaft nut to the specified torque setting, and secure it in position with the locking clip **(see illustration)**.

11   Align the pedal hole with the pushrod end, and insert the clevis pin. Secure the pin in position with the spring clip **(see illustration)**.

12   Hook the return spring over the pedal, and check the operation of the brake pedal.

Right-hand drive models

13   Refit the brake pedal as described above in paragraphs 9 to 12.

14   Refit the clutch pedal mounting bracket, tightening its retaining nuts and bolts securely.

15   Where necessary, connect the clutch cable to the clutch pedal, and hook the return spring back into position on the pedal. Adjust the clutch cable as described in Chapter 1.

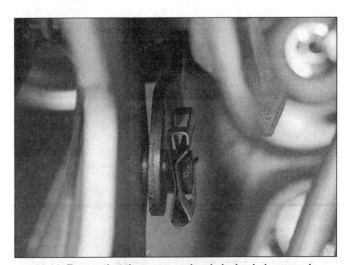

11.11 Ensure that the servo pushrod clevis pin is securely
retained by its spring clip

9

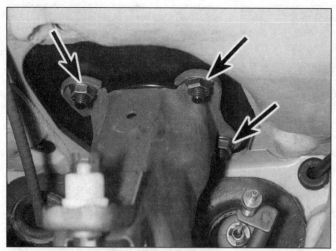

12.16 Servo unit retaining nuts (arrowed, one hidden) - right-hand drive models

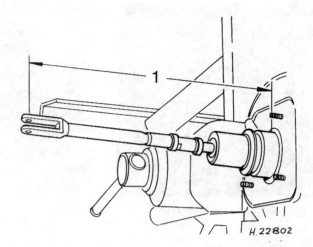

12.19 Prior to refitting the servo unit, ensure that the pushrod length (1) is correctly set - see text

12 Vacuum servo unit - testing, removal and refitting

Testing

1   To test the operation of the servo unit, with the engine off, depress the footbrake several times to exhaust the vacuum. Now start the engine, keeping the pedal firmly depressed. As the engine starts, there should be a noticeable "give" in the brake pedal as the vacuum builds up. Allow the engine to run for at least two minutes, then switch it off. The brake pedal should now feel normal, but further applications should result in the pedal feeling firmer, the pedal stroke decreasing with each application.

2   If the servo does not operate as described, first inspect the servo unit check valve as described in Section 13.

3   If the servo unit still fails to operate satisfactorily, the fault lies within the unit itself. Repairs to the unit are not possible; if faulty, the servo unit must be renewed.

Removal

Left-hand drive models

4   On models with ABS, remove the master cylinder as described in Section 10.

5   On models without ABS, undo the two master cylinder retaining nuts, and disengage the unit from the front of the vacuum servo unit. Release the brake pipes from their retaining clips on the bulkhead and body, and position the master cylinder clear of the servo unit, ensuring that no excess strain is placed on the brake pipes. Keep the master cylinder upright, to prevent fluid loss. Discard the retaining nuts; new ones must be used on refitting.

6   Carefully ease the vacuum hose out of the servo unit, taking care not to displace the sealing grommet.

7   Release the cooling system expansion tank from the bulkhead, and position it clear of the servo.

8   Release the clutch cable from its retainer, and remove the retainer. Also remove the frame.

9   Working from inside the vehicle, slide off the spring clip and withdraw the clevis pin securing the brake pedal to the servo unit pushrod.

10   Slacken and remove the nuts securing the servo unit to the brake pedal mounting bracket, then return to the engine compartment and manoeuvre the servo unit out of position. Recover the gasket from the rear of the servo unit. Discard the gasket and retaining nuts; new ones should be used on refitting.

Right-hand drive models

11   Remove the windscreen wiper motor assembly as described in Chapter 12.

12   Remove the master cylinder as described in Section 10. On some

models, it may prove sufficient to unbolt the master cylinder and position it clear of the servo, taking great care not to strain the brake pipes. This removes the need to disconnect the brake pipes and open the hydraulic system.

13   On models with manual transmission, detach the clutch cable from the pedal as described in Chapter 6, and unhook the return spring from the pedal.

14   Working in the engine compartment, unscrew the clutch pedal mounting bracket retaining nuts and washers. From inside the vehicle, undo the bracket retaining bolt(s) and remove the bracket from the vehicle. **Note:** *This bracket is fitted on models with automatic transmission, even though the clutch pedal is not present.*

15   Unhook the return spring from the brake pedal, then slide off the spring clip and withdraw the clevis pin securing the pedal to the servo unit pushrod.

16   Slacken and remove the nuts securing the servo unit to the pedal mounting bracket, and remove the bracket **(see illustration)**.

17   Return to the engine compartment, and lift the servo unit out of position. Recover the gasket from the rear of the servo unit. Discard the gasket and retaining nuts; new ones should be used on refitting.

Refitting

18   Before refitting the servo, check that the pushrod fork dimension is correct, as follows.

19   Measure the distance from the end face of the servo casing to the centre of the clevis pin hole in the pushrod fork **(see illustration)**. This distance should be 141.5 mm on left-hand drive models and 133.0 mm on right-hand drive models. To make accurate measurement easier, insert a bolt or bar of suitable diameter through the pivot pin hole, and measure to the centre of the bolt or bar.

20   If adjustment is necessary, slacken the locknut, and turn the fork to give the specified dimension. Hold the fork and securely tighten the locknut.

21   Inspect the servo unit check valve sealing grommet for signs of damage or deterioration, and renew if necessary. Proceed as described under the relevant sub-heading.

Left-hand drive models

22   Ensure that the servo and bulkhead mating surfaces are clean and dry

23   Fit a new gasket to the rear of the servo, and reposition the unit in the engine compartment.

24   From inside the vehicle, ensure that the servo unit pushrod is correctly engaged with the brake pedal, then offer up the pedal mounting bracket and fit the new servo unit mounting nuts. Tighten the nuts to the specified torque setting.

25   Refit the servo unit pushrod-to-brake pedal clevis pin, and secure

13.1 Vacuum servo unit check valve is integral with the hose, and cannot be renewed separately

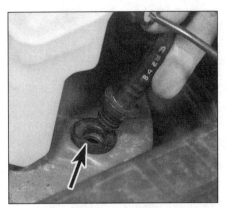

13.2 Ease the vacuum hose out from the servo unit, taking care not to displace the grommet (arrowed)

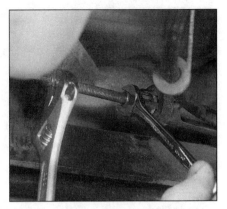

14.4 Adjusting the handbrake cable - Corsa and Corsavan models

it in position with the spring clip.

26 Install the frame and clutch cable retainer. Clip the clutch cable back into position.

27 Refit the expansion tank in its original position.

28 Ease the vacuum hose end piece into place in the servo unit, taking great care not to displace or damage the grommet.

29 On models without ABS, refit the master cylinder to the front of the servo unit, ensuring that the servo pushrod enters the master cylinder squarely. Fit the new master cylinder mounting nuts, and tighten them to the specified torque setting. Ensure that the brake pipes are correctly clipped back into position in all the relevant retaining clips.

30 On models with ABS, refit the master cylinder as described in Section 10.

31 On completion, start the engine and check for air leaks at the vacuum hose-to-servo unit connection. Check the operation of the braking system.

Right-hand drive models

32 Install the servo unit as described above in paragraphs 22 to 24.

33 Refit the clutch pedal mounting bracket, tightening its retaining nuts and bolts securely.

34 Where necessary, reconnect the clutch cable to the pedal, and hook the return spring back over the pedal (see Chapter 6). Adjust the clutch cable as described in Chapter 1.

35 Refit the master cylinder as described in Section 10.

36 Refit the windscreen wiper motor as described in Chapter 12.

37 On completion, start the engine and check for air leaks at the vacuum hose-to-servo unit connection. Check the operation of the braking system.

---

13 Vacuum servo unit check valve - removal, testing and refitting

1 The check valve is located in the vacuum hose running from the inlet manifold to the brake servo. Although the valve is available separately from the hoses, in order to remove the valve, the hoses must be cut, and therefore renewed on reassembly. If the valve is to be renewed, it is therefore easier to remove the complete hose/valve assembly, and renew it complete **(see illustration)**.

Removal

2 Carefully ease the vacuum hose out of the servo unit, taking care not to displace the grommet **(see illustration)**.

3 Note the correct routing of the hose, then undo the union nut securing the hose to the inlet manifold and remove the hose assembly from the vehicle.

Testing

4 Examine the check valve and vacuum hose for signs of damage,

and renew if necessary.

5 The valve may be tested by blowing through it in both directions. Air should flow through the valve in one direction only; when blown through from the servo unit end of the valve. Renew the valve if this is not the case.

6 Examine the servo unit rubber sealing grommet for signs of damage or deterioration, and renew as necessary.

Refitting

7 Ensure that the sealing grommet is correctly fitted to the servo unit.

8 Ease the hose union into position in the servo, taking great care not to displace or damage the grommet.

9 Ensure that the hose is correctly routed, and connect it to the inlet manifold, tightening its union nut securely.

10 On completion, start the engine and check for air leaks at the check valve-to-servo unit connection.

---

14 Handbrake - adjustment

1 To check the handbrake adjustment, fully release the handbrake lever, and apply the footbrake firmly several times. This will establish correct shoe-to-drum clearance, and ensure that the self-adjust mechanism is fully adjusted. Applying normal, moderate pressure, pull the handbrake lever to the fully-applied position, counting the number of clicks emitted from the handbrake ratchet mechanism. If adjustment is correct, there should be 8 clicks before the handbrake is fully applied; if this is not the case, adjust as follows.

2 Chock the front wheels, then jack up the rear of the vehicle, and support securely on axle stands.

3 On Corsa and Corsavan models, the handbrake cable adjuster nut is situated above the rear axle crossmember. On Combo Van models, the handbrake cable adjuster nut is situated directly underneath the handbrake lever; if necessary, unscrew the retaining nuts and remove the exhaust heat shield to improve access to the nut.

4 With the handbrake set on the fourth notch of the ratchet mechanism, rotate the adjusting nut until a reasonable amount of force is required to turn each wheel/hub **(see illustration)**. **Note:** *The force required should be equal for each wheel.* Once this is so, fully release the handbrake lever and check that the wheels/hubs rotate freely. Check the adjustment by applying the handbrake fully whilst counting the clicks emitted from the handbrake ratchet and, if necessary, re-adjust.

5 On completion of adjustment, check the handbrake cables for free movement, and apply a little grease to the adjuster threads and exposed cable ends to prevent corrosion.

6 Refit the exhaust heat shield and/or roadwheels (as applicable) and lower the vehicle to the ground. If the roadwheels have been removed, tighten the roadwheel bolts to the specified torque setting.

9

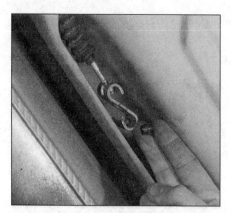

15.3 On Corsa and Corsavan models, remove the grommet and free the cable and connecting link from the handbrake lever

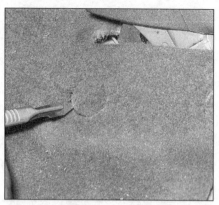

15.6 Note that will probably be necessary to cut holes in the carpet to gain access to the handbrake lever retaining bolts

15.7a Unscrew the two retaining bolts . . .

15.7b . . . and remove them through the access holes . . .

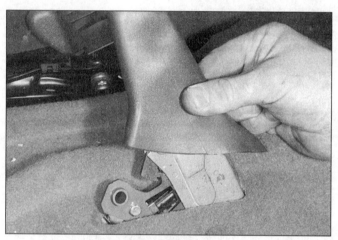

15.7c . . . then lift the handbrake lever out of position

15   Handbrake lever - removal, overhaul and refitting

Removal

1   Chock the front wheels, then jack up the rear of the vehicle, and support securely on axle stands.

2   Undo the retaining nuts, and remove the exhaust heat shield from underneath the vehicle to gain access to the underside of the handbrake lever.

3   On Corsa and Corsavan models, fully slacken the handbrake cable adjuster nut. Remove the grommet from the connecting link joining the front end of the cable to the handbrake lever, and detach the cable **(see illustration)**. Detach the connecting joint from the handbrake lever rod, and remove it from underneath the vehicle.

4   On Combo Van models, slacken and remove the handbrake cable adjuster nut, and detach the cable equaliser plate from the handbrake rod.

5   Remove the left-hand front seat as described in Chapter 11.

6   Peel back the carpet situated at the base of the handbrake lever, to gain access to the handbrake lever mounting bolts via the holes in the vehicle body. If necessary, cut flaps in the carpet using a sharp knife **(see illustration)**.

7   Unscrew the handbrake lever mounting bolts and withdraw the lever, disconnecting the wiring connector from the handbrake warning light switch as it becomes accessible **(see illustrations)**.

Overhaul

8   A worn ratchet segment can be renewed by driving the securing sleeve from the handbrake lever, using a metal rod or a bolt of suitable

diameter.

9   Drive the new sleeve supplied with the new segment into the lever, to permit a little play between the segment and lever.

10   If desired, a new pawl can be fitted after drilling out the original pivot rivet.

11   Rivet the new pawl so that it is still free to move.

12   The handbrake warning light switch can be removed from the lever assembly after unscrewing its retaining bolt.

Refitting

13   Refitting is a reversal of the removal procedure, adjusting the cable as described in Section 14.

16   Handbrake cables - removal and refitting

Corsa and Corsavan

1   The handbrake cable consists of two sections, a long cable (complete with equaliser plate) linking the handbrake lever to the left-hand drum brake, and a short cable linking the right-hand drum brake to the equaliser plate. The equaliser plate links both cables together, and is situated above the rear axle crossmember. Each cable can be renewed individually as follows.

Long cable

2   Undo the retaining nuts, and remove the exhaust heat shield from underneath the vehicle to gain access to the underside of the handbrake lever.

3   Unscrew the handbrake cable adjuster nut, and detach the short

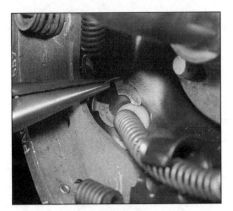

16.6 Each handbrake cable is secured to the backplate by a retaining clip

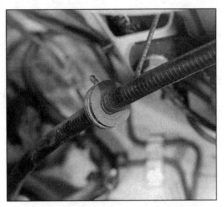

16.7 Free the cable from any relevant clips or brackets securing it to the vehicle underbody

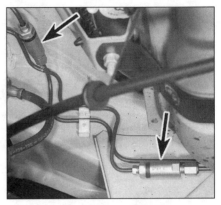

17.1 Rear brake pressure-regulating valves (arrowed) - 1.2 litre models

cable from the equaliser plate.

4   Remove the left-hand rear brake drum as described in Section 7.

5   Referring to Section 5, remove the upper and lower return springs, then remove the spring cup, spring and retainer pin, and remove the rear brake shoe. Note that the front shoe and adjuster strut mechanism can be left in position on the backplate.

6   Free the handbrake cable from the retaining clip on the shoe lower pivot, then remove the retaining clip and withdraw the cable from the rear of the backplate **(see illustration)**.

7   Work back along the cable, releasing it from any relevant retaining clips and ties, whilst noting its correct routing **(see illustration)**.

8   Remove the grommet from the connecting link, and detach the front end of the cable from the connecting joint. Remove the cable from underneath the vehicle. Free the connecting link from the handbrake lever rod, and store it with the cable for safe-keeping.

9   On refitting, attach the connecting link to the handbrake lever, then hook the cable into the connecting link. Secure the cables in position with the grommet.

10   Work back along the cable, securing it in position with all the relevant clips and ties, and routing it as noted on removal.

11   Insert the cable through the backplate, and secure it in position with the clip. Insert the short cable in the equaliser plate, and screw the adjuster nut onto the cable threads.

12   Ensure that the cable is securely retained by the clip on the shoe lower pivot point, and refit the rear brake shoe as described in Section 5.

13   Ensure that the brake shoes and adjuster strut components are correctly fitted, then refit the brake drum as described in Section 7.

14   Adjust the handbrake cable as described in Section 14.

Short cable

15   Remove the cable as described above in paragraphs 3 to 7, removing the right-hand brake drum instead of the left-hand drum.

16   Refit the cable as described in paragraphs 10 to 14.

Combo Van

17   The handbrake cable consists of two sections of equal length, which run from each rear brake to the equaliser plate. The equaliser plate is secured to the handbrake lever rod by the adjuster nut. The cables cannot be separated from the equaliser plate, and therefore the cable arrangement can only be removed and refitted as an assembly.

Removal

18   Undo the retaining nuts, and remove the exhaust heat shield from underneath the vehicle to gain access to the underside of the handbrake lever.

19   Unscrew the handbrake cable adjuster nut, and detach the equaliser plate from the handbrake lever.

20   Remove the left-hand rear brake drum as described in Section 7.

21   Referring to Section 5, remove the upper and lower return springs, then remove the spring cup, spring and retainer pin, and re-

move the rear brake shoe. Note that the front shoe and adjuster strut mechanism can be left in position on the backplate.

22   Free the handbrake cable from the retaining clip on the shoe lower pivot, then remove the retaining clip and withdraw the cable from the rear of the backplate.

23   Repeat the operations in paragraphs 20 to 22 on the right-hand rear brake.

24   Work back along both cables, releasing them from any relevant retaining clips and ties, whilst noting the correct routing. Remove the cable/equaliser plate assembly from the underneath the vehicle.

Refitting

25   Connect the equaliser plate to the handbrake lever, and screw on the adjuster nut.

26   Work back along both cables, securing them in position with all the relevant clips and ties, and routing them as noted on removal.

27   Insert the cable through the left-hand backplate, and secure it in position with the clip.

28   Ensure that the cable is securely retained by the clip on the shoe lower pivot point, and refit the rear brake shoe as described in Section 5.

29   Ensure that the brake shoes and adjuster strut components are correctly fitted, then refit the left-hand brake drum as described in Section 7. **Note:** *Do not apply the brake pedal until the right-hand drum has also been installed.*

30   Repeat the operations in paragraphs 27 to 29 on the right-hand brake.

31   Once both drums are in position, with the handbrake fully released, adjust the lining-to-drum clearance by repeatedly depressing the brake pedal at least 20 to 25 times. Whilst depressing the pedal, have an assistant listen to the rear drums, to check that the adjuster strut is functioning correctly; if so, a clicking sound will be emitted by the strut as the pedal is depressed

32   Adjust the handbrake cable as described in Section 14.

---

17   Rear brake pressure-regulating valve(s) - removal and refitting

---

Note: *Before starting work, refer to the warning at the beginning of Section 2 concerning the dangers of hydraulic fluid.*

Removal

1.2 litre models

1   On 1.2 litre models, the rear brake pressure-regulating valves are of the pressure-dependent type, and are located underneath the vehicle, directly above the rear axle on the left-hand side of the vehicle **(see illustration)**. There are two valves, one for each rear brake. The purpose of the valves is to prevent the rear wheels locking up under

9

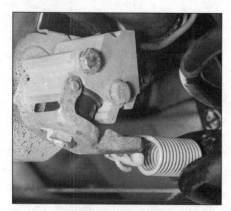

17.8 Rear brake pressure-regulating valve assembly - 1.4 and 1.6 litre Corsa and Corsavan models

17.18 On Corsa and Corsavan models, slacken the pivot bolt . . .

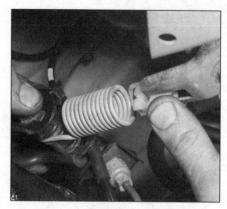

17.19a . . . and adjust the valve as described in the text

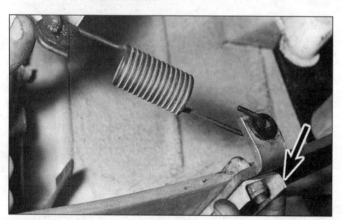

17.19b On Combo van models, adjust the valve as described in the text by repositioning the clamp (arrowed) on the leaf spring

heavy braking.

2   Chock the front wheels, then jack up the rear of the vehicle and support it on axle stands.

3   Minimise fluid loss by first removing the master cylinder reservoir cap, then tightening it down onto a piece of polythene to obtain an airtight seal.

4   Wipe clean the area around the brake pipe unions on the relevant valve, and place absorbent rags beneath the pipe unions to catch any surplus fluid.

5   Retain the relevant pressure-regulating valve with a suitable open-ended spanner, slacken the union nuts and disconnect both brake pipes, and remove the valve from underneath the vehicle. Plug or tape over the pipe ends and valve orifices, to minimise the loss of brake fluid and to prevent the entry of dirt into the system. Wash off any spilt fluid immediately with cold water.

6   Where necessary, remove the other valve in the same way.

7   If renewal is necessary, both valves should be renewed as a matched pair. The lead and switching pressures are stamped on the body of each valve (lead pressure in front of the slash, and switching pressure after the dash). Ensure that both valves are stamped with exactly the same pressures.

1.4 and 1.6 litre models

8   On 1.4 and 1.6 litre models, the pressure-regulating valve is of the load-dependent type, and is mounted underneath the rear of the vehicle. The valve is mounted onto the vehicle underbody, and is connected to the rear axle (Corsa and Corsavan) or leaf spring (Combo Van) by a spring **(see illustration)**. As the load being carried by the vehicle is altered, the suspension moves in relation to the vehicle body, altering the tension in the spring. The spring then adjusts the pressure-regulating valve lever so that the correct pressure is applied to the rear brakes to suit the load being carried. The purpose of the valve is to

prevent the rear wheels locking up under heavy braking.

9   Minimise fluid loss by first removing the master cylinder reservoir cap, then tightening it down onto a piece of polythene to obtain an airtight seal.

10   Using pliers, carefully unhook the spring and detach it from the valve.

11   Wipe clean the area around the brake pipe unions on the valve, and place absorbent rags beneath the pipe unions to catch any surplus fluid. Make identification marks on the brake pipes; these marks can then be used on refitting to ensure that each pipe is correctly reconnected.

12   Slacken the union nuts, and disconnect the brake pipes from the valve. Plug or tape over the pipe ends and valve orifices, to minimise the loss of brake fluid and to prevent the entry of dirt into the system. Wash off any spilt fluid immediately with cold water.

13   Undo the two bolts, and remove the pressure-regulating valve from underneath the vehicle.

Refitting

1.2 litre models

14   Refitting is the reverse of the removal procedure, tightening the pipe union nuts to the specified torque setting. On completion, bleed the complete hydraulic system as described in Section 2.

1.4 and 1.6 litre models

15   Refitting is the reverse of the removal procedure, noting the following points:

(a)   Tighten the valve mounting bolts to the specified torque.

(b) · Ensure that the brake pipes are correctly connected to the valve, and tighten the union nuts to the specified torque settings.

(c)   Coat the ends of the spring with grease prior to installation.

(d)   Bleed the complete hydraulic system as described in Section 2.

16   On completion, adjust the valve as follows.

17   With the vehicle completely unladen, position the car over an inspection pit, or drive it onto ramps so that it is resting on all four wheels.

18   On Corsa and Corsavan models, slacken the front pivot bolt, which secures the valve spring to the axle **(see illustration)**. On Combo Van models, slacken the nuts securing the spring clamp to the right-hand leaf spring.

19   Remove all tension from the spring, then push the pressure-regulating valve lever towards the pivot bolt/clamp (as applicable) until the lever reaches its stop. Hold it there, then position the pivot bolt/clamp so that all clearance between the spring and valve is removed, without tensioning the spring **(see illustrations)**.

20   On Corsa and Corsavan models, hold the bolt in this position and tighten it to the specified torque setting. On Combo Van models, tighten the spring clamp nuts to the specified torque setting.

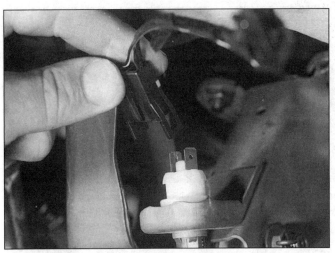

18.2a Disconnect the wiring connector from the stop-light switch . . .

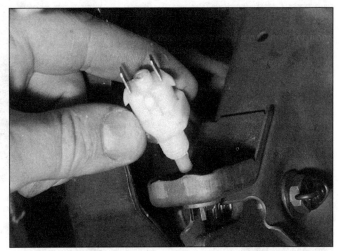

18.2b . . . and unscrew the switch from the pedal bracket

18 Stop-light switch - removal, refitting and adjustment

Removal

1   The stop-light switch is located on the pedal bracket behind the facia. To remove the switch, first disconnect the battery negative lead.
2   Disconnect the wiring plug from the stop-light switch, then un-screw the switch from its mounting bracket **(see illustrations)**.

Refitting and adjustment

3   Refitting is a reversal of removal, adjusting the switch as follows.
4   The switch should be positioned so that the stop-lights are illumi-nated after the brake pedal has travelled approximately 5 mm. Adjust the position of the switch as required until the stop-lights are function-ing correctly.

19 Anti-lock braking system (ABS) - general information

1   ABS is fitted as standard to all 1.6 litre DOHC models, and is available as an option on some other models in the range. The main system component is the modulator assembly, which contains the four solenoid and governor valve assemblies (one for each brake), the elec-trically-driven return pump, and the fluid reservoir. In addition to the modulator assembly, there is an electronic control unit (ECU) and four roadwheel sensors; one fitted to each wheel. The purpose of the sys-tem is to prevent wheel(s) locking during heavy braking. This is achieved by automatic release of the brake on the relevant wheel if it is on the point of locking, followed by reapplication of the brake.
2   The solenoid valves are controlled by the ECU, which receives signals from the four wheel sensors (one fitted on each hub), which monitor the speed of rotation of each wheel. By comparing these speed signals from the four wheels, the computer can determine the speed at which the vehicle is travelling. It can then use this information to determine when a wheel is decelerating at an abnormal rate com-pared to the speed of the vehicle, and thus predict when a wheel is about to lock.
3   During normal operation, the solenoid valves in the modulator as-sembly are closed, and the governor valves are in the at-rest position. The system then functions in the same way as a non-ABS braking sys-tem does.
4   If the ECU senses that a wheel is about to lock, the system enters the "pressure-reduction" phase. The ECU opens the relevant solenoid valve in the modulator assembly. This forces the governor valve against its spring, which then isolates the brake from the master cylin-der. The excess fluid in the brake hydraulic line returns from the brake

to the modulator reservoir via the restrictor, reducing the hydraulic pressure and releasing the brake. At the same time, the return pump is switched on, to return the fluid to the master cylinder reservoir.
5   Once the danger of the wheel locking has decreased below the critical point, the system enters the "pressure-increase" phase, and the ECU closes the solenoid valve. The governor valve then returns under spring pressure, allowing hydraulic pressure from the master cylinder to act on the brake at a reduced pressure, via the restrictor in the mod-ulator. When the pressure in the brake line is equal to the that in the master cylinder, the governor valve returns to the at-rest position, and the braking system returns to normal operation. This cycle can be car-ried out several times a second.
6   The action of the solenoid valves and return pump creates pulses in the hydraulic circuit. When the system is functioning, these pulses can be felt through the brake pedal. This is quite normal, and should not be misinterpreted as the brake discs being warped, for example.
7   The operation of the system is entirely dependent on electrical signals. To prevent the system responding to any inaccurate signals, a built-in safety circuit monitors all signals received by the ECU. The first time the vehicle exceeds 5 mph (7 kmh) after the ignition has been switched on, the ECU tests the readings from each wheel sensor, and the operation of the modulator solenoid valves. If a fault is detected, the system is automatically shut down by the ECU, and the warning light on the instrument panel is illuminated to inform the driver that the system is not operational. Normal braking should still be available, however.
8   If a fault does develop in the system, the vehicle must be taken to a Vauxhall/Opel dealer for fault diagnosis and repair at the earliest pos-sible opportunity. The ECU will store a fault code, which can be ac-cessed by the dealer using special electronic test equipment.

20 Anti-lock Braking system (ABS) components - removal and refitting

9

Modulator assembly

Note: *Before starting work, refer to the note at the beginning of Section 2 concerning the dangers of hydraulic fluid.*

Romoval

1   Disconnect the battery negative terminal.
2   Unclip the relay cover from the front of the modulator assembly **(see illustration)**.
3   Lift the retaining clip, and disconnect the wiring connector from the modulator assembly **(see illustration)**.
4   Unscrew the master cylinder reservoir filler cap, and top-up the

20.2 Remove the relay cover from the ABS modulator assembly . . .

20.3 . . . then lift up the retaining clip and disconnect the wiring connector

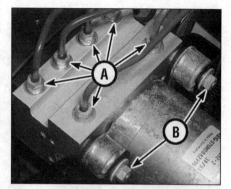

20.5 Modulator brake pipe unions (A) and mounting nuts (B)

20.7 Modulator earth lead retaining nut (arrowed)

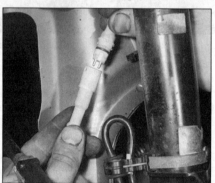

20.17 Disconnect the wiring connector . . .

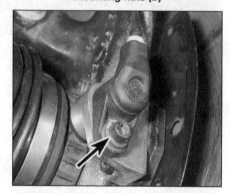

20.18a . . . then undo the retaining bolt (arrowed) . . .

reservoir to the "MAX" mark (see Chapter 1). Place a piece of polythene over the filler neck, and securely refit the cap. This will minimise brake fluid loss during subsequent operations. As a precaution, place absorbent rags beneath the modulator brake pipe unions when unscrewing them.

5   Wipe clean the area around the modulator brake pipe unions, then make a note of how the pipes are arranged, to use as a reference on refitting. Unscrew the union nuts, and carefully withdraw the pipes **(see illustration)**.

6   Plug or tape over the pipe ends and modulator orifices, to minimise the loss of brake fluid and to prevent the entry of dirt into the system. Wash off any spilt fluid immediately with cold water.

7   Slacken and remove the mounting nuts, and release the modulator assembly from its mounting bracket. Undo the retaining nut, and disconnect the earth lead from the modulator **(see illustration)**. Remove the assembly from the engine compartment. **Note:** *Do not attempt to dismantle the modulator block hydraulic assembly; overhaul of the unit is not possible.*

Refitting

8   Refitting is the reverse of the removal procedure, noting the following points:

(a) *Tighten the modulator block mounting nuts to the specified torque setting.*

(b) *Refit the brake pipes to their respective unions, and tighten the union nuts to the specified torque.*

(c) *Ensure that the wiring is correctly routed, and that the connector is firmly pressed into position.*

(d) *On completion, and prior to refitting the battery, bleed the complete hydraulic system as described in Section 2. Ensure that the system is bled in the correct order, to prevent air entering the modulator return pump.*

Electronic control unit (ECU)

Removal

9   The ABS electronic control unit (ECU) is mounted beneath the facia, behind the left-hand front footwell side panel. Prior to removing the

ECU, disconnect the battery negative lead.

10   On right-hand drive models, remove the storage compartment (where fitted) from underneath the passenger side of the facia. The compartment is secured in position by a retaining screw and clip.

11   Release the retaining clips, and unclip the left-hand front footwell side panel from underneath the facia to gain access to the ECU.

12   Release the ECU from its mounting bracket.

13   Release the retaining clip, disconnect the wiring connector, and remove the ECU from the vehicle.

Refitting

14   Refitting is a reversal of the removal procedure, ensuring that the wiring connector is securely reconnected, and that the ECU is clipped securely into its retaining bracket.

Front wheel sensor

Removal

15   Disconnect the battery negative terminal.

16   Chock the rear wheels, firmly apply the handbrake, then jack up the front of the vehicle and support on axle stands. Remove the appropriate front roadwheel, marking its correct fitted position on the wheel hub.

17   Trace the wheel sensor wiring back to its wiring connector, and release it from its retaining clip. Disconnect the connector **(see illustration)**, and work back along the sensor wiring, freeing it from all the relevant retaining clips and ties.

18   Slacken and remove the bolt securing the sensor to the mounting bracket, and remove the sensor and lead assembly from the vehicle **(see illustrations)**.

Refitting

19   Prior to refitting, apply a thin coat of multi-purpose grease to the sensor mounting bracket.

20   Ensure that the sensor and mounting bracket sealing faces are clean, then fit the sensor to the hub. Refit the retaining bolt, and tighten it to the specified torque.

20.18b ... and remove the front wheel sensor from the vehicle

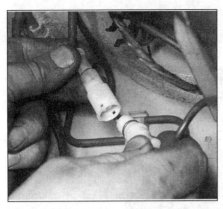

20.24 Disconnecting a rear wheel sensor wiring connector

20.26 Removing the sensor from the rear of the backplate

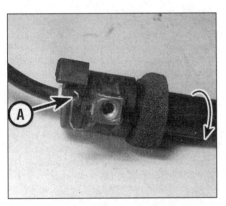

20.28 Turn the sensor in the direction of the arrow, so that the retaining clip (A) is freed from the mounting bracket

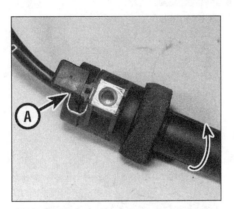

20.29 With the sensor in position and the screw tightened, turn the sensor in the direction of the arrow so that the clip (A) engages with the mounting bracket and the correct air gap is set

20.33 Rear wheel sensor toothed ring is an integral part of the brake drum

21   Ensure that the sensor wiring is correctly routed, and retained by all the necessary clips. Reconnect it to its wiring connector, and fit the connector into the retaining clip.

22   Refit the roadwheel, aligning the marks made on removal, then lower the vehicle to the ground and tighten the roadwheel bolts to the specified torque.

Rear wheel sensor

Removal

23   Chock the front wheels, then jack up the rear of the vehicle and support it on axle stands.

24   Trace the wiring back from the sensor to its wiring connector, which is situated just near the spare wheel well. Free the connector from its retaining clip, and disconnect the wiring from the main wiring loom **(see illustration)**.

25   Work back along the sensor wiring, and free it from any relevant retaining clips.

26   Slacken and remove the screw securing the sensor unit to the backplate, and withdraw the sensor from the backplate. Remove the sensor and lead assembly from the vehicle **(see illustration)**.

Refitting

27   Prior to refitting, apply a thin coat of multi-purpose grease to the sensor tip. Ensure that the sensor and backplate mating faces are clean.

28   Turn the sensor anti-clockwise to release it from the retaining clip on the mounting bracket. This is vital to ensure that the sensor is correctly positioned on refitting **(see illustration)**.

29   Push the sensor in lightly until it seats, then refit its retaining

screw and tighten it to the specified torque setting. With the screw tightened, rotate the sensor clockwise until it engages with the retaining clip **(see illustration)**. As the sensor engages with the clip, it will move out slightly, to leave the correct air gap between the sensor tip and toothed ring on the drum.

30   Ensure that the sensor wiring is correctly routed and retained by all the necessary retaining clips. Reconnect the wiring connector, and fit it back into the retaining clip.

31   Lower the vehicle to the ground.

Front wheel sensor toothed rings

32   The front toothed rings are an integral part of the driveshaft outer constant velocity (CV) joints, and cannot be renewed separately. Examine the rings for such damage as chipped or missing teeth. If renewal is necessary, the complete outer constant velocity joint must be renewed, as described in Chapter 8.

Rear wheel sensor toothed rings

33   The rear toothed rings are an integral part of the rear brake drum, and cannot be renewed separately **(see illustration)**. Examine the rings for signs of damage such as chipped or missing teeth. If renewal is necessary, the rear brake drum must be renewed as described in Section 7.

Relays

34   Disconnect the battery negative lead.

35   Both the solenoid relay and return pump relay are located on the front of modulator assembly. To gain access to them, unclip the relay cover from the front of the modulator (see illustration 20.2).

9

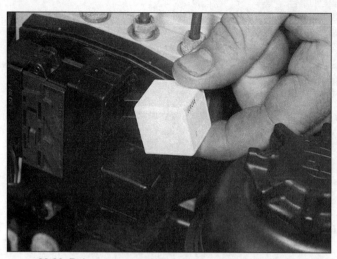

20.36 Relays are a push fit in the modulator assembly

36　Either relay can then be simply pulled out of position **(see illustration)**. The return pump relay is the top relay, and the solenoid valve relay the bottom relay. Refer to Chapter 12 for further information on relays.

37　When refitting, ensure that the relay is securely pushed into position, then refit the cover and connect the battery negative lead.

Chapter 10 Suspension and steering

Contents

Specifications

Front suspension

Type.. Independent, with MacPherson struts and forward-facing tie-bars. Anti-roll bar fitted to most models

Rear suspension

Type:

Corsa and Corsavan .... Semi-Independent torsion beam, with trailing arms, coil springs and telescopic shock absorbers. Anti-roll bar on some models

Combo Van models.. Tubular axle and leaf springs with telescopic shock absorbers

Steering

Type.. Rack-and-pinion. Power assistance standard on certain models, optional on others

10

Wheel alignment and steering angles

Front wheels:
Camber angle:
1.2 and 1.4 litre models:
Corsa and Corsavan... -35' ± 45'
Combo Van.. -45' ± 45'
1.6 litre DOHC models... -55' ± 45'
Maximum difference between sides... 1°
Castor angle:
1.2 and 1.4 litre models:
Corsa and Corsavan... 1°50' ± 1°
Combo Van.. 1°15' ± 1°
1.6 litre DOHC models... 1°55' ± 1°
Maximum difference between sides... 1°
Toe setting... -10' ± 10' (1.0 mm toe-out ± 1.0 mm)
Rear wheels:
Camber angle:
Corsa and Corsavan .... -1°30' ± 30'
Combo Van .... -25' ± 25'
Maximum difference between sides .... 30'
Toe setting:
Corsa and Corsavan .... 10' +30' -15' (1.0 mm toe-in +3 mm -1.5 mm)
Combo Van .... 15' ± 10' (1.5 mm toe-in ± 1.0 mm)

Roadwheels

Type... Pressed-steel or aluminium alloy (depending on model)
Size.. 5J x 13, 5.5J x 13 and 5.5J x 14

Tyres

Size:
1.2 litre and 1.4 litre models:
Corsa and Corsavan:
Standard fitment .... 145 R 13
Optional .... 165/70 R 13 or 165/65 R 13
Combo Van .... 165/70 R 13
1.6 litre DOHC models .... 185/60 R 14 or 165/65 R 14
Pressures - refer to Chapter 1 Specifications

Torque wrench settings

	Nm	lbf ft
Front suspension		
Lower arm balljoint clamp bolt nut	30	22
Suspension strut upper mounting nuts	30	22
Suspension strut-to-swivel hub bolts:		
Stage 1	50	37
Stage 2	90	66
Stage 3	Angle-tighten a further 45 to 60°	
Lower arm-to-balljoint/tie-bar bolts	100	74
Lower arm pivot bolt	60	44
Tie-bar bush bracket bolts:		
Stage 1	50	37
Stage 2	Angle-tighten a further 90 to 105°	
Tie-bar front nut	90	66
Anti-roll bar clamp nuts	20	15
Rear suspension - Corsa and Corsavan models		
Hub nut	25	18
Stub axle bolts:		
Stage 1	50	37
Stage 2	Angle-tighten a further 30 to 45°	
Shock absorber upper nut	20	15
Shock absorber lower bolt	65	48
Trailing arm pivot bolts:		
Stage 1	50	37
Stage 2	Angle-tighten a further 45 to 60°	
Anti-roll bar bolts:		
Stage 1	60	44
Stage 2	Angle-tighten a further 60 to 75°	

	Nm	lbf ft
Rear suspension - Combo Van models		
Hub nut	25	18
Shock absorber upper bolt	70	52
Shock absorber lower bolt	65	48
Leaf spring pivot bolts	65	48
Shackle nut	35	26
U-bolt nuts	45	33
Bump stop bolt	50	37
Bump stop seat nut	20	15
Steering		
Steering wheel nut	25	18
Steering column bolts	22	16
Column clamp bolt	22	16
Intermediate shaft clamp bolt	22	16
Steering gear	22	16
Power steering pipe union nuts	28	21
Power steering pump bolts	28	21
Track rod balljoint-to-swivel hub nut	35	26
Track rod balljoint locknut	50	37
Roadwheels		
Roadwheel bolts	110	81

1 General information

1   The independent front suspension is of the MacPherson strut type, incorporating coil springs and integral telescopic shock absorbers **(see illustration)**. The MacPherson struts are located by transverse lower suspension arms, which utilise rubber inner mounting bushes, and incorporate a balljoint at the outer ends. The front swivel hubs, which carry the wheel bearings, brake calipers and the hub/disc assemblies, are bolted to the MacPherson struts, and connected to the lower arms via the balljoints. A forward-facing tie-bar connects each lower suspension arm to the vehicle body. On most models, a front anti-roll bar is fitted. The anti-roll bar is rubber-mounted onto the tie-bars by mounting clamps.

2   On Corsa and Corsavan models, the rear suspension is of semi-independent type, consisting of a torsion beam axle and trailing arms, with double-conical coil springs and telescopic shock absorbers **(see**

illustration). The front ends of the trailing arms are attached to the vehicle underbody by horizontal bushes; the rear ends are located by the shock absorbers, which are bolted to the underbody at their upper ends. The coil springs are mounted independently of the shock absorbers, and act directly between the trailing arms and the underbody. Certain models are fitted with an anti-roll bar, which is bolted onto the underside of each trailing arm.

3   On Combo Van models, the rear suspension consists of a tubular axle and leaf spring arrangement, with telescopic shock absorbers **(see illustration)**. The front end of each leaf spring is bolted directly to the vehicle underbody, and the rear end is attached by a shackle arrangement to allow movement of the spring. The axle is secured to each leaf spring by two U-bolts. The shock absorber upper ends are bolted to the vehicle underbody; the lower ends are bolted to the axle.

4   The steering column is linked to the steering gear by an intermediate shaft. The intermediate shaft has a universal joint fitted to its upper end, and is secured to the column by a clamp bolt. The lower end of

10

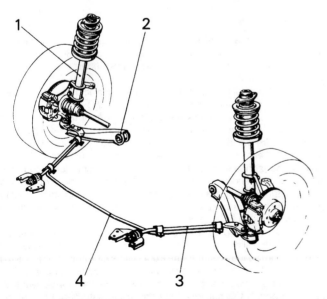

1.1 Front suspension components

1	MacPherson strut	3	Tie-bar
2	Lower arm	4	Anti-roll bar

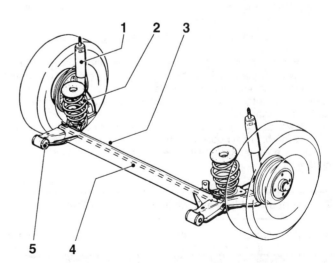

1.2 Rear suspension components - Corsa and Corsavan models

1	Shock absorber	4	Anti-roll bar (where
2	Coil spring		fitted)
3	Torsion beam axle	5	Trailing arm

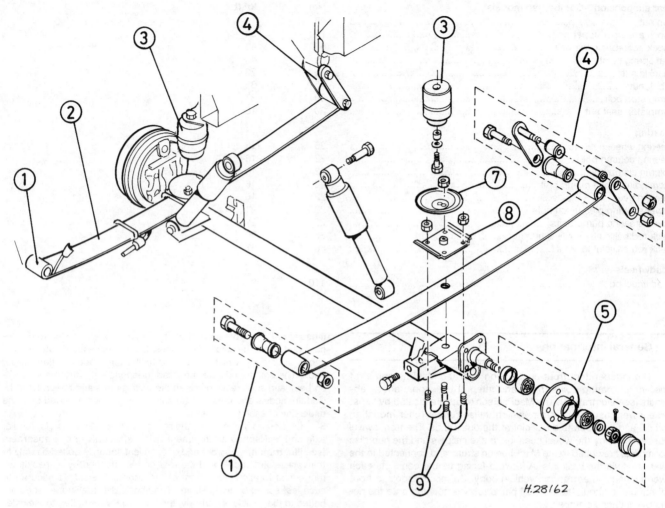

H.28162

1.3 Rear suspension components - Combo Van models

1	Leaf spring front pivot and bush	4	Shackle	7	Bump stop seat
2	Leaf spring	5	Rear hub assembly	8	Retaining plate
3	Bump stop	6	Shock absorber	9	U-bolts

the intermediate shaft is attached to the steering gear pinion by means of a clamp bolt.

5   The rack and pinion type steering gear is rubber-mounted onto the engine compartment bulkhead, and is connected by two track rods, with balljoints at their outer ends, to the steering arms projecting rearwards from the swivel hubs. The track rod ends are threaded, to facilitate adjustment.

6   Power-assisted steering is fitted as standard on some models, and is available as an option on most others. The hydraulic steering system is powered by a belt-driven pump, which is driven off the crankshaft pulley.

2   Front swivel hub assembly - removal and refitting

Note: *When fitting a new driveshaft, new lower arm balljoint and track rod balljoint nuts must be fitted. The brake caliper bracket mounting bolts and suspension strut-to-swivel hub nuts and bolts should also be renewed.*

Removal

Tip: *If work is being carried out without the aid of an assistant, remove the wheel trim/hub cap (as applicable), then withdraw the split pin and slacken the driveshaft retaining nut prior to jacking up the vehicle.*

1   Chock the rear wheels, firmly apply the handbrake, then jack up the front of the vehicle and support it on axle stands. Remove the appropriate front roadwheel, marking its correct fitted position on the wheel hub.

2   Extract the split pin from the driveshaft retaining nut and discard it; a new one must be used on refitting.

3   Refit at least two roadwheel bolts to the front hub, and tighten them securely. Have an assistant firmly depress the brake pedal to prevent the front hub from rotating, then using a socket and extension bar, slacken and remove the driveshaft retaining nut. Alternatively, a tool can be fabricated from two lengths of steel strip (one long, one short) and a nut and bolt; the nut and bolt forming the pivot of a forked tool. Bolt the tool to the hub using two wheel bolts, and hold the tool to prevent the hub from rotating as the driveshaft retaining nut is undone (see illustration 8.3 in Chapter 8).

4   Unscrew the two bolts securing the brake caliper assembly to the swivel hub, and slide the caliper assembly off the disc. Using a piece of wire or string, tie the caliper to the front suspension coil spring to avoid placing any strain on the hydraulic brake hose **(see illustrations)**. Discard the caliper mounting bolts - they must be renewed whenever they are disturbed. If the hub bearings are to be disturbed, remove the brake disc as described in Chapter 9.

5   Unscrew the driveshaft retaining nut, and remove the washer. Discard the nut; a new one must be used on refitting.

2.4a Undo the bolts (arrowed) securing the caliper bracket to the swivel hub . . .

2.4b . . . then slide the caliper off the disc, and hook it onto the strut spring using a piece of wire

2.6 Withdraw the clamp bolt, and free the lower arm balljoint from the swivel hub

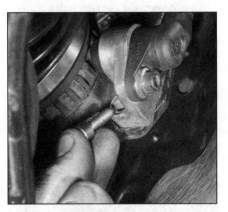

2.7a On models with ABS, slacken and remove the retaining bolt . . .

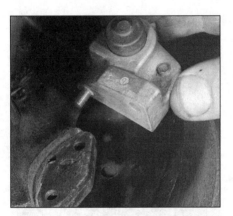

2.7b . . . and release the wheel sensor mounting bracket from the swivel hub

2.9 Unscrew the nuts and withdraw the bolts securing the suspension strut to the swivel hub

6   Slacken and remove the lower arm balljoint clamp nut and bolt, and free the lower arm from the swivel hub **(see illustration)**. Discard the clamp bolt nut; a new one must be used on refitting.

7   On models with ABS, undo the bolt securing the wheel sensor mounting bracket to the swivel hub, and position the sensor assembly clear of the hub **(see illustrations)**.

8   On all models, slacken and remove the nut securing the steering gear track rod balljoint to the swivel hub, and release the balljoint tapered shank using a universal balljoint separator. Discard the nut; it should be renewed whenever it is disturbed.

9   Slacken and remove the two nuts and bolts securing the suspension strut to the swivel hub, noting which way around the bolts are inserted **(see illustration)**. Discard the nuts and bolts; they should be renewed whenever they are disturbed.

10   Carefully pull the swivel hub assembly outwards, and withdraw the driveshaft outer constant velocity joint from the hub assembly. If necessary, the shaft can be tapped out of the hub using a soft-faced mallet. Support the driveshaft by suspending it with wire or string, and do not allow it to hang under its own weight. Remove the hub assembly from the vehicle **(see illustration)**.

Refitting

11   Ensure that the driveshaft outer constant velocity joint and hub splines are clean, then slide the hub onto the driveshaft splines. Fit the washer and new driveshaft retaining nut, tightening it by hand only at this stage **(see illustration)**.

12   Engage the swivel hub with the suspension strut, and insert the new bolts from the rear of the strut so that their threads are facing forwards (see illustration 4.8a). Fit the new nuts, tightening them by hand only at this stage.

13   Locate the lower arm balljoint in the swivel hub. Insert the clamp bolt from the rear of the swivel hub, so that its threads are facing forwards. Fit the new nut to the clamp bolt, and tighten it to the specified torque setting **(see illustration)**.

14   With the hub correctly located, tighten the strut-to-swivel hub bolts through the various stages given in the Specifications at the start of this Chapter.

15   Engage the track rod balljoint in the swivel hub, then fit the new retaining nut and tighten it to the specified torque setting.

2.10 Free the swivel hub from the end of the driveshaft, and withdraw it from the vehicle

10

2.11 Engage the swivel hub with the driveshaft constant velocity joint, and fit the washer and new retaining nut

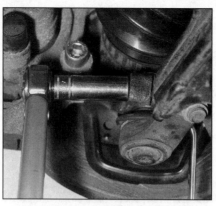

2.13 Fit a new nut to the lower arm balljoint clamp bolt, and tighten it to the specified torque setting

2.17 In the absence of a suitable tap, one of the old caliper mounting bolts with slots cut in its threads (arrowed) can be used to clean the old thread-locking compound from the holes

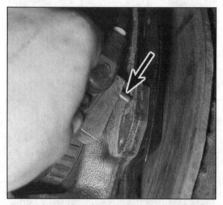

2.19 On models with ABS, ensure that the sensor bracket pin (arrowed) is correctly located in the hub hole when refitting the bracket to the swivel hub

3.2 Disc shield retaining screws are accessed through holes in the hub flange

3.4 Hub bearing is retained by a circlip (arrowed)

16   Refit the brake disc (where removed) to the hub, referring to Chapter 9 for further information.

17   Remove all traces of old thread-locking compound from the brake caliper holes in the swivel hub, ideally by running a tap of the correct size and pitch through them. **Tip:** *If a suitable tap is not available, cut two slots into the threads of one of the original mounting bolts, and use the bolt to remove the locking compound from the threads* **(see illustration)**.

18   If the threads of the new caliper mounting bolts are not already pre-coated with thread-locking compound, apply a suitable locking compound to them. Slide the caliper assembly into position over the disc, then fit the mounting bolts and tighten them to the specified torque setting (Chapter 9 Specifications).

19   Where necessary, refit the ABS wheel sensor bracket to the hub, making sure its locating peg is correctly engaged **(see illustration)**, and tighten the mounting bracket retaining bolt to the specified torque (Chapter 9 Specifications).

20   Using the method employed on removal to prevent rotation, tighten the driveshaft retaining nut through the stages given in the Specifications shown in Chapter 8 .

21   With the nut correctly tightened, secure it in position with a new split pin. If the holes in the driveshaft are not aligned with any of the slots in the nut, loosen (**do not** tighten) the nut by the *smallest possible amount* until the split pin can be inserted.

22   Refit the roadwheel, aligning the marks made on removal, then lower the vehicle to the ground and tighten the roadwheel bolts to the specified torque. Refit the wheel trim/hub cap, where applicable.

3   Front hub bearings - renewal

Note: *The bearing is sealed, pre-adjusted and pre-lubricated. Never overtighten the driveshaft nut beyond the specified torque wrench setting in an attempt to "adjust" the bearing.*

Note: *A press will be required to dismantle and rebuild the assembly; if such a tool is not available, a large bench vice and spacers (such as large sockets) will serve as an adequate substitute. The bearing's inner races are an interference fit on the hub; if the inner race remains on the hub when it is pressed out of the hub carrier, a knife-edged bearing puller will be required to remove it.*

1   Remove the swivel hub assembly as described in Section 2.

2   Undo the screws and remove the brake disc shield from the hub **(see illustration)**. Discard the screws; new ones should be used on refitting.

3   Support the swivel hub securely on blocks or in a vice. Using a tubular spacer which bears only on the inner end of the hub flange, press the hub flange out of the bearing. If the bearing's outboard inner race remains on the hub, remove it using a bearing puller (see note above).

4   Extract the bearing retaining circlips from the swivel hub assembly **(see illustration)**.

5   Where necessary, refit the inner race back in position over the ball cage, and securely support the inner face of the swivel hub. Using a tubular spacer which bears only on the inner race, press the complete bearing assembly out of the swivel hub.

4.2 On models with ABS, free the sensor wiring from its clip on the base of the strut

4.4a On some models, it may be necessary to undo the nuts (arrowed) . . .

4.4b . . . and reposition the wiring loom tray to gain access to the strut upper mounting nuts (arrowed)

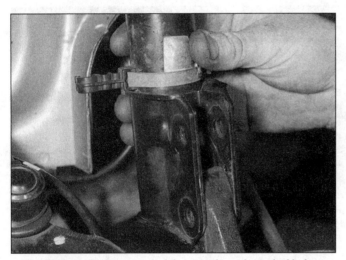

4.5a Release the lower end of the strut from the swivel hub . . .

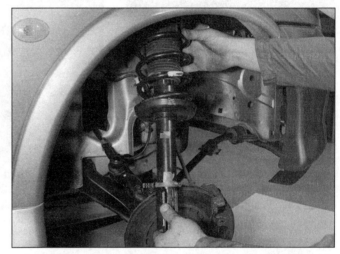

4.5b . . . and manoeuvre the strut out from underneath the wheelarch

6   Thoroughly clean the hub and swivel hub, removing all traces of dirt and grease. Polish away any burrs or raised edges which might hinder reassembly. Check both assemblies for cracks or any other signs of wear or damage, and renew as necessary. Renew the circlips regardless of their apparent condition.
7   On reassembly, apply a light film of oil to the bearing outer race and hub flange shaft, to aid installation of the bearing. Remove all traces of old thread-locking compound from the disc shield retaining screw holes, ideally by running a tap of the correct size and pitch through them.
8   Install the new outer circlip in the swivel hub. Make sure that the circlip is correctly located in its groove, with its holes situated at the bottom of the hub.
9   Securely support the swivel hub, and locate the bearing in the hub. Press the bearing fully into position, ensuring that it enters the hub squarely, using a tubular spacer which bears only on the bearing outer race.
10   Once the bearing is correctly seated against the outer circlip, se-cure the bearing in position with the new inner circlip. Make sure that the circlip is correctly located in its groove, with its holes situated at the bottom of the hub.
11   Securely support the outer face of the hub flange, and locate the swivel hub bearing inner race over the end of the hub flange. Press the bearing onto the hub, using a tubular spacer which bears only on the inner race of the hub bearing, until it seats against the hub shoulder. Check that the hub flange rotates freely, and wipe off any excess oil or grease.
12   Fit the disc shield to the hub assembly, and apply a few drops of

thread-locking compound to the new screws. Fit the screws, and tighten them to securely.
13   Refit the swivel hub assembly as described in Section 2.

---

4   **Front suspension strut - removal, overhaul and refitting**

Note: *When refitting, new strut-to-swivel hub bolts and nuts, and strut upper mounting nuts, will be required.*

Removal

1   Chock the rear wheels, firmly apply the handbrake, then jack up the front of the vehicle and support on axle stands. Remove the appro-priate roadwheel, marking its correct fitted position on the hub.
2   On models with ABS, release the front wheel sensor wiring from its clip on the suspension strut **(see illustration)**.
3   Slacken and remove the two nuts and bolts securing the suspen-sion strut to the swivel hub. Discard both nuts and bolts; these must be renewed whenever they are disturbed.
4   From within the engine compartment, unscrew the two suspen-sion strut upper mounting nuts and discard them; new ones should be used on refitting. On some models, it may be necessary to reposition the wiring loom tray to improve access to the strut upper mounting; the tray is retained by plastic nuts **(see illustrations)**.
5   Release the strut from the swivel hub, and withdraw it from under the wheel arch **(see illustrations)**.

10

4.7 Tighten the strut upper mounting nuts to the specified torque setting

4.8a Insert the new bolts from the rear of the strut, so their threads are facing forwards

4.8b Tighten the bolts first to the specified torque settings . . .

4.8c . . . and then through the specified angle

5.4 Examine the lower arm pivot bush for signs of damage or deterioration, and if necessary renew

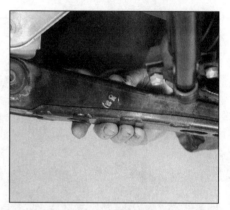

5.6 Engage the outer end of the lower arm with the balljoint and tie-bar, and insert the new bolts . . .

Overhaul

6   Overhaul of the strut should be entrusted to a Vauxhall/Opel dealer or garage having access to a spring compressor. Any attempt to dismantle the strut without such a tool is likely to result in damage or personal injury.

Refitting

7   Manoeuvre the strut assembly into position, ensuring that the top mounting plate is correctly located. Fit the washers and new strut upper mounting nuts, and tighten them to the specified torque setting **(see illustration)**. Refit the wiring loom tray to its original location, where applicable.
8   Engage the lower end of the strut with the swivel hub. Insert the new bolts from the rear of the strut so that their threads are facing forwards. Fit the new nuts to the bolts, and tighten them through the various stages given in the Specifications at the start of this Chapter **(see illustrations)**.
9   On models with ABS, clip the sensor wiring back into its retaining clip.
10   Refit the roadwheel. aligning the marks made on removal, then lower the vehicle to the ground and tighten the roadwheel bolts to the specified torque.

---

5   Front suspension lower arm - removal, overhaul and refitting

Note: *When refitting, a new pivot bolt nut, and new lower arm-to-balljoint/tie-bar nuts and bolts, will be required.*

Removal

1   Chock the rear wheels, firmly apply the handbrake, then jack up the front of the vehicle and support on axle stands. Remove the appropriate front roadwheel, making alignment marks between the wheel and hub.
2   Unscrew the nut and withdraw the pivot bolt securing the lower arm to the vehicle body. Discard the nut; a new one should be used on refitting.
3   Slacken and remove the two nuts and bolts securing the balljoint and tie-bar to the lower arm, and remove the lower arm from the vehicle. Discard the nuts and bolts; new ones should be used on refitting.

Overhaul

4   Thoroughly clean the lower arm and the area around the arm mountings, removing all traces of dirt and underseal if necessary. Check carefully for cracks, distortion, or any other signs of wear or damage, paying particular attention to the pivot bush **(see illustration)**. If bush renewal is necessary, the lower arm should be taken to a Vauxhall/Opel dealer or suitably-equipped garage. A hydraulic press and spacers are required to press the bush out of the arm, and to install the new one.
5   Examine the shank of the pivot bolt for signs of wear or scoring, and renew if necessary.

Refitting

6   Offer up the lower arm, aligning it with the tie-bar and balljoint, and install the new bolts and nuts **(see illustration)**.
7   Align the inner end of the arm with its mounting, and insert the pivot bolt from the front of the vehicle, so that its threads are facing towards the rear of the vehicle **(see illustration)**.

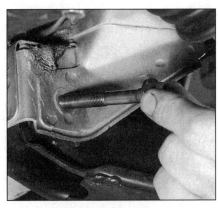

5.7 . . . then align the inner end of the arm, and insert the pivot bolt so its threads are facing towards the rear of the vehicle

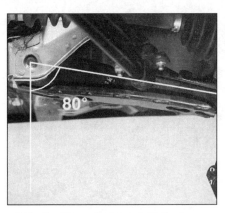

5.9a Position a jack beneath the lower arm, and raise it until the angle at the arm is at 80° to the vertical . . .

5.9b . . . then fit a new nut to the pivot bolt, and tighten it to the specified torque setting

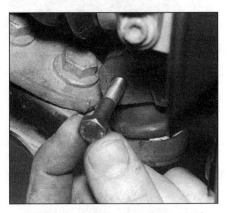

6.2 Slacken and remove the nut and clamp bolt . . .

6.3 . . . then remove the balljoint-to-lower arm/tie-bar bolts (arrowed) . . .

6.4 . . . and withdraw the balljoint from the end of the lower arm

8   Tighten the balljoint/tie-bar-to-lower arm bolt nuts to the specified torque setting.
9   Position a jack underneath the outer end of the lower arm. Raise the jack so that the lower arm is positioned as shown in **illustration 5.9a**. With the arm correctly positioned, fit the new nut to the pivot bolt, and tighten it to the specified torque setting **(see illustrations)**.
10   Remove the jack from underneath the arm, then refit the roadwheel, aligning the marks made on removal.
11   Lower the vehicle to the ground, and tighten the roadwheel bolts to the specified torque setting.

6   Front suspension lower arm balljoint - removal and refitting

Note: *When refitting, a new clamp bolt nut and new balljoint/tie-bar to lower arm nuts and bolts will be required.*

Removal

1   Chock the rear wheels, firmly apply the handbrake, then jack up the front of the vehicle and support on axle stands. Remove the appropriate front roadwheel, making alignment marks between the wheel and hub.
2   Slacken and remove the lower arm balljoint clamp nut and bolt, and free the balljoint from the swivel hub **(see illustration)**. Discard the clamp bolt nut; a new one must be used on refitting.
3   Slacken and remove the two nuts and bolts securing the balljoint and tie-bar to the lower arm **(see illustration)**. Discard the nuts and bolts; these should be renewed whenever they are disturbed.

4   Withdraw the balljoint from the lower arm, and remove it from the vehicle **(see illustration)**.

Refitting

5   Align the balljoint with the lower arm and tie-bar, then insert the new bolts **(see illustration)**. Fit the new nuts to the bolts, tightening them by hand only at this stage.

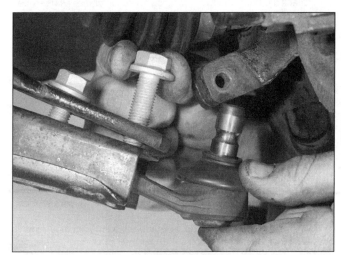

6.5 Insert the balljoint into the end of the lower arm, and fit the new retaining bolts

10

6.7 Fit a new nut to the balljoint clamp bolt, and tighten it to the specified torque setting

7.4a Unscrew the retaining nut from the front end of the tie-bar . . .

7.4b . . . and remove the washer from the end of the bar

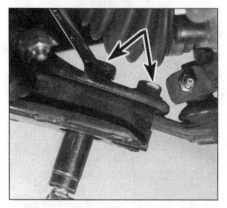

7.5 Slacken and remove the two bolts (arrowed) securing the tie-bar and balljoint to the lower arm . . .

7.6 . . . then free the front end of the bar from its mounting bush, and recover the washer (arrowed)

7.8 Tie-bar front mounting bush bracket is retained by three bolts (arrowed)

6   Locate the balljoint shank in the swivel hub, and insert the clamp bolt from the rear of the swivel hub, so that its threads are facing forwards.

7   Fit the new nut to the balljoint clamp bolt, and tighten it to the specified torque setting **(see illustration)**. Tighten the balljoint-to-lower arm/tie-bar bolt nuts to the specified torque.

8   Refit the roadwheel, aligning the marks made on removal, then lower the vehicle to the ground and tighten the roadwheel bolts to the specified torque setting.

9   Check the front wheel alignment and steering angles as described in Section 27.

7   Front suspension tie-bar - removal, overhaul and refitting

Note: *When refitting, a new tie-bar front mounting nut and anti-roll bar mounting clamp nuts will be required. The balljoint/tie-bar-to-lower arm nuts and bolts must also be renewed, as must the front mounting bracket bolts if they are disturbed.*

Removal

1   Chock the rear wheels, firmly apply the handbrake, then jack up the front of the vehicle and support on axle stands.

2   Prior to removal, mark the position of the anti-roll bar mounting clamp rubbers on the tie-bar.

3   Unscrew the two nuts from each anti-roll bar clamp, and remove both halves of the clamp. Discard the nuts; new ones must be used on refitting.

4   Slacken the nut securing the front of the tie-bar to its mounting bracket, and remove the nut along with its washer **(see illustrations).**

Discard the nut; a new one should be used on refitting.

5   Slacken and remove the two nuts and bolts securing the tie-bar and balljoint to the lower arm **(see illustration)**. Discard the nuts and bolts; these should be renewed whenever they are disturbed. **Note:** *On some models, it may be necessary to disconnect the lower arm balljoint from the swivel hub to enable the bolts to be withdrawn (see Section 6).*

6   Free the front end of the tie-bar from its mounting bush, and remove it from the vehicle **(see illustration)**. Slide the washer off the end of the tie-bar.

Overhaul

7   Inspect the tie-bar for signs of damage, paying particular attention to the threads, and renew if necessary. If the anti-roll bar clamp rubbers show any signs of damage or deterioration, they must also be renewed.

8   Examine the front mounting bush and bracket for signs of wear and damage. If renewal is necessary, undo the three bolts securing the bracket to the crossmember **(see illustration)**, and take the bracket to a Vauxhall/Opel dealer or suitably-equipped garage. A hydraulic press and spacers are required to press the bush out of position, and to install the new one. Discard the bracket retaining bolts; they must be renewed whenever they are disturbed. On refitting, remove all traces of old thread-locking compound from the retaining bolt holes in the crossmember, ideally by running a tap of the correct size and pitch through them. Apply a suitable locking compound to the new bracket retaining bolt threads, and screw in the new bolts. Tighten them first to the specified torque setting, and then through the specified angle given in the Specifications at the start of this Chapter. **Tip:** *If a suitable tap is not available, cut two slots into the threads of one of the original mounting bolts, and use the bolt to remove the locking compound from the threads.*

Refitting

9   Fit the washer to the threaded end of the tie-bar, and insert the tie-bar into its mounting bush.

10   Align the tie-bar with the lower arm and balljoint, and insert the new retaining bolts. Fit new nuts to the bolts, and tighten them to the specified torque setting.

11   Fit the washer and new nut to the front of the tie-bar, and tighten it to the specified torque setting.

12   Install the anti-roll bar mounting clamps as described in Section 8, then lower the vehicle to the ground.

8   Front suspension anti-roll bar - removal and refitting

Note: *When refitting, new anti-roll bar mounting clamp nuts will be required.*

Removal

1   Chock the rear wheels, firmly apply the handbrake, then jack up the front of the vehicle and support on axle stands.

2   Prior to removal, mark the position of each anti-roll bar mounting clamp rubber on the control arms.

3   Unscrew the two nuts from each mounting clamp, and remove both halves of the clamp. As the last clamp is removed, support the anti-roll bar and remove it from underneath the vehicle **(see illustrations)**. Discard all clamp nuts; new ones must be used on refitting.

4   Inspect the mounting clamp rubbers for signs of damage and deterioration, and renew if necessary **(see illustration)**.

Refitting

5   Align all the mounting rubbers with the marks made on the tie-bars prior to removal. Ensure that the flat edge of each rubber is facing downwards.

6   Fit the upper half of each mounting clamp to its relevant rubber.

7   Offer up the anti-roll bar, and fit the lower half of the mounting clamp. Ensure that the clamp half is correctly engaged with the anti-roll bar flats, then couple both halves of each clamp together **(see illustration)**. Fit the new clamp nuts, tightening them by hand only at this stage.

8   With all the clamps loosely installed, check that the distance between the right-and left-hand rear clamps and the tie-bar inner bolt is as shown **(see illustration)**. Reposition the anti-roll bar as required until both the right- and left-hand clamps are correctly positioned, then go around and tighten all the clamp nuts to the specified torque setting.

9   Lower the vehicle to the ground.

9   Rear hub assembly - removal and refitting

Removal

Corsa and Corsavan models

1   On Corsa and Corsavan models, the rear hub is an integral part of the brake drum. Refer to Chapter 9 for drum removal and refitting details.

8.3a Unscrew the anti-roll bar clamp retaining nuts . . .

8.3b . . . and free the bar and lower clamp halves from the tie-bar

8.3c Recover the upper half of each clamp . . .

8.4 . . . and remove the mounting rubber from the tie-bar

8.7 When refitting, ensure that each lower clamp is correctly engaged with the anti-roll bar flats

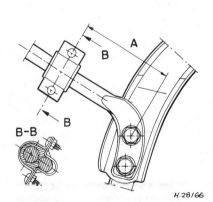

H.28166

8.8 Position the anti-roll bar so that the distance between the left- and right-hand rear clamp and each tie-bar inner bolt (A) is 121 mm. Inset (B) shows cross-sectional view of anti-roll bar and tie-bar

10

10.3 Lever the oil seal out from the hub with a flat-bladed screwdriver

10.5 Support the hub on blocks of wood, and drift out the outer races using a hammer and punch

10.9a Insert the outer race into the hub . . .

2   Check the hub bearing for signs of roughness or damage, and re-new if necessary as described in Section 10.

3   With the hub removed, examine the stub axle shaft for signs of wear or damage and, if necessary, renew it as described in Section 11.

Combo Van models

4   Remove the rear brake drum as described in Chapter 9. Prise out the cap from the centre of the hub.

5   Extract the split pin from the hub nut, then slacken and remove the nut.

6   Slide the hub assembly, complete with the toothed washer and outer bearing, off the stub axle.

7   Check the hub bearing for signs of roughness or damage, and re-new if necessary as described in Section 10.

8   With the hub removed, examine the stub axle shaft for signs of wear or damage. If renewal is necessary, the complete rear axle must be renewed; it is not possible to separate the stub axles from the axle.

Refitting

Corsa and Corsavan models

9   Refit the brake drum as described in Chapter 9.

Combo Van models

10   Ensure that the stub axle is clean, and apply a smear of grease to the lip of the hub oil seal.

11   Slide the hub, outer bearing and toothed washer onto the stub axle, ensuring that the toothed washer is correctly engaged with the stub axle slot.

12   Refit the hub nut, tightening it to the specified torque setting whilst rotating the hub to settle the bearings in position. Gradually slacken the hub nut until the position is found where it is just possible to move the toothed washer from side-to-side using a screwdriver. **Note:** *Only a small amount of force should be needed to move the washer.* When the hub nut is correctly positioned, secure it in position with a new split pin.

13   If the stub axle holes are not aligned with any of the slots in the hub nut, tighten the nut by the *smallest possible amount* until the split pin can be inserted. With the nut in this position, check that it is still possible to move the toothed washer. If it is, insert the split pin and se-cure it in position. If it is not possible to move the washer, slacken the nut slightly until the next hub nut slot/axle hole aligns. Check that it is possible to move the toothed washer, then secure the hub nut in posi-tion with the new split pin.

14   Fit the cap to the centre of the hub.

15   Install the brake drum as described in Chapter 9.

10 Rear hub bearings - renewal

1   On Corsa and Corsavan models, remove the rear brake drum as

described in Chapter 9. On Combo Van models, remove the hub as described in Section 9.

2   If not already done, remove the toothed washer from the drum/hub, and lift out the outer taper roller bearing.

3   Using a suitable flat-bladed screwdriver, lever the oil seal out of the rear of the drum/hub, noting which way around it is fitted **(see il-lustration)**.

4   Remove the inner taper roller bearing from the inside of the drum/hub.

5   Support the drum/hub, and tap the outer bearing outer race out of position, using a hammer and metal drift which just passes through the centre of the inner bearing outer race **(see illustration)**.

6   Turn the drum/hub over, and tap the inner bearing outer race out of position.

7   Thoroughly clean the hub, removing all traces of dirt and grease. Polish away any burrs or raised edges which might hinder reassembly. Check the drum/hub surface for cracks or any other signs of wear or damage, and renew it if necessary. The bearings and oil seal must be renewed whenever they are disturbed, as removal will almost certainly damage the outer races. Obtain new bearings, an oil seal, and a small quantity of the special bearing grease (90 001 812 / 19 41 574) from your Vauxhall/Opel dealer. In the absence of the special grease, a good-quality lithium-based grease may be used instead.

8   On reassembly, apply a light film of clean engine oil to each bear-ing outer race, to aid installation.

9   Securely support the drum/hub, and locate the outer bearing outer race in the hub. Tap the outer race fully into position, using a tubular spacer which bears only on the outer edge of the race, and en-suring that it enters the hub squarely **(see illustrations)**.

10.9b . . . and drift it into position using a hammer and tubular drift

10.12a Work the grease well into the roller bearings . . .

10.12b . . . and smear the outer race surfaces

10.13 Fit the taper roller bearing to the innermost outer race . . .

10.14 . . . then press the oil seal into position

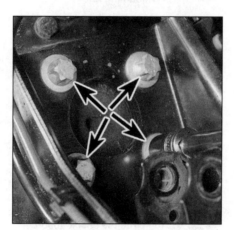

11.4a On Corsa and Corsavan models, undo the four retaining bolts (arrowed) . . .

11.4b . . . and remove the stub axle (shown with brake shoes removed)

10 Turn the drum/hub over, and install the inner bearing outer race in the same way.

11 Ensure that both outer races are correctly seated in the hub, and wipe them clean.

12 Work the grease well into both the taper roller bearings, and apply a smear of grease to the outer races **(see illustrations)**.

13 Fit the taper roller bearing to the innermost outer race **(see illustration)**.

14 Press the oil seal into the rear of the drum/hub, ensuring that its sealing lip is facing inwards **(see illustration)**. Position the seal so that it is flush with the hub face, or until its lip abuts the rear of the drum/hub. If necessary, the seal can be tapped into position using a suitable tubular drift which bears only on the hard outer edge of the seal.

15 Turn the drum/hub over, fit the taper roller bearing to the outer race, and install the toothed washer.

16 Pack the hub bearings with grease.

17 On Corsa and Corsavan models, install the brake drum as described in Chapter 9.

18 On Combo Van models, refit the hub assembly as described in Section 9.

11 Rear stub axle - removal and refitting

Corsa and Corsavan models

Note: *When refitting, new stub axle retaining bolts must be used.*

Removal

1 Remove the brake drum as described in Chapter 9.

2 Position a jack underneath the relevant trailing arm, and raise the jack until it is just supporting the weight of the arm.

3 Undo the lower shock absorber mounting bolt, and swing the shock absorber away from the trailing arm to gain access to the stub axle retaining bolts.

4 Slacken and remove the retaining bolts, and remove the stub axle from the trailing arm **(see illustrations)**. Discard the retaining bolts; new ones must be used on refitting.

5 Inspect the stub axle surface for signs of damage such as scoring, and renew if necessary.

Refitting

6 Ensure that the mating surfaces of the stub axle and backplate are clean and dry. Check the backplate for signs of damage, and remove any burrs with a fine file or emery cloth.

7 Offer up the stub axle, and fit the new retaining bolts. Tighten the retaining bolts first to the specified torque setting, then tighten them through the specified angle given in the Specifications at the start of this Chapter.

8 Align the shock absorber with the trailing arm, then fit its lower mounting bolt, tightening it to the specified torque.

9 Remove the jack from underneath the trailing arm, and refit the brake drum as described in Chapter 9.

Combo Van models

10 On Combo Van models, the stub axles are an integral part of the rear axle, and cannot be removed separately. If a stub axle is damaged, the complete axle assembly must be renewed. Refer to Section 15 for axle removal and refitting details.

10

12.3a On Corsa models, unclip the trim cover . . .

12.3b . . . and remove the cap to gain access to the shock absorber upper mounting nut

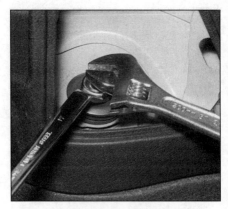

12.4 Slacken the mounting nut whilst retaining the piston with an open-ended spanner

12.5a Remove the lower mounting bolt . . .

12.5b . . . then free the shock absorber from the trailing arm, and manoeuvre it out from underneath the vehicle

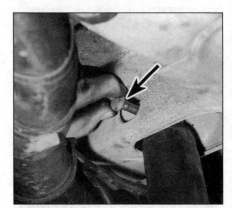

12.9a On Combo Van models, slacken and remove the upper (arrowed) . . .

12 Rear shock absorber - removal, testing and refitting

Removal

Corsa and Corsavan models

1   Chock the front wheels, then jack up the rear of the vehicle and support it on axle stands.
2   Position a jack underneath the relevant trailing arm, and raise the jack until it is just supporting the weight of the arm.
3   Working in the luggage compartment, prise out the trim cover and/or remove the trim cap (as applicable) to gain access to the shock absorber upper mounting nut **(see illustrations)**.
4   Slacken and remove the nut, and lift off the plate and rubber mounting damper. If necessary, to prevent the shock absorber piston rotating as the nut is slackened, retain it using an open-ended spanner on the flats on the upper end of the piston **(see illustration)**.
5   Slacken and remove the lower shock absorber mounting bolt, then lower the shock absorber out of position and remove it from underneath the vehicle **(see illustrations)**.
6   Remove the rubber damper, spacer and dust cover from the shock absorber piston.

Combo Van

7   Chock the front wheels, then jack up the rear of the vehicle and support it on axle stands.
8   Position a jack underneath the axle, and raise the jack until it is just supporting the weight of the axle.
9   Note the orientation of the shock absorber, then slacken and re-move the upper and lower shock absorber mounting bolts, and remove the shock absorber from underneath the vehicle **(see illustrations)**.

Testing

10   Examine the shock absorber for signs of fluid leakage or damage. Test the operation of the strut, while holding it in an upright position, by moving the piston through a full stroke, and then through short strokes of 50 to 100 mm. In both cases, the resistance felt should be smooth and continuous. If the resistance is jerky, or uneven, or if there is any visible sign of wear or damage to the strut, renewal is necessary. Also check the rubber mounting bush(es) for damage and deterioration. If the bushes are damaged or worn, the complete shock absorber will have to be renewed, as the mounting bushes are not available separately. Inspect the shanks of the mounting bolts for signs of wear or damage, and renew as necessary.
11   On Corsa and Corsavan models, examine the upper mounting rubber dampers for signs of damage or deterioration, and renew if necessary.

Refitting

Corsa and Corsavan

12   Ensure that the rubber bump stops are in position on the piston, then operate the piston fully through several strokes to prime it.
13   Fully extend the piston, then slide the dust cover, spacer and rub-ber damper onto the piston.
14   Manoeuvre the shock absorber into position, ensuring that the piston is correctly located in the hole in the vehicle body.
15   Insert the shock absorber lower mounting bolt, and tighten it to the specified torque setting **(see illustration)**.
16   From inside the luggage compartment, refit the rubber mounting damper and plate to the piston.
17   Fit the upper mounting nut, and tighten it to the specified torque setting. If necessary, prevent the piston rotating as described in para-

12.9b . . . and lower mounting bolts . . .

12.9c . . . and remove the shock absorber from underneath the vehicle

12.15 Tightening the shock absorber lower mounting bolt (Corsa)

12.21 Tightening the shock absorber lower mounting bolt (Combo Van)

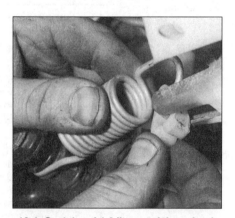

13.4 On 1.4 and 1.6 litre models, unhook the spring from the rear brake pressure-regulating valve

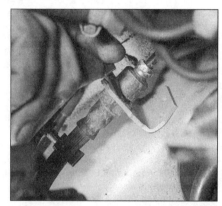

13.5a Slide out the retaining clips . . .

graph 4.

18 Refit the trim cap/cover (as applicable).

19 Remove the jack from underneath the trailing arm, and lower the vehicle to the ground.

Combo Van

20 Operate the shock absorber fully through several strokes to prime it, then manoeuvre it into position underneath the vehicle.

21 Ensure that the shock absorber is positioned the correct way up, and insert both the upper and lower mounting bolts. Tighten both mounting bolts to their specified torque settings **(see illustration)**.

22 Remove the jack from underneath the axle, and lower the vehicle to the ground.

---

13 Rear suspension coil spring (Corsa and Corsavan) - removal and refitting

---

Note: *Both coil springs are removed at the same time.*

Removal

1 Chock the front wheels, then jack up the rear of the vehicle and support it on axle stands. Remove both rear roadwheels, making alignment marks between the wheels and hubs.

2 Position a jack underneath the right-hand trailing arm, and raise the jack until it is just supporting the weight of the arm.

3 Undo the shock absorber lower mounting bolt, and disengage the right-hand shock absorber from the trailing arm.

4 On 1.4 and 1.6 litre models, remove the spring connecting the rear brake pressure-regulating valve to the axle (Chapter 9) **(see illustration)**.

5 Detach the rear brake pipes from their clips on the vehicle underbody and axle **(see illustrations)**, then slowly lower the jack until it is no longer supporting the trailing arm. With the trailing arm unsupported, check that no excess strain is being placed on the brake pipes.

6 Position the jack underneath the left-hand trailing arm, and raise the jack until it is supporting the weight of the arm.

7 Undo the lower shock absorber mounting bolt, and disengage the left-hand shock absorber from the trailing arm.

8 Slowly lower the jack, keeping watch on the brake pipes to ensure no excess strain is placed on them, until it is possible to withdraw the right-hand coil spring. Note which way around the spring is installed, and recover the upper and lower spring seats.

10

13.5b . . . and free the rear brake pipes from the vehicle underbody brackets

13.9a Lower the rear axle, then remove the coil springs . . .

13.9b . . . and recover the upper . . .

13.9c . . . and lower spring seats

9   Remove the left-hand spring, noting which way around it is installed, and recover both the upper and lower spring seats **(see illustrations)**.

10   If the vehicle is to be left for some time with the springs removed, lift up the trailing arms and refit the shock absorber lower mounting bolts. **Note:** *Do not allow the rear axle assembly to hang unsupported.*

11   Inspect the springs closely for signs of damage, such as cracking, and check the spring seats for signs of wear or damage. Renew worn components as necessary.

Refitting

12   If the shock absorber lower bolts were refitted in paragraph 10, remove them now, and lower the trailing arms.

13   Install the upper and lower spring seats in position on the underbody and trailing arms.

14   Manoeuvre the left-hand coil spring into position, noting that the smaller-diameter end of the spring must be uppermost (towards the vehicle body). Ensure that the spring is correctly located in both the upper and lower seats.

15   Fit the right-hand spring in the same way.

16   With both springs correctly seated, lift the left-hand trailing arm up on the jack, and align the shock absorber with its mounting bracket. Refit the shock absorber lower mounting bolt, and tighten it to the specified torque setting.

17   Repeat the operation on the right-hand side, and remove the jack.

18   Locate the rear brake pipes back in position, and secure them with the retaining clips.

19   On 1.4 and 1.6 litre models, refit the brake pressure-regulating valve spring, and adjust the valve as described in Chapter 9.

20   Refit the roadwheels, aligning the marks made on removal. Lower the vehicle to the ground, and tighten the roadwheel bolts to the specified torque.

14   Rear suspension leaf spring and bump stop (Combo Van) - removal, inspection and refitting

Removal

1   Chock the front wheels, then jack up the rear of the vehicle and support it on axle stands. Remove the relevant rear roadwheel, making alignment marks between the wheel and hub. Proceed as described under the relevant sub-heading

Leaf spring

2   Unscrew the two retaining nuts, and release the handbrake cable bracket from the spring **(see illustrations)**.

3   If the right-hand leaf spring is being removed, unscrew the two retaining nuts, and detach the rear brake pressure-regulating valve spring clamp from the leaf spring **(see illustration)**.

4   Place a jack underneath the rear axle, and raise the jack so that it is supporting the weight of the axle.

5   Slacken and remove the front pivot bolt securing the leaf spring to the vehicle body, and the rear pivot bolt securing the spring to the shackle **(see illustrations)**.

6   Lower the axle slightly, then unscrew the nut and remove the bump stop seat from the top of the leaf spring **(see illustration)**.

7   Unscrew the four U-bolt retaining nuts, then remove both U-bolts and the retaining plate **(see illustrations)**.

8   Remove the leaf spring from underneath the vehicle.

9   Undo the shackle nut, and remove both halves of the shackle from underneath the vehicle **(see illustration)**.

Bump stop

10   Unscrew the bump stop retaining bolt, and remove the stop from the vehicle **(see illustration)**. Withdraw the bolt, and recover the spacer and washer.

14.2a Undo the two retaining nuts (arrowed) . . .

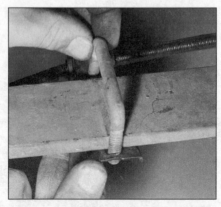

14.2b . . . and detach the handbrake cable bracket from the leaf spring

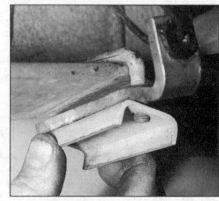

14.3 If the right-hand spring is being removed, also remove the brake pressure-regulating valve spring clamp

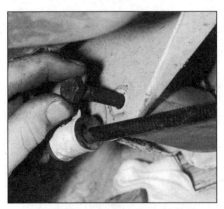

14.5a Slacken and remove the
front pivot bolt . . .

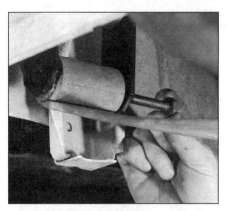

14.5b . . . and the rear bolt securing the
spring to the shackle

14.6 Undo the nut (arrowed) and remove
the bump stop seat from the spring

14.7a Undo the retaining nuts, then
withdraw both U-bolts . . .

14.7b . . . and remove the retaining plate

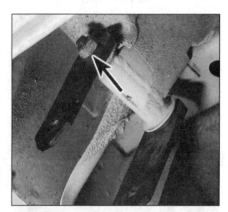

14.9 Undo the nut (arrowed) and remove
the shackle

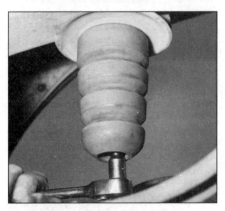

14.10 Unscrew the retaining bolt from the
centre of the bump stop, and remove the
stop from the vehicle

14.12 Remove the shackle bushes from
the vehicle, and inspect them for wear

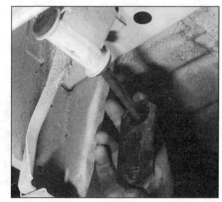

14.15a Insert the shackle plate from the
inboard side . . .

Inspection

11   Closely inspect the leaf spring and shackle for signs of damage, such as cracking, especially around the pivot points. Renew components as necessary.

12   Inspect the spring and shackle pivot bushes for signs of wear, and renew if necessary. A hydraulic press and spacers will be required to renew the leaf spring bushes, but the shackle-to-body bush halves can be easily levered out of position and the new ones installed (see illustration).

13   Examine the pivot bolts and shackle stud for signs of scoring, and renew worn components as necessary.

14   Check the rubber bump stop, and renew it if the rubber shows signs of damage or deterioration.

Refitting

15   Insert the shackle plate with the stud through from the inboard side of the bracket, and fit the plain plate on the outside. Fit the nut, tightening it by hand only at this stage (see illustrations).

16   Engage the leaf spring with the shackle and front mounting bracket. Note that the locating pin on the base of the spring is offset. Make sure that the spring is fitted with the shorter distance between the spring pivot bush and locating pin facing towards the front of the vehicle.

17   Insert the front and rear spring pivot bolts, and tighten the pivot bolts and shackle nut to the specified torque setting (see illustrations).

18   Lift the axle into position, ensuring its hole is correctly engaged

10

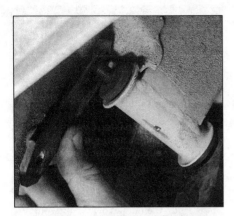

14.15b . . . and fit the plain plate on the outside

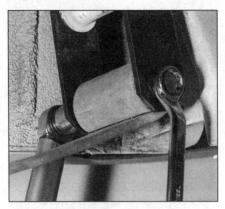

14.17a Tighten the rear pivot bolt. . .

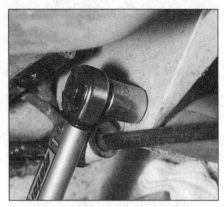

14.17b . . . and the front pivot bolt to the specified torque

14.18 Lift the axle into position, making sure that the spring locating pin is correctly located in the axle hole (arrowed) - shown with spring removed

14.19 Tighten the U-bolt retaining nuts to the specified torque as described in text

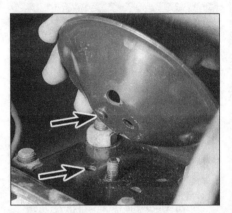

14.20 Fit the bump stop seat, making sure its locating peg is engaged with the inner retaining plate hole (arrowed)

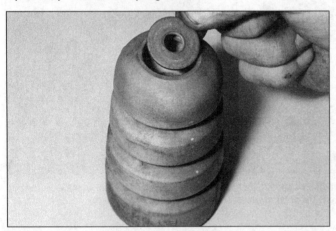

14.24a When refitting the bump stop, do not omit the washer from inside the stop . . .

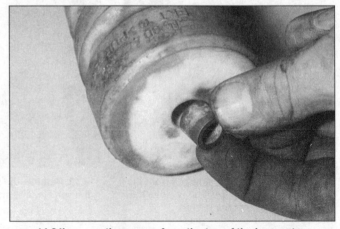

14.24b . . . or the spacer from the top of the bump stop

with the locating pin on the base of the leaf spring **(see illustration)**.

19 Refit the retaining plate to the top of the spring, and install both the U-bolts and retaining nuts. Tighten the retaining nuts evenly and progressively to the specified torque **(see illustration)**, ensuring that an equal length of thread is visible above each nut. If there is a difference of more than 3 mm between any two, slacken the retaining nuts and repeat the tightening sequence.

20 Fit the bump stop seat to the retaining plate, aligning its locating peg with innermost retaining plate hole, and tighten its retaining nut to the specified torque **(see illustration)**.

21 Refit the handbrake cable clamp to the leaf spring, and securely tighten its retaining nuts.

22 On the right-hand spring, refit the brake pressure-regulating valve clamp to the spring, and adjust the valve as described in Chapter 9.

23 Refit the roadwheel, aligning the marks made on removal. Lower the vehicle to the ground, and tighten the roadwheel bolts to the specified torque.

Bump stop

24 Insert the washer into the bump stop, and fit the spacer and retaining bolt **(see illustrations)**.

25   Fit the bump stop to the vehicle, and tighten the retaining bolt to the specified torque.
26   Refit the roadwheel, aligning the marks made on removal. Lower the vehicle to the ground, and tighten the roadwheel bolts to the specified torque.

15   Rear axle - removal and refitting

Removal

1   Chock the front wheels, then jack up the rear of the vehicle and support it on axle stands. Remove both rear roadwheels, making alignment marks between the wheels and hubs.
2   Unscrew the brake master cylinder fluid reservoir cap, then tighten the cap down onto a piece of polythene, to minimise fluid loss during the following procedure. Proceed as described under the relevant sub-heading.

Corsa and Corsavan models

Note: *New trailing arm pivot bolts and nuts will be required when refitting.*

3   Undo the retaining nuts, and remove the exhaust heat shield from underneath the vehicle to gain access to the underside of the handbrake lever.
4   Referring to Chapter 9, unscrew the handbrake cable adjuster nut, then remove the grommet from the connecting link, and detach the front end of the cable from the connecting joint. Work back along the cable, releasing it from any relevant retaining clips and ties, so that the cable is free to be removed with the axle.
5   On models with ABS, disconnect the rear wheel sensors at the wiring connectors. Free the sensor wiring from all its retaining clips, so that it is free to be removed with the axle.
6   Trace the brake pipes back from the backplates to their unions situated directly above the axle. Slacken the union nuts, and disconnect the pipes. Plug the pipe ends, to minimise fluid loss and prevent the entry of dirt into the hydraulic system. Remove the retaining clips, and release the pipes from the axle/vehicle body.
7   Remove the left- and right-hand coil springs as described in Section 13, then place the jack underneath the centre of the axle.
8   Slacken and remove the nut and pivot bolt securing each trailing arm to the vehicle underbody **(see illustration)**. Discard the nuts and bolts; new ones should be used on refitting.
9   Make a final check that all necessary components have been disconnected and positioned so that they will not hinder the removal procedure. Carefully lower the axle assembly out of position, and remove it from underneath the vehicle.
10   Inspect the trailing arm bushes for signs of damage or deterioration, and renew if necessary. Bush renewal should be entrusted to a

Vauxhall/Opel dealer, or to a suitably-equipped garage with access to a hydraulic press and spacers.

Combo Van

11   Undo the retaining nuts, and remove the exhaust heat shield from underneath the vehicle to gain access to the underside of the handbrake lever and cable.
12   Referring to Chapter 9, unscrew the handbrake cable adjuster nut, then remove the equaliser plate from the handbrake lever. Work back along each cable, releasing it from any relevant retaining clips and ties, so that the cable assembly is free to be removed with the axle.
13   Trace the brake pipes back from the backplates to their unions on the top of the axle. Slacken the union nuts, and disconnect the pipes. Plug the pipe ends, to minimise fluid loss and prevent the entry of dirt into the hydraulic system. Remove the retaining clips, and release the pipes from the axle **(see illustration)**.
14   Unscrew both the left- and right-hand shock absorber lower mounting bolts, and free both shock absorbers from the axle.
15   Position a jack beneath the centre of the axle, and raise the jack until it is supporting the weight of the axle.
16   Unscrew the nut, and remove the bump stop seat from the top of the both the left- and right-hand leaf springs.
17   Unscrew the four U-bolt retaining nuts, then remove both U-bolts and the retaining plate from the left-hand leaf spring. Remove the U-bolts and retaining plate from the right-hand leaf spring in the same way.
18   Make a final check that all necessary components have been disconnected and positioned so that they will not hinder the removal procedure. Carefully lower the axle assembly out of position, and remove it from underneath the vehicle.

Refitting

Corsa and Corsavan models

19   Refitting is a reverse of the removal procedure, bearing in mind the following points:

   (a)   Ensure that the trailing arm and mounting bracket surfaces are clean and dry. Raise the axle assembly into position, and insert the new trailing arm pivot bolts, tightening them by hand only at this stage.

   (b)   Ensure that the brake pipes, handbrake cables and wiring (as applicable) are correctly routed, and retained by all the necessary retaining clips.

   (c)   Tighten all the brake pipe union nuts to the specified torque, and bleed the braking system, with reference to Chapter 9.

   (d)   Adjust the handbrake cable as described in Chapter 9. On 1.4 and 1.6 litre models, also adjust the rear brake pressure-regulating valve once the vehicle is on the ground.

10

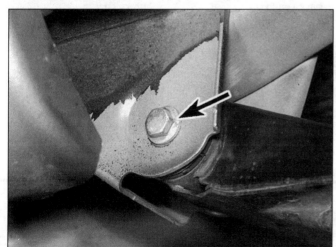

**15.8   Trailing arm pivot bolt (arrowed)
- Corsa and Corsavan models**

**15.13   Remove the retaining clips (arrowed), and release the brake
pipes from the top of the axle**

(e) On completion, lower the vehicle to the ground, and tighten the roadwheel bolts to the specified torque.

(f) With the vehicle resting on its wheels and two assistants seated in the front seats, tighten the trailing arm pivot bolts first to the specified torque setting, and then through the specified angle given in the Specifications.

Combo Van models

20 Refitting is a reverse of the removal procedure, bearing in mind the following points:

(a) Ensure that the holes in the axle are correctly aligned with the locating pegs on the leaf springs when raising the axle into position.

(b) Install the U-bolts, retaining plates and bump stop seats as described in Section 14.

(c) Ensure that the brake pipes, handbrake cables and wiring (as applicable) are correctly routed and retained by all the necessary retaining clips.

(d) Tighten all the brake pipe union nuts to the specified torque, and bleed the braking system, with reference to Chapter 9.

(e) Adjust the handbrake cable and rear brake pressure-regulating valve as described in Chapter 9.

(f) On completion, lower the vehicle to the ground, and tighten the roadwheel bolts to the specified torque.

---

16 Rear suspension anti-roll bar (Corsa and Corsavan) - removal and refitting

---

Note: New retaining bolts will be required on refitting.

Removal

1 Chock the front wheels, then jack up the rear of the vehicle, and support securely on axle stands. Remove one of the rear roadwheels, making alignment marks between the wheel and hub.

2 Prior to removal, mark the position of the rubber dampers on the axle crossmember **(see illustration)**.

3 Slacken and remove the bolts securing the anti-roll bar to the trailing arms **(see illustration)**. Discard the bolts; new ones must be used on refitting.

4 Withdraw the bar from the side on which the roadwheel has been removed. If the bar is tight, remove the opposite roadwheel, and drift the bar out using a hammer and soft metal drift. Recover the dampers from the bar as they are released **(see illustrations)**.

5 Inspect the rubber dampers for signs of damage or deterioration, and renew as necessary.

Refitting

6 To ease installation, coat the anti-roll bar with soapy water.

7 Insert the anti-roll bar in through the trailing arm, and locate the rubber dampers on the bar. Align the rubber dampers with the marks made prior to removal, and seat them in the axle crossmember.

8 Slide the anti-roll bar fully into position, so that it is correctly engaged in the opposite trailing arm.

9 Install the new retaining bolts, then refit the washers and nuts. Tighten both bolts first to the specified torque, and then through the specified angle given in the Specifications at the start of this Chapter **(see illustrations)**.

10 Refit the roadwheel(s), aligning the marks made on removal. Lower the vehicle to the ground, and tighten the roadwheel bolts to the specified torque.

16.2 Prior to removal, mark the positions (arrowed) of the rubber dampers on the axle crossmember

16.3 Slacken and remove the nut and bolt securing the anti-roll bar to each trailing arm . . .

16.4a . . . then withdraw the anti-roll bar . . .

16.4b . . . and recover the rubber dampers

16.9a Insert the new anti-roll bar retaining bolts . . .

16.9b . . . and tighten them to the specified torque, and then through the specified angle

17.3 Ease the horn button out from the steering wheel, and disconnect its wiring

17.4 Using a screwdriver, bend down the tabs of the lockwasher from the steering wheel nut

17.7 With the steering wheel removed, lift the spring from the column

17.8 Removing the indicator cancelling lug/horn button contact pad from the steering wheel

17.11 Fit the new lockwasher, engaging its tabs with the wheel cut-outs (arrowed)

17 Steering wheel - removal and refitting

Note: *A puller will be required to draw the steering wheel off the column splines. A new retaining nut lockwasher will be required when refitting.*

Models without an air bag

Removal

1   Disconnect the battery negative terminal.
2   Set the front wheels in the straight-ahead position, and release the steering lock by inserting the ignition key.
3   Carefully ease the horn button out from the steering wheel, and disconnect its wiring **(see illustration)**.
4   Using a screwdriver, prise back the tabs on the retaining nut lockwasher **(see illustration)**.
5   Unscrew the retaining nut, and lift off the lockwasher. Discard the lockwasher; a new one should be used on refitting.
6   Make alignment marks between the steering wheel and steering column shaft.
7   A 2-legged puller will now be required to free the steering wheel from its splines. Locate the legs of the puller in the holes in the centre of the wheel, and draw the steering wheel off the column splines. Lift off the steering wheel, and remove the spring from the column shaft **(see illustration)**.

Refitting

8   Check that the indicator cancelling lug/horn button contact pad fitted to the rear of steering wheel is in good condition, and if neces-

sary renew it. To release the pad, depress the two clips located inside the steering wheel **(see illustration)**.
9   Ensure that the indicator switch stalk is in its central (OFF) position. Failure to do this could lead to the steering wheel lug breaking the switch tab as the steering wheel is refitted.
10   Fit the spring to the column, then locate the wheel on the column splines, aligning the marks made on removal.
11   Fit the new lockwasher, and screw on the retaining nut **(see illustration)**. Tighten the retaining nut to the specified torque, and secure it in position with the lockwasher tabs.
12   Reconnect the wiring connectors to the horn button, and refit the button in the centre of the steering wheel.
13   Reconnect the battery, and check the operation of the horn.

Models with an air bag

Warning: *Make sure that the safety recommendations given in Chapter 12 are followed, to prevent personal injury.*

Removal

14   Remove the air bag as described in Chapter 12.
15   Set the front wheels in the straight-ahead position, then lock the column in position after removing the ignition key.
16   Slacken and remove the two screws securing the wiring contact unit to the steering wheel.
17   Release the horn wiring connector from the steering wheel, and disconnect it.
18   Remove the steering wheel as described above in paragraphs 4 to 7, taking great care not to damage the wiring contact unit.
19   Disconnect the contact unit wiring connectors, and slide the contact unit off the steering column, noting its correct fitted position.

10

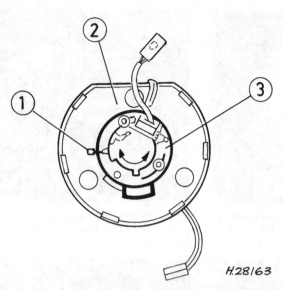

H.28/63

17.20 Air bag wiring contact unit. Centralise the unit as described in text before fitting it to the steering wheel

1 Arrow markings
2 Contact unit

3 Centre

Refitting

20   Prior to installation, it is necessary to set the contact unit to its centre position. To do this, hold the outside of the unit, and rotate the centre of the contact unit anti-clockwise until sharp resistance is felt. From this point, turn the centre back through two-and-a-half turns in a clockwise direction, and align the arrow markings on the centre and outer parts of the contact unit **(see illustration)**.

21   With the contact unit correctly centralised, install the unit in the rear of the steering wheel, routing the wiring connectors through the relevant wheel aperture, and secure it in position with the retaining screws. Reconnect the horn wiring connector and clip it into the steering wheel recess.

22   Ensure that the indicator switch stalk is in its central (OFF) position, then refit the steering wheel to the column, aligning the marks made prior to removal. When locating the steering wheel on the splines, make sure that the contact unit is correctly engaged with both the steering column and indicator switch.

23   Fit the new lockwasher, and screw on the retaining nut. Tighten the retaining nut to the specified torque, and secure it in position with the lockwasher tabs.

24   Reconnect the contact unit wiring connectors, and clip them into position on the steering column.

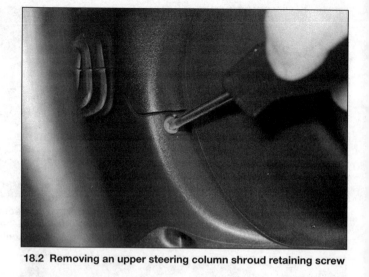

18.2 Removing an upper steering column shroud retaining screw

25   Release the steering lock, and refit the air bag as described in Chapter 12.

18   Ignition switch/steering column lock - removal and refitting

Removal

1   Disconnect the battery negative lead.

2   With the steering wheel in the straight-ahead position, turn the wheel 90° to the left, then prise off the trim cap and remove the left upper shroud screw **(see illustration)**. Turn the wheel 180° to the right and remove the right upper screw. Remove the rubber seal from the ignition switch/lock, then undo the lower retaining screws and remove the lower steering column shroud. Proceed as described under the relevant sub-heading.

Lock cylinder

3   Insert the ignition key into the ignition switch/lock, and turn it to position "I".

4   Insert a thin rod into the hole in the lock housing, press the rod to release the detent spring, and pull out the lock cylinder using the key **(see illustrations)**. If the lock cylinder will not come out easily, turn the key to position "II" and try and withdraw it.

Ignition switch wiring block

5   Disconnect the wiring connector from the ignition switch wiring block **(see illustration)**.

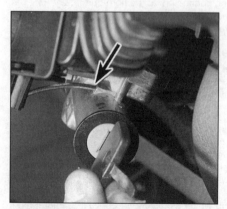

18.4a Insert the rod (arrowed) into the lock housing hole, then with the ignition key correctly positioned (see text) . . .

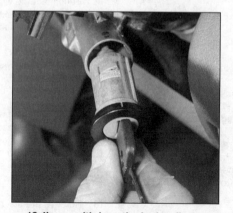

18.4b . . . withdraw the lock cylinder

18.5 Disconnect the wiring connector . . .

18.6a ... then undo the grub screws ...

18.6b ... and remove the ignition switch wiring block

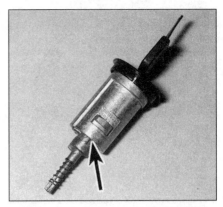

18.7 Later type of lock cylinder. Early types have a hook cast onto the end of the lock cylinder in the position indicated by the arrow

18.8 Prior to installing the lock cylinder, depress the steering lock mechanism block with a screwdriver

19.5 Depress the retaining clips, and slide the combination switches out from the column ...

19.6 ... and disconnect the wiring connector from the horn contact pin (arrowed)

6   Slacken the two grub screws (one at the front and one at the rear), and withdraw the wiring block from the end of the switch housing **(see illustrations)**.

Refitting

Lock cylinder

7   Insert the ignition key into the lock cylinder. There are two different types of lock cylinder; early types have a hook on the inner end of the lock cylinder housing, and later types do not **(see illustration)**. The early-type cylinder must be installed with the key in position "II", while the later type is installed with the key in position "I".

8   Ensure that the centre of the ignition switch wiring block is correctly aligned with the lock cylinder rod flats. If necessary, rotate the switch centre using a suitable screwdriver. If the steering column lock has been actuated, release the lock by depressing the locking mechanism block in the column housing **(see illustration)**.

9   Insert the cylinder into the housing until the detent spring clicks into position, then check the operation of the lock cylinder and steering lock.

10   Refit the steering column shroud, tightening its retaining screws securely, and fit the rubber to the switch/lock. Reconnect the battery.

Ignition switch wiring block

11   Refit the ignition switch to the housing, ensuring that the switch centre is correctly engaged with lock cylinder rod flats.

12   Insert both grub screws, and tighten them securely.

13   Reconnect the wiring connector to ignition switch.

14   Refit the steering column shroud, tightening its retaining screws securely. Refit the rubber to the switch/lock, and the trim caps to the upper screws.

15   Reconnect the battery negative terminal, and check the operation of the switch.

19   Steering column - removal, inspection and refitting

Note: *A new column mounting shear-head bolt will be required when refitting.*

Removal

1   Disconnect the battery negative terminal.

2   Remove the steering wheel as described in Section 17. On models with an air bag, also remove the contact unit from the steering column.

3   On models without an air bag, remove the rubber seal from the ignition switch/lock, then undo the retaining screws and remove the upper and lower steering column shrouds.

4   Where necessary, undo the nut and release the support bar from the column.

5   Depress the retaining clips, and release the left- and right-hand combination switches from the column. Disconnect the wiring connectors, and remove the switches from the vehicle **(see illustration)**.

6   Disconnect the wiring connectors from the ignition switch wiring block and the horn contact, then release the wiring from the steering column **(see illustration)**.

7   Using paint or similar, make alignment marks between the steering column and intermediate shaft, then slacken and remove the clamp bolt securing the intermediate shaft to the steering column **(see illustration)**.

10

19.7 Steering column-to-intermediate shaft clamp bolt (arrowed)

19.8 Steering column lower mounting bolt

19.9 Steering column upper mounting nut (A) and shear-head bolt (B)

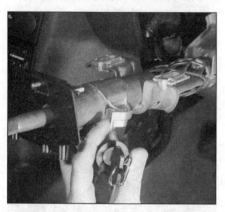

19.11 Removing the steering column

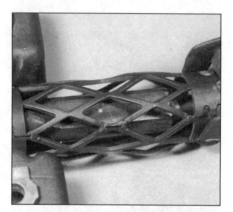

19.12 Inspect the collapsible section of the column for signs of damage, and renew the column assembly if necessary

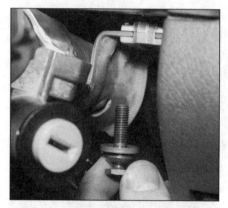

19.14 Use a new shear-head bolt when refitting the column

8   Unscrew the lower mounting bolt securing the steering column to the bulkhead **(see illustration)**.

9   Two fasteners must now be extracted from the column upper mounting bracket. A conventional nut is used on one side of the column, and a shear-head type bolt is used on the other side **(see illustration)**.

10   The shear-head bolt must be removed by drilling down the centre of the bolt, and then using a suitable bolt/stud extractor (sometimes called "easy-outs"). When drilling the bolt, take care not to damage the facia panel or steering column.

11   Release the column assembly from its mountings, then detach it from the intermediate shaft and remove it from the vehicle **(see illustration)**. Handle the column carefully, avoiding knocks or impact of any kind, which may damage the collapsible section of the column housing.

Inspection

12   The steering column incorporates a telescopic safety section. In the event of a front-end crash, the shaft housing collapses, and prevents the steering wheel injuring the driver. Before refitting the steering column, examine the column and mountings for signs of damage and deformation, and check the steering shaft for signs of free play in the column bushes **(see illustration)**. If there are signs of damage or play, the column must be renewed. On models not fitted with an air bag, overhaul of the column is possible, but this is a fiddly task which should really be entrusted to a Vauxhall/Opel dealer. Consult your dealer for further information.

Refitting

13   Manoeuvre the steering column into position, and engage it with the intermediate shaft universal joint, aligning the marks made on removal.

14   Refit the column upper and lower mounting nut/bolts, and the new shear-head bolt. Tighten all bolts by hand only at this stage **(see illustration)**.

15   Align the intermediate shaft bolt hole with the steering column shaft cutout so that the clamp bolt can be slid into position. Tighten the bolt by hand only.

16   Tighten the column mounting bolts to the specified torque setting. Tighten the shear-head bolt until its head breaks off.

17   Tighten the clamp bolt to the specified torque setting.

18   Ensure that the wiring is correctly routed, and reconnect it to the ignition switch wiring block and horn contact.

19   Clip the left-and right-hand switches back into position, and reconnect their wiring connectors.

20   Where necessary, refit the support strut to the column, and securely tighten its retaining nut.

21   On models without an air bag, clip the steering column shrouds into position, and securely tighten the retaining screws. Refit the rubber seal to the ignition switch/lock, then refit the steering wheel as described in Section 17.

22   On models with an air bag, refit the contact unit and steering wheel as described in Section 17.

20   Steering column intermediate shaft - removal, inspection and refitting

Removal

1   Set the front wheels in the straight-ahead position.

2   Using paint or a suitable marker pen, make alignment marks between the intermediate shaft joints and the steering column and steering gear shafts.

20.3a Slacken and remove the steering column-to-intermediate shaft clamp bolt . . .

20.3b . . . and the intermediate shaft-to-steering gear clamp bolt and nut (arrowed)

20.4 Free the intermediate shaft from the column and steering gear, and remove it from under the facia

3   Slacken and remove the upper clamp bolt and the lower clamp bolt and nut **(see illustrations)**.

4   Disengage the shaft universal joint from the steering column, then slide the shaft from the steering gear pinion and remove it from the vehicle **(see illustration)**.

Inspection

5   Inspect the intermediate shaft universal joint for signs of roughness in its bearings and ease of movement. If either joint is damaged in any way, the complete shaft assembly must be renewed.

Refitting

6   Check that the front wheels are still in the straight-ahead position, and that the steering wheel is correctly positioned.

7   Aligning the marks made on removal, engage the shaft with the steering gear pinion, then locate the universal joint on the steering column end. Install both clamp bolts, tightening them to the specified torque setting.

---

21 Steering gear assembly - removal, overhaul and refitting

Note: *New track rod balljoint nuts will be required when refitting.*

Removal

1   Chock the rear wheels, firmly apply the handbrake, then jack up the front of the vehicle and support on axle stands. Remove both front roadwheels, making alignment marks between the wheels and hubs.

Manual steering gear

2   Referring to Chapter 2A, support the weight of the engine/transmission unit, and remove the rear engine/transmission mounting rubber and bracket from the vehicle.

3   On models with manual transmission, disconnect the gearchange linkage from the transmission as described in Chapter 7A.

4   Slacken and remove the nuts securing the steering gear track rod balljoints to the swivel hubs **(see illustration)**, and release the balljoint tapered shanks using a universal balljoint separator. Discard the nuts; they should be renewed whenever they are disturbed.

5   Remove the intermediate shaft as described in Section 20.

6   Prior to removal, mark the position of the mounting rubbers on the steering gear housing. These marks can then be used on refitting to ensure that the steering gear is correctly positioned in the clamps.

7   Slacken and remove the four nuts and washers securing the steering gear to the bulkhead. Note the correct fitted locations of any relevant brackets retained by the nuts, then remove the steering gear mounting clamp(s) **(see illustration)**.

8   Detach the rubber gaiter from the bulkhead, and free the steering gear pinion from the intermediate shaft.

9   Move the steering gear towards the right-hand side of the engine compartment, then lower the left-hand end of the assembly, and manoeuvre the assembly out from underneath the vehicle. Note that it may be necessary to lower the engine slightly to gain the necessary clearance for removal.

Power-assisted steering gear

10   On left-hand drive models, to improve access to the steering gear, remove the braking system vacuum servo unit as described in Chapter 9.

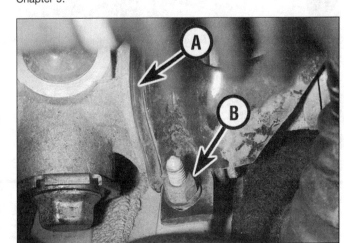

21.4 Unscrew the retaining nuts securing each track rod balljoint to the swivel hubs

21.7 Steering gear mounting rubber (A) and mounting clamp and nut (B) - viewed from underneath

10

11   Remove the intermediate shaft as described in Section 20.

12   On models with manual transmission, disconnect the gearchange linkage from the transmission as described in Chapter 7A, and unbolt the clutch cable bracket from the bulkhead.

13   Slacken and remove the nuts securing the steering gear track rod balljoints to the swivel hubs, and release the balljoint tapered shanks using a universal balljoint separator. Discard the nuts; they should be renewed whenever they are disturbed.

14   Using brake hose clamps, clamp both the supply and return hoses near the power steering fluid reservoir. This will minimise fluid loss during subsequent operations.

15   Mark the unions to ensure that they are correctly positioned on reassembly, then unscrew the feed and return pipe union nuts from the steering gear assembly; be prepared for fluid spillage, and position a suitable container beneath the pipes whilst unscrewing the union nuts **(see illustration)**. Disconnect both pipes, and plug the pipe ends and steering gear orifices, to prevent excessive fluid leakage and the entry of dirt into the hydraulic system.

16   Free the power steering pipes from any relevant retaining clips, and position them clear of the steering gear so that they will not hinder the removal procedure.

17   Referring to Chapter 2A, support the weight of the engine/transmission unit, and remove the rear engine/transmission mounting rubber and bracket from the vehicle.

18   Prior to removal, mark the position of the mounting rubbers on the steering gear housing. These marks can then be used on refitting to ensure that the steering gear is correctly positioned in the clamps.

19   Slacken and remove the four nuts and washers securing the steering gear to the bulkhead. Note the correct fitted locations of any relevant brackets retained by the nuts, then remove the steering gear mounting clamp(s).

20   On models with air conditioning, release the refrigerant pipes from their retaining clips on the bulkhead. **Note:** *Refer to the warning notes in Chapter 3 - do not attempt to disconnect any of the pipes.*

21   Release the rubber gaiter from the bulkhead, then move the steering gear fully towards the right on right-hand drive models, or the left on left-hand drive models. Lower the opposite end of the steering gear, and manoeuvre the assembly out from underneath the vehicle. Note that on 1.6 litre DOHC engine models, it may be necessary to unbolt the remaining engine/transmission mountings and lower the engine slightly to gain the necessary clearance for removal (see Chapter 2A).

Overhaul

22   Examine the steering gear assembly for signs of wear or damage, and check that the rack moves freely throughout the full length of its travel, with no signs of roughness or excessive free play between the steering gear pinion and rack. It is possible to overhaul the steering gear assembly housing components, but this task should be entrusted

21.15 Power-assisted steering gear fluid feed and return pipe unions (arrowed) - shown with engine removed for clarity

to a Vauxhall/Opel dealer. The only components which can be renewed easily by the home mechanic are the steering gear gaiters, the track rod balljoints and the track rods. Steering gear gaiter, track rod balljoint and track rod renewal procedures are found in Sections 24, 25 and 26 respectively.

23   On models with power-assisted steering, inspect all the steering gear fluid unions for signs of leakage, and check that all union nuts are securely tightened.

24   Inspect the rubber mountings and pinion gear rubber gaiter, and renew them if they show signs of wear or deterioration.

Refitting

Manual steering gear

25   Fit the mounting rubbers to the steering gear, and align them with the marks made prior to removal. If a new steering gear assembly is being installed, transfer the marks from the original onto the new assembly.

26   Manoeuvre the steering gear assembly back into position on the bulkhead. With the pinion correctly located in the bulkhead aperture, refit the mounting clamps and retaining nuts, not forgetting to fit the necessary brackets to steering gear mounting studs.

27   Ensure that the rubbers are correctly aligned with the marks made on removal, and tighten the mounting clamp nuts to the specified torque setting.

28   The remainder of refitting is reverse of the removal procedure, noting the following points:

(a)   *Refit the intermediate shaft as described in Section 20.*

(b)   *Locate the track rod balljoints in position, fit the new nuts and tighten them to the specified torque.*

(c)   *Connect the gearchange linkage as described in Chapter 7A.*

(d)   *Refit the engine/transmission mounting as described in Chapter 2A.*

(e)   *On completion, check and, if necessary, adjust the front wheel alignment as described in Section 27.*

Power-assisted steering gear

29   Install the steering gear as described above in paragraphs 25 to 27.

30   Wipe clean the feed and return pipe unions, and refit them to their respective unions on the steering gear. Tighten the union nuts to the specified torque setting, and ensure that the pipes are securely retained by all the necessary retaining clips.

31   The remainder of the refitting procedure is a direct reversal of the removal sequence, noting the following points:

(a)   *Refit the intermediate shaft as described in Section 20, and ensure that the rubber gaiter is correctly seated in the bulkhead.*

(b)   *On models with air conditioning, ensure that the refrigerant pipes are securely retained by all the necessary clips.*

(c)   *Locate the track rod balljoints in position, fit the new nuts and tighten them to the specified torque.*

(d)   *Connect the gearchange linkage as described in Chapter 7A.*

(e)   *Refit the engine/transmission mounting(s) as described in Chapter 2A.*

(f)   *On completion, remove the clamps from the hoses, and bleed the hydraulic system as described in Section 23.*

(g)   *Check and, if necessary, adjust the front wheel alignment as described in Section 27.*

---

22 Power steering pump - removal and refitting

Removal

1   Remove the auxiliary drivebelt as described in Chapter 1. On 1.6 litre DOHC models, remove the exhaust manifold heat shield (see Chapter 4A) to improve access to the rear of the pump.

2   Using brake hose clamps, clamp both the supply and return hoses near the power steering fluid reservoir. This will minimise fluid loss during subsequent operations.

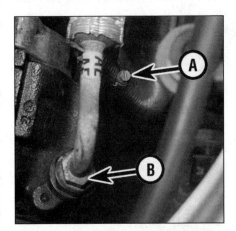

22.3 Power steering pump fluid supply hose retaining clip (A) and feed pipe union nut (B)

22.4 Power steering pump rear mounting bolts (arrowed) - shown with coolant hose removed

25.4 Release the track rod balljoint from the swivel hub using a universal balljoint separator

3   Slacken the retaining clip, and disconnect the fluid supply hose from the rear of the pump. Slacken the union nut, and disconnect the feed pipe from the pump, along with its O-ring **(see illustration)**. Be prepared for some fluid spillage as the pipe and hose are disconnected, and plug the hose/pipe end and pump unions, to minimise fluid loss and prevent the entry of dirt into the system.

4   Slacken and remove the front and rear retaining bolts securing the power steering pump to its mounting bracket **(see illustration)**, and remove the pump from the engine compartment.

Refitting

5   Manoeuvre the pump into position and refit its mounting bolts, tightening them to the specified torque setting.

6   Fit a new O-ring to the feed pipe union, then reconnect the pipe to the pump, and tighten the union nut to the specified torque setting. Refit the supply hose to the pump, and securely tighten its retaining clip. Remove the brake hose clamps used to minimise fluid loss.

7   Refit the auxiliary drivebelt as described in Chapter 1.

8   On completion, bleed the hydraulic system as described in Section 23.

23 Power steering system - bleeding

1   With the engine stopped, fill the fluid reservoir right up to the brim with the specified type of fluid. This is more important if fluid has been lost after work has been carried out, or if the system has been leaking. Otherwise, top the level up to the relevant mark (see paragraph 5).

2   Have an assistant start the engine, while you keep watch on the fluid level. Be prepared to add more fluid as the engine starts, as the fluid level may drop quickly. The fluid level must be kept above the "MIN" mark at all times, or air will be drawn into the system.

3   With the engine running at idle speed, turn the steering wheel slowly two or three times approximately 45° to the left and right of the centre, then turn the wheel twice from lock to lock. Do not hold the wheel on either lock, as this places strain on the hydraulic system. Repeat this procedure until bubbles cease to appear in fluid reservoir, topping-up as necessary.

4   If, when turning the steering, an abnormal noise is heard from the fluid lines, it indicates that there is still air in the system. Check this by turning the wheels to the straight-ahead position and switching off the engine. If the fluid level in the reservoir rises, then air is present in the system, and further bleeding is necessary.

5   Once all air is removed from the system, stop the engine and check the fluid level. With the fluid at operating temperature (80°C), the level should be on the "MAX" mark; with the fluid cold (20°C), the level should be on the "MIN" mark. Correct the level by topping-up, or by removing fluid using a syringe or similar, as necessary.

24 Steering gear rubber gaiters - renewal

1   Remove the track rod balljoint as described in Section 25.

2   Mark the correct fitted position of the gaiter on the track rod, then release the retaining clips, and slide the gaiter off the steering gear housing and track rod end.

3   Thoroughly clean the track rod and the steering gear housing, using fine abrasive paper to polish off any corrosion, burrs or sharp edges which might damage the new gaiter's sealing lips on installation. Scrape off all grease from the old gaiter, and apply to the track rod inner balljoint.

4   Carefully slide the new gaiter onto the track rod end, and locate it on the steering gear housing. Align the outer edge of the gaiter with the mark made on the track rod prior to removal, then secure it in position with new retaining clips.

5   Refit the track rod balljoint as described in Section 25.

25 Track rod balljoint - removal and refitting

Note: A new track rod balljoint nut will be required when refitting.

Removal

1   Chock the rear wheels, apply the handbrake, then jack up the front of the vehicle and support it on axle stands. Remove the appropriate front roadwheel, making alignment marks between the wheel and hub.

2   If the balljoint is to be re-used, use a straight-edge and a scriber, or similar, to mark its relationship to the track rod.

3   Hold the track rod, and unscrew the balljoint locknut by a quarter of a turn.

4   Slacken and remove the nut securing the track rod balljoint to the swivel hub, and release the balljoint tapered shank using a universal balljoint separator **(see illustration)**. Discard the nut; a new one must be used of refitting.

5   Counting the **exact** number of turns necessary to do so, unscrew the balljoint from the track rod end.

6   Count the number of exposed threads between the end of the track rod and the locknut, and record this figure. If a new gaiter is to be fitted, unscrew the locknut from the track rod.

7   Carefully clean the balljoint and the track rod threads. Renew the balljoint if its movement is sloppy or too stiff, if it is excessively worn, or if it is damaged in any way; carefully check the stud taper and threads. If the balljoint gaiter is damaged, the complete balljoint assembly must be renewed; it is not possible to obtain the gaiter separately.

Refitting

8   If it was removed, screw the locknut onto the track rod threads, and position it so that the same number of exposed threads are visible as was noted prior to removal.

9   Screw the balljoint into the track rod by the number of turns noted on removal. This should bring the balljoint locknut to within a quarter of a turn from the locknut, with the alignment marks that were made (if applicable) on removal lined up.

10   Refit the balljoint shank to the swivel hub, then fit a new retaining nut and tighten it to the specified torque setting.

11   Refit the roadwheel, aligning the marks made on removal, then lower the vehicle to the ground and tighten the roadwheel bolts to the specified torque setting.

12   Check and, if necessary, adjust the front wheel toe setting as described in Section 27. Tighten the balljoint locknut to the specified torque setting on completion.

---

26 Track rod - renewal

Manual steering gear

Note: *When refitting, a new track rod balljoint nut and new gaiter retaining clips will be required.*

1   Remove the track rod balljoint as described in Section 25.

2   Release the retaining clips, and slide the steering gear gaiter off the end of the track rod as described in Section 24.

3   Extend the steering rack from the housing. Prevent the rack from rotating using an open-ended spanner located on the rack flats, and slacken the track rod inner balljoint from the rack end.

4   Unscrew the track rod assembly, and remove it along with its spacer.

5   Remove the track rod assembly, and examine the track rod inner balljoint for signs of slackness or tight spots. Check that the track rod itself is straight and free from damage. If necessary, renew the track rod; it is also recommended that the steering gear gaiter/dust cover is renewed.

6   Locate the spacer on the end of the steering rack, and screw the balljoint into the steering rack. Tighten the track rod balljoint to the specified torque, whilst retaining the steering rack with an open-ended spanner.

7   Install the steering gaiter and track rod balljoint as described in Sections 24 and 25.

Power-assisted steering gear

8   At the time of writing, on models with power-assisted steering, the track rods are not available separately. If a track rod balljoint is worn, or the rod is damaged, the complete steering gear assembly must be renewed. Refer to your Vauxhall/Opel dealer for further information on parts availability.

---

27 Wheel alignment and steering angles - general information

1   Accurate front wheel alignment is essential for precise steering and handling, and for even tyre wear. Before carrying out any checking or adjusting operations, make sure that the tyres are correctly inflated, that all steering and suspension joints and linkages are in sound condition, and that the wheels are not buckled or distorted, particularly around the rims. It will also be necessary to have the vehicle positioned on flat, level ground, with enough space to push the car backwards and forwards through about half its length.

2   Front wheel alignment consists of four factors **(see illustration)**:

Camber is the angle at which the roadwheels are set from the vertical, when viewed from the front or rear of the vehicle. Positive camber is the angle (in degrees) that the wheels are tilted outwards at the top from the vertical.

Castor is the angle between the steering axis and a vertical line

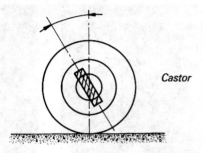
Castor

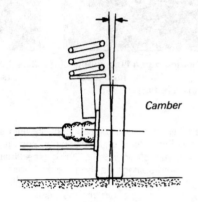
Camber

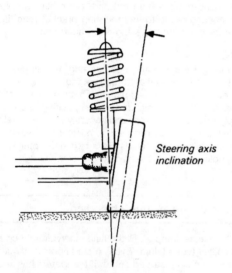
Steering axis inclination

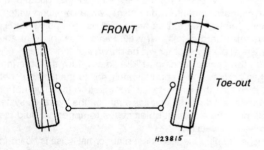
FRONT   *Toe-out*

H23815

27.2 Wheel alignment and steering angles

when viewed from each side of the vehicle. Positive castor is indicated when the steering axis is inclined towards the rear of the vehicle at its upper end.

Steering axis inclination is the angle, when viewed from the front or rear of the vehicle, between the vertical and an imaginary line drawn between the upper and lower front suspension strut mountings.

Toe setting is the amount by which the distance between the front inside edges of the roadwheels differs from that between the rear inside edges, when measured at hub height. If the distance between the front edges is less than at the rear, the wheels are said to "toe-in". If it is greater than at the rear, the wheels are said to "toe-out".

3   Camber, castor and steering axis inclination are set during manufacture, and are not adjustable. Unless the vehicle has suffered accident damage, or there is gross wear in the suspension mountings or joints, it can be assumed that these settings are correct. If for any reason it is believed that they are not correct, the task of checking them should be left to a Vauxhall/Opel dealer, who will have the necessary special equipment needed to measure the small angles involved.

4   It is, however, within the scope of the home mechanic to check and adjust the front wheel toe setting. To do this, a tracking gauge must first be obtained. Two types of gauge are available, and can be obtained from motor accessory shops. The first type measures the distance between the front and rear inside edges of the roadwheels, as previously described, with the vehicle stationary. The second type, known as a "scuff plate", measures the actual position of the contact surface of the tyre, in relation to the road surface, with the vehicle in motion. This is achieved by pushing or driving the front tyre over a plate, which then moves slightly according to the scuff of the tyre, and shows this movement on a scale. Both types have their advantages and disadvantages, but either can give satisfactory results if used correctly and carefully.

5   Many tyre specialists will also check toe settings free, or for a nominal charge.

6   Make sure that the steering is in the straight-ahead position when making measurements.

7   If adjustment is necessary, chock the rear wheels, apply the handbrake, then jack up the front of the vehicle and support it securely on axle stands. Turn the steering wheel onto full-left lock, and record the number of exposed threads on the right-hand track rod end. Now turn the steering onto full-right lock, and record the number of threads on the left-hand side. If there are the same number of threads visible on both sides, then subsequent adjustment should be made equally on both sides. If there are more threads visible on one side than the other, it will be necessary to compensate for this during adjustment. It is most important that, after adjustment, the same number of threads are visible on each track rod end.

8   First clean the track rod threads; if they are corroded, apply penetrating fluid before starting adjustment. Release the rubber gaiter outer clips, then peel back the gaiters and apply a smear of grease, so that the gaiters will not be twisted or strained as their respective track rods are rotated.

9   Use a straight-edge and a scriber, or similar, to mark the relationship of each track rod to its balljoint then, holding each track rod in turn, unscrew its locknut fully.

10   Alter the length of the track rods, bearing in mind the note made in paragraph 7, screwing them into or out of the balljoints by rotating the track rod using an open-ended spanner fitted to the track rod flats provided. Shortening the track rods (screwing them into their balljoints) will reduce toe-in/increase toe-out.

11   When the setting is correct, hold the track rods and securely tighten the balljoint locknuts. Check that the balljoints are seated correctly in their sockets, and count the exposed threads to check the length of both track rods. If they are not the same, then the adjustment has not been made equally, and problems will be encountered with tyre scrubbing in turns; also, the steering wheel spokes will no longer be horizontal when the wheels are in the straight-ahead position.

12   If the track rod lengths are the same, check that the toe setting has been correctly adjusted by lowering the vehicle to the ground and re-checking the toe setting; re-adjust if necessary. If the setting is correct, tighten the track rod balljoint locknuts to the specified torque setting. Ensure that the rubber gaiters are seated correctly and are not twisted or strained, and secure them in position with the retaining clips.

Notes

Chapter 11 Bodywork and fittings

Contents

Specifications

Torque wrench settings

	Nm	lbf ft
Tailgate lock cylinder/handle nuts	4	3
Front seat bolts	20	15
Rear seat:		
Corsa and Corsavan (split rear seat):		
Seat back-to-bracket bolts	30	22
Seat back-to-hinge bolts	20	15
Combo Van:		
Seat back bolts	20	15
Seat belt anchorage bolts	35	26
Seat belt inertia reel bolt	35	26
Seat belt height adjuster ratchet bolts	20	15
Facia fasteners:		
Facia-to-bulkhead nuts	22	16
Facia end screws	6	4
Support bracket screws	6	4

11

1 General information

1   The bodyshell is made of pressed-steel sections, and is available in three- and five-door Hatchback versions, as well as two different forms of Van. Most components are welded together, but some use is made of structural adhesives; the front wings are bolted on.
2   The bonnet, doors, and some other vulnerable panels, are made of zinc-coated metal, and are further protected by being coated with an anti-chip primer, prior to being sprayed.
3   Extensive use is made of plastic materials, mainly on the interior, but also in exterior components. The front and rear bumpers are injection-moulded from a synthetic material which is very strong and yet light. Plastic components such as wheelarch liners are fitted to the underside of the vehicle, to improve the body's resistance to corrosion.

2 Maintenance - bodywork and underframe

The general condition of a vehicle's bodywork is the one thing that significantly affects its value. Maintenance is easy, but needs to be regular. Neglect, particularly after minor damage, can lead quickly to further deterioration and costly repair bills. It is important also to keep watch on those parts of the vehicle not immediately visible, for instance the underside, inside all the wheel arches, and the lower part of the engine compartment.

The basic maintenance routine for the bodywork is washing - preferably with a lot of water, from a hose. This will remove all the loose solids which may have stuck to the vehicle. It is important to flush these off in such a way as to prevent grit from scratching the finish. The wheel arches and underframe need washing in the same way, to remove any accumulated mud which will retain moisture and tend to encourage rust. Paradoxically enough, the best time to clean the underframe and wheel arches is in wet weather, when the mud is thoroughly wet and soft. In very wet weather, the underframe is usually cleaned of large accumulations automatically, and this is a good time for inspection.

Periodically, except on vehicles with a wax-based underbody protective coating, it is a good idea to have the whole of the underframe of the vehicle steam-cleaned, engine compartment included, so that a thorough inspection can be carried out to see what minor repairs and renovations are necessary. Steam-cleaning is available at many garages, and is necessary for the removal of the accumulation of oily grime, which sometimes is allowed to become thick in certain areas. If steam-cleaning facilities are not available, there are some excellent grease solvents available, such as Holts Engine Degreasant, which can be brush-applied; the dirt can then be simply hosed off. Note that these methods should not be used on vehicles with wax-based underbody protective coating, or the coating will be removed. Such vehicles should be inspected annually, preferably just prior to Winter, when the underbody should be washed down, and any damage to the wax coating repaired using Holts Undershield. Ideally, a completely fresh coat should be applied. It would also be worth considering the use of such wax-based protection for injection into door panels, sills, box sections, etc, as an additional safeguard against rust damage, where such protection is not provided by the vehicle manufacturer.

After washing paintwork, wipe off with a chamois leather to give an unspotted clear finish. A coat of clear protective wax polish like the many excellent Turtle Wax polishes, will give added protection against chemical pollutants in the air. If the paintwork sheen has dulled or oxidised, use a cleaner/polisher combination such as Turtle Wax Hard Shell to restore the brilliance of the shine. This requires a little effort, but such dulling is usually caused because regular washing has been neglected. Care needs to be taken with metallic paintwork, as special non-abrasive cleaner/polisher is required to avoid damage to the finish. Always check that the door and ventilator opening drain holes and pipes are completely clear, so that water can be drained out. Brightwork should be treated in the same way as paintwork. Windscreens and windows can be kept clear of the smeary film which often appears, by the use of proprietary glass cleaner like Holts Mixra. Never use any form of wax or other body or chromium polish on glass.

3 Maintenance - upholstery and carpets

Mats and carpets should be brushed or vacuum-cleaned regularly, to keep them free of grit. If they are badly stained, remove them from the vehicle for scrubbing or sponging, and make quite sure they are dry before refitting. Seats and interior trim panels can be kept clean by wiping with a damp cloth and Turtle Wax Carisma. If they do become stained (which can be more apparent on light-coloured upholstery), use a little liquid detergent and a soft nail brush to scour the grime out of the grain of the material. Do not forget to keep the headlining clean in the same way as the upholstery. When using liquid cleaners inside the vehicle, do not over-wet the surfaces being cleaned. Excessive damp could get into the seams and padded interior, causing stains, offensive odours or even rot. If the inside of the vehicle gets wet accidentally, it is worthwhile taking some trouble to dry it out properly, particularly where carpets are involved. *Do not leave oil or electric heaters inside the vehicle for this purpose.*

4 Minor body damage - repair

The colour bodywork repair photographic sequences between pages 0-32 and 1-1 illustrate the operations detailed in the following sub-sections.

For more detailed information about bodywork repair, Haynes Publishing produce a book by Lindsay Porter called "The Car Bodywork Repair Manual". This incorporates information on such aspects as rust treatment, painting and glass-fibre repairs, as well as details on more ambitious repairs involving welding and panel-beating.

Repairs of minor scratches in bodywork

If the scratch is very superficial, and does not penetrate to the metal of the bodywork, repair is very simple. Lightly rub the area of the scratch with a paintwork renovator like Turtle Wax Color Back, or a very fine cutting paste like Holts Body+Plus Rubbing Compound, to remove loose paint from the scratch, and to clear the surrounding bodywork of wax polish. Rinse the area with clean water.

Apply touch-up paint to the scratch using a fine paint brush; continue to apply fine layers of paint until the surface of the paint in the scratch is level with the surrounding paintwork. Allow the new paint at least two weeks to harden, then blend it into the surrounding paintwork by rubbing the scratch area with a paintwork renovator or a very fine cutting paste, such as Holts Body+Plus Rubbing Compound or Turtle Wax Color Back. Finally, apply wax polish from one of the Turtle Wax range of wax polishes.

Where the scratch has penetrated right through to the metal of the bodywork, causing the metal to rust, a different repair technique is required. Remove any loose rust from the bottom of the scratch with a penknife, then apply rust-inhibiting paint such as Turtle Wax Rust Master, to prevent the formation of rust in the future. Using a rubber or nylon applicator, fill the scratch with bodystopper paste like Holts Body+Plus Knifing Putty. If required, this paste can be mixed with cellulose thinners such as Holts Body+Plus Cellulose Thinners, to provide a very thin paste which is ideal for filling narrow scratches. Before the stopper-paste in the scratch hardens, wrap a piece of smooth cotton rag around the top of a finger. Dip the finger in cellulose thinners, and quickly sweep it across the surface of the stopper-paste in the scratch; this will ensure that the surface of the stopper-paste is slightly hollowed. The scratch can now be painted over as described earlier in this Section.

Repairs of dents in bodywork

When deep denting of the vehicle's bodywork has taken place, the first task is to pull the dent out, until the affected bodywork almost attains its original shape. There is little point in trying to restore the original shape completely, as the metal in the damaged area will have stretched on impact, and cannot be reshaped fully to its original contour. It is better to bring the level of the dent up to a point which is about 3 mm below the level of the surrounding bodywork. In cases where the dent is very shallow anyway, it is not worth trying to pull it out at all. If the underside of the dent is accessible, it can be hammered out gently from behind, using a mallet with a wooden or plastic head. Whilst doing this, hold a suitable block of wood firmly against the outside of the panel, to absorb the impact from the hammer blows and thus prevent a large area of the bodywork from being "belled-out".

Should the dent be in a section of the bodywork which has a double skin, or some other factor making it inaccessible from behind, a different technique is called for. Drill several small holes through the metal inside the area - particularly in the deeper section. Then screw long self-tapping screws into the holes, just sufficiently for them to gain a good purchase in the metal. Now the dent can be pulled out by pulling on the protruding heads of the screws with a pair of pliers.

The next stage of the repair is the removal of the paint from the damaged area, and from an inch or so of the surrounding "sound" bodywork. This is accomplished most easily by using a wire brush or abrasive pad on a power drill, although it can be done just as effectively by hand, using sheets of abrasive paper. To complete the preparation for filling, score the surface of the bare metal with a screwdriver or the tang of a file, or alternatively, drill small holes in the affected area. This will provide a really good "key" for the filler paste.

To complete the repair, see the Section on filling and respraying.

Repairs of rust holes or gashes in bodywork

Remove all paint from the affected area, and from an inch or so of the surrounding "sound" bodywork, using an abrasive pad or a wire brush on a power drill. If these are not available, a few sheets of abrasive paper will do the job most effectively. With the paint removed, you will be able to judge the severity of the corrosion, and therefore decide whether to renew the whole panel (if this is possible) or to repair the affected area. New body panels are not as expensive as most people think, and it is often quicker and more satisfactory to fit a new panel than to attempt to repair large areas of corrosion.

Remove all fittings from the affected area, except those which will act as a guide to the original shape of the damaged bodywork (eg headlight shells etc). Then, using tin snips or a hacksaw blade, remove all loose metal and any other metal badly affected by corrosion. Hammer the edges of the hole inwards, in order to create a slight depression for the filler paste.

Wire-brush the affected area to remove the powdery rust from the surface of the remaining metal. Paint the affected area with rust-inhibiting paint such as Turtle Wax Rust Master; if the back of the rusted area is accessible, treat this also.

Before filling can take place, it will be necessary to block the hole in some way. This can be achieved by the use of aluminium or plastic mesh, or aluminium tape.

Aluminium or plastic mesh, or glass-fibre matting, is probably the best material to use for a large hole. Cut a piece to the approximate size and shape of the hole to be filled, then position it in the hole so that its edges are below the level of the surrounding bodywork. It can be retained in position by several blobs of filler paste around its periphery.

Aluminium tape should be used for small or very narrow holes. Pull a piece off the roll, trim it to the approximate size and shape required, then pull off the backing paper (if used) and stick the tape over the hole; it can be overlapped if the thickness of one piece is insufficient. Burnish down the edges of the tape with the handle of a screwdriver or similar, to ensure that the tape is securely attached to the metal underneath.

Bodywork repairs - filling and respraying

Before using this Section, see the Sections on dent, deep scratch, rust holes and gash repairs.

Many types of bodyfiller are available, but generally speaking, those proprietary kits which contain a tin of filler paste and a tube of resin hardener are best for this type of repair, like Holts Body+Plus or Holts No-Mix, which can be used directly from the tube. A wide, flexible plastic or nylon applicator will be found invaluable for imparting a smooth and well-contoured finish to the surface of the filler.

Mix up a little filler on a clean piece of card or board - measure the hardener carefully (follow the maker's instructions on the pack), otherwise the filler will set too rapidly or too slowly. Alternatively, Holts No-Mix can be used straight from the tube without mixing, but daylight is required to cure it. Using the applicator, apply the filler paste to the prepared area; draw the applicator across the surface of the filler to achieve the correct contour and to level the surface. As soon as a contour that approximates to the correct one is achieved, stop working the paste - if you carry on too long, the paste will become sticky and begin to "pick-up" on the applicator. Continue to add thin layers of filler paste at 20-minute intervals, until the level of the filler is just proud of the surrounding bodywork.

Once the filler has hardened, the excess can be removed using a metal plane or file. From then on, progressively-finer grades of abrasive paper should be used, starting with a 40-grade production paper, and finishing with a 400-grade wet-and-dry paper. Always wrap the abrasive paper around a flat rubber, cork, or wooden block - otherwise the surface of the filler will not be completely flat. During the smoothing of the filler surface, the wet-and-dry paper should be periodically rinsed in water. This will ensure that a very smooth finish is imparted to the filler at the final stage.

At this stage, the "dent" should be surrounded by a ring of bare metal, which in turn should be encircled by the finely "feathered" edge of the good paintwork. Rinse the repair area with clean water, until all of the dust produced by the rubbing-down operation has gone.

Spray the whole area with a light coat of primer, either Holts Body+Plus Grey or Red Oxide Primer - this will show up any imperfections in the surface of the filler. Repair these imperfections with fresh filler paste or bodystopper, and once more smooth the surface with abrasive paper. If bodystopper is used, it can be mixed with cellulose thinners, to form a really thin paste which is ideal for filling small holes. Repeat this spray-and-repair procedure until you are satisfied that the surface of the filler, and the feathered edge of the paintwork, are perfect. Clean the repair area with clean water, and allow to dry fully.

The repair area is now ready for final spraying. Paint spraying must be carried out in a warm, dry, windless and dust-free atmosphere. This condition can be created artificially if you have access to a large indoor working area, but if you are forced to work in the open, you will have to pick your day very carefully. If you are working indoors, dousing the floor in the work area with water will help to settle the dust which would otherwise be in the atmosphere. If the repair area is confined to one body panel, mask off the surrounding panels; this will help to minimise the effects of a slight mis-match in paint colours. Bodywork fittings (eg chrome strips, door handles etc) will also need to be masked off. Use genuine masking tape, and several thicknesses of newspaper, for the masking operations.

Before commencing to spray, agitate the aerosol can thoroughly, then spray a test area (an old tin, or similar) until the technique is mastered. Cover the repair area with a thick coat of primer; the thickness should be built up using several thin layers of paint, rather than one thick one. Using 400-grade wet-and-dry paper, rub down the surface of the primer until it is really smooth. While doing this, the work area should be thoroughly doused with water, and the wet-and-dry paper periodically rinsed in water. Allow to dry before spraying on more paint.

Spray on the top coat using Holts Dupli-Color Autospray, again building up the thickness by using several thin layers of paint. Start spraying in the centre of the repair area, and then, using a circular motion, work outwards until the whole repair area and about 2 inches of the surrounding original paintwork is covered. Remove all masking material 10 to 15 minutes after spraying on the final coat of paint.

Allow the new paint at least two weeks to harden, then, using a paintwork renovator or a very fine cutting paste such as Turtle Wax Color Back or Holts Body+Plus Rubbing Compound, blend the edges of the paint into the existing paintwork. Finally, apply wax polish.

Plastic components

With the use of more and more plastic body components by the vehicle manufacturers (eg bumpers, spoilers, and in some cases major body panels), rectification of more serious damage to such items has become a matter of either entrusting repair work to a specialist in this field, or renewing complete components. Repair of such damage by

11

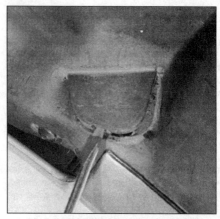

6.2a Unclip the access cover in the wheelarch liner . . .

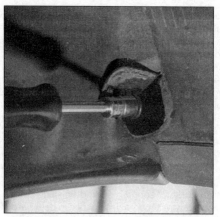

6.2b . . . to gain access to the bumper retaining nut (viewed from underneath the wheelarch liner)

6.3 Slacken and remove the bolts securing the radiator grille section of the bumper to the crossmember

the DIY owner is not really feasible, owing to the cost of the equipment and materials required for effecting such repairs. The basic technique involves making a groove along the line of the crack in the plastic, using a rotary burr in a power drill. The damaged part is then welded back together, using a hot air gun to heat up and fuse a plastic filler rod into the groove. Any excess plastic is then removed, and the area rubbed down to a smooth finish. It is important that a filler rod of the correct plastic is used, as body components can be made of a variety of different types (eg polycarbonate, ABS, polypropylene).

Damage of a less serious nature (abrasions, minor cracks etc) can be repaired by the DIY owner using a two-part epoxy filler repair material, such as Holts Body+Plus or Holts No-Mix, which can be used directly from the tube. Once mixed in equal proportions (or applied directly from the tube in the case of Holts No-Mix), this is used in similar fashion to the bodywork filler used on metal panels. The filler is usually cured in twenty to thirty minutes, ready for sanding and painting.

If the owner is renewing a complete component himself, or if he has repaired it with epoxy filler, he will be left with the problem of finding a suitable paint for finishing which is compatible with the type of plastic used. At one time, the use of a universal paint was not possible, owing to the complex range of plastics encountered in body component applications. Standard paints, generally speaking, will not bond to plastic or rubber satisfactorily, but Holts Professional Spraymatch paints, to match any plastic or rubber finish, can be obtained from dealers. However, it is now possible to obtain a plastic body parts finishing kit which consists of a pre-primer treatment, a primer and coloured top coat. Full instructions are normally supplied with a kit, but basically, the method of use is to first apply the pre-primer to the component concerned, and allow it to dry for up to 30 minutes. Then the primer is applied, and left to dry for about an hour before finally applying the special-coloured top coat. The result is a correctly-coloured component, where the paint will flex with the plastic or rubber, a property that standard paint does not normally possess.

5   Major body damage - repair

Where serious damage has occurred, or large areas need renewal due to neglect, it means that complete new panels will need welding-in, and this is best left to professionals. If the damage is due to impact, it will also be necessary to check completely the alignment of the bodyshell, and this can only be carried out accurately by a Vauxhall/Opel dealer, using special jigs. If the body is left misaligned, it is primarily dangerous as the car will not handle properly, and secondly, uneven stresses will be imposed on the steering, suspension and possibly transmission, causing abnormal wear, or complete failure, particularly to such items as the tyres.

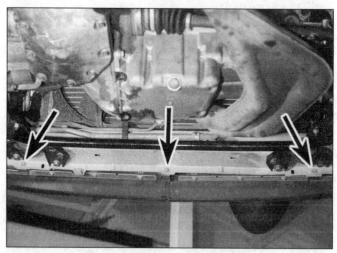

6.4 Front bumper-to-body bolts (arrowed)

6   Front bumper - removal and refitting

Removal

1   Chock the rear wheels, apply the handbrake, then jack up the front of the vehicle and support it on axle stands.

2   Unclip the access covers, situated at the top of each wheelarch liner, and unscrew the two plastic nuts (one on each side) securing either end of the bumper to the vehicle (see illustrations). Note that the plastic retaining nuts should be discarded, and new ones used on refitting.

3   Open the bonnet, and undo the two bolts securing the radiator grille section of the bumper to the body crossmember (see illustration).

4   Slacken and remove the three bolts securing the bottom of the bumper to the vehicle body (see illustration).

5   On models with front foglights, disconnect the wiring connector from each light unit.

6   Undo the four screws (two on either side) securing the ends of the bumper to the wheelarch liner (see illustration).

7   With the aid of an assistant, release the bumper ends from the wheelarch outer trim covers, and remove the bumper from the front of the vehicle (see illustration). On models with headlight washers, note that it will be necessary to disconnect the supply hose from the T-piece as it becomes accessible.

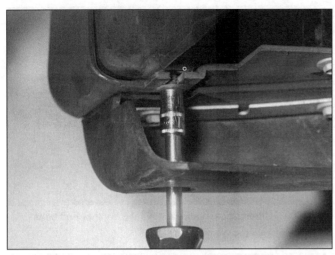

6.6 Unscrewing a bumper-to-wheelarch liner lower screw

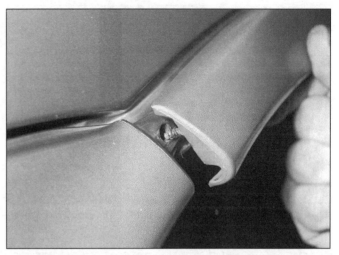

6.7 Carefully ease the wheelarch outer trim covers away from the vehicle, then release the bumper ends and remove the bumper from the vehicle

Refitting

8   Refitting is a reversal of the removal procedure, using new plastic nuts, and ensuring that all bumper fasteners are securely tightened.

7   Rear bumper - removal and refitting

Removal

Corsa and Corsavan

1   Remove the number plate light unit as described in Chapter 12.

2   Open the tailgate, and undo the three screws securing the top of the bumper to the vehicle **(see illustration)**.

3   Slacken and remove the four screws securing the bottom of the bumper to the vehicle body **(see illustration)**.

4   Unscrew the two plastic nuts (one on either side) securing the ends of the bumper to the inside of the wheelarch **(see illustration)**. Note that the plastic nuts should be discarded, and new ones used on refitting.

5   With the aid of an assistant, unclip the bumper ends from the wheelarch outer trim covers, and remove the bumper from the rear of the vehicle **(see illustration)**.

Combo Van

6   Remove both rear number plate light units as described in

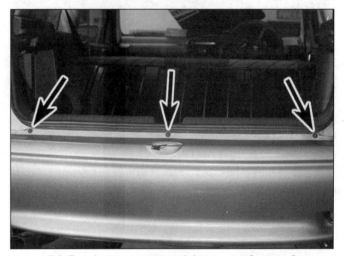

7.2 Rear bumper upper retaining screws (arrowed)

Chapter 12.

7   Prise out the trim plug from either end of the bumper to gain access to the bumper retaining bolts, then slacken and remove the two

7.3 Unscrew the four screws securing the bottom of the bumper to the vehicle . . .

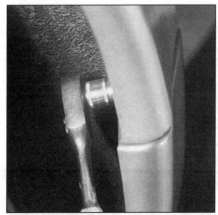

7.4 . . . and the plastic nut securing each end of the bumper to the wheelarch

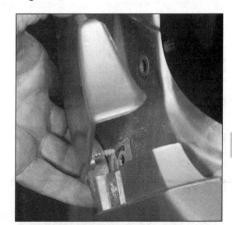

7.5 Release the bumper ends from the wheelarch outer trim covers, and remove the rear bumper

11

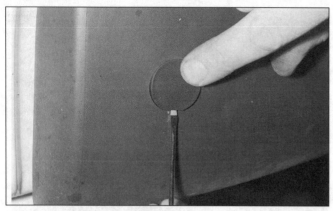

7.7a On Combo Van models, prise out the trim plug from either end of the bumper . . .

7.7b . . . then slacken and remove the bumper end bolts

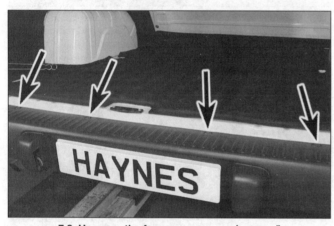

7.8 Unscrew the four upper screws (arrowed) and the lower screws . . .

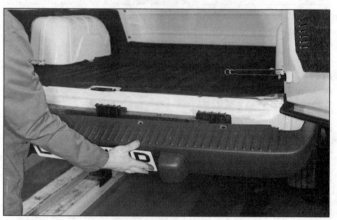

7.9 . . . and remove the bumper

mounting bolts (one on either end) **(see illustrations)**.
8   Undo the three screws securing the bottom of the bumper to the vehicle, and the four screws securing the top of the bumper to the vehicle **(see illustration)**.
9   Lift the bumper away from the rear of the vehicle **(see illustration)**.
10   If necessary, slide the foam wedges out from between the bumper mountings, and unbolt the mountings from the vehicle body. Each mounting is retained by two bolts **(see illustrations)**.

Refitting

11   Refitting is a reverse of the relevant removal procedure, ensuring

that all disturbed fasteners are securely tightened. Before bolting the bumper in position, ensure that the number plate light wiring is fed through the bumper aperture(s).

---

8   Bonnet - removal, refitting and adjustment

Removal

1   Open the bonnet, and get an assistant to support it. Using a pencil or felt-tip pen, mark the outline position of each bonnet hinge rela-

7.10a Remove the foam wedges . . .

7.10b . . . then undo the two retaining bolts (arrowed) . . .

7.10c . . . and unhook the bumper mounting from the vehicle

8.2 Disconnect the washer hose from the reservoir pump . . .

8.3a . . . then undo the bonnet retaining bolts . . .

8.3b . . . and lift the bonnet away from the vehicle with the aid of an assistant

9.1 Slackening the bonnet release cable clamp screw

10.1 Bonnet lock hook is removed by drilling out its pivot pin (arrowed)

tive to the bonnet, to use as a guide on refitting.
2   Undo the retaining screws, and lift the left-hand windscreen cowl panel to improve access to the washer reservoir. Undo the reservoir retaining nut, then disconnect the windscreen washer supply pipe from the reservoir pump, and release it from the bonnet hinge **(see illustration)**.
3   Undo the bonnet retaining bolts and, with the help of an assistant, carefully lift the bonnet clear **(see illustrations)**. Store the bonnet out of the way, in a safe place. Inspect the hinge for signs of wear or damage. If hinge renewal is necessary, the vehicle must be taken to a Vauxhall/Opel dealer, as renewal requires the windscreen to be removed (see Section 20).

Refitting and adjustment

4   With the aid of an assistant, offer up the bonnet, and loosely fit the retaining bolts. Align the hinges with the marks made on removal, then tighten the retaining bolts securely. Reconnect the windscreen washer supply pipe.
5   Close the bonnet, and check for alignment with the adjacent panels. If necessary, slacken the bonnet support bolts, and realign the bonnet to suit. Once the bonnet is correctly aligned, securely tighten the bolts.
6   Once the bonnet is correctly aligned, check that the bonnet fastens and releases in a satisfactory manner, and if necessary adjust the lock striker as described in Section 10.

9   Bonnet release cable - removal and refitting

Removal

1   Open the bonnet, and unscrew the release cable retaining clamp screw from the body crossmember **(see illustration)**.
2   Release the outer cable from the clamp, then detach the inner

cable from the lock spring.
3   Work back along the cable, releasing it from all the relevant retaining clips and ties, whilst noting its correct routing. Release the rubber sealing grommet from the engine compartment bulkhead, and tie a piece of string to the cable end, this can then be used to draw the cable back into position.
4   From inside the vehicle, unclip the bonnet release lever from the side of the driver's footwell.
5   Withdraw the lever and cable assembly from inside the vehicle. Once the cable end appears, untie the string and leave it in position in the vehicle; the string can then be used to draw the new cable back into position.

Refitting

6   Tie the string to the end of the cable, and use the string to draw the bonnet release cable through from inside the vehicle into the engine compartment. Once the cable is through, untie the string.
7   Ensure that the cable is correctly routed and retained by all the relevant clips and ties, then seat the outer cable grommet in the engine compartment bulkhead.
8   Connect the inner cable to the lock spring, and seat the outer cable in its retaining clamp. Position the outer cable so that all free play is removed from the inner cable, then securely tighten its clamp screw.
9   Check the operation of the bonnet release lever before shutting the bonnet.

10   Bonnet lock components - removal and refitting

Bonnet lock hook

1   Drill out the pivot pin, and remove the lock hook and return spring from the bonnet **(see illustration)**.

11

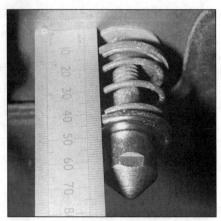

10.5 When refitting, adjust the position of the bonnet lock striker as described in text

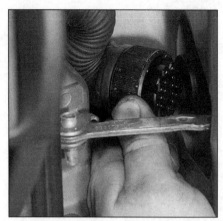

11.2 Release the locking ring, and disconnect the wiring connector from the door

11.3 Tap out the check link roll pin using a suitable hammer and punch

11.4a Remove the upper plastic cover . . .

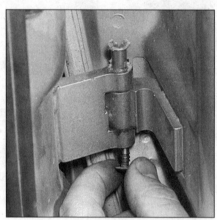

11.4b . . . and lower plastic cover . . .

11.4c . . . then tap out the hinge pins whilst an assistant supports the weight of the door

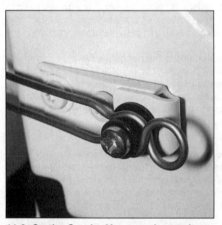

11.6 On the Combo Van rear door, release the check link spring from the door pin

11.7a Unclip the wiring from the vehicle body . . .

11.7b . . . then release the grommet . . .

2   On refitting, locate the hook and spring in the bonnet bracket, and insert a new pivot pin. Secure the pin in position by flattening its end with a suitable pair of pliers.

Lock striker

3   Slacken the striker locknut, then unscrew the striker from the bonnet and recover the washer. If necessary, unscrew the locknut from the end of the striker, and remove the spring and spring seats.

4   Where necessary, fit the spring and spring seats to the striker, and screw on the locknut. Fit the washer to the striker, and screw the striker into position in the bonnet, tightening it only lightly at this stage.

5   Hold the locknut, and adjust the position of the striker so that the distance from the lower spring seat to the inside of the bonnet is 40 to 45 mm **(see illustration)**.

6   When the striker is correctly positioned, securely tighten the locknut.

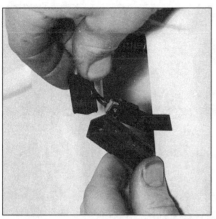

11.7c ... and disconnect the relevant rear door wiring

11.8 Unscrew the hinge retaining bolts and remove the door

11.15a Rear door lock striker - Combo Van

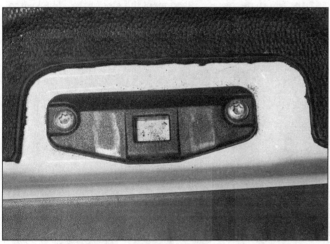

11.15b Rear door latch striker - Combo Van

Lock spring

7   Unhook the spring from the body crossmember, then free it from the release cable and remove it from the vehicle.
8   On refitting, ensure that the spring is correctly engaged with the cable and crossmember. Check the operation of the bonnet release lever before shutting the bonnet.

11   Door - removal, refitting and adjustment

Removal

Front door (all models) and rear door (five-door models)

1   Open the door to gain access to the wiring connector which is fitted to the front edge of the door.
2   Disconnect the wiring connector from the front edge of the door. To do this, unscrew the connector locking ring, then pull the connector away from the door **(see illustration)**.
3   Using a suitable hammer and punch, tap out the roll pin securing the door check link to the vehicle body **(see illustration)**.
4   Remove the plastic covers (where fitted) from the door hinge pins. Have an assistant support the door, then drive both hinge pins out of position using a hammer and suitable punch **(see illustrations)**. Remove the door from the vehicle.
5   Inspect the hinge pins for signs of wear or damage, and renew if necessary. The check link roll pin should be renewed as a matter of course.

Rear door - Combo Van

6   Open the rear door, and release the check link spring from the door pin **(see illustration)**.
7   Where necessary, trace the wiring back from the door to its wiring connectors in the main vehicle body. Disconnect the wiring connectors, then free the grommet from the vehicle body, and withdraw the wiring loom so that it is free to be removed with the door **(see illustrations)**.
8   Have an assistant support the door, then slacken and remove the four hinge retaining bolts and remove the door from the vehicle **(see illustration)**.
9   If necessary, the hinge(s) can then be unbolted and removed.

Refitting

Front door (all models) and rear door (five-door models)

10   Refitting is the reversal of removal, using a new check link roll pin.

Rear door - Combo Van

11   Refitting is a reversal of the removal procedure, tightening the hinge bolts securely, and ensuring that the wiring is securely reconnected.

Adjustment

Front door (all models) and rear door (five-door models)

12   Adjustment of the door position is not possible; the hinges are welded to the vehicle body and door, and cannot be repositioned. Misalignment of the door can only be caused by accident damage or wear of the hinge pins.
13   Door closure may be adjusted by altering the position of the door lock striker on the body. Slacken the striker retaining bolts, reposition the striker as required, then securely retighten the bolts.

Rear door - Combo Van

14   Slight adjustment of the doors can be achieved by slackening the hinge retaining bolts and repositioning the hinge/door.
15   Door closure may be adjusted by altering the position of the door lock striker on the door/body (as applicable). Slacken the striker retaining bolts, reposition the striker as required, then securely retighten the bolts **(see illustrations)**.

12   Door inner trim panel - removal and refitting

Removal

Front door

1   Unscrew the door pocket retaining screws, and pull the pocket downwards and away from the door to release its retaining clips. On

11

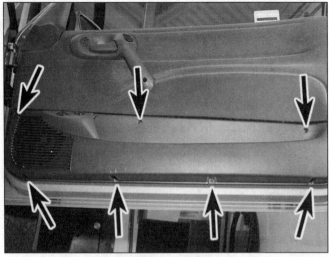

12.1a   Undo the retaining screws (arrowed) and remove the door pocket

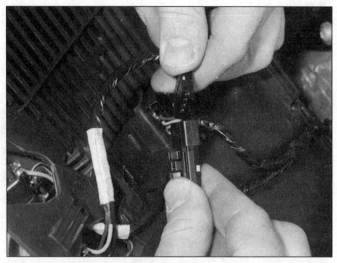

12.1b   Where necessary, disconnect the electric window switch wiring connectors as the pocket is removed

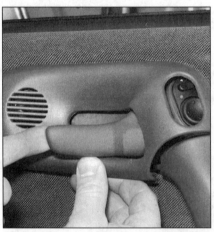

12.2   Lift the handle, and unclip the handle trim cover from the door panel

12.3   Where necessary, carefully prise the exterior mirror switch out of the armrest

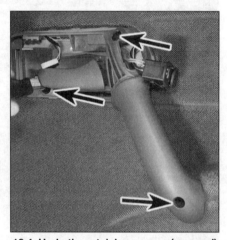

12.4   Undo the retaining screws (arrowed) and remove the armrest - three-door model shown

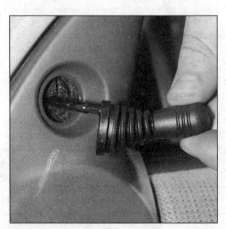

12.5a   On models with manually-operated exterior mirrors, it will be necessary to remove the knob from the adjusting lever . . .

12.5b   . . . in order to remove the inner trim panel

12.6   On models with manual windows, unhook the regulator handle retaining clip using a piece of welding rod

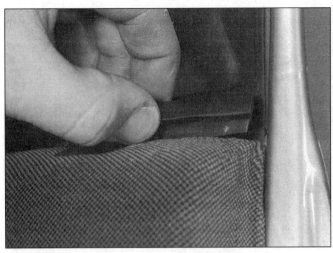

12.7 Carefully prise out the window sealing strip from the top of the inner trim panel

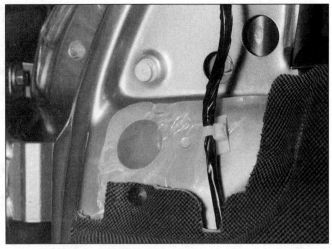

12.8a Undo the front . . .

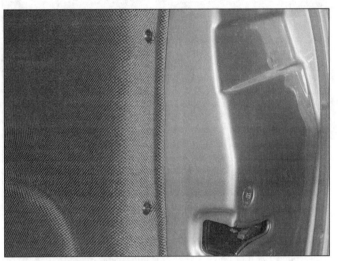

12.8b . . . and rear retaining screws from the trim panel . . .

models with electric windows, disconnect the window switch wiring connectors as the pocket is removed **(see illustrations)**.

2 Lift the inner door lock handle, and carefully prise the handle trim cover out from the door trim panel **(see illustration)**.

3 Where necessary, remove the loudspeaker from the armrest handle as described in Chapter 12, and free the electric exterior mirror or passenger side window switch (as applicable) from the armrest **(see illustration)**.

4 Undo the three retaining screws, and remove the armrest handle from the door **(see illustration)**.

5 Undo the retaining screw (where fitted) and unclip the exterior mirror inner trim panel from the door. On models with manually-operated mirrors, it will be necessary to pull the knob off the adjusting lever in order to remove the panel **(see illustrations)**.

6 On models with manual windows, release the retaining clip and remove the window regulator handle. To release the clip, fabricate a hook from a piece of welding rod, and use the rod to hook the clip out from between the handle and bezel **(see illustration)**. Slide the handle off the regulator, and remove the handle bezel.

7 Carefully prise the window inner sealing strip from the top edge of the door trim panel **(see illustration)**.

8 Slacken and remove the retaining screws on the rear edge of the panel, and at the front of the panel, directly below the exterior mirror, and remove the trim panel from the door **(see illustrations)**.

Rear door

9 Undo the retaining screws, and remove the handle from the rear door **(see illustration)**.

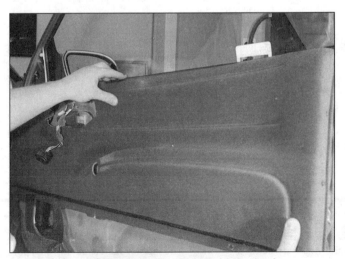

12.8c . . . and remove the trim panel from the door - three-door model shown

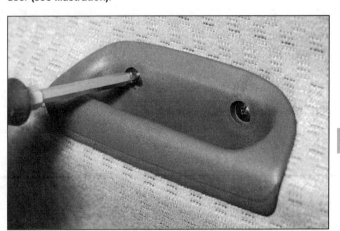

12.9 Undo the two screws, and remove the handle from the rear door

11

12.10 Unclip the trim cover from the door inner handle

12.12 Unclip the inner trim panel from the rear door . . .

12.13 . . . then prise out the window sealing strip from the top of the door

10   Lift the inner door lock handle, and carefully prise the handle trim cover out from the door trim panel **(see illustration)**.
11   Remove the window regulator handle as described in paragraph 6.
12   Carefully prise the inner trim panel away from the rear of the door **(see illustration)**.
13   Carefully prise the window inner sealing strip from the top edge of the door trim panel **(see illustration)**. The strip retaining clips should stay in position on the door; if they are loose, remove then and store with the sealing strip.
14   Unscrew the retaining screws from the edge of the door trim panel, and remove the panel from the door **(see illustration)**.

Refitting

15   Refitting is the reverse of the relevant removal procedure. On models with manual windows, fit the retaining clip to the regulator handle before fitting the handle onto the regulator **(see illustration)**.

---

13   Door handle and lock components - removal and refitting

Removal

Interior door handle

1   Remove the door inner trim panel as described in Section 12.
2   Peel the polythene weathershield away from the door to gain access to the door lock components **(see illustration)**. Where necessary,

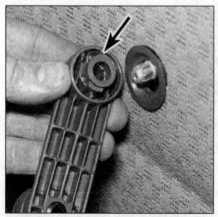

12.15 When refitting, fit the clip (arrowed) to the regulator handle before fitting the handle to the door

12.14 Undo the retaining screws (arrowed) and remove the inner trim panel from the rear door

cut around the trim panel screw brackets, using a sharp knife, to release the weathershield.
3   Release the retaining clip by pivoting it away from the link rod, and detach the rod from the lock assembly.
4   Unclip the interior handle from the door, and remove it complete with the rod **(see illustration)**.

13.2 Carefully peel the weathershield away from the door to gain access to the lock components

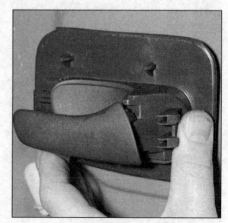

13.4 The interior handle simply unclips from the door

13.8a Undo the two nuts . . .

13.8b . . . then free the lock cylinder mounting plate from the rear of the exterior door handle

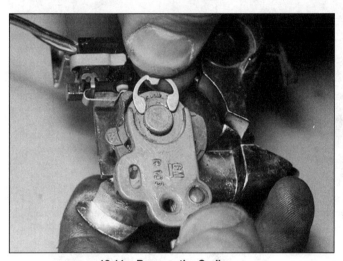

13.11a Remove the C-clip . . .

base of the window guide, and manoeuvre the guide out from the door.

7   Release the retaining clips by pivoting them away from the link rods, and free the link rods from the lock assembly.

8   Unscrew the two handle retaining nuts, and detach the lock cylinder mounting plate from the rear of the handle (see illustrations).

9   Lift the retaining clips on the base of the handle, and remove the handle from the outside of the door.

Front lock cylinder

10   Remove the exterior door handle as described above, then manoeuvre the lock cylinder mounting plate out of the door. Where necessary, trace the wiring back from the central locking/alarm microswitch, and disconnect it at the wiring connector to enable the plate to be removed.

11   With the mounting plate removed, insert the key into the lock cylinder, then prise off the C-clip from rear of the mounting plate. Lift off the link rod bracket and spring, noting their correct fitted locations, and withdraw the lock cylinder (see illustrations).

Front door lock

12   Remove the door inner trim panel as described in Section 12, and peel back the weathershield (see paragraph 2).

13   Remove the window guide as described in paragraph 6.

14   Undo the three retaining screws, and manoeuvre the lock assembly out of the door. On models with central locking, disconnect the wiring connector from the servo unit as it becomes accessible (see illustrations).

Front exterior door handle

5   Remove the door inner trim panel as described in Section 12, and peel back the weathershield (see paragraph 2).

6   With the window fully raised, undo the retaining bolt(s) from the

13.11b . . . then lift off the link rod bracket and spring, noting its correct fitted position . . .

13.11c . . . and withdraw the lock cylinder

13.14a Undo the three retaining screws . . .

11

13.14b ... then remove the lock assembly from the door

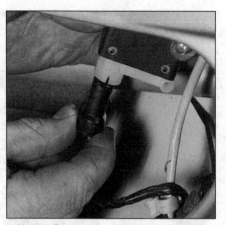

13.14c On models with central locking, disconnect the wiring connector from the servo unit before removing the lock

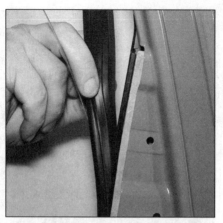

13.16 Free the sealing strip from the rear of the door to gain access to the guide upper retaining bolt

13.17a Slacken and remove the upper window guide retaining bolt ...

13.17b ... and lower retaining bolt ...

13.17c ... and manoeuvre the guide upwards and out of the rear door

13.18 Pivot the retaining clip (arrowed) away from each link rod, and disconnect the rods from the lock

13.19 Undo the two nuts, and free the mounting plate from the rear of the exterior handle

Rear exterior door handle - five-door models

15   Remove the door inner trim panel as described in Section 12, and peel back the weathershield (see paragraph 2). Carefully prise the outer trim panel away from the door.

16   Wind the window fully down, and release the window sealing strip from the rear of the door and guide, to gain access to the retaining bolt **(see illustration)**.

17   Undo the two guide retaining bolts, and manoeuvre the guide

upwards and out from the door **(see illustrations)**.

18   Release the retaining clips by pivoting them away from the link rods, and free the link rods from the lock assembly **(see illustration)**.

19   Undo the two nuts, and free the mounting plate assembly from the rear of the handle **(see illustration)**.

20   Lift the retaining clips on the base of the handle, then remove the handle from the outside of the door, freeing its link rod from the lock **(see illustration)**.

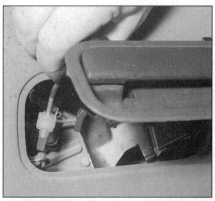

13.20 Remove the exterior handle from the door, freeing its link rod from the lock

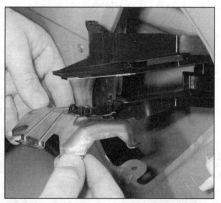

13.21 Remove the lock cylinder mounting plate from the door to improve access to the rear door lock

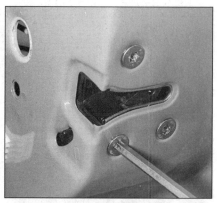

13.22a Undo the three retaining screws . . .

13.22b . . . and remove the lock assembly from the rear door

13.23a On Combo Van models, prise out the access cover . . .

13.23b . . . and remove the trim panel to gain access to the lock

13.24 Link rod pivot clips (arrowed) are released by pivoting them away from the rod

13.25a Free the lock cylinder mounting plate from the handle . . .

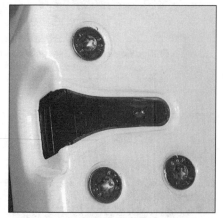

13.25b . . . then undo the three lock retaining screws . . .

11

Rear door lock - five-door models

21   Remove the exterior handle as described above, and manoeuvre out the mounting plate assembly **(see illustration)**.

22   Undo the three retaining screws, and remove the lock assembly **(see illustrations)**. On models with central locking, disconnect the wiring connector from the servo unit as it becomes accessible.

Rear door lock and lock cylinder - Combo Van models

23   Carefully prise the access cover out from the rear door. To further improve access, prise out the retaining clips and remove the trim panel from the centre of the door **(see illustrations)**.

24   Release the retaining clips by pivoting them away from the link rods, and free the link rods from the lock assembly **(see illustration)**.

25   Undo the two retaining nuts, then free the lock cylinder mounting plate from the rear of the handle. Undo the three lock assembly retaining screws, and manoeuvre the lock and cylinder mounting plate assembly out of the door **(see illustrations)**.

26   Release the retaining clip, and separate the lock and mounting

13.25c . . . and manoeuvre the lock and cylinder mounting plate assembly out of the door

13.26 Release the retaining clip (arrowed), and separate the lock from the lock cylinder mounting plate

13.27 Lock cylinder and associated components are retained by a C-clip

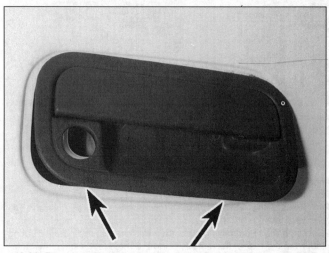

13.29 Door handle is retained by two clips (locations arrowed)

plate **(see illustration)**.

27   If necessary, to remove the lock cylinder, insert the key into the lock cylinder, then prise off the C-clip from rear of the mounting plate. Lift off the link rod bracket and spring, noting their correct fitted locations, and withdraw the lock cylinder **(see illustration)**.

Rear door handle - Combo Van models

28   Remove the lock and lock cylinder mounting plate as described above.

29   Lift the retaining clips on the base of the handle, and remove the handle from the outside of the door **(see illustration)**.

Rear door latch lock - Combo Van models

30   Carefully prise the access cover from the rear door **(see illustration)**. To further improve access, prise out the retaining clips and remove the trim panel from the centre of the door.

31   Release the retaining clip, and pull the knob off the latch handle **(see illustration)**.

32   Release the retaining clips by pivoting them away from the link rods, and free both link rods from the lock **(see illustration)**.

33   Undo the three retaining screws, and manoeuvre the latch lock out from the door **(see illustration)**.

Rear door latches - Combo Van

34   Remove the access cover and trim panel as described in paragraph 30.

35   Release the relevant retaining clip by pivoting it away from the link rod, and free the link rod from the lock.

36   Undo the screws securing the latch to the door, and guide the latch and link rod out of position **(see illustrations)**.

37   If necessary, remove the second latch in the same way.

Refitting

38   Refitting is the reverse of the removal sequence, noting the following points:

(a)   If a lock cylinder has been removed, on refitting ensure that the spring and link rod bracket are correctly positioned and are securely held by the C-clip. Check the operation of the lock cylinder, making sure that the spring returns the cylinder to its central position, before refitting the plate to the door.

(b)   Ensure that all link rods are securely held in position by their retaining clips.

(c)   Apply grease to all lock and link rod pivot points.

(d)   Before installing the relevant trim panel, thoroughly check the operation of all the door lock handles and, where necessary, the central locking system, and ensure that the weathershield is correctly positioned.

13.30 Remove the access cover to reveal the latch lock

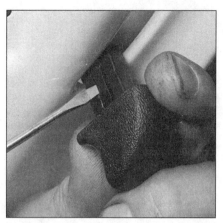

13.31 Release the retaining clip, and slide the knob off the latch lock handle

13.32 Detach both link rods (arrowed) from the lock . . .

13.33 . . . and manoeuvre the lock out from the door

13.36a Undo the two bolts . . .

13.36b . . . and slide the latch and link rod out from the door

14 Door window glass and regulator - removal and refitting

Removal

1 Remove the door inner trim panel as described in Section 12.
2 Peel the polythene weathershield away from the door to gain access to the door lock components. Where necessary, cut around the trim panel screw brackets, using a sharp knife, to release the weathershield. Proceed as described under the relevant sub-heading.

Front door window glass - manual window
3 With the window fully raised, undo the retaining bolt(s) from the base of the window rear guide, and manoeuvre the guide out from the door.
4 Wind the window down, and position it so its guide is in the centre of the door aperture.
5 Mark the position of the regulator guide retaining bolts on the door, then undo the two bolts and release the regulator bracket from the door. The marks can then be used on refitting to make sure the bracket is correctly positioned.
6 Release the regulator rollers from the ends of the window glass guide rail, then lift the glass and manoeuvre it out from the door.

Front door window glass - electric window
7 Remove the regulator assembly as described below. The glass can then be lifted out from the door **(see illustration)**.

Rear door window glass - five-door models
8 Carefully prise the outer trim panel away from the door.

14.7 Removing the front door window glass

9 Wind the window fully down, then release the window sealing strip from the rear of the door and guide, to gain access to the guide retaining bolt.
10 Undo the two bolts, and remove the window guide from the door (see illustrations 13.17a, 13.17b and 13.17c).
11 Tilt the window glass forwards, and free the window guide from the regulator mechanism. The glass can then be manoeuvred out from the door.

11

14.12a Undo the two retaining bolts (arrowed) . . .

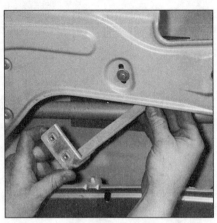

14.12b . . . then manoeuvre the window guide out from the door

14.14a Mark the position of the regulator guide bolts on the door, then undo the bolts . . .

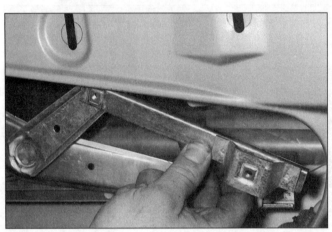

14.14b . . . and remove the guide

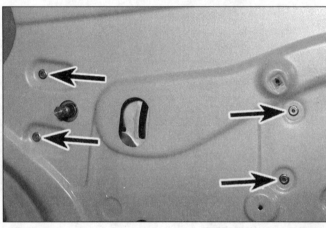

14.15a Front door window regulator retaining rivets (arrowed) - manual window

Front door window regulator

Note: *A pop-rivet gun and suitable rivets will be required when refitting. The rivet heads should be approximately 4.8 mm in diameter and 11 mm in length.*

12 With the window fully raised, undo the retaining bolt(s) from the base of the window guide, and manoeuvre the guide out from the door **(see illustrations)**.

13 Position the window so that its guide rail is in the centre of the door aperture, and wedge it in position with a suitable wooden or rubber wedge.

14 Mark the position of the regulator guide retaining bolts on the door, then undo the two bolts and remove the guide **(see illustrations)**.

15 Using an 8.5 mm drill bit, drill out the rivets securing the regulator assembly to the door, taking great care not to damage the door panel. With all the rivets removed, free the regulator rollers from the ends of the window glass guide rail, and manoeuvre the regulator assembly out through the door aperture. On models with electric windows,

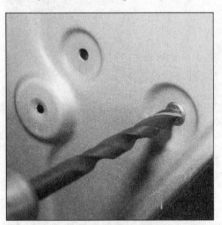

14.15b Carefully drill out the rivets with a suitable drill . . .

14.15c . . . then free the regulator rollers from the window glass . . .

14.15d . . . and remove the regulator assembly from the door

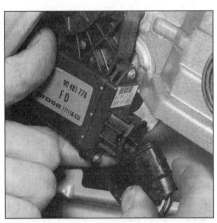

14.15e On models with electric windows, disconnect the wiring connector from the regulator as it is removed

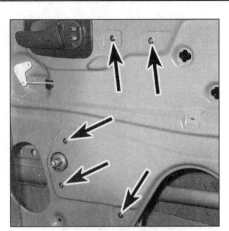

14.17 Rear door window regulator retaining rivets (arrowed) - five-door models

15.2 Undo the retaining screws, and remove the parcel shelf lifter hooks from the tailgate . . .

disconnect the wiring connector from the regulator as it becomes accessible **(see illustrations)**.

Rear door window regulator - five-door models
Note: *A pop-rivet gun and suitable rivets will be required when refitting. The rivet heads should be approximately 4.8 mm in diameter and 11 mm in length.*
16   Position the window so that its guide rail is in the centre of the lower door aperture, and wedge it in position with a suitable wooden or rubber wedge.
17   Using an 8.5 mm drill bit, drill out the rivets securing the regulator assembly to the door, taking great care not to damage the door panel **(see illustration)**.
18   With all the rivets removed, free the regulator from the glass guide rail, and manoeuvre it out through the door aperture.

Refitting

19   Refitting is the reverse of the removal procedure, noting the following points:
   (a)   *Where the regulator has been removed, remove the remains of the old rivets before fitting the regulator to the door. Engage the regulator with the window glass, and secure it in position with new pop-rivets.*
   (b)   *On the front window, align the regulator guide bolts with the marks made on removal, then tighten them securely.*
   (c)   *Check the window moves smoothly and easily up and down, without any sign of tight spots. If the window movement is stiff, trace and rectify the cause. On the front window, movement is*

adjustable by slackening the regulator guide bolts and moving the bolts up and down the slotted holes. Find the position where the window movement is the easiest, then securely tighten the bolts.
   (d)   *Refit the weathershield, making sure it is securely stuck to the door, then install the trim panel as described in Section 12.*

15   Tailgate and support struts - removal and refitting

Removal

Tailgate
1   Disconnect the battery negative terminal.
2   Open the tailgate, and detach the parcel shelf cords. Undo the retaining screws, and remove the lifter hooks from the tailgate **(see illustration)**.
3   Carefully prise out the retaining clips, and remove the inner trim panel from the tailgate **(see illustration)**.
4   Disconnect the wiring connectors from the tailgate wiper motor, central locking components and/or courtesy light switch (as applicable). Undo the relevant tailgate wiper motor bolt, and free the earth lead. Also disconnect the wiring connector from the heated rear window element. Tie a suitable length of string to the end of the wiring loom, then free the grommet from the top of the tailgate and withdraw the wiring loom **(see illustrations)**. When the end of the loom appears, untie the string and leave it in position in the tailgate; it can then be used to draw the wiring back into position when refitting.

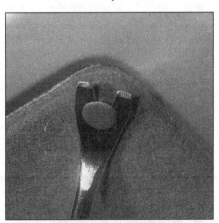

15.3 . . . then prise out the retaining clips and remove the inner trim panel

15.4a Disconnect the various wiring connectors situated behind the trim panel . . .

15.4b . . . and the heated rear window wiring connector . . .

11

15.4c . . . then remove the grommet and withdraw the wiring from the tailgate

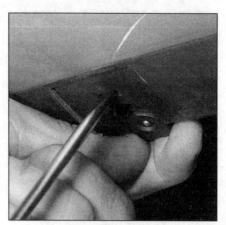

15.5a Prise the washer jet out from the tailgate . . .

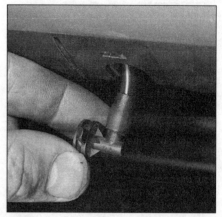

15.5b . . . and disconnect it from the hose (1.6 litre DOHC model shown - jet mounted in spoiler)

5   Where necessary, prise out the washer jet from the tailgate/spoiler (as applicable), and disconnect it from the washer hose **(see illustrations)**. Tie a suitable length of string to the hose end, then withdraw the hose, leaving the string in position in the same way as for the wiring.

6   Have an assistant support the tailgate, then raise the spring clips and pull the support struts off their balljoint mountings on the tailgate. Prise out the hinge pin retaining clips, then tap both hinge pins out of position and remove the tailgate from the vehicle **(see illustrations)**.

7   Examine the hinge pins for signs of wear or damage, and renew if necessary.

Support struts

8   Support the tailgate in the open position using a stout piece of wood, or with the help of an assistant.

9   Raise the spring clips, and pull the support strut off its balljoint mountings on the tailgate and vehicle body **(see illustration)**.

Refitting

Tailgate

10   Refitting is a reversal of the removal procedure, noting the following points:

  (a) *Prior to refitting, apply a smear of multi-purpose grease to the hinge pins.*

  (b) *Ensure that the hinge pins are securely retained by their clips, and that the support struts are securely held in position by their spring clips.*

  (c) *Use the string to draw the wiring loom and washer hose through into position, and ensure that all wiring connectors are correctly reconnected.*

Support struts

11   Refitting is a reverse of the removal procedure, ensuring that the strut is securely retained by its spring clips.

---

16   Tailgate lock components - removal and refitting

Removal

1   Release the rear parcel shelf lifting cords from the tailgate, then unclip the shelf and remove it from the vehicle.

2   Undo the retaining screws, and remove the parcel shelf lifting cord hooks from the tailgate trim panel.

3   Carefully prise out the retaining clips, and remove the trim panel from the tailgate. Proceed as described under the relevant sub-heading.

Tailgate lock

4   From inside the tailgate, release the retaining clip by pivoting it away from the link rod, and detach the rod from the lock assembly.

5   Slacken and remove the three screws, and remove the lock from the tailgate **(see illustration)**.

Tailgate lock cylinder

6   From inside the tailgate, release the retaining clip by pivoting it away from the link rod, and detach the rod from the lock cylinder **(see illustration)**.

7   Where necessary, release the retaining clip and detach the central locking/alarm microswitch from the top of the lock cylinder **(see illustration)**.

8   Undo the three nuts and remove the exterior handle; the lock

15.6a Remove the retaining clips . . .

15.6b . . . then withdraw the hinge pin and lift off the tailgate

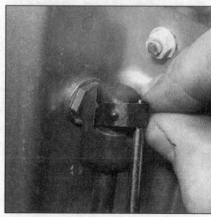

15.9 Lift the retaining clip, and free the support strut from its balljoints

16.5 Tailgate lock is retained by three screws (arrowed)

16.6 Release the retaining clip (arrowed) and detach the link rod from the tailgate lock cylinder casting

cylinder casting can then be manoeuvred out of the tailgate **(see illustrations)**.

9   To dismantle the assembly, insert the key into the lock cylinder, then tap out the roll pin from the rear of the cylinder housing using a suitable pin punch, and remove the link rod bracket from the rear of the cylinder **(see illustration)**. Note which way around the bracket is fitted. Discard the roll pin; a new one should be used on refitting.

10   Release the retaining catches, remove the trim cover, and free the lock cylinder housing from the casting. The lock cylinder can then be withdrawn from its housing.

Refitting

Tailgate lock

11   Refitting is a reverse of the removal procedure.

Tailgate lock cylinder

12   Insert the lock cylinder into its housing, and insert the housing and spring into the main casting. Refit the link rod bracket, making sure it is fitted the correct way around, and secure it in position with a new roll pin. Check the operation of the lock, then refit the trim cover.

13   Refit the lock cylinder casting and exterior handle to the tailgate, then fit the retaining nuts and tighten them to the specified torque. On models with central locking, make sure that the casting is correctly engaged with the servo unit rod before tightening the retaining nuts.

14   Connect the link rod, and secure it in position with the clip.

16.7 Where necessary, release the microswitch from the top of the casting

15   Where necessary, clip the alarm/central locking switch back onto the lock assembly.

16   Refit the trim panel and parcel shelf.

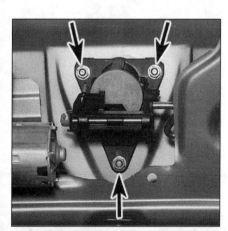

16.8a Undo the three nuts (arrowed), then remove the lock cylinder casting from inside the tailgate . . .

16.8b . . . and the exterior handle from the outside

16.9 Lock cylinder roll pin can be tapped out with a suitable punch

11

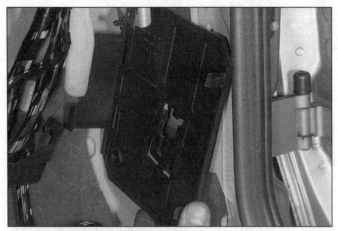

17.2a Unclip the ECU mounting bracket . . .

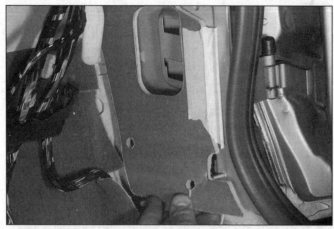

17.2b . . . and remove the insulation panel . . .

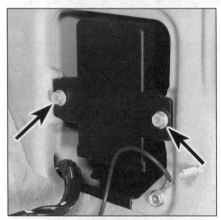

17.3 . . . to gain access to the central
locking control unit (retaining bolts
arrowed)

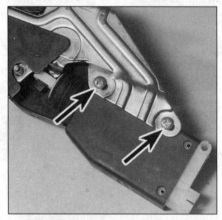

17.6 Front door lock servo unit is retained
by two screws (arrowed)

17.11a On Combo Van rear door, unclip
the access cover . . .

17.11b . . . and remove the trim panel to
improve access to the servo unit

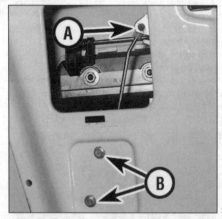

17.13a Detach the link rod (A) and undo
the retaining screws (B) . . .

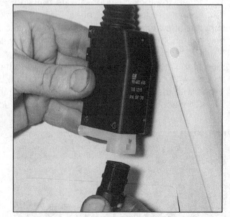

17.13b . . . then remove the servo unit
and disconnect its wiring connector

17 Central locking components - removal and refitting

Electronic control unit

1   Ensure that the ignition is switched off. Remove the fuel injection ECU as described in Chapter 4A.
2   Release the retaining clip, then remove the ECU mounting bracket from the side of the footwell and withdraw the insulation panel **(see illustrations)**.

3   Undo the two bolts and remove the central locking ECU from the vehicle, disconnecting the wiring connector as it becomes accessible **(see illustration)**.
4   Refitting is the reverse of removal.

Front door servo unit

5   Remove the relevant lock assembly as described in Section 13.
6   Undo the two retaining screws, and detach the servo unit from the lock **(see illustration)**.
7   Refitting is the reverse of removal.

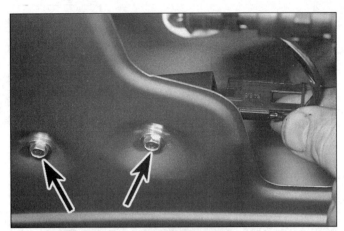

17.16a Disconnect the wiring connector, then undo the retaining bolts (arrowed) . . .

17.16b . . . and remove the servo unit from the tailgate

17.17 When refitting, ensure that the servo unit rod (arrowed) is correctly engaged with the lock

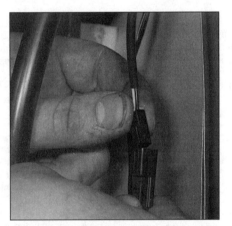

17.19a Disconnect the wiring connector . . .

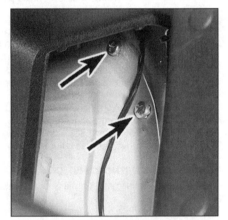

17.19b . . . then undo the two retaining screws (arrowed) . . .

17.19c . . . and remove the fuel filler cap servo unit

Rear door servo unit - five-door models

8 Remove the relevant lock assembly as described in Section 13.
9 Undo the two retaining screws, and detach the servo unit from the lock.
10 Refitting is the reverse of removal.

Rear door servo unit - Combo Van models

11 Carefully prise the access cover out from the rear door. To further improve access, prise out the retaining clips and remove the trim panel from the centre of the door (see illustrations).

12 Release the retaining clip by pivoting it away from the link rod, and free the servo unit link rod from the lock assembly.
13 Undo the two retaining screws and remove the servo unit from the door, disconnecting its wiring connector as it becomes accessible (see illustrations).
14 Refitting is the reverse of removal. Prior to installing the trim panel, check the operation of the servo unit.

Tailgate servo unit

15 Remove the tailgate inner trim panel as described in paragraphs 1 to 3 of Section 16.
16 Undo the two bolts and manoeuvre the servo unit out of position, disconnecting the wiring connector as it becomes accessible (see illustrations).
17 Refitting is the reverse of removal, ensuring that the servo rod is correctly engaged with the lock casting (see illustration). Prior to installing the trim panel, check the operation of the servo unit.

Fuel filler cap servo unit

18 Remove the right-hand rear light unit as described in Chapter 12.
19 Disconnect the servo unit wiring connector, then undo the retaining screws and manoeuvre the servo out through the rear light aperture (see illustrations).
20 Refitting is the reverse of removal, ensuring that the servo unit rod is correctly engaged with the filler cap hole. Check the operation of the servo unit before refitting the light unit.

Door microswitch

21 Remove the door inner trim panel as described in Section 12.
22 Peel the polythene weathershield away from the door to gain

11

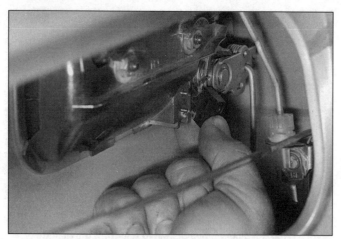

17.24a When refitting, ensure that the microswitch is correctly located on the pins . . .

17.24b . . . and secure it in position with the retaining clip

access to the door lock. Where necessary, cut around the trim panel screw brackets, using a sharp knife, to release the weathershield.

23   Using a suitable screwdriver, prise off the switch retaining clip, and disengage the switch from the lock cylinder mounting plate. Trace the wiring back to its connector, then disconnect it and remove the switch from the door.

24   Refitting is the reverse of the removal, making sure that the switch is correctly located on the mounting plate pins. Also ensure that the wiring is routed around the back of the window guide so that it doesn't foul the window movement **(see illustrations)**.

Tailgate lock microswitch

25   Remove the tailgate trim panel as described in paragraphs 1 to 3 of Section 16.

26   Using a suitable screwdriver, prise off the switch retaining clip, and disengage the switch from the lock cylinder mounting plate **(see illustration)**. Trace the wiring back to its connector, then disconnect it and remove the switch from the tailgate.

27   Refitting is the reverse of the removal, making sure that the switch is correctly located and securely retained by its clip.

---

18   Electric window components - removal and refitting

Note: *Every time the battery is disconnected, or the electric window motors are disconnected, it will be necessary when reconnecting to re-programme the motors, to restore the one-touch function of the buttons. To do this, fully close both front windows. With the windows closed, depress the up button of the driver's side window for approximately 5 seconds, then release it and depress the passenger side window up button for approximately 5 seconds.*

Window switches

1   Refer to Chapter 12.

Window winder motors

2   Remove the regulator mechanism as described in Section 14.

3   Prior to removing the motor, it is necessary to secure the regulator arm to the mounting bracket, to prevent it moving as the motor is removed. The arm is spring-loaded, and if it is not secured in position, it will be forcibly twisted as the motor is removed, and could severely damage your hands.

4   With the regulator arm secured, slacken and remove the three retaining screws, and separate the motor and regulator **(see illustration)**. Do not attempt to dismantle the motor assembly, as it is a sealed unit.

5   Fit the motor assembly to the regulator, and securely tighten its retaining screws.

6   Release the regulator arm, and install the regulator mechanism as described in Section 14.

---

19   Exterior mirror and associated components - removal and refitting

Note: *There are two different manufacturers of the exterior mirrors fitted to Corsa models, and the individual mirror components are not in-*

17.24c Make sure that the switch wiring is correctly routed, and reconnect the wiring connector

17.26 Release the retaining clip and remove the microswitch from the tailgate lock

18.4 Electric window motor retaining screws (arrowed)

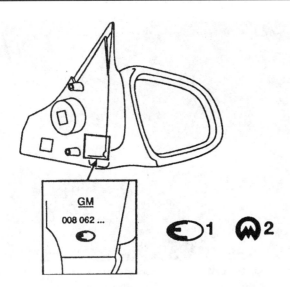

19.1 Exterior mirror manufacturer's identification markings

1   Engelmann   2   Fico

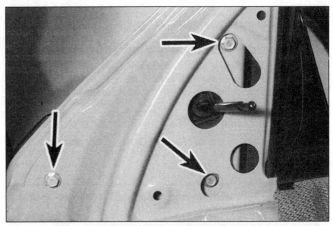

**19.3 Exterior mirror retaining bolts (arrowed) -
manually-operated mirror**

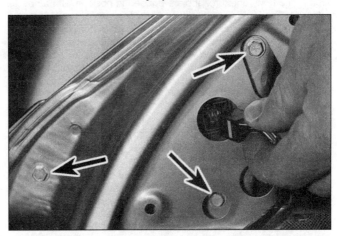

**19.5 Disconnect the wiring connector, then undo the
three retaining bolts (arrowed) . . .**

terchangeable between the two types. This mirror type is indicated by a symbol on the rubber seal located on the inside of the mirror (the mirror must be removed to see this) **(see illustration)**. *Identify the mirror type before ordering mirror spares.*

Manually-operated mirror

1   Pull off the knob from the mirror adjusting lever.
2   Undo the screw (where fitted), and unclip the inner trim panel from the door.
3   Undo the retaining bolts, and remove the mirror assembly from the outside of the door **(see illustration)**.
4   Refitting is the reverse of removal.

Electrically-operated mirror

5   Undo the retaining screw (where fitted), and unclip the exterior mirror inner trim panel from the door. Disconnect the wiring connector from the mirror **(see illustration)**.
6   Undo the three retaining bolts, and remove the mirror assembly from the outside of the door **(see illustration)**.
7   Refitting is a reverse of the removal procedure.

Mirror glass

8   Insert a wide plastic or wooden wedge between the mirror glass

and mirror housing, and carefully prise the glass from its balljoints **(see illustration)**. Take great care when removing the glass; do not use excessive force, as the glass is easily broken (wear thick gloves, particularly if removing an already-broken mirror glass).
9   Remove the glass from the mirror. On models with electric mirrors, disconnect the wiring connectors from the mirror heating element as they become accessible **(see illustration)**.

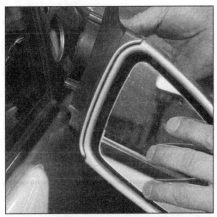

**19.6 . . . and remove the mirror
from the door**

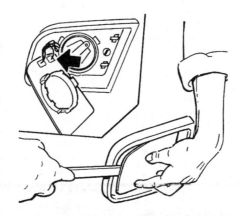

**19.8 Using a wooden wedge to prise the
window glass out of position. Inset shows
heating element wiring connections on
electrically-operated mirror**

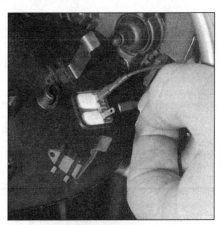

**19.9 Disconnecting the heating
element wiring connections -
electrically-operated mirrors**

11

10   When refitting, carefully clip the glass back into position, ensuring that it is correctly located on each of its balljoints **(see illustration)**.

Mirror motor - electrically-operated mirror

11   Remove the mirror glass as described above.
12   Undo the three screws and remove the motor assembly, disconnecting its wiring connectors as they become accessible **(see illustration)**.
13   Refitting is the reverse of removal.

Mirror switch - electrically-operated mirror

14   Refer to Chapter 12.

20 Windscreen, tailgate and fixed window glass - general information

1   These areas of glass are secured by the tight fit of the weather-strip in the body aperture, and are bonded in position with a special adhesive. The removal and refitting of these areas of fixed glass is a difficult, messy and time-consuming task, which is considered beyond the scope of the home mechanic. It is difficult, unless one has plenty of practice, to obtain a secure, waterproof fit. Furthermore, the task carries a high risk of breakage; this applies especially to the laminated glass windscreen. In view of this, owners are strongly advised to have this sort of work carried out by one of the many specialist windscreen fitters, or a Vauxhall/Opel dealer.

21 Sunroof - general information

1   A manual or electric sunroof was offered as an optional extra on most models, and is fitted as standard equipment on some models.
2   Due to the complexity of the sunroof mechanism, considerable expertise is needed to repair, replace or adjust the sunroof components successfully. Removal of the roof first requires the headlining to be removed, which is a complex and tedious operation in itself, and not a task to be undertaken lightly (See Section 26). Therefore, any problems with the sunroof should be referred to a Vauxhall/Opel dealer.
3   On models with an electric sunroof, if the sunroof motor fails to operate, first check the relevant fuse. If the fault cannot be traced and rectified, the sunroof can be opened and closed manually using a suitable Allen wrench to turn the motor spindle. To gain access to the motor spindle, carefully prise out the trim cover situated at the rear of the sunroof. Insert the Allen key in the motor spindle, and turn to move the sunroof to the required position. A suitable Allen key is supplied with the vehicle, and should be found in the glovebox.

22 Body exterior fittings - removal and refitting

Wheel arch liners and body under-panels

1   The various plastic covers fitted to the underside of the vehicle are secured in position by a mixture of screws, nuts and retaining clips, and removal will be fairly obvious on inspection. Work methodically around the liner/panel, removing its retaining screws and releasing its retaining clips until it is free to be removed from the underside of the vehicle. Most clips used on the vehicle, with the exception of the fasteners which are used to secure the wheelarch liners, are simply prised out of position. The wheelarch liner clips are released by tapping their centre pins through the clip, and then removing the outer section of the clip; new clips will be required on refitting if the centre pins are not recovered.
2   When refitting, renew any retaining clips that may have been broken on removal, and ensure that the panel is securely retained by all the relevant clips, nuts and screws. Vauxhall/Opel also recommend that plastic nuts (where used) are renewed, regardless of their apparent condition, whenever they are disturbed.

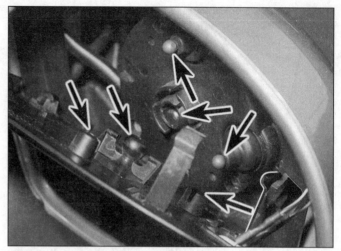

19.10 Align the balljoints and sockets (arrowed) when refitting the mirror glass

Body trim strips and badges

3   The various body trim strips and badges are held in position with a special adhesive tape. Removal requires the trim/badge to be heated, to soften the adhesive, and then cut away from the surface. Due to the high risk of damage to the vehicle's paintwork during this operation, it is recommended that this task should be entrusted to a Vauxhall/Opel dealer.

23 Seats - removal and refitting

Warning: *The seat belt tensioners fitted to the front seat assemblies may cause injury if triggered accidentally. Before carrying out any work on the front seats, always ensure that the safety fork is inserted into the seat belt tensioner cylinder, to prevent the possibility of the tensioner being accidentally triggered (see paragraphs 2 and 3 below). Seats should always be transported and installed with the safety fork in place. If a seat is to be disposed of, the tensioner must be triggered before the seat is removed from the vehicle, by striking the tensioner tube sharply with a hammer. If the tensioner has been triggered due to a sudden impact or accident, the unit must be renewed, as it cannot be reset. A triggered tensioner mechanism can be identified by the yellow tongue which will be visible on the seat belt stalk buckle. Due to safety considerations, tensioner renewal should be entrusted to a Vauxhall/Opel dealer.*

Removal

Front seat
1   Undo the retaining screws, and remove the trim panel from the outside of the seat to gain access to the outer seat guide rail bolt.
2   Locate the plastic safety fork, which is clipped onto the rear of the tensioner. Insert the safety fork into the slot provided in the tensioner cylinder, ensuring that the fork engages securely **(see illustrations)**.
3   Where necessary, on models with heated seats, disconnect the wiring connector which is situated underneath the seat.
4   Slide the seat fully forwards, then slacken and remove the seat rear retaining bolts.
5   Move the seat forwards to disengage the seat guide rails from the floor brackets, and lift the seat out of the vehicle.

Rear seat cushion - Corsa and Corsavan
6   Prise off the trim covers from the rear seat cushion hinges.
7   Slacken and remove the two retaining bolts, then release the seat cushion clips and remove the cushion from the vehicle.

One-piece rear seat backrest - Corsa and Corsavan
8   Open up the tailgate, and remove the rear parcel shelf.

19.12 Motor retaining screws (arrowed) - electrically-operated mirror

23.2a Unclip the safety fork from the rear of the seat belt tensioner . . .

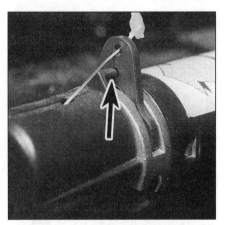

23.2b . . . and insert it into the slot, making sure that it is correctly engaged with the tensioner pin (arrowed)

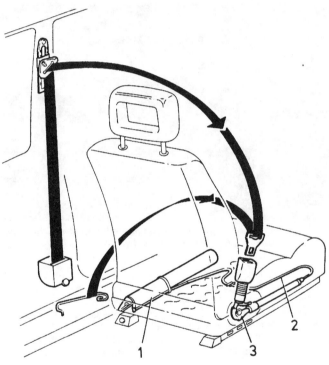

24.1 Seat belt tensioner mechanism components

1   Tensioner unit, containing pre-tensioned spring
2   Cable
3   Pivot

9   Fold the rear seat backrest forwards, and remove the spring clip from the left- and right-hand seat backrest pivot pins.
10   Using a small flat-bladed screwdriver, release the retaining clips, and remove the left- and right-hand pivot pin guides from the vehicle. The seat backrest can then be manoeuvred out of the vehicle.

Two-piece (split folding) rear seat backrest - Corsa and Corsavan
11   Open up the tailgate, and remove the rear parcel shelf.
12   Unclip the trim covers from the left- and right-hand seat backrest hinges.
13   Prise out the retaining clips, and peel back the carpet from the rear of the seats to gain access to the centre pivot of the seat. Undo the four retaining screws, and remove the hinge.
14   Undo the left- and right-hand seat backrest retaining bolts, and remove the seat assembly.

Rear seat cushion - Combo Van
15   Fold back the carpet from front of the seat to gain access to the seat pivot pins.
16   Prise off the C-clip from each pin, then withdraw both pins and remove the seat cushion from the vehicle.

Rear seat backrest - Combo Van
17   Where necessary, undo the retaining bolts and remove the luggage compartment grille from the vehicle.
18   Fold the seat backrest forwards, then undo the retaining bolts from the left- and right-hand seat hinges and remove the backrest from the vehicle.

Refitting

Front seats
19   Refitting is a reverse of the removal procedure, noting the following points:

(a)   *Remove all traces of old thread-locking compound from the threads of the seat retaining bolts, and clean the threaded holes in the vehicle floor, ideally by running a tap of the correct size and pitch down them.*
(b)   *Apply a suitable thread-locking compound to the threads of the seat bolts. Refit the bolts, and tighten them to the specified torque setting.*
(c)   *Prior to refitting the trim panel, remove the safety fork from the seat belt tensioner, and clip it back into position on the outside of the tensioner.*

Rear seats - all models
20   Refitting is a reverse of the removal procedure, tightening the seat mounting bolts to the specified torque (where applicable).

24   Front seat belt tensioning mechanism - general information

All models covered in this manual are fitted with a front seat belt tensioner system. The system is designed to instantaneously take up any slack in the seat belt in the case of a sudden frontal impact, therefore reducing the possibility of injury to the front seat occupants. Each front seat is fitted with its own system, the components of which are mounted in the seat frame **(see illustration)**.
The seat belt tensioner is triggered by a frontal impact causing a deceleration of six times the force of gravity or greater. Lesser impacts, including impacts from behind, will not trigger the system.
When the system is triggered, a pre-tensioned spring draws back the seat belt via a cable which acts on the seat belt stalk. The cable can move by up to 80.0 mm, which therefore reduces the slack in the

11

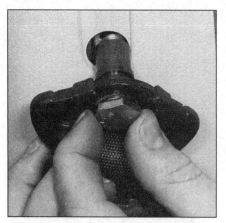

25.1 On three-door models, unscrew the front seat belt upper mounting bolt, and recover the spacer and washer from behind the belt anchorage

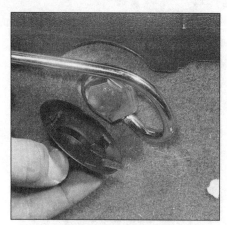

25.2a Remove the trim cap . . .

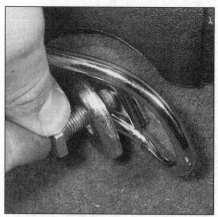

25.2b . . . then unscrew the retaining bolt and washer . . .

seat belt around the shoulders and waist of the occupant by a similar amount.

There is a risk of injury if the system is triggered inadvertently when working on the vehicle, and it is therefore strongly recommended that any work involving the seat belt tensioner system is entrusted to a Vauxhall/Opel dealer. Refer to the warning given at the beginning of Section 23 before contemplating any work on the front seats.

25 Seat belt components - removal and refitting

Removal

Front seat belt - three-door models

1   Prise off the trim cover from the upper seat belt mounting. Unscrew the mounting bolt, and recover the washer and spacer from behind the belt anchorage **(see illustration)**.
2   Remove the trim cap, then slacken and remove bolt and washer securing the seat belt mounting rail to the floor. Disengage the rail from the floor and the seat belt, and remove it **(see illustrations)**.
3   Remove the rear seat backrest as described in Section 23.
4   If the left-hand seat belt is to be removed, remove the interior light unit from the luggage compartment trim panel as described in Chapter 12.
5   Remove the rear shock absorber access panel from the relevant luggage compartment side trim panel. Where necessary, undo the retaining nut and washer, and remove the seat pin and washer from the vehicle **(see illustrations)**.

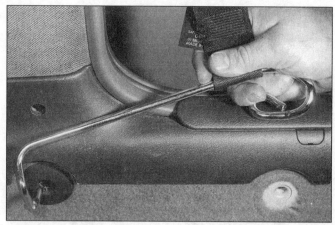

25.2c . . . and disengage the seat belt mounting rail from the floor and seat belt, and remove it from the vehicle

6   Prise out the retaining clips from the rear of the panel, and the circular plug/seat stop buffer (as applicable) from the front of the panel. Slacken and remove all the panel retaining screws, then release the panel from the vehicle body and disconnect the speaker wiring connector (where fitted) **(see illustrations)**.
7   Position the luggage compartment panel clear of the rear seat side trim panel. There is no need to undo the rear seat belt anchorages.

25.5a Unscrew the retaining nut and washer . . .

25.5b . . . and remove the seat pin and washer (where fitted)

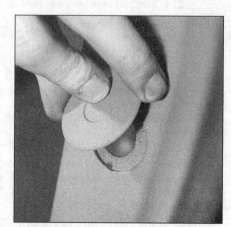

25.6a Prise out the circular plug (where fitted) from the front of the luggage compartment side trim panel

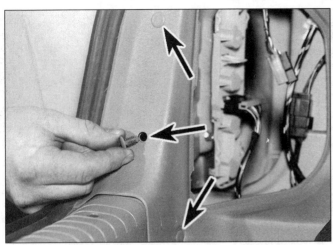

25.6b Prise out the three retaining clips (arrowed) from the rear of the panel . . .

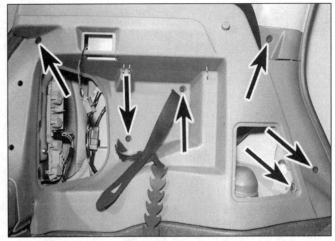

25.6c . . . then undo the retaining screws (arrowed) and remove the panel

25.8 Undo the two screws, and release the sill trim panel from the rear seat side trim panel

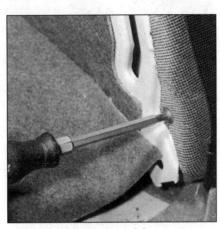

25.9 Undo the rear retaining screw . . .

25.10a . . . then peel the door sealing strip away from the front of the panel . . .

8   Undo the two screws, and release the sill trim panel from the front edge of the rear seat side trim panel **(see illustration)**.

9   Slacken and remove the rear retaining screw from the base of the panel **(see illustration)**.

10   Peel the door sealing strip away from the front edge of the rear seat side panel, then unclip the top of the panel and remove it from the vehicle **(see illustrations)**.

11   Undo the inertia reel retaining bolt, and remove the seat belt assembly from the vehicle. If necessary, the seat belt height adjuster ratchet can be removed as follows.

12   Prise out the hook from the top of the door pillar panel. Undo the upper and lower retaining screws, and remove the trim panel to gain access to the seat belt height adjuster ratchet. Undo the two bolts and remove the ratchet **(see illustrations)**.

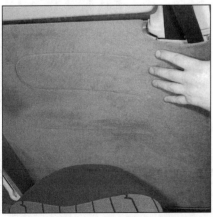

25.10b . . . and unclip the panel from the vehicle

25.12a Remove the hook from the door pillar panel, and unscrew the upper retaining screw . . .

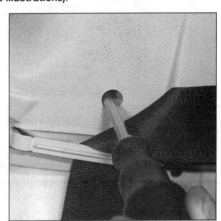

25.12b . . . then undo the lower retaining screw . . .

11

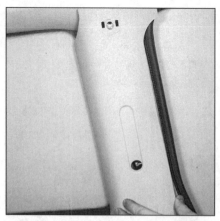

25.12c ... and remove the door pillar trim panel

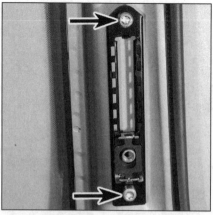

25.12d Seat belt height adjuster ratchet is retained by two bolts (arrowed)

25.13a Unclip the trim cap ...

25.13b ... then unscrew the mounting bolt, and recover the washer and spacer from behind the belt anchorage

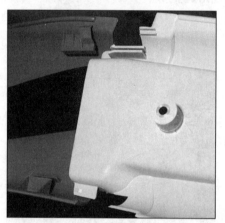

25.14 Unclip the two halves of the door pillar trim panel, and remove them

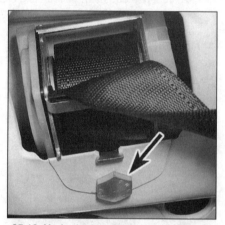

25.16 Undo the inertia reel retaining bolt (arrowed) and remove the seat belt assembly

25.18 Unscrew the rear seat belt upper mounting bolt, noting the correct fitted position of the washer and spacer

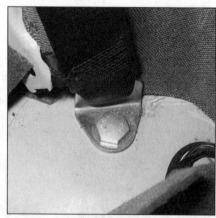

25.19a Unscrew the lower mounting bolt ...

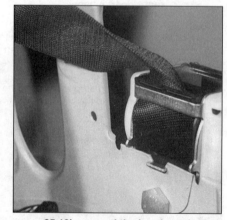

25.19b ... and the inertia reel retaining bolt ...

Front seat belt - five-door and Combo Van models

13   Prise off the trim cap from the seat belt upper mounting. Unscrew the mounting bolt, and recover the washer and spacer from behind the belt anchorage **(see illustrations)**.

14   Remove the trim caps from the door pillar trim panel to reveal the retaining screws, then undo both screws and free the panels. Unclip the two panel sections, and remove them from the vehicle **(see illustration)**.

15   Prise off the trim cap from the lower seat belt mounting. Unscrew

the mounting bolt, and recover the washer, spacer and trim cover from behind the belt anchorage.

16   Undo the inertia reel retaining bolt, and remove the seat belt assembly from the vehicle **(see illustration)**. If necessary, undo the retaining bolts and remove the seat belt ratchet mechanism from the door pillar.

Rear seat side belt - three-door and five-door models

17   Carry out the operations described above in paragraphs 3 to 6.

25.19c ... then remove the guide, and feed the belt through the luggage compartment trim panel

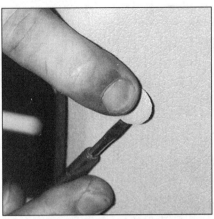

25.20a On three-door models, prise out the trim cap ...

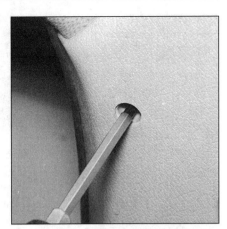

25.20b ... then undo the upper retaining screw ...

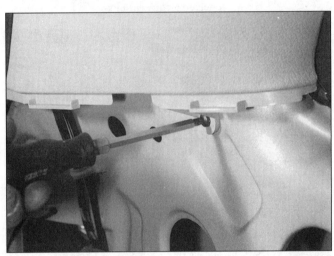

25.20c ... and the lower retaining screw ...

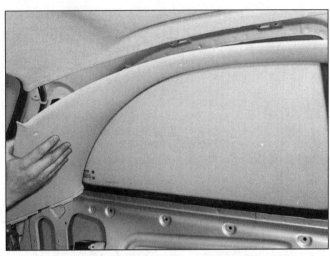

25.20d ... and unclip the trim panel from the vehicle

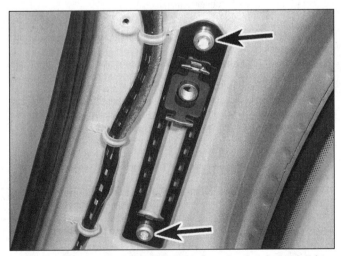

25.21 Rear seat belt height adjuster mechanism is retained by two bolts (arrowed)

18   Prise off the trim cover from the upper seat belt mounting. Unscrew the mounting bolt, and recover the washer and spacer from behind the belt anchorage **(see illustration)**.

19   Unscrew the lower seat belt mounting bolt and washer, then undo the inertia reel retaining bolt. Remove the guide from the luggage compartment trim panel, then free the belt and remove it from the vehicle **(see illustrations)**. If necessary, the seat belt height adjuster ratchet can be removed as follows.

20   On three-door models, prise out the trim cap from the top of the rear window trim panel, then undo both the upper and lower panel retaining screws. Unclip the retaining clips, situated along the top edge of the panel, and free it from the door pillar trim panel **(see illustrations)**. **Note:** *It may be necessary to remove the hook and undo the door pillar panel upper screw first (see paragraph 12).* Undo the two retaining bolts and remove the ratchet.

21   On five-door models, prise out the trim caps, then undo the retaining screws and remove the rear quarter window trim panel. Undo the two retaining bolts, and remove the ratchet **(see illustration)**.

Rear seat side belt - Combo Van models

22   Where necessary, undo the retaining bolts and remove the luggage compartment grille from the vehicle.

23   Fold the rear seat cushion forwards, then prise out the retaining clips and remove the trim panel from either side of the seat belt inertia reel.

24   Undo the retaining screws, and remove the cover from the inertia reel.

25   Unclip the trim cover from the upper belt mounting. Undo the bolt, and recover the washer and spacer from behind the belt anchorage.

26   Undo the lower seat belt and inertia reel retaining bolts, and remove the seat belt from the vehicle.

11

25.27 Rear seat belt buckle retaining bolt

25.28 When refitting, tighten the seat belt mounting bolts to their specified torque settings

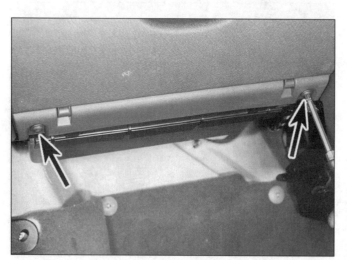

26.6 Unscrew the glovebox lower retaining screws (arrowed) . . .

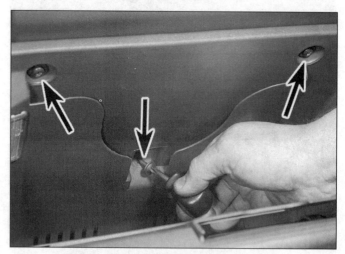

26.7a . . . then undo the three upper retaining screws (arrowed) . . .

Rear seat centre belt and buckles - all models

27   Fold the rear seat cushion forwards, and unscrew the relevant bolt securing the belt or buckle to the floor **(see illustration)**.

Refitting

28   Refitting is a reversal of the removal procedure, ensuring that all the mounting bolts are tightened to the specified torque, where applicable **(see illustration)**. Make sure that any trim panels disturbed during removal are securely retained by all the relevant retaining clips.

26   Interior trim - removal and refitting

Interior trim panels

1   The interior trim panels are secured using either screws or various types of trim fasteners, usually studs or clips.
2   Check that there are no other panels overlapping the one to be removed; usually there is a sequence that has to be followed that will become obvious on close inspection.
3   Remove all obvious fasteners, such as screws. If the panel will not come free, it is held by hidden clips or fasteners. These are usually situated around the edge of the panel, and can be prised up to release them; note, however, that they can break quite easily, so replacements should be available. The best way of releasing such clips (in the absence of the correct type of tool) is to use a large flat-bladed

screwdriver. Note in many cases that the adjacent sealing strip must be prised back to release a panel.
4   When removing a panel, **never** use excessive force, or the panel may be damaged; always check carefully that all fasteners have been removed or released before attempting to withdraw a panel.
5   Refitting is the reverse of the removal procedure; secure the fasteners by pressing them firmly into place, and ensure that all disturbed components are secured correctly, to prevent rattles.

Glovebox

6   Slacken and remove the two glovebox lower retaining screws **(see illustration)**.
7   Open up the glovebox lid, and undo the three upper retaining screws situated inside the glovebox. Slide the glovebox out of position, disconnecting the wiring connector from the glovebox illumination light (where fitted) as it becomes accessible **(see illustrations)**.
8   Refitting is the reverse of removal.

Carpets

9   The passenger compartment floor carpet is in one piece, and is secured at its edges by screws or clips, usually the same fasteners used to secure the various adjoining trim panels.
10   Carpet removal and refitting is reasonably straightforward, but very time-consuming. All adjoining trim panels must be removed first, as must components such as the seats, the centre console and seat belt lower anchorages.

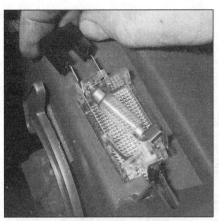

26.7b ... and withdraw the glovebox, disconnecting the wiring connector from the illumination light as it becomes accessible

27.2a Prise out the trim cap from the centre console storage compartment ...

27.2b ... to gain access to the retaining screw

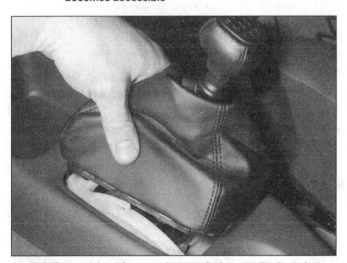

27.3 On models with manual transmission, unclip the gaiter and fold it back over the gear lever

27.4 Move the centre console to the rear to free it from its retaining clips, and lift it over the gear lever

Headlining

11   The headlining is clipped to the roof, and can only be withdrawn once all fittings such as the grab handles, sunvisors, sunroof (if fitted), windscreen and rear quarterwindows and related trim panels have been removed, and the door, tailgate and sunroof aperture sealing strips have been prised clear.

12   Note that headlining removal requires considerable skill and experience if it is to be carried out without damage, and is therefore best entrusted to an expert.

27 Centre console - removal and refitting

Removal

1   Firmly apply the handbrake, and slide both front seats fully rearwards.

2   Prise out the trim cap from the front of the centre console storage compartment, and unscrew the retaining screw **(see illustrations)**.

3   On models with manual transmission, unclip the gear lever gaiter from the centre console, and fold it back over the gear lever **(see illustration)**.

4   On all models, slide the console to the rear to disengage it from its retaining clip, and lift it upwards and over the gear/selector lever **(see illustration)**.

Refitting

5   Refitting is the reverse of removal.

28 Facia panel assembly - removal and refitting

Tip: Label each wiring connector as it is disconnected from its relevant component. The labels will prove useful when refitting, as a guide to routing the wiring and feeding it through the facia apertures.

Removal

1   Disconnect the battery negative terminal.

2   Remove the following components as described in Chapter 12:

   (a) Instrument panel.
   (b) Windscreen wiper motor.
   (c) Radio/cassette player.
   (d) Clock/multi/function unit display.
   (e) Steering column combination switches.

3   Remove the following components as described in Chapter 3:

   (a) Heater/ventilation control unit.
   (b) Driver's side vent housing.
   (c) Passenger side heater duct.

4   Remove the glovebox as described in Section 26.

5   Remove the storage compartment (where fitted) from underneath the passenger side of the facia. The compartment is secured in

11

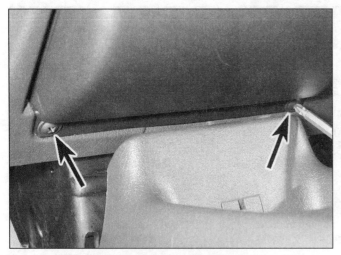

28.6a Undo the two lower retaining screws . . .

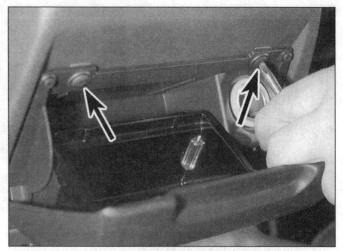

28.6b . . . then open up the ashtray, and undo the two upper retaining screws

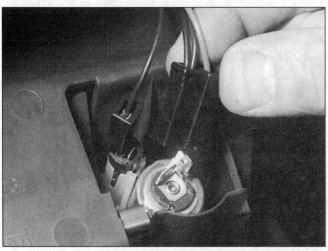

28.6c Withdraw the ashtray from the facia, and disconnect its wiring connectors

28.10a Prise out the two retaining clips . . .

28.10b . . . then turn the combination switch mounting bracket anti-clockwise, and slide it off the steering column

28.12 Removing the support bracket from the centre of the facia

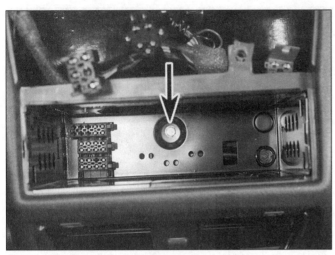

28.13a Undo the retaining screw (arrowed) . . .

28.13b . . . then slide out the radio/cassette bracket, freeing the wiring connector . . .

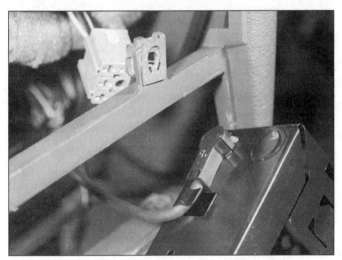

28.13c . . . and aerial lead from the rear of the bracket

position by a retaining screw and clip.

6　Undo the two lower ashtray retaining screws, then open up the ashtray and remove the two upper retaining screws. Withdraw the ashtray from the centre of the facia, disconnecting the wiring connectors from the rear of the unit as they become accessible **(see illustrations)**.

7　Remove the centre console as described in Section 27.

8　Undo the retaining screws, and release the fusebox from the driver's side of the facia, and the relay carrier from the top of the glovebox aperture. See Section 3 of Chapter 12 for further information. There is no need to disconnect any of the above components - they can be left in position

9　Remove the steering wheel as described in Chapter 10.

10　Prise out the two retaining clips from the combination switch mounting bracket, then twist the bracket anti-clockwise and slide it off the top of the steering column **(see illustrations)**.

11　Disconnect the wiring connector from the stop-light switch.

12　Undo the retaining screws, and remove the support bracket from the base of the centre of the facia **(see illustration)**.

13　Where necessary, undo the screw securing the radio/cassette mounting bracket in position, then slide out the bracket, freeing it from the aerial lead and wiring connector **(see illustrations)**.

14　Release the retaining clips and, noting its correct routing, free the wiring loom from the metal frame of the facia panel. Also slide the instrument panel wiring connector out from its clip on the facia **(see illustrations)**.

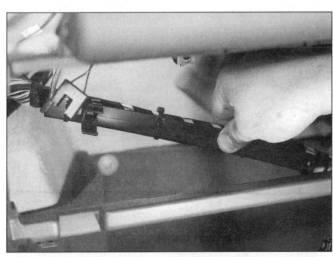

28.14a Release the retaining clips and ties, and free the wiring from the facia metal frame . . .

28.14b . . . and the instrument panel wiring connector from the facia

11

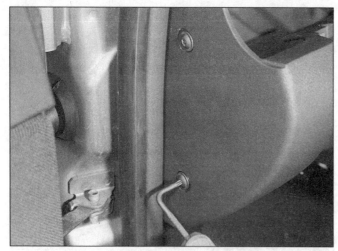

28.15 Undo the facia side retaining screws . . .

28.16 . . . then undo the nuts securing the facia assembly to the engine compartment bulkhead

15   Undo the two retaining screws from the left-hand end of the facia panel, and the two screws from the facia right-hand end **(see illustration)**.

16   Return to the engine compartment, and undo the three retaining nuts securing the facia to the bulkhead **(see illustration)**.

17   The facia panel is now free to be removed. Pull the panel away from the bulkhead, then remove the facia assembly, noting the correct routing of the wiring harnesses, and feeding the wiring back through the facia apertures **(see illustration)**.

Refitting

18   Refitting is a reversal of the removal procedure, noting the following points:

(a)   *Manoeuvre the facia into position and, using the labels stuck on during removal, ensure that the wiring is correctly routed and fed through the relevant facia apertures.*

(b)   *Clip the facia back into position, then refit all the facia fasteners and tighten them to their specified torque settings.*

(c)   *On completion, reconnect the battery and check that all the electrical components and switches function correctly.*

28.17 The facia panel can then be removed from the vehicle

Chapter 12 Body electrical systems

Contents

Specifications

System type .... 12-volt negative earth

Fuses

Fuse	Rating (amps)	Circuit(s) protected
1	20	Hazard warning lights, horn, anti-theft alarm and interior lights
2	10	Automatic transmission
3	30	Heated rear window
4	10	Daytime driving lights
5	10	Automatic transmission
6	10	Rear foglights
7	30	Air conditioning
8	10	Left-hand sidelight and tail light, and headlight beam adjustment system

12

Fuses (continued)

Fuse	Rating (amps)	Circuit(s) protected
9	20	Front foglights
10	10	Left-hand main beam
11	30	Headlight washer system
12	10	Left-hand dipped beam and headlight beam adjustment system
13	20	Central locking system
14	-	Not used
15	30	Heater blower motor, radiator cooling fan and air conditioning system
16	30	Windscreen wipers
17	10	Radio and multi-function display unit, instrument panel,glovebox light and electric exterior mirrors
18	20	Central locking system, reversing lights, cigarette lighter and automatic transmission
19	20	Electric sunroof
20	30	Radiator cooling fan
21	15	Stop-lights and hazard warning lights
22	10	Anti-lock braking system (ABS)
23	10	Right-hand sidelight and tail light, and headlight beam adjustment system
24	-	Not used
25	10	Right-hand main beam
26	20	Fuel injection system
27	10	Right-hand dipped beam and headlight beam adjustment system
28	30	Electric windows
*	10	Anti-theft alarm

Note: *Not all items fitted to all models*
Located in the engine compartment junction box

Relays

Relay and wiring diagram component number	Location
Air conditioning (K6)	Relay carrier above glovebox
Air conditioning cooling fan (K7)	Relay carrier above glovebox
Air conditioning compressor relay (K60)	Engine compartment junction box
Anti-theft alarm horn (K63)	Fusebox
Anti-theft alarm immobiliser (K3)	Fusebox
Cooling fan (K26)	Relay carrier above glovebox
Cooling fan (K51)	Relay carrier above glovebox
Cooling fan (K52)	Relay carrier above glovebox
Cooling fan high speed (K67)	Relay carrier above glovebox
Daytime driving light (K59)	Behind fusebox
Exterior mirror heating (K35)	Fusebox
Front foglight (K5)	Fusebox
Fuel pump (K58)	Behind right-hand footwell trim panel
Headlight washer pump (K97)	Fusebox
Heated rear screen (K1)	Fusebox
"Lights-on" buzzer (H19)	Fusebox
Rear foglight (K89)	Fusebox
Tailgate wiper (K30)	Fusebox
Turn signal (K10)	Fusebox
Windscreen wiper (K8)	Fusebox

Bulbs	Wattage
Headlight	60/55
Front foglight	55
Front sidelight	5
Direction indicator	21
Direction indicator side repeater	5
Stop/tail light	21/5
Reversing light	21
Rear foglight	21
Number plate light	10
Interior lights	10
Instrument panel illumination lights	2
Instrument panel warning lights	1.2

Torque wrench settings

	Nm	lbf ft
Windscreen wiper motor	25	18
Air bag unit retaining screws	10	7

1 General information and precautions

Warning: *Before carrying out any work on the electrical system, read through the precautions given in "Safety first!" at the beginning of this manual, and in Chapter 5.*

1   The electrical system is of the 12-volt negative earth type. Power for the lights and all electrical accessories is supplied by a lead/acid type battery, which is charged by the engine-driven alternator.

2   This Chapter covers repair and service procedures for the various electrical components not associated with engine. Information on the battery, alternator and starter motor can be found in Chapter 5.

3   It should be noted that, prior to working on any component in the electrical system, the battery negative terminal should first be disconnected, to prevent the possibility of electrical short-circuits and/or fires.

Caution: *If the radio/cassette player fitted to the vehicle is equipped with an anti-theft security code (as the standard unit is) refer to "Radio/cassette unit anti-theft system - precaution" at the beginning of this manual before disconnecting the battery.*

2 Electrical fault-finding - general information

Note: *Refer to the precautions given in "Safety first!" and in Section 1 before starting work. The following tests relate to testing of the main electrical circuits, and should not be used to test delicate electronic circuits (such as the anti-lock braking system or fuel injection system), particularly where an electronic control module is used.*

General

1   A typical electrical circuit consists of an electrical component, any switches, relays, motors, fuses, fusible links or circuit breakers related to that component, and the wiring and connectors which link the component to both the battery and the vehicle body. To help to pinpoint a problem in an electrical circuit, wiring diagrams are included at the end of this manual.

2   Before attempting to diagnose an electrical fault, first study the appropriate wiring diagram to obtain a complete understanding of the components included in the particular circuit concerned. The possible sources of a fault can be narrowed down by noting if other components related to the circuit are operating properly. If several components or circuits fail at one time, the problem is likely to be related to a shared fuse or earth connection.

3   Electrical problems usually stem from simple causes, such as loose or corroded connections, a faulty earth connection, a blown fuse, a melted fusible link, or a faulty relay (refer to Section 3 for details of testing relays). Inspect the condition of all fuses, wires and connections in a problem circuit before testing the components. Use the wiring diagrams to determine which terminal connections will need to be checked in order to pinpoint the trouble-spot.

4   The basic tools required for electrical fault-finding include a circuit tester or voltmeter (a 12-volt bulb with a set of test leads can also be used for certain tests); a self-powered test light (sometimes known as a continuity tester); an ohmmeter (to measure resistance); a battery and set of test leads; and a jumper wire, preferably with a circuit breaker or fuse incorporated, which can be used to bypass suspect wires or electrical components. Before attempting to locate a problem with test instruments, use the wiring diagram to determine where to make the connections.

5   To find the source of an intermittent wiring fault (usually due to a poor or dirty connection, or damaged wiring insulation), a "wiggle" test can be performed on the wiring. This involves wiggling the wiring by hand to see if the fault occurs as the wiring is moved. It should be possible to narrow down the source of the fault to a particular section of wiring. This method of testing can be used in conjunction with any of the tests described in the following sub-Sections.

6   Apart from problems due to poor connections, two basic types of fault can occur in an electrical circuit - open-circuit, or short-circuit.

7   Open-circuit faults are caused by a break somewhere in the circuit, which prevents current from flowing. An open-circuit fault will prevent a component from working, but will not cause the relevant circuit fuse to blow.

8   Short-circuit faults are caused by a "short" somewhere in the circuit, which allows the current flowing in the circuit to "escape" along an alternative route, usually to earth. Short-circuit faults are normally caused by a breakdown in wiring insulation, which allows a feed wire to touch either another wire, or an earthed component such as the bodyshell. A short-circuit fault will normally cause the relevant circuit fuse to blow.

Finding an open-circuit

9   To check for an open-circuit, connect one lead of a circuit tester or voltmeter to either the negative battery terminal or a known good earth.

10   Connect the other lead to a connector in the circuit being tested, preferably nearest to the battery or fuse.

11   Switch on the circuit, bearing in mind that some circuits are live only when the ignition switch is turned to a particular position.

12   If voltage is present (indicated either by the tester bulb lighting or a voltmeter reading, as applicable), this means that the section of the circuit between the relevant connector and the battery is problem-free.

13   Continue to check the remainder of the circuit in the same fashion.

14   When a point is reached at which no voltage is present, the problem must lie between that point and the previous test point with voltage. Most problems can be traced to a broken, corroded or loose connection.

Finding a short-circuit

15   To check for a short-circuit, first disconnect the load(s) from the circuit (loads are the components which draw current from a circuit, such as bulbs, motors, heating elements, etc).

16   Remove the relevant fuse from the circuit, and connect a circuit tester or voltmeter to the fuse connections.

17   Switch on the circuit, bearing in mind that some circuits are live only when the ignition switch is turned to a particular position.

18   If voltage is present (indicated either by the tester bulb lighting or a voltmeter reading, as applicable), this means that there is a short-circuit.

19   If no voltage is present, but the fuse still blows with the load(s) connected, this indicates an internal fault in the load(s).

Finding an earth fault

20   The battery negative terminal is connected to "earth" - the metal of the engine/transmission unit and the car body - and most systems are wired so that they only receive a positive feed, the current returning via the metal of the car body. This means that the component mounting and the body form part of that circuit. Loose or corroded mountings can therefore cause a range of electrical faults, ranging from total failure of a circuit, to a puzzling partial fault. In particular, lights may shine dimly (especially when another circuit sharing the same earth point is in operation), motors (eg. wiper motors or the radiator cooling fan motor) may run slowly, and the operation of one circuit may have an apparently-unrelated effect on another. Note that on many vehicles, earth straps are used between certain components, such as the engine/transmission and the body, usually where there is no metal-to-metal contact between components, due to flexible rubber mountings, etc.

21   To check whether a component is properly earthed, disconnect the battery, and connect one lead of an ohmmeter to a known good earth point. Connect the other lead to the wire or earth connection being tested. The resistance reading should be zero; if not, check the connection as follows.

22   If an earth connection is thought to be faulty, dismantle the connection, and clean back to bare metal both the bodyshell and the wire terminal or the component earth connection mating surface. Be careful to remove all traces of dirt and corrosion, then use a knife to trim away any paint, so that a clean metal-to-metal joint is made. On reassembly, tighten the joint fasteners securely; if a wire terminal is being refitted, use serrated washers between the terminal and the bodyshell, to ensure a clean and secure connection. When the connection is remade, prevent the onset of corrosion in the future by applying a coat of petroleum jelly or silicone-based grease. Alternatively, at regular intervals, spray on a proprietary ignition sealer such as Holts Damp Start, or a water-dispersant lubricant such as Holts Wet Start.

12

3.1a Unclip the cover from the driver's side of the facia to gain access to most of the fuses

3.1b A few odd fuses and relays are located in the junction box in the engine compartment (right-hand drive model shown)

3   Fuses and relays - general information

Fuses

1   Most of the fuses are located behind the driver's side lower facia panel, with a few odd fuses on some models being located in the junction box in the engine compartment **(see illustrations)**. The junction box is located next to the master cylinder brake fluid reservoir.

2   To gain access to fusebox, unclip the access panel from the driver's side of the facia. To gain access to those in the junction box, unclip the junction box lid.

3   The fuse number is marked on the fusebox next to each fuse. A list of the circuits each fuse protects is given in the Specifications at the start of this Chapter.

4   To remove a fuse, first switch off the circuit concerned (or the ignition), then pull the fuse out of its terminals. The wire within the fuse is clearly visible; if the fuse is blown, it will be broken or melted.

5   Always renew a fuse with one of an identical rating; never use a fuse with a different rating from the original, nor substitute anything else. Never renew a fuse more than once without tracing the source of the trouble. The fuse rating is stamped on top of the fuse; note that the fuses are also colour-coded for easy recognition.

6   If a new fuse blows immediately, find the cause before renewing it again; a short to earth as a result of faulty insulation is most likely. Where a fuse protects more than one circuit, try to isolate the defect by switching on each circuit in turn (if possible) until the fuse blows again. Always carry a supply of spare fuses of each relevant rating on the vehicle, a spare of each rating should be clipped into the base of the fusebox.

Relays

7   The majority of relays are located in the top of the fusebox panel behind the driver's side lower facia panel. On some models, some relays (mainly those involved with the air conditioning system) are located on the relay carrier which is situated behind the facia, directly above the glovebox. Full details of relay locations are given in the Specifications at the start of this Chapter, and in the accompanying illustrations **(see illustrations)**.

8   To gain access to the fusebox relays, unclip the fusebox access panel from the facia, then undo the two retaining screws and lower the fusebox out from the facia **(see illustrations)**.

9   To gain access to the relay carrier relays, remove the glovebox as described in Section 26 of Chapter 11. Undo the two retaining screws, and lower the anti-theft alarm control unit (where fitted) out from the top of the glovebox aperture. Undo the two screws, and lower the relay carrier plate out from the top of the glovebox aperture **(see illustrations)**.

10   If a circuit or system controlled by a relay develops a fault and the

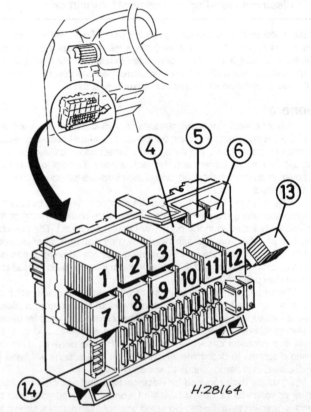

3.7a Fusebox relay locations and identification numbers

1   Exterior mirror heating timer relay (K35)
2   Turn signal relay (K10)
3   Tailgate wiper relay (K30)
4   Not used
5   Front foglight relay (K5)
6   Rear foglight relay (K89)
7   Windscreen wiper relay (K8)
8   Heated rear window relay (K1)
9   "Lights-on" warning buzzer (H19)
10   Anti-theft alarm horn relay (K63)
11   Headlight washer system relay (K97)
12   Anti-theft alarm immobiliser relay (K3)
13   Daytime driving light relay (K59)
14   Diagnostic plug (for use by Vauxhall/Opel dealer)

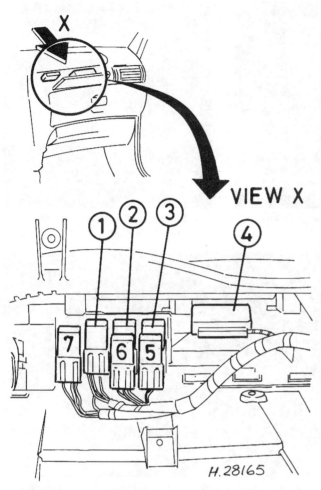

3.7b Relay carrier relay locations and identification numbers

1   Cooling fan relay (K51)
2   Cooling fan relay (K52)
3   Cooling fan relay (K26)
4   Anti-theft alarm control unit
5   Air conditioning relay (K6)
6   Air conditioning cooling fan relay (K7)
7   Cooling fan relay (high-speed) (K67)

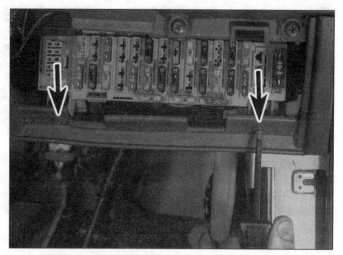

3.8a Undo the two retaining screws (arrowed) . . .

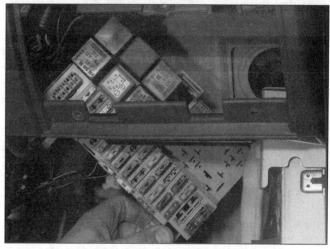

3.8b . . . and lower the fusebox out of position to gain
access to the relays

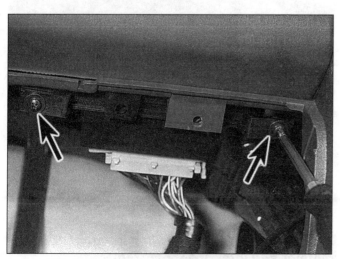

3.9a Undo the two retaining screws (arrowed) . . .

3.9b . . . and lower the anti-theft alarm control unit out of position
to gain access to the relay carrier

12

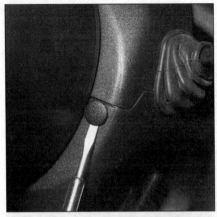

4.2a Prise out the trim plugs from the top of the steering column shrouds . . .

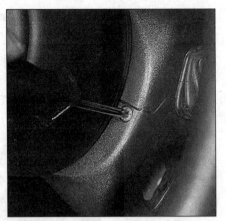

4.2b . . . and unscrew the upper shroud screws

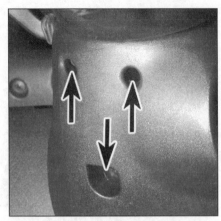

4.2c Unscrew the three lower shroud retaining screws (arrowed) . . .

4.2d . . . then remove the rubber seal from the ignition switch/lock . . .

4.2e . . . and remove the both shrouds from the column

relay is suspect, operate the system; if the relay is functioning, it should be possible to hear it click as it is energised. If this is the case, the fault lies with the components or wiring of the system. If the relay is not being energised, then either the relay is not receiving a main supply or a switching voltage or the relay itself is faulty. Testing is by the sub-stitution of a known good unit, but be careful; while some relays are identical in appearance and in operation, others look similar but per-form different functions.

11   To renew a relay, first ensure that the ignition switch is off. The re-lay can then simply be pulled out from the socket and the new relay pressed in.

4   Switches - removal and refitting

Note: *Disconnect the battery negative lead before removing any switch, and reconnect the lead after refitting.*

Ignition switch/steering column lock

1   Refer to Chapter 10, Section 18.

Steering column combination switches

2   With the steering wheel in the straight-ahead position, turn the wheel 90° to the left, then prise off the trim cap and remove the left up-per shroud screw. Turn the wheel 180° to the right, and remove the right upper screw. Remove the rubber seal from the ignition switch/lock, then undo the lower retaining screws and remove the steering column shrouds **(see illustrations)**.

3   Depress the retaining clips, and release the relevant switch as-sembly from the column bracket. Disconnect the wiring connector, and

4.3a Depress the retaining clips, then slide out the switch (shown with steering wheel removed for clarity) . . .

remove the switch assembly from the vehicle **(see illustrations)**.

4   If necessary, remove the opposite switch assembly in the same way.

5   Refitting is a reversal of the removal procedure.

Lighting switch (incorporating instrument panel dimmer and interior light switch)

6   Turn the knob to the headlight "on" position, and pull the knob out.

4.3b ... and disconnect its wiring connector

4.7 Release the retaining clip with a flat-bladed screwdriver, and pull off the lighting switch knob

4.8 Depress the retaining clips, and withdraw the lighting switch from the facia

4.12 Using the hooked tool to withdraw the front foglight switch

4.15 Removing the hazard warning light switch. Note the use of a piece of card to avoid marking the switch surround

4.18 Release the retaining clip with a suitable screwdriver, and pull off the knob

4.19 Depress the retaining clips, and withdraw the heated rear window/blower motor switch from the facia

7   Insert a small screwdriver or suitable rod through the hole in the bottom of the knob, then depress the switch knob retaining clip and remove the knob **(see illustration)**.

8   Depress the switch retaining clips, pull the switch out from the facia, and disconnect the wiring connector **(see illustration)**.

9   Note that the switch assembly cannot be dismantled; if any of its functions are faulty, the complete assembly must be renewed.

10   Refitting is a reversal of the removal procedure.

Foglight, heated seat and headlight beam adjuster switches

11   To remove the facia pushbutton switches, a suitable hooked tool is needed. A suitable tool can be fabricated from a strip of 2 mm steel which is approximately 5 mm in width (a small hacksaw blade works well). Bend the end of the strip through 90° so that there is a hook approximately 4 mm in length at a right-angle to the strip.

12   Manoeuvre the strip into position, taking great care not to damage the switch or facia panel. Locate the hook behind the switch, and use it to pull the switch out of position **(see illustration)**.

13   On refitting, push the switch into position until it clicks into position.

Hazard warning switch

14   Depress the switch so that it is set in the "on" position.

15   Using a small flat-bladed screwdriver, carefully lever the switch out of position, taking great care not to mark the switch or vent panel **(see illustration)**.

16   On refitting, push the switch in until it clicks into position.

Heated rear window/blower motor switch

17   Pull the switch out so that it is set in the "on" position.

18   Insert a small screwdriver or suitable rod through the hole in the bottom of the knob, then depress the switch knob retaining clip and remove the knob **(see illustration)**.

19   Depress the switch retaining clips, and pull the switch out from the facia **(see illustration)**.

20   Refitting is the reverse of removal.

12

4.22 Undo the retaining bolt, and remove the handbrake warning light switch from the lever

4.25 Withdraw the courtesy light switch from the door pillar, and disconnect its wiring connector

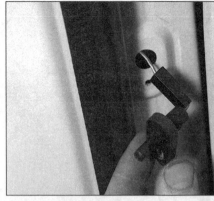

4.28 Removing the luggage compartment light switch - Combo Van models

Handbrake warning light switch

21　Remove the handbrake lever as described in Chapter 9.
22　Undo the bolt, and remove the switch from the lever **(see illustration)**.
23　Install the new switch, securely tightening its retaining bolt, and refit the handbrake lever as described in Chapter 9.

Stop-light switch

24　Refer to Chapter 9.

Courtesy light switches

25　Open the door, then undo the switch retaining screw. Withdraw the switch from the pillar, disconnecting its wiring connector as it becomes accessible **(see illustration)**. Tie a piece of string to the wiring, to prevent it falling back into the door pillar.
26　Refitting is a reverse of the removal procedure.

Luggage compartment light switch

27　On Corsa and Corsavan models, the switch is fitted to the bottom of the tailgate. On Combo Van models, the switch is fitted to the right-hand side of the vehicle body, on the outside edge of the rear door.
28　Undo the retaining screw, then withdraw the switch and disconnect it from its wiring connector **(see illustration)**. Tie a piece of string to the wiring, to prevent it falling back into the tailgate/vehicle body (as applicable).
29　Refitting is a reverse of the removal procedure.

Driver's door electric window switches

30　Unscrew the door pocket retaining screws, and pull the pocket downwards and away from the door to release its retaining clips **(see illustration)**. Disconnect the switch wiring connectors.
31　Release the retaining clips, and remove the relevant switch from the panel **(see illustration)**.
32　Refitting is the reverse of removal, ensuring that the wiring is correctly routed inside the door pocket.

Passenger door electric window switch

33　Remove the door inner trim panel as described in Chapter 11.
34　Disconnect the switch wiring connector, and remove the switch from the vehicle.
35　Refitting is the reverse of removal.

Electric mirror switch

36　Remove the door inner trim panel as described in Chapter 11.
37　Disconnect the switch wiring connector, and remove the switch from the vehicle **(see illustration)**.
38　Refitting is the reverse of removal.

Electric sunroof switch

39　Carefully prise the sunroof switch out of position, and disconnect it from its wiring connector.

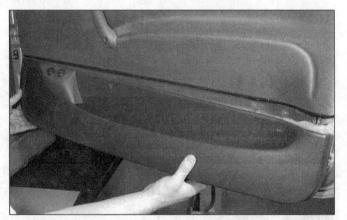

4.30 To remove the driver's door electric window switches, remove the door pocket . . .

40　When refitting, connect the wiring connector, and clip the switch back into position.

Air conditioning system control switch

41　The air conditioning system control switch is an integral part of the heating/ventilation control unit, and cannot be removed. Should the switch become faulty, the complete control unit assembly must be renewed (see Chapter 3).

5　Bulbs (exterior lights) - renewal

General

1　Whenever a bulb is renewed, note the following points:

(a)　Disconnect the battery negative lead before starting work.
(b)　Remember that if the light has just been in use, the bulb may be extremely hot.
(c)　Always check the bulb contacts and holder, ensuring that there is clean metal-to-metal contact between the bulb and its live(s) and earth. Clean off any corrosion or dirt before fitting a new bulb.
(d)　Wherever bayonet-type bulbs are fitted (see Specifications) ensure that the live contact(s) bear firmly against the bulb contact.
(e)　Always ensure that the new bulb is of the correct rating, and that it is completely clean before fitting it; this applies particularly to headlight/foglight bulbs (see below).

Headlight

2　Working in the engine compartment, disconnect the wiring connector from the rear of the headlight, then remove the rubber dust

4.31 ... then release the retaining clips, and slide the relevant switch out of the pocket

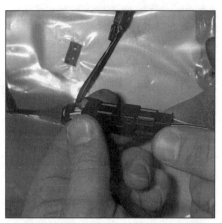

4.37 Disconnect the wiring connector, and remove the electric mirror switch from the door

5.2a To improve access to the right-hand headlight unit, release the fastener ...

5.2b ... and remove the intake duct from the air cleaner housing

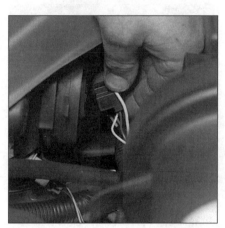

5.2c Disconnect the wiring connector ...

5.2d ... and remove the rubber cover from the rear of the headlight

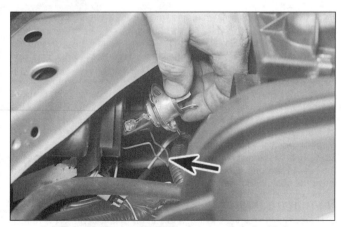

5.4 Release the retaining clip (arrowed) and withdraw the headlight bulb

5.8 Removing the sidelight bulbholder from the headlight unit

cover. Note that if the right-hand bulb is being replaced, it will be necessary to unclip the intake duct from the air cleaner housing to improve access **(see illustrations)**.

3 Unhook and release the ends of the bulb retaining clip, and release it from the rear of the light unit.

4 Withdraw the bulb **(see illustration)**.

5 When handling the new bulb, use a tissue or clean cloth to avoid touching the glass with the fingers; moisture and grease from the skin can cause blackening and rapid failure of this type of bulb. If the glass is accidentally touched, wipe it clean using methylated spirit.

6 Install the new bulb, ensuring that its locating tabs are correctly located in the light cutouts.

7 Refit the dust cover to the rear of the light unit, and reconnect the wiring connector.

Front sidelight

8 Working in the engine compartment, push the bulbholder inwards, then twist it anti-clockwise to release it from the rear of the headlight unit **(see illustration)**. Note that if the right-hand bulb is being replaced, it will be necessary to unclip the intake duct from the air

12

5.12 Front direction turn signal bulb is a bayonet fit in its holder

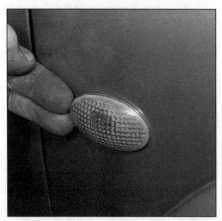

5.14 Lift the rear of the indicator side repeater light to release it from the wing

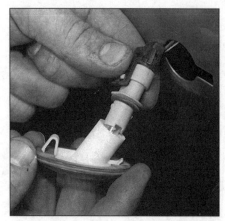

5.15a Release the bulbholder from the rear of the light unit . . .

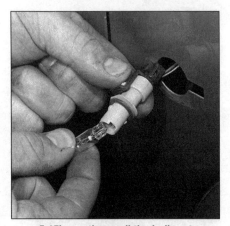

5.15b . . . then pull the bulb out of the holder

5.18 Twist the cover anti-clockwise to release it from the rear of the foglight

5.19a Disconnect the bulb from the cover . . .

cleaner housing to improve access.

9   The bulb is of the capless (push-fit) type, and can be removed by simply pulling it out of the bulbholder.

10   Refitting is the reverse of the removal procedure, ensuring that the bulbholder is securely clipped into position.

Front direction indicator

11   Working in the engine compartment, twist the bulbholder anti-clockwise, and remove it from the rear of the headlight unit. Note that if the right-hand bulb is being replaced, it will be necessary to unclip the intake duct from the air cleaner housing to improve access.

12   The bulb is a bayonet fit in the holder, and can be removed by pressing it and twisting in an anti-clockwise direction **(see illustration)**.

13   Refitting is a reverse of the removal procedure.

Front direction indicator side repeater

14   Carefully prise the rear edge of the indicator side repeater light out from the wing, if necessary using a suitable plastic wedge, taking great care not damage the painted finish of the wing **(see illustration)**.

15   Withdraw the light unit from the wing, and pull the bulbholder out of the light unit. The bulb is of the capless (push-fit) type, and can be removed by simply pulling it out of the bulbholder **(see illustrations)**.

16   Refitting is a reverse of the removal procedure.

Front foglight

17   Raise and support the front of the vehicle, If necessary, to improve access to the rear of the foglight; firmly apply the handbrake, then jack up the front of the vehicle and support it on axle stands.

18   Disconnect the wiring connector from the rear of the foglight unit.

Twist the cover anti-clockwise, and free it from the rear of the foglight **(see illustration)**.

19   Disconnect the bulb wire from the cover terminal, then release the spring clip and withdraw the foglight bulb from the rear of the light unit **(see illustrations)**.

20   When handling the new bulb, use a tissue or clean cloth to avoid touching the glass with the fingers; moisture and grease from the skin can cause blackening and rapid failure of this type of bulb. If the glass is accidentally touched, wipe it clean using methylated spirit.

21   Insert the new bulb, making sure it is correctly located, and secure it in position with the spring clip.

22   Connect the bulb wire to the cover terminal, then refit the cover to the rear of the unit. Connect the wiring connector to the cover, and lower the vehicle to the ground (where applicable).

Rear light cluster

23   From inside the vehicle luggage compartment, depress the retaining catches, and open the trim panel flap to gain access to the rear of the light unit **(see illustration)**.

24   Release the rear light cluster retaining catch(es), and free the bulbholder assembly from the rear of the light unit **(see illustration)**.

25   The relevant bulb can then be renewed; all bulbs have a bayonet fitting **(see illustration)**. Note that the stop/tail light bulb has offset locating pins, to prevent it being installed incorrectly.

26   Refitting is the reverse of the removal sequence, ensuring that the bulbholder is securely clipped into position.

Number plate light - Corsa and Corsavan models

27   Using a small flat-bladed screwdriver, carefully prise the light out

5.19b . . . then release the retaining clip . . .

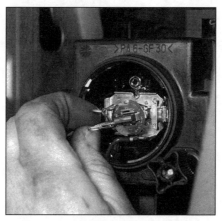

5.19c . . . and withdraw the foglight bulb from the rear of the unit

5.23 Release the retaining clips, and remove the trim cover to gain access to the rear of the rear light cluster (Combo Van shown)

5.24 Depress the retaining catches (arrowed) . . .

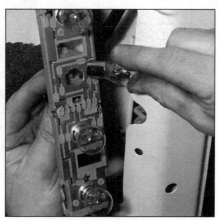

5.25 . . . then withdraw the bulbholder and remove the relevant bulb

5.27 On Corsa and Corsavan models, carefully prise the rear number plate light out from the bumper . . .

5.28a . . . then unclip the lens . . .

5.28b . . . and remove the bulb, which is a bayonet fit in the light unit

5.30 On Combo Van models, release the relevant number plate light from the bumper as described in the text . . .

12

from the rear bumper **(see illustration)**.
28   Unclip the lens from the light unit, and remove the bulb. The bulb is a bayonet fit in the holder, and can be removed by pressing it and twisting anti-clockwise **(see illustrations)**.
29   Refitting is a reverse of the removal procedure.

Number plate light - Combo Van models

30   On the left-hand side, lift up the light unit, and prise out the base of the unit from the bumper. On the right-hand side, push down on the light unit, and prise out the top of the unit from the bumper **(see illustration)**.
31   Withdraw the light unit, then release the retaining clips and open it

5.31a . . . then unclip the cover . . .

5.31b . . . and remove the bulb

6.2a Carefully prise the courtesy light
unit out of position using a
small screwdriver . . .

up. The bulb is a bayonet fit in the holder, and can be removed by pressing it and twisting anti-clockwise **(see illustrations)**.

32   Refitting is a reverse of the removal procedure.

6   Bulbs (interior lights) - renewal

General

1   Refer to Section 5, paragraph 1.

Front courtesy light

2   Using a suitable screwdriver, carefully prise the light unit out of position, and release the bulb from the light unit contacts **(see illustrations)**.

3   Install the new bulb, ensuring that it is securely held in position by the contacts, and clip the light unit back into position.

Rear courtesy light

4   Using a small flat-bladed screwdriver, carefully prise the light unit out from is surround. Disconnect the wiring connector, and remove the light.

5   Unclip the heat shield from the light unit, and release the bulb from its contacts.

6   Install the new bulb, ensuring that it is securely held in position by the contacts, and clip the heat shield back into position.

7   Connect the wiring connector, and clip the light back into position in the surround.

Luggage compartment light

8   Refer to the information given above in paragraphs 2 and 3.

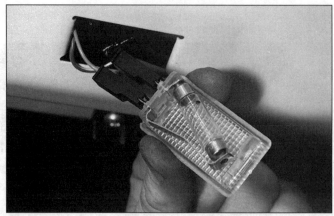

6.2b . . . and release the bulb from its wiring contacts

Instrument panel illumination/warning lights

9   Remove the instrument panel as described in Section 9.

10   Twist the relevant bulbholder anti-clockwise, and withdraw it from the rear of the panel **(see illustration)**.

11   All bulbs are integral with their holders. Be very careful to ensure that the new bulbs are of the correct rating, the same as those removed; this is especially important in the case of the ignition/no-charge warning light.

12   Refit the bulbholder to the rear of the instrument panel, then refit the instrument panel as described in Section 9.

6.10 Removing an instrument panel illumination/warning
light bulb

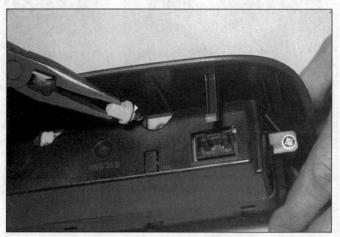

6.14 Removing the clock/multi-function display illumination bulb

6.17 Withdraw the ashtray unit from the facia . . .

6.18 . . . then disconnect the wiring connectors and remove the illumination bulb from the rear of the unit

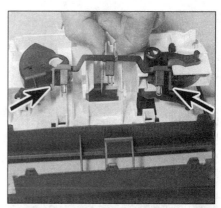

6.21 Release the retaining clips (arrowed), and withdraw the bulbholder from the rear of the heater control panel

Clock/multi-function display illumination bulb

13   Remove the clock/multi-function display unit as described in Section 11.
14   Twist the bulbholder anti-clockwise, and withdraw it from the rear of the clock **(see illustration)**. The bulb is integral with its holder.
15   Refit the bulbholder to the rear of the unit, then refit the unit as described in Section 11.

Cigarette light/ashtray illumination bulb

16   Open the ashtray, and remove the cigarette lighter insert.
17   Undo the retaining screws, and withdraw the ashtray from the centre of the facia, disconnecting the wiring connectors from the rear of the unit as they become accessible **(see illustration)**.
18   Slide the illumination bulbholder out of the panel, and renew the bulb **(see illustration)**. The bulbs is of the capless (push-fit) type; pull the old bulb out of the holder, and press the new one into position.
19   Slide the illumination bulbholder back into position, and refit the ashtray by reversing the removal procedure.

Heater control panel illumination bulb

20   Withdraw the heater control panel as described in Section 9 of Chapter 3, so that access to the rear of the panel can be gained. Note there is no need to remove the panel completely; the control cables can be left attached.
21   Unclip the bulbholder from the rear of the control unit **(see illustration)**. The bulbs are of the capless (push-fit) type; pull the relevant bulb out of the holder, and press the new one into position.
22   Refit the bulbholder, and install the control panel as described in Section 9 of Chapter 3.

Glovebox illumination light bulb

23   Open the glovebox. Using a small flat-bladed screwdriver, carefully prise the light unit out of position, then release the bulb from its contacts.
24   Install the new bulb, ensuring it is securely held in position by the contacts, and clip the light unit back into position.

Switch illumination bulbs

25   All the switches are fitted with illumination bulbs; some are also fitted with a bulb to show when the circuit concerned is operating. These bulbs are an integral part of the switch assembly, and cannot be obtained separately. Bulb replacement will therefore require the renewal of the complete switch assembly.

---

7   Exterior light units - removal and refitting

Note: *Disconnect the battery negative lead before removing any light unit, and reconnect the lead after refitting*

Headlight

1   Unscrew the two screws securing the relevant end of the front bumper to the wheelarch liner. Unclip the access cover from the top of the liner, and unscrew the plastic nut securing the bumper to the vehicle. Discard the nut; a new one should be used on refitting.
2   Open the bonnet, then slacken and remove the bolts securing the radiator grille section of the bumper to the crossmember, and the two bolts securing the headlight to the crossmember **(see illustrations)**.
3   Release the bumper end from the wheelarch outer trim cover,

12

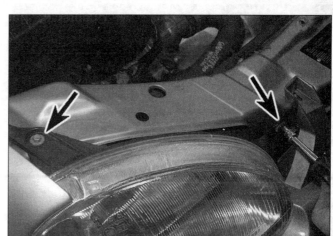

7.2a Undo the bolts securing the radiator grille section of the front bumper to the crossmember . . .

7.2b . . . then undo the two headlight unit retaining bolts (arrowed)

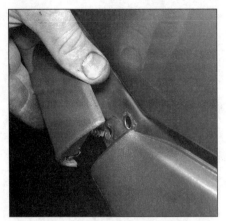

7.3a Release the end of the bumper from the wheelarch outer trim cover . . .

7.3b . . . then push the bumper down and withdraw the headlight unit . . .

7.3c . . . disconnecting the wiring connectors as they become accessible

7.4 Where fitted, remove the headlight beam adjustment motor as described in text

7.11a Disconnect the foglight wiring connector . . .

7.11b . . . then undo the three retaining screws (arrowed) . . .

then hold and push down on the bumper end, and manoeuvre the headlight out of position. Disconnect the wiring connectors from rear of the unit as they become accessible, and remove the headlight unit from the vehicle **(see illustrations)**.

4   On models with a headlight beam adjustment system, if necessary, rotate the adjustment motor clockwise to free the motor from the rear of the headlight unit, and pull the motor squarely away to disconnect its

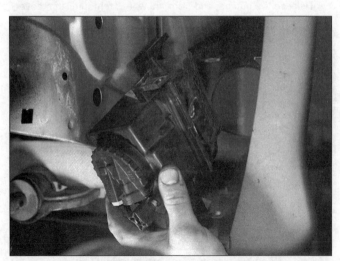

7.11c . . . and remove the light unit from the rear of the bumper

balljoint **(see illustration)**. On refitting, align the motor balljoint with the light unit socket, and clip it into position. Engage the motor assembly with the light, and twist it anti-clockwise to secure it in position.

5   Refitting is a direct reversal of the removal procedure. On completion, check the headlight beam alignment using the information given in Section 8.

Front direction indicator light

6   The front direction indicator lights are integral with the headlight units. Removal and refitting is as described above.

Front direction side repeater light

7   Carefully prise the rear edge of the indicator side repeater light out from the wing, if necessary using a suitable plastic wedge, taking great care not damage the painted finish of the wing.

8   Withdraw the light unit from the wing, and disconnect its wiring connector. Tie a piece of string to the wiring, to prevent it falling back into the wing.

9   On refitting, connect the wiring connector, and clip the light unit back into position.

Front foglight

10   Release the relevant end of the front bumper from the vehicle, as described above in paragraphs 1 to 3, ignoring the references to the headlight. If necessary, jack up the front of the vehicle and support it on axle stands to improve access to the foglight.

11   Disconnect the wiring connector, then undo the three foglight retaining screws and remove the light unit from the bumper **(see illustrations)**.

7.13 Foglight aim is adjusted using the adjuster on the rear of the unit

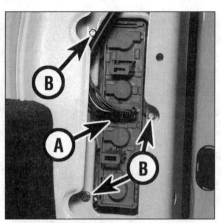

7.16 Rear light unit wiring connector (A) and retaining bolts (B) (Combo Van shown)

7.18 Removing the rear number plate light unit - Corsa and Corsavan models

7.21 Removing a rear number plate light unit - Combo Van models

8.2 Adjusting the headlight horizontal beam using a suitable screwdriver (vertical beam adjuster arrowed)

12 Refit the light unit to the bumper, and securely tighten its retaining screws.

13 Secure the front bumper in position, and adjust the foglight aim using the adjuster on the rear of the light unit **(see illustration)**.

Rear light cluster

14 From inside the luggage compartment, depress the retaining catches and open up the trim panel flap to gain access to the rear of the light unit.

15 Disconnect the wiring connector from the rear of the bulbholder.

16 Slacken and remove the rear light unit retaining bolts, and withdraw the light unit from the rear of the vehicle **(see illustration)**.

17 Refitting is a reverse of the removal procedure, tightening the retaining bolts securely.

Number plate light - Corsa and Corsavan models

18 Using a small flat-bladed screwdriver, carefully prise the light out from the rear bumper, and disconnect it from the wiring connectors **(see illustration)**.

19 When refitting, connect the wiring connector, and clip the light back into the bumper.

Number plate light - Combo Van models

20 On the left-hand side, lift up the light unit, and prise out the base of the unit from the bumper. On the right-hand side, push the light unit

down, and prise out the top of the unit from the bumper.

21 Withdraw the light unit, and disconnect the wiring connectors **(see illustration)**.

22 When refitting, connect the wiring connectors, and clip the light back into the bumper.

8 Headlight beam alignment - general information

1 Accurate adjustment of the headlight beam is only possible using optical beam-setting equipment, and this work should therefore be carried out by a Vauxhall/Opel dealer or suitably-equipped workshop.

2 For reference, the headlights can be adjusted using the adjuster assemblies fitted to the top and bottom of each light unit. The top adjuster, accessed through a hole in the crossmember, alters the horizontal position of the beam. The bottom adjuster alters the vertical aim of the beam **(see illustration)**.

3 Some models have an electrically-operated headlight beam adjustment system, controlled via a switch in the facia. The recommended settings are as follows.

Corsa and Corsavan (with rear seats)

0 Front seat(s) occupied
1 All seats occupied
2 All seats occupied, and load in luggage compartment
3 Driver's seat occupied and load in the luggage compartment

12

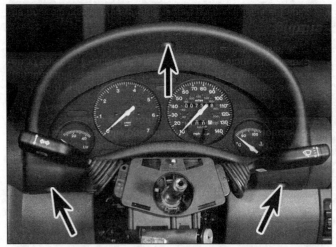

9.3a Undo the three instrument panel shroud retaining screws (shown with steering wheel removed for clarity) . . .

9.3b . . . and manoeuvre the shroud out of position

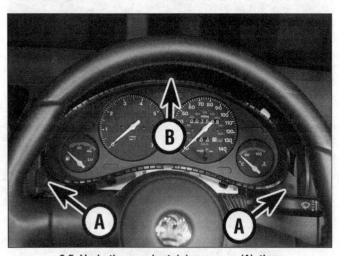

9.5 Undo the panel retaining screws (A), then release the clip (B) . . .

9.6 . . . and withdraw the instrument panel from the facia

Combo Van and Corsavan (without rear seats)

0   *Seat(s) occupied*
1   *Seats occupied and load compartment approximately half-loaded*
2   *Seats occupied and luggage compartment fully loaded*
3   *Driver's seat only occupied and luggage compartment fully loaded*

Note: *When adjusting the headlight aim, ensure that the switch is set to position "0".*

---

9   Instrument panel - removal and refitting

Removal

1   Disconnect the battery negative terminal.
2   With the steering wheel in the straight-ahead position, turn the wheel 90° to the left, then prise off the trim cap and remove the left upper shroud screw. Turn the wheel 180° to the right, and remove the right upper screw. Remove the rubber seal from the ignition switch/lock, then undo the lower retaining screws and remove the steering column shrouds.
3   Undo the three retaining screws, and remove the instrument panel shroud from the facia **(see illustrations)**. Recover the two shroud retaining clips.
4   Unscrew the speedometer cable lower end from the transmission

unit. If necessary, remove the battery, then jack up the front of the vehicle and support it on axle stands to improve access to the cable.
5   Unscrew the two retaining screws from the base of the instrument panel **(see illustration)**.
6   Using a small flat-bladed screwdriver, depress the panel upper retaining clip, and withdraw the panel from the facia. The wiring connector disconnects automatically as the panel is removed **(see illustration)**.
7   Depress the retaining clip, disconnect the speedometer cable, and remove the instrument panel from the vehicle.

Refitting

8   Connect the speedometer cable to the rear of the panel, making sure it is securely retained by the clip, and connect the panel wiring connectors.
9   Clip the panel back into position, aligning it with its wiring connector, and secure it in position with the two retaining screws.
10   Refit the instrument panel shroud, and securely tighten its retaining screws.
11   Install the upper and lower steering column shrouds, and securely tighten all the retaining screws. Fit the rubber seal to the ignition switch/lock and the trim caps to the upper screws.
12   Connect the lower end of the speedometer cable to the transmission, and tighten it securely.
13   Reconnect the battery, and check the operation of the panel warning lights to ensure that they are functioning correctly.

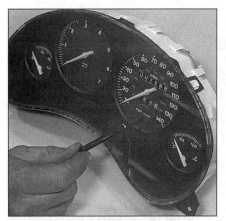

10.2a Pull out the trip odometer reset pin . . .

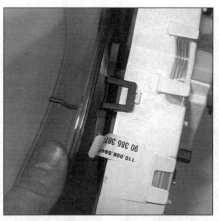

10.2b . . . then release the retaining clips and remove the lens from the front of the instrument panel

10.3 Carefully detach the printed circuit from the top of the speedometer housing

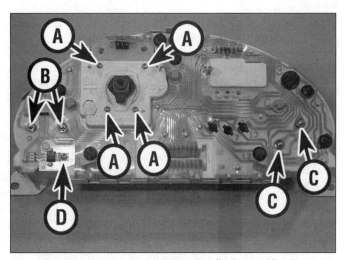

10.4 Instrument panel components (high-specification panel with tachometer)

A   Speedometer retaining screws
B   Temperature gauge nuts
C   Fuel gauge nuts
D   Voltage stabiliser

10 Instrument panel components - removal and refitting

General

1   Remove the instrument panel as described in Section 9, then proceed as described under the relevant sub-heading.

Speedometer

2   Remove the reset pin for the trip odometer, then carefully release the retaining clips and remove the lens from the front of the instrument panel **(see illustrations)**.
3   Carefully detach the printed circuit from the speedometer housing **(see illustration)**.
4   Undo the retaining screws, and remove the speedometer from the rear of the instrument panel **(see illustration)**.
5   Refitting is a reverse of the removal procedure. Do not overtighten the instrument panel fasteners, as the plastic is easily cracked.

Tachometer

6   Remove the lens from the panel as described in paragraph 2.
7   Undo the retaining screws, and lift the tachometer out from the

10.15 Undo the retaining screw (arrowed) and disconnect the voltage stabiliser from the rear of the instrument panel

panel assembly.
8   When refitting, ensure that the tachometer pins are correctly aligned with the panel housing, then refit the retaining screws. Do not overtighten the screws, as the plastic is easily cracked. Clip the lens back onto the panel, and refit the trip odometer reset pin.

Temperature gauge

9   Remove the lens from the panel as described in paragraph 2.
10   Undo the retaining nuts securing the wiring to the temperature gauge terminals, and lift the gauge out from the panel (see illustration 10.4).
11   Refitting is the reverse of removal. Do not overtighten the retaining nuts, as the plastic is easily cracked.

Fuel gauge

12   Remove the lens from the panel as described in paragraph 2.
13   Undo the retaining nuts securing the wiring to the fuel gauge terminals, and lift the gauge out from the panel (see illustration 10.4).
14   Refitting is the reverse of removal. Do not overtighten the retaining nuts, as the plastic is easily cracked.

Voltage stabiliser

15   Undo the retaining screw, then carefully pull the stabiliser from the instrument panel wiring pins **(see illustration)**.
16   When refitting, ease the stabiliser onto the pins, and secure it in position with the retaining screw.

12

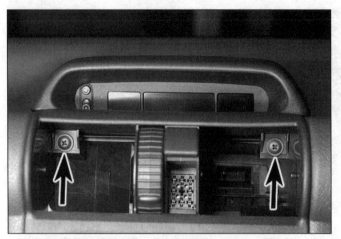

11.4a Undo the two retaining screws (arrowed) . . .

11.4b . . . then lift the multi-function display away from the facia . . .

Printed circuit

17 Remove all the instruments and the voltage stabiliser as described above.

18 Remove all the bulbholders from the rear of the case by twisting them in an anti-clockwise direction. Release the printed circuit from its retaining pins, and remove it from the rear of the case.

19 Refitting is a reversal of the removal procedure, ensuring that the printed circuit is correctly located on all the necessary retaining pins.

11 Clock/multi-function display components - removal and refitting

1 The clock/multi-function display unit is fitted to the centre of the facia. The display panel shows the time; on higher-specification models, it also shows the outside air temperature and/or the radio station.

Clock/multi-function display unit

Removal

2 Disconnect the battery negative terminal

3 Remove both the centre heater/ventilation vents from the facia, as described in Chapter 3.

4 Undo the two retaining screws located in the vent apertures, then withdraw the clock/multi-function display from the facia **(see illustrations)**.

5 Disconnect the wiring connector, and remove the unit from the vehicle **(see illustration)**.

Refitting

6 Reconnect the wiring connector, then manoeuvre the unit back into position.

7 Securely tighten the screws, and install the vents as described in Chapter 3.

8 Reconnect the battery negative terminal, then reset the clock and enter the radio security code.

Air temperature sensor

Removal

9 The multi-function unit air temperature sensor is mounted in the front of the vehicle, directly behind the centre of the bumper. The sensor is accessible through the bumper grille.

10 Depress the retaining clips, then free the sensor from the rear of its bracket. Disconnect the sensor from its wiring connector, and remove it from the vehicle.

Refitting

11 Connect the sensor to the wiring connector, and clip it back into position in the bumper.

12 "Lights-on" warning system - general information

1 Most vehicles covered in this manual are equipped with a "lights-on" warning system. The purpose of the system is to warn the driver that the lights have been left on. Once the ignition switch has been turned off; the buzzer will sound when a door is opened. The system consists of a buzzer unit which is linked to the driver's door courtesy light switch.

2 To gain access to the buzzer unit, unclip the fusebox access panel from the facia, then undo the two retaining screws and lower the fusebox out from the facia. The buzzer is the third unit from the left in the lower row of relays. The unit is a push fit in the fusebox.

3 Refer to Section 4 for information on courtesy light switch removal.

13 Cigarette lighter - removal and refitting

Removal

1 Open up the ashtray, and remove the cigarette lighter insert.

2 Undo the retaining screws, and withdraw the ashtray from the centre of the facia. Disconnect the wiring connectors from the rear of the unit as they become accessible.

3 Release the retaining tangs and push out the metal insert, then remove the plastic outer section of the lighter.

Refitting

4 Refitting is a reversal of the removal procedure.

14 Horn - removal and refitting

Removal

1 Remove the front bumper as described in Chapter 11.

2 Undo the retaining bolt and remove the horn, disconnecting its wiring connectors as they become accessible **(see illustration)**.

Refitting

3 Refitting is the reverse of removal.

15 Speedometer drive cable - removal and refitting

Removal

1 Remove the instrument panel as described in Section 9. Tie a

11.5 ... and disconnect its wiring connector

14.2 Horn unit is retained by a single bolt (arrowed)

16.3 Lift the nut cover, then undo the retaining nut and lift off the wiper arm

17.3 Removing the right-hand windscreen cowl panel

17.5 Unscrew the large plastic nut from each wiper spindle . . .

piece string to the upper end of the cable; this can then be used to draw the cable back into position.

2   Free the speedometer cable from any relevant retaining clips and ties, noting its correct routing.

3   Release the cable grommet from the engine compartment bulkhead, and withdraw the cable forwards and out through the bulkhead. Once the cable is free, untie the string and leave it in position in the vehicle; the string can then be used to draw the new cable back into position.

Refitting

4   Tie the string to the end of the cable, then use the string to draw the speedometer cable through from the engine compartment and into position. Once the cable is through, untie the string.

5   Ensure that the cable is correctly routed, and retained by all the relevant clips and ties, then seat the outer cable grommet in the engine compartment bulkhead.

6   Refit the instrument panel as described in Section 9.

16 Wiper arm - removal and refitting

Removal

1   Operate the wiper motor, then switch it off so that the wiper arm returns to the at-rest (parked) position.

2   Stick a piece of masking tape along the edge of the wiper blade, to use as an alignment aid on refitting.

3   Lift up the wiper arm spindle nut cover, then slacken and remove

the spindle nut. Lift the blade off the glass, and pull the wiper arm off its spindle **(see illustration)**. If necessary, the arm can be levered off the spindle using a suitable flat-bladed screwdriver.

Note: If both windscreen wiper arms are to be removed at the same time, mark them for identification. The arms are not interchangeable; the passenger-side wiper arm is longer than the driver's-side arm, and its shaft is also cranked slightly.

Refitting

4   Ensure that the wiper arm and spindle splines are clean and dry, then refit the arm to the spindle, aligning the wiper blade with the tape fitted on removal. Refit the spindle nut, tightening it securely, and clip the nut cover back in position.

17 Windscreen wiper motor and linkage - removal and refitting

Removal

1   Disconnect the battery negative terminal.

2   Remove the wiper arms as described in the previous Section.

3   Undo the retaining screws, and remove both halves of the windscreen cowl panel from the vehicle **(see illustration)**.

4   Peel the bonnet seal off the engine compartment bulkhead, and remove it from the vehicle.

5   Unscrew the large plastic nut from each wiper spindle **(see illustration)**.

12

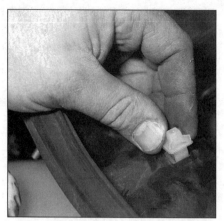

17.6a . . . then prise out the two clips . . .

17.6b . . . and remove the water deflector shield from the vehicle

17.7a Disconnect the wiring connector . . .

17.7b . . . then undo the three retaining bolts (arrowed) . . .

17.7c . . . and remove the wiper motor and linkage assembly from the vehicle (right-hand drive model shown)

6   Prise out the two clips from the centre of the water deflector shield. Release the shield from the engine compartment bulkhead and wiper spindles, and remove it from the vehicle **(see illustrations)**.

7   Disconnect the wiring connector from the wiper motor. Undo the three retaining bolts, and remove the wiper motor and linkage assembly out from the vehicle **(see illustrations)**.

8   If necessary, mark the relative positions of the motor shaft and linkage arm, then unscrew the retaining nut from the motor spindle. Free the wiper linkage from the spindle, then remove the three motor retaining bolts, and separate the motor and linkage **(see illustration)**. **Note:** *It is not necessary to remove the linkage assembly from the vehicle to remove the motor.*

Refitting

9   Where necessary, assemble the motor and linkage, and securely tighten the motor retaining bolts. Locate the linkage arm on the motor spindle, aligning the marks made prior to removal, and securely tighten its retaining nut.

10   Manoeuvre the motor assembly back into position in the vehicle. Refit the three retaining bolts, and tighten them to the specified torque setting.

11   Reconnect the wiper motor wiring connector.

12   Refit the water deflector, making sure it is correctly located on the bulkhead and wiper spindles, and secure it in position with the two clips and wiper spindle nuts.

13   Install both halves of the windscreen cowl, and securely tighten the retaining screws.

14   Refit the bonnet seal to the engine compartment bulkhead.

15   Install both the wiper arms as described in Section 16, and reconnect the battery negative terminal.

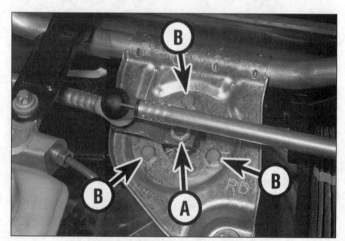

17.8 Windscreen wiper motor spindle nut (A) and retaining bolts (B)

18 Tailgate wiper motor - removal and refitting

Removal

1   Remove the wiper arm as described in Section 16.

2   Remove the plastic cover from the wiper spindle, then unscrew the retaining nut, and lift the washer and outer mounting rubber off the spindle **(see illustrations)**.

18.2a Remove the plastic cover from the tailgate wiper motor spindle . . .

18.2b . . . then undo the retaining nut . . .

18.2c . . . and lift off the washer and outer mounting rubber (arrowed)

18.3 Undo the retaining screws, and remove the parcel shelf lifter cords from the tailgate

18.6a Undo the wiper motor mounting bolts, noting the correct fitted positions of the earth leads (arrowed)

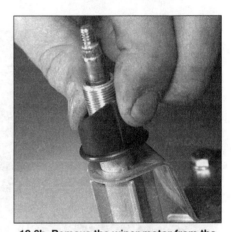

18.6b Remove the wiper motor from the tailgate, and slide off the inner mounting rubber

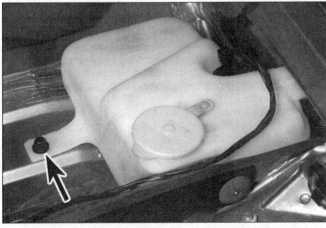

19.2 Undo the retaining nut (arrowed) . . .

Recover the collars from either side of each motor mounting rubber, and slide the inner mounting rubber off the motor spindle **(see illustrations)**.
7   Examine the motor mounting rubbers for signs of damage or deterioration, and renew as necessary.

Refitting

8   Slide the inner mounting rubber onto the motor spindle, and ensure that the rubbers are correctly fitted to the motor mountings.
9   Position a collar on each side of the motor mounting rubbers, and refit the motor to the tailgate. Fit the mounting bolts, not forgetting to fit the earth leads to the bolts, and tighten them securely.
10   Reconnect the wiper motor wiring connector.
11   Refit the trim panel to the tailgate, ensuring that it is securely retained by all of its clips. Install the lifter cords.
12   Slide the outer mounting rubber and washer onto the wiper spindle, then fit the retaining nut. Securely tighten the retaining nut, and refit the plastic cover.
13   Refit the wiper arm as described in Section 16, and reconnect the battery.

19 Windscreen/tailgate washer system components - removal and refitting

Washer system reservoir

1   Remove both the windscreen cowl panels as described in paragraphs 1 to 4 of Section 17.
2   Unscrew the fluid reservoir retaining nut **(see illustration)**, then release the reservoir from its retaining bracket.

3   Open the tailgate, and detach the parcel shelf cords. Undo the retaining screws, and remove the lifter hooks from the tailgate **(see illustration)**.
4   Carefully prise out the retaining clips, and remove the inner trim panel from the tailgate.
5   Disconnect the wiper motor wiring connector, and release the wiring from any relevant retaining clips.
6   Slacken and remove the wiper motor mounting bolts, noting the correct fitted location of the earth leads, and remove the wiper motor.

12

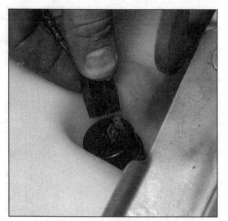

19.3a ... disconnect the washer pump wiring connector ...

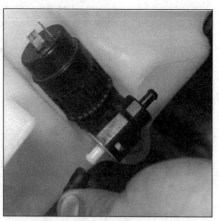

19.3b ... then lift out the washer reservoir, and disconnect hoses from the pump

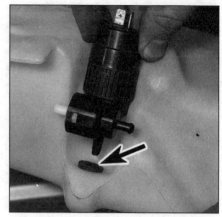

19.6 Ease the pump out of the reservoir, and recover the sealing grommet (arrowed)

21.4 Removing the radio/cassette player using the special DIN tools

3   Disconnect the wiring connector from the washer pump, then disconnect the hose(s) from the base of the pump and remove the reservoir from the vehicle **(see illustrations)**. Wash off any spilt fluid with cold water.
4   Refitting is the reverse of removal, ensuring that the washer hose(s) are securely connected.

Washer pump

5   Remove the washer reservoir as described above.
6   Tip out the contents of the reservoir, then carefully ease the pump out from the reservoir and recover its sealing grommet **(see illustration)**.
7   Refitting is the reverse of removal, using a new sealing grommet if the original one shows signs of damage or deterioration.

Windscreen washer jets

8   Carefully prise the nozzle from the bonnet, taking great care not to damage the paintwork.
9   Disconnect the nozzle from its fluid hose, and remove it from the vehicle. Tie a piece of string to the hose, to prevent it falling back into the bonnet.
10 On refitting, securely connect the nozzle to the hose, and clip it into position in the bonnet. Check the operation of the jet. If necessary, adjust the nozzle using a pin, aiming the spray to a point slightly above the centre of the swept area.

Tailgate washer jet

11 Carefully prise the washer jet out of the top of the tailgate/spoiler

(as applicable), and disconnect it from its supply pipe. Whilst the jet is removed, tie a piece of string to the supply pipe, to ensure that it does not fall back into the tailgate.
12 When refitting, ensure that the jet is clipped securely in position. Check the operation of the jet. If necessary, adjust the nozzle using a pin, aiming the spray to a point slightly above the centre of the swept area.

20 Headlight washer system components - removal and refitting

Washer system reservoir

1   Firmly apply the handbrake, then jack up the front of the vehicle and support it on axle stands. Remove the left-hand front roadwheel, making alignment marks between the wheel and hub.
2   Undo the retaining nuts and screws, then release the retaining fasteners and remove the left-hand wheelarch liner (see Chapter 11, Section 22). Discard the nuts and fasteners; new ones should be used on refitting.
3   Remove the front bumper as described in Chapter 11.
4   Slacken and remove the retaining bolts, then lower the reservoir out from underneath the wing to gain access to the washer pump.
5   Slacken the retaining clip, and disconnect the hose from the washer pump. Disconnect the pump wiring connector, and remove the reservoir from the vehicle.
6   Refitting is the reverse of removal.

Washer pump

7   Remove the washer reservoir as described above.
8   Tip out the contents of the reservoir, then carefully ease the pump out from the reservoir and recover its sealing grommet.
9   Refitting is the reverse of removal. Use a new sealing grommet if the original one shows signs of damage or deterioration.

Washer nozzles

10 Remove the front bumper as described in Chapter 11.
11 Undo the two retaining bolts, and remove the nozzle from the bumper.
12 On refitting, securely tighten the retaining bolts and refit the bumper as described in Chapter 11.

21 Radio/cassette player - removal and refitting

Note: *The following removal and refitting procedure is for the range of radio/cassette units which Vauxhall/Opel fit as standard equipment.*

22.2a Unclip the small (treble) loudspeaker from the door panel . . .

22.2b . . . and disconnect its wiring connector

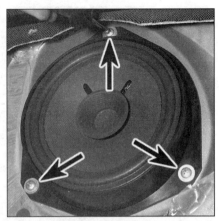

22.5a Undo the three retaining screws (arrowed) . . .

Removal and refitting procedures of non-standard units may differ slightly. Before starting work, refer to "Radio/cassette unit anti-theft system - precaution" at the beginning of this manual.

Removal

1   All the radio/cassette players fitted by Vauxhall/Opel have DIN standard fixings. Two special tools, obtainable from most car accessory shops, are required for removal. Alternatively, suitable tools can be fabricated from 3 mm diameter wire, such as welding rod.
2   Disconnect the battery negative lead.
3   Unscrew the four grub screws from the corners of the radio/cassette player, using a suitable Allen key.
4   Insert the tools into the holes exposed by removal of the grub screws, and push them until they snap into place. The radio/cassette player can then be slid out of the facia **(see illustration)**.

Refitting

5   To refit the radio/cassette player, simply push the unit into the facia until the retaining lugs snap into place, then refit the grub screws. On completion, reconnect the battery and enter the radio security code, where applicable.

22.5b . . . then withdraw the large (bass) loudspeaker from the door, and disconnect its wiring connector

22   Speakers - removal and refitting

Front small (treble) speaker

1   Lift the front door inner handle, and carefully prise the handle trim cover out from the door trim panel.
2   Unclip the speaker from the handle, disconnecting its wiring connectors as they become accessible **(see illustrations)**.
3   Refitting is the reverse of removal.

Front large (bass) speaker

4   Undo the retaining screws, and free the door pocket from the inner trim panel, disconnecting the window switch wiring connector(s) (where applicable) as they become accessible.
5   Undo the retaining screws, then free the speaker from the door. Disconnect the wiring connectors and remove the speaker **(see illustrations)**.
6   Refitting is the reverse of removal.

Rear speaker

7   Remove the rear parcel shelf. If the left speaker is to be removed, remove the interior light unit from the trim panel as described in Section 6.
8   Remove the rear shock absorber access panel from the trim panel.
9   Prise out the retaining clips from the rear of the panel, and the

22.9a Release the luggage compartment trim panel from the vehicle . . .

12

circular plug/seat stop buffer (as applicable) from the front of the panel. Slacken and remove all the panel retaining screws, and release the panel from the vehicle body. Disconnect the speaker wiring connector, and turn the panel around to gain access to the speaker **(see illustrations)**. Note that it is not necessary to detach the seat belt unless the

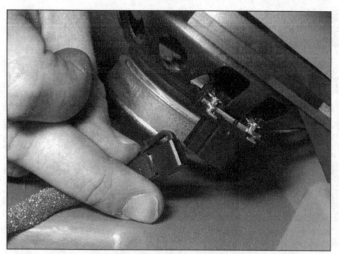

22.9b . . . then turn it around and disconnect the wiring connector from the rear loudspeaker

22.10 Undo the three retaining screws, and remove the speaker from the trim panel

trim panel is to be removed.

10   Undo the three retaining screws, and remove the speaker from the trim panel **(see illustration)**.

11   Refitting is a reverse of the removal procedure. Make sure that the trim panel is securely retained by all the relevant clips and screws. If the left trim panel is being installed, do not forget to feed the interior light wiring through the trim panel aperture before fastening the panel in position.

23   Radio aerial - removal and refitting

Corsa and Corsavan

Removal

1   Open the tailgate, then prise out the trim clips and release the rear of the headlining from the roof. Carefully peel the headlining back until access is gained to the aerial retaining nut and wiring connectors.

2   Disconnect both wiring connectors, then undo the retaining nut and remove the aerial from the roof.

Refitting

3   Locate the aerial in roof hole and refit its retaining nut, tightening it securely. Reconnect the wiring connectors, then clip the headlining back into position

Combo Van

Removal

4   Chock the rear wheels, firmly apply the handbrake, then jack up the front of the vehicle and support it on axle stands. Remove the left-hand front roadwheel, making alignment marks between the wheel and hub.

5   Undo the retaining nuts and screws, then release the retaining fasteners and remove the left-hand wheelarch liner (refer to Chapter 11, Section 22). Discard the nuts and fasteners; new ones should be used when refitting.

6   From inside the vehicle, release the retaining clips and remove the trim panel from the left-hand front footwell.

7   Reach up behind the facia, and disconnect the aerial lead from the rear of the radio/cassette player. Work back along the aerial lead, releasing it from the all the relevant retaining clips and ties, noting how the lead is routed. If necessary, to improve access, remove the storage compartment from underneath the facia; the compartment is retained by a single screw and retaining clip.

8   From underneath the wing, release the grommet and withdraw the aerial lead. Unscrew the aerial nut, remove the washer and rubber,

then release the aerial from its lower retaining clip. Remove the aerial and lead from underneath the wing.

Refitting

9   Insert the aerial from underneath the wing, and clip it into position. Fit the rubber and washer onto the aerial, and securely tighten the retaining nut.

10   Pass the aerial lead through into the vehicle, and seat the rubber grommet in the vehicle body.

11   From inside the vehicle, ensure that the lead is correctly routed, and secure it in position with all the necessary clips and ties. Reconnect the lead to the rear of the radio/cassette player. Where necessary, refit the storage compartment.

12   Refit the footwell trim panel, making sure that it is securely retained by its clips.

13   Install the wheelarch liner, securing it in position with new nuts and clips.

14   Refit the roadwheel, aligning the marks made on removal, then lower the vehicle to the ground and tighten the roadwheel bolts to the specified torque.

24   Anti-theft alarm system - general information

Note: *This information is applicable only to the anti-theft alarm system fitted by Vauxhall/Opel as standard equipment.*

1   Some models in the range are fitted with an anti-theft alarm system as standard equipment. The alarm is automatically armed and disarmed when the deadlocks are locked and unlocked using the driver's door lock. The alarm has switches on all the doors (including the tailgate), the bonnet, the radio/cassette player and the ignition and starter circuits. If the tailgate, bonnet or any of the doors are opened whilst the alarm is set, the alarm horn will sound and the hazard warning lights will flash. The alarm also has an immobiliser function which makes the ignition and starter circuits inoperable whilst the alarm is triggered.

2   The alarm system performs a self-test every time it is switched on; this test takes approximately 10 seconds. During the self-test, the LED (light emitting diode) in the hazard warning light switch will come on. If the LED flashes, then either the tailgate, bonnet or one of the doors is open, or there is a fault in the circuit. After the initial 10-second period, the LED will flash to indicate that the alarm is switched on. On unlocking the driver's door lock, the LED will illuminate for approximately 1 second, then go out, indicating that the alarm has been switched off.

3   With the alarm set, if the tailgate is unlocked, the tailgate switch sensing will automatically be switched off, but the door and bonnet switches will still be active. Once the tailgate is shut and locked again,

the tailgate switch sensing will be switched back on after approximately 10 seconds.

4   Should the alarm system develop a fault, the vehicle should be taken to a Vauxhall/Opel dealer for examination.

25 Heated front seat components - removal and refitting

Heater mats

1   On models with heated front seats, a heater mat is fitted to the both the seat back and seat cushion. Renewal of either heater mat involves peeling back the upholstery, removing the old mat, sticking the new mat in position and then refitting the upholstery. Note that upholstery removal and refitting requires considerable skill and experience if it is to be carried out successfully, and is therefore best entrusted to your Vauxhall/Opel dealer. In practice, it will be very difficult for the home mechanic to carry out the job without ruining the upholstery.

Heated seat switches

2   Refer to Section 4.

26 Air bag system - general information and precautions

1   A driver's side air bag is fitted to some models in the Corsa range. These models have the word AIRBAG stamped on the air bag unit, which is fitted to the centre of the steering wheel, and a warning label is stuck onto the rear edge of the driver's door. The air bag system comprises of the air bag unit (complete with gas generator) which is fitted to the steering wheel, an impact sensor, the control unit, and a warning light in the instrument panel.

2   The air bag system is triggered in the event of a frontal impact at a speed of approximately 19 mph (30 kmh) or more; depending on the point of impact. The air bag is inflated within milliseconds, and forms a safety cushion between the driver's upper body and the wheel, and therefore greatly reduces the risk of injury. The air bag then deflates almost immediately.

3   Every time the ignition is switched on, the air bag control unit performs a self-test. The self-test takes approximately 4 seconds; during this time, the air bag warning light in the instrument panel will come on. After the self-test has been completed, the warning light should go out. If the warning light fails to come on, remains illuminated after the initial 4-second period, or comes on at any time when the vehicle is being driven, there is a fault in the air bag system, and the vehicle be taken to a Vauxhall/Opel dealer for examination at the earliest opportunity.

Precautions

4   To ensure that the air bag will operate correctly should it ever be needed, and to avoid the risk of personal injury from it being accidentally triggered, the following precautions must be observed:

(a)   *Before carrying out any operations on the air bag system, disconnect the battery negative terminal, and wait at least 1 minute to ensure that the system capacitor has been discharged.*

(b)   *Note that the air bag must not be subjected to temperatures in excess of 90°C (194°F). When the air bag is removed, ensure that it is stored the correct way up to prevent possible inflation.*

(c)   *Do not allow any solvents or cleaning agents to contact the air bag assembly. The unit must be cleaned using only a damp cloth.*

(d)   *The air bag and control unit are both sensitive to impact. If either is dropped from a height of more than 50 cm (20 in), they must be renewed.*

(e)   *Disconnect the air bag control unit wiring plug prior to using arc-welding equipment on the vehicle.*

27 Air bag system components - removal and refitting

Note: *Refer to the precautions given in the previous Section before carrying out the following operations.*

1   Disconnect the battery negative terminal, then wait at least 1 minute. Proceed as described under the relevant heading.

Air bag

2   With the steering wheel in the straight-ahead position, turn the wheel 90° to the left, then prise off the trim cap and remove the left upper shroud screw. Turn the wheel 180° to the right, and remove the right upper screw. Remove the rubber seal from the ignition switch/lock, then undo the lower retaining screws and remove the steering column shrouds.

3   With the steering wheel positioned in the straight-ahead position, turn the wheel 90° to the right to gain access to the left-hand air bag retaining bolt. Unscrew the bolt from the rear of the steering wheel, then turn the wheel 180° to the left to gain access to the right-hand air bag retaining bolt. Unscrew the right-hand retaining bolt, then return the steering wheel to the straight-ahead position.

4   Carefully lift the air bag assembly away from the steering wheel, and disconnect the wiring connector from the rear of the unit. Note that the air bag must not be knocked or dropped, and should be stored the correct way up, with its padded surface uppermost.

5   Refitting is a reversal of the removal procedure. Tighten the air bag retaining screws to the specified torque setting.

Air bag control unit

6   Remove the centre console as described in Chapter 11.

7   Disconnect the control unit wiring connector, then undo the retaining screws and remove the control unit from the vehicle.

8   Refitting is the reverse of removal. If a new control unit is being installed, the vehicle must be taken to a Vauxhall/Opel dealer for the control unit to be reprogrammed at the earliest possible opportunity. **Note:** *The air bag system will not be operational until the new control unit is reprogrammed; this will be indicated by the warning light in the instrument panel being illuminated.*

Air bag wiring contact unit

9   The wiring contact unit is fitted to the underside of the steering wheel, and provides the electrical supply to both the air bag and horn buttons. The unit is removed and refitted with the steering wheel. See Chapter 10, Section 17.

28 Wiring diagrams - explanatory notes

1   The wiring diagrams are of the current flow type, each circuit being shown in the simplest possible form. Note that since the diagrams were originally produced in Germany (to the DIN standard), all wire colours and abbreviations used on the diagrams are in German; refer to the information given in the diagram keys for clarification.

2   The bottom line of the diagram represents the earth (or negative) connection; the numbers below this line are track numbers, enabling circuits and components to be located using the key.

3   The lines at the top of the diagram represent live feed (or positive) connection points. The line marked "30" is live at all times, that marked "15" is live only when the ignition is switched on.

4   A number in a square box at the end of a wire is the track number (see paragraph 2) at which that particular wire is continued. At the point indicated, another framed number will appear, referring back to the previous circuit.

Key to wiring diagrams

Not all items fitted to all models

No	Description	Track
E1	Left sidelight	504
E2	Left tail light	502
E3	Number plate light	513 to 517
E4	Right sidelight	509
E5	Right tail light	511
E7	Left main beam	527
E8	Right main beam	529
E9	Left dipped beam	528
E10	Right dipped beam	530
E11	Instrument lights	452, 454
E12	Selector lever light	296, 297
E13	Boot light	587
E14	Passenger compartment light	589
E15	Glovebox light	854
E16	Cigarette lighter light	853
E17	Left reversing light	598
E18	Right reversing light	599
E19	Heated rear window (Corsa and Corsavan)	749
E20	Left foglight	556
E21	Right foglight	557
E24	Left rear foglight	551
E25	Left front seat heating mat	856
E27	Rear passenger compartment reading light	592
E30	Right front seat heating mat	860
E34	Heating adjustment light	760
E39	Right rear foglight	552
E60	Left-hand heated rear window (Combo Van)	745
E63	Multi-function unit	429
E64	Right-hand heated rear window (Combo Van)	747
F1 onwards	Fuses	Various
F35	Voltage stabiliser	
G1	Battery	101
G2	Alternator (petrol engines)	118
G6	Alternator (Diesel engines)	202 to 205
H1	Radio	401 to 417
H2	Horn	661
H3	Direction indicator warning light	455
H4	Oil pressure warning light	461
H5	Brake fluid warning light	463
H6	Hazard flasher warning light	574
H7	Charging indicator light	466
H8	Main beam warning light	457
H9	Left stop-light	563
H10	Right stop-light	564
H11	Left front direction indicator	575
H12	Left rear direction indicator	576
H13	Right front direction indicator	583
H14	Right rear direction indicator	584
H15	Fuel warning light	451
H16	Preheating time warning light (Diesel)	439
H19	"Lights on" warning buzzer	595, 596
H22	Rear foglight warning light	444
H23	Air bag warning light	435
H25	Exterior mirror heating warning light	842
H26	ABS warning light	437
H30	Engine warning light	458
H33	Left direction indicator repeater	579
H34	Right direction indicator repeater	581
H37	Left front speaker	405, 406
H38	Right front speaker	409, 410
H39	Left rear speaker	405, 406
H40	Right rear speaker	409, 410
H42	Auto transmission "power" programme warning light	438
H47	Anti-theft alarm horn	652

No	Description	Track
H52	Left front treble speaker	406
H53	Right front treble speaker	409
K1	Heated rear window relay	749, 750
K3	Anti-theft alarm immobiliser relay	113, 114
K5	Foglight relay	557, 558
K6	Air conditioning relay	763, 764
K7	Air conditioning cooling fan relay	772, 773
K8	Windscreen wiper relay	703 to 706
K10	Flasher unit	570 to 572
K18	Air bag relay	665, 666
K20	Ignition coil module	235 to 237
K26	Cooling fan relay	785 to 787
K30	Tailgate wiper relay	713 to 715
K31	Air bag control unit	669 to 674
K35	Exterior mirror heating timer relay	847 to 849
K37	Central locking control unit	605 to 611
K50	ABS control unit	803 to 818
K51	Cooling fan relay	791 to 792
K52	Cooling fan relay	794 to 796
K57	Multec control unit	172 to 196, 241 to 263, 308 to 332, 363 to 398
K58	Fuel pump relay	198, 199, 265, 266, 336, 337, 398, 399
K59	Daytime driving light relay	517 to 523
K60	Air conditioning compressor relay	780, 781
K63	Anti-theft alarm horn relay	655, 656
K67	Cooling fan relay - high-speed	798, 799
K76	Glow time control unit (Diesel)	210 to 216
K77	Glow plugs relay (Diesel)	216, 217
K79	Charge indicator relay	205 to 207
K80	Filter heating relay (Diesel)	223, 224
K85	Automatic transmission control unit	271 to 294
K89	Rear foglight relay	545 to 547
K94	Anti-theft alarm control unit	637 to 652
K97	Headlight washer pump relay	720 to 722
L1	Ignition coil	237
L2	Ignition coil	166 to 169, 301 to 303, 359 to 362
M1	Starter	105, 106
M2	Windshield wiper motor	700 to 704
M3	Heating blower motor	754 to 757
M4	Radiator cooling fan motor	123 to 130, 786
M8	Tailgate wiper motor	711 to 713
M10	Air conditioning fan motor	769 to 772
M11	Radiator cooling fan motor	787
M15	Passenger door window motor	694, 697
M18	Driver's door central locking motor	606 to 609
M19	Left rear door central locking motor	617 to 619
M20	Right rear door central locking motor	621 to 623
M21	Fuel pump	340
M24	Headlight washer pump	722
M30	Driver's side exterior mirror	838 to 841
M31	Passenger side exterior mirror	844 to 847
M32	Passenger door central locking motor	617 to 620
M39	Left headlight levelling motor	534 to 536
M40	Right headlight levelling motor	538 to 540
M41	Fuel filler flap central locking motor	625 to 626
M47	Driver's door window motor	685 to 688
M55	Windscreen and tailgate washer pump	717
M60	Tailgate central locking motor	626, 628
M66	Idle air stepper motor	180 to 183, 245 to 248, 315 to 318, 372 to 375
P1	Fuel gauge	450
P2	Coolant temperature gauge	448
P4	Fuel sensor	450
P5	Coolant temperature sensor	448
P7	Tachometer	442

Key to wiring diagrams (continued)

Not all items fitted to all models

No	Description	Track	No	Description	Track
P13	Outside temperature sensor	422	S41	Driver's door deadlock switch	602 to 604
P17	ABS left front wheel sensor	807	S42	Passenger door central locking switch	614
P18	ABS right front wheel sensor	811	S47	Driver's door contact switch	595, 596
P19	ABS left rear wheel sensor	815	S52	Hazard flasher switch	571 to 576
P20	ABS right rear wheel sensor	817	S55	Right front seat heating switch	860 to 862
P21	Distance sensor	445, 446	S64	Horn switch	661, 666
P23	Intake manifold absolute pressure sensor	254 to 256, 320 to 322, 381 to 383	S68	Exterior mirror switch	
P29	Intake manifold temperature sensor	377	S68.1	Exterior mirror adjustment switch	836 to 840
P30	Coolant temperature sensor	181, 251, 318, 379	S68.2	Exterior mirror heating switch	842
P32	Heated exhaust oxygen sensor	196, 197	S68.3	Left/right exterior mirror switch	836 to 841
P33	Exhaust oxygen sensor	254, 324, 392	S78	Passenger door window switch	694 to 697
P34	Throttle valve potentiometer	187 to 189, 268 to 260, 323 to 325, 385 to 387	S88	2-stage coolant temperature switch	126 to 131
P35	Crankshaft impulse sensor	172 to 174, 307 to 309, 368 to 370	S98	Headlight levelling switch	533 to 535
			S101	Air conditioning compressor switch	773, 776
P45	Transmission input revolution sensor	287, 288	S104	Kickdown switch	291
P46	Knock control sensor	179, 330	S105	Start-up assistance switch	293 to 295
P47	Cylinder identification - Hall sensor	177, 178	S106	Economy/power programme switch	290
P48	Automatic transmission distance sensor	285, 286	S109	Air conditioning switch	782
P52	Airflow meter	174, 175	S114	Coolant temperature switch	212
R3	Cigarette lighter	852	S120	Bonnet anti-theft alarm switch	641
R5	Glow plugs (Diesel)	217 to 219	S127	Tailgate central locking switch	634
R19	Blower motor resistor	126, 130	S128	Coolant temperature switch	787, 788
R23	Air bag unit	672	U4	ABS modulator assembly	
S1	Starter switch	105, 106	U4.1	Pump motor relay	802 to 805
S2	Light switch assembly		U4.2	Solenoid valves relay	811 to 815
S2.1	Light switch	504 to 507	U4.3	Pump motor	801
S2.2	Passenger compartment light switch	589	U4.4	Diode	813
S2.3	Instrument lighting dimmer	431	U4.5	Left front solenoid valve	807
S3	Heater blower switch	753 to 758	U4.6	Right front solenoid valve	809
S5.2	Dipped beam switch	528, 529	U4.7	Left rear solenoid valve	806
S5.3	Direction indicator switch	582 to 584	U4.8	Right rear solenoid valve	808
S7	Reversing light switch	598	U12	Filter heater (Diesel)	
S8	Stop-light switch	564	U12.1	Temperature switch	223
S9	Wiper unit switch		U12.2	Filter heater	224
S9.2	Intermittent wipe switch	701 to 704	U13	Automatic transmission	
S9.5	Tailgate wash/wipe switch	714 to 716	U13.1	Solenoid valve (shift 1)	279
S10	Automatic transmission switch	271 to 277	U13.2	Solenoid valve (shift 2)	280
S11	Brake fluid control switch	463	U13.3	Solenoid valve (lock-up control)	281
S13	Handbrake "on" switch	464	U13.4	Solenoid valve (pressure control)	282
S14	Oil pressure switch	461	U13.5	Transmission fluid temperature sensor	285
S15	Boot light switch	587	U14	Multi-function unit (dual display)	421 to 431
S17	Passenger door contact switch	594	U15	Multi-function unit (triple display)	421 to 431
S20	Air conditioning pressure switch		U17	Roof aerial amplifier	414, 415
S20.1	Low pressure compressor switch	776	V3	Anti-theft alarm LED	571
S20.2	High pressure compressor switch	776	V8	Air conditioning compressor diode	778
S20.3	High pressure blower compressor switch	794	V14	Knock sensor module	331, 332
S21	Front foglight switch	558 to 560	V15	Exhaust gas recirculation (EGR) amplifier	331 to 334
S22	Rear foglight switch	551 to 553			
S24	Air conditioning blower switch	767 to 771	X1 onwards	Wiring connectors	Various
S29	Coolant temperature switch	123, 791	Y1	Air conditioning compressor clutch	780
S30	Left front seat heating switch	856 to 858	Y5	Fuel solenoid valve	201
S31	Rear left door contact switch	591	Y7	Fuel injection valves	185 to 192, 383 to 391
S32	Rear right door contact switch	592	Y10	Hall sensor - ignition distributor	238 to 244
S37.1	Left window switch	686, 687	Y18	Exhaust gas recirculation valve	326 to 329
S37.2	Right window switch	684 to 689	Y32	Fuel injection valve	246, 312
			Y34	Tank ventilation valve	196, 310

12

Explanation of abbreviations used

Note: *The following list is included for guidance only - a comprehensive list was not available at time of writing.*

AB	Air bag	M1.5.2	Fuel injection (Bosch Motronic M1.5.2)
ABS	Anti-lock braking system	M2.7	Fuel injection (Bosch Motronic M2.7)
AC	Air conditioning	M2.8	Fuel injection (Bosch Motronic M2.8)
AT	Automatic transmission	MID	Multi-information display (multi-function unit)
ATC	Automatic temperature control	MOT	Motronic system (general)
AZV	Trailer hitch	MT	Manual transmission
BR	On-board computer	MUL	Fuel injection (Multec)
CC	Check control	NS	Front foglight
CRC	Cruise control	NSL	Rear foglight
D	Diesel	OEL	Oil level check (oil pressure)
DID	Dual information display (multi-function unit)	OPT	Optional equipment
DIS	Distributorless ignition system	PBSL	Parking/brake lockout
DS	Theft protection	P/N	Park/Neutral (starter inhibitor - automatic transmission)
DWA	Anti-theft warning system	POT	Potentiometer
DZM	Tachometer	RC	Ride control
EFC	Electric folding roof (Convertible)	RFS	Reversing lights
EKP	Fuel pump	RHD	Right-hand drive
EKS	Pinch guard (electric windows)	SD	Sliding sunroof
EMP	Radio/cassette	SH	Seat heating
EZ+	EZ Plus ignition with self-diagnosis	SRA	Headlight washer
FH	Electric windows	TANK	Fuel gauge
HRL	Luggage compartment light	TD	Turbodiesel
HS	Heated rear window	TEMP	Temperature gauge
HW	Tailgate wiper	TFL	Day running lights
HZG	Heating	TIP	Triple information display (multi-function unit)
INS	Instrument	TKS	Door courtesy light switch
IRL	Interior light	TSZI	Transistor ignition (Inductive)
KAT	Catalytic converter	WEG	Odometer (mileometer) frequency sensor
KBS	Wiring harness	WHR	Vehicle level control
KV	Contact, distributor	WS	Warning buzzer
L3.1	Fuel injection (Bosch L3.1-Jetronic)	ZV	Central locking
LHD	Left-hand drive	ZYL	Cylinder
LWR	Headlight beam range control	4WD	Four-wheel-drive
M1.5	Fuel injection (Bosch Motronic M1.5)		

Wiring identification

Example: GE WS 1.5

GE - Basic colour
WS - Identification colour
1.5 - Wire cross-section (mm^2)

Colour code

BL	Blue
BR	Brown
GE	Yellow
GN	Green
GR	Grey
HBL	Light blue
LI	Lilac
RT	Red
SW	Black
VI	Violet
WS	White

Circuit interconnections

A boxed number - eg 180 - refers to a grid reference (track number) at which the circuit is continued.

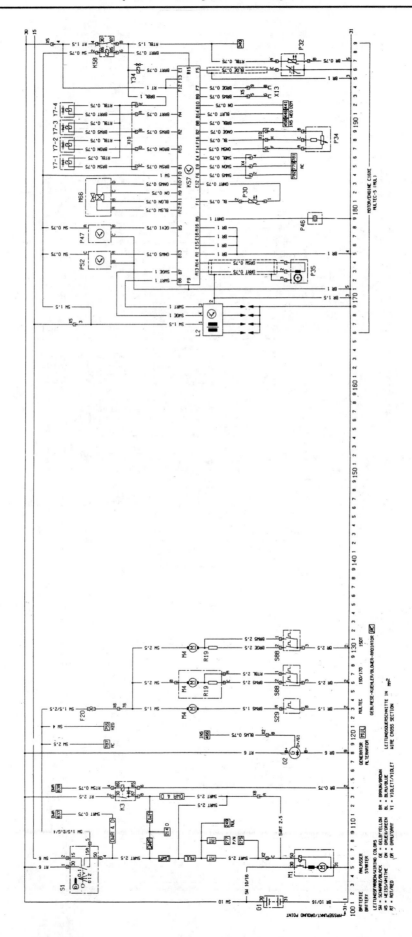

Wiring diagram (all models)

12

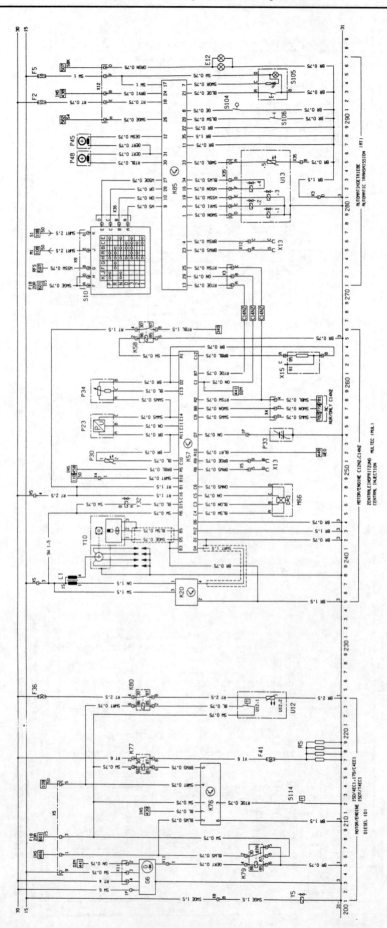

Wiring diagram (all models) - continued

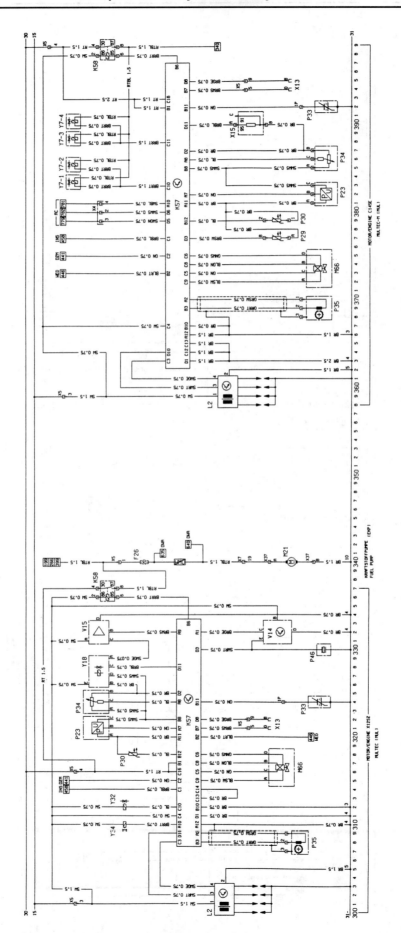

Wiring diagram (all models) - continued

12

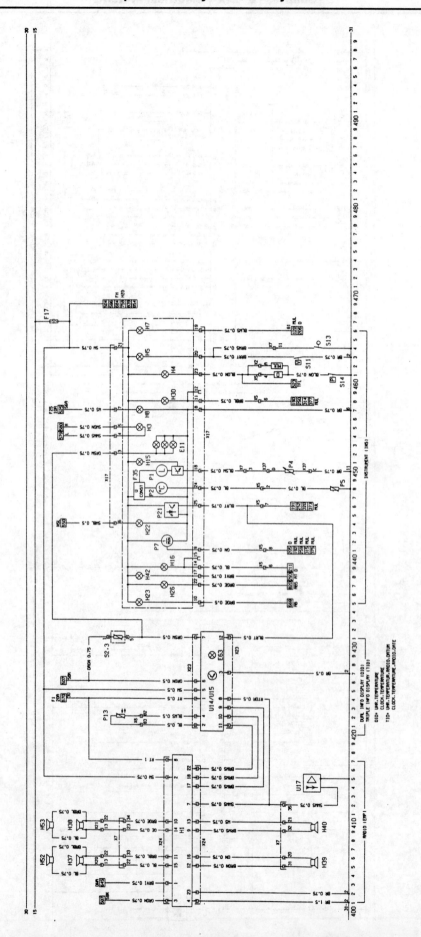

Wiring diagram (all models) - continued

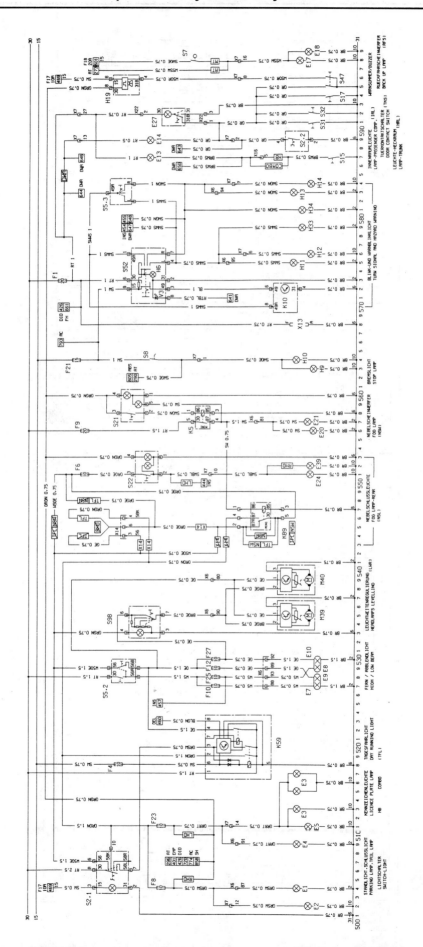

Wiring diagram (all models) - continued

12

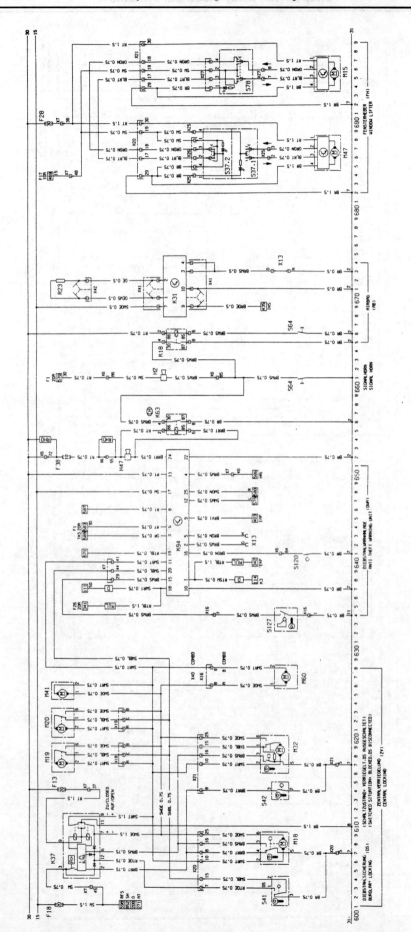

Wiring diagram (all models) - continued

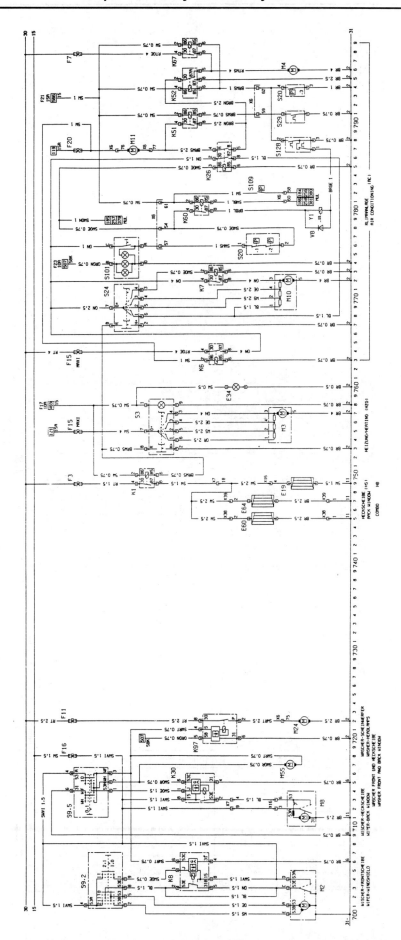

Wiring diagram (all models) - continued

12

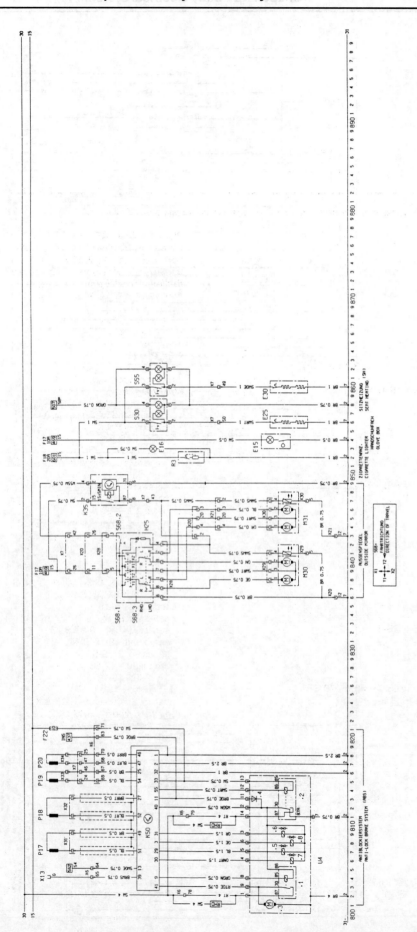

Wiring diagram (all models) - continued

Index

Note: *References throughout this index relate to Chapter and page numbers, separated by a hyphen.*